London

timeout.com/london

Time Out Guides Ltd
Universal House
251 Tottenham Court Road
London W1T 7AB
United Kingdom
Tel: +44 (0)20 7813 3000
Fax: +44 (0)20 7813 6001
Email: guides@timeout.com
www.timeout.com

Published by Time Out Guides Ltd, a wholly owned subsidiary of Time Out Group Ltd.
Time Out and the Time Out logo are trademarks of Time Out Group Ltd.

This edition first published in Great Britain in 2011 by Ebury Publishing.
A Random House Group Company
20 Vauxhall Bridge Road, London SW1V 2SA

Random House Australia Pty Ltd 20 Alfred Street, Milsons Point, Sydney, New South Wales 2061, Australia

Random House New Zealand Ltd 18 Poland Road, Glenfield, Auckland 10, New Zealand

Random House South Africa (Pty) Ltd Isle of Houghton, Corner Boundary Road & Carse O'Gowrie, Houghton 2198, South Africa

Random House UK Limited Reg. No. 954009

Distributed in the US and Latin America by Publishers Group West (1-510-809-3700)
Distributed in Canada by Publishers Group Canada (1-800-747-8147)
For further distribution details, see www.timeout.com.

ISBN: 978-1-84670-207-5

A CIP catalogue record for this book is available from the British Library.

Printed and bound by Firmengruppe APPL, aprinta druck, Wemding, Germany.

The Random House Group Limited supports The Forest Stewardship Council (FSC), the leading international forest certification organisation. All our titles that are printed on Greenpeace approved FSC certified paper carry the FSC logo. Our paper procurement policy can be found at http://www.rbooks.co.uk/environment.

Time Out carbon-offsets its flights with Trees for Cities (www.treesforcities.org).

Contents

Introduction

This past year there's been a real buzz about London. Not only in the music, style and foodie mags, where the Big Smoke is an almost permanent presence, but on mainstream television and the radio too, on which variously sober or idiosyncratic personalities have sought to uncover the mysteries of this city's distant past, recent past or immediate future, dissecting its culture and its people in the process.

Why the interest? Of course, the rapid approach of the London 2012 Olympic and Paralympic Games has much to do with it. In this edition, we've dedicated a whole section to the venues and context of the Games – as well as sharing some interesting facts, figures and personalities we've chanced upon along the way. The Olympic Park itself remains closed to the public until the Opening Ceremony on 27 July 2012, but there's lots to explore in this transformed area of east London. There are also many already-functioning London 2012 venues, spread right across town, that are open to the public as usual.

The attention that is being paid to east London – from the hipster fiefdom of Shoreditch (under constant attack, the bleeding-edge artists and nightlife gurus there grumble, from moneyed types from its 2,000-year-old neighbour banking district, the City) to hitherto overlooked stretches of post-industrial marshland where the Olympic Park has grown – shouldn't distract you from the rest of the city. This is a big town. Bigger than you can satisfactorily explore in a holiday... bigger than you could satisfactorily explore in several lifetimes, in fact. The sheer wealth of attractions – world-class museums and art galleries that still charge no entry free, several World Heritage Sites, any number of niche attractions for fans of fashion, terrifying surgical techniques, ancient Egyptian ephemera, children's toys, steam engines or the bones of long-dead creatures – might make it possible for curmudgeons to entirely ignore London 2012, were they so minded.

And we haven't yet touched on London's astonishingly various nightlife, music, theatre or gastronomy: St John restaurant, where this city pioneered the revival in traditional cooking now called 'modern British', or a tiny Islington bar that's bringing 'molecular gastronomy' to cocktails. Whatever your pleasure, London truly satisfies. *Simon Coppock, Editor*

London in Brief

IN CONTEXT
Recession is only the latest trauma to afflict London, a city that's survived more than 2,000 years of turbulence. From old buildings adapted for modern needs to the sudden expansion of cycling, the capital is meeting new challenges with renewed creativity, as we suggest in this series of features.
▶ *For more, see pp14-40.*

LONDON 2012
Whether you want to explore the waterways around the Olympic Park as it closes in on its summer 2011 completion date, or to plan a visit to the London 2012 Olympic & Paralympic Games itself, this dedicated section gives details on all the London venues and events, as well as historical and cultural context, and practical information.
▶ *For more, see pp42-67.*

SIGHTS
Some of London's attractions write their own headlines: the British Museum or the riverside Tates. But such major sights come nowhere near accounting for all the city's wealth of attractions: within these pages, you'll also find everything from ancient palaces to shiny new developments, quirky museums to expansive parks.
▶ *For more, see pp70-180.*

CONSUME
London's reputation for lousy cooking is no longer justified, as a visit to St John and its followers will prove, but whether you're eating, drinking or shopping, variety is the keynote. Elegant bars jostle with ancient pubs, a traditional umbrella shop plies its trade near hip boutiques, and the city's hotels and B&Bs are all getting spruced up.
▶ *For more, see pp182-276.*

ARTS & ENTERTAINMENT
London's nightlife is famously lively, with new venues such as XOYO enhancing already stellar options. Head to Shoreditch for clubs and the best gay nights, and to pretty much anywhere in town for music and contemporary art. Add compelling theatre, exciting comedy and uniquely hybrid dance shows, and you have a superb cultural scene.
▶ *For more, see pp278-348.*

ESCAPES & EXCURSIONS
When trying to get round the innumerable attractions of London has started to feel too much like hard work, take a break. Breezy Brighton is an easy train ride from the city and nothing but cheery seaside fun; other escapes covered here range from austere Dungeness to the discreet joys of Cambridge and Canterbury.
▶ *For more, see pp350-360.*

London in 48 Hours

Day 1 Trafalgar, Tradition and the Thames

10AM Start the day in **Trafalgar Square** (*see p129*). The centre of London is a rather impressive sight, especially when it's not too full of tourists snapping themselves with the lions. The masterpieces of the **National Gallery** (*see p129*) are on the square's pedestrianised northern side.

10.45AM Head south down Whitehall, keeping an eye out for the cavalryman on sentry duty. You should arrive in time to see Horse Guards with shiny swords and helmets go through the daily **Changing of the Guard** (*see p279* **Standing on Ceremony**; it's an hour earlier on Sunday). The **Household Cavalry Museum** (*see p137*) is just off the parade ground if you want to learn more; otherwise, head into **St James's Park** (*see p136*) to feed the ducks and admire **Buckingham Palace** (*see p137*) at the end of the lake.

NOON Just out of the park's southern corner is Parliament Square. Admire the tobacco-yellow stone of **Westminster Abbey**, **Parliament** and **Big Ben** (*see pp131-134*), then cross Westminster Bridge for County Hall and the **London Eye** (*see p71*). This walk is modern London's biggest tourist cliché, but it's wonderful to stroll along the South Bank. Busy places to eat surround the **Southbank Centre** (*see p317*).

3PM Go with the flow past **BFI Southbank** (*see p300*) and the **National Theatre** (*see p342*) to **Tate Modern** and **Shakespeare's Globe** (for both, *see p76*), and finish your afternoon by crossing the Millennium Bridge for the slow climb up to **St Paul's Cathedral** (*see p87*), handily close to St Paul's tube station.

7PM Enough history and culture. Head north into Clerkenwell for brilliant food: modern British at **St John** or Antipodean fusion at the **Modern Pantry** (for both, *see p213*). If you're in town at the weekend and you've still got some energy, join the queue for London's coolest superclub, **Fabric** (*see p329*).

NAVIGATING THE CITY

London is a wonderful place to visit, but its size can be overwhelming. Don't worry: with a little understanding of the geography and transport, not to mention reliable street maps (*see pp388-416*), it becomes much easier to navigate.

The tube is the most straightforward way to get around town – you're rarely far from a station in central London. Mix your tube journeys with bus rides to get a handle on London's topography; free bus maps are available at many tube stations and from the Britain & London Visitor Centre (*see p374*). And don't forget the river: commuter and tourist boats run all day on the Thames. For more on travel, *see pp362-366*; for our selection of guided tours, *see p366*.

SEEING THE SIGHTS

To escape queues and overcrowding, try to avoid visiting major attractions at the weekend – and using any form of public

Day 2 Culture and Clubbing from West to East

10AM Start at one of the world's finest museums – early enough to avoid the crowds. The **British Museum** (see p102) is so full of treasures you may not know where to begin: try left out of the stunning central courtyard for the monumental antiquities.

NOON Wander south to the boutiques around Seven Dials until lunch. **Great Queen Street** (see p215) is a good option if you didn't try St John; **Wahaca** (see p216) and **Food for Thought** (see p215) are handy on a budget. Covent Garden market is here, but the excellent **London Transport Museum** and the opulent **Royal Opera House** (for both, see p109) are the principal reasons to linger.

3PM If the weather's fine, head to Bank station and get the DLR all the way east to Pudding Mill Lane station. From there, it's a short walk to the **View Tube** (see p160) for a brilliant vista over the **Olympic Park** (see pp53-59), which is racing towards completion in summer 2011, and intriguing riverside walks. On a rainy day, Covent Garden station puts you on the right tube line for South Kensington's trio of superb museums: the **Victoria & Albert Museum** (see p145), **Natural History Museum** (see p143) and **Science Museum** (see p144). If there's still some walking left in you, head to Hyde Park for the **Albert Memorial** (see p143) and Kensington Gardens for the understated **Serpentine Gallery** (see p146).

7PM By now, you'll need food. Take on a sturdy refuel at **Madsen** (see p223) or, if you're in the park, head to **Le Café Anglais** (see p224) or the cheaper **Kiasu** (see p225).

9PM Not yet ready for your bed? Grown-ups head a little further west: **Notting Hill Gate** is the place for civilised cocktailing (see p241). Hip kids and the young at heart should get to a tube station and take the Central (red) underground line east: Liverpool Street station is the gateway to bleakly nondescript **Shoreditch**. Here you'll find a plethora of concept bars (see pp245-248), trend-setting clubs (see pp331-332) and wispily mustachioed youths.

transport during rush hour (8-9.30am and 4.30-7pm, Monday to Friday). Many attractions, including all the big museums, offer free admission, so if you're on a budget you can tick off large numbers of places on your must-see list just for the price of getting there.

We've given last-entry times where they precede an attraction's closing time by more than an hour. Some smaller venues may close early when they're quiet, and many places close all day on certain public holidays (notably Christmas). Call ahead before making a special trip.

PACKAGE DEALS

The **London Pass** (www.londonpass.com) gives pre-paid access to more than 50 sights and attractions. Unless you're prepared to visit several sights a day for four or five days, you're unlikely to get your money's worth. However, you will be able to jump the queues at such ultra-popular sights as the Tower of London.

London in Profile

THE SOUTH BANK & BANKSIDE

Running along the Thames from the London Eye to Gabriel's Wharf, the **South Bank** is the centre of the nation's arts scene. Directly east is **Bankside**, which has risen to prominence thanks to Tate Modern and Borough Market.
▶ For more, see pp70-80.

THE CITY

Reminders of London's long, ramshackle and occasionally great history jostle with latter-day citadels of high finance in the City, the fascinating 'square mile' (it's actually slightly over a mile) that essentially *was* London for centuries.
▶ For more, see pp81-97.

HOLBORN & CLERKENWELL

Just west of the City lie two different, distinct locales. Quietly historic **Clerkenwell** boasts some of London's best bars and restaurants. Adjacent **Holborn**, meanwhile, is the city's legal quarter, and sits on the fringes of London's West End.
▶ For more, see pp98-100.

BLOOMSBURY & KING'S CROSS

North-west of Holborn, literary **Bloomsbury** draws millions to the British Museum. North of Bloomsbury is fast-improving **King's Cross**, while to the west the restaurant-packed area of **Fitzrovia** concerns itself only with its media-industry locals.
▶ For more, see pp101-106.

COVENT GARDEN & THE STRAND

Covent Garden, just south of Bloomsbury, is a genuine visitor-magnet: tourists adore its open-plan piazza and wearingly cheery street entertainers. Between here and the Thames lies the traffic-choked, theatre-lined **Strand**.
▶ For more, see pp107-111.

SOHO & LEICESTER SQUARE

The hub of the West End, **Soho** is London's most notorious district. These days, it's far more civilised than its naughty reputation suggests, but is still fun to wander. Just south sit bustling **Chinatown** and touristy **Leicester Square**.
▶ For more, see pp112-116.

OXFORD STREET & MARYLEBONE

London's shoppers get to choose from countless different shopping areas, but chain-heavy **Oxford Street** is where most of the money is spent. Oxford Street separates Soho and Mayfair from Fitzrovia and **Marylebone**, an agreeably villagey district dotted with boutiques and restaurants.
▶ For more, see pp117-121.

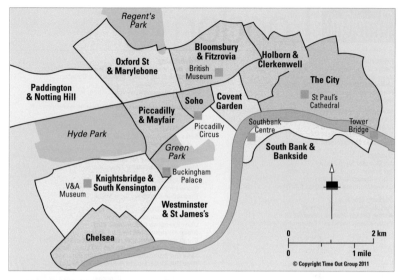

© Copyright Time Out Group 2011

PADDINGTON & NOTTING HILL
Millions have been spent improving north-westerly **Paddington** in recent years, but the area still lacks focus. It's better to head west to the market, bars and boutiques of **Notting Hill**.
▶ *For more, see pp122-123.*

PICCADILLY & MAYFAIR
The flashing neon beguiles small-town tourists, but **Piccadilly Circus** is little more than a charmless traffic island nowadays. Instead of lingering there, stroll west into **Mayfair**, home to London's most upmarket shops and prestigious hotels.
▶ *For more, see pp124-128.*

WESTMINSTER & ST JAMES'S
With the northern edge of Trafalgar Square pedestrianised, the centre of London is a pleasant place to be. Just south is historic **Westminster**, the home of government; go south-west and you'll reach immaculate, aristocratic **St James's**.
▶ *For more, see pp129-138.*

CHELSEA
Chelsea starts in earnest at Sloane Square, before stretching west and ebbing outwards off the shop-lined King's Road. Its southern border is the Thames.
▶ *For more, see pp139-141.*

KNIGHTSBRIDGE & SOUTH KENSINGTON
Knightsbridge draws devotees with a welter of high-class, high-priced shops. Adjoining **South Kensington** is where the throngs pile into London's three palatial Victorian museums.
▶ *For more, see pp142-146.*

Time Out London

Editorial
Editor Simon Coppock
Copy Editor Edoardo Albert
Listings Editors William Crow, Jamie Warburton
Proofreader Tamsin Shelton
Indexer Ismay Atkins

Managing Director Peter Fiennes
Editorial Director Ruth Jarvis
Business Manager Dan Allen
Editorial Manager Holly Pick
Assistant Management Accountant Ija Krasnikova

Design
Art Director Scott Moore
Art Editor Pinelope Kourmouzoglou
Senior Designer Kei Ishimaru
Group Commercial Designer Jodi Sher

Picture Desk
Picture Editor Jael Marschner
Acting Deputy Picture Editor Liz Leahy
Picture Desk Assistant/Researcher Ben Rowe

Advertising
New Business & Commercial Director Mark Phillips
Magazine & UK Guides Commercial Director
  St John Betteridge
Account Managers Jessica Baldwin, Michelle Daburn,
  Ben Holt
Production Controller Chris Pastfield
Copy Controller Alison Bourke

Marketing
Sales & Marketing Director, North America
  & Latin America Lisa Levinson
Senior Publishing Brand Manager Luthfa Begum
Group Commercial Art Director Anthony Huggins
Marketing Co-ordinator Alana Benton

Production
Group Production Manager Brendan McKeown
Production Controller Katie Mulhern

Time Out Group
Director & Founder Tony Elliott
Chief Executive Officer David King
Group Financial Director Paul Rakkar
Group General Manager/Director Nichola Coulthard
Time Out Communications Ltd MD David Pepper
Time Out International Ltd MD Cathy Runciman
Time Out Magazine Ltd Publisher/MD Mark Elliott
Group Commercial Director Graeme Tottle
Group IT Director Simon Chappell

Contributors
Introduction Simon Coppock. **History** Simon Coppock (*Time Machine* Museum of London curators; *Thanks for the Memories* Peter Watts). **London Today** Peter Watts. **Architecture** Simon Coppock (*Spotter's Guides* Simon Coppock, Peter Watts). **London 2012** Edoardo Albert, Simon Coppock, Hugh Graham. **Sights** Simon Coppock, Charlie Godfrey-Faussett, Peter Watts (*Profile: London Eye* Ronnie Haydon; *Snapshots* Simon Coppock, Sally Harrild; *Profile: Museum of London, Walk: The New City, Walk: Book Stops, Death and Dignity* Peter Watts; *Plaques, Decay, On Routie, Profile: Science Museum, Sounds of the Sea* Simon Coppock; *Gay Superhighway* Patrick Welch; *Walk: The Sidestreet Shuffle* Helen Walasek; *Artistic Revival* Nuala Calvi). **Hotels** Simon Coppock. **Restaurants & Cafés** contributors to *Time Out Eating & Drinking* (*Eating In… and Eating Out, Prime Locations* Charmaine Mok; *Front Row Seats* Simon Coppock). **Pubs & Bars** contributors to *Time Out Bars, Pubs & Clubs* (*In the Mix* Charlie Godfrey-Faussett; *Bigging Up the Beer* Simon Coppock). **Shops & Services** Anna Norman (*Profile: Selfridges* Simon Coppock). **Calendar & Directory** Jamie Warburton, William Crow (*Standing on Ceremony* Charlie Godfrey-Faussett). **Children** Jamie Warburton, William Crow (*Meet the Mascots* Edoardo Albert). **Comedy** Patrick Welch (*Our Own Edinburgh?* Edoardo Albert). **Dance** Lyndsey Winship. **Film** John Watson. **Galleries** Martin Coomer, Ossian Ward. **Gay & Lesbian** Patrick Welch (*Get the Look* Simone Baird). **Music** Simon Coppock, Chris Parkin. **Nightlife** Kate Hutchinson. **Sport & Fitness** Simon Coppock, Patrick Welch (*Cycle City* Patrick Welch). **Theatre** Nuala Calvi. **Escapes & Excursions** Anna Norman & contributors to *Time Out Great Days Out*.

The Editor would like to thank Carol Baker for timely questions; Andy Atkin, Malcolm Brockwell, Kerri Chambers, John Hopkins and Ken Swaby for interesting answers; and all contributors to previous editions of *Time Out London* and *Time Out* magazine, whose work forms the basis for parts of this book.

Maps john@jsgraphics.co.uk

Cover Photograph: Photolibrary.com
Back Cover Photography by Getty Images, Britta Jaschinski, Ed Marshall, 2007 ODA/Getty Images/London 2012.

Photography by pages 4, 5 (top right), 7, 8 (top left and centre right), 9 (top right), 13, 40, 69, 89 (left), 71, 72, 93, 100, 108, 123, 125, 133, 135, 136, 137, 146, 148, 161, 166, 175, 179, 209, 215, 242, 254, 277, 288, 292, 295, 309, 311, 313, 327, 331 Jonathan Perugia; 5 (top left), 41, 45, 57, 62, 66 © ODA/London 2012; 5 (centre right) Barry J. Holmes; 5 (centre left and bottom right), 86, 96, 126, 153, 154, 193, 196, 199, 235, 243, 249, 253, 259, 261, 266, 267, 269, 274, 287, 318, 329, 330, 346, 347 Michelle Grant; 6, 77 (right), 99, 109, 134, 140, 162 (bottom), 183, 302, 303, 315, 317 Andrew Brackenbury; 8 (top right), 9 (top left), 150 Elisabeth Blanchet; 8 (centre right and bottom right), 78, 79, 90 (bottom), 143, 157 (bottom left), 225, 227, 239, 240, 245, 250, 252 (centre), 262, 276, 320, 335, 341, 352 Rob Greig; 8 (centre), 270 Craig Deane; 8 (bottom left), 30, 33, 34, 35, 113, 114, 119, 144, 158, 176, 290, 298, 299, 305, 308, 312, 325, 339, 340 Ben Rowe; 9 (centre), 164, 221, 286 Heloise Bergman; 9 (bottom right), 74 (top left and right), 184 Emma Wood; 9 (bottom left), 226 Michael Franke; 14 Chalmers Butterfield; 15, 17, 19, 24, 25 Museum of London; 16 Time Life Pictures/Getty Images; 18 Hulton Archive/Getty Images; 20 MEPL; 23 Peter Watts; 26 Bert Hardy/Picture Post/Getty Images; 38 Andreas Schmidt; 42 AFP/ Getty Images; 47, 48, 49, 50 copyright of and reproduced with the consent of the International Olympic Committee; 52 © ODA 2008/London 2012; 53 (top), 59, 63, 64 (top) © ODA 2008; 53 (bottom) 2007 ODA/Getty Images/London 2012; 56 MCC; 61, 64 London 2012; 73 (top), 105, 152, 233, 246, 281 (top) Scott Wishart; 73 (centre and bottom), 111 simonleigh.com; 77 (left), 169 Olivia Rutherford; 82, 87, 89 (right), 92 Laurence Davis; 90 (top) Nigel Tradewell; 115 Paul Mattson; 74 (bottom), 116, 216, 218, 252 (top and bottom), 260 Ming Tang-Evans; 118, 127, 147, 157 (top and bottom right), 171, 187, 190, 195, 200, 207, 211, 247, 273, 334, 343, 356 Britta Jaschinski; 149 Oliver Knight; 162 (top) Tove K. Breitstein; 167 Susannah Stone; 172 Susie Rae; 180, 285 Belinda Lawley; 181, 251, 256, 258 Ed Marshall; 182, 203 (top) Chris Tubbs; 188 Nerida Howard; 212 Jason Lowe; 223 Tricia de Courcy de Ling; 236 Hayley Harrison; 268 Alys Tomlinson; 280 Jon Enoch; 281 (bottom) Nick Ballon; 282 Getty Images; 289 (left) Mandeville TM © LOCOG 2009-10, (right) Wenlock TM © LOCOG 2009-10; 293 Warren King; 297 Johan Persson; 333 Tim Motion; 349 Markabond; 350 Karen Gentry; 355 Amra Pasic; 359 (top) Mark William Penny; 359 (bottom) Adrian Zenz; 361 David Axelbank.

The following images were provided by the featured establishments/artists: pages 84, 104, 130, 189, 203 (bottom), 228, 230, 279, 283, 301, 328, 344, 345, 353.

About the Guide

GETTING AROUND

The back of the book contains street maps of London, as well as overview maps of the city and its surroundings. The maps start on page 388; on them are marked the locations of hotels (❶), restaurants and cafés (❶), and pubs and bars (❶). The majority of the businesses listed in this guide are located in the areas we've mapped; the grid-square references included throughout the listings refer to these maps.

THE ESSENTIALS

For practical information, including visas, disabled access, emergency numbers, lost property, useful websites and local transport, please see the Directory. It begins on page 362.

THE LISTINGS

Addresses, phone numbers, websites, transport information, hours and prices are all included in our listings, as are selected other facilities. All were checked and correct at press time. However, business owners can alter their arrangements at any time, and fluctuating economic conditions can cause prices to change rapidly.

The very best venues in the city, the must-sees and must-dos in every category, have been marked with a red star (★). In the Sights chapters, we've also marked venues with free admission with a FREE symbol.

PHONE NUMBERS

The area code for London is 020. You don't need to use the code when calling from within London: simply dial the eight-digit number as listed in this guide.

From outside the UK, dial your country's international access code (011 from the US) or a plus symbol, followed by the UK country code (44), 20 for London (dropping the initial zero) and the eight-digit number as listed in the guide. So, to reach the British Museum, dial +44 20 7323 8000. For more on phones, including information on calling abroad from the UK and details of local mobile-phone access, see pp373-374.

FEEDBACK

We welcome feedback on this guide, both on the venues we've included and on any other locations that you'd like to see featured in future editions. Please email us at guides@timeout.com.

TIME OUT GUIDES

Founded in 1968, Time Out has grown from humble beginnings into the leading resource for anyone wanting to know what's happening in the world's greatest cities. Alongside our influential weeklies in London, New York and Chicago, we publish more than 20 magazines in cities as varied as Beijing and Beirut; a range of travel books, with the City Guides now joined by the newer Shortlist series; and an information-packed website. The company remains proudly independent, still owned by Tony Elliott more than four decades after he launched *Time Out London*.

Written by local experts and illustrated with original photography, our books also retain their independence. No business has been featured because it has advertised, and all restaurants and bars are visited and reviewed anonymously.

The complete range of Time Out guidebooks is available for purchase online at www.timeout.com/shop.

ABOUT THE CONTRIBUTORS

Based in east London, **Simon Coppock** has edited more than a dozen books about London for Time Out and contributed to many more, as well as writing travel features on his favourite city for publications including the *Sunday Telegraph* and the *Sunday Times*. A full list of the book's contributors can be found opposite, but we've also included details of writers in selected chapters through the guide.

Time Out Guides is proud to be the official book publisher of travel and tourism guides for the **London 2012 Olympic Games and Paralympic Games**.

The London 2012 shop

London 2012 merchandise

Official shops now open in London at:
St Pancras International and Paddington stations

london2012.com/shop

In Context

30 St Mary Axe. *See p39.*

History

Plague, fire and disaster – enjoy
2,000 years of London.

TEXT: SIMON COPPOCK

Over the 2,000 years since London was born, a small trading station by a broad and marshy river, the city has faced plagues and invasions, fires and wars, religious turbulence and financial turmoil. Its history is a sequence of wars, natural disasters and acts of terrorism, borne by Londoners with their characteristic upbeat pessimism and gloomily forthright moaning until the moment arrives when the frenzy of commerce can begin again. Once-beloved leaders are cruelly dismissed, then their departure lamented. Booms beget depressions beget booms. More than anything, this city's past is a tale of resilience, of locals grinning while bearing their burdens of disaster.

In the City, Wren churches – built from the ruins of the Great Fire – have walls still blackened by the German incendiary bombs dropped during the Blitz, and shrapnel scars around Cleopatra's Needle beside the Thames remain from a World War I biplane raid. A fragment of glass, deeply embedded in a wall at the Old Bailey, tells of an IRA terrorist attack back in 1973, while 52 austere steel columns in Hyde Park commemorate those killed by suicide bombers in the summer of 2005.

Evidence of strife is everywhere in this city and the true Londoner will cheerfully insist there's more and worse to come. Just don't bet against them handling their portion of strife with aplomb.

LATIN LESSONS

The city's origins are hardly grand. Celtic tribes lived in scattered communities along the banks of the Thames before the Romans arrived in Britain, but there's no evidence of a settlement on the site of the future metropolis before the invasion of the Emperor Claudius in AD 43. During the Roman conquest, they forded the Thames at its shallowest point (probably near today's London Bridge) and, later, built a timber bridge there. A settlement developed on the north side of this crossing.

Over the next two centuries, the Romans built roads, towns and forts in the area. Progress was halted in AD 61 when Boudicca, the widow of an East Anglian chieftain, rebelled against the imperial forces who had seized her land, flogged her and raped her daughters. She led the Iceni in a revolt, destroying the Roman colony at Colchester before marching on London. The Romans were massacred and their settlement razed.

After order was restored, the town was rebuilt; around AD 200, a two-mile, 18-foot wall was put up around it. Chunks of the wall survive today; the early names of the original gates – Ludgate, Newgate, Bishopsgate and Aldgate – are preserved on the map of the modern city, with the street known as London Wall tracing part of its original course. But through to the fourth century, racked by invasions and internal strife, the Roman Empire was clearly in decline (*see below* **Time Machine**). In 410, the last troops were withdrawn, and London became a ghost town.

INTO THE DARK

During the fifth and sixth centuries, history gives way to legend. The Saxons crossed the North Sea; apparently avoiding the ruins of London, they built farmsteads and trading posts outside the city walls. Pope Gregory sent Augustine to convert the English to Christianity in 596; Mellitus, one of his missionaries, was appointed the first Bishop of London, founding a cathedral dedicated to St Paul inside the old city walls in 604.

From this period, the history of London is one of expansion. Writing in 731, the Venerable Bede described 'Lundenwic' as 'the mart of many nations resorting to it by land and sea'. Yet the city faced a new danger during the ninth century: the Vikings. The city was ransacked in 841 and again in 851, when Danish raiders returned with 350 ships. It was not until 886 that King Alfred of Wessex, Alfred the Great, regained the city, re-establishing London as a major trading centre.

Throughout the tenth century the city prospered. Churches were built, parishes established and markets set up. However, the 11th century brought more harassment

IN CONTEXT

Time Machine AD 290s

By Jenny Hall, Roman curator at the Museum of London.

Who's in control? Carausius declares Home Rule for Britain in AD 293 and makes London his base; Constantius Chlorus, junior emperor of the Roman Empire, is charged with returning Britain to Roman control.

Average wage Unskilled labourer, 25 to 50 silver denarii a day.

Life expectancy 26 to 45.

Key concerns How long could this unofficial empire last? What would happen to Londoners who sided with Carausius and Allectus if the Roman Empire won back Britain?

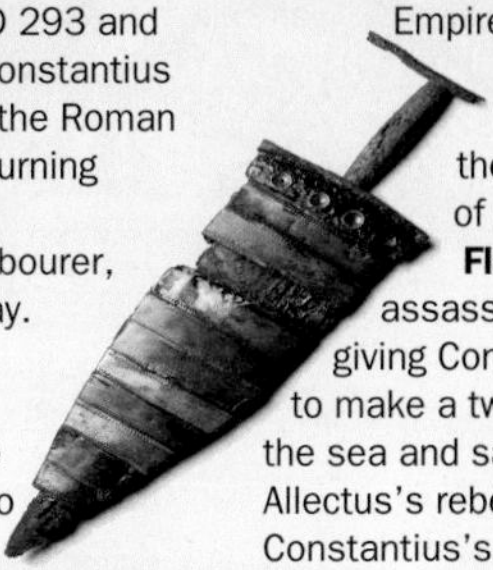

Local legislation Coins are minted in London for the first time after a period of rampant inflation.

Flash point Allectus assassinates Carausius, giving Constantius the opportunity to make a two-pronged attack from the sea and save London from Allectus's rebel army in AD 296. Constantius's son was Constantine.

IN CONTEXT

William the Conqueror's coronation at **Westminster Abbey**.

from the Vikings, and the English were forced to accept a Danish king, Cnut (Canute, 1016-35), during whose reign London replaced Winchester as the capital of England.

After a brief spell under Danish rule, the country reverted to English control in 1042 under Edward the Confessor, who devoted himself to building England's grandest church two miles west of the City on an island in the river marshes at Thorney: 'the West Minster' (Westminster Abbey; see p133). Just a week after the consecration, he died. London now had two hubs: Westminster, centre of the royal court, government and law; and the City of London, centre of commerce.

On Edward's death, foreigners took over. Duke William of Normandy was crowned king on Christmas Day 1066, having defeated Edward's brother-in-law Harold at the Battle of Hastings. The pragmatic Norman resolved to win over the City merchants by negotiation rather than force, and in 1067 granted the burgesses and the Bishop of London a charter – still available to researchers in the London Metropolitan Archives – that acknowledged their rights and independence in return for taxes. He also ordered strongholds to be built at the city wall 'against the fickleness of the vast and fierce population', including the White Tower (the tallest building in the Tower of London; see p97) and the now-lost Baynard's Castle that stood at Blackfriars.

PARLIAMENT AND RIGHTS

In 1295, the Model Parliament, held at Westminster Hall by Edward I and attended by barons, clergy and representatives of knights and burgesses, agreed the principles of English government. The first step towards establishing personal rights and political liberty, not to mention curbing the power of the king, had already been taken in 1215 with the signing of the Magna Carta by King John (see below **Time Machine**). Then, in the 14th century, subsequent assemblies gave rise to the House of Lords and the House of Commons. During the 12th and 13th centuries, the king and his court travelled the kingdom, but the Palace of Westminster was now the permanent seat of law and government; noblemen and bishops began to build palatial houses along the Strand from the City to Westminster, with gardens stretching down to the river.

Relations between the monarch and the City were never easy. Londoners guarded their privileges, and resisted attempts by kings to squeeze money out of them to finance wars and construction projects. Subsequent kings were forced to turn to Jewish and Lombard moneylenders, but the City merchants were intolerant of foreigners too.

The self-regulation privileges granted to the City merchants under Norman kings were extended by the monarchs who followed – in return for finance. In 1191, the City of London was recognised by Richard I as a self-governing community; six years later, it won control of the Thames. King John had in 1215 confirmed the city's right 'to elect every year a mayor', a position of authority with power over the sheriff and the Bishop of London. A month later, the mayor joined the rebel barons in signing the Magna Carta.

IN CONTEXT

Time Machine 1210s

By Jackie Keily, medieval curator at the Museum of London.

Who's in control? Nominally, King John.
Average wage Unskilled labourer, 2d a day; skilled craftsman, 3d to 5d a day.
Key concerns Fire, fighting, Frenchmen.
Local legislation After a Southwark fire in 1212, straw roofs are banned.
Flash point In 1215, the inhabitants of London side with the barons against

King John; and in 1216, they support Prince Louis of France when he arrives in the city. Never crowned king, Louis is defeated at the Battle of Lincoln in 1217.

Over the next two centuries, the power and influence of the trade and craft guilds (later known as the City Livery Companies) increased as dealings with Europe grew. The City's markets drew produce from miles around: livestock at Smithfield, fish at Billingsgate, poultry at Leadenhall. The street markets ('cheaps') around Westcheap (now Cheapside) and Eastcheap were crammed with a variety of goods. The population within the city walls grew from about 18,000 in 1100 to well over 50,000 in the 1340s.

WAKE UP AND SMELL THE ISSUE

Lack of hygiene became a serious problem. Water was provided in cisterns, but the supply, more or less direct from the Thames, was limited and polluted. The street of Houndsditch was so named because Londoners threw their dead animals into the furrow there; in the streets around Smithfield (the Shambles), butchers dumped entrails into the gutters. These conditions helped foster the greatest catastrophe of the Middle Ages: the Black Death of 1348 and 1349, which killed about 30 per cent of England's population. The plague came to London from Europe, carried by rats on ships, and was to recur in London several times during the next three centuries.

Disease left the harvest short-handed, causing unrest among the peasants whose labour was in such demand. Then a poll tax of a shilling a head was imposed. It was all too much: the Peasants' Revolt began in 1381. Thousands marched on London, led by Jack Straw from Essex and Wat Tyler from Kent; the Archbishop of Canterbury was murdered and hundreds of prisoners were set free. After meeting the Essexmen near Mile End, the 14-year-old Richard II rode out to the rioters at Smithfield and spoke with Tyler. During their discussion, Tyler was fatally stabbed by the Lord Mayor; the revolt collapsed and the ringleaders were hanged. But no more poll taxes were imposed.

IN CONTEXT

Peasants' Revolt.

Time Machine 1480s

By Jackie Keily, medieval curator at the Museum of London.

Who's in control? Complicated! Four kings in three years: Edward IV and his son, Edward V, both die in 1483 and are succeeded by Edward IV's brother Richard III, who is defeated and killed at Bosworth Field in 1485 by Henry Tudor, the future Henry VII.

Average wage Unskilled labourer, 4d a day.

Unusual imports In 1480-81, Portuguese ships bring 300,000 oranges; a single Venetian galley brings a mixed cargo including coral beads, pepper, sponges, ginger, satin, silk, Corinth raisins and two apes.

Key concerns Avoiding major unrest.

Local legislation In 1484, statutes are passed to stop the importation of certain foreign manufactured goods, so as to protect local jobs.

Flash point In June 1483, London supports Richard III as king instead of the 12-year-old Edward V, who is in prison. The young prince never leaves the Tower of London (*see p97*) – he and his brother, Richard of Shrewsbury, are later known as the 'Princes in the Tower'.

ROSES, WIVES AND THE ROYAL DOCKS

Its growth spurred by the discovery of America and the opening of ocean routes to Africa and the Orient, London became one of Europe's largest cities under the Tudors (1485-1603). The first Tudor monarch, Henry VII, had ended the Wars of the Roses by might, defeating Richard III at the Battle of Bosworth, and policy, marrying Elizabeth of York, a daughter of his rivals (*see above* **Time Machine**). By the time his son took the throne, the Tudor dynasty was firmly established. But progress under Henry VIII was not without its hiccups. His first marriage to Catherine of Aragon failed to produce an heir, so in 1527 he determined the union should be annulled. When the Pope refused to co-operate, Henry defied the Catholic Church, demanding to be recognised as Supreme Head of the Church in England and ordering the execution of anyone who opposed the plan (including Sir Thomas More, his otherwise loyal chancellor). The subsequent dissolution of the monasteries transformed the face of the medieval city.

When not transforming the politico-religious landscape, Henry found time to develop a professional navy, founding the Royal Dockyards at Woolwich in 1512. He also established palaces at Hampton Court (*see p173*) and Whitehall, and built a residence at St James's Palace. Much of the land he annexed for hunting became today's Royal Parks, among them Greenwich Park, Hyde Park and Regent's Park.

RENAISSANCE MEANS REBIRTH

Elizabeth I's reign (1558-1603) saw the founding of the Royal Exchange in 1566, which enabled London to emerge as Europe's commercial hub. Merchant venturers and the first joint-stock companies established new trading enterprises, as pioneering seafarers Francis Drake, Walter Raleigh and Richard Hawkins sailed to the New World. As trade grew, so did London: it was home to some 200,000 people in 1600, many living in dirty, overcrowded conditions. The most complete picture of Tudor London is given in John Stow's *Survey of London* (1598), a fascinating first-hand account by a diligent Londoner whose monument stands in the church of St Andrew Undershaft.

These were the glory days of English drama. The Rose (1587) and the Globe (1599, now recreated; *see p76*) were erected at Bankside, providing homes for the works of popular playwrights Christopher Marlowe and William Shakespeare. Deemed officially

Carousing during the **Plague**.

'For all its devastation, the Great Fire of 1666 at least allowed planners the chance to rebuild London as a modern city.'

'a naughty place' by royal proclamation, 16th-century Bankside was a vibrant mix of entertainment and 'sport' (bear-baiting, cock-fighting), drinking and whoring – and all within easy reach of the City, which had outlawed theatres in 1575.

In 1605, two years after the Tudor dynasty ended with Elizabeth's death, her Stuart successor, James I, escaped assassination on 5 November, when Guy Fawkes was found underneath the Palace of Westminster. Commemorated with fireworks each year as Bonfire Night, the Gunpowder Plot was hatched in protest at the failure to improve conditions for the persecuted Catholics, but only resulted in an intensification of anti-papist sentiment. James I is more positively remembered for hiring Inigo Jones to design court masques (musical dramas) and London's first influential examples of the classical Renaissance architectural style: the Queen's House (1616; *see p167*), the Banqueting House (1619; *see p132*) and St Paul's Covent Garden (1631; *see p109*).

ROYALISTS AND ROUNDHEADS

Charles I succeeded his father in 1625, but gradually fell out of favour with the City of London and an increasingly independent-minded Parliament over taxation. The country slid into civil war (1642-49), the supporters of Parliament (the Roundheads, led by Puritan Oliver Cromwell) opposing the supporters of the King (the Royalists).

Both sides knew that control of the country's major city and port was vital for victory, and London's sympathies were with the Parliamentarians. In 1642, 24,000 citizens assembled at Turnham Green to face Charles's army, but the King withdrew. The move proved fatal: Charles never threatened the capital again, and was eventually found guilty of treason. Taken to the Banqueting House in Whitehall on 30 January 1649, he declared himself a 'martyr of the people' and was beheaded. A commemorative wreath is still laid at the site of the execution on the last Sunday in January each year.

For the next decade, the country was ruled as a Commonwealth by Cromwell. But his son Richard's subsequent rule was brief: due to the Puritans closing theatres and banning Christmas (a Catholic superstition), the Restoration of the exiled Charles II in 1660 was greeted with great rejoicing. The Stuart king had Cromwell exhumed from Westminster Abbey, and his body was hung in chains at Tyburn (near modern-day Marble Arch). His severed head was displayed on a pole outside the abbey until 1685.

PLAGUE, FIRE AND REVOLUTION

The year 1665 saw the most serious outbreak of bubonic plague since the Black Death, killing nearly 100,000. Then, on 2 September 1666, a second disaster struck. The fire that spread from a carelessly tended oven in Thomas Farriner's baking shop on Pudding Lane raged for three days and consumed four-fifths of the City.

The Great Fire at least allowed planners the chance to rebuild London as a modern city. Many blueprints were considered, but Londoners were so impatient to get on with business that the City was reconstructed largely on its medieval street plan (albeit in brick and stone rather than wood). The prolific Sir Christopher Wren oversaw work on 51 of the 54 rebuilt churches. Among them was his masterpiece: the new St Paul's (*see p87*), completed in 1710 and effectively the world's first Protestant cathedral.

In the wake of the Great Fire, many well-to-do City dwellers moved to new residential developments west of the old quarters, an area subsequently known as the West End. In the City, the Royal Exchange was rebuilt, but merchants increasingly used the new

IN CONTEXT

coffeehouses to exchange news. With the expansion of the joint-stock companies and the chance to invest capital, the City emerged as a centre not of manufacturing but of finance. Even at this early stage, economic instability was common: the 1720 financial disaster known as the South Sea Bubble ruined even Sir Isaac Newton.

Anti-Catholic feeling still ran high. The accession in 1685 of Catholic James II aroused such fears of a return to papistry that a Dutch Protestant, William of Orange, was invited to take the throne with his wife, Mary Stuart (James's daughter). James fled to France in 1688 in what became known (by its beneficiaries) as the 'Glorious Revolution'. It was during William's reign that the Bank of England was founded, initially to finance the King's religious wars with France.

Thanks for the Memories

The plaques that honour London's lost notables.

The first blue plaque celebrating a notable Londoner was erected in 1867, when the Royal Society of Arts put up a memorial at the (now-demolished) birthplace of Lord Byron. The low-key scheme found increased popularity under the auspices of the London County Council (1901-65) and the Greater London Council (1965-85); when the GLC was shut, the scheme passed to English Heritage (www.english-heritage.org.uk). To be eligible for consideration for a blue plaque, a person must have been dead for 20 years or born more than a century ago (so, for instance, nothing yet celebrating Paul McCartney), and a building associated with them must survive (which is why there's no blue plaque honouring Shakespeare).

The popularity of the scheme has been such that it's spawned imitators. Some are operated by councils: Westminster City Council has a green plaque scheme, while Camden prefers brown and Southwark favours a rich, dark blue. And they aren't all round: the City of London goes for square plaques (often placed at eccentric heights – down by your ankles or way up above your head), while Croydon has a nice green oval. Other schemes are run by groups such as Equity and the British Film Institute, and some companies have got in on the act: HMV unveiled one after they left their old Oxford Street store, while Bentley erected one for the first car they produced (near Baker Street). There's even a black plaque: on Porchester Square, for Szmul Zygielbojm, a Polish trade unionist who killed himself 'nearby' in 1943 in despair at the world's indifference to Jewish suffering.

Many plaques look official but aren't: check out the perfect tones and font of the blue plaque to 'film-maker Monty Python' above the comic troupe's old HQ in Neal's Yard. There are even plaques to fictional characters, such as Great Russell Street's tribute to Charles Kitterbell from Charles Dickens' *Sketches by Boz*. Dickens, incidentally, is London's most plaqued resident: there are ten devoted to him, erected by the LCC, the Dickens Fellowship, Southwark Council and Haringey Council. And increasing numbers of plaques have even been privately erected, either by local enthusiasts or by businesses hoping to improve the prestige of their property – publicising the fact that a famous architect built your terraced house could easily bump the value up by a few grand.

CREATION OF THE PRIME MINISTER

In 1714, the throne passed to George, the Hanover-born great-grandson of James I. The German-speaking king (he never learned English) became the first of four long-reigning Georges in the Hanoverian line.

During George I's reign (1714-27), and for several years after, Sir Robert Walpole's Whig party monopolised Parliament. Their opponents, the Tories, supported the Stuarts and had opposed the exclusion of the Catholic James II. On the king's behalf, Walpole chaired a group of ministers (the forerunner of today's Cabinet), becoming, in effect, Britain's first prime minister. Walpole was presented with 10 Downing Street (built by Sir George Downing) as a residence; it remains the official prime ministerial home.

During the 18th century, London grew with astonishing speed. New squares and terraced streets spread across Soho, Bloomsbury, Mayfair and Marylebone, as wealthy landowners and speculative developers cashed in on the new demand for leasehold properties. South London also became more accessible with the opening of the first new bridges for centuries: Westminster Bridge (opened 1750) and Blackfriars Bridge (completed 1769) joined London Bridge, previously the only Thames crossing.

GIN-SOAKED POOR, NASTY RICH

In London's older districts, people were living in terrible squalor. Some of the most notorious slums were located around Fleet Street and St Giles's (north of Covent Garden), only a short distance from fashionable residences. To make matters worse, gin ('mother's ruin') was readily available at low prices; many poor Londoners drank excessive amounts in an attempt to escape the horrors of daily life. The well-off seemed complacent, amusing themselves at the popular Ranelagh and Vauxhall Pleasure Gardens or with trips to mock the patients at the Bedlam lunatic asylum. Public executions at Tyburn were popular events in the social calendar; it's said that 200,000 people gathered to see the execution (after he had escaped from prison four times) of the folk-hero thief Jack Sheppard in 1724.

The outrageous imbalance in the distribution of wealth encouraged crime, and there were daring daytime robberies in the West End. Reformers were few, though there were exceptions. Henry Fielding, author of the picaresque novel *Tom Jones*, was also an enlightened magistrate at Bow Street Court. In 1751, he and his blind half-brother John set up a volunteer force of 'thief-takers' to back up the often ineffective efforts of the parish constables and watchmen who were, until then, the city's only law-keepers. This crime-busting group of proto-cops, known as the Bow Street Runners, were the earliest incarnation of today's Metropolitan Police (established in 1829).

Meanwhile, five major new hospitals were founded by private philanthropists. St Thomas's and St Bartholomew's were long-established monastic institutions for the care of the sick, but Westminster (1720), Guy's (1725), St George's (1734), London (1740) and the Middlesex (1745) went on to become world-famous teaching hospitals. Thomas Coram's Foundling Hospital (*see p104*) was another remarkable achievement.

INDUSTRY AND CAPITAL GROWTH

It wasn't just the indigenous population of London that was on the rise. Country folk, whose common land had been replaced by sheep enclosures, were faced with a choice between starvation wages or unemployment, and so drifted into the towns. Just outside the old city walls, the East End drew many poor immigrant labourers to build the docks towards the end of the 18th century. London's total population had grown to one million by 1801, the largest of any city in Europe. By 1837, when Queen Victoria came to the throne (*see p24* **Time Machine**), five more bridges and the capital's first passenger railway (from Greenwich to London Bridge) gave hints of huge expansion.

As well as being the administrative and financial capital of the British Empire, London was its chief port and the world's largest manufacturing centre. On one hand, it had splendid buildings, fine shops, theatres and museums; on the other, it was a

IN CONTEXT

Time Machine 1830s

By Alex Werner, head of history at the Museum of London.

Who's in control? In 1837, 18-year-old Queen Victoria arrives on the throne. Prime Minister Lord Melbourne holds together a divided cabinet and mentors the young Queen, who turns a blind eye to past indiscretions (and his wife's affair with Lord Byron). **Population** About two million. **Average wage** Tailor, 5s a day; about half of the total female labour force are servants.

Key concerns Stopping cholera: many die in epidemics during the 1830s. **Local legislation** The London to Birmingham Railway opens in 1837, but the line is not yet ready; early riders can only get as far as Hemel Hempstead.

city of poverty, pollution and disease. Residential areas were polarised into districts of fine terraces maintained by squads of servants and overcrowded, insanitary slums.

The growth of the metropolis in the century before Victoria came to the throne had been spectacular, but during her reign (1837-1901), thousands more acres were covered with roads, houses and railway lines. If you visit a street within five miles of central London, its houses will be mostly Victorian. By the end of the 19th century, the city's population had swelled to more than six million, an incredible growth of five million in just 100 years.

Despite social problems of the Victorian era, memorably depicted in the writings of Charles Dickens, steps were being taken to improve conditions for the majority of Londoners by the turn of the century. The Metropolitan Board of Works installed an efficient sewerage system, street lighting and better roads. The worst slums were replaced by low-cost building schemes funded by philanthropists such as the American George Peabody, whose Peabody Donation Fund continues to provide subsidised housing to the working classes. The London County Council (created in 1888) also helped to house the poor.

The Victorian expansion would not have been possible without an efficient public transport network with which to speed workers into and out of the city from the new suburbs. The horse-drawn bus appeared on London's streets in 1829, but it was the opening of the first passenger railway seven years later that heralded the commuters of the future. The first underground line, which ran between Paddington and Farringdon Road, opened in 1863 and proved an instant success, attracting 30,000 travellers on the first day. The world's first electric track in a deep tunnel – the 'tube' – opened in 1890 between the City and Stockwell, later becoming part of the Northern line.

THE CRYSTAL PALACE

If any single event symbolised this period of industry, science, discovery and invention, it was the Great Exhibition of 1851. Prince Albert, the Queen's Consort, helped organise the triumphant showcase, for which the Crystal Palace, a vast building of iron and glass, was erected in Hyde Park. It looked like a giant greenhouse; hardly surprising as it was designed not by a professional architect but by the Duke of Devonshire's gardener, Joseph Paxton. Condemned by art critic John Ruskin as the model of dehumanisation in design, the Palace came to be presented as the prototype of modern architecture. During the five months it was open, the Exhibition drew six million visitors. The profits were used by the Prince Consort to establish a permanent centre for the study of the applied arts and sciences; the enterprise survives today in the South Kensington museums of natural history, science, and decorative and applied arts (*see pp143-145*), and in three colleges (of art, music and science). After the Exhibition, the Palace was moved to Sydenham and used as an exhibition centre until it burned down in 1936.

ZEPPELINS ATTACK FROM THE SKIES

London entered the 20th century as the capital of the largest empire in history. Its wealth and power were there for all to see in grandstanding monuments such as Tower Bridge (*see p97*) and the Midland Grand Hotel at St Pancras Station (*see p106*), both of which married the retro stylings of High Gothic with modern iron and steel technology. During the brief reign of Edward VII (1901-10), London regained some of the gaiety and glamour it had lacked in the later years of Victoria's reign. Parisian chic came to London with the opening of the Ritz (*see p197*); Regent Street's Café Royal hit the heights as a meeting place for artists and writers; gentlemen's clubs proliferated; and 'luxury catering for the little man' was provided at the new Lyons Corner Houses (the Coventry Street branch held 4,500 people).

Road transport, too, was revolutionised. By 1911, horse-drawn buses were abandoned, replaced by motor cars, which put-putted around the city's streets, and the motor bus, introduced in 1904. Disruption came in the form of devastating air raids during World War I (1914-18). Around 650 people lost their lives in Zeppelin raids, but the greater impact was psychological – the mighty city had experienced helplessness.

CHANGE, CRISIS AND SHEER ENTERTAINMENT

Political change happened quickly after the war. At Buckingham Palace (*see p137*), the suffragettes had fiercely pressed the case for women's rights before hostilities began (*see below* **Time Machine**) and David Lloyd George's government averted revolution in 1918-19 by promising 'homes for heroes' (the returning soldiers). It didn't deliver, and in 1924 the Labour Party, led by Ramsay MacDonald, formed its first government.

A live-for-today attitude prevailed in the Roaring '20s among the young upper classes, who flitted from parties in Mayfair to dances at the Ritz. But this meant little to the mass of Londoners, who were suffering in the post-war slump. Civil disturbances, brought on by the high cost of living and rising unemployment, resulted in the nationwide General

IN CONTEXT

Time Machine 1910s

By Jenny Hall, curator of social history at the Museum of London.

Who's in control? In 1910, the London County Council assumes greater responsibility for governing London, particularly in areas such as education, health and housing.

Life expectancy Men, 52; women, 55.

Average wage 31s 6d.

Prices The maximum retail price of a 4lb loaf in 1912 is 6d.

Key concerns The death of a whole generation of young men during World War I: about 60,000 Londoners will die in the trenches.

Local legislation In 1918, the Representation of the People Act gives eight million women over 30 the right to vote in parliamentary elections for the first time, and also enfranchises all adult males over the age of 21 who are resident householders.

Flash point In May 1914, police stop suffragettes entering Buckingham Palace (*see p137*) in a bid to present a 'Votes for Women' petition to the King; 66 women are arrested, among them Emmeline Pankhurst.

Soho. *See p28*.

Strike of 1926, when the working classes downed tools en masse in support of striking miners. Prime Minister Baldwin encouraged volunteers to take over the public services, and the streets teemed with army-escorted food convoys, aristocrats running soup kitchens and students driving buses. After nine days of chaos, the strike was called off.

The economic situation only worsened in the early 1930s following the New York Stock Exchange crash of 1929. By 1931, more than three million Britons were jobless. During these years, the London County Council (LCC) began to have a greater impact on the city, clearing slums and building new houses, creating parks and taking control of public services. All the while, London's population increased, peaking at nearly 8.7 million in 1939. To accommodate the influx, the suburbs expanded, particularly to the north-west with the extension of the Metropolitan line to an area that became known as 'Metroland'. Identical gabled houses sprang up in their thousands.

At least Londoners were able to entertain themselves with film and radio. Not long after London's first radio broadcast was beamed from the roof of Marconi House in the Strand in 1922, families were gathering around huge Bakelite wireless sets to hear the BBC (the British Broadcasting Company; from 1927 the British Broadcasting Corporation). TV broadcasts started on 26 August 1936, when the first telecast went out from Alexandra Palace, but few Londoners could afford televisions until the 1950s.

BLITZKRIEG

Abroad, events had taken on a frightening impetus. Neville Chamberlain's policy of appeasement towards Hitler's Germany collapsed when the Germans invaded Poland. Britain duly declared war on 3 September 1939. The government implemented precautionary measures against air raids, including the evacuation of 600,000 children and pregnant mothers, but the expected bombing raids didn't happen during the autumn and winter of 1939-40 (the so-called 'Phoney War'). Then, in September 1940, hundreds of German bombers dumped explosives on east London and the docks, destroying entire streets and killing or injuring more than 2,000 in what was merely an opening salvo. The Blitz had begun. Raids on London continued for 57 consecutive nights, then intermittently for a further six months. Londoners reacted with stoicism, famously asserting 'business as usual'. After a final raid on 10 May 1941, the Nazis had left a third of the City and the East End in ruins.

From 1942 onwards, the tide began to turn, but Londoners had a new terror to face: the V1 or 'doodlebug'. Dozens of these deadly, explosive-packed, pilotless planes descended on the city in 1944, causing widespread destruction. Later in the year, the more powerful V2 rocket was launched. The last fell on 27 March 1945 in Orpington, Kent, around six weeks before Victory in Europe (VE Day) was declared on 8 May 1945.

'NEVER HAD IT SO GOOD'

World War II left Britain almost as shattered as Germany. Soon after VE Day, a general election was held and Winston Churchill was defeated by the Labour Party under Clement Attlee. The new government established the National Health Service in 1948, and began a massive nationalisation programme that included public transport, electricity, gas, postal and telephone services. For most people, however, life remained regimented and austere. In war-ravaged London, local authorities struggled with a critical shortage of housing. Prefabricated bungalows provided a temporary solution for some (60 years later, six prefabs on the Excalibur estate in Catford, south-east London, were given protection as buildings of historic interest), but the huge new high-rise housing estates that the planners devised proved unpopular with their residents.

There were bright spots. London hosted the Olympics in 1948; three years later came the Festival of Britain, resulting in the first full redevelopment of the riverside site into the South Bank (now Southbank) Centre (*see p73*). As the 1950s progressed, life and prosperity returned, leading Prime Minister Harold Macmillan in 1957 to proclaim that 'most of our people have never had it so good'. However, many Londoners were leaving. The population dropped by half a million in the late 1950s, causing a labour shortage that prompted huge recruitment drives in Britain's former colonies. London Transport and the National Health Service were both particularly active in encouraging West Indians to emigrate to Britain. Unfortunately, as the Notting Hill race riots of 1958 illustrated, the welcome these new immigrants received was rarely friendly. Still, there were several areas of tolerance: Soho (*photo p26*), for instance, which became famous for its mix of cultures and the café and club life they brought with them.

THE SWINGING '60S
By the mid 1960s, London had started to swing. The innovative fashions of Mary Quant and others broke the stranglehold Paris had on couture: boutiques blossomed along the King's Road, while Biba set the pace in Kensington. Carnaby Street (*see p115*) became a byword for hipness as the city basked in its new-found reputation as music and fashion capital of the world – made official, it seemed, when *Time* magazine devoted its front cover to 'swinging London' in 1966. The year of student unrest in Europe, 1968, saw the first issue of *Time Out* hit the streets in August; it was a fold-up sheet, sold for 5d. The decade ended with the Rolling Stones playing a free gig in Hyde Park that drew around 500,000 people.

Then the bubble burst. Many Londoners remember the 1970s as a decade of economic strife, the decade in which the IRA began its bombing campaign on mainland Britain. After the Conservatives won the general election in 1979, Margaret Thatcher instituted an economic policy that cut public services and widened the gap between rich and poor. Riots in Brixton (1981) and Tottenham (1985) were linked to unemployment and heavy-handed policing, keenly felt in London's black communities. The Greater London Council (GLC), led by Ken Livingstone, mounted vigorous opposition to the government with a series of populist measures, but it was abolished in 1986.

The replacement of Thatcher by John Major in October 1990 signalled a short-lived upsurge of hope among Londoners. A riot in Trafalgar Square had helped to see off both Maggie and her inequitable Poll Tax, yet the early 1990s were scarred by continuing recession and more IRA terrorist attacks.

THINGS CAN ONLY GET BETTER?
In May 1997, the British people ousted the Tories and gave Tony Blair's Labour Party the first of three election victories, but enthusiasm waned. The government hoped the Millennium Dome (now the O2; *see p320*) would be a 21st-century rival to the 1851 Great Exhibition. It wasn't, and ate £1 billion on the way to becoming a national joke.

The millennium saw Ken Livingstone return to power as London's first directly elected mayor and head of the new Greater London Assembly (GLA). Livingstone was re-elected in 2004 for a second term, a thumbs-up for first-term policies that included a congestion charge that sought to ease traffic by forcing drivers to pay £5 (now more) to enter the city centre. Summer 2005 brought elation, as London won the bid to host the 2012 Olympic and Paralympic Games (*see pp42-45* **And the Winner Is...**), and devastation, as bombs on tube trains and a bus killed 52 people and injured 700.

Aided by support from the suburbs that Livingstone had neglected, thatch-haired Conservative Boris Johnson became mayor in 2008 with a healthy majority. His rule so far has been characterised by flashy new schemes – a ban on alcohol consumption on public transport, the introduction of Cycle Superhighways and a cheap bike rental scheme – but doubts remain about his substance and ability to deliver more than an entertaining speech. The cuts to public services being instituted by the country's new government, a coalition of Conservatives and Liberals that took power when the 2010 General Election resulted in a hung parliament, may make things difficult for Johnson (*see pp30-33* **London Today**), since the Labour vote remained strong in London. But ensuring a smooth run-up to the 2012 Games will remain his sternest test, as 'two years to go' turns rapidly into just one.

Key Events

London in brief.

43 The Romans invade; the settlement of Londinium is founded.
61 Boudicca burns Londinium; the city is rebuilt and made provincial capital.
200 A city wall is built.
410 Roman troops evacuate Britain.
c600 Saxon London is built to the west.
841 The Norse raid for the first time.
c871 The Danes occupy London.
886 Alfred the Great takes London.
1013 The Danes take back London.
1042 Edward the Confessor builds a palace and 'West Minster' upstream.
1066 William I is crowned in Westminster Abbey.
1078 The Tower of London is begun.
1123 St Bart's Hospital is founded.
1197 Henry Fitzalwin is the first mayor.
1215 The mayor signs the Magna Carta.
1240 First Parliament at Westminster.
1290 Jews are expelled from London.
1348 The Black Death arrives.
1381 The Peasants' Revolt.
1397 Richard Whittington is Lord Mayor.
1476 William Caxton sets up the first printing press at Westminster.
1534 Henry VIII cuts Britain off from the Catholic Church.
1555 Martyrs burned at Smithfield.
1565 Sir Thomas Gresham proposes the Royal Exchange.
1572 First known map of London.
1599 The Globe Theatre opens.
1605 Guy Fawkes's plot to blow up James I fails.
1642 The start of the Civil War.
1649 Charles I is executed; Cromwell establishes Commonwealth.
1664 Beginning of the Great Plague.
1666 The Great Fire.
1675 Building starts on the new St Paul's Cathedral.
1694 The Bank of England is set up.
1710 St Paul's is completed.
1766 The city wall is demolished.
1773 The Stock Exchange is founded.
1824 The National Gallery is founded.
1833 The London Fire Brigade is set up.

1836 The first passenger railway opens; Charles Dickens publishes *The Pickwick Papers*, his first novel.
1843 Trafalgar Square is laid out.
1851 The Great Exhibition takes place.
1858 The Great Stink: pollution in the Thames reaches hideous levels.
1863 The Metropolitan line opens as the world's first underground railway.
1866 London's last major cholera outbreak; the Sanitation Act is passed.
1868 The last public execution is held at Newgate prison (now the Old Bailey).
1884 Greenwich Mean Time is established as a global standard.
1888 Jack the Ripper prowls the East End; London County Council is created.
1890 The Housing Act enables the LCC to clear the slums; the first electric underground railway opens.
1897 Motorised buses are introduced.
1908 London hosts the Olympic Games for the first time.
1915 Zeppelins begin three years of bombing raids on London.
1940 The Blitz begins.
1948 London again hosts the Olympic Games; forerunner of the Paralympics, the Stoke Mandeville Games are organised in Buckinghamshire by neurologist Sir Ludwig Guttman.
1951 The Festival of Britain is held.
1952 The last 'pea-souper' smog.
1953 Queen Elizabeth II is crowned.
1981 Riots in Brixton.
1982 The last London docks close.
1986 The GLC is abolished.
1992 One Canada Square tower opens on Canary Wharf.
2000 Ken Livingstone becomes London's first directly elected mayor; Tate Modern and the London Eye open.
2005 The city wins its bid to host the 2012 Games; suicide bombers kill 52 on public transport.
2008 Boris Johnson becomes mayor.
2010 Hung parliament leads to new Conservative–Liberal coalition.

IN CONTEXT

London Today

Which way will London look as it climbs out of recession?

TEXT: PETER WATTS

London doesn't know which way to look at the moment. Certainly towards the London 2012 development (*see pp53-59*), which stands like a beacon on the banks of the River Lee, drawing the eye – and the city's focus – to the east. The city is also looking backwards, enviously over its shoulder to the recent past when money flowed and anything seemed possible. When it looks forward – which it does, this is still a forward-looking city – it does so nervously, anticipating a difficult future of rising unemployment and increasing inequality, where harsh financial realities will have an impact on key areas such as transport and the arts.

London is even starting to look a little southwards. The extended East London Line was reopened in summer 2010, crossing the River Thames to join Crystal Palace in the south with Dalston in the north-east. The line is due to be further extended to Highbury & Islington this spring, providing a rare means of linking north, east and south London.

On opening, the East London Line was hastily marketed as the Culture Line in laboured celebration of the various museums and galleries along its length (and skating over the fact that London has so many museums and galleries, any tube line could be rechristened thus). It is tempting to see this as a valedictory salute to the early 2000s, a golden age when it seemed there was cash enough to fund any cultural or transport scheme. Things look very different now.

Peter Watts is a freelance journalist who writes for Prospect *and the* New Statesman, *and blogs about London at http:// greatwenlondon. wordpress.com.*

HIGHS AND LOWS

These days in London, things are done on the cheap. Numerous tube improvements have been put back until the gravy train returns, while many museums and galleries – Tate Modern and the National Maritime Museum among them – will be thankful their ambitious plans for redevelopments and extensions were instigated before recession began to bite into arts funding. Others have been less fortunate, such as the British Film Institute, whose plans for new offices and a cinema have been stymied by the withdrawal of government support. It's the same story in the City, where the rush to build iconic high-rise tower blocks along the lines of the Gherkin is beginning to look like childish attention-seeking, even as Heron Tower – currently the tallest building in the City – approaches completion and the nearby Pinnacle begins its 945-foot ascent.

The most vainglorious of all is across the river from the City in London Bridge. When the Shard is completed in 2012, it will be the largest building in the European Union. It's part funded by money from Qatar, the Gulf State whose investment arm bought Harrods in 2010 and has an interest in a number of other London developments. Rich Russians and Arabs continue to treat London as both playground and investment opportunity, but the morality of this no longer goes unchallenged. London's increasing inequality became the focus of a newspaper campaign, when its only daily, the *Evening Standard* – not known as a friend to poorer Londoners – launched a campaign about 'the dispossessed', looking at the extremes of poverty present in most London boroughs. This isn't something likely to get better soon.

The state of the country's finances has meant that Boris Johnson, London's Conservative mayor, has found himself in the curious – but not unfamiliar – position – of having to defend the city he represents against the party he stands for. Not that Johnson doesn't enjoy such contradictions, or miss any opportunity to continue his impish rivalry with old schoolchum, Prime Minister David Cameron. Johnson has found that being mayor of a cosmopolitan, anti-authoritarian and largely liberal city like London means he often has to stand to the left of typical Conservative policy, while his own fondness for mischief-making has seen him make a number of statements that directly challenge party policy – arguing, for example, that it would be 'madness' to 'starve' the city of funding. For his part, Cameron isn't shy of making things difficult for his potential rival, Johnson being the only Tory with the charisma and popular support to be able to present a challenge to the PM should the occasion arise.

ON YOUR BIKES

Despite all this potential for fun and grandstanding, and given his all-or-nothing verbal style, Johnson's policies for London continue to be disappointingly limp. Bikes were the focus of 2010, as London strived to become as bike-friendly as some of its counterpart European cities. (London is always trying, in different ways, to be more European.) First Johnson introduced two 'Cycle Superhighways', a series of routes from outer to inner London that look like giant blue cycle lanes. They are meant to provide a safe and direct way into town for cyclists, but have been called 'pointless', 'ludicrously bad' and 'actively dangerous' by the *Telegraph*'s Andrew Gilligan, usually one of Boris's biggest cheerleaders. Thirteen more superhighways, sponsored by Barclays at a time when banks are hardly at their most popular, are due to be painted on our roads by 2015.

More promising is the £140m Cycle Hire Scheme (*see p339* **Cycle City**). Despite teething troubles, the scheme was quickly dubbed 'the bikes that saved Boris' by 853, a well-reputed London blogger. Hailed as Johnson's flagship policy, Boris's Bikes could be his answer to predecessor Ken Livingstone's era-defining Congestion Charge – fittingly, since Livingstone who proposed the cycle hire idea before he was unseated.

Johnson's other big idea, his 'new Routemaster', a bus specially designed to replace the beloved hop-on, hop-off double-deckers of a thousand cheesy films, is due to hit our streets by 2012. Early impressions on that particular white elephant have been underwhelming (*see p130* **On Routie to the Future**).

NEW MONEY AND GETTING CLEAN

The Cycle Hire Scheme is heavily marketed by Barclays (which paid £25m for the privilege), one of the corporate sponsors that both Johnson and Cameron hope will help fill the funding hole left by a retreating state. It is surely no coincidence that shortly after the severity of the cuts in public funding became clear, art collector Charles Saatchi made a big splash by announcing he was giving his Chelsea gallery and 200 works of contemporary art (among them key works by Damien Hirst and Tracey Emin) to the nation, perhaps as a way of chivvying along other patrons who the government hopes will take over the state's role in funding the arts. For their part, potential patrons have pointed out that they are already helping as much as they can in the absence of US-style tax breaks and given the effect of the country's flatlining economy on their own businesses. This is one circle that can't be squared. The details of Saatchi's largesse are proving difficult to work out, but he plans a major retrospective – showing the works the grateful nation is about to receive – in 2012.

The hand of state investment can be seen, carrying over from the Labour government ousted in May 2010, in some of the city's major construction works. One example, of course, is the London 2012 Olympic and Paralympic Games (*see pp53-59*). The other is Crossrail, a new train line due for completion in 2017 that will link east and west London. Crossrail is currently responsible for much of the building work you'll see around the place, most notably at the east end of Oxford Street but also at critical points including Canary Wharf and Farringdon. Various local regeneration schemes are also under way, among them a long-awaited £18m scheme to clean up tatty Leicester Square, which has resulted in two promising new hotels – the luxury chain W Hotel and a boutique hotel by restaurateur Fergus Henderson, whose original St John restaurant was integral to helping people recognise that London's centre had drifted east from the West End to beyond Farringdon Road.

The west isn't quite dead, at least as far as chasing the tourist dollar is concerned. In the very heart of the old West End, Soho is facing one of its periodic delousings. Drug users and dealers are being targeted alongside sex workers in a Westminster Council scheme that intends to clean up Soho by, yes, 2012. It's a future-looking policy, but also a blast from the past. Campaigners have been trying to get the grime out of Soho since the Victorian era. In that sense, it's typical of this confused climate, in which Londoners simultaneously look east and south, backwards and forwards. No wonder we're all feeling a bit dizzy.

The **Shard**.

IN CONTEXT

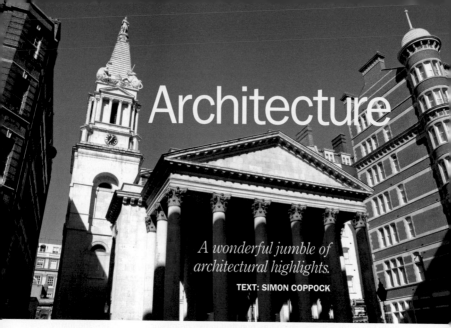

Architecture

A wonderful jumble of architectural highlights.

TEXT: SIMON COPPOCK

For the first decade of this century, it seemed every central London street was obliged by some arcane law to engage a cluster of cranes. Then the recession made loans expensive, property returns unpredictable and investors wary. Suddenly, the city's mania for redevelopment seemed to be over.

After the shock, some reality. News of projects – notably any tall buildings – hits the press when planning permission is sought, but the buildings might take three years from site-clearance to topping out. So several monster blocks that outraged columnists are only now becoming visible. Renzo Piano's 1,004-foot Shard is one of them, now looming over London Bridge despite completion not being due until 2012.

For all the annual top ten lists of loathed new buildings, the best modern architecture is taken to the city's heart. Some is swiftly loved (the Gherkin a classic example), other buildings become favourites over time: Centre Point, the BT Tower, the Barbican and the National Theatre are once-hated structures that increasingly find themselves dearly loved.

None of this is new. In the 17th century, the authorities objected to Sir Christopher Wren's magnificent St Paul's Cathedral because it looked far too Roman Catholic for their Anglican sensibilities. This year, other sensibilities will be offended by Jean Nouvel's 'groundscraper' One New Change, a block of shops and offices right opposite the cathedral.

In fact, this city's defining characteristic is its aesthetically unhappy mix of buildings. As it always has been, London is a mess of historic bits and modern bobs, giving the city's built landscape a unique capacity to surprise and delight.

THE NEW CITY

Modern London sprang into being after the Great Fire of 1666. The Fire destroyed four-fifths of the City of London, burning 13,200 houses and 89 churches. The devastation was commemorated by Sir Christopher Wren's 202-foot **Monument** (*see p96*), recently renovated, but many of the finest buildings in the City still stand as testament to the talents of Wren, the architect of the great remodelling, and his successors.

London was a densely populated place built largely of wood, and fire control was primitive. It was only after the three-day inferno that the authorities insisted on a few basic regulations. Brick and stone became the construction materials of choice, and key streets were widened to act as firebreaks. Despite grand, classical proposals from several architects, Wren among them, London reshaped itself around its old street pattern, with buildings that survived the Fire standing as monuments to earlier ages. Chief of these was the Norman **Tower of London** (*see p97*), begun soon after William's 1066 conquest and extended over the next 300 years; the Navy saved the Tower from the flames by blowing up surrounding houses before the inferno could reach it.

Another longstanding building, **Westminster Abbey** (*see p133*) was begun in 1245 when the site lay far outside London's walls; it was completed in 1745 by Nicholas Hawksmoor's west towers. The abbey is the most French of England's Gothic churches, but the chapel begun by Henry VII is pure Tudor. Centuries later, Washington Irving gushed: 'Stone seems, by the winning labour of the chisel, to have been robbed of its weight and density, suspended aloft, as if by magic.'

St Bartholomew-the-Great.

IN CONTEXT

Spotter's Guide to Tudor Windows

An ancient architectural style made new friends in the 19th century.

Reputedly built so he could keep tabs on his monks praying without having to leave his quarters, Prior Bolton's oriel window at **St Bartholomew-the-Great** (*see p88*) is a classic example of the characteristic Renaissance design. The bay window bears the Prior's rebus (an arrow from a crossbow piercing a wine barrel; bolt + tun = bolton), and shows a parabolic arch (a flatter curve than the more steeply curving Gothic arch) with a plain trefoil design at the top of the upper panes. The form found popularity with Victorian architects, as they sought a style sufficiently British to support their imperial aims; this is why oriel windows are so common in London's institutional buildings.

A LATE FLOWERING

The European Renaissance came late to Britain, making its London debut with Inigo Jones's 1622 **Banqueting House** (see p132). The sumptuously decorated ceiling, added in 1635 by Rubens, celebrated the Stuart monarchy's Divine Right to rule, although 14 years later King Charles I provided a greater spectacle as he was led from the room and beheaded on a stage outside. Tourists also have Jones to thank for **St Paul's Covent Garden** (see p109) and the immaculate **Queen's House** (see p167), but they're not his only legacies. He mastered the art of piazzas (such as the one at Covent Garden), porticos and pilasters, changing British architecture forever. His work influenced the careers of succeeding generations of architects and introduced a habit of venerating the past that it would take 300 years to kick.

Nothing cheers a builder like a natural disaster, and one can only guess at the relish with which Wren and co began rebuilding after the Fire. They brandished classicism like a new broom: the pointed arches of English Gothic were duly rounded off, Corinthian columns made an appearance and church spires became as complex, frothy and multi-layered as a wedding cake.

Wren blazed the trail with his daring plans for **St Paul's Cathedral** (see p87), spending an enormous (for the time) £500 on the oak model of his proposal. But the scheme, incorporating a Catholic dome rather than a Protestant steeple, was too Roman for the establishment and the design was rejected. Wren quickly produced a redesign and gained planning permission by incorporating a spire, only to set about a series of mischievous U-turns to give us the building, domed and heavily suggestive of an ancient temple, that's survived to this day.

Wren's baton was picked up by Nicholas Hawksmoor and James Gibbs, who benefited from a 1711 decree that 50 extra churches should be built (see below **Spotter's Guide**). Gibbs became busy around Trafalgar Square with the steepled Roman temple of **St Martin-in-the-Fields** (see p131), as well as the Baroque **St Mary-le-Strand** and the tower of **St Clement Danes** (for both, see pp110-111). His work was well received, but the more experimental Hawksmoor had a rougher ride. For one thing, not everyone admired his stylistic innovations; for another, even fewer approved of his financial planning, or lack of it: **St George's Bloomsbury** (see p105) cost three times its £10,000 budget and took 15 years to build.

Spotter's Guide to Baroque Spires

How Hawksmoor reinvented the English church.

Under the Fifty New Churches Act of 1711, which used a coal tax to fund the building of 'churches of stone… with Towers and Steeples', Nicholas Hawksmoor designed, in whole or part, eight new places of worship. Like Wren, Hawksmoor loved the classical temple, a style at odds with the Act's Anglican insistence on spires. **St George-in-the-East**, **St Anne Limehouse** and **St Mary Woolnoth** (see p91) are all unorthodox resolutions of this contradiction, but the 'spire' of **St George's Bloomsbury** (see p105; photo p34) is the barmiest. Aping the Mausoleum of Halicarnassus,

Hawksmoor created a peculiar stepped pyramid design, plopped a giant statue of George I in a toga on top and then added unicorns and lions.

Hawksmoor's ruinous overspends (St Anne's was so costly no money was left for the rector's salary) was one reason why just a dozen of the proposed 50 churches were built. Still, the four corner towers of Thomas Archer's **St John's, Smith Square** (see p317) and the spire 'portholes' of **St Martin-in-the-Fields** (see p131) today provide further delightful evidence of Baroque invention.

One of a large family of Scottish architects, Robert Adam found himself at the forefront of a movement that came to see Italian Baroque as a corruption of the real thing, with architectural exuberance dropped in favour of a simpler interpretation of ancient forms. The best surviving work of Adam and his brothers James, John and William can be found in London's great suburban houses **Osterley Park**, **Syon House** (see p179) and **Kenwood House** (see p151), but the project for which they're most famous no longer stands: the cripplingly expensive Adelphi housing estate off the Strand. Most of the complex was pulled down in the 1930s and replaced by an office block, and only a small part of the original development survives; it's now the **Royal Society of Arts** (8 John Adam Street, Covent Garden, WC2N 6EZ).

SOANE AND NASH

Just as the first residents were moving into the Adelphi, a young unknown called John Soane was embarking on a domestic commission in Ireland. It was never completed, but Soane eventually returned to London and went on to build the **Bank of England** (see p92) and **Dulwich Picture Gallery** (see p163). The Bank was demolished between the wars, leaving only the perimeter walls and depriving us of Soane's masterpiece, though his gracious Stock Office has been reconstructed in the museum. A further glimpse of what those bankers might have enjoyed can be gleaned from his house, the quirky **Sir John Soane's Museum** (see p99), an exquisite architectural experiment.

A near-contemporary of Soane's, John Nash was a less talented architect, but his contributions – among them the inner courtyard of **Buckingham Palace** (see p137), the **Theatre Royal Haymarket** (Haymarket, SW1Y 4HT) and **Regent Street** (W1) – have proved comparable to those of Wren. Regent Street began as a proposal to link the West End to the planned park further north, as well as a device to separate the toffs of Mayfair from the riff-raff of Soho; in Nash's own words, a 'complete separation between the Streets occupied by the Nobility and Gentry, and the narrow Streets and meaner houses occupied by mechanics and the trading part of the community'.

By the 1830s, the classical form of building had been established in England for some 200 years, but this didn't prevent a handful of upstarts from pressing for change. In 1834, the **Houses of Parliament** (see p132) burned down, leading to the construction of Sir Charles Barry's Gothic masterpiece. Barry sought out Augustus Welby Northmore Pugin. Working alongside Barry, if not always in agreement with him (of Barry's symmetrical layout, he famously remarked, 'All Grecian, sir. Tudor details on a classic body'), Pugin created a Victorian fantasy that would later be condemned as the Disneyfication of history.

GETTING GOTHIC

This was the beginning of the Gothic Revival, a move to replace what was considered foreign and pagan with something that was native and Christian. Architects would often decide that buildings weren't Gothic enough; as with the **Guildhall**'s 15th-century Great Hall (see p92), which gained its corner turrets and central spire only in 1862. The argument between Classicists and Goths erupted in 1857, when the government hired Sir George Gilbert Scott, a leading light of the Gothic movement, to design a new home for the Foreign Office. Scott's design incensed anti-Goth Lord Palmerston, then prime minister, whose diktats prevailed. But Scott exacted his revenge by building an office in which everyone hated working, and by going on to construct Gothic edifices all over town, among them the **Albert Memorial** (see p143) and the impressive frontage of what is now **St Pancras International** train station (see p106), due to be returned to its original function as a hotel this year.

St Pancras was completed in 1873, after the Midland Railway commissioned Scott to build a London terminus that would dwarf that of its rivals next door at King's Cross. Using the project as an opportunity to show his mastery of the Gothic form, Scott built an asymmetrical castle that obliterated views of the train shed behind, itself an engineering marvel completed earlier by William Barlow. Other charming and imposing neo-Gothic buildings around the city include the **Royal Courts of Justice** (*see p83*), the **Natural History Museum** (*see p143*) and **Tower Bridge** (*see p97*). Under the influence of the Arts and Crafts movement, medievalism morphed into such mock Tudor buildings as the wonderful half-timbered **Liberty** department store (*see p253*).

BEING MODERN

World War I and the coming of modernism led to a spirit of renewal and a starker aesthetic. **Freemasons' Hall** (*see p110*) and the BBC's **Broadcasting House** (*see p118*) are good examples of the pared-down style of the 1920s and '30s, but perhaps the finest example of between-the-wars modernism can be found at **London Zoo** (*see p121*). Built by Russian émigré Bertold Lubetkin and the Tecton group, the spiral ramps of the Penguin Pool were a showcase for the possibilities of concrete. The material was also put to good use on the London Underground, enabling the quick, cheap building of cavernous spaces with sleek lines and curves. There was nothing quick or cheap about the art deco **Daily Express** building (*see below* **Spotter's Guide**).

The bombs of World War II left large areas of London ruined, providing another opportunity for builders to cash in. Lamentably, the city was little improved by the

Daily Express Building.

Spotter's Guide to Art Deco

London wasn't short of curves in the Roaring '20s.

Dating from the mid 1920s, the art deco architectural style favoured streamlined geometrical simplicity, in keeping with the Jazz Age's wide-eyed belief in a bright and beautiful future. From tube stations to cinemas, London has some prime examples of the style, but one of the best art deco buildings is the old **Daily Express Building** (121-128 Fleet Street, the City). Built in 1931, it's an early example of 'curtain wall' construction, its radical black vitrolite and glass façade (by Sir Owen Williams) hung on an internal frame, and demonstrates the modernist belief that form should reflect function. Public access is restricted to very occasional tours (sometimes during Open-City events; *see p283*), but stick your head around the door to glimpse the Robert Atkinson interior of plaster reliefs, with an oval staircase and lots of silver and gilt. The *Architects' Journal* called it a 'defining monument of 1930s London'.

rebuild; in many cases, it was left worse off. The destruction left the capital with a dire housing shortage, so architects were given a chance to demonstrate the grim efficiency with which they could house large numbers of families in tower blocks.

There were post-war successes, however, including the **Royal Festival Hall** (*see p73*) on the South Bank. The sole survivor of the 1951 Festival of Britain, the RFH was built to celebrate the end of the war and the centenary of the Great Exhibition, held in 1851 and responsible for the foundation in South Kensington of the Natural History Museum, the Science Museum and the V&A. Next door to the RFH, the **Hayward** gallery (*see p75*) is an exemplar of the 1960s vogue for Brutalist architecture, a style more thoroughly explored at the **Barbican** (*see p89*), loved by many but never fully rehabilitated from the vilification it received in the years after it opened in 1982.

HERE COME THE STARCHITECTS

The 1970s and '80s offered up a pair of alternatives to concrete: postmodernism and high-tech. The former is represented by César Pelli's blandly monumental **One Canada Square** (*see p158*) in Docklands, an oversized obelisk that's perhaps the archetypal expression of late '80s architecture. Richard Rogers' high-tech **Lloyd's of London** building (*see p93*) is much more widely admired. A clever combination of commercial and industrial aesthetics that adds up to one of the most significant British buildings since the war, it was mocked on completion in 1986, but outclasses newer projects.

Apart from Rogers, the city's most visible contemporary architect has been Norman Foster, whose **City Hall** and **30 St Mary Axe** (aka 'the Gherkin'; *see p40* **Spotter's Guide**) have caught up with Big Ben and black taxis as movie shorthand for 'Welcome to London!'. His prolific practice set new standards in sports design with the soaring arch of the new **Wembley Stadium** (*see p335*); the exercise in complexity that is the £100 million Great Court at the **British Museum** (*see p102*) did the same for London's cultural gem. The Great Court is the largest covered square in Europe, but every one of its 3,300 triangular glass panels is unique.

Much new architecture is to be found cunningly inserted into old buildings. Herzog & de Meuron's fabulous transformation of a Bankside power station into **Tate Modern** (*see p76*) is perhaps the most famous example – the firm aims to repeat its success with an ambitious new extension. Due to be completed in 2012, it will look something like a pyramid folded out of origami. Equally ground-breaking was Future Systems' NatWest Media Centre at **Lord's Cricket Ground** (*see p149*). Built from aluminium in a boatyard and perched high above the pitch, it's one of London's most daring constructions to date, especially given the traditional setting. More recently, the arty new **Town Hall Hotel & Apartments** (*see p204*) redeveloped an Edwardian town hall in Bethnal Green by adding a new top floor under a laser-cut metal 'veil', but keeping intact as many characterful aspects of the exterior and interior as possible, right down to brass fire-hose reels and lift numbers.

LOCAL COLOUR AND OLYMPIC FEATS

Architecture hasn't all been about headline projects and eye-troubling commercial developments. Will Alsop's multicoloured **Peckham Library** (122 Peckham Hill Street, SE15 5JR) has helped redefine community architecture, as did David Adjaye's later **Idea Stores** (www.ideastore.co.uk) in Poplar (1 Vesey Path, East India Dock Road, E14 6BT) and Whitechapel (321 Whitechapel Road, E1 1BU); the crisp aesthetic of these buildings is a world away from the traditional Victorian library. Adjaye's inspiration in shop design is even more explicit in the **Rivington Place** gallery (Rivington Place, Shoreditch, EC2A 3BA), with the main entrance tucked to the side so that passers-by are drawn into the main gallery by a display window – just like that of a department store. The subtle Robbrecht en Daem expansion of **Whitechapel Gallery** (*see p155*) into the stylistically very different former library next door reversed the process, giving a new democratic openness to a pair of landmark Victorian buildings.

IN CONTEXT

PLANNING THE FUTURE

With so much going on in so many parts of town, it's difficult to get a grip on the whole picture. The magnificent Open-City London festival (*see p283*) does a terrific job of getting locals engaged with their built environment, but for an overview of what the city might look like in a few years' time, get off the tube at Goodge Street and visit **New London Architecture** (*see p307* **Inside Track**). The centre's impressive centrepiece is a 39-foot-long scale model of London, stretching from Battersea Power Station in the south, north up to King's Cross and out to Docklands and Stratford in the east. Currently, the dozens of unbuilt schemes on the model include **One Blackfriars Road**, a spectacular 560-foot hotel and residential building (topped off with a public gallery) that will appear near Tate Modern, probably by 2012.

On the model, you'll note two huge areas of development, one in the north, one in the east. In the north, the transformation of King's Cross is continuing apace. St Pancras International Station and **Kings Place** (*see p318* **Profile**) – the first of a series of cultural edifices, to be joined by the University of the Arts London, which takes over a redeveloped Victorian granary in 2012 – are just the vanguard of the 67-acre brownfield redevelopment known as King's Cross Central. As well as the arts and education, two dozen new streets are being built to service 2,000 new homes. Even more impressive is the **Olympic Park** (*see pp53-59*). The new stadiums that have sprung up in this formerly disregarded corner of east London are already structurally complete, and the tours and cultural events at the site have been hugely popular. With London 2012 large on the horizon, it looks like London's builders and developers will be kept busy for quite a while longer.

Spotter's Guide to City Skyscrapers

The City shoots for the skies.

When some wag dubbed Lord Foster's 40-storey Swiss Re Tower, now **30 St Mary Axe**, 'the Erotic Gherkin' in 2004, it wasn't with fondness. Yet the name became such a badge of honour that the City planners now give every new skyscraper a nickname: the Walkie-

30 St Mary Axe.

Talkie, the Helter Skelter, Darth Vader's Helmet. **Lloyd's of London**, completed to rival architect Lord Rogers' design in 1986, has never had a nickname and never been as loved as the Gherkin, despite its innovative inside-out design. Perhaps Rogers' 48-storey **122 Leadenhall Street** ('the Cheese Grater'), under way right opposite, will win his work some affection. But our money's on the City's current tallest building at 110 Bishopsgate, standing a proud 755 feet (including radio mast) and 46 storeys tall. Due to open this year, **Heron Tower** is by no means as beautiful as Lloyd's or the Gherkin, but – like ugly **Tower 42** (*see p93*), just over the junction – has the advantage of regular public access. The designers thoughtfully included a 'Restaurant & Sky Bar' on Levels 38-40, reached by half a dozen exterior glass lifts that promise exhilarating views.

London 2012

Aquatics Centre. *See p56.*

And the Winner Is...

London 2012, now and the future.

TEXT: REBECCA TAYLOR

The date is 6 July 2005; the place Trafalgar Square. At precisely 12.49pm, the face of International Olympic Committee President Jacques Rogge beams out across the square, live from Singapore, on an enormous screen erected beneath Nelson's Column. The thousands of expectant Londoners who have turned up today to witness history in the making hold their breath. 'The Games of the XXXth Olympiad in 2012 are awarded to the city of...', Rogge pauses, '... London.' The square erupts with yelps of delight. 'Well done, London,' he adds later at a press conference. 'It will be a superb Games and will strengthen the Olympics.'

Anyone who was in Trafalgar Square amid the noise and celebrations of that momentous day would be forgiven for thinking that the city had won through force of will alone. In fact, the win was the culmination of years of preparation, with the final vote only wrestled from the bookies' favourite, Paris, at the last, nail-biting, minute (54 votes to Paris's 50). So how did London do it?

Rebecca Taylor is the news editor of Time Out *magazine.*

'Give us the Games, and one of the world's great capital cities will be transformed.'

WINNING THE BID

The city's energetic and visionary bid owed much of its success to the efforts of one man: Lord Coe. Coe, plain Sebastian when he claimed double Olympic 1500m gold in 1980 and 1984, expertly combined his athletics experience with political nous, culminating in a passionate final plea to the IOC voters in Singapore. There, Coe emphasised the importance of youth participation to the future of sport, introducing 30 young people from the capital to the audience as a means of illustrating the Olympic Movement's ability to inspire.

There were other influential ambassadors on board: Nelson Mandela and David Beckham had helped promote the bid, the Queen spoke to the IOC inspectors over dinner at Buckingham Palace, former mayor Ken Livingstone buried his differences with the then prime minister Tony Blair to present a united front. Blair even flew to Singapore to meet an estimated 30 members of the IOC in person.

The bid itself was impressive. Its aim: to revitalise sport for a new generation of Britons. It offered a new Athletics Stadium, Aquatics Centre and Velodrome (*see pp53-59* **Olympic Park**), but promised there would be no white elephants. It would also use famous landmarks (among them, The Royal Artillery Barracks, *see p60*) and existing venues (such as Wimbledon, *see p63*). It promised state-of-the-art transport links, such as the Javelin®, a high-speed rail service running from St Pancras International to Stratford Regional in just seven minutes. Plans already under way to link Hackney to the tube network via the East London Line, upgrades to the North London Line and the Javelin® link contributed to a transport package that convinced inspectors the Games would be accessible. And an ambitious Cultural Olympiad, with events running across the country, would celebrate the best of UK arts and culture.

REGENERATION AND A SUSTAINABLE GAMES

If there was one buzzword that symbolised the bid, it was 'legacy'. The Olympic Park (*see p53*) was to be built in the deprived area of Stratford in east London. Neglected by developers and largely unvisited by tourists, east London had long been characterised by a mix of grimy urban decay, grey industrial estates and stubby wasteland. The five boroughs that would incorporate the Olympic Park and other venues – Hackney, Waltham Forest, Newham, Greenwich and Tower Hamlets – accounted for the 'greatest cluster of deprivation in England and Wales', according to a report commissioned by the boroughs. The site for the Olympic Park was a wasteland of abandoned industrial buildings.

'The most enduring legacy of the Olympics will be the regeneration of an entire community for the direct benefit of everyone who lives there,' read London's 2004 bid. Once the Games were over, the aim was to use the park for thousands of new homes and businesses. The message was simple: give us the Games, and one of the world's great capital cities will be transformed.

It was a vision that chimed with the idea of a non-wasteful Games – 'the greenest Games in modern times', according to David Higgins, then Chief Executive of the Olympic Delivery Authority (ODA), the body responsible for building the venues. Environmental pledges included providing 20 per cent of electricity from renewable sources, avoiding sending waste to landfill, creating wildlife habitats (*see p45* **London Remade**) and transporting half of all building materials by rail. London was the only contender that proposed locating the Athletes' Village within the Olympic Park, allowing half of the competitors to walk to their events.

LONDON 2012

The bid's environmental aspirations were innovative as well as ambitious. The level of planning detail alone is staggering. The 80,000-seat Olympic Stadium (*see p53*), for example, uses a quarter of the steel that built its equivalent for Beijing 2008, thereby massively reducing the environmental costs of transport. There's a 'black water' treatment plant within the Park that converts sewage from under the Greenway (a cycling and walking route that runs along the huge Northern Outfall Sewer) into water that can be used for irrigation and flushing the toilets. Paving stones are porous to ensure water is caught in natural cleansing ponds. Footpaths are kept strictly to no more than a 1:21 gradient, with benches at regular intervals, so that the whole area is accessible to wheelchair-users and child buggies. An electricity generator reroutes its own waste heat to use elsewhere on the site for heating and cooling.

MAKING IT HAPPEN

The bid's far-reaching vision swung the vote, but the real test was to come: could a desolate chunk of east London be transformed into a stage for the best athletes on Earth? Just six years ago, the site of the Olympic Park was little more than a post-industrial sprawl. Today, the Olympic Stadium already seems long established. Its 'inside-out' design, with many amenities housed in pods surrounding the stadium, gives it a minimalist, functional look – a fitting symbol for a sleek, stripped-down Games. Nearby, the train line from Stratford International swerves close to the undulating line of the Aquatics Centre (*see p56*); the Athletes' Village sits against the curving backdrop of the Velodrome (*see p56*). The total visual effect is stunning.

Huge expanses of wetland, parks and wildflower meadows are taking root in what will become a spectacular green oasis. Toxins have been removed from the earth. The giant electrical pylons that once towered over the landscape have been demolished, their cables now buried below ground. What's more, the construction is likely to come in under the £9.3 billion budget – as well as being on time.

THE FUTURE

What of the bid-winning regeneration legacy? So far, the Athletes' Village looks very promising. Of the planned 2,818 new homes, 1,379 will be 'affordable housing', aimed at those on lower incomes. A new education campus will offer nursery, primary and secondary education; a state-of-the-art health centre will include a children's clinic, dentistry and optometry services. All are linked by courtyards, open spaces and parks.

The future of the Olympic Stadium will be announced in spring 2011. A number of bidders submitted proposals by the September 2010 deadline, among them two Premiership football clubs, West Ham and Tottenham Hotspur. Bids have also been sought for the International Broadcast Centre/Main Press Centre (IBC/MPC). The hope is that the IBC/MPC will attract high-profile companies that can provide media or high-tech employment to locals after the Games are over.

London 2012's environmental pledges have given impetus to emerging green technologies: Transport for London hopes to boost its current fleet of five emission-free, hydrogen-powered single-decker buses by 2012, and it is working on finding a manufacturer for a fleet of hydrogen-powered black taxi cabs in time to serve the Games. In addition, plans to extend the city's popular new cycle hire scheme – Boris Bikes (*see p339* **Cycle City**) – to include the Olympic Park have been announced.

As tickets for the sporting events go on sale in spring 2011, a palpable sense of excitement is beginning to build in a city that usually prides itself on its cynicism. One key remaining component for a truly successful Games is the spectators. It is here, perhaps, that London really has a chance to shine. Kofi Annan, former Secretary General of the United Nations, has suggested that the 2012 Games had a special advantage. This is a city, he said, where visiting competitors from countries all over the globe would be able to find willing support from London residents who share the same roots as them. London 2012 should be one heck of a party.

LONDON 2012

London Remade

How the 2012 Games are creating a whole new area of London.

John Hopkins, Project Sponsor for Parklands and Public Realm for the Olympic Delivery Authority (ODA), is justifiably proud: 'It will be very different to any park that anyone's seen before.' He's describing the extraordinarily complex work that has been going on in the Olympic Parklands, work that was almost entirely unnoticed until the wild flowers of the 'golden meadow' bloomed into the headlines in 2010.

From Hopkins' perspective, the Olympic Park (*see p53*) can be divided into two sections. Through the northern part, there's a single river, which he says was almost lost under 'factories, warehouses and dereliction – it was a huge Victorian tip site', the leftovers from a hundred years of damage caused by the Industrial Revolution. There the ODA is creating 45 hectares of intricate marshland habitat. Flood modelled to cope with 'a 100-year storm' (in effect, a rise in water levels of 4m), the new habitat protects 4,000 buildings from extreme weather. It also returns the area to an earlier natural state: 'It's really ironic,' says Hopkins,

'that when we ran the flood models, the only places that didn't flood were the marshes.'

In the southern part of the Olympic Park are the major sporting venues – set on islands between three rivers or channels: the Waterworks River, City Mill River and the River Lea. Here the difficulties are as much structural as environmental, with vast bridges to be built over railways and watercourses, and ground to be made accessible to every active user.

The traditions of even this largely neglected area of London have to be carefully negotiated, too, whether it's a matter of ensuring treasured war memorials are returned to Eton Manor (*see p57*) after redevelopment or protecting the area's industrial heritage. Hopkins mentions Carpenters Lock, which dates to the 1930s. It has been covered by one of the huge new Olympic Park bridges, but this particular bridge was designed with holes that encourage you to view the old lock beneath. A fit metaphor, in several ways, for the Olympic Park itself.

Discover the best of Britain...

Olympic City

London has proper Games pedigree.

On 27 July 2012, London will become the first city to host the modern Olympic Games for a third time. Yes, the Games originated in Athens in 776 BC, were revived there in 1896 and returned in 2004, but the London Games of 1908 and 1948 were pivotal in establishing the character and some cherished traditions of the modern Olympic Movement.

Nor is the United Kingdom's role confined to those two years. Key to the revival of the Games was the work of Dr William Penny Brookes, a Victorian educationist and believer in physical exercise as a means for moral improvement. He began staging a sporting competition inspired by the ancient Olympic Games in the tiny Shropshire hamlet of Much Wenlock from the 1850s. In 1890, this annual event was attended by Baron Pierre de Coubertin, who was inspired to organise the first modern Games.

The Paralympic Games also have their origins in this country: at Stoke Mandeville Hospital in Buckinghamshire the first wheelchair games were organised in 1948 by Sir Ludwig Guttmann, a doctor who worked with World War II veterans suffering from spinal injuries.

Peter Watts is a freelance journalist who writes for Prospect *and the* New Statesman, *and blogs about London at greatwenlondon. wordpress.com.*

Women's Archery at the **1908 Games**.

VOLCANIC INTERRUPTION

It isn't just the faded black-and-white photos of the 1908 Olympic Games that make it seem they were from a distant era. There was the inclusion of keenly contested events that from this distance seem rather quaint: Bicycle Polo (recently revived by Shoreditch hipsters), Tug-of-War, the Standing Long Jump. There was the sheer dominance of the hosts, who won 99 more medals than the second-placed United States. But the most amazing thing is that the 1908 Games happened at all.

The Games had originally been allocated to Rome but, when Vesuvius erupted in 1906, the Italian government felt it couldn't afford the cost. So London stepped in to save the day, hastily building an athletics stadium at White City, which was being redeveloped for the Franco-British Exhibition. It was an impressive arena, able to hold 70,000 spectators and with a swimming pool in the centre. Other venues included the All England Club at Wimbledon for Tennis (a role it will reprise for London 2012; *see p63*), Hurlingham for Polo and Queen's Club for Real Tennis.

There was a great deal about the 1908 Games that was novel. For the first time, athletes competed not as individuals, but in national teams (the first ever national flag parade inaugurated these Games). Many regulations were still being worked out, from

the length of running shorts to the rules for the 400m. Indeed, disagreement about whether a runner had to stay in lane in the 400m led to all three US competitors boycotting a re-run of the four-man final. British athlete Wyndham Halswelle thus won the only walkover in Olympic history. A make-it-happen attitude pervaded the Games: British middleweight Johnny Douglas won gold in the Boxing on a split decision decided by his father, who happened to be the referee, and the American Tug-of-War team was defeated by a team of Liverpudlian policemen.

The event that defined the 1908 Games was the Marathon. This was to begin at Windsor Castle, and King Edward VII and Queen Alexandra wanted it to end at the stadium. Problem. The accepted Marathon distance was 25 miles – that's the distance between Athens and Marathon, after all – but Windsor Castle was 26 miles from White City. So the length of the race was increased to accommodate the Royal Couple, plus an extra 385 yards so it could finish directly beneath the Royal Box. This became the established distance from 1924, but it was a mile too far for several competitors in the un-British summer heat of 1908. The race leader, Italian baker Dorando Pietri, collapsed inches from the end. He was helped over the finishing line by supporters –

and promptly disqualified. (As a consolation prize, Queen Alexandra gave Pietri a silver cup.) The race favourite, an Onondaga Indian from Canada called Tom Longboat, lasted just 19 miles, perhaps due to the champagne runners routinely supped.

THE AUSTERITY GAMES

If there is something charming about the can-do brio of competitors in 1908, the 1948 Olympic Games were played out against a much graver backdrop. Their predecessor had been the infamous Berlin Games of 1936, while the 1940 event would have been held, at the height of World War II, in Tokyo. After the war, it was felt Europe needed something to celebrate and London duly volunteered as host. Intended to be called the Reconciliation Games, the '48 Olympics became, in British folklore, the Austerity Games.

In Britain, rationing was even worse after 1945 than it had been during the war. To help out, all participants were asked to bring food: the United States team flew in white flour daily and ate steak, and it's said the French brought champagne. British athletes were given double rations, 5,467 calories a day – the same as dockers and miners, almost double the amount for ordinary Londoners. London was desperately short of housing after years of bombing and there was no money to build an Olympic Village, so male athletes lived in RAF camps in Richmond and Uxbridge, while the women stayed at Southlands College in West Drayton. A volunteer programme was for the first time established to help run the Games, and Wembley (*see p63*), the principal venue, was hastily converted into an athletics stadium. Other surviving venues include Earls Court (which London 2012 revisits, *see p59*) and the Herne Hill Velodrome (*see p338*).

The Opening Ceremony on 29 July was seen as a landmark occasion for the post-war world – many had believed there would never be another Games after '36 – and 2,500 pigeons were released as a symbol of its significance. Technological advances were also being made: the ceremony was broadcast live by the BBC (these were the first televised Games) and the result of the 100m final was the first determined by photo-finish (the equipment was in place, but unused, in '32 and '36).

The 1948 Games uncovered several heroes. One was Károly Takács, a Hungarian, who won gold in the Rapid-Fire Pistol event. Takacs' favoured right hand had been shattered by a grenade in the war, so he trained himself to shoot with his left. Another success was Bob Mathias, an American who

Jack Heid, USA, and Argentina's Clodomiro Cortoni in the 1,000m Sprint at **London 1948**; (*inset*) photo-finish timing at Wembley Stadium.

LONDON 2012

Micheline Ostermeyer – Discus champion and concert pianist.

LONDON 2012

won the Decathlon four months after taking up the sport. At 17, he became the youngest man to win an Olympic Athletics event. British weightlifter Jim Haldaway was more than a mere sporting hero: he weighed just four and a half stones when he was liberated from a Japanese prisoner-of-war camp, but won a bronze in the lightweight class.

The undoubted king and queen of the 1948 Games were Emil Zatopek and Fanny Blankers-Koen. Zatopek was a Czech long-distance runner, one of the best of all time, and he first made an impact at London 1948, winning the 10,000m in only his second ever race at the distance. His achievements four years later were even more impressive – golds at the 5,000m, 10,000m and Marathon.

Blankers-Koen was Dutch and probably the first great female athlete. Nicknamed the Flying Housewife, she won four gold medals (in the 100m, 200m, 400m and 4x100m relay) despite being (gasp) 30, (wince) married and (gulp) a mother of two. Another female success story was France's Micheline Ostermeyer, who won the Shot Put and Discus. Her day job: a concert pianist.

Birth of the Paralympic Games

How a global movement grew from one doctor's vision.

While the 1948 Games were happening in London, a small event took place in nearby Buckinghamshire that would later become the Paralympic Games. The 1948 International Wheelchair Games were organised at Stoke Mandeville Hospital for 16 ex-soldiers by Dr Ludwig Guttmann. Guttmann was responsible for a special unit treating those who had suffered spinal injuries in World War II.

A German-Jewish neurologist who fled the Nazis in the 1930s, Guttmann used sport as part of his rehabilitation programme. 'Paraplegia is not the end of the way,' he said. 'It is the beginning of a new life.' He encouraged the ex-servicemen to participate in sports including darts, billiards, skittles, polo and basketball. 'We're so bloody busy in this place, we haven't got time to be ill,' a patient is said to have remarked.

The Games began on 29 July, the same day as the London Olympic Games. The Stoke Mandeville Games were then held every year in the last week of July. Word spread quickly: the arrival in 1952 of Dutch athletes made it an international competition, and by 1960 it was no longer reserved for war veterans, with Guttmann taking 400 athletes in wheelchairs to compete alongside the Olympic Games in Rome.

From this, the new competition took its name – 'Paralympics' is an abbreviated form of 'Parallel Olympics' – and the Paralympic Games have followed every Olympic Games since. In 2012, 162 countries and 4,200 athletes are expected to take part in 20 sports.

Athletes are of mixed disabilities and events are split into different classes, depending on the capabilities of the competitors. For instance, Archery is open to amputees, those with cerebral palsy and wheelchair-users, and has three classes, two for standing athletes and one for wheelchair-users. There are also sports unique to the Paralympic Games, such as Boccia – pronounced 'botcha', it is a game like boules that was specifically designed to be played by those with cerebral palsy.

The Games returned to Stoke Mandeville in 1984 in a dual event shared with New York. The British section was at Stoke Mandeville Stadium, the national centre for disability sport where such home Paralympians as Baroness Tanni Grey-Thompson, multi-gold medallist, have trained. The street on which the stadium is located is called Guttmann Road, in tribute to the pioneering doctor who made the Paralympic Games possible.

LONDON 2012

Explore

What's where for the London 2012 Games.

An extraordinary transformation has been made to the mostly derelict, former industrial land between Stratford International station and the River Lea. In just a few years, a cluster of remarkable stadiums have sprung up – all due for completion in summer 2011 and already impressive in scale and design.

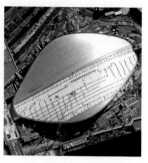

Unless you're lucky enough to get a place on a guided tour of the site, there's no access to the **Olympic Park** (*see right*) until the London 2012 Olympic and Paralympic Games are under way, but its riverside location makes for a fascinating day out on foot or by bicycle.

You can, of course, already visit the several historic venues that are also to be used in the 2012 Games. **Horse Guards Parade** (*see p59*), **Hyde Park** (*see p59*) and **Greenwich Park** (*see p60*), **Wimbledon** (*see p63*), **Lord's Cricket Ground** (*see p59*) and **Wembley Stadium** (*see p63*) are among them.

THE LAY OF THE LAND

The London 2012 Games are divided into three principal areas – the Olympic Park, the Central Zone and the River Zone – with a number of satellite venues around them.

The **Olympic Park** (*see pp53-59*) is quite staggering – as an architectural, environmental and logistical achievement, for sure, but also in its sheer scale as you walk or cycle beside it. More than half the bridges were complete by summer 2010, and planting in the parklands was well under way – the 'golden meadow', carefully planted to flower in July and August 2012, first bloomed in summer 2010. In this chapter, we list the sporting venues and the events they will host in 2012, but there are many other significant structures in the Park. The innovative, eco-friendly **Energy Centre** will be operational from the end of 2010, while the 'brown roof' of the **Main Press Centre** is being made out of wood and seeds recycled from the developing parkland habitat around it. In **Stratford City**, to the west of the Olympic Park, Phase I of the development of the vast

> ⚡ Pictograms in this colour represent events in the **Olympic Games**.
> ♿ Pictograms in this colour represent events in the **Paralympic Games**.

Westfield shopping mall should be complete in 2011, while the apartment blocks that will house some 17,000 athletes and officials during the Games have taken shape in the Athletes' Village. It is a rare boon for competitors that they'll be staying within walking distance of the major competition venues for London 2012. Everything will be connected to central London by the new Javelin® shuttle service, promising journey times of just seven minutes to St Pancras International come the Games.

The **Central Zone** (*see p59*) brings events for the 2012 Games into the part of the city that most visitors will recognise as 'London': **Horse Guards Parade** is just down the road from Buckingham Palace (*see p137*), while **Hyde Park** is alongside the posh shops, hotels and embassies of Mayfair (*see pp125-127*). Visitors interested in getting a flavour of London 2012 venues prior to the events themselves are able to explore all of these – given good weather, a day spent watching a cricket match at **Lord's Cricket Ground**, for example, is a holiday highlight for many sports fans.

The Olympic Park has transformed a vast, once-decrepit area of east London, but the **River Zone** (*see pp59-61*) may prove to have a subtler long-term influence on how Londoners understand their city. Locals generally conceive of London as divided by the River Thames into south and north, but infrastructure improvements, linking south bank venues such as **Greenwich Park** (*see p60*) and the **North Greenwich Arena** (*see p60*) to **ExCeL** (*see p59*) on the north bank, may encourage them to consider the Thames as less of an absolute barrier. Whatever your level of interest in the Games, the UNESCO World Heritage Site of Maritime Greenwich (*see pp164-168*) is likely to be included on your list of must-sees.

Beyond these three major zones, the 2012 Games will visit two further historic London venues – **Wembley and Wimbledon** (*see p63*), respectively the heart of English football and the centre of world tennis – and a number of improved or purpose-built sites **outside London** (*see pp63-64*).

For succinct advice about planning your trip, *see p67* **Visit**. For details on general transport around London, *see pp362-366* **Getting Around**.

OLYMPIC PARK

Stratford tube/DLR/rail or West Ham tube/rail. **Map** pp54-55.

The centre of the Games is the combination of permanent stadiums and temporary venues that make up the **Olympic Park** in east London. This has already become a major destination for both locals and tourists. A self-guided tour is the best way to enjoy the last stages of the Park's development. The raised Greenway foot- and cyclepath, and towpaths north and south along the River Lea, make casual viewing from outside the perimeter fence a pleasure, with the **View Tube** (*see p160*) near Pudding Mill Lane DLR supplying fine vistas over the Park and good-quality café food.

BUILDING THE PARK ANDY ATKIN, THE TRACTOR DRIVER

'Every day, when I walk on site, I look up at the roof of the **Aquatics Centre** (*see p56*) and I just think: how on earth is that staying up there? So much steel – and there's only three pillars actually holding the roof up. I don't think there's another construction like it anywhere in the world.

'I can't wait for 2012, now. I mean, the last time we had the Olympics here was the year I was born: 1948.'

Olympic Stadium

On Stadium Island, in the south section of the Park, across the Central Concourse from the Aquatics Centre.

The focal venue in the Olympic Park – host to the Opening and Closing Ceremonies, as well as both the Olympic and the Paralympic Athletics – looks like a kind of giant mechanical lotus flower, especially when you see its 14 stanchions of floodlights, open like 60m-long petals, reflected in the junction of the Lea Navigation and Hertford Union Canal. It sits on an island between three rivers, crossed by a total of five bridges. When the stadium is complete, its top

Olympic Stadium.

Olympic Park at Games Time
(Provisional)

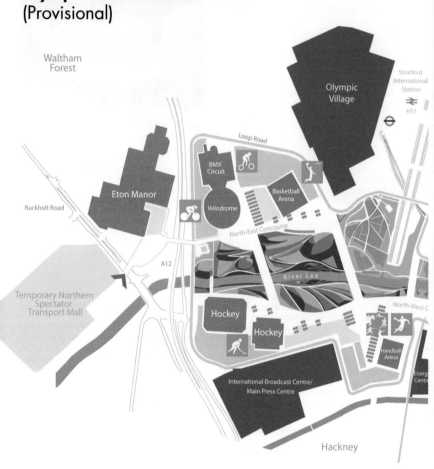

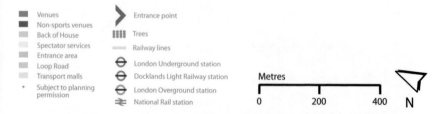

Lord's Cricket Ground. *See p59.*

LONDON 2012

layer will be covered by material stretched over a cable-net roof to provide perfect conditions for the competitors and shelter for two-thirds of the 80,000 spectators in the stands.

By the time you read this, all the seats should be in place, and the flattening and resurfacing well under way, but the actual track won't be laid until summer 2011. Within the Stadium, there are 700 rooms (medical facilities, changing rooms, toilets) and a 60m warm-up track, but most of the normal stadium functions have been moved outside: refreshments, merchandising and information desks are to be stationed in a 'village' around the perimeter, giving the Park a festival feel.

This – and the division of seating into 25,000 permanent seats below temporary stands for a further 55,000 spectators – has allowed the weight of materials to be kept low, reducing the carbon footprint created by their manufacture and transport.

Athletics
Paralympic Athletics

Aquatics Centre & Water Polo Arena

In the south-east of the Park, between the Olympic Stadium and Stratford City.

Another of the Olympic Park's iconic buildings, the Aquatics Centre will be the first building many spectactors see – it's on the approach from Stratford Regional station, with visitors crossing a vast bridge that conceals the training pool, a river and a railway line. The Aquatics Centre was designed by Iraqi-born starchitect Zaha Hadid in typically uncompromising style. Its talking point is the huge, wave-shaped roof – steel and glass on the outside, treated timber within – that is flanked by 42m-high temporary stands on either side. These will accommodate 15,000 people, with a further 2,500 seated on

permanent concrete terracing. Inside, there are a 50m competition pool, 25m competition diving pool and a 50m warm-up pool. The first of 180,000 pool tiles was laid by world record-holding swimmer Mark Foster on 23 September 2010; the venue as a whole will use more than 800,000 ceramic tiles.

Located next door to the Aquatics Centre, the 5,000-capacity Water Polo Arena is to be one of several temporary structures in the Olympic Park. Work on it is due to begin in spring 2011.

Aquatics – Diving
Aquatics – Swimming
Aquatics – Synchronised Swimming
Aquatics – Water Polo
Modern Pentathlon – Swimming
Paralympic Swimming

Velodrome & BMX Circuit

At the northern end of the North-East Concourse, between the Basketball Arena and Eton Manor.

Until the Olympic Park opens to ticket-holders, the Velodrome will remain the least accessible of the three key venues to curious onlookers: the Stadium (*see p53*) and Aquatics Centre (*see left*) can be admired from the riverbank, but the Velodrome is set back from the river beside a major arterial road. It's a shame, because this 6,000-seater venue, shaped like a Pringle crisp, is a stunner. Sir Chris Hoy – with three gold medals, a major part of the UK's cycling triumph at Beijing 2008 – helped to select the winning design team for the Velodrome. Inside, the slope of the track and the best temperature have been carefully worked out to produce the optimal conditions for fast rides. The track is made of sustainable Siberian pine wood and the whole structure built from lightweight materials (including another cable-net roof) to keep transport and manufacture emissions low. Great pains have been taken to use daylight, rather than artificial lighting, and natural ventilation. The Velodrome even catches rainwater for recycling. Unimpressed by the engineering? Aesthetes will get great views of east London via a glass wall between upper and lower seating.

Work starts on the BMX Circuit, right next door, in spring 2011. There will be temporary seating for 6,000 during the Games, and afterwards the track is to be relocated to form part of the VeloPark.

Cycling – BMX
Cycling – Track
Paralympic Cycling – Track

Basketball Arena
In the north-east of the Park, between the Velodrome and the Athletes' Village, on the North-East Concourse.

It will accommodate 12,000 spectators, making it the Olympic Park's third-largest venue, and is going to be one of the busiest parts of the Park, with events daily throughout the Games, but the Basketball Arena is only temporary. In fact, it's one of the largest impermanent structures built for any Games. Erected in only three months, it is covered with a stretched white material that will be used for light projections during London 2012, in a style perhaps reminiscent of the Beijing 2008 Water Cube.

Basketball (preliminary rounds; women's quarter-finals)
Handball (men's quarter-finals; men's & women's semi-finals, finals)
Wheelchair Basketball
Wheelchair Rugby

Eton Manor
In the most northerly section of the Olympic Park.
Perhaps the lowest profile of the Park's new, permanent constructions, this venue is on the site of the early 20th-century Eton Manor Sports Club, which had fallen into disuse by 2001. For the Games themselves, it will contain three 50m training pools for the Swimming and smaller pools for the other Aquatics disciplines, as well as a 5,000-capacity show court set aside for the Wheelchair Tennis. Memorials to sportsmen from the original club who died in World War I and II, moved off-site during construction, will return once work is complete – and remain here after the Games, when Eton Manor will become a sports centre with facilities for tennis, hockey and five-a-side football.

Wheelchair Tennis

Handball Arena
On the west side of the Park, just off the North-West Concourse, between the Olympic Stadium and the Hockey Centre.

The Handball Arena is a sleek, boxy modernist structure, but its appearance is designed to change over time: the exterior is adorned with around 3,000sq m of copper cladding that is intended to age and weather. Green initiatives include 88 pipes through the roof to let in natural light and reduce the need for artificial lighting, and rainwater pipes for recycling water. The sportsmen and -women might be more excited about the sprung wood floor in the competition area.

After the Games, a combination of permanent and retractable seating will enable the venue to be converted into a flexible indoor sports centre.

Handball (preliminary rounds; women's quarter-finals)
Modern Pentathlon – Fencing
Goalball

Hockey Centre
At the north end of the North-West Concourse, west of the Velodrome.

LONDON 2012

Velodrome.

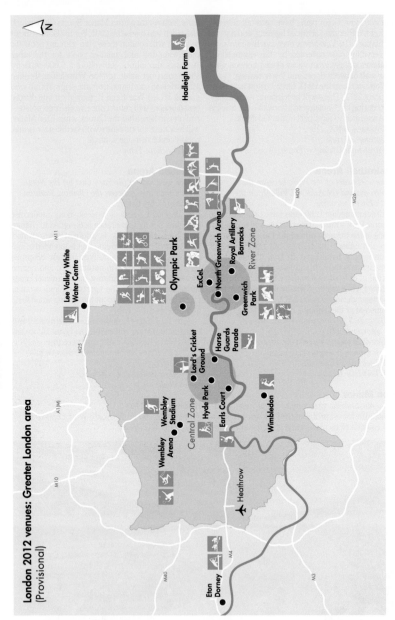

LONDON 2012

London 2012 venues: Greater London area (Provisional)

N

Hadleigh Farm

Lee Valley White Water Centre

Olympic Park

ExCeL

North Greenwich Arena

Royal Artillery Barracks

River Zone

Greenwich Park

Lord's Cricket Ground

Horse Guards Parade

Central Zone

Wembley Stadium

Wembley Arena

Hyde Park

Earls Court

Wimbledon

Heathrow

Eton Dorney

M11

M25

M20

M26

M1(M)

M10

M40

M4

M3

The Hockey Centre will have two pitches: the main one will have 16,000 seats, while the smaller – principally intended for warming up – will have 300. It is hoped that, after the Games, both pitches will be moved north to Eton Manor (*see p57*).
🏑 *Hockey*
⚽ *Paralympic 5-a-side & 7-a-side Football*

CENTRAL ZONE

Taking the 2012 Games right into the heart of tourist London, the Central Zone mixes sightseeing (**Horse Guards Parade**, **Hyde Park**) and sporting history (**Lord's Cricket Ground**, **Earls Court**).

Earls Court Exhibition Centre

Warwick Road, SW5 9TA. Earl's Court or West Brompton tube. **Map** left.
Usually associated with trade shows and concerts (this is where Pink Floyd built *The Wall*), the concrete Exhibition Centre has a strong Olympic past: it hosted the Boxing, Gymnastics, Weightlifting and Wrestling for the 1948 Games. Built in 1937, the building has a certain retro flair: its architect also designed 1920s movie palaces. It will seat 15,000.
🏐 *Volleyball*

Horse Guards Parade

Horse Guards Road, SW1A 2BJ. Charing Cross tube/rail or Westminster tube. **Map** left.
Best known for the Changing of the Guard and Trooping the Colour (*see p279* **Standing on Ceremony**), this large parade ground is open along its eastern side to sleepy St James's Park (*see p136*). For London 2012, it brings 15,000 fans to watch the Beach Volleyball – which might bring a smile to the lips of even the legendarily deadpan Horse Guards.
🏐 *Volleyball – Beach*

Hyde Park

Hyde Park, W2 2UH. Hyde Park Corner, Lancaster Gate, Knightsbridge or Queensway tube. **Map** left.
London's largest Royal Park (*see p145*) will provide one of the most scenic backdrops for London 2012. Triathletes will swim 1,500m in the Serpentine boating lake, run 10,000m around the lake in four equal laps, and then cycle 40,000m over seven laps of the park's perimeter, taking in Constitution Hill and Buckingham Palace. A 3,000-seat grandstand will have a clear view of the finish line. The Marathon Swimmers will do six 1,670m laps of the Serpentine.
🏊 *Aquatics – Swimming (Marathon Swimming)*
🏃 *Triathlon*

Lord's Cricket Ground

St John's Wood Road, NW8 8QN. St John's Wood tube. **Map** left.
Established in 1814, Lord's is the spiritual home of cricket (*see p335*). But, while much of the world

remains immune to the charms of our summer sport, the 2012 Games will use this splendid setting instead to showcase a sport of far longer pedigree: Archery. The juxtaposition of the regal Victorian pavilion and the strikingly modern white pod of the media centre should be enjoyed by 6,500 spectators. *Photo p56*.
🎯 *Archery*

RIVER ZONE

This selection of venues is scattered north and south across the traditionally inviolable divide of the River Thames, with **Greenwich Park** (*see p60*), **North Greenwich Arena** (*see p60*) and **The Royal Artillery Barracks** (*see p60*) on the southern side, and **ExCeL** (*see below*) among the docks to the north.

ExCeL

1 Western Gateway, Royal Victoria Dock, E16 1XL. Custom House or Prince Regent DLR. **Map** left.
Located between Canary Wharf and London City Airport, this convention centre (*see p158*) is right on Royal Victoria Dock. For the London 2012 Games, ExCeL's 45,000sq m and two halls will be divided

BUILDING THE PARK KERRI CHAMBERS, THE APPRENTICE

'I started at the **Stadium** (*see p53*) when it was all brick, working on the underneath. Now there's all the seats and steel on top.

'I'm only 5'1" – anything I stand by looks big, but those machines... I was amazed even by the size of the wheels. I'd never seen anything so big. They had this crane – the biggest crane in Europe – lifting up steels. They lifted up this steel [post] right in front of me: if you see it from a distance you think it's nothing, but if you're standing there and it's up in the air above you... it was amazing.

'Just being here was exciting, I was getting on with my career anyway, and to be on site, and then to actually be working on the Stadium – I really enjoyed it.'

LONDON 2012

Factfile 2012

Some things you might not know.

The Games
10,500 Olympic athletes competing for 205 nations
4,200 Paralympic athletes competing for 162 nations
302 Olympic events over 19 days
500 Paralympic events over 11 days
34 venues, with five new permanent venues within the Olympic Park
70,000 volunteers
10.2 million tickets available for the Olympic and Paralympic Games, 75% of which are available to members of the public

The venues
More than 10,000 workers involved at the peak of construction on the Olympic Park and Athletes' Village
1mm – the accuracy to which the Olympic Stadium running track will be laid
723 inches – size of the two Panasonic TV screens inside the Olympic Stadium
More than 800,000 tiles used in the Aquatics Centre
26°C – the temperature (plus or minus 1°C) of the Aquatics Centre pools
28°C temperature at track level during races at the Velodrome

The equipment
510 adjustable hurdles
600 basketballs, **800** Water Polo balls and **2,400** footballs
275,000 clay targets (Shotgun)
1,630 metal discs (Weightlifting)
150 sets of Paralympic black-out goggles
200 gate poles for the Canoe Slalom

The Olympic parklands
250 different species in the London 2012 Garden
300,000 wetland plants and more than **30 bridges** to span the rivers and railways in the Olympic Park
100 hectares of open space
1.8m tonnes of material delivered to the Olympic Park by rail
98% of construction waste has been reused, recycled or recovered

The coverage
4 billion global audience
20,000 accredited media, to be served around **50,000 meals** a day

into five arenas accommodating 13 sports – it is to host the largest number of events of any venue outside the Olympic Park.

Boxing
Fencing
Judo
Table Tennis
Taekwondo
Weightlifting
Wrestling
Boccia
Paralympic Judo
Paralympic Powerlifting
Paralympic Table Tennis
Volleyball – Sitting
Wheelchair Fencing

Greenwich Park
Greenwich Park, Greenwich, SE10 8XJ. Cutty Sark DLR or Greenwich DLR/rail. **Map** p58.
Greenwich Park (*see p164*) was, appropriately enough, a former royal hunting ground. An anticipated crowd of 23,000 people will pack an arena set behind the National Maritime Museum and the wonderfully grand colonnades of the Old Royal Naval Hospital (for both, *see p166*).

Equestrian – Dressage
Equestrian – Eventing
Equestrian – Jumping
Modern Pentathlon – Riding
Paralympic Equestrian

North Greenwich Arena
Millennium Way, North Greenwich, SE10 0PH. North Greenwich tube. **Map** p58.
Derided as an exorbitant New Labour vanity project when it opened in 2000, Lord Rogers' striking Millennium Dome has made a major comeback (*see p320* **O2 Arena**). As the North Greenwich Arena, it will play a major role in London 2012. A proposed cable-car link with ExCeL (*see p59*) across the Thames remains an exciting possibility.

Basketball (men's quarter-finals; men's & women's semi-finals, finals)
Gymnastics – Artistic
Gymnastics – Trampoline
Wheelchair Basketball

The Royal Artillery Barracks
Greenwich, SE18 4BH. Woolwich Arsenal rail. **Map** p58.
Built in 1776, The Royal Artillery Barracks has the country's longest Georgian façade. To convert the area for Shooting and Paralympic Archery, a 62ft-high safety screen will be erected. Outdoor ranges are being built for Trap and Skeet; the Pistol and Rifle shooting will be held indoors. Grandstands, seating 7,500 spectators, will be built for each range.

Shooting
Paralympic Archery
Paralympic Shooting

ExCeL (*see p59*), above right, and the **North Greenwich Arena**, above rear left.

Wimbledon.

WEMBLEY AND WIMBLEDON

Providing a counterweight to the east London focus of the 2012 Games, these iconic sporting venues are in the city's north-west (**Wembley**) and west (**Wimbledon**).

Wembley Stadium
Stadium Way, Wembley, Middx HA9 0WS. Wembley Park tube or Wembley Stadium rail. **Map** p58.
Lord Foster's reworked Wembley Stadium (*see p335*) will be an impressively grand setting for the finals of the London 2012 Football. With a 90,000-seat capacity, it is Europe's second-largest stadium, and its 317m arch became an instant landmark when the new stadium opened back in 2007.
Football

Wembley Arena
Arena Square, Engineers Way, Wembley, Middx HA9 0DH. Wembley Park tube. **Map** p58.
Most Londoners know Wembley Arena as a music venue (*see p321*), but it was built, in 1934, to host the Empire Games (forerunner of the Commonwealth Games). It has good Olympic credentials, having been the location for the Swimming in the 1948 Games. For London 2012, the Arena will seat 6,000 people.
Badminton
Gymnastics – Rhythmic

Wimbledon
All England Lawn Tennis Club, Church Road, Wimbledon, SW19 5AE. Southfields tube. **Map** p58.
There could only be one setting for the London 2012 Tennis: the world's only world-class grass-court venue, home of the game's most prestigious Grand Slam tournament (*see p334*). The revamped Centre Court, first used in 2009, seats 13,800 spectators.
Tennis

OUTSIDE LONDON

The following venues range from those on the fringes of London (**Hadleigh Farm**, *see right*; **Eton Dorney Rowing Centre**, *see below*; **Lee Valley White Water Centre**, *see p64*) to the south coast, a hundred miles away (**Weymouth & Portland**; *see p64*). The Olympic Football competition might take you further yet: preliminary rounds will take place in Scotland (**Hampden Park**, Glasgow) and Wales (the **Millennium Stadium**, Cardiff), as well as the north of England (**Old Trafford**, Manchester; **St James' Park**, Newcastle) and the Midlands (**City of Coventry Stadium**).

Eton Dorney Rowing Centre
Dorney Lake, off Court Lane, Dorney, Windsor, Berks SL4 6QP. Maidenhead, Slough or Windsor

BUILDING THE PARK MALCOLM BROCKWELL, THE FALCONER

'We go straight to the **Olympic Stadium** (*see p53*), park the van up, and then walk straight into it – so you don't see a lot of the other facilities. Because the Stadium's all open, we work there: the **Velodrome** and the **Aquatics Centre** (for both, *see p56*) are roofed off, so you don't get nothing inside them.

'All the time you're looking for what Willow [Malcolm's Harris hawk] is looking at, 'cause she can see a mouse at the far side of the Stadium and you can't.

'At the moment, it's just a job – you're going around, checking for pigeons, that sort of thing – but you can see the site change... you stand and look at it, and say, ooh yeah, that's progressing, that's coming. When you looked at those floodlight towers still on the ground they looked massive, but now they're up they don't look so big.'

& Eton Riverside rail (approx 15-45mins from London Paddington station). **Map** p58.
The London 2012 Games should liven things up at Eton College, posh alma mater of Prime Minister David Cameron and London Mayor Boris Johnson. The lake, set in 400 acres of park, had a dry run for the Games when it hosted the 2006 Rowing World Championships, but further improvements to the eight-lane, 2,200m course and the warm-up lanes were completed in summer 2010, along with a new cut-through and two bridges. The venue is expecting 30,000 visitors daily. *Photo p64.*
Canoe Sprint
Rowing
Paralympic Rowing

Hadleigh Farm
Castle Lane, Benfleet, Essex SS7 2AP. Leigh-on-Sea or Benfleet rail (approx 45-50mins from London Fenchurch Street station). **Map** p58.
Hadleigh Farm is a lovely mix of woodland, pasture, hay meadow and marsh, with views of the Thames

LONDON 2012

BUILDING THE PARK
KEN SWABY, THE FOREMAN

'When I first came on the Park, we laid all the pipes on a muddy field that is now the **Velodrome** (*see p56*). I went from doing all the cable-pulling, then the roads and bridges, and now I'm on the landscaping. I'm working in places I've already worked before, so I get to see the whole picture.

'I'm lucky: I'm in a vehicle. I'm at high points looking down on the Park; I'm at low points looking up at the bridges. But my route into work changes every day. You get used to going on to autopilot and then suddenly that road's blocked and you have to go another way 'cause construction's started there.

'Without a doubt, my favourite building is the **Aquatics [Centre]** (*see p56*). It looks like a whale's tail coming out of the water.'

Estuary and even a ruined 13th-century castle. The hilly terrain is ideal for the Mountain Bike competition; 3,000 spectators are expected.
Cycling – Mountain Bike

Lee Valley White Water Centre
Station Road, Waltham Cross, Herts EN9 1AB.
Waltham Cross rail (approx 30mins from
London Liverpool Street station). **Map** p58.
The brand-new White Water Centre is at the far northern end of Lee Valley Regional Park (*see p159*). The first new London 2012 venue to open to the public in spring 2011, it has two white-water courses. The 300m competition course and 160m training course are both fed from a starting lake filled with 25,000 cubic metres of water – enough to fill 5,000 Olympic-sized swimming pools. The lake pumps 15 cubic metres of water per second down the course, with parts of the course reaching 7mph.
Canoe Slalom

Weymouth & Portland
Weymouth & Portland National Sailing Academy,
Osprey Road, Portland, Dorset DT5 1SA.
Weymouth rail (approx 2hrs 40mins to 3hrs
from London Waterloo station).
Improvements to the Weymouth & Portland National Sailing Academy were ready for competition by 2008 – making this the first London 2012 venue of any type to be finished. The new slipway, moorings and other facilities have already been used for several international events.
Sailing
Paralympic Sailing

LONDON 2012

Eton Dorney Rowing Centre. *See p63.*

London 2012 Olympic Games Schedule

SPORT	VENUE	JULY							AUGUST											
		W 25	Th 26	F 27	Sa 28	Su 29	M 30	Tu 31	W 1	Th 2	F 3	Sa 4	Su 5	M 6	Tu 7	W 8	Th 9	F 10	Sa 11	Su 12
Opening Ceremony	Olympic Stadium p53			•																
Closing Ceremony	Olympic Stadium p53																			•
Archery	Lord's Cricket Ground p59				•	•	•	•	•	•	•									
Athletics	Olympic Stadium p53										•	•	•	•	•	•	•	•	•	•
Athletics – Marathon	London													•						•
Athletics – Race Walk	London											•						•		
Badminton	Wembley Arena p63				•	•	•	•	•	•	•	•								
Basketball	Basketball Arena p57				•	•	•	•	•	•	•	•	•	•						
	North Greenwich Arena p60															•	•	•	•	•
Beach Volleyball	Horse Guards Parade p59				•	•	•	•	•	•	•	•	•	•	•					
Boxing	ExCeL p59				•	•	•	•	•	•	•	•	•	•	•	•	•	•	•	•
Canoe Slalom	Lee Valley White Water Centre p64					•	•	•	•											
Canoe Sprint	Eton Dorney p63													•	•	•	•	•	•	
Cycling – BMX	BMX Circuit p56															•	•	•		
Cycling – Mountain Bike	Hadleigh Farm p63																		•	•
Cycling – Road	London				•	•			•											
Cycling – Track	Velodrome p56									•	•	•	•	•	•					
Diving	Aquatics Centre p56					•	•	•	•							•	•	•	•	
Equestrian – Dressage	Greenwich Park p60								•	•		•			•					
Equestrian – Eventing	Greenwich Park p60				•	•	•	•												
Equestrian – Jumping	Greenwich Park p60													•		•	•		•	
Fencing	ExCeL p59				•	•	•	•	•	•	•	•								
Football	City of Coventry Stadium, Coventry	•	•		•	•		•	•		•					•				
	Hampden Park, Glasgow	•	•		•				•		•									
	Millennium Stadium, Cardiff	•	•		•			•	•		•			•						
	Old Trafford, Manchester				•		•		•		•		•	•						
	St James' Park, Newcastle				•		•		•		•		•							
	Wembley Stadium p63				•		•		•		•		•		•		•			
Gymnastics – Artistic	North Greenwich Arena p60				•	•	•	•	•	•				•	•	•				
Gymnastics – Rhythmic	Wembley Arena p63																	•	•	•
Gymnastics – Trampoline	North Greenwich Arena p60													•	•					
Handball	Handball Arena p57				•	•	•	•	•	•	•	•	•	•	•					
	Basketball Arena p57															•	•	•	•	•
Hockey	Hockey Centre p57					•	•	•	•	•	•	•	•	•	•	•	•	•	•	
Judo	ExCeL p59				•	•	•	•	•	•	•									
Modern Pentathlon	Handball Arena p57, Aquatics Centre p56 & Greenwich Park p60																		•	•
Rowing	Eton Dorney p63				•	•	•	•	•	•	•	•								
Sailing	Weymouth & Portland p64					•	•	•	•	•	•	•	•	•	•	•	•			
Shooting	Royal Artillery Barracks p60				•	•	•	•	•	•	•	•	•							
Swimming	Aquatics Centre p56				•	•	•	•	•	•	•									
Swimming – Marathon	Hyde Park p59																	•	•	
Synchronised Swimming	Aquatics Centre p56													•	•	•		•	•	
Table Tennis	ExCeL p59					•	•	•	•	•	•	•	•	•	•					
Taekwondo	ExCeL p59																•	•	•	•
Tennis	Wimbledon p63					•	•	•	•	•	•	•	•	•						
Triathlon	Hyde Park p59													•		•				
Volleyball	Earls Court p59				•	•	•	•	•	•	•	•	•	•	•	•	•	•	•	•
Water Polo	Water Polo Arena p56					•	•	•	•	•	•	•	•	•	•	•	•	•	•	•
Weightlifting	ExCeL p59					•	•	•	•		•	•	•	•	•					
Wrestling – Freestyle	ExCeL p59															•	•	•	•	•
Wrestling – Greco-Roman	ExCeL p59														•	•	•			

NOTES

Correct as at 15 October 2010; final schedule to be released March 2011; see www.london2012.com.

LONDON 2012

Velodrome & BMX Circuit. *See p56.*

After London 2012: the **Aquatics Centre**.
See p56.

Visit

TICKETS

Tickets for the London 2012 Olympic Games will go on sale in March 2011. Tickets for the London 2012 Paralympic Games will go on sale separately in autumn 2011. To be among the first to hear about future ticketing news, events and offers, register at **www.tickets.london2012.com**. Creating an account now will also save you time when tickets go on sale.

A wide range of prices, starting from £20, are available across all 26 Olympic sports. 'Pay your age' tickets will be available to under-16s (at 27 July 2012) for one-third of the 640-plus events; over-60s (at 27 July 2012) will pay £16 for a ticket to these events.

All UK residents and residents of designated European countries can apply for tickets. If you're not resident in these countries, apply for tickets through your National Olympic Committee or National Paralympic Committee in 2011.

GETTING AROUND

For transport options to see the venues in 2011, *see pp362-366*. If you're planning your visit for 2012, you will need to think about your travel arrangements when deciding which tickets to apply for:
● Always allow plenty of time to travel to and between venues.

● National rail across the country will be very busy during the Games. We strongly recommend pre-booking rail tickets.
● Some of the co-host city venues are a significant distance from London and from each other.
● London will be significantly busier than usual, so plan carefully, allowing two to three hours' travel time between venues.

There will be no public parking at venues, other than for disabled spectators, so whenever possible walk, cycle and use public transport or park-and-ride services to get to venues. During the Games, the venues will be served by:
● London's extensive public transport network, which includes London Underground, London Overground, the Docklands Light Railway (DLR), and mainline rail, bus, tram and river services.
● Public transport, such as rail, underground, metro, tram and bus services, in the co-host cities.
● Dedicated park-and-ride, shuttle bus and direct coach services to the various venues.
● The national network of train, coach and bus services for people travelling around the UK.

In London, operational hours for public transport will be extended, with the Underground, Overground, DLR and some mainline rail services running until around 1.30am. Many buses will operate 24 hours a day.

Public transport systems will be busy, and other factors could add to the total time it takes to get to your seat in each venue. These include walking from rail stations to the venue entrance, walking within large venues (such as the Olympic Park) and queues at security/ticket checks. We recommend planning your journeys as early as possible.

Ticket holders for Games events in London will receive free travel on public transport for the day of the event. This will include London Underground, London Overground, DLR, bus, tram and some mainline rail services, but not the Heathrow, Stansted or Gatwick Express trains or taxis. Ticket holders for Games events in London will also be entitled to a one-third discount on travel using boat services in London.

For full details on how to use London's transport system, *see pp362-366* **Getting Around**.

ACCOMMODATION

New hotels are starting to appear near the Olympic Park – and there are plenty of business chains around Greenwich. If you are staying in central London, we advise that you plan your journey carefully and allow plenty of time for travelling around the city.

For our favourite places to stay, across town and to suit all pockets, *see pp182-208* **Hotels**.

CULTURAL CALENDAR

Throughout the run-up to London 2012, the **Cultural Olympiad** is supporting and promoting cultural and artistic activities alongside the sport. Projects already under way include 'Artists Taking the Lead' – country-wide art installations (Alfie Dennen and Paula Le Dieu will be putting LED panels on London bus stops, for example) – and 'Film Nation:Shorts', which trains young people with state-of-the-art Panasonic equipment to make short films that could be screened at London 2012 Olympic and Paralympic Games venues; www.london2012.com/

culture has the latest news. For sporting events through 2011, including several at the London 2012 venues, *see pp333-335*.

NPG / BT ROAD TO 2012
A National Portrait Gallery (*see p131*) exhibition of photos of Olympians, Paralympians and the people behind the Games. **Date** summer 2011.

OPEN WEEKEND
Supported by BP, Open Weekend will celebrate two years to go to the London 2012 Games and include hundreds of events across the UK – from sport to art. **Date** 23-25 July 2011.

BP PORTRAIT AWARDS
The National Portrait Gallery (*see p131*) also presents the world's most prestigious portrait competition, displaying fine examples of the genre by contemporary painters. **Date** June-Sept 2011.

LIBERTY FESTIVAL
A free annual celebration of deaf and disabled Londoners in Trafalgar Square (*see p129*). **Date** early Sept 2011.

PEACE ONE DAY CONCERT
Charity concert at the O2 Arena (*see p320*). Film Nation: Shorts – work by 14- to 25-year-olds – will be screened. **Date** 21 Sept 2011.

Get the local experience

Over 50 of the world's top destinations available.

Sights

Albert Memorial. *See p143.*

The South Bank & Bankside

You haven't been to London until you've walked the South Bank.

An estimated 14 million people come this way each year, and it's easy to see why. Between the **London Eye** and **Tower Bridge**, the south bank of the Thames offers a two-mile procession of diverting, largely state-funded arts and entertainment venues, while also affording breezy, traffic-free views of a succession of city landmarks (Big Ben, St Paul's, the Tower of London) that lie on the other side of the water.

The area's modern-day life began in 1951 with the Festival of Britain, staged in a bid to boost morale in the wake of World War II. The **Royal Festival Hall** stands testament to the inclusive spirit of the project; it was later expanded into the Southbank Centre, alongside **BFI Southbank** and the concrete ziggurat of the **National Theatre**. However, it wasn't until the new millennium that the riverside really took off, with the threefold arrival of the **London Eye**, **Tate Modern** and the **Millennium Bridge**. Ever since, the area has been top of most tourists' itineraries.

Map p399 & pp402-403	**Restaurants & cafés** pp209-211
Hotels pp183-185	**Pubs & bars** p235

THE SOUTH BANK

Lambeth Bridge to Hungerford Bridge

Embankment or Westminster tube, or Waterloo tube/rail.

Thanks to the sharp turn the Thames makes around Waterloo, **Lambeth Bridge** lands you east of the river, not south, opposite the Tudor gatehouse of **Lambeth Palace**. Since the 12th century, it's been the official residence of the Archbishops of Canterbury. The palace is not normally open to the public, except on holidays. The church next door, St Mary at Lambeth, is now the **Garden Museum** (*see p71*).

The benches along the river here are great for viewing the Houses of Parliament opposite, before things get crowded after **Westminster Bridge**, where London's major riverside tourist zone begins. Next to the bridge is **County Hall**, once the residence of London's city government, now home to the revamped **Sea Life London Aquarium** (*see p73*) and the **London Film Museum** (*see p71*). The massive wheel of the **London Eye** (*see p71*) rotates slowly in front of you.

Florence Nightingale Museum

St Thomas's Hospital, 2 Lambeth Palace Road, SE1 7EW (7620 0374, www.florence-nightingale. co.uk). Westminster tube or Waterloo tube/rail. **Open** 10am-5pm daily. **Admission** £5.80; £4.80 reductions; £16 family; free under-5s. **Credit** AmEx, MC, V. **Map** p399 M9.

The nursing skills and campaigning zeal that made Nightingale a Victorian legend are honoured here. Reopened after refurbishment for the centenary of her death in 2010, the museum is a chronological tour through a remarkable life under three key themes: family life, the Crimean War, health reformer. Among the period mementoes – clothing, furniture, books, letters and portraits – are Nightingale's lantern and stuffed pet owl, Athena.

Garden Museum
Lambeth Palace Road, SE1 7LB (7401 8865, www.gardenmuseum.org.uk). Lambeth North tube or Waterloo tube/rail. **Open** 10.30am-5pm Mon-Fri; 10.30am-4pm Sat. **Admission** £6; £5 reductions; free under-16s. **Credit** AmEx, MC, V. **Map** p399 L10.

The world's first horticulture museum (formerly the Museum of Garden History) fits neatly into the old church of St Mary's. A 'belvedere' gallery (built from eco-friendly Eurban wood sheeting) contains the permanent collection of artworks, antique gardening tools and horticultural memorabilia, while the ground floor is used for interesting temporary exhibitions. In the small back garden, the replica of a 17th-century knot garden was created in honour of John Tradescant, intrepid plant hunter and gardener to Charles I; Tradescant is buried here. A stone sarcophagus contains the remains of William Bligh, the captain of the mutinous HMS *Bounty*.

▶ *The breadfruit that ruined Bligh's expedition can be seen at Kew Gardens; see p172.*

★ London Eye
Jubilee Gardens, SE1 7PB (0870 500 0600, www.londoneye.com). Westminster tube or Waterloo tube/rail. **Open** *Oct-Apr* 10am-8pm daily. *May, June* 10am-9pm Mon-Thur, Sun; 10am-9.30pm Fri, Sat. *July, Aug* 10am-9.30pm Mon, Sun; 10am-9pm Tue-Sat. *Sept* 10am-9pm daily. **Admission** £17.95; £9.50-£14.30 reductions; free under-4s. **Credit** AmEx, MC, V. **Map** p399 M8.
See p77 **Profile**. *Photos p77.*

INSIDE TRACK
COFFEE AND A VIEW

Overlooking the river outside the London Film Museum and the five-star Marriott hotel, the **Balcony Terrace** at County Hall offers seating for a breather or a BYO sandwich, well above the scrum on the riverside pavement in front of the building. It's easily missed but worth seeking out.

London Film Museum
County Hall, Riverside Building, SE1 7PB (7202 7040, www.londonfilmmuseum.com). Westminster tube or Waterloo tube/rail. **Open** 10am-5pm Mon-Fri; 10am-6pm Sat, Sun. **Admission** £12; free-£10 reductions. **Credit** MC, V. **Map** p399 M8.

Dedicated to British film since the 1950s (the brief is for films that were *made* in Britain, which allows unexpected blockbusters like *Star Wars* and the Indiana Jones movies to be sneaked in alongside the more obvious *Kind Hearts and Coronets* and *Brief Encounter*), the London Film Museum is at the heart of the former home of London's metropolitan government, County Hall. The interactive displays tell the stories of great studios such as Pinewood and Ealing, discussing David Lean and other major directors, and detail different types of movie that have come from these islands. The box-like offices lining the corridors contain sets and props – among thousands of original artefacts, you can see the Rank gong. 'Charlie Chaplin: The Great Londoner' explores the Tramp's life, while 'Ray Harryhausen: Myths & Legends' (to June 2011) looks at his pioneering stop-motion techniques.

SIGHTS

London Film Museum.

SIGHTS

Hungerford Bridge.

Sea Life London Aquarium

County Hall, Riverside Building, Westminster
Bridge Road, SE1 7PB (0871 663 1678, 7967
8007 tours, www.sealife.co.uk). Westminster tube
or Waterloo tube/rail. **Open** *July, Aug* 10am-8pm
daily. *Sept-June* 10am-7pm Mon-Thur, Sun; 10am-
8pm Fri, Sat. **Admission** £18; £12.50-£16.50
reductions; £55 family; free under-3s. **Credit**
MC, V. **Map** p399 M8.

This is one of Europe's largest aquariums and a
huge hit with kids. The inhabitants are grouped by
geographical origin, beginning with the Atlantic,
where blacktail bream swim alongside the Thames
Embankment. The new 'Rainforests of the World'
exhibit has introduced poison arrow frogs, croco-
diles and piranha. The Ray Lagoon is still popular,
though touching the friendly flatfish is no longer
allowed (it's bad for their health). Starfish, crabs and
anenomes can be handled in special open rock pools
instead, and the clown fish still draw crowds.
There's a mesmerising Seahorse Temple and a tank
full of turtles. The centrepieces, though, are the two
massive Pacific and Indian Ocean tanks, with menacing sharks quietly circling fallen Easter Island
statues and dinosaur bones.

Topolski Century

150-152 Hungerford Arches, behind the
Royal Festival Hall, SE1 8XU (7620 1275,
www.topolskicentury.org.uk). Waterloo tube/
rail. **Open** 11am-7pm Mon-Sat; noon-6pm Sun.
Admission free. **Credit** MC, V. **Map** p399 M8.
Underneath the arches near Waterloo, this extensive
mural depicts an extraordinary procession of 20th-
century events and faces, from Bob Dylan to
Winston Churchill via Chairman Mao and Malcolm
X. It's the work of Feliks Topolski, a Polish-born
artist who travelled the world from 1933 until his
death in 1989, popping up at just about every major
event from the liberation of Bergen-Belsen to the
coronation of Queen Elizabeth II. Refurbished, the
space has lost some of its bombed-out atmosphere,
but it's much better annotated and easier to decipher.

Hungerford Bridge to
Blackfriars Bridge

Embankment or Temple tube, Blackfriars rail
or Waterloo tube/rail.

When the **Southbank Centre** (*see p317*) was
built in the 1950s, the big concrete boxes that
together contain the Royal Festival Hall (RFH),
the Queen Elizabeth Hall (QEH) and the Purcell
Room were hailed as a daring statement of
modern architecture. Along with the Royal
National Theatre and the Hayward, they
comprise one of the largest and most popular
arts centres in the world.

The centrepiece is Sir Leslie Martin's **Royal
Festival Hall** (1951), given a £75 million

Southbank Centre.

SIGHTS

Garden Museum. *See p71.*

overhaul in 2007. The main auditorium has had its acoustics enhanced and seating refurbished; the upper floors include an improved Poetry Library, and event rooms in which readings are delivered against the backdrop of the Eye and, on the far side of the river, Big Ben. Behind the hall on Belvedere Road, **Festival Square** now hosts off-beat but crowd-pulling events, markets and exhibitions, and there are busy cafés and chain restaurants all around.

Next door, just across from the building housing the QEH and the Purcell Room, the **Hayward** (*see below*) is a landmark of Brutalist architecture. *Waterloo Sunset*, the gallery's elliptical glass pavilion, was designed in collaboration with light artist Dan Graham. Tucked under Waterloo Bridge is **BFI Southbank** (*see p300*); the UK's premier arthouse cinema, it's run by the British Film Institute. At the front is a second-hand book market – fun, but not brilliant for real finds. Due to its relative height and location just where the Thames bends from north–south to east–west, **Waterloo Bridge** provides some of the finest views of London, especially at dusk. It was designed by Sir Giles Gilbert Scott, the man behind Tate Modern (*see p76*), in 1942.

East of the bridge is Denys Lasdun's terraced **National Theatre** (*see p342*), another Brutalist concrete structure, and one that still divides opinion like few other London buildings (*see also p78* **Snapshot**). There are popular free performances outside in the summer and free chamber music within during winter. Shaded by trees dotted with blue LEDs, the river path leads past a rare sandy patch of riverbed, busy with sculptors in warm weather, to **Gabriel's Wharf**, a collection of small independent shops that range from stylish to kitsch.

Next door, the deco tower of **Oxo Tower Wharf** was designed to circumvent advertising regulations for the stock-cube company that used to own the building. Saved by local action group Coin Street Community Builders, it now provides affordable housing, interesting designer shops and galleries, and restaurants (including a rooftop restaurant and bistro with more wonderful views). Behind, **Bernie Spain Gardens** is great for a break from the crowds.

Shortly after the Oxo Tower, the path along the south bank path is blocked by current redevelopment to Blackfriars station – by 2012, it is to have become a single station spanning both sides of the river. Until then, you'll have to divert inland to ugly Southwark Street if you're continuing to Bankside.

Hayward
Southbank Centre, Belvedere Road, SE1 8XX, (0844 875 0073, www.southbankcentre.co.uk). Embankment tube or Waterloo tube/rail. **Open**
10am-6pm Mon-Thur, Sat, Sun; 10am-10pm Fri. **Admission** varies, check website for details. **Credit** AmEx, MC, V. **Map** p399 M8.
This versatile gallery continues its excellent programme of exhibitions, loaned from around the world. It's carved out a particular niche for itself with participatory installations – Antony Gormley's fog-filled chamber for 'Blind Light', the rooftop rowing boat for group show 'Psycho Buildings' and, in for summer 2010, Ernesto Neto's swimming pool – but there's plenty of variety offered. Visitors can hang out in the industrial-look café downstairs (it's a bar at night), aptly called Concrete, before visiting free contemporary exhibitions at the inspired Hayward Project Space; take the stairs to the first floor from the glass foyer extension.

Around Waterloo

Waterloo tube/rail.

Surprisingly, perhaps, there's plenty of interest around the stone-meets-glass rail terminus of London Waterloo. The most obvious attraction is the massive **BFI IMAX** (*see p301*), located in the middle of a roundabout at the southern end of Waterloo Bridge. The £20m cinema makes imaginative use of a desolate space that, in the 1990s, was notorious for its 'Cardboard City' population of homeless residents.

South, on the corner of Waterloo Road and the Cut, is the restored Victorian façade of the **Old Vic** theatre (*see p343*), now overseen by Kevin Spacey. Further down the Cut is the renovated home of the **Young Vic** (*see p348*), a hotbed of theatrical talent with a stylish balcony bar. Both bring a touch of West End glamour across the river. To the north of the Cut, off Cornwall Road, are a number of atmospheric terraces made up of mid 19th-century artisans' houses.

BANKSIDE

Borough or Southwark tube, or London Bridge tube/rail.

INSIDE TRACK ANCIENT GODS

In a corridor of the Millennium Buildings at **Southwark Cathedral** (*see p79*), there's a small statue of a Roman hunter god that dates back to the early fourth century AD. It was discovered at the bottom of a well in the crypt in 1977. Alongside the statue, a 'window on the past' takes you through the archaeological evidence including a Roman road and a 13th-century stone coffin, dotted now with well-wishers' coins.

SIGHTS

In Shakespeare's day, the area known as Bankside was the centre of bawdy Southwark, neatly located just beyond the jurisdiction of the City fathers. As well as playhouses such as the Globe and the Rose, there were the famous 'stewes' (brothels) presided over by the Bishops of Winchester, who made a tidy income from the fines they levied on the area's 'Winchester Geese' (or, in common parlance, prostitutes). There's less drinking, carousing and mischief-making here these days, but the area's cultural heritage remains alive thanks to the reconstructed **Shakespeare's Globe** (*see right*) and, pretty much next door to it, **Tate Modern** (*see right*), a former power station that's now a gallery.

Spanning the river in front of the Tate, the **Millennium Bridge** opened in 2000, when it became the first new Thames crossing in London since Tower Bridge (1894). Its early days were fraught with troubles; after just two days, the bridge was closed because of a pronounced wobble, and didn't reopen until 2002. Its troubles long behind it, the bridge is an extremely elegant structure; a 'ribbon of steel' in the words of its conceptualists, architect Lord Foster and sculptor Anthony Caro. Cross it and you're at the foot of the stairs leading up to St Paul's Cathedral (*see p87*).

Continuing past the Globe and Southwark Bridge, you'll reach the **Anchor Bankside** pub (34 Park Street, 7407 1577). Built in 1775 on the site of an even older inn, the Anchor has, at various points, been a brothel, a chapel and a ship's chandlers. The outside terrace, across the pathway, offers fine river views – a fact lost on no one each summer, when it's invariably crammed with people.

All that's left of the Palace of Winchester, home of successive bishops, is the ruined rose window of the Great Hall on Clink Street. It stands next to the site of the bishops' former Clink prison, where thieves, prostitutes and debtors all served their sentences; it's now the **Clink Prison Museum** (1 Clink Street, SE1 9DG, 7403 0900, www.clink.co.uk). Around the corner is the entrance to the wine showcase **Vinopolis** (*see p78*). At the other end of Clink Street, St Mary Overie's dock contains a terrific full-scale replica of Sir Francis Drake's ship, the **Golden Hinde** (*see right*).

FREE Bankside Gallery

48 Hopton Street, SE1 9JH (7928 7521, www.banksidegallery.com). Southwark or London Bridge tube/rail. **Open** 11am-6pm daily. **Admission** free; donations appreciated. **Credit** MC, V. **Map** p402 O7.
In the shadow of Tate Modern, this tiny gallery is the home of the Royal Watercolour Society and the Royal Society of Painter-Printmakers. The gallery

runs a frequently changing programme of delightful print and watercolour exhibitions throughout the year; many of the works on show are for sale. Both societies hold frequent events here, including talks and demonstrations.

Golden Hinde

St Mary Overie Dock, Cathedral Street, SE1 9DE (7403 0123, www.goldenhinde.com). London Bridge tube/rail. **Open** 10am-5.30pm daily. **Admission** £6; £4.50 reductions; £18 family. **Credit** MC, V. **Map** p402 P8.
This meticulous replica of Sir Francis Drake's 16th-century flagship is thoroughly seaworthy: the ship has even reprised the privateer's circumnavigatory voyage. 'Living History Experiences' (some overnight) allow participants to dress in period clothes, eat Tudor fare and learn the skills of the Elizabethan seafarer; book well in advance. On weekends, it swarms with children dressed up as pirates for birthday dos.

★ Shakespeare's Globe

21 New Globe Walk, SE1 9DT (7401 9919, www.shakespeares-globe.org). Southwark tube or London Bridge tube/rail. **Open** *Exhibition* 10am-5pm daily. *Globe Theatre tours* Oct-Apr 10am-5pm daily. May-Sept 9.30am-12.30pm Mon-Sat; 9.30-11.30am Sun. *Rose Theatre tours* May-Sept 1-5pm Mon-Sat; noon-5pm Sun. *Tours* every 30mins. **Admission** £10.50; £8.50 reductions; £6.50 children; £28 family. **Credit** AmEx, MC, V. **Map** p402 O7.
The original Globe Theatre, where many of William Shakespeare's plays were first staged and which he co-owned, burned to the ground in 1613 during a performance of *Henry VIII*. Nearly 400 years later, it was rebuilt not far from its original site, using construction methods and materials as close to the originals as possible, and is now open to the public for 90-minute tours throughout the year. During matinées, the tours go to the site of the Rose (21 New Globe Walk, SE1 9DT, 7261 9565, www.rosetheatre.org.uk), built by Philip Henslowe in 1587 as the first theatre on Bankside; red lights show the position of the original theatre. Funds are being sought to continue excavations and preserve the site.

Under the adventurous artistic directorship of Dominic Dromgoole, the Globe is also a fully operational theatre. From 23 April, conventionally regarded as the bard's birthday, into early October, Shakespeare's plays and the odd new drama are performed. For more on the theatre, *see p344*.

★ FREE Tate Modern

Bankside, SE1 9TG (7887 8888, www.tate.org.uk). Southwark tube or London Bridge tube/rail. **Open** 10am-6pm Mon-Thur, Sun; 10am-10pm Fri, Sat. *Tours* 11am, noon, 2pm, 3pm daily. **Admission** free. *Temporary exhibitions* vary. **Credit** AmEx, MC, V. **Map** p402 O7.

Profile London Eye

It took less than a decade for the Eye to become an icon of modern London.

At the hub of the South Bank's millennial makeover rolls the **London Eye** (for listings, *see p71*), here only since 2000 but already up there with Tower Bridge and the Houses of Parliament as the capital's most postcard-friendly tourist asset. Assuming you choose a clear day, a 30min circuit on the Eye affords predictably great views of the city. Take a few snaps from the comfort of your pod and that's your sightseeing done.

The London Eye was the vision of husband-and-wife architect team Julia Barfield and David Marks, who entered a 1992 competition to design a structure auspicious enough to mark the millennium. The Marks' giant wheel idea came second in the contest; the winning entry is conspicuous by its absence. The Eye was planned as a temporary structure but its removal now seems unthinkable. Indeed, the wheel's popularity is such that owner Merlin Entertainments has seen fit to future-proof its investment with a three-year renovation for London 2012.

Before then, each of the wheel's 32 pods (there's one for every London borough) will be in turn unpinned from its cantilevered moorings. The first ten-ton pod was detached in 2009, placed on to a pontoon and floated down the Thames on the tide to Tilbury Docks, from where it was loaded on to a truck and escorted by road to a Worcester workshop. So the wheel can keep its balance, a dummy capsule is put in place of the one that is missing. The renovation has been a knotty problem for Merlin; a spokesman tells us that more than 20 companies have been involved in the project.

So what can we expect from the shiny new Eye pods? They will be, said a press spokesman, more high-tech with improved climate control. Some will be given screens, so business folk can hire them for high-level presentations. So while it's not exactly a case of Pimp my Eye (the attraction won't look any different), we're promised a snappier, happier ride.

THREE MORE VIEWS
The Monument
Over the City.
See p96.

Wolfe Monument, Greenwich Park
The Thames and beyond.
See p164.

Richmond Park
Sprawl to the east, 'burbs to the west.
See p172.

Snapshot
Post-war London

Where to see how London lived.

After the Blitz, vast tracts of land were left desolate and thzousands of London residents needed rehousing. The city's saviour was surprising and divisive: concrete. Cheap, quick and strong enough to create extraordinary geometric buildings, it was loved by architects and hated by pretty much everyone else. The saw-tooth towers of the huge Barbican Centre are the most frequently debated example; just as visible, though, is the still-controversial **National Theatre** (*see p342*), right on the South Bank.

Thanks to its industrial architecture, this power-house of modern art is awe-inspiring even before you enter. Built after World War II as Bankside Power Station, it was designed by Sir Giles Gilbert Scott, architect of Battersea Power Station (*see p170*). The power station shut in 1981; nearly 20 years later, it opened as an art museum, and has enjoyed spectac-ular popularity ever since. The gallery attracts five million visitors a year to a building intended for half that number; work on the hugely ambitious, £215m TM2 extension began in 2010. You can see how far the workers have got in constructing the vast new origami structure, designed by Herzog & de Meuron who were behind the original conversion, by taking a peek through hoardings at the back of the power station. It isn't due for completion until 2012, but won't interrupt normal service in the main galleries.

The original cavernous turbine hall is used to jaw-dropping effect as the home of large-scale, tempo-rary installations. Beyond, the permanent collection draws from the Tate's collections of modern art (international works from 1900) and features heavy hitters such as Matisse, Rothko and Beuys. There are vertiginous views down inside the building from outside the galleries, which group artworks accord-ing to movement (Surrealism, Minimalism, Post-war abstraction) rather than theme.

If you don't know where to start, take one of the tours (ask at the information desk).

▶ *The polka-dotted Tate-to-Tate boat zooms to Tate Britain (see p135) every 40 minutes, with a stop-off at the London Eye (see p71). Tickets are available at both Tates, on board, online or by phone (7887 8888; £5, £1.65-£3.75 reductions).*

Vinopolis

1 Bank End, SE1 9BU (020 7940 8300, www.vinopolis.co.uk). London Bridge tube/rail. **Open** noon-10pm Thur, Fri; noon-10pm Sat; noon-6pm Sun. **Admission** £21-£40. **Credit** AmEx, MC, V. **Map** p402 P8.

Glossy Vinopolis is more of an introduction to wine-tasting than a resource for cognoscenti, but you do need to have some prior interest to get a kick out of it. Participants are furnished with a wine glass and an audio guide. Exhibits are set out by country, with opportunities to taste wine or champagne from dif-ferent regions. Gin crashes the party courtesy of a Bombay Sapphire cocktail, and you can also sample Caribbean rum, whisky, beer from the venue's microbrewery and even different types of absinthe.

BOROUGH

Borough or Southwark tube, or London Bridge tube/rail.

At Clink Street, the route cuts inland, skirting the edge of the district of Borough. The landmark here is the Anglican **Southwark Cathedral** (*see p79*), formerly St Saviour's and

SIGHTS

before that the monastic church of St Mary Overie. Shakespeare's brother Edmund was buried in the graveyard; there's a monument to the playwright inside.

Just south of the cathedral you'll find the roof of **Borough Market**, a busy food market dating from the 13th century. It's wholesale only for most of the week, but hosts London's foodiest public food market (*see p268*) on Thursdays, Fridays and Saturdays (when it gets very crowded). It's surrounded by good places to eat and drink. Not far away, the quaint **George** (77 Borough High Street, 7407 2056) is London's last surviving galleried coaching inn.

Around London Bridge station, tourist attractions clamour for attention. One of the grisliest, with its body parts and surgical implements, is the **Old Operating Theatre, Museum & Herb Garret** (*see right*), but it's the less scary **London Dungeon** (*see below*) that draws the biggest queues. Underneath the arches almost opposite the Dungeon is a rival gore-fest: the **London Bridge Experience** (*see below*). Competing with the blood-curdling shrieks from the Dungeon's entrance are the dulcet tones of Vera Lynn, broadcast from **Winston Churchill's Britain at War Experience** (*see p80*). And soon to tower over them all is the vast, 1,017ft **Shard** development at London Bridge station. By 2012, it will be Britain's tallest building.

London Bridge Experience

2-4 Tooley Street, SE1 2SY (0844 847 2287, www.thelondonbridgeexperience.com). London Bridge tube/rail. **Open** 10am-5pm Mon-Fri; 10am-6pm Sat, Sun. **Admission** £21.95; £16.95-£17.95 reductions; £64.95 family. **Credit** MC, V. **Map** p403 Q8.

Billing itself as two shows for the price of one, this costumed whistle-stop tour comprises a family-friendly lesson on the history of London Bridge, as well as a scary walk through the haunted foundations of the bridge for over-11s only. Upstairs, it's all good, smoke-filled fun as actors ham it up in front of wobbly sets and a bewildered, rapidly bonding audience. A Viking warrior urges us to heave on hawsers to pull the bridge down; a chamber of gore is hosted by the chap in charge of putting chopped-off heads on poles. Downstairs, pestilential corridors are peopled by crazed zombies, animatronic torture victims and a Hannibal Lecter-esque butcher wielding a chainsaw. The calmness of Peter Jackson's London Bridge artefacts comes as a real relief.

London Dungeon

28-34 Tooley Street, SE1 2SZ (0871 423 2240, www.thedungeons.com). London Bridge tube/rail. **Open** times vary; check website for details. **Admission** £23.00; £17.00-£21.00 reductions. **Credit** AmEx, MC, V. **Map** p403 Q8.

Borough Market.

Enter the Victorian railway arches of London Bridge for this jokey and rather expensive celebration of torture, death and disease. Visitors are led through a dry-ice fog past gravestones and hideously rotting corpses to experience nasty symptoms from the Great Plague exhibition: an actor-led medley of corpses, boils, projectile vomiting, worm-filled skulls and scuttling rats. The death-dealing exploits of Bloody Mary are explored alongside those of Sweeney Todd and the Ripper. Extremis: Drop Ride to Doom re-enacts an execution – with you as victim.

★ Old Operating Theatre, Museum & Herb Garret

9A St Thomas's Street, SE1 9RY (7188 2679, www.thegarret.org.uk). London Bridge tube/rail. **Open** 10.30am-5pm daily. **Admission** £5.80; £3.25-£4.80 reductions; £13.75 family. **No credit cards. Map** p403 Q8.

The tower that houses this reminder of surgical practice used to be part of the chapel of St Thomas's Hospital. Visitors enter via a vertiginous spiral staircase to view a pre-anaesthetic operating theatre dating from 1822, with tiered viewing seats for students. The operating tools look like torture implements.

FREE Southwark Cathedral

London Bridge, SE1 9DA (7367 6700, www.southwark.anglican.org). London Bridge tube/rail. **Open** 9am-6pm daily (closing times vary on religious holidays). *Services* 8am, 8.15am, 12.30pm, 12.45pm, 5.30pm Mon-Fri; 9am, 9.15am, 4pm Sat; 8.45am, 9am, 11am, 3pm, 6.30pm Sun. Choral Evensong 5.30pm Mon, Thur (girls); 5.30pm Tue (boys & men); Fri (men only). **Admission** free; suggested donation £4. **Credit** MC, V. **Map** p402 P8.

SIGHTS

The oldest bits of this building date back more than 800 years. The retro-choir was the setting for several Protestant martyr trials during the reign of Mary Tudor. The courtyard is one of the area's prettiest places for a rest, especially during the summer. Inside, there are memorials to Shakespeare, John Harvard (benefactor of the American university) and Sam Wanamaker (the force behind the reconstruction of the Globe); Chaucer features in the stained glass. The Millennium Buildings, including a refectory, explain the place's history.

Winston Churchill's Britain at War Experience

64-66 Tooley Street, SE1 2TF (7403 3171, www.britainatwar.co.uk). London Bridge tube/rail. **Open** *Apr-Oct* 10am-5pm daily. *Nov-Mar* 10am-4.30pm daily. **Admission** £12.95; free-£6.50 reductions; £29 family. **Credit** AmEx, MC, V. **Map** p403 Q8.
This old-fashioned exhibition recalls the privations endured by the British during World War II. Visitors descend from street level in an ancient lift to a reconstructed tube station shelter. The experience continues with displays about London during the Blitz, including bombs, rare documents, photos and reconstructed shopfronts. The displays on rationing, food production and Land Girls are fascinating, and the set-piece walk-through bombsite is quite disturbing.

LONDON BRIDGE TO TOWER BRIDGE

Bermondsey tube/London Bridge tube/rail.

Across the street from the Dungeon is **Hay's Galleria**. Once an enclosed dock, it's now dominated by a peculiar kinetic sculpture called *The Navigators*. Exiting on the riverside, you can walk east past the great grey hulk of **HMS Belfast** (*see right*) to Tower Bridge. Beyond the battleship you pass the pristine, but rather soulless environs of **City Hall**, home of London's current government. There's a pleasant outside 'amphitheatre' called the Scoop, used for lunch breaks, sunbathing and outdoor events. It's part of a massive corporate development with the rather asinine name of **More London**.

South of here, many of the historic houses on Bermondsey Street now host hip design studios or funky shops. This is also where you'll find the **Fashion & Textile Museum** (*see right*). At the street's furthest end, the redevelopment of Bermondsey Square created an arthouse cinema and the Bermondsey Square Hotel (*see p183*), but old-timers linger on. There's the eel and pie shop M Manze (*see p210*) and a Friday antiques market (6am-2pm) – great for browsing, even though the best of the bargains have usually gone before breakfast.

Back on the riverfront, a board announces when **Tower Bridge** is next due to be raised, which happens several hundred times a year. The bridge is one of the lowest to span the Thames, hence its twin lifting sections or bascules. The original steam-driven machinery can still be seen at the **Tower Bridge Exhibition** (*see p97*), which also offers the visitor fantastic views from the top. Further east, the former warehouses of **Butler's Wharf** are now mainly given over to expensive riverside dining; one of them currently houses the **Design Museum** (*see below*).

Design Museum

Shad Thames, SE1 2YD (7403 6933, www. designmuseum.org). Tower Hill tube or London Bridge tube/rail. **Open** 10am-5.45pm daily. **Admission** £8.50; £5-£6.50 reductions; free under-12s. **Credit** AmEx, MC, V. **Map** p403 S9.
Exhibitions in this white 1930s building, formerly a banana warehouse, focus on modern and contemporary design. The temporary shows run from major installations to prize-winning design artefacts, from architects' travel photographs to retrospectives of key modernist theorists of the built environment. The Blueprint Café has a balcony overlooking the Thames, and you can buy designer books and items relating to the current show in the museum shop.

Fashion & Textile Museum

83 Bermondsey Street, SE1 3XF (7407 8664, www.ftmlondon.org). London Bridge tube/rail. **Open** 11am-6pm Wed-Sun. **Admission** £6.50; free-£3.50 reductions. **Credit** AmEx, MC, V. **Map** p403 Q9.
As flamboyant as its founder, fashion designer Zandra Rhodes, this pink and orange museum holds 3,000 of Rhodes's garments, some on permanent display, and her archive of paper designs, sketchbooks, silk screens and show videos. Temporary shows explore the work of particular trend-setters or themes such as the development of underwear. A quirky shop sells ware by new designers.

HMS Belfast

Morgan's Lane, Tooley Street, SE1 2JH (7940 6300, www.iwm.org.uk). London Bridge tube/rail. **Open** *Mar-Oct* 10am-6pm daily. *Nov-Feb* 10am-5pm daily. **Admission** £12.95; £10.40 reductions; free under-16s (must be accompanied by an adult). **Credit** MC, V. **Map** p403 R8.
This 11,500-ton 'Edinburgh' class large light cruiser is the last surviving big gun World War II warship in Europe. A floating branch of the Imperial War Museum (*see p161*), it makes an unlikely playground for children, who tear around its complex of gun turrets, bridge, decks, and engine room. The *Belfast* was built in 1938, ran convoys to Russia, and supported the Normandy Landings. She also helped UN forces in Korea, before being decommissioned in 1965.

The City

Where London began – and where much of its wealth is made.

The City's current fame merely as the financial heart of London does no justice to its 2,000 years of history. This was where the Romans founded the city they called Londinium, building a bridge to the west of today's **London Bridge**. Here were a forum-basilica, an amphitheatre, public baths and, eventually, the surrounding defensive wall that still more or less defines the area we call the Square Mile (actually an area of 1.21 square miles).

Although the City has just over 9,000 residents, 330,000 people arrive each weekday to work as bankers, brokers, lawyers and traders, taking over 85 million square feet of office space. Tourists come, too, to see **St Paul's Cathedral** and the **Tower of London**, but there's much else besides. No area of London offers quite so much to see in so small a space. Roman ruins? Medieval remains? Iconic 21st-century offices? You've come to the right place.

Map pp400-403	Restaurants
Hotels p185	& cafés p211
	Pubs & bars p236

INTRODUCING THE CITY

London has long been divided in two, with Westminster the centre of politics and the City the capital of commerce. Many of the City's administrative affairs are still run on a feudal basis under the auspices of the City of London, Britain's richest local authority. The wealth of the area has always been hard to comprehend; this is, after all, an area that was able to bounce back after losing half its population to the Black Death and half its buildings first to the Great Fire and, later, to Nazi bombs during the Blitz.

To understand the City properly, visit on a weekday when the great economic machine is running at full tilt. At weekends, many of the streets fall quiet, although the key areas – around **St Paul's** (*see p87*), say – are these days busy all week.

FREE **City of London Information Centre**
St Paul's Churchyard, EC4M 8BX (7332 1456, www.cityoflondon.gov.uk). St Paul's tube. **Open** 9.30am-5.30pm Mon-Sat; 10am-4pm Sun. **Credit** (shop) MC, V. **Map** p402 O6.
Run by the City of London, this spiky-roofed modern tourist office is just opposite St Paul's, at the top of the stairs that lead up from the Millennium

Bridge. As well as information and brochures on sights, events, walks and talks, it offers tours with well-trained specialist guides.

TEMPLE & THE INNS OF COURT

Temple tube.

At its western end, the Strand (*see p110*) becomes Fleet Street (*see p83*) at **Temple Bar**, the City's ancient western boundary and once the site of Wren's great gateway (now relocated to Paternoster Square beside St Paul's; *see p85*). A newer, narrower, but still impressive griffin-topped monument marks the original spot. The area has long been linked to the law, and here, on the edge of Holborn (*see p98*), stands the splendid neo-Gothic **Royal Courts of Justice** (*see p83*). On the other side of the road, stretching almost to the Thames, are the several courtyards that make up **Middle Temple** (7427 4800, www.middle temple.org.uk) and **Inner Temple** (7797 8250, www.innertemple.org.uk), two of the Inns of Court that provided training and lodging for London's medieval lawyers. Anybody may visit the grounds, but access to the grand, collegiate

St Paul's Cathedral. *See p87.*

buildings is reserved for lawyers and barristers. Tours of Inner Temple cost £10 per person (minimum five people; book on 7797 8241).

The site was formerly the headquarters of the Knights Templar, an order of warrior monks founded in the 12th century to protect pilgrims travelling to the Holy Land. The Templars built the original **Temple Church** (*see below*) in 1185, but they fell foul of Catholic orthodoxy during the Crusades and the order was disbanded for heresy. Dan Brown used the Temple Church as a setting for his bestselling conspiracy novel *The Da Vinci Code* (2003). Robin Griffith-Jones, the master of Temple Church, has produced a robust response to his claims at www.beliefnet.com/templechurch.

FREE Royal Courts of Justice

Strand, WC2A 2LL (7947 6000, 7947 7684 tours, www.hmcourts-service.gov.uk). Temple tube. **Open** 9am-4.30pm Mon-Fri. **Admission** free. *Tours* £10. **Credit** MC, V. **Map** p397 M6.
Two of the highest civil courts in the land sit in these imposing buildings: the High Court and the Appeals Court, justice at its most bewigged and ermine-robed. Visitors are welcome to observe the process of law in any of the 88 courtrooms, but very little happens in August and September. There are also two-hour tours on the first and third Tuesday of the month (11am or 2pm; pre-book on 7947 7684 or rcj-tours@talktalk.net). Cameras and children under 14 are not allowed on the premises.

FREE Temple Church

Fleet Street, EC4Y 7BB (7353 8559, www. templechurch.com). Chancery Lane or Temple tube. **Open** 2-4pm Tue-Fri; phone or check website for details. *Services* 1.15pm Thur; 8.30am, 11.15am Sun. **Admission** free. **No credit cards. Map** p402 N6.
Inspired by Jerusalem's Church of the Holy Sepulchre, the Temple Church was the private chapel of the mystical Knights Templar. The rounded apse contains the worn gravestones of several Crusader knights, but the church was refurbished by Wren and the Victorians, and was damaged in the Blitz. Not that it puts off the wild speculations of avid *Da Vinci Code* fans. There are organ recitals most Wednesdays (phone for details).
▶ *There's a Crusader altar in All Hallows by the Tower; see p96. For the Hospitallers, try the Museum of the Order of St John; see p100.*

FLEET STREET

Temple tube or Blackfriars rail.

Without Fleet Street, the daily newspaper might never have been invented. Named after the vanished River Fleet, Fleet Street was a major artery for the delivery of goods

into the City, including the first printing press, which was installed behind **St Bride's Church** (*see p85*) in 1500 by William Caxton's assistant, Wynkyn de Worde, who also set up a bookstall in the churchyard of St Paul's. London's first daily newspaper, the *Daily Courant*, rolled off the presses in 1702; in 1712, Fleet Street saw the first of innumerable libel cases when the *Courant* leaked the details of a private parliamentary debate.

By the end of World War II, half a dozen offices were churning out scoops and scandals between the Strand and Farringdon Road. Most of the newspapers moved away after Rupert Murdoch won his war with the print unions in the 1980s; the last of the news agencies, Reuters, finally followed suit in 2005. Until recently, the only periodical published on Fleet Street was a comic, the much-loved *Beano*. However, in 2009, left-wing weekly the *New Statesman* moved into offices around the corner from Fleet Street on Carmelite Street. Interesting relics from the media days remain: the Portland-stone **Reuters building** (no.85), the Egyptian-influenced **Daily Telegraph building** (no.135) and the sleek, black **Daily Express building** (nos.121-128), designed by Owen Williams in the 1930s and arguably the only art deco building of note in London. Tucked away on an alley behind St Bride's Church is the **St Bride Foundation Institute**, its library (7353 4660, www.st bride.org; open noon-5.30pm Tue, Thur; noon-9pm Wed) dedicated to printing and typography. The library mounts temporary exhibitions showing off its collections, which include rare works by Eric Gill and maquettes for Kinnear and Calvert's distinctive road signs.

At the top of Fleet Street itself is the church of **St Dunstan-in-the-West** (7405 1929, www.stdunstaninthewest.org; free tours 11am-3pm Tue), where the poet John Donne was rector in the 17th century. The church was rebuilt in the 1830s, but the eye-catching clock dates to 1671. The clock's chimes are beaten by clockwork giants who are said to represent Gog and Magog, tutelary spirits of the City. Next door, no.186 is the house where Sweeney Todd,

INSIDE TRACK
PRIVATE PROPERTY

If you'd like to see inside the City's most interesting buildings but are keen to avoid the queues at September's **Open-City London** weekend (*see p283*), try the **City of London Festival** (*see p316* **Festivals**). There are special tours at Mansion House, Bank and St Paul's Cathedral.

Profile Museum of London

The story of London's past, gloriously told.

When a museum opening is attended not just by Mayor Boris Johnson, who sometimes seems happy to open anything at all if he's asked nicely enough, but by Sir Michael Caine (born in Rotherhithe) and Barbara Windsor, MBE (Shoreditch), you know it's somewhere special. And the **Museum of London** (for listings, *see p90*) is certainly that.

A five-year, £20 million refurbishment finally came to completion last year with the unveiling of a thrilling lower-ground-floor gallery that covers the city from 1666 to the present day. The new space features everything from an unexploded World War II bomb, suspended in a room where the understated and very moving testimony of ordinary Blitz survivors is screened, to clothes by the late Alexander McQueen.

The museum's biggest obstacle has always been its tricky location: the entrance is two floors above street level, hidden behind a grim wall. To solve this, a new space was created on the ground floor, allowing one key exhibit – the Lord Mayor's gold coach – to be seen from the outside. The architects Wilkinson Eyre also managed to increase gallery space by a quarter, enabling the museum to focus on the

city's relationship with the rest of the world and how it was changed by trade, war and empire. There are displays and brilliant interactives on poverty (they've reconstructed an actual debtor's cell, complete with graffiti), finance, shopping and 20th-century fashion, including a re-created Georgian pleasure garden, with mannequins that sport Philip Treacy masks and hats. Some displays are grand flourishes – the suspended installation that chatters London-related web trivia in the Sackler Hall, a printing press gushing changing newsheets – but others ingeniously solve problems: games to engage the kids, glass cases in the floors to maximise display space.

ON THE DOCKS
The MoL's younger, river-obsessed sibling, the **Museum of London Docklands** (*see p159*), stopped charging for admission in 2010.

Upstairs, the chronological displays begin with 'London Before London', where artefacts include flint axes from 300,000 BC, found near Piccadilly, and the bones of an aurochs. 'Roman London' includes an impressive reconstructed dining room complete with mosaic floor. Windows overlook a sizeable fragment of the City wall, whose Roman foundations have clearly been built upon many times over the centuries. Sound effects and audio-visual displays illustrate the medieval, Elizabethan and Jacobean city, with particular focus on the plague and the Great Fire.

the 'demon barber of Fleet Street', reputedly murdered his customers before selling their bodies to a local pie shop. The legend, sadly, is a porky pie: Todd was invented by the editors of a Victorian penny dreadful in 1846 and propelled to fame rather later by a stage play.

Fleet Street was always known for its pubs; half the newspaper editorials in London were composed over liquid lunches, but there were also more literary imbibers. If you walk down Fleet Street, you'll see **Ye Olde Cheshire Cheese** (no.145, 7353 6170; *photo p87*), a favourite of Dickens and Yeats. In its heyday, it hosted the bibulous literary salons of Dr Samuel Johnson, who lived nearby at 17 Gough Square (*see below* **Dr Johnson's House**). It also had a famous drinking parrot, the death of which prompted hundreds of newspaper obituaries. At no.66, the **Tipperary** (7583 6470) is the oldest Irish pub outside Ireland: it sold the first pint of Guinness on the British mainland in the 1700s.

Dr Johnson's House

17 Gough Square, off Fleet Street, EC4A 3DE (7353 3745, www.drjohnsonshouse.org). Chancery Lane tube or Blackfriars rail. **Open** *May-Sept* 11am-5.30pm Mon-Sat. *Oct-Apr* 11am-5pm Mon-Sat. *Tours* by arrangement, groups of 10 or more only. **Admission** £4.50; £1.50-£3.50 reductions; £10 family; free under-5s. *Tours* free. **No credit cards. Map** p402 N6.

Famed as the author of one of the first – as well as surely the most significant and unquestionably the wittiest – dictionaries of the English language, Dr Samuel Johnson (1709-84) also wrote poems, a novel and one of the earliest travelogues, an acerbic account of a tour of the Western Isles with his indefatigable biographer James Boswell. You can tour the stately Georgian townhouse off Fleet Street where Johnson came up with his inspired definitions – 'to make dictionaries is dull work,' was his definition of the word 'dull'. The house has been open to the public since 1911 – its centenary will be celebrated with a variety of exhibitions.

▶ *A neat statue of Johnson's cat Hodge sits contentedly in the square outside.*

FREE St Bride's Church

Fleet Street, EC4Y 8AU (7427 0133, www.st brides.com). Temple tube. **Open** 8am-6pm Mon-Fri; 11am-3pm Sat; 10am-6.30pm Sun. Times vary Mon-Sat, so phone ahead to check. *Services* 8.30am Mon, Tue, Thur, Fri; 8.30am, 1.15pm Wed; 11am, 5.30pm Sun. **Admission** free. **No credit cards. Map** p402 N6.

Hidden down an alley south of Fleet Street, St Bride's is known as the journalists' church: in the north aisle, a shrine is dedicated to hacks killed in action. Down in the crypt a surprisingly interesting little museum displays fragments of the churches that have existed on this site since the sixth century.

▶ *The Wren-designed spire is said to have inspired the traditional tiered wedding cake.*

ST PAUL'S & AROUND

St Paul's tube.

The towering dome of **St Paul's Cathedral** (*see p87*) is, excluding the Big Ben clocktower, probably the definitive symbol of traditional London. It was also an architectural two fingers to the Great Fire and, later, to the Nazi bombers that pounded the city in 1940 and 1941. Immediately north of the cathedral itself is the redeveloped **Paternoster Square**, a modern plaza incorporating a sundial that only rarely tells the time. The name harks to the days when priests from St Paul's walked the streets chanting the Lord's Prayer (*Pater noster* is Latin for 'Our Father', the first words of that prayer).

Also of interest is Wren's statue-covered **Temple Bar**. It once stood at the intersection of Fleet Street and the Strand (*see p110*), marking the boundary between the City and neighbouring Westminster; during the Middle Ages, the monarch was only allowed to pass through the Temple Bar into the City with the approval of the Lord Mayor of London. The archway was dismantled as part of a Victorian road-widening programme in 1878 and became a garden ornament for a country estate in Hertfordshire, before being installed in its current location, as the gateway between St Paul's and Paternoster Square, in 2004. The gold-topped pillar in the centre of the square looks as if it commemorates something important, but's just an air vent for the Underground. Victorians would admire such spirited decoration of the mundane.

South of St Paul's, a cascade of steps runs down to the **Millennium Bridge**, which spans the river to Tate Modern (*see p76*) and now offers the main gateway to the City for tourists. The stairs take you close to the 17th-century **College of Arms** (*see p87*), the official seat of British heraldry.

East of the cathedral, the huge **One New Change** shopping mall and office development (www.onenewchange.com) was due to have opened in autumn 2010. Designed by French starchitect Jean Nouvel, the most interesting aspects are a gash that gives views straight through the building to St Paul's and the sixth-floor public terrace. Meekly hidden among the alleys behind it, you'll find narrow Bow Lane. At one end sits **St Mary-le-Bow** (7248 5139, www.stmarylebow.co.uk; open 7am-6pm Mon, Tue; 7am-6.30pm Wed; 7am-4pm Fri), built by Wren between 1671 and 1680. The church bell's peals once defined anyone born within earshot as a true Cockney. At the other end of Bow Lane

SIGHTS

Monument. *See p96.*

is **St Mary Aldermary** (7248 9902, www.st
maryaldermary.co.uk; open 11am-3pm Mon-
Fri). With a pin-straight spire designed by
Wren's office, this was the only Gothic church
by him to survive World War II. Inside, there's
a fabulous moulded plaster ceiling and original
wooden sword rest (London parishioners
carried arms until the late 19th century). Roman
coins are sold here to fund renovation work.

There are more Wren creations south of St
Paul's. On Garlick Hill, named for the medieval
garlic market, is **St James Garlickhythe**
(7236 1719, www.stjamesgarlickhythe.org.uk;
open 10.30am-4pm Mon-Fri). The official church
of London's vintners and joiners, it was built
by Wren in 1682. Hidden in the tower are the
naturally mummified remains of a young man,
nicknamed Jimmy Garlick, discovered in the
vaults in 1855. The church was hit by bombs
in both World Wars, and partly ruined by a
falling crane in 1991, but the interior has been
convincingly restored. Off Victoria Street, **St
Nicholas Cole Abbey** was the first church
rebuilt after the Great Fire.

Built on the site of the infamous Newgate
Prison to the north-west of the cathedral is the
Old Bailey (*see below*). A remnant of the
prison's east wall can be seen in Amen Corner.

Ye Olde Cheshire Cheese. *See p85.*

▶ *A blocked-up door in St Sepulchre Without is
the visible remains of a priest tunnel into the
court; the Newgate Execution Bell is also there.*

FREE College of Arms

*130 Queen Victoria Street, EC4V 4BT (7248
2762, www.college-of-arms.gov.uk). St Paul's
tube or Blackfriars rail.* **Open** 10am-4pm Mon-
Fri. *Tours* by arrangement. **Admission** free.
No credit cards. Map p402 O7.
Originally created to identify competing knights at
medieval jousting tournaments, coats of arms soon
became an integral part of family identity for the
landed gentry of Britain. Scriveners still work here
to create beautiful heraldic certificates. Only the Earl
Marshal's Court is open to the general public, but
visitors can book for evening tours (Mon-Fri) around
the historic interior, led by a herald who will usually
be able to show you documents from the archive.

FREE Old Bailey
(Central Criminal Court)

*Corner of Newgate Street & Old Bailey,
EC4M 7EH (7248 3277). St Paul's tube.*
Open *Public gallery* 10am-1pm, 2-4.30pm
Mon-Fri. **Admission** free. No under-14s;
14-16s only if accompanied by adults.
No credit cards. Map p402 O6.
A gilded statue of blind (meaning impartial) justice
stands atop London's most famous criminal court.
The current building was completed in 1907; the site
itself has hosted some of the most famous trials in
British history, including that of Oscar Wilde.
Anyone is welcome to attend a trial, but bags,
cameras, dictaphones, mobile phones and food are
banned (and no storage facilities are provided).

★ St Paul's Cathedral

*Ludgate Hill, EC4M 8AD (7236 4128, www.st
pauls.co.uk). St Paul's tube.* **Open** 8.30am-4pm
Mon-Sat. *Galleries, crypt & ambulatory* 9.30am-
4.15pm Mon-Sat. Special events may cause
closure; check before visiting. *Tours of cathedral
& crypt* 10.45am, 11.15am, 1.30pm, 2pm Mon-Sat.
Services 7.30am, 8am, 12.30pm, 5pm Mon-Sat;
8am, 10.15am, 11.30am, 3.15pm, 6pm Sun.
Admission *Cathedral, crypt & gallery* £12.50;
£4.50-£11.50 reductions; £29.50 family; free
under-6s. *Tours* £3; £1-£2.50 reductions.
Credit AmEx, MC, V. **Map** p402 O6.
The first cathedral to St Paul was built on this site
in 604, but fell to Viking marauders. Its Norman
replacement, a magnificent Gothic structure with a
490ft spire (taller than any London building until the
1960s), burned in the Great Fire. The current church
was commissioned in 1673 from Sir Christopher
Wren as the centrepiece of London's resurgence from
the ashes. Modern buildings now encroach on the
cathedral from all sides, but the passing of three centuries has done nothing to diminish the appeal of
London's most famous cathedral.

Start with the exterior. Over the last decade, a
£40m restoration project has painstakingly removed
most of the Victorian grime from the walls and the
extravagant main façade looks as brilliant today as
it must have when the last stone was placed in 1708.
On the south side of the cathedral, an austere park
has been laid out, tracing the outline of the medieval
chapter house whose remains lie 4ft under it.

SIGHTS

SIGHTS

The vast open spaces of the interior contain memorials to national heroes such as Wellington and Lawrence of Arabia. The statue of John Donne, metaphysical poet and former Dean of St Paul's, is often overlooked, but it's the only monument to have been saved from Old St Paul's. There are also more modern works, including a Henry Moore sculpture and temporary Arts Project displays of major contemporary art. The Whispering Gallery, inside the dome, is reached by 259 steps from the main hall; the acoustics here are so good that a whisper can be bounced clearly to the other side of the dome. Steps continue up to first the Stone Gallery (119 tighter, steeper steps), with its high external balustrades, then outside the Golden Gallery (152 steps), with its giddying views. Come here to orient yourself before setting off in search of other City monuments.

Before leaving St Paul's, head down to the maze-like crypt (through a door whose frame is decorated with skull and crossbones), which contains a shop and café and memorials to such dignitaries as Alexander Fleming, William Blake and Admiral Lord Nelson, whose grand tomb (purloined from Wolsey by Henry VIII but never used by him) is right beneath the centre of the dome. To one side is the small, plain tombstone of Christopher Wren himself, inscribed by his son with the epitaph, 'Reader, if you seek a monument, look around you'; at their request, Millais and Turner were buried near him.

As well as tours of the main cathedral and self-guided audio tours (£4, £3.50 reductions), you can join special tours of the Triforium, visiting the library and Wren's 'Great Model', at 11.30am and 2pm on Monday and Tuesday and at 2pm on Friday (pre-book on 7246 8357, £16 incl admission).

▶ *The crypt now also houses Oculus – a 270° film that tells the cathedral's history and flies you up the dome, past the Whispering Gallery, to look out over the City from the Golden Gallery.*

NORTH TO SMITHFIELD

Barbican or St Paul's tube.

North of St Paul's Cathedral on Foster Lane is **St Vedast-alias-Foster** (7606 3998; open 8am-6pm Mon-Fri), another finely proportioned Wren church, restored after World War II using spare trim from other churches in the area. Off nearby Aldersgate Street, peaceful **Postman's**

Park contains the Watts Memorial to Heroic Sacrifice: a wall of ceramic plaques, each of which commemorates a heroic but doomed act of bravery. Most date to Victorian times – pantomime artiste Sarah Smith, for example, who received 'terrible injuries when attempting in her inflammable dress to extinguish the flames which had engulfed her companion (1863)' – but the first new plaque for 70 years was added in 2009. It was dedicated to Leigh Pitt, who died in 2007 while saving a child from drowning in Thamesmead.

Further west on Little Britain (named after the Duke of Brittany) is **St Bartholomew-the-Great** (*see below*), founded along with **St Bartholomew's Hospital** in the 12th century. Popularly known as St Bart's, the hospital treated air-raid casualties throughout World War II; shrapnel damage from German bombs is still visible on the exterior walls. Scottish nationalists now come here to lay flowers at the monument to William Wallace, executed in front of the church on the orders of Edward I, in 1305. Just beyond St Bart's is the handsome ironwork of Smithfield Market (*see p100*).

FREE Museum of St Bartholomew's Hospital

St Bartholomew's Hospital, North Wing, West Smithfield, EC1A 7BE (3456 5798, www.barts andthelondon.nhs.uk/museums). Barbican tube or Farringdon tube/rail. **Open** 10am-4pm Tue-Fri. **Admission** free; donations welcome. **No credit cards. Map** p400 O5.

Be glad you're living in the 21st century. Many of the displays in this small museum inside St Bart's Hospital relate to the days before anaesthetics, when surgery and carpentry were kindred occupations. Every Friday at 2pm, visitors can take a guided tour of the museum (£5; for information, call 7837 0546) that takes in the Hogarth paintings in the Great Hall, the little church of St Bartholomew-the-Less, neighbouring St Bartholomew-the-Great and Smithfield.

St Bartholomew-the-Great

West Smithfield, EC1A 9DS (7606 5171, www. greatstbarts.com). Barbican tube or Farringdon tube/rail. **Open** 8.30am-5pm Mon-Fri (until 4pm Nov-Feb); 10.30am-4pm Sat; 8.30am-8pm Sun. *Services* 12.30pm Tue; 8.30pm Thur; 9am, 11am, 6.30pm Sun. **Admission** £4; £3 reductions; £10 family. **Credit** AmEx, MC, V. **Map** p400 O5.

This atmospheric medieval church was built over the remains of the 12th-century priory hospital of St Bartholomew, founded by Prior Rahere, a former courtier of Henry I. The church was chopped about during Henry VIII's reign and the interior is now firmly Elizabethan, although it also contains donated works of modern art. You may recognise the main hall from *Shakespeare in Love* or *Four Weddings and a Funeral*.

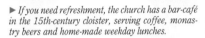

St Paul's Cathedral. *See p87.*

▶ *If you need refreshment, the church has a bar-café in the 15th-century cloister, serving coffee, monastry beers and home-made weekday lunches.*

NORTH OF LONDON WALL

Barbican tube or Moorgate tube/rail.

From St Bart's, the road known as London Wall runs east to Bishopsgate, following the approximate route of the old Roman walls. Tower blocks have sprung up here like daisies, but the odd lump of weathered stonework can still be seen poking up between the office blocks, marking the path of the old City wall. You can patrol the remaining stretches of the wall, with panels (some barely legible) pointing out highlights on a route of two miles. The walk starts near the brilliant **Museum of London** (*see p84* **Profile**) and runs to the Tower of London.

The area north of London Wall was reduced to rubble by German bombs in World War II. In 1958, the City of London and London County Council clubbed together to buy the land for the construction of 'a genuine residential neighbourhood, with schools, shops, open spaces and amenities'. What Londoners got was the **Barbican** (*photo p90*), a vast concrete estate of 2,000 flats that feels a bit like a university campus after the students have gone home. Casual visitors may get the eerie feeling they have been miniaturised and transported into a giant architect's model, but design enthusiasts will recognise the Barbican as a prime example of 1970s Brutalism, softened a little by time and rectangular ponds of friendly resident ducks.

The main attraction here is the Barbican arts complex, with its library, cinema, theatre and concert hall – each reviewed in the appropriate chapters – plus an art gallery (*see below*) and the **Barbican Conservatory** (open noon-5pm Sun), a huge greenhouse full of exotic plants. Sadly, pedestrian access wasn't high on the architects' list of priorities: the Barbican is a maze of blank passages and dead-end walkways. Marooned amid the towers is the only pre-war building in the vicinity: the restored 16th-century church of **St Giles Cripplegate** (7638 1997, www.stgilescripplegate.com; open 11am-4pm Mon-Fri), where Oliver Cromwell was married and John Milton buried.

North-east of the Barbican on City Road are **John Wesley's House** (*see p90*) and **Bunhill Fields**, the nonconformist cemetery where William Blake, the preacher John Bunyan and novelist Daniel Defoe are buried.

Barbican Art Gallery

Barbican Centre, Silk Street, EC2Y 8DS (7638 8891, www.barbican.org.uk). Barbican tube or Moorgate tube/rail. **Open** 11am-8pm Mon, Fri-Sun; 11am-6pm Tue, Wed; 11am-10pm Thur. **Admission** £10; £6-£8 reductions; under-12s free. **Credit** AmEx, MC, V. **Map** p400 P5.

The art gallery at the Barbican Centre on the third floor isn't quite as 'out there' as it would like you to think, but the exhibitions on design, architecture and pop culture are usually pretty diverting, as are their often attention-grabbing titles.

▶ *On the ground floor, the Curve is a long, thin gallery (yes, it's curved) that commissions free large-scale installations. They're often superb.*

SIGHTS

FREE John Wesley's House & the Museum of Methodism

Wesley's Chapel, 49 City Road, EC1Y 1AU (7253 2262, www.wesleyschapel.org.uk). Moorgate or Old Street tube/rail. **Open** 10am-4pm Mon-Sat; after the service until 1.45pm Sun. *Tours* arrangements on arrival; groups of 10 or more phone ahead. **Admission** free; donations welcome. **Credit** AmEx, MC, V. **Map** p401 Q4. John Wesley (1703-91), the founder of Methodism, was a man of legendary self-discipline. You can see the minister's nightcap, preaching gown and personal experimental electric-shock machine on a tour of his austere home on City Road. The adjacent chapel has a small museum on the history of Methodism and fine memorials of dour, sideburn-sporting preachers. Downstairs (to the right) are some of the finest public toilets in London, built in 1899 with original fittings by Sir Thomas Crapper.

★ FREE Museum of London

150 London Wall, EC2Y 5HN (7001 9844, www.museumoflondon.org.uk). Barbican or St Paul's tube. **Open** 10am-6pm daily. **Admission** free; suggested donation £3. **Credit** MC, V. **Map** p400 P5. *See p84* **Profile**.

BANK & AROUND

Mansion House tube or Bank tube/DLR.

Above Bank station, seven streets come together to mark the symbolic heart of the Square Mile, ringed by some of the most important buildings in the City. Constructed from steely Portland stone, the Bank of England, the Royal Exchange and Mansion House form a stirring monument to the power of money: most decisions about the British economy are still made within this small precinct. Few places in London have quite the same sense of pomp and circumstance.

Easily the most dramatic building is the **Bank of England**, founded in 1694 to fund William III's war against the French. It's a fortress, with no accessible windows and just one public entrance (leading to the **Bank of England Museum**; *see p92*). The outer walls were designed in 1788 by Sir John Soane, whose own museum can be seen in Holborn (*see p99* **Sir John Soane's Museum**). Millions have been stolen from its depots elsewhere in London, but the bank itself has never been robbed. Today, it's responsible for printing the nation's banknotes and setting the base interest rate.

On the south side of the junction is the Lord Mayor of London's official residence, **Mansion House** (7626 2500, group visits by written application to Diary Office, Mansion House, Walbrook, EC4N 8BH, or by phone), an imposing neoclassical building constructed

SIGHTS

Barbican. *See p89.*

by George Dance in 1753. It's the only private residence in the country to have its own court and prison cells for unruly guests. Just behind Mansion House is the superbly elegant church of **St Stephen Walbrook** (7626 9000, www.ststephenwalbrook.net; open 11am-4pm Mon-Fri), built by Wren in 1672. Its gleaming domed, coffered ceiling was borrowed from Wren's original design for St Paul's; other features include an incongruous modernist altar, sculpted by Sir Henry Moore and cruelly dubbed 'the camembert'. The Samaritans were founded here in the 1950s.

To the east of Mansion House is the **Royal Exchange**. It's the Parthenon-like former home of the London Stock Exchange, founded back in 1565 to facilitate the newly invented trade in stocks and shares with Antwerp. In 1972, the exchange shifted to offices on Threadneedle Street, thence to Paternoster Square in 2004; today, the Royal Exchange houses a posh champagne bar and some expensive fashion and gift shops. Flanking the Royal Exchange are statues of James Henry Greathead, who invented the machine that cut the tunnels for the London Underground, and Paul Reuter, who founded the Reuters news agency here in 1851.

The period grandeur is undermined by the monstrosity on the west side of the square, **No.1 Poultry**. The name fits: it's a turkey. A short walk down Queen Victoria Street will lead you to the eroded foundations of the **Temple of Mithras**, built by Roman soldiers in AD 240-250. Beliefs from the cult of Mithras were incorporated into Christianity when Rome abandoned paganism in the fourth century, but what remains of the site is rather unimpressive. Further south, on Cannon Street, you can see the **London Stone**. Depending who you talk to, it marks the Roman's measuring point for distances across Britain, it's a druidic altar or it's just a lump of rock. Whichever way, it's a small thing, easily missed and preserved behind a grille in the wall. Nearby Cannon Street station is being refurbished beneath a new eight-storey office, Cannon Place, due for completion this year.

Nearby on College Hill is the late Wren church of **St Michael Paternoster Royal** (7248 5202; open 9am-5pm Mon-Fri), the final resting place of Richard 'Dick' Whittington. Later transformed into a rags-to-riches pantomime hero, the real Dick Whittington was a wealthy merchant who was elected Lord Mayor of London four times between 1397 and 1420. The role of Dick Whittington's cat is less clear – many now believe that 'cat' was actually slang for a ship – but an excavation to find Whittington's tomb in 1949 did uncover a mummified medieval moggy. The happy pair are shown in the stained-glass windows.

Returning to Bank, stroll north along Prince's Street, beside the Bank of England's blind wall. Look right along Lothbury to find **St Margaret Lothbury** (7726 4878, www.stml.org.uk; open 7am-5.15pm Mon-Fri). The grand screen dividing the choir from the nave was designed by Wren himself; other works here by his favourite woodcarver, Grinling Gibbons, were recovered from various churches damaged in World War II. Lothbury also features a beautiful neo-Venetian building, now apartments, built by 19th-century architect Augustus Pugin, who worked with Charles Barry on the Houses of Parliament.

South-east of Bank on Lombard Street is Hawskmoor's striking, twin-spired church of **St Mary Woolnoth** (7626 9701; open 9.30am-4.30pm Mon-Fri), squeezed in between what were 17th-century banking houses. Only their gilded signboards now remain, a hanging heritage artfully maintained by the City's planners. The gilded grasshopper at 68 Lombard Street is the heraldic emblem of Sir Thomas Gresham, who founded the Royal Exchange and **Gresham College**.

Further east on Lombard Street is Wren's **St Edmund the King** (7621 1391, www.spiritualitycentre.org; open 10am-6pm Mon-Fri), which now houses a centre for modern spirituality. Other significant churches in the area include Wren's handsome red-brick **St Mary Abchurch**, off Abchurch Lane, and **St Clement**, on Clement's Lane, immortalised in the nursery rhyme 'Oranges and Lemons'. Over on Cornhill are two more Wren churches: **St Peter-upon-Cornhill**, mentioned by Dickens in *Our Mutual Friend*, and **St Michael Cornhill**, which contains a bizarre statue of a pelican feeding its young with pieces of its own body – a medieval symbol for the Eucharist, it was sculpted by someone who had plainly never seen a pelican.

North-west of the Bank of England is the **Guildhall**, the City of London headquarters. 'Guildhall' can either describe the original banqueting hall or the cluster of buildings around it, of which the **Guildhall Art Gallery**, the **Clockmakers' Museum & Library** (for all three, *see p92*) and the church of **St Lawrence Jewry** (7600 9478, www.stlawrencejewry.org.uk; open 8am-4pm Mon-Fri), opposite the hall, are also open to the public. St Lawrence is another restored Wren, with an impressive gilt ceiling. Within, you can hear the renowned Klais organ at lunchtime organ recitals (usually from 1pm Tue).

Glance north along Wood Street to see the isolated tower of **St Alban**, built by Wren in 1685 but ruined in World War II and now an eccentric private home. At the end of the street is **St Anne & St Agnes** (7606 4986; open

SIGHTS

Leadenhall Market.

British banknotes, the museum offers a rare chance to lift nearly 30lbs of gold bar (you reach into a secure box, closely monitored by CCTV). One exhibit looks at the life of Kenneth Grahame, author of *The Wind in the Willows* and a long-term employee of the bank. Child-friendly temporary exhibitions take place in the museum lobby.

FREE Clockmakers' Museum & Guildhall Library
Aldermanbury, EC2V 7HH (Guildhall Library 7332 1868, www.clockmakers.org). St Paul's tube or Bank tube/DLR. **Open** 9.30am-5pm Mon-Sat. **Admission** free. **No credit cards.** **Map** p402 P6.

Hundreds of ticking, chiming clocks and watches are displayed in this single-room museum, from the egg-sized Elizabethan pocket watches to marine chronometers via a 'fuse for a nuclear device'. Highlights include Marine Chronometer H5, built by John Harrison (1693-1776) to solve the problem of longitude, and the plain Smith's Imperial wristwatch worn by Sir Edmund Hillary on the first (Rolex-sponsored) ascent of Everest. Just down the corridor, the library has books, manuscripts and prints relating to the history of London – original historic works can be requested for browsing (bring ID), but much of the archive has been moved to the London Metropolitan Archives. The bookshop stocks loads of London books and maps.

FREE Guildhall
Gresham Street, EC2P 2EJ (7606 3030, www. guildhall.cityoflondon.gov.uk). St Paul's tube or Bank tube/DLR. **Open** May-Sept 10am-5pm daily. Oct-Apr 10am-5pm Mon-Sat. Closes for functions; phone ahead. **Admission** free. **No credit cards. Map** p402 P6.

The City of London and its progenitors have been holding grand ceremonial dinners in this hall for eight centuries. Memorials to national heroes line the walls, shields of the 100 livery companies grace the ceiling, and every Lord Mayor since 1189 gets a namecheck on the windows. Many famous trials have taken place here, including the treason trial of 16-year-old Lady Jane Grey, 'the nine days' queen', in 1553. Above the entrance to the Guildhall are statues of Gog and Magog. Born of the union of demons and exiled Roman princesses, these two mythical giants are said to protect the City of London. The current statues replaced 18th-century forebears that were destroyed during the Blitz.

10.30am-5pm Mon-Fri, Sun), laid out in the form of a Greek cross. Recitals take place here on weekday lunchtimes.

FREE Bank of England Museum
Entrance on Bartholomew Lane, EC2R 8AH (7601 5545, www.bankofengland.co.uk/museum). Bank tube/DLR. **Open** 10am-5pm Mon-Fri. **Admission** free. **No credit cards.** **Map** p403 Q6.

Housed inside the former Stock Offices of the Bank of England, this engaging and surprisingly lively museum explores the history of the national bank. As well as ancient coins and original artwork for

★ Guildhall Art Gallery
Guildhall Yard, off Gresham Street, EC2P 2EJ (7332 3700, www.guildhall-art-gallery.org.uk). St Paul's tube or Bank tube/DLR. **Open** 10am-4.30pm Mon-Sat; noon-4pm Sun. **Admission** £2.50; £1 reductions; free under-16s. Free to all from 3.30pm daily, all day Fri. **Credit** MC, V. **Map** p402 P6.

The City of London's gallery contains numerous dull or unimpressive portraits of royalty and long-gone mayors, but also some wonderful surprises, including a brilliant Constable, some superbly camp Pre-Raphaelite works (Clytemnestra looks mighty riled) and a number of absorbing paintings of London, from moving depictions of war and melancholy working streets to the likes of the grandiloquent (and never-enacted) George Dance plan for a new London Bridge. The collection's centrepiece is the massive *Siege of Gibraltar* by John Copley, which spans two entire storeys of the purpose-built gallery. A sub-basement contains the scant remains of London's 6,000-seater Roman amphitheatre, built around AD 70; Tron-like figures and crowd sound effects give a quaint inkling of scale.

MONUMENT & THE TOWER OF LONDON

Aldgate or Monument tube, Liverpool Street tube/rail, Tower Hill tube or Tower Gateway DLR.

From Bank, King William Street runs south-east towards London Bridge, passing the small square containing the **Monument** (*see p96*). South on Lower Thames Street is the moody-looking church of **St Magnus the Martyr** (*see p97*); nearby are several relics from the days when this area was a busy port, including the old Customs House and **Billingsgate Market**, London's main fish market until 1982 (when it was relocated to east London).

North of the Monument along Gracechurch Street is the atmospheric **Leadenhall Market**, constructed in 1881 by Horace Jones (who also built the market at Smithfield; *see p100*). The vaulted roof was restored to its original Victorian finery in 1991 and City workers come here in droves to lunch at the pubs, cafés and restaurants, including the historic Lamb Tavern. Fantasy fans may recognise the market as Diagon Alley in *Harry Potter & the Philosopher's Stone*.

Behind the market is Lord Rogers' high-tech **Lloyd's of London** building, constructed in 1986, with all its ducts, vents, stairwells and lift shafts on the outside, like an oil rig dumped in the heart of the City. The original Lloyd's Register of Shipping, decorated with evocative bas-reliefs of sea monsters and nautical scenes, is on Fenchurch Street. South on Eastcheap (derived from the Old English 'ceap' meaning 'barter') is Wren's **St Margaret Pattens**, with an original 17th-century interior.

Several of the City's tallest buildings are nearby. To the north, the ugly and rather dated **Tower 42** (25 Old Broad Street) was the tallest building in Britain until the construction of 1 Canada Square in Docklands in 1990. And

30 St Mary Axe.

topped out at 755ft (including a radio mast), **Heron Tower** (110 Bishopsgate, www.heron tower.com) became the UK's tallest building at the end of 2009. Its 46 storeys are to include a restaurant and bar, a bit under 600ft up. Also on Bishopsgate, behind Tower 42, is **Gibson Hall**, the ostentatious former offices of the National Provincial Bank of England.

A block south, St Mary Axe is an insignificant street named after a vanished church that is said to have contained an axe used by Attila the Hun to behead English virgins. It is now known for Lord Foster's **30 St Mary Axe**, arguably London's finest modern building. The building is known as 'the Gherkin' (and, occasionally, more suggestive nicknames) for reasons that are obvious. On curved stone benches either side of 30 St Mary Axe are inscribed the 20 lines of Scottish poet Ian Hamilton Finlay's 'Arcadian Dream Garden', a curious counterpart to Lord Foster's popular building. Nearby are two more medieval churches that survived the Great Fire: **St Helen's Bishopsgate** (*see p97*) and **St Andrew Undershaft** (*see left* **Inside Track**).

The north end of St Mary Axe intersects with two interesting streets. The more northerly, Houndsditch, is where Londoners threw dead

SIGHTS

Walk The New City

Peter Rees, the City Planning Officer, tells us about the area's best new buildings.

Along Gresham Street and Aldermanbury are three new buildings that blend in with the existing City. There's Lord Foster's at **10 Gresham Street**, all dark metal and stone corners; the stone acts as buttresses to encase escape stairs, and the roof is thrown back to provide light for surrounding buildings. At **20 Gresham Street** is a building by Kohn Pedersen Fox in metal and stone that looks very modern; from afar, it looks like a basket. And the building at **30 Gresham Street**, designed by Sidell Gibson Architects, follows the curve of the street. The street curves because it was originally going round an amphitheatre, the remains of which you can see in the **Guildhall Art Gallery** (*see p92*).

Walk down Gresham Street towards the Bank of England (*see p90*). Most of these buildings have been refurbished: some have retained façades, others have been stretched. On your right, look out for the two buildings either side of **Ironmonger Lane**: one is new and one is old, they complement each other perfectly.

Along Throgmorton Street at the site of the old Stock Exchange, we've put an alleyway – **Threadneedle Walk** – between two new buildings at **125 Old Broad Street** and **60 Threadneedle Street**. It's on your right. Walk down it and look at the building opposite on the angle of Threadneedle Street and Old Broad Street. It has three new floors, but the average Joe would never notice. In fact, it fits in much better with the neighbours now. Planning means you can put right things that went wrong before.

Head along Threadneedle Street to **22-24 Bishopsgate**. Work has begun on Kohn Pederson Fox's Bishopsgate Tower, the 'Helter Skelter'. It will be the tallest building in the City when completed. Next door is **122 Leadenhall**, the proposed site of the wedge-shaped 'Cheesegrater'. At the north end of Bishopsgate, **Heron Tower** (*see p93*) should be finished in spring 2011.

Head south. At **20 Gracechurch Street** you can see something we got wrong in the past: this building has been described as 'mating jukeboxes'. We've put retail in the

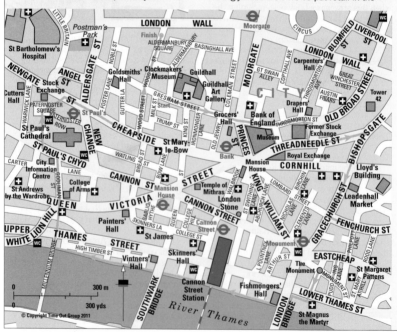

bottom and taken off some of the more ephemeral decoration, but there's not much you can do with it. Sometimes you get saddled with bad buildings.

Nearby, **10 Fenchurch Street** is by Denys Lasdun, the architect of the National Theatre (*see p342*). It's a sympathetic restoration of a classic 1960s design. **20 Fenchurch Street** is the site of what will be the 'Walkie Talkie', where clearance is complete and core construction should begin in 2011. Head down towards the Monument and cross Lower Thames Street; turn right past St Magnus the Martyr (*see p97*) and left on to Riverside Walk.

Walk east by the Thames and you'll pass two adjacent new buildings, David Walker's **Riverbank House** and Fletcher Priest Architects' **Watermark Place**. The latter is on the site of Mondial House, the BT building Prince Charles described as like a 'giant word processor'. Keep on through the tunnel under Southwark Bridge until you reach Arup & Foster's **Millennium Bridge**. Head up to St Paul's (*see p87*). Here's our exciting **visitor centre** (*see p81*), by Ken Shuttleworth. It's amazing how quickly it has settled in.

Head north past St Paul's, through Temple Bar and into Paternoster Square. Turn right and make your way out on to Cheapside. **One New Change** (*see p85*) is the centrepiece of our new Cheapside strategy that will make the area a seven-day-a-week retail destination. When Jean Nouvel came into my office, he produced an Airfix construction kit of a stealth bomber and said, 'We have to come under the radar of St Paul's.'

Proceed down Cheapside and turn left up Wood Street. Halfway along on your left, note the alleyway, **St Alban's Court**, created in the wall of no.100 by Norman Foster, with a glass walkway above. Next, **5 Aldermanbury Square** was designed by Eric Parry and nominated for the 2009 Stirling Prize. From its curved, shiny metal façade you can see the Foster and the Parry, a Farrell (the brown-striped towers of **125 London Wall**), a Rogers (**88 Wood Street**, with its primary-coloured funnels) and even a Wren: the church tower of **St Alban** remains in the centre of Wood Street at no.35.

dogs and other rubbish in medieval times – the ditch ran outside the London Wall (*see p89*), dividing the City from the East End. The southerly one is Bevis Marks, home to the superbly preserved **Bevis Marks Synagogue** (7626 1274; open 10.30am-2pm Mon, Wed, Thur; 10.30am-1pm Tue, Fri; 10.30am-12.30pm Sun), founded in 1701 by Sephardic Jews fleeing the Spanish Inquisition. Services are still held in Portuguese as well as Hebrew. On neighbouring Heneage Lane is the classy kosher **Bevis Marks Restaurant** (no.4, 7283 2220, www.bevismarkstherestaurant.com).

South along Bevis Marks are **St Botolph's-without-Aldgate** (*see p96*) and the tiny stone church of **St Katharine Cree** (7283 5733; open 9.30am-4pm Mon-Fri) on Leadenhall Street, one of only eight churches to survive the Great Fire. Inside is a memorial to Sir Nicholas Throckmorton, Queen Elizabeth I's ambassador to France, who was imprisoned for treason on numerous occasions, despite – or perhaps because of – his friendship with the temperamental queen. Just north of St Katharine is Mitre Square, site of the fourth Jack the Ripper murder.

Further south, towards the Tower of London, streets and alleys have evocative names: Crutched Friars, Savage Gardens, Pepys Street and the like. The famous diarist lived in nearby Seething Lane and observed the Great Fire of London from **All Hallows by the Tower** (*see p96*). Pepys is buried in the church of **St Olave** on Hart Street, nicknamed 'St Ghastly Grim' by Dickens for the skulls at the entrance.

Marking the eastern edge of the City, the **Tower of London** (*see p97*) was the palace of the medieval kings and queens of England. Home to the Crown Jewels and the Royal Armoury, it's one of Britain's best-loved tourist attractions and, accordingly, is mobbed by visitors seven days a week. Overlooking the Tower from the north, beside the tube station, **Trinity Square Gardens** are a humbling memorial to the tens of thousands of merchant seamen killed in the two World Wars, and across the road is a small square in which London's druids celebrate each spring equinox with an elaborate ceremony. Just beyond is one of the City's finest Edwardian buildings: the former **Port of London HQ** at 10 Trinity Square, with a huge neoclassical façade and gigantic statues symbolising Commerce, Navigation, Export, Produce and Father Thames. It's now being turned into a luxury hotel. Next door is **Trinity House**, the home of the General Lighthouse Authority, founded by Henry VIII for the upkeep of shipping beacons along the river.

At the south-east corner of the Tower is **Tower Bridge** (*see p97*), built in 1894 and

SIGHTS

still London's most distinctive bridge. Used as a navigation aid by German bombers, it escaped the firestorm of the Blitz. East across Bridge Approach is **St Katharine Docks**, the first London docks to be formally closed. The restaurants around the marina, slightly hidden behind modern office blocks, offer more dignified dining than those around the Tower.

FREE All Hallows by the Tower
Byward Street, EC3R 5BJ (7481 2928, www. ahbtt.org.uk). Tower Hill tube or Tower Gateway DLR. **Open** 9am-5pm Mon-Fri; 10am-4pm Sat, Sun. *Tours* phone for details; donation requested. *Services* 6pm Wed; 11am Sun. **Admission** free; donations appreciated. **No credit cards. Map** p403 R7.
Often described as London's oldest church, All Hallows is built on the foundations of a seventh-century Saxon church. Much of what survives today was reconstructed after World War II, but several Saxon details can be seen in the main hall, where the Knights Templar were tried by Edward II in 1314. The undercroft contains a museum with Roman and Saxon relics and a Crusader altar. William Penn, the founder of Pennsylvania, was baptised here in 1644.

★ Monument
Monument Street, EC3R 8AH (7626 2717, www.themonument.info). Monument tube. **Open** 9.30am-5pm daily. **Admission** £3; £1-£2 reductions; free under-5s. **No credit cards. Map** p403 Q7.
One of 17th-century London's most important landmarks, the Monument reopened in 2009 after an 18-month refurbishment – the column's magnificent Portland stone was cleaned and repaired, and the golden orb at the top restored with more than 30,000 leaves of gold. The Monument was designed by Sir Christopher Wren and his (often overlooked) associate Robert Hooke as a memorial to the Great Fire. The world's tallest free-standing stone column, it measures 202ft from the ground to the tip of its golden flames, exactly the distance east to Farriner's bakery in Pudding Lane, where the fire is supposed to have begun on 2 September 1666. New lighting has been installed, and the cumbersome old iron bars of the viewing platform replaced with a new, lightweight mesh cage – you still have to walk the 311 steps up the internal spiral staircase to enjoy the sights, though. At least everyone who makes it to

Tower Bridge.

the top gets a certificate. A stone and glass pavilion at the bottom has been specially designed to reflect the gleaming orb and gilded flames from its roof.

FREE St Botolph's-without-Aldgate
Aldgate High Street, EC3N 1AB (7283 1670, www.stbotolphs.org.uk). Aldgate tube. **Open** 10am-3pm Mon, Wed, Thur; 11am-3pm Tue; 10am-12.30pm Sun. *Eucharist* 1.05pm Tue, Thur; 10.30am Sun. **Admission** free; donations appreciated. **No credit cards. Map** p403 R6.
The oldest of three churches of St Botolph in the City, this handsome monument was built at the gates of Roman London as a homage to the patron saint of travellers. The building was reconstructed by George Dance in 1744 and a beautiful ornamental ceiling was added in the 19th century by John Francis Bentley, who also created Westminster Cathedral.

FREE St Ethelburga Centre for Reconciliation & Peace
78 Bishopsgate, EC2N 4AG (7496 1610, www. stethelburgas.org). Bank tube/DLR or Liverpool Street tube/rail. **Open** 11am-3pm Fri. **Admission** free; donations appreciated. **No credit cards. Map** p403 R6.
Built around 1390, the tiny church of St Ethelburga was reduced to rubble by an IRA bomb in 1993 and rebuilt as a centre for peace and reconciliation. Behind the chapel is a Bedouin tent where events are held to promote dialogue between the faiths (phone or check the website for details), an increasingly

INSIDE TRACK RIVER WALK

Much of the north bank of the Thames can now be accessed by the public. The **Riverside Walk** offers a splendid and tourist-free counterpoint to the more popular South Bank.

heated issue in modern Britain. Meditation classes are held here on Tuesdays and Thursdays.

FREE St Helen's Bishopsgate

Great St Helen's, off Bishopsgate, EC3A 6AT (7283 2231, www.st-helens.org.uk). Bank tube/ DLR or Liverpool Street tube/rail. **Open** 9.30am-12.30pm Mon-Fri, afternoons by appointment only. *Services* 10.30am, 4pm, 6pm Sun. *Lunchtime meetings* 1-2pm Tue, Thur. **Admission** free. **No credit cards. Map** p403 R6.

Founded in 1210, St Helen's Bishopsgate is actually two churches knocked into one, which explains its unusual shape. The church survived the Great Fire and the Blitz, but was partly wrecked by IRA bombs in 1992 and 1993. The hugely impressive 16th- and 17th-century memorials inside include the grave of Thomas Gresham, founder of the Royal Exchange (*see p91*).

FREE St Magnus the Martyr

Lower Thames Street, EC3R 6DN (7626 4481, www.stmagnusmartyr.org.uk). Monument tube. **Open** 10am-4pm Tue-Fri; 10am-1pm Sun. *Mass* 12.30pm Tue, Thur, Fri; 11am Sun. *Evensong* 6.30pm 2nd Wed of mth. **Admission** free; donations appreciated. **No credit cards. Map** p403 Q7.

Downhill from the Monument, this looming Wren church marked the entrance to the original London Bridge. A cute scale model of the old bridge is displayed inside the church, along with a statue of axe-wielding St Magnus, the 12th-century Earl of Orkney. The church is mentioned at one of the climaxes of TS Eliot's *The Waste Land*: 'Where the walls/Of Magnus Martyr hold/Inexplicable splendour of Ionian white and gold.'

▶ *St Mary Woolnoth (see p91) is another star of* The Waste Land*: keeping 'the hours/With a dead sound on the final stroke of nine'.*

Tower Bridge Exhibition

Tower Bridge, SE1 2UP (7403 3761, www.tower bridge.org.uk). Tower Hill tube or Tower Gateway DLR. **Open** *Apr-Sept* 10am-6.30pm daily. *Oct-Mar* 9.30am-6pm daily. **Admission** £7; £3-£5 reductions; £11 family; free under-5s. **Credit** AmEx, MC, V. **Map** p403 R8.

Opened in 1894, this is the 'London Bridge' that wasn't sold to America. Originally powered by steam, the drawbridge is now opened by electric rams when big ships need to venture upstream (check when the bridge is next due to be raised on the bridge's website or follow the feed on Twitter). An entertaining exhibition on the history of the bridge is displayed in the old steamrooms and the west walkway, which provides a superb crow's-nest view along the Thames.

▶ *The bridge is enjoying a three-year restoration, but will remain open. There's a website dedicated to the work: www.thetowerbridge.info.*

★ Tower of London

Tower Hill, EC3N 4AB (0844 482 7777, www. hrp.org.uk). Tower Hill tube or Tower Gateway DLR. **Open** *Mar-Oct* 10am-5.30pm Mon, Sun; 9am-5.30pm Tue-Sat. *Nov-Feb* 10am-4.30pm Mon, Sun; 9am-4.30pm Tue-Sat. **Admission** £17; £9.50-£14.50 reductions; £47 family; free under-5s. **Credit** AmEx, MC, V. **Map** p403 R8.

If you haven't been to the Tower of London before, go now. Despite the exhausting crowds and long climbs up inaccessible stairways, this is one of Britain's finest historical attractions. Who would not be fascinated by a close-up look at the crown of Queen Victoria or the armour (and prodigious codpiece) of King Henry VIII? The buildings of the Tower span 900 years of history and the bastions and battlements house a series of interactive displays on the lives of British monarchs, and the often excruciatingly painful deaths of traitors. There's easily enough to do here to fill a whole day, and it's worth joining one of the highly recommended and entertaining free tours led by the Yeoman Warders (or Beefeaters).

Make the Crown Jewels your first stop, and as early in the day as you possibly can: if you wait until you've pottered around a few other things and generally got your bearings, the queues are usually immense. Beyond satisfyingly solid vault doors, you get to glide along a set of travelators (each branded with the Queen's official 'EIIR' badge) past such treasures of state as the Monarch's Sceptre, mounted with the Cullinan I diamond, and the Imperial State Crown, which is worn by the Queen each year for the opening of Parliament.

The other big draw to the tower is the Royal Armoury in the central White Tower, with its swords, armour, poleaxes, halberds, morning stars (spiky maces) and other gruesome tools for separating human beings from their body parts. Kids are entertained by swordsmanship games, coin-minting activities and even a child-sized long bow. The garderobes (medieval toilets) also seem to appeal.

Back outside, Tower Green – where executions of prisoners of noble birth were carried out, continuing until 1941 – is marked by a poem and a stiff glass pillow, sculpted by poet and artist Brian Catling. Overlooking the green, Beauchamp Tower, dating to 1280, has an upper floor full of intriguing graffiti by the prisoners that were held here (including Anne Boleyn, Rudolf Hess and the Krays).

Towards the entrance, the 13th-century Bloody Tower is another must-see that gets overwhelmed by numbers later in the day. The ground floor is a reconstruction of Sir Walter Raleigh's study, the upper floor details the fate of the Princes in the Tower. In the riverside wall is the unexpectedly beautiful Medieval Palace, with its reconstructed bedroom and throne room, and spectacularly complex stained glass in the private chapel. The whole palace is deliciously cool if you've been struggling round on a hot summer's day.

Holborn & Clerkenwell

Lawyers, clubbers and meat-market porters.

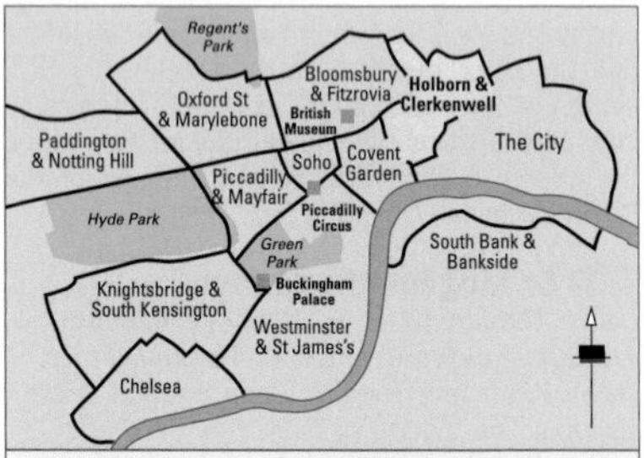

Along Fleet Street and Holborn, the West End dives into the City of London and heads for St Paul's. The newspapers that once called **Fleet Street** home have long since jumped ship for Docklands and Kensington, but some of their grand old offices remain, flanked by the collegiate quiet of the barristers' ancient **Inns of Court**.

Meanwhile, across Farringdon Road, the boom years have transmogrified **Clerkenwell** from an earnest and shabby suburb of Grub Street into a playground for afterwork City boys, bambi-eyed clubbers and design-led media businesses. And in a typically startling juxtaposition, the butchers of **Smithfield Market** still ply their bleeding trade right in the thick of the party.

Map p397 & p400
Pubs & bars pp236-237
Hotels pp185-186
Restaurants & cafés pp212-213

HOLBORN

Holborn tube.

A sharp left out of Holborn tube and left again leads into the unexpectedly lovely **Lincoln's Inn Fields**. Surely London's largest square (indeed, it's more of a park), it's blessed with gnarled oaks casting dappled shade over a tired bandstand. In summer, book an outside seat for Caribbean-accented modern European food at the **Terrace** (7430 1234, www.theterrace.info), an airy, eco-friendly building by the tennis courts. On the south side of the square, the neoclassical façade of the Royal College of Surgeons hides the **Hunterian Museum**; facing it from the north is the magical **Sir John Soane's Museum** (for both, *see right*).

East of the square lies **Lincoln's Inn** (7405 1393, www.lincolnsinn.org.uk), one of the city's four Inns of Court. Its grounds are open to the public, ogling an odd mix of Gothic, Tudor and Palladian buildings. On nearby Portsmouth Street lies the **Old Curiosity Shop** (nos.13-14, WC2A 2ES, 7405 9891, www.curiosityuk.com),

its timbers apparently known to Charles Dickens, but now selling Daita Kimura's decidedly modern shoes. Nearby, Gray's Inn Road runs north beside the second Inn of Court. The sculpted gardens at **Gray's Inn** (7458 7800, www.graysinn.org.uk), dating to 1606, are open on weekdays, 10am-2.30pm.

Opened in 1876 on Chancery Lane as a series of strongrooms in which the upper classes could secure their valuables, the **London Silver Vaults** (7242 3844, www.thesilvervaults.com) are now a hive of dealers buying, selling and repairing silverware. There are also glittering window displays on **Hatton Gardens**, the jewellery and diamond centre of London. It's a short walk but a million miles from the Cockney fruit stalls and sock merchants of the market on **Leather Lane** (10am-2.30pm Mon-Fri).

Further on is **Ely Place**, its postcode absent from the street sign as a result of it technically falling under the jurisdiction of Cambridgeshire. The church garden of ancient **St Etheldreda** (*see right*) produced strawberries so delicious that they made the pages of Shakespeare's *Richard III*; a celebratory Strawberrie Fayre is still held on the street each June. The 16th-century **Ye Old Mitre** (1 Ely Court, EC1N 6SJ, 7405 4751) remains an atmospheric pub.

FREE Hunterian Museum

Royal College of Surgeons, 35-43 Lincoln's Inn Fields, WC2A 3PE (7869 6560, www.rcseng. ac.uk/museums). Holborn tube. **Open** 10am-5pm Tue-Sat. **Admission** free. **No credit cards.** **Map** p397 M6.

The collection of medical specimens once held by John Hunter (1728-93), physician to King George III, can be viewed in this museum. The sparkling glass cabinets of the main room offset the goriness of the exhibits, which include Charles Babbage's brain and Winston Churchill's dentures, as well as shelf after shelf of diligently classified pickled body parts. The upper floor holds a brutal account of surgical techniques. Kids' activities include occasional demonstrations by a 'barber surgeon' (book on 7869 6560).

FREE St Etheldreda

14 Ely Place, EC1N 6RY (7405 1061, www.st etheldreda.com). Chancery Lane tube. **Open** 8am-5pm Mon-Sat; 8am-1pm Sun. **Admission** free; donations appreciated. **No credit cards.** **Map** p400 N5.

Dedicated to the saintly seventh-century Queen of Northumbria, this is Britain's oldest Catholic church, London's only surviving example of 13th-century Gothic architecture; it was saved from the Great Fire by a change in the wind. The crypt is darkly atmospheric, untouched by traffic noise, and the stained glass (actually from the 1960s) is stunning.

Hunterian Museum.

★ FREE Sir John Soane's Museum

13 Lincoln's Inn Fields, WC2A 3BP (7405 2107, www.soane.org). Holborn tube. **Open** 10am-5pm Tue-Sat; 10am-5pm, 6-9pm 1st Tue of mth. *Tours* 11am Sat. **Admission** free; donations appreciated. *Tours* £5; free reductions. **Credit** AmEx, MC, V. **Map** p397 M5.

When he wasn't designing notable buildings, among them the original Bank of England, Sir John Soane (1753-1837) obsessively collected art, furniture and architectural ornamentation. In the 19th century, he turned his house into a museum to which he said, 'amateurs and students' should have access. The result is this perfectly amazing place.

Much of the museum's appeal derives from the domestic setting. The modest rooms were modified by Soane with ingenious devices to channel and direct daylight, and to expand space, including walls that open out like cabinets to display some of his many paintings (Canaletto, Turner, Hogarth). The Breakfast Room has a beautiful domed ceiling, inset with convex mirrors. The extraordinary Monument Court contains a sarcophagus of alabaster, so fine that it's almost translucent, that was carved for the pharaoh Seti I (1291-78 BC) and discovered in his tomb in Egypt's Valley of the Kings. There are also numerous examples of Soane's eccentricity, not least the cell for his imaginary monk 'Padre Giovanni'.

The museum has launched an appeal that will open Soane's top-floor 'private apartments', recreated from contemporary watercolours, with Phase I due to be completed by 2012.

CLERKENWELL & FARRINGDON

Farringdon tube/rail.

Few places encapsulate London's capacity for reinvention quite like Clerkenwell, an erstwhile religious centre that takes its name from the parish clerks who once performed Biblical mystery plays on its streets. The most lasting holy legacy is that of the 11th-century knights of the **Order of St John**; the remains of their

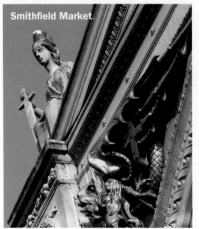

Smithfield Market.

priory can still be seen at St John's Gate, a crenellated gatehouse that dates from 1504 and is home to the **Museum & Library of the Order of St John** (*see below*).

By the 17th century, this was a fashionable locale, but the Industrial Revolution soon buried it under warehouses and factories. Printing houses were established, and the district gained a reputation as a safe haven for radicals, from 16th-century Lollards to 19th-century Chartists. In 1903, Lenin is believed to have met Stalin for a drink in what is now the **Crown Tavern** (43 Clerkenwell Green, 7253 4973), one year after moving the publication of *Iskra* to neighbouring 37A (now the **Marx Memorial Library**; 7253 1485, www.marx-memorial-library.org).

Industrial dereliction and decay were the theme until property development in the 1980s and '90s turned Clerkenwell into a desirable area. The process was aided by a slew of artfully distressed gastropubs (following the lead of the **Eagle**; *see p212*), and the food stalls, fashion boutiques, restaurants and bars along the colourful strip of **Exmouth Market**.

INSIDE TRACK
LOVELY LEARNING

Maintaining a 400-year-old tradition started by Sir Thomas Gresham, founder of the Stock Exchange, **Gresham College** lays on a series of free evening lectures on a wide variety of subjects throughout the year at Barnards Inn Hall, Holborn, and elsewhere in the City, especially at the Museum of London (*see p84* **Profile**). Check www.gresham.ac.uk for details.

FREE Islington Museum

245 St John Street, Finsbury, EC1V 4NB (7527 3235, www.islington.gov.uk). Angel tube. **Open** 10am-5pm Mon, Tue, Thur-Sat. **Admission** free. **No credit cards. Map** p400 O3.

The Islington Museum covers local history and the political and ethical credentials of the borough, exemplified by local residents such as reformist preacher John Wesley, playwright Joe Orton and eminent feminist Mary Wollstonecraft.

FREE Museum of the Order of St John

St John's Gate, St John's Lane, Clerkenwell, EC1M 4DA (7324 4005, www.sja.org.uk/museum). Farringdon tube/rail. **Open** 10am-5pm Mon-Sat. *Tours* 11am, 2.30pm Tue, Fri, Sat. **Admission** free. *Tours* free. Suggested donation £5; £4 reductions. **Credit** MC, V. **Map** p400 O4.

This museum celebrates the Order of St John. Now best known for its ambulance service, the Order's roots lie in the Christian medical practices developed during the Crusades of the 11th to 13th centuries. Artefacts related to the Order of Hospitaller Knights, from Jerusalem, Malta and the Ottoman Empire, is displayed; there's a separate collection relating to the evolution of the modern ambulance service. The museum was due to reopen at the end of 2010, after major refurbishment reorganised the galleries in the Tudor gatehouse and, across St John's Square, opened the Priory Church, its garden and its 12th-century crypt to the public for the first time. A 'pavement museum' will help visitors visualise the contours of the lost medieval priory.

SMITHFIELD

Farringdon tube/rail.

Smithfield Market provides a colourful link to an age when the quality of British beef was a symbol of national virility and good humour. Meat has been traded here for a millennium or more; the current market, designed by Horace Jones, opened in 1868, though it's since been altered (in part out of necessity, thanks to World War II bombs). Meat trucks start arriving around 11pm; early risers will find traders setting up stalls at first light.

The meat traders are joined at night these days by revellers settling in for dinner at vast **Smiths of Smithfield** (67-77 Charterhouse Street, EC1M 6HJ, 7251 7950, www.smithsof smithfield.co.uk) or nearby **St John** (*see p213*), tucking into a glass or two at **Vinoteca** (*see p237*) or taking to the dancefloor at superclub **Fabric** (*see p329*). For a little peace and quiet, stroll by the **Charterhouse**. This Carthusian monastery, founded in 1370, is now Anglican almshouses that retain the original 14th-century chapel and a 17th-century library. It's now right beside the **Malmaison** (*see p185*).

Bloomsbury
& King's Cross

Culture – global, intellectual and literary bohemian – is celebrated here.

London's neighbourhoods north of
Oxford Street are full of bookishness
and bohemianism. **Bloomsbury** is
best known as the home of the **British
Museum** (*see p102*), but the presence
of University College London (UCL)
also helps lend the area a youthful,
if studious, tone. The unofficial heart of
the area is the redeveloped **Brunswick
Centre** and the buzzing network of
surrounding streets.

Next door to the west, **Fitzrovia** is
a favourite source of stories for London
nostalgists, but those days of postwar
spivs and never-knowingly-sober poets have almost vanished beneath a tide of
new media offices. Centred on Charlotte Street, they at least keep the pubs lively
and the restaurants high-quality.

To the north of Bloomsbury, the legendarily seedy **King's Cross** may be going
the way of raffish Fitzrovia. The arrival of the **British Library** (*see p105*) and
the later rebirth of **St Pancras station** (*see p106*) as an international rail hub
are leading the redevelopment of a former blackspot into a destination.

Map pp396-397	Restaurants &
& p416	cafés pp213-214
Hotels pp186-189	Pubs & bars p237

BLOOMSBURY

*Euston Square, Holborn, Russell Square
or Tottenham Court Road tube.*

Bloomsbury's florid name is, prosaically, taken
from 'Blemondisberi' – the manor ('bury') of
William Blemond, who acquired the area in the
13th century. It remained rural until the 1660s,
when the fourth Earl of Southampton built
Bloomsbury Square around his house. The
Southamptons intermarried with the Russells,
the Dukes of Bedford; together, they developed
the area as one of London's first planned suburbs.

Over the next two centuries, the group built
a series of grand squares. **Bedford Square**
(1775-80) is London's only complete Georgian
square (regrettably, its garden is closed to the
public); huge **Russell Square** has been
restored as a public park with a popular café.

To the east, the cantilevered postwar
Brunswick Centre is full of shops, flats,
restaurants and a cinema. The nearby streets,
particularly **Marchmont Street**, are some
of the most characterful in the West End.

Bloomsbury's charm is the sum of its parts,
best experienced on a meander through its
bookshops (many on **Great Russell Street**)
and pubs. The blue plaques are a *Who's Who*
of literary modernists (*see p103* **Walk**), with
a few interlopers from more distant history:
Edgar Allan Poe (83 Southampton Row),
Anthony Trollope (6 Store Street) and, of
course, Dickens (48 Doughty Street; *see p104*
Charles Dickens Museum).

On Bloomsbury's western border, Malet
Street, Gordon Street and Gower Street are
dominated by the **University of London**.
The most notable building is Gower Street's
University College, founded in 1826. Inside is

SIGHTS

INSIDE TRACK
SECRET GARDEN

Between Malet Street and the north-west corner of Russell Square, SOAS (the University of London's School of Oriental and African Studies) has a fine exhibition space, the Brunei Gallery (open to the public 10.30am-5pm Tue-Sat). Head through it and, up on the roof, you'll find a delightful little Japanese Garden, unknown even to many students.

the 'autoicon' of utilitarian philosopher and founder of the university Jeremy Bentham: his preserved cadaver, fully clothed, sits in a glass-fronted cabinet. The university's main library is housed in towering **Senate House** on Malet Street, one of the city's most imposing examples of monumental art deco. It was the model for Orwell's Ministry of Truth in *1984*.

South of the university sprawls the **British Museum** (*see below*), the must-see of all London must-sees. Running off Great Russell Street, where you'll find the museum's main entrance, are three attractive parallel streets (Coptic, Museum and Bury) and, nearby, the **Cartoon Museum** (*see right*); also close by, Bloomsbury Way is home to Hawksmoor's restored **St George's Bloomsbury** (*see p105*). Across from here, **Sicilian Avenue** is a fancy-pants, Italianate, pedestrian precinct of colonnaded shops.

North-east of the British Museum, **Lamb's Conduit Street** is a convivial neighbourhood lined with interesting shops. At the top of the street is **Coram's Fields** (*see p291*), a delightful children's park on the grounds of the former Thomas Coram's Foundling Hospital. Coram's legacy is commemorated in the beautiful **Foundling Museum** (*see p104*).

★ FREE British Museum

Great Russell Street, WC1B 3DG (7323 8299, www.britishmuseum.org). Russell Square or Tottenham Court Road tube. **Open** *Galleries* 10am-5.30pm Mon-Wed, Sat, Sun; 10am-8.30pm Thur, Fri. *Great Court* 9am-6pm Mon-Wed, Sun; 9am-11pm Thur-Sat. *Multimedia guides* 10am-4.30pm Mon-Wed, Sat, Sun; 10am-7.30pm Thur, Fri. *Eye Opener tours* (40mins) phone for details. **Admission** free; donations appreciated. *Temporary exhibitions* prices vary. *Multimedia guides* £4.50; £3-£4 reductions. *Eye Opener tours* free. **Credit** (shop) AmEx, DC, MC, V. **Map** p397 K5.
Officially the country's most popular tourist attraction, the British Museum opened to the public in 1759 in Montagu House, which then occupied this

site. The current building is a neoclassical marvel built in 1847 by Robert Smirke, one of the pioneers of the Greek Revival style. The most high profile addition since then was Lord Foster's popular if rather murky glass-roofed Great Court, open since 2000 and now claimed to be 'the largest covered public square in Europe'. This £100m landmark surrounds the domed Reading Room (used by the British Library until its move to King's Cross; *see p105*), where Marx, Lenin, Dickens, Darwin, Hardy and Yeats once worked.

Star exhibits include ancient Egyptian artefacts – the Rosetta Stone on the ground floor (with a barely noticed, perfect replica in the King's Library), mummies upstairs – and Greek antiquities, including the marble friezes from the Parthenon known as the Elgin Marbles. The Celts gallery upstairs has Lindow Man, killed in 300 BC and so well preserved in peat you can see his beard, while the Wellcome Gallery of Ethnography holds an Easter Island statue and regalia from Captain Cook's travels. The King's Library provides a calming home to a permanent exhibition entitled 'Enlightenment: Discovering the World in the 18th Century', a 5,000-piece collection devoted to the extraordinary formative period of the museum. The remit covers archaeology, science and the natural world; the objects displayed range from Indonesian puppets to a beautiful orrery.

You won't be able to see everything in one day, so buy a souvenir guide and pick out the showstoppers, or plan several visits. Highlights tours focus on specific aspects of the huge collection; Eye Opener tours offer specific introductions to world cultures. There are also regular blockbuster exhibitions, for which it may be necessary to book. A planned extension is aimed in part to provide more spacious accommodation for such shows.

▶ *The historic Museum Tavern (49 Great Russell Street, 7242 8987), by the front gate, is no mere tourist trap. It has a fine range of ales.*

Cartoon Museum

35 Little Russell Street, WC1A 2HH (7580 8155, www.cartoonmuseum.org). Tottenham Court Road tube. **Open** 10.30am-5.30pm Tue-Sat; noon-5.30pm Sun. **Admission** £5.50; free-£4 reductions. **Credit** (shop) MC, V. **Map** p416 Y1.
The best of British cartoon art is displayed on the ground floor of this former dairy. The displays start in the early 18th century, when high-society types back from the Grand Tour introduced the Italian practice of *caricatura* to polite company. From Hogarth, it moves through Britain's cartooning 'golden age' (1770-1830) to examples of wartime cartoons, ending up with modern satirists such as Gerald Scarfe and the wonderfully loopy Ralph Steadman. Upstairs is a celebration of UK comic art, with original 1921 *Rupert the Bear* artwork by Mary Tourtel, Frank Hampson's Dan Dare, Leo Baxendale's Bash Street Kids and a painted *Asterix* cover by that well-known Briton, Albert Uderzo.

Walk Book Stops

A stroll round Bloomsbury's fine array of modern literary luminaries.

One of Britain's most important publishing houses, **Faber & Faber** was founded in 1929 on the north-west corner of Russell Square (no.24), where this walk begins. The poet TS Eliot was appointed literary advisor, and pored over the work of authors and poets such as Ted Hughes and Sylvia Plath. Eliot romanced his secretary Valerie Fletcher for eight years at the **Russell Hotel** (nos.1-8), marrying her in 1957 to the astonishment of his fellow staff.

Head south along Southampton Row and turn left down Cosmo Place until you reach Queen Square. No.3 served as Faber's home from 1971 to 2008. And on the right is **St George-the-Martyr** (www.stgeorges bloomsbury.org.uk), where Plath and Hughes married on 16 June 1956.

No.44 **Mecklenburgh Street** was home to Hilda Doolittle, an imagist poet. Doolittle's husband was the writer Richard Aldington; his mistress, Dorothy Yorke, lived in another part of the house. Yorke was friends with DH Lawrence, who came here in 1917 to write *Women in Love*.

Head through the alleyway that skirts around the Coram Trust, then weave your way through to **Woburn Walk**. From 1895 to 1919, no.5 (marked by a square metal plaque) was home to WB Yeats, who later became one of Faber's 11 Nobel laureates.

Down the road, Virginia Woolf lived for a time at 52 Tavistock Square (now the **Tavistock Hotel**). Woolf published Eliot's *Poems* in 1919. Close by, Woolf and her assorted Bloomsbury Group cohorts (the likes of EM Forster, Lytton Strachey and Duncan Grant) would discuss literature, art, politics and, above all, each other at **50 Gordon Square**; many were Faber authors.

Go past **Senate House**, then left behind the **British Museum** (*see p102*). From here, cross the corner of Russell Square to **28 Bedford Place**; Eliot briefly lived in this 'cheap boarding house' in 1914.

Turn right on to Great Russell Street and stop outside nos.74-77: **Bloomsbury House**, the current home of Faber & Faber. Congratulations: you've just completed 80 years of literary history in an hour.

SIGHTS

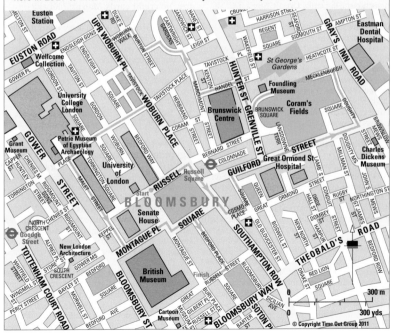

Snapshot Iron Age London

Where to see how London lived.

Even before the Romans transformed a cluster of settlements into the walled city of Londinium, there was civilisation on the site that is now London. The Iron Age treasures displayed in the Britain and Europe room of the **British Museum** (*see p102*) testify to the flamboyance and complexity of life here prior to the invasion of AD 43. The Battersea Shield – unearthed from the Thames at Battersea Bridge in 1857, but dating back as far as 350 BC – is more pretty than protective. Too short and flimsy to have been used in battle, it was more likely to have been thrown or placed in the river as a showy sacrifice for someone of high status. Its intricate design is a clear indication of the sophistication of the tribal craftsmen.

SIGHTS

Charles Dickens Museum
48 Doughty Street, WC1N 2LX (7405 2127, www.dickensmuseum.com). Chancery Lane or Russell Square tube. **Open** 10am-5pm daily. *Tours* by arrangement. **Admission** £6; £3-£4.50 reductions; £15 family. **Credit** AmEx, DC, MC, V. **Map** p397 M4.

London is scattered with plaques marking addresses where Dickens lived, but this is the only building still standing. He lived here from 1837 to 1840, writing *Nicholas Nickleby* and *Oliver Twist* while in residence. Ring the doorbell to gain access to four floors of Dickensiana, collected over the years from various former residences. Some rooms are arranged as they might have been when he lived here; others deal with different aspects of his life, from struggling hack to famous performer.

Foundling Museum
40 Brunswick Square, WC1N 1AZ (7841 3600, www.foundlingmuseum.org.uk). Russell Square tube. **Open** 10am-5pm Tue-Sat; 11am-5pm Sun. **Admission** £7.50; £5 reductions; free under-16s. **Credit** MC, V. **Map** p397 L4.

The Foundling Museum recalls the social history of the Foundling Hospital, set up in 1739 by shipwright and sailor Thomas Coram. Returning to England from America in 1720, Coram was appalled by the number of abandoned children he saw. Securing royal patronage, he persuaded Hogarth and Handel to become governors; it was Hogarth who made the building Britain's first public art gallery; works by artists as notable as Gainsborough and Reynolds are on display. The most heart-rending display is a tiny case of mementoes that were all mothers could leave the children they abandoned here.

FREE Grant Museum
Rockefeller Building, 21 University Street, WC1E 6JJ (7679 2647, www.ucl.ac.uk/museums/zoology). Goodge Street tube. **Open** phone or check website for details. **Admission** free. **No credit cards. Map** p397 K4.

The Grant Museum of Zoology & Comparative Anatomy used to be hidden away down the alley from the Petrie Museum of Egyptian Archaeology (*see below*) and was, once you found it, an absolute joy. Due to reopen in more prominent new premises as this guide hits the shelves, we're assured that the array of Victorian animal skeletons, crammed into wooden cabinets, will retain their wonderfully creepy atmosphere.

▶ *If the grisliness of body parts in jars appeals, check out the Hunterian as well; see p99.*

FREE Petrie Museum of Egyptian Archaeology
University College London, Malet Place, WC1E 6BT (7679 2884, www.petrie.ucl.ac.uk). *Goodge Street or Warren Street tube.* **Open** 1-5pm Tue-Sat. **Admission** free; donations appreciated. **No credit cards. Map** p397 K4.

Set up in 1892 by eccentric traveller and diarist Amelia Edwards, the refurbished (and now much easier to find) museum is named after Flinders Petrie, tireless excavator of ancient Egypt. Where the British Museum's Egyptology collection is strong on the big stuff, the Petrie is dim case after dim case of minutiae: pottery shards, grooming accessories, beads. Highlights include artefacts from the heretic pharaoh Akhenaten's capital Tell el Amarna. Wind-up torches illuminate gloomy corners and computers offer 3D views of select objects.

FREE St George's Bloomsbury
Bloomsbury Way, WC1A 2HR (7242 1979,
www.stgeorgesbloomsbury.org.uk). Holborn or
Tottenham Court Road tube. **Open** times vary;
phone for details. *Services* 1.10pm Wed, Fri;
10.30am Sun. **Admission** free. **No credit**
cards. Map p397 L5.
Consecrated in 1730, St George's is a grand and disturbing Hawksmoor church, with an offset, stepped spire inspired by Pliny's account of the Mausoleum at Halicarnassus. Highlights of its recent renovation include the mahogany reredos and the sculptures of lions and unicorns clawing at the base of the steeple. The hours are erratic, but on Sundays, the church always remains open for visitors after the regular service. Check online for details of concerts.
▶ *For Christ Church Spitalfields, another*
wonderful Hawksmoor church, see p153.

★ **FREE Wellcome Collection**
183 Euston Road, NW1 2BE (7611 2222,
www.wellcomecollection.org). Euston Square
tube or Euston tube/rail. **Open** 10am-6pm Tue,
Wed, Fri, Sat; 10am-10pm Thur; 11am-6pm Sun.
Library 10am-6pm Mon-Wed, Fri; 10am-8pm
Thur; 10am-4pm Sat. **Admission** free. **Credit**
MC, V. **Map** p397 K4.
Sir Henry Wellcome, a pioneering 19th-century pharmacist, amassed a vast and idiosyncratic collection of implements and curios relating to the medical trade, now displayed here. In addition to these fascinating and often grisly items – ivory carvings of pregnant women, used guillotine blades, Napoleon's toothbrush – there are several serious works of modern art, most on display in a smaller room to one side of the main chamber of curiosities. The temporary exhibitions are wonderfully interesting ('Identity', 'Skin', 'Things') and come with all manner of associated events, from lectures and walks to gigs and experimental food.

KING'S CROSS & ST PANCRAS

King's Cross tube/rail.

North-east of Bloomsbury, King's Cross is becoming a major European transport hub, thanks to a £500m makeover of the area. The renovated and restored **St Pancras International** (*see p106*) was the key arrival, but neighbouring King's Cross station will itself be getting an expanded station concourse and, in front of the original 1851 façade, a new public square. The gaping badlands to the north are being transformed into a mixed-use nucleus called **King's Cross Central**, with the University of the Arts London due to take up residence in a converted granary building by 2012. Before that's complete, there are already several places to explore: the **London Canal Museum** (*see right*), north of King's Cross

Station by the **Kings Place** arts complex (*see p318* **Profile**); kids' favourite, **Camley Street Natural Park** (*see p290*); and charming **St Pancras Old Church** (*see p106*).

★ **FREE British Library**
96 Euston Road, NW1 2DB (7412 7332,
www.bl.uk). Euston or King's Cross tube/rail.
Open 9.30am-6pm Mon, Wed-Fri; 9.30am-
8pm Tue; 9.30am-5pm Sat; 11am-5pm Sun.
Admission free; donations appreciated.
Credit (shop) AmEx, MC, V. **Map** p397 K3.
'One of the ugliest buildings in the world,' opined a Parliamentary committee on the opening of the new British Library in 1997. But don't judge a book by its cover: the interior is a model of cool, spacious functionality, the collection is unmatched (150 million items and counting), and the reading rooms (open only to cardholders) are so popular that regular users are now complaining that they can't find a seat. The focal point of the building is the King's Library, a six-storey glass-walled tower housing George III's collection, but the library's main treasures are displayed in the John Ritblat Gallery: Magna Carta, the Lindisfarne Gospels, original Beatles lyrics. There is also a great programme of temporary exhibitions and associated events.

London Canal Museum
12-13 New Wharf Road, off Wharfdale Road,
N1 9RT (7713 0836, www.canalmuseum.org.uk).
King's Cross tube/rail. **Open** 10am-4.30pm Tue-
Sun; 10am-7.30pm 1st Thur of mth. **Admission**
£3; £1.50-£2 reductions; free under-8s. **No**
credit cards. Map p397 M2.
Housed in a former 19th-century ice warehouse, the little London Canal Museum has a barge cabin to sit in and models of boats, but the displays (photos and

BT Tower. *See p106.*

videos about ice-importer Carlo Gatti) on the history of the ice trade are perhaps the most interesting. The installation of new, low-energy lighting should help make the most of the collections. The canalside walk from here to Camden Town is pleasant.

FREE St Pancras International

Pancras Road, NW1 2QP (7843 4250, www.stpancras.com). King's Cross tube/rail. **Open** 24hrs daily. **Admission** free. **No credit cards. Map** p397 L3.

William Barlow's gorgeous Victorian glass and iron train shed welcomes high-speed Eurostar trains from Paris. The redeveloped station has become somewhere to linger, but for all the public art, 'the longest champagne bar in Europe', the high-end boutiques, the gastropubs, the restaurants and the farmers' market, St Pancras is really worth a diversion because of the beauty of the original structure. ▶ *Sir George Gilbert Scott's magnificent neo-Gothic hotel building at the front of the station is also being refurbished – it will reopen as a Renaissance Marriott hotel perhaps in 2012.*

FREE St Pancras Old Church & St Pancras Gardens

St Pancras Road, NW1 1UL (7387 4193). Mornington Crescent tube or King's Cross tube/rail. **Open** *Gardens* 7am-dusk daily. *Services* 9am Mon-Fri; 7pm Tue; 9.30am Sun. **Admission** free. **No credit cards. Map** p397 K2.

St Pancras Old Church has been ruined and rebuilt many times. The current structure is handsome, but it's the churchyard that delights. Among those buried here are writer William Godwin and his wife, Mary Wollstonecraft; over their grave, their daughter Mary Godwin (author of *Frankenstein*) told her love for poet Percy Bysshe Shelley. Also here is the last resting place of Sir John Soane, one of only two Grade I-listed tombs (the other is Karl Marx's, in Highgate Cemetery; *see p151*). Designed for his wife, the tomb's dome influenced Gilbert Scott's design for the red British phone box.

FITZROVIA

Goodge Street or Tottenham Court Road tube.

Squeezed in between Tottenham Court Road, Oxford Street, Great Portland Street and Euston Road, Fitzrovia isn't as famous as Bloomsbury, but its history is just as rich. The origins of the name are hazy: some believe it comes from **Fitzroy Square**, named after Henry Fitzroy (son of Charles II); others insist it's due to the famous **Fitzroy Tavern** (16 Charlotte Street, 7580 3714), focal venue for London bohemia of the 1930s and '40s and a favourite with the likes of Dylan Thomas and George Orwell. Fitzrovia also had its share of artists: James McNeill

Whistler lived at 8 Fitzroy Square, later taken over by British Impressionist Walter Sickert, while Roger Fry's Omega Workshops, blurring the distinction between fine and decorative arts, had its studio at no.33. However, this raffish image is largely a thing of the past, and the area is better known as a high-powered media hub.

The district's icon is the **BT Tower** (*photo p105*), completed in 1964 as the Post Office Tower. Its revolving restaurant and observation deck featured in any film that wanted to prove how much London was swinging (*Bedazzled* is just one example). The restaurant is now reserved for corporate functions, but **Charlotte Street** and neighbouring byways have plenty of good options for earthbound food and drink.

FREE All Saints

7 Margaret Street, W1W 8JG (7636 1788, www.allsaintsmargaretstreet.org.uk). Oxford Circus tube. **Open** 7am-7pm daily. *Services* 7.30am, 8am, 1.10pm, 6pm, 6.30pm Mon-Fri; 7.30am, 8am, 6pm, 6.30pm Sat; 8am, 10.20am, 11am, 5.15pm, 6pm Sun. **Admission** free. **No credit cards. Map** p416 U1.

Respite from the tumult of Oxford Street, this 1850s church was designed by William Butterfield, one of the great Gothic Revivalists. The church looks as if it has been lowered into its tiny site, so tight is the fit; its lofty spire is the second-highest in London. Behind the polychromatic brick façade, the shadowy, lavish interior is one of the capital's finest ecclesiastical triumphs, with luxurious marble, flamboyant tile work and glittering stones built into its pillars.

Pollock's Toy Museum

1 Scala Street, W1T 2HL (7636 3452, www.pollockstoymuseum.com). Goodge Street tube. **Open** 10am-5pm Mon-Sat. **Admission** £5; £2-£4 reductions; free under-3s. **Credit** AmEx, MC, V. **Map** p396 J5.

Housed in a creaky Georgian townhouse, Pollock's is named after Benjamin Pollock, the last of the Victorian toy theatre printers. By turns beguiling and creepy, it's a nostalgia-fest of old board games, tin trains, porcelain dolls and Robertson's gollies. It's fascinating for adults but less so for children, for whom the displays may seem a bit static; describing a pile of painted woodblocks stuffed in a cardboard box as a 'Build a skyscraper' kit may make them feel lucky to be going home to their Wii.

INSIDE TRACK STREET ART

Many of Fitzrovia's more rakish characters and most familiar buildings appear in the 60 foot **Fitzrovia Mural**, painted on a wall next to Goodge Street tube off Tottenham Court Road in 1980.

Covent Garden & the Strand

A covered market with more buskers than Cockney barrow boys.

From the capital's wholesale fruit and veg market, decades-since relocated to Vauxhall, to the Royal Opera House, still regal overlord of the market's north-east corner, **Covent Garden** has always been an index of the extremes of London life. At which end of the slippery scale you think it sits will depend on your tolerance for crowds. The masses descend daily on the restored 19th-century market and its cobbled 'piazza' to peruse the la-di-da shops and gawp at the street entertainment. Yet even the most crowd-averse Londoner finds

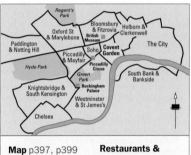

| **Map** p397, p399 & p416 | **Restaurants & cafés** pp214-216 |
| **Hotels** pp189-191 | **Pubs & bars** p238 |

plenty that's irresistible: the **London Transport Museum** (*see p109*); the **Royal Opera House** (*see p109*), eager nowadays to draw in all kinds of visitor; and, down towards the river on the grubbily historic **Strand**, the **Courtauld Gallery** just off the vast courtyard of **Somerset House** (for both, *see p111*).

SIGHTS

COVENT GARDEN

Covent Garden or Leicester Square tube.

Covent Garden was once the property of the medieval Abbey ('convent') of Westminster. When Henry VIII dissolved the monasteries, it passed to John Russell, first Earl of Bedford, in 1552; his family still owns land hereabouts. During the 16th and 17th centuries, they developed the area: the fourth Earl employed

Inigo Jones to create the Italianate open square that remains the area's centrepiece.

Market activity in Covent Garden was first documented in 1640 on the south side of the square, with stalls selling fruit and vegetables. The market grew until it had become London's pre-eminent fruit and vegetable wholesaler, employing over 1,000 porters; its success led to the opening of coffeehouses, theatres, gambling dens and brothels in the surrounding streets. A flower market was added (where the London Transport Museum now stands); the main market building itself was redesigned in the 19th century by Charles Fowler.

In the second half of the 20th century, it became obvious that the congested streets of central London were unsuitable for such market traffic and the decision was taken to move the traders out; for a look at the market shortly before it closed, watch Alfred Hitchcock's 1972 thriller *Frenzy*. In 1974, with the market gone, the threat of property development loomed for the empty stalls and offices. It was only through demonstrations that the

INSIDE TRACK
THAT'S THE WAY TO DO IT

On 9 May 1662, Samuel Pepys observed what is thought to be Britain's first Punch & Judy show ('an Italian puppet play', as he described it) just by **St Paul's Covent Garden** (*see p109*). This glorious event is celebrated yearly at the **Covent Garden May Fayre & Puppet Festival**; *see p280*.

area was saved. It's now a pleasant place for a stroll, especially if you catch it early on a fine morning before the crowds descend.

Covent Garden Piazza

Centred on Covent Garden Piazza, the area now offers a combination of gentrified shops, restaurant and cafés, supplemented by street artists and busking musicians in the lower courtyard. The majority of the entertainment takes place under the portico of **St Paul's Covent Garden** (*see right*).

Tourists favour the 180-year-old **covered market** (7836 9136, www.coventgardenlondon uk.com), which combines upmarket chain stores such as **Hobbs**, **Whistles** and **Crabtree &**

Evelyn with a collection of small, sometimes quirky but often rather twee independent shops. On the way down to the market, on the right, a whole historic building has been given over to the swanky new **Apple Store** (1-7 The Piazza, WC2E 8HB, 7447 1400, www.apple.com), an indication, perhaps, of the kind of upmarket tenants the market's organisers hope to pursue. The market building is best viewed from the Amphitheatre Café Bar's terrace loggia at the **Royal Opera House** (*see right*).

Change is barely evident elsewhere. The **Apple Market**, in the North Hall, still has arts and crafts stalls from Tuesday to Sunday, and antiques on Monday. Across the road, the tackier **Jubilee Market** deals mostly in novelty T-shirts and other tat.

Plaques, Decay

London's lost actors and their testaments to mortality.

St Paul's Covent Garden (*see right*) is justly known as the Actors' Church. Thespians commemorated on its walls range from those lost in obscurity – step forward Percy Press the Punch & Judy man – to those destined for immortality – Charlie Chaplin. Perhaps most charming are the numerous sublunary figures. Hello, William Henry Pratt, his birth name forgotten to all but devotees, yet – as Boris Karloff – universally famous as the real flesh behind unforgettable monsters. Take a bow too, Hattie Jacques, archetypal matron in the interminable series of *Carry On...* films. The Jacques memorial is so very plain you wonder if the inscriber felt that any embellishment would seem impertinence in the face of such a big comic persona.

There are plenty of inadvertently comic and inescapably tragic memorials across London, not least in the tranquil, lovely Postman's Park (*see p88*), but surely no more romantic tribute is paid anywhere in the city than here to Vivien Leigh. Her plaque is simply inscribed with words from Shakespeare's *Antony & Cleopatra*: 'Now boast thee, death, in thy possession lies a lass unparallel'd.'

Whenever we visit this church, however, our first homage is always paid to the memory of the mysterious 'Pantopuck the Puppetman', one AR Philpott. Who was he? Why is he here? We choose to imagine him wooing Edna Best, who is remembered not far away as 'The Constant Nymph'. Was ever name so charming as Edna? How could our Mr Philpott have resisted?

★ London Transport Museum
Covent Garden Piazza, WC2E 7BB (7379 6344, www.ltmuseum.co.uk). Covent Garden tube. **Open** 10am-6pm Mon-Thur, Sat, Sun; 11am-6pm Fri. **Admission** £10; £6-£8 reductions; free under-16s. **Credit** AmEx, DC, MC, V. **Map** p416 Z3.

Reopened in 2007 after the most thorough refurbishment since its move to Covent Garden in 1980, the London Transport Museum traces the city's transport history from the horse age to the present day. As well as a remodelled interior, the museum emerged with a much more confident focus on social history and design, illustrated by a superb array of preserved buses, trams and trains, and backed up by some brilliant temporary exhibitions.

The collections are in broadly chronological order, beginning with the Victorian gallery, where a replica of Shillibeer's first horse-drawn bus service in 1829 takes pride of place. Another gallery is dedicated to the museum's truly impressive collection of poster art. Under the leadership of Frank Pick, in the early 20th century London Transport developed one of the most coherent brand identities in the world. The new museum also raises some interesting and important questions about the future of public transport in the city, with a display on ideas that are 'coming soon'.
▶ *For occasional opening of the museum's huge Acton depot, see p175* **Inside Track**.

Royal Opera House
Bow Street, WC2E 9DD (7304 4000, www.roh.org.uk). Covent Garden tube. **Open** 10am-3.30pm Mon-Sat. **Admission** free. *Stage tours* £10; £7-£9 reductions. **Credit** AmEx, DC, MC, V. **Map** p416 Y3.

The Royal Opera House was founded in 1732 by John Rich on the profits of his production of John Gay's *Beggar's Opera*; the current building, constructed roughly 150 years ago but extensively remodelled since, is the third on the site. Visitors can explore the massive eight-floor building as part of an organised tour, including the main auditorium, the costume workshops and sometimes even a rehearsal. Certain parts of the building are also open to the general public, including the glass-roofed Floral Hall, the Crush Bar (so named because in Victorian times, the only thing served during intermissions was orange and lemon crush) and the Amphitheatre Café Bar.
▶ *For the Royal Opera House's primary function as a music venue, see p319.*

FREE St Paul's Covent Garden
Bedford Street, WC2E 9ED (7836 5221, www.actorschurch.org). Covent Garden or Leicester Square tube. **Open** 8.30am-5pm Mon-Fri; 9am-1pm Sun. Times vary Sat; phone for details. *Services* 1.10pm Tue, Wed; 6am Thur; 11am Sun. *Choral Evensong* 4pm 2nd Sun of mth. **Admission** free; donations appreciated. **No credit cards. Map** p416 Y3.

Covent Garden Piazza.

Known as the Actors' Church for its long association with Covent Garden's theatres, this pleasingly spare building was designed by Inigo Jones in 1631. A lovely limewood wreath by the 17th-century master carver Grinling Gibbons hangs inside the front door as a reminder that he and his wife are interred in the crypt. For the many thespians commemorated on its walls, *see left* **Plaques, Decay**.

Elsewhere in Covent Garden

Outside Covent Garden Piazza, the area offers a mixed bag of entertainment, eateries and shops. Nearest the markets, most of the more unusual shops have been superseded by a homogeneous mass of cafés, while big fashion chains – and the new **St Martin's Courtyard** mall (www.stmartinscourtyard.co.uk) – have all but domesticated Long Acre. There are more interesting stores north of here on Neal Street and Monmouth Street; Earlham Street is also home to the **Donmar Warehouse** (*see p347*), a former banana-ripening depot that's now an intimate and groundbreaking theatre. On tiny Shorts Gardens next door is the **Neal's Yard Dairy** (*see p269*), purveyor of exceptional UK cheeses; down a passageway one door along is Neal's Yard itself, known for its co-operative cafés, herbalists and head shops.

South of Long Acre and east of the Piazza, historical depravity is called to account at the former **Bow Street Magistrates Court**. Once home to the Bow Street Runners, the precursors of the Metropolitan Police, this was also where Oscar Wilde entered his plea when arrested for 'indecent acts' in 1895. It's currently being converted into a hotel. To the south, Wellington and Catherine streets mix restaurants and theatres, including the grand

SIGHTS

Theatre Royal. Other diversions in and
around Covent Garden include the museum
at **Freemasons' Hall** (7831 9811, www.
freemasonry.london.museum; call for details
of tours), the eye-catchingly bombastic white
stone building where Long Acre becomes Great
Queen Street; and, at opposite ends both of St
Martin's Lane and the cultural spectrum, lap-
dancing club **Stringfellows** (16-19 Upper St
Martin's Lane, 7240 5534) and the **Coliseum**
(*see p317*), home of the English National Opera.

THE STRAND & EMBANKMENT

Embankment tube or Charing Cross tube/rail.

Until as recently as the 1860s, the Strand ran
beside the Thames; indeed, it was originally
the river's bridlepath. In the 14th century, it
was lined with grand residences with gardens
that ran down to the water. It wasn't until
the 1870s that the Thames was pushed back
with the creation of the Embankment and its
adjacent gardens. By the time George Newnes's
famed *Strand* magazine was introducing its
readership to Sherlock Holmes (1891), the street
boasted the Cecil Hotel (long since demolished),
Simpson's, **King's College** and **Somerset
House** (*see right*). Prime Minister Benjamin
Disraeli described it as 'perhaps the finest street
in Europe'. Nobody would make such a claim
today – there are too many overbearing office
blocks and underwhelming restaurants – but
there's still plenty to interest visitors.

In 1292, the body of Eleanor of Castile,
consort to King Edward I, completed its
funerary procession from Lincoln in the small
hamlet of Charing, at the western end of what
is now the Strand. The occasion was marked by
the erection of the last of 12 elaborate crosses. A
replica of the Eleanor Cross (originally set just
south of nearby Trafalgar Square; *see p129*)
was placed in 1865 on the forecourt of **Charing
Cross Station**; it remains there today, looking
like the spire of a sunken cathedral. It emerged
from under tarpaulins in summer 2010 after
major refurbishments. Across the road, behind

St Martin-in-the-Fields (*see p131*), is
Maggie Hambling's weird memorial to a more
recent queen, *A Conversation with Oscar Wilde*.
The Embankment itself can be reached down
Villiers Street. Pass through the tube station
to the point at which boat tours with on-board
entertainment depart. Just to the east stands
Cleopatra's Needle, an obelisk presented
to the British nation by the viceroy of Egypt,
Mohammed Ali, in 1820 but not set in place
by the river for a further 59 years. The obelisk
was originally erected around 1500 BC by the
pharaoh Tuthmosis III at a site near modern-
day Cairo, before being moved to Alexandria,
Cleopatra's capital, in 10 BC. By this time,
however, the great queen was 20 years dead.

Back on the Strand, the majestic **Savoy**
hotel (*see p191*) has just reached the end of
tortuously thorough refurbishment. The hotel
first opened in 1889, financed by profits from
Richard D'Oyly Carte's productions of Gilbert
and Sullivan's light operas at the neighbouring
Savoy Theatre (*see p345* **Legally Blonde**).
The theatre, which pre-dates the hotel by eight
years, was the first to use electric lights.

Benjamin Franklin House

*36 Craven Street, the Strand, WC2N 5NF
(7925 1405, www.benjaminfranklinhouse.org).
Charing Cross tube/rail or Embankment tube.*
Open pre-book tours by phone or online. *Box
office* 10.30am-5pm Wed-Sun. **Admission** £7;
£5 reductions; free under-16s. **Credit** AmEx,
MC, V. **Map** p416 Y5.

This is the house where Franklin – scientist, diplo-
mat, philosopher, inventor and Founding Father of
the US – lived between 1757 and 1775. It isn't a
museum in the conventional sense, but can be
explored on pre-booked 'experiences' lasting a short
but intense 45 minutes (noon, 1pm, 2pm, 3.15pm and
4.15pm Wed-Sun). The tours are led by an actress
playing Franklin's landlady Margaret Stevenson,
using projections and sound to conjure up the world
and times in which Franklin lived. From noon on
Mondays, the house offers more straightforward,
20-minute tours given by house interns (£3.50).

THE ALDWYCH

Temple tube.

At the eastern end of the Strand is the Aldwych.
This grand crescent dates only from 1905, but
the name 'ald wic' (old settlement or market)
has its origins in the 14th century. To the south
is **Somerset House** (*see right*); even if you
aren't interested in the galleries, it's worth
visiting the regal fountain courtyard. Almost
in front of it is **St Mary-le-Strand** (7836 3126,
open 11am-4pm Tue-Sat, 10am-3pm Sun), James
Gibbs's first public building, completed in 1717.

Original plans called for a statue of Queen Anne on a column beside it, but she died before it could be built and the plan was scrapped. On Strand Lane, reached via Surrey Street, is the so-called **'Roman' bath** where Dickens took the waters – you have to peer through a dusty window.

On a traffic island just east of the Aldwych is **St Clement Danes** (7242 2380). It's believed that a church was first built here by the Danish in the ninth century, but the current building is mainly Wren's handiwork. It's the principal church of the RAF. Just beyond the church are the Royal Courts of Justice (*see p83*) and the original site of Temple Bar (*see p81*).

★ Courtauld Gallery

The Strand, WC2R 1LA (7848 2526, www. courtauld.ac.uk/gallery). Temple tube or Charing Cross tube/rail. **Open** *10am-6pm daily. Tours* phone for details. **Admission** *£5; £4 reductions. Free 10am-2pm Mon; students & under-18s daily.* **Credit** MC, V. **Map** p399 M7.

Located for the last two decades in the north wing of Somerset House (*see right*), the Courtauld has one of Britain's greatest collections of paintings, and contains several works of world importance. Although there are some outstanding early works (Cranach's wonderful *Adam & Eve*, for one), the collection's strongest suit is in Impressionist and Post-Impressionist paintings. Popular masterpieces include Manet's astonishing *A Bar at the Folies-Bergère*, alongside plenty of superb Monets and Cézannes, important Gauguins (such as *Nevermore*), and some Van Goghs and Seurats. On the top floor, there's a selection of gorgeous Fauvist works, a lovely room of Kandinskys and plenty more besides.

Hidden downstairs, the sweet little gallery café is frequently forgotten, but it feels delightfully separate from the rest of Somerset House. Make a free

Monday morning visit to the art collection and finish with a relaxed lunch. Note that bulky backpacks must be carried, not worn, through the collection; there are a few coin-operated lockers downstairs.

FREE Somerset House & the Embankment Galleries

The Strand, WC2R 1LA (7845 4600, www. somersethouse.org.uk). Temple tube or Charing Cross tube/rail. **Open** *10am-6pm (last entry 5.15pm) daily. Tours* phone for details. **Admission** *Courtyard & terrace free. Embankment Galleries prices vary; check* website for details. *Tours* phone for details. **Credit** MC, V. **Map** p399 M7.

The original Somerset House was a Tudor palace commissioned by the Duke of Somerset. In 1775, it was demolished to make way for a new building, effectively the first purpose-built office block in the world. The architect Sir William Chambers spent the last 20 years of his life working on the neoclassical edifice overlooking the Thames, built to accommodate learned societies such as the Royal Academy. Various governmental offices also took up residence.

The taxmen are still here, but the rest of the building is open to the public. Attractions include a formidable art gallery (the wonderful Courtauld; *see left*), the handsome fountain court, and a terraced café and a classy restaurant, both taken over in 2010 by Tom Aikens (*see p222* **Tom's Kitchen**). The Embankment Galleries explore connections between art, architecture and design in temporary exhibitions, and at Christmas usually host an adventurous market; downstairs, a ceremonial Thames barge and information boards explain the place's history, to the accompaniment of Handel's *Water Music*. In summer, children never tire of running through the choreographed fountains; in winter, a popular ice rink is erected on top of them.

SIGHTS

Somerset House

Soho & Leicester Square

The bohemians are not yet entirely banished from the city's core.

For more than two centuries, poseurs, spivs, tarts, toffs, drunks and divas have gathered in **Soho** to ply their trades. Many of the area's music, film and advertising businesses have moved on, but the gay scene still thrives, and now drives a non-stop party atmosphere.

Hemmed in by Oxford Street to the north, Charing Cross Road to the east, Shaftesbury Avenue to the south and Regent Street to the west, Soho is packed with a huge range of restaurants, clubs and bars, sharing the streets with a sizeable residential community. Just to the south, beyond tiny **Chinatown**, **Leicester Square** is many a drunken exhibitionist's favourite late-night stamping ground – the council hopes it will soon return to more general favour.

| Map p416 | Hotels pp191-192 |
| Pubs & bars pp239-240 | Restaurants & cafés pp216-218 |

SOHO SQUARE

Tottenham Court Road tube.

Forming the area's northern gateway, **Soho Square** was laid out in 1681. It was initially called King's Square; a weather-beaten statue of Charles II stands just north of the centre. On warmer days, the grassy spaces are filled with courting couples as snacking workers occupy its benches; one of these benches is dedicated to singer Kirsty MacColl, in honour of her song named after the square. The denominations of

INSIDE TRACK SO LONG, SOHO

With so much of Soho lost except to history, it's pleasing to see someone is trying to keep track of the ephemera: **www.themuseumofsoho.org.uk** has the stories of the Colony Room, Windmill Girls, the Pierpoint Monument and all sorts of interesting odds and ends.

the two churches on the square testify to the area's long-standing European credentials: as well as the French Protestant church, you'll find St Patrick's, one of the first Catholic churches built in England after the Reformation.

Two classic Soho streets run south from the square. **Greek Street**, its name a nod to a church that once stood here, is lined with restaurants and bars, among them 50-year-old Hungarian eaterie the **Gay Hussar** (no.2, 7437 0973) and the nearby **Pillars of Hercules** pub (no.7, 7437 1179), where the literati once enjoyed long liquid lunches. Just by the Pillars, an arch leads to Manette Street and the Charing Cross Road, where you'll find **Foyles** (*see p257*). Back on Greek Street, no.49 was once Les Cousins, a folk venue (note the heldover mosaic featuring a musical note); Casanova lived briefly at no.46.

Parallel to Greek Street is **Frith Street**, once home to Mozart (1764-65, no.20) and painter John Constable (1810-11, no.49). Humanist essayist William Hazlitt died in 1830 at no.6, now a discreet hotel named in his memory (*see p191* **Hazlitt's**). Further down the street are **Ronnie Scott's** (*see p326*), Britain's best-known jazz club, and, across from Ronnie's, the similarly mythologised **Bar Italia** (no.22, 7437 4520). A large portrait of Rocky Marciano dominates Italia's narrow, chrome bar, but it's the place's 24-hour opening that makes it likely you'll have to fight for a seat.

OLD COMPTON STREET & AROUND

Leicester Square or Tottenham Court Road tube.

Linking Charing Cross Road to Wardour Street and crossed by Greek, Frith and Dean streets, **Old Compton Street** is London's gay catwalk (*see below* **Gay Superhighway**). Tight T-shirts congregate around **Balans** (*see p309*), **Compton's** (nos.51-53) and the **Admiral**

Duncan (no.54). However, the street has an interesting history that dates back long before rainbow flags were hung above its doors. Now the **Boulevard Bar & Dining Room**, 59 Old Compton Street was formerly the 2i's Coffee Bar, the skiffle venue where stars and svengalis mingled in the late 1950s and early '60s at the dawn of the British rock 'n' roll scene. Around this time, the street drew a raffish collection of chancers, ne'er-do-wells and criminals, two of whom – Jack Spot and Albert Dimes – faced off in a famous knife fight at the intersection of Old Compton Street and Frith Street in 1955.

Visit Old Compton Street in the morning for a sense of the mostly vanished immigrant Soho of old. Cheeses and cooked meats from **Camisa** (no.61, 7437 7610) and roasting beans from the **Algerian Coffee Stores** (*see p267*) scent the air, as **Pâtisserie Valerie** (no.44, 7437 3466,

Gay Superhighway

The scene has moved elsewhere, but Old Compton Street is still pure theatre.

Walk down **Old Compton Street** (*see above*) and it's obvious that you're in Europe's queerest quarter. Coffeeshops overflow with orange-hued queens, tag teams hand out flyers and drinks promos, and there's plenty of covert and not-so-covert checking-out. In short, it's fagtastic. So why have London's boys and girls been emigrating en masse to Shoreditch and Vauxhall?

Soho's perma-tanned princes and showtunes are seen as a little bridge-and-tunnel by your average Shoreditch fashion

gay, while Vauxhall marys tend to baulk at Westminster Council's limited opening hours ('Closed by 1am? We haven't even snorted dessert yet.'). But talk of Soho going the way of Earl's Court – the city's one-time queer quarter, of which few traces remain – is premature.

For one thing, out east and down south there's basically nothing to do and no one to look at during the day. Not so in Soho. Old Compton Street's coffeeshops (**Caffè Nero** at the Frith Street corner, **Balans** at no.60, **Costa** at no.39) are prime perches. Or check out the **Admiral Duncan** (no.54), **Freedom** (66 Wardour Street) or **Friendly Society** (79 Wardour Street). When night falls, there are venues such as **Heaven** (*see p310*), a scene institution whose credentials were reinforced when the G-A-Y night moved there a couple of years ago.

In short, Soho's queer credentials remain strong because of its location. This is London's cosmopolitan heartland and it overflows with theatres, production companies and publishing houses, hornets' nests of homosexuality. There's a real mix of people, which means there's none of the scenester snootiness of the east or the crazed-eye sweatiness of the south. You get all sorts in Soho – tourists talking to recently-popped-out-the-closets, out-of-towners mixing with post-work drinkers – and that's the real attraction. In a city as notoriously cold as London, Soho's gay venues are some of its friendliest corners.

SIGHTS

www.patisserie-valerie.co.uk) does a brisk trade in croissants and cakes. Its traditional French rival is the older **Maison Bertaux** (*see p217*), an atmospheric holdover from the 19th century that sits near the southern end of Greek Street.

Maison Bertaux is far from the only point of interest on the roads south of Old Compton Street. At the corner of Greek and Romilly Streets sits the **Coach & Horses** (no.29, 7437 5920), where irascible Soho flâneur Jeffrey Bernard held court for decades. It's almost opposite the members' club **Soho House** (no.40, 7734 5188), where a current crop of wannabes hopes to channel the same vibe. Two streets along, Dean Street holds the **French House** (*see p239*); formerly the York Minster pub, it was De Gaulle's London base for French resistance in World War II and in later years became a favourite of painters Francis Bacon and Lucian Freud.

North of Old Compton Street on Dean Street sits the **Groucho Club** (no.45), a members-only media hangout that was founded in the mid 1980s and named in honour of the familiar Groucho Marx quote about not wanting to join any club that would have him as a member. A few doors along, **Quo Vadis** (nos.26-29) has a costly grill room and an upstairs bar for members; Karl Marx, who lived in the garret at no.28 from 1850 to 1856, would probably not have approved. To the north is the **Soho Theatre** (*see p348*), which programmes comedy shows and new plays.

WARDOUR STREET & AROUND

Leicester Square or Tottenham Court Road tube.

Parallel to Dean Street, **Wardour Street** provides offices for film and TV production

---

A Better Leicester Square?

Central London's least appealing space begins to pull its socks up.

Locals have for many years scorned the fast food, expensive cinemas and tacky pavement artists of **Leicester Square**. Apart from the **tkts** booth (*see p342* **The Cheap Seats**), selling cut-price, same-day theatre tickets, and Leicester Place's unlikely neighbours the **Prince Charles** cinema (*see p300*) and the French Catholic church of **Notre Dame de France** (no.5, 7437 9363, www.notredamechurch.co.uk), with its Jean Cocteau murals, there was no reason to venture here. The green patch in the centre might be bearable on a sunny day, but woe betide anyone caught in the jostle of drunken suburban idiots and lost tourists at night.

When Westminster Council announced plans for an £18m redevelopment in 2008, there were serious doubts that the fortunes of the square could be turned round. The idea of a new layout for the square's centre (improved lighting, modish 'ribbon' seating doubtless designed to prevent drunks and the homeless getting a good kip) conjured visions of another clean, characterless, commerce-friendly space. Certainly the pitch is high-end: the Grade II-listed, Frank Matcham-designed **Hippodrome** (*see p116*; *pictured*) on the north-east corner is to reopen as a casino, while two new hotels are appearing in the north-west, a swish boutique **W** property from Starwood and an outpost of the brilliant **St John** restaurant (*see p189* **Come and St John the Fun**),

with beds upstairs. But not all memories of the square's cheerfully tacky phase will be erased: the glockenspiel clock that used to command the attention of crowds outside the Swiss Centre every hour will return, redesigned (27 bells, mechanical mountain farmers) but still chiming out the time on behalf of Switzerland Tourism.

companies, but is also known for its rock history. What's now upscale tapas joint **Meza** (no.100) was, for nearly three decades, the Marquee, where Led Zeppelin played their first London gig and Hendrix appeared four times. The latter's favourite Soho haunt was the nearby **Ship** pub (no.116), still with a sprinkling of music-themed knick-knacks. There's more music history at Trident Studios on nearby **St Anne's Court**: Lou Reed recorded *Transformer* here, and David Bowie cut both *Hunky Dory* and *The Rise and Fall of Ziggy Stardust* on the site.

Back when he was still known as David Jones, Bowie played a gig at the Jack of Clubs on Brewer Street, now **Madame JoJo's** (*see p329*). But this corner of Soho is most famous not for music but for its position at the heart of Soho's dwindling but still notorious sex trade. The **Raymond Revuebar** opened on the neon alleyway of Walker's Court in 1958, swiftly becoming London's most famous strip club. It closed in 2004, but numerous smaller, seedier establishments continue to tout for business close by on Brewer Street and Tisbury Court, despite the council's efforts to winkle every trace of malfeasance out of Soho.

North of here, **Berwick Street** is a lovely mix of old-school London raffishness and new-Soho style. The former comes courtesy of an amiable street food market, with stalls offering sweets, nuts, fruit, vegetables and even fresh fish (9am-6pm Mon-Sat), and the egalitarian, old-fashioned and unceasingly popular **Blue Posts** pub (no.22, 7437 5008), where builders, post-production editors, restaurateurs and market traders gabble and glug as one beneath a portrait of Berwick Street-born star of stage and radio Jessie Matthews (1907-81). It's quite a contrast with the **Endurance** (no.90, 7437 2944), the street's gastropub; **Flat White** (no.17, 7734 0370), a shabby-chic coffee bar; and **Yauatcha** (*see p218*), a design-led teahouse and pioneering all-day dim sum eaterie, with its Christian Liagre interior.

WEST SOHO

Piccadilly Circus tube.

West of Berwick Street, Soho has been branded 'West Soho' in a misplaced bid to give some kind of upmarket identity to its shops. **Brewer Street** does have some interesting places; among them is the **Vintage Magazine Store** (nos.39-43, 7439 8525), offering everything from retro robots to pre-war issues of *Vogue*. Star restaurant **Hix** (*see p212* **Hix Oyster & Chop House**) is also here. On Great Windmill Street is the **Windmill Theatre** (nos.17-19), which gained fame in the 1930s and '40s for its

Berwick Street Market.

'revuedeville' shows with erotic 'tableaux' – naked girls who remained stationary in order to stay within the law. The place is now a lap-dancing joint. North of Brewer Street is **Golden Square**. Developed in the 1670s, it became the political and ambassadorial district of the late 17th and early 18th centuries, and remains home to some of the area's grandest residential buildings (many now home to media firms).

Just north of Golden Square is **Carnaby Street**, which became a fashion mecca shortly after John Stephen opened His Clothes here in 1956; Stephen, who went on to own more than a dozen fashion shops on the street, is now commemorated with a plaque at the corner with Beak Street. After thriving during the Swinging Sixties, Carnaby Street went on to become a rather seamy commercialised backwater. However, along with nearby **Newburgh Street** and **Kingly Court** (*see p255*), it's undergone a revival, with the tourist traps and chain stores joined by a wealth of independent stores. Kingly Street, now full of fashionable bars such as **Two Floors** (no.3, 7439 1007), has a chequered past (*see p116* **Inside Track**).

CHINATOWN & LEICESTER SQUARE

Leicester Square tube.

Shaftesbury Avenue is the very heart of Theatreland. The Victorians built seven grand

SIGHTS

INSIDE TRACK BAD BOYS

Celebrities and criminals have long rubbed shoulders in Soho. On boutique-friendly Kingly Street, no.7 was once a brothel owned by the Messini brothers, five Maltese siblings who ran the vice trade from the 1930s until their empire was cracked by a crusading journalist in the '50s. Two doors down at no.9 was the Bag O Nails, the nightclub where Paul met Linda and Jimi Hendrix played his official introduction to the press in 1966.

theatres here, six of which still stand. The most impressive is the gorgeous **Palace Theatre** on Cambridge Circus, which opened in 1891 as the Royal English Opera House; when grand opera flopped, the theatre reopened as a music hall two years later. Appropriately, it's most famous for the musicals it has staged: *The Sound of Music* (1961) and *Jesus Christ Superstar* (1972) had their London premières here, and *Les Misérables* racked up 7,602 performances between 1985 and 2004. The current resident is *Priscilla, Queen of the Desert*.

Just opposite the Palace Theatre, what's now the Med Kitchen occupies premises that were

Chinatown.

once home to Marks & Co, the shop made famous by Helene Hanff's *84 Charing Cross Road*. A few second-hand bookshops line **Charing Cross Road** to the south, heading towards Leicester Square, where **Cecil Court** (*see p257* **Inside Track**) is a better bet for bibliophiles. West of Charing Cross Road and south of Shaftesbury Avenue, and officially just outside Soho, is the city's **Chinatown**.

The Chinese are relative latecomers to this part of town. London's original Chinatown was set around Limehouse in east London, but hysteria about Chinese opium dens and criminality led to 'slum clearances' in 1934 (interestingly, the surrounding slums were deemed to be in less urgent need of clearance). It wasn't until the 1950s that the Chinese put down roots here, attracted by the cheap rents along Gerrard and Lisle streets.

The ersatz oriental gates, stone lions and pagoda-topped phone boxes around Gerrard Street suggest a Chinese theme park, but this remains a close-knit residential and working enclave, a genuine focal point for the Chinese community in London. The area is crammed with restaurants, Asian grocery stores and a host of small shops selling iced-grass jelly, speciality teas and cheap air tickets to Beijing.

South of Chinatown, **Leicester Square** was one of London's most exclusive addresses in the 17th century; in the 18th, it became home to the royal court of Prince George (later George II). Satirical painter William Hogarth had a studio here (1733-64), as did 18th-century artist Sir Joshua Reynolds; both are commemorated by busts in the small gardens that lie at the heart of the square, although it's the statue of a tottering Charlie Chaplin that gets all the attention. There's no particular reason for Chaplin to be here, other than the fact that Leicester Square is considered the home of British film thanks to its numerous cinemas. The monolithic **Odeon Leicester Square** (*see p299*) once boasted the UK's largest screen, and probably still has the UK's highest ticket prices. Like the neighbouring **Empire**, it's regularly used for movie premières.

The **Hippodrome**, on the corner of Cranbourn Street and Charing Cross Road beside the tube station, is an impressive red-brick edifice designed by the prolific theatre architect Frank Matcham. It became famous as the 'Talk of the Town' cabaret venue in the 1960s, featuring the likes of Shirley Bassey and Judy Garland. It is currently being refurbished to reopen as a casino, perhaps before the end of 2011. This, and the arrival of two new hotels on the north-western corner of the square, are encouragement for the council in its attempts to revivify a square most locals cordially loathe (*see p114* **A Better Leicester Square?**).

SIGHTS

Oxford Street
& Marylebone

Genteel sidestreets and a pedestrian-crazed shopping thoroughfare.

Oxford Street is working hard to stay top of London's shopping destinations. A revamped roundabout at **Marble Arch** (*see below*), wider pavements, innovative pedestrian crossings and an all-new 'eastern gateway' development should, come London 2012, make sunset on 'London's High Street' memorable for more of the right reasons. Until then, crowd-phobic locals will continue to favour the luxury cafés and boutiques of **Marylebone**, the flowering green acres of **Regent's Park** (*see p120*) and, on occasion, **London Zoo** (*see p121*).

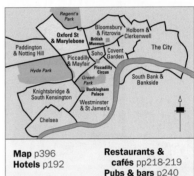

Map p396	**Restaurants &**
Hotels p192	**Cafés** pp218-219
	Pubs & bars p240

Map p396
Hotels p192
Restaurants & Cafés pp218-219
Pubs & bars p240

OXFORD STREET

Bond Street, Marble Arch, Oxford Circus or Tottenham Court Road tube.

Official estimates put the annual footfall at somewhere near 200 million people per year, but few Londoners love **Oxford Street**. A shopping district since the 19th century, it's unmanageably busy on weekends and in the run-up to Christmas. Even outside these times, it's never pretty, lined with over-familiar chain stores and choked with bus traffic. The New West End Company (www.newwestend.com) has been charged with changing all that, and Oxford Circus, Marble Arch and Regent Street are feeling the benefits.

The street gets smarter as you walk from east to west. The eastern end around Tottenham Court Road station is under major redevelopment for Crossrail, but has anyway lacked destination shops for years. The string of big department stores – **John Lewis** (nos.278-306, 7629 7711), **Debenhams** (nos.334-348, 0844 561 6161) and **Selfridges** (no.400; *see p252* **Profile**) – are west of chaotic **Oxford Circus**. Apart from the art deco splendour of Selfridges, architectural interest along Oxford Street is largely limited to Oxford Circus's four identical convex corners,

constructed between 1913 and 1928. The crowds and rush of traffic hamper investigations, a problem the council attempted to address a couple of years ago by widening pavements, removing street clutter and creating Tokyo Shibuya-style diagonal crossings. The success of the plan has led to it proposing the same measures at Piccadilly Circus (*see p124*), at the southern end of Regent Street. Further Crossrail-related redevelopment will begin at Bond Street station in 2011.

Oxford Street gained notoriety as the route by which condemned men were conveyed from Newgate Prison to the old Tyburn gallows, stopping only for a last pint at the **Angel** (61-62 St Giles High Street, 7240 2876). Thousands gathered to watch the countless executions that were held at Tyburn over six centuries; held in 1783, the final execution to be carried out here is marked by an X on a traffic island at the junction of the Edgware and Bayswater roads. Close by, at the western end of Oxford Street, stands **Marble Arch**, with its Carrara marble cladding and sculptures celebrating Nelson and Wellington. It was designed by John Nash in 1827 as the entrance to a rebuilt Buckingham Palace, but the arch was moved here in 1851, after – it is said – a fuming Queen Victoria found it to be too narrow for her coach. Now

SIGHTS

Broadcasting House and **All Souls**.

SIGHTS

given a £2m revamp, it's been joined by renovated water fountains and gardens that contain an ongoing series of public sculpture commissions. The current incumbent is Nic Fiddian-Green's giant *Horse at Water*, a vast horse's head poised on its lips amid the lawns.

North of Oxford Circus

Great Portland Street, Oxford Circus or Regent's Park tube.

North of Oxford Circus runs **Langham Place**, notable for the Bath stone façade of John Nash's **All Souls Church** (Langham Place, 2 All Souls Place, 7580 3522, www.allsouls.org). Its bold combination of a Gothic spire and classical rotunda wasn't popular: in 1824, a year after it opened, the church was condemned in the House of Commons as 'deplorable and horrible'.

Opposite the church you'll find the BBC's **Broadcasting House**, an oddly asymmetrical art deco building that's shipshape in more ways than one. Prominent among the carvings is a statue of Shakespeare's Prospero and Ariel, his spirit of the air – or, in this case, the airwaves. The statue caused controversy when it was unveiled due to the flattering size of the airy sprite's manhood; artist Eric Gill was recalled and asked to make it more modest. Major renovations are under way, due to completion

in 2011. Over the road is the **Langham Hotel** (1C Portland Place, Regent Street, W1B 1JA, 7636 1000, http://london.langhamhotels.co.uk). It opened in 1865 as Britain's first grand hotel and has been home at various points to Mark Twain, Napoleon III and Oscar Wilde.

North, Langham Place turns into **Portland Place**, designed by Robert and James Adam as the glory of 18th-century London. Its Georgian terraced houses are now mostly occupied by embassies and swanky offices. At no.66 is the **Royal Institute of British Architects** (RIBA; *see p307*). Parallel to Portland Place are **Harley Street**, famous for its high-cost dentists and doctors, and **Wimpole Street**, erstwhile home to the poet Elizabeth Barrett Browning (no.50) and Sir Arthur Conan Doyle (2 Upper Wimpole Street).

MARYLEBONE

Baker Street, Bond Street, Marble Arch, Oxford Circus or Regent's Park tube.

North of Oxford Street, the fashionable district known to its boosters as 'Marylebone Village' has become a magnet for moneyed Londoners. Many visitors to the area head directly for the waxworks of **Madame Tussauds** (*see right*); there's also a small and oft-overlooked museum at the neighbouring **Royal Academy of Music** (7873 7300, www.ram.ac.uk). However, the area's beating heart is **Marylebone High Street**, teeming with interesting shops.

St Marylebone Church stands in its fourth incarnation at the northern end of the street. The name of the neighbourhood is a contraction of the church's earlier name, St Mary by the Bourne; the 'bourne' in question, Tyburn stream, still filters into the Thames near Pimlico, but its entire length is now covered. The church's lovely garden hosts designer clothing and artisan food stalls at the **Cabbages & Frocks** market on Saturdays (www.cabbagesandfrocks.co.uk).

More lovely boutiques can be found on winding **Marylebone Lane**, along with the **Golden Eagle** (no.59, 7935 3228), which hosts regular singalongs around its piano. There's fine food here, too, with smart, often upmarket eateries snuggling alongside delicatessens such as **La Fromagerie** (2-6 Moxon Street, 7935 0341, www.lafromagerie.co.uk) and century-old lunchroom **Paul Rothe & Son** (35 Marylebone Lane, 7935 6783). **Marylebone Farmers' Market** takes place in the Cramer Street car park every Sunday.

Further south, the soaring neo-Gothic interior of the 19th-century **St James's Roman Catholic Church** (22 George Street) is lit dramatically by stained-glass windows; Vivien

Leigh (née Hartley) married barrister Herbert Leigh Hunt here in 1932. Other cultural diversions include the **Wallace Collection** (*see below*) and the **Wigmore Hall** (*see p317*).

Madame Tussauds

Marylebone Road, NW1 5LR (0870 400 3000, www.madametussauds.com/london). Baker Street tube. **Open** 9.30am-6pm daily. **Admission** £28; £24 reductions; £99 family; free under-4s. **Credit** MC, V. **Map** p396 G4.

Streams of humanity jostle excitedly here for the chance to take pictures of each other planting a smacker on the waxen visage of fame and fortune. Madame Tussaud brought her show to London in 1802, 32 years after it was founded in Paris, and it's been expanding ever since, on these very premises since 1884. There are some 300 figures in the collection now, under various themes: 'A-list Party' (Brad, Keira, Kate Moss, Will Smith), 'Première Night' (Monroe, Chaplin, Arnie as the Terminator), 'Sports Zone' (Tendulkar, Rooney, Muhammad Ali), 'By Royal Appointment' and so on. If you're not already overheating, your palms will be sweating by the time you descend to the Chamber of Horrors in 'Scream', where only teens claim to enjoy the floor drops and scary special effects. Much more pleasant is the kitsch 'Spirit of London' ride, whisking you through 400 years of London life in a taxi pod.

Since summer 2010, Tussauds has also been host to Marvel Super Heroes 4D. Interactives and waxworks of Iron Man, Spiderman and an 18ft Hulk provide further photo opportunities, but the highlight is the nine-minute film in '4D' (as well as 3D projections, there are 'real' effects such as a shaking floor

and smoke in the auditorium) in the dome that used to house the planetarium.

▶ *Get here before 10am to avoid the enormous queues, and book online in advance to make the steep admission price more palatable.*

★ FREE Wallace Collection

Hertford House, Manchester Square, W1U 3BN (7935 0687, www.wallacecollection.org). Bond Street tube. **Open** 10am-5pm daily. **Admission** free. **Credit** (shop) AmEx, MC, V. **Map** p396 G5.

Built in 1776, this handsome house contains an exceptional collection of 18th-century French furniture, painting and objets d'art, as well as an amazing array of medieval armour and weaponry. It all belonged to Sir Richard Wallace, who, as the illegitimate offspring of the fourth Marquess of Hertford, inherited in 1870 the treasures his father had amassed in the last 30 years of his life. Room after grand room contains Louis XIV and XV furnishings and Sèvres porcelain; the galleries are hung with

ZSL London Zoo. *See p121.*

paintings by Gainsborough, Velázquez, Fragonard, Titian and Reynolds; Franz Hals's *Laughing Cavalier* (neither laughing nor a cavalier) is one of the best known, along with Fragonard's *The Swing*. Since summer 2010, refurbished West Galleries have displayed the museum's 19th-century and Venetian works, including paintings by Canaletto, and the collections of miniatures and gold boxes have been on show in the Boudoir Cabinet; new East Galleries should be complete by early 2012.

▶ *The museum restaurant is beautifully set in a glass-roofed courtyard, but service can be slow.*

REGENT'S PARK

Baker Street or Regent's Park tube.

Regent's Park (open 5am-dusk daily) is one of London's most delightful open spaces. Originally a hunting ground for Henry VIII, it

---

Walk The Sidestreet Shuffle

Avoid Oxford Street's clogged pavements with a trail through the back streets.

When it comes to shopping on Oxford Street, the average Londoner doesn't. But if a visit is unavoidable, you can escape the crowds by diving into the streets that fringe the main drag. This hour-long walk introduces the hinterlands of Oxford Street, prized by locals; walk the whole thing or, just as easily, pick it up and leave it at any point.

Rathbone Place marks the lower reaches of Fitzrovia, where the worlds of media and design collide with the rag trade. The fun begins at Hobgoblin (no.24, 7323 9040), a folk music store where musicians test-drive zithers, banjos and ukuleles. Close by on Percy Street, **Contemporary Applied Arts** (*see p271*) sells outstanding British crafts, from jewellery to furniture.

Keep north up restaurant-lined Charlotte Street, buzzing with media types, then turn left beside the suave **Charlotte Street Hotel** (*see p186*) through Percy Passage. Cross the dog-leg of Rathbone Street, and head on via Dickensian Newman Passage

to emerge in Newman Street. Pause for a snap of the **BT Tower**, then go left and right on to Eastcastle Street. Detour up Margaret Street to **All Saints** church (*see p106*).

Back on Eastcastle Street sits cutting-edge gallery **Stuart Shave/Modern Art** (*see p304*). Over the road, **Fever** (no.52, 7636 6326) mixes cute retro-inspired clothing and accessories with vintage, while the **Getty Images Gallery** (no.46, 7291 5380) holds great photography exhibitions. Market Place opens ahead, a mellow collection of sidewalk cafés yards from the frenzy of Oxford Street. Stop for refreshment and then head across Oxford Street down Argyll Street, aiming for the half-timbered **Liberty** building (*see p253*).

Next, cross Regent Street towards Conduit Street, where a visit to **Vivienne Westwood**'s flamboyant flagship store (no.44, 7439 1109, www.vivienne westwood.com) provides a taste of punky London couture. Continue to

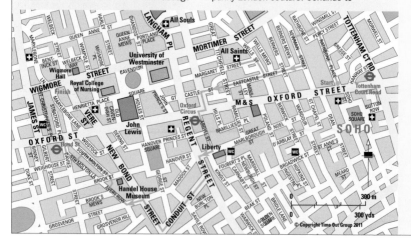

© Copyright Time Out Group 2011

remained a royals-only retreat long after it was formally designed by John Nash in 1811; only in 1845 did it open to the public as a spectacular shared space. Attractions run from the animal noises and odours of **ZSL London Zoo** (*see below*) to the enchanting **Open Air Theatre** (*see p343*); rowing boat hire, beautiful rose gardens, ice-cream stands and the **Garden Café** (7935 5729, www.thegardencafe.co.uk) complete the postcard-pretty picture.

New Bond Street into Grosvenor Street, then right up Avery Row. This is the land of Victorian London's great aristocratic estates, where narrow service alleys brought tradesmen to the rear entrances of the grand residences. The alleys still offer services to the gentry, but they're now exclusive little boutiques and restaurants that are hidden from the dazed tourists wandering nearby. On Avery Row, check out the **Paul Smith Sale Shop** (*see p263*).

Adjoining Lancashire Court is home to restaurants and the **Handel House Museum** (*see p126*), which faces Brook Street and, close by, Italian design legend **Alessi** (no.22, 7518 9091). Move on to pedestrianised South Molton Street and its strong mix of chain stores, cafés and independents, among them glittery **Butler & Wilson** (no.20, 7409 2955). Take the passage to the left of fashion queen **Browns** (*see p260*) and pop out by the imposing terracotta structure of **Grays Antique Market** (*see p274*).

Cross Oxford Street again, battling your way to the freestanding clock signposting the narrow entrance to St Christopher's Place. This warren of little streets houses a traffic-free complex of cafés and shops, among them handbag specialist **Ollie & Nic** (no.5, 7935 2185) and Finnish designer **Marimekko** (nos.16-17, 7486 6454). There's also a fountain and a flower-decked Victorian WC.

Need a rest? Head north to Wigmore Street for one last stop at **Robert Clergerie Shoes** (no.67, 7935 3601), before heading a couple of doors down to **Comptoir Libanais** (no.65, 7935 1110, www.lecomptoir.co.uk). This colourful and inviting Lebanese eaterie is the perfect place to mull over your purchases with a rosewater macaroon and a mint tea.

West of Regent's Park rises the golden dome of the **London Central Mosque** (www.iccuk.org), while the northern end of **Baker Street** is unsurprisingly heavy on nods of respect to the world's favourite freelance detective. At the **Sherlock Holmes Museum** (no.221B, 7935 8866, www.sherlock-holmes.co.uk), Holmes stories are earnestly re-enacted using mannequins, but serious fans may find more of interest among the books and photos of the **Sherlock Holmes Collection** at Marylebone Library (7641 1206, by appointment only); or, for that matter, at Arthur Conan Doyle's former home on Upper Wimpole Street and the Langham Hotel (for both, *see p118*), which plays a role in a number of the Holmes stories.

The Beatles painted 94 Baker Street with a psychedelic mural before opening it in December 1967 as the Apple Boutique, a clothing store run on such whimsical hippie principles that it had to close within six months due to financial losses. Fab Four pilgrims head to the **London Beatles Store** (no.231, 7935 4464, www.beatlesstorelondon.co.uk), where the ground-floor shop offers a predictable array of Beatles-branded accessories alongside genuine collectibles. Next door, **Elvisly Yours** (7486 2005) caters to the blue-suede-shoed fraternity.

★ ZSL London Zoo

Regent's Park, NW1 4RY (7722 3333, www. zsl.org/london-zoo). Baker Street or Camden Town tube then 274, C2 bus. **Open** 10am-6pm daily. **Admission** £18-£19.80; £15-£18.30 reductions; free under-3s. **Credit** AmEx, MC, V. **Map** p396 G2.

London Zoo has been open in one form or another since 1826. Spread over 36 acres and containing more than 600 species, it cares for many of the endangered variety – part of the entry price (pretty steep at nearly £20, in peak season and including the voluntary donation) goes towards the ZSL's projects around the world. The emphasis is on upbeat education. Regular events include 'animals in action' and keeper talks; explanations are simple, short and lively. Exhibits are entertaining: look out, in particular, for the re-creation of a kitchen overrun with large cockroaches. The relaunched 'Rainforest Life' biodome and the 'Meet the Monkeys' attractions allow visitors to walk through enclosures that recreate the natural habitat of, respectively, tree anteaters and sloths, and black-capped Bolivian squirrel monkeys, while personal encounters of the avian kind can be had in the Victorian Blackburn Pavilion. 'Gorilla Kingdom' is another highlight, and the reptile house delights and horrifies in equal measure. Bring a picnic basket and you could easily spend the entire day here. *Photo p119.*

▶ *Excellent for children, the petting zoo in Battersea Park is half the price; see p289.*

Paddington & Notting Hill

Middle Eastern kitchens, mazy markets and media darlings.

Sprawled beneath the Westway flyover, with its railway terminus and branch of the Grand Union Canal, **Paddington** is where central London meets the west of England. It's not an attractive area, but it holds appeal thanks to the Arab influence around the Edgware Road and the goodies hidden away in Alfie's Antique Market. There's nothing hidden away about **Notting Hill**, where **Portobello Market** is surrounded by some of the most desirable addresses in west London, one of which houses the inimitable **Museum of Brands, Packaging & Advertising**.

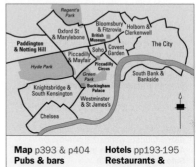

| **Map** p393 & p404 | **Hotels** pp193-195 |
| **Pubs & bars** pp240-241 | **Restaurants & cafés** pp224-225 |

SIGHTS

EDGWARE ROAD & PADDINGTON

Edgware Road, Lancaster Gate or Marble Arch tube, or Paddington tube/rail.

Part of the Romans' Watling Street from Dover to Wales, **Edgware Road** rules a definite north–south line marking where the West End stops and central west London begins. It's now the heart of the city's Middle East end: if you want to pick up your copy of *Al Hayat*, cash a cheque at the Bank of Kuwait or catch Egyptian football, head here. North of the Marylebone Road, **Church Street** is home to the wondrous **Alfie's Antique Market** (*see p274*).

INSIDE TRACK MARKET FINDS

Portobello Green Market has the area's best vintage fashion stalls. Look out for the excellent second-hand boot and shoe stall and brilliant vintage handbag stall (usually outside Falafel King), along with vintage clothing stall Sage Femme, often outside the Antique Clothing Shop.

The fact that the name Paddington has been immortalised by a certain small, ursine Peruvian émigré is appropriate, given that the area has long been home to refugees and immigrants. It was a country village until an arm of the Grand Union Canal arrived in 1801, linking London to the Midlands, followed in the 1830s by the railway. **Paddington Station**, with its fine triple roof of iron and glass, was built in 1851 to the specifications of the great engineer Isambard Kingdom Brunel.

Paddington's proximity to central London eventually drew in developers. To the east of the station, gleaming **Paddington Central** now provides a million square feet of office space, canalside apartments and restaurants. In St Mary's Hospital, the old-fashioned **Alexander Fleming Laboratory Museum** gives a sense of what the district used to be like.

Alexander Fleming Laboratory Museum
St Mary's Hospital, Praed Street, W2 1NY (7886 6528, www.imperial.nhs.uk/aboutus/museumsand archives/index.htm). Paddington tube/rail. **Open** 10am-1pm Mon-Thur. *By appointment* 2-5pm Mon-Thur; 10am-5pm Fri. **Admission** £4; £2 reductions; free under-5s. **No credit cards.** **Map** p393 D5.

Kensal Green Cemetery

Buzz in at the entrance on your left as you enter hospital and head up the stairs to find this tiny, dusty, instrument-cluttered lab. Enthusiastic guides conjure up the professor who, in 1928, noticed that mould contamination had destroyed some staphylococcus bacteria on a set-aside culture plate: he had discovered penicillin. The keen entrepreneurs across the street immediately began to advertise their pub's healthful properties, claiming the miracle fungus had blown into the lab from them. The video room has a documentary on Fleming's life and discovery.

NOTTING HILL

Notting Hill Gate, Ladbroke Grove or Westbourne Park tube.

Head north up Queensway from Kensington Gardens and turn west along **Westbourne Grove**. The road starts humble but gets posher the further west you go; cross Chepstow Road and you're in upmarket **Notting Hill**. A host of fashionable restaurants and bars exploit the lingering street cred of the fast-disappearing black and working-class communities; posh shops are a better reflection of the area's current character. **Notting Hill Gate** isn't a pretty street, but the leafy avenues to the south are; so is **Pembridge Road**, to the north, leading to the boutique-filled streets of Westbourne Grove and Ledbury Road, and to **Portobello Road** and its renowned market (*see p255*).

Halfway down, **Blenheim Crescent** boasts three notable independent booksellers. The **Travel Bookshop** (nos.13-15, 7229 5260, www.thetravelbookshop.com) is the store on which Hugh Grant's bookshop was based in the movie *Notting Hill*, a film that did more to undermine the area's bohemian credentials than a fleet of Starbucks. You'll often see a group of tourists here, listening intently to their guide. Under the Westway, that elevated section of the M40 motorway linking London with Oxford,

is the small but busy **Portobello Green Market** (*see left* **Inside Track**).

North of the Westway, Portobello's vitality fizzles out. It sparks back to life at **Golborne Road**, the heartland of London's North African community and the address of the excellent, no-frills Moroccan **Tagine** café (no.95, 8968 8055). Here, too, is a fine Portuguese café-deli, the **Lisboa Pâtisserie** (no.57, 8968 5242). At the north-eastern end of the road stands **Trellick Tower**, an architecturally significant, like-it-or-loathe-it piece of Ernö Goldfinger modernism. At its western end, Golborne Road connects with Ladbroke Grove, which can be followed north to spooky **Kensal Green Cemetery**.

FREE Kensal Green Cemetery

Harrow Road, Kensal Green, W10 4RA (8969 0152, www.kensalgreen.co.uk). Kensal Green tube. **Open** *Apr-Sept* 9am-6pm Mon-Sat; 10am-6pm Sun. *Oct-Mar* 9am-5pm Mon-Sat; 10am-5pm Sun. **Tours** *Mar-Oct* 2pm Sun. *Nov-Feb* 2pm 1st & 3rd Sun of mth. **Admission** free. *Tours* £5 (£4 reductions) donation. **No credit cards**.
Behind a neoclassical gate is a green oasis of the dead. It's the resting place of both the Duke of Sussex, sixth son of George III, and his sister, Princess Sophia; also buried here are Wilkie Collins, Anthony Trollope and William Makepeace Thackeray.

Museum of Brands, Packaging & Advertising

Colville Mews, Lonsdale Road, W11 2AR (7908 0880, www.museumofbrands.com). Notting Hill Gate tube. **Open** 10am-6pm Tue-Sat; 11am-5pm Sun. **Admission** £6.50; £2.50-£4 reductions; free under-7s. **Credit** MC, V. **Map** p404 Y4.
Robert Opie began collecting the things others throw away when he was 16. His collection now includes anything from milk bottles to vacuum cleaners and cereal packets. The emphasis is on the last century of British consumerism, design and domestic life, but there are older items, such as an ancient Egyptian doll.

SIGHTS

Piccadilly Circus & Mayfair

Neon lights and the calm of moneyed streets.

Top dog since the 1930s, when it was a playground for London's aristocracy, **Mayfair** oozes wealth. The area is now the haunt of hedge funders, who defy the lingering recession as they flash cash in restaurants and hotel bars. There are vestiges of old Mayfair: the tailors of Savile Row, marginally destuffed; the galleries of Cork Street; the bijou shopping rookery of Shepherd Market. To the south-east, the neon-lit roundabout of **Piccadilly Circus** remains the one part of town that every Londoner does their best to avoid.

Map p396, p398	**Restaurants &**
& p416	**cafés** pp219-220
Hotels pp196-198	**Pubs & bars** p241

PICCADILLY CIRCUS & REGENT STREET

Oxford Circus or Piccadilly Circus tube.

Frantic **Piccadilly Circus** is an uneasy mix of the tawdry and the grand, a mix with little to do with the vision of its architect. John Nash's 1820s design for the intersection of Regent Street and Piccadilly, two of the West End's most elegant streets, was a harmonious circle of curved frontages. But 60 years later, Shaftesbury Avenue muscled in, creating the lopsided and usually pandemonious traffic junction still in place today. This might have all changed by the end of 2011:

INSIDE TRACK ROCK ROUTE

Just off Regent Street, **Heddon Street** is where the iconic photograph that graces the cover of David Bowie's *Rise and Fall of Ziggy Stardust* was taken. The building against which Bowie leans is now the Moroccan-flavoured **Mô Tea Room**, next door to famed North African eaterie Momo (*see p220*). For this and other classic London sleeves, *see p322* **Picture This**.

a £14m revamp is planned, due to begin at the end of 2010. Almost a mile of ugly, pedestrian-funnelling and cyclist-shredding railings are to be ripped out by the same design consultants who successfully remodelled Oxford Circus.

Alfred Gilbert's memorial fountain in honour of child-labour abolitionist Earl Shaftesbury was erected in 1893. It's properly known as the **Shaftesbury Memorial**, with the statue on top intended to show the Angel of Christian Charity, but critics and public alike recognised the likeness of **Eros** and their judgement has stuck. The illuminated advertising panels around the intersection appeared late in the 19th century and have been present ever since: a Coca-Cola ad has been here since 1955, making it the world's longest-running advertisement. Running Sky News broadcasts indicate the likely media-saturated future for the illuminations.

Opposite the memorial, the **Trocadero Centre** (www.londontrocadero.com) has seen several ventures come and go, driven out by high rents and low footfall in a prime but tired location. Tween magnet **Funland** (www.funland.co.uk) seems to be a fixture, and newcomer **Ripley's Believe It or Not!** (*see right*) seems already to be well established. Plans for a massive revamp of the site, including a huge new hotel, had drifted off the radar as we went to press.

Connecting Piccadilly Circus to Oxford Circus to the north and Pall Mall to the south, the broad curve of **Regent Street** was designed by Nash in the early 1800s with the aims of improving access to Regent's Park and bumping up property values in Haymarket and Pall Mall. Much of Nash's architecture was destroyed in the early 20th century, but the grandeur of the street remains impressive. Among the highlights are the mammoth children's emporium **Hamleys** (nos.188-196, 0871 704 1977, www.hamleys.com), landmark department store **Liberty** (*see p253*) and, perhaps the first of a new Regent Street pedigree, **Anthropologie** (*see p262*).

Ripley's Believe It or Not!
1 Piccadilly Circus, W1J 0DA (3238 0022, www. ripleyslondon.com). Piccadilly Circus tube. **Open** *July, Aug* 9am-midnight daily (last entry 11pm). *Sept-June* 10am-midnight daily (last entry 11pm). **Admission** £25.95; £19.95-£23.95 reductions; £81.95 family; free under-4s. **Credit** MC, V. **Map** p416 W4.
This 'odditorium' follows a formula more or less unchanged since Robert Ripley opened his first display at the Chicago World Fair in 1933: an assortment of 800 curiosities is displayed, ranging from the world's smallest road-safe car to da Vinci's *Last Supper* painted on a grain of rice – via the company's signature shrunken heads.

MAYFAIR

Bond Street or Green Park tube.

The gaiety suggested by the name of Mayfair, derived from a long-gone spring celebration, isn't matched by its latter-day atmosphere today. Even on Mayfair's busy shopping streets, you may feel out of place without the reassuring heft of a platinum card. Nonetheless, there are many pleasures to enjoy if you fancy a stroll, not least the concentration of blue-chip commercial galleries – a stroll to **White Cube Mason's Yard** (*see p304*) is a good taster.

The Grosvenor and Berkeley families bought the rolling green fields that would become Mayfair in the middle of the 17th century. In the 1700s, they developed the pastures into a posh new neighbourhood, focused on a series of landmark squares. The most famous of these, **Grosvenor Square** (1725-31), is dominated by the supremely inelegant US Embassy, its only decorative touches a fierce eagle and a mass of post-9/11 protective barricades. Out front, pride of place is taken by a statue of President Dwight Eisenhower, who stayed in nearby **Claridge's** (*see p196*) when in London; Roosevelt is in the park nearby. Plans are in place to move the embassy to the much less salubrious (but apparently more secure) environs of Vauxhall – in 2017.

Brook Street has impressive musical credentials: GF Handel lived and died at no.25, and Jimi Hendrix roomed briefly next door at no.23, adjacent buildings that have been combined into the **Handel House Museum** (*see p126*). For most visitors, however, this part of town is all about shopping. Connecting Brook Street with Oxford Street to the north, **South Molton Street** is home to the fabulous boutique-emporium **Browns** (*see p260*) and the excellent **Grays Antique Market** (*see p274*), while **New Bond Street** is an A-Z of top-end, mainstream fashion houses.

Beyond New Bond Street, **Hanover Square** is another of the area's big squares, now a busy traffic chicane. Just to the south is **St George's Church**, built in the 1720s and once everyone's favourite place to be seen and to get married. Handel, who married nobody, attended services

SIGHTS

Royal Institution & Faraday Museum. *See p127.*

here. South of St George's, salubrious **Conduit Street** is where fashion shocker Vivienne Westwood (no.44) faces staid Rigby & Peller (no.22A), corsetière to the Queen.

Running south off Conduit Street is the most famous Mayfair shopping street of all, **Savile Row**. Gieves & Hawkes (no.1) is a must-visit for anyone interested in the history of British menswear; at no.15, the estimable Henry Poole & Co has cut suits for clients including Napoleon III, Charles Dickens and 'Buffalo' Bill Cody. No.3 was the home of the Beatles' Apple Records and their rooftop farewell concert.

Two streets west, **Cork Street** is known as the heart of the West End art scene; more than half a dozen galleries are strung along its few hundred feet of shopfront. A couple of streets

over is Albemarle Street, where you'll find the handsomely rejuvenated **Royal Institution**, home to the **Faraday Museum** (*see right*).

★ **Handel House Museum**
25 Brook Street (entrance in Lancashire Court), W1K 4HB (7399 1953, www.handelhouse.org). Bond Street tube. **Open** 10am-6pm Tue, Wed, Fri, Sat; 10am-8pm Thur; noon-6pm Sun. **Admission** £5; £2-£4.50 reductions; free under-5s. **Credit** MC, V. **Map** p396 H6.
The composer George Frideric Handel moved to Britain from his native Germany aged 25 and settled in this house 12 years later, remaining here until his death in 1759. The house has been beautifully restored with original and recreated furnishings, paintings and a welter of the composer's scores (in

Death and Dignity

London remembers those killed in recent terrorist attacks.

There was outrage among the victims' families as the fifth anniversary of the 7 July 2005 terrorist attack came and went without official ceremony – understandable, given how keen the politicians were to capitalise on those families' grief when it suited their agenda a short time before. The city has, however, a calm, surprisingly unrhetorical memorial to the tube and bus passengers killed by those suicide bombs. In the south-east corner of Hyde Park between the Lovers' Walk and busy Park Lane, the £1m monument consists of 52 ten-foot-tall, square steel columns, one for each of the fatalities. Each is marked with the date, time and location of that person's death; they're arranged in four groups, according to which of the four explosions killed the person in question. Designed by architects Carmody Groarke in close consultation with the victims' families, with Antony Gormley as an independent adviser, the monument is an austerely beautiful, quietly modern and human-scale tribute.

Elsewhere, London has a memorial to the 202 victims of the 2002 Bali bombings (just by the Churchill War Rooms, *see p132*), as well as a memorial garden for the victims of 9/11 (Grosvenor Square, near the US Embassy). Interestingly, and despite widespread commemoration events for the 70th anniversary of the beginning of the Blitz (57 consecutive nights of German bombing which began on 7 September 1940), there is still no unified memorial to the perhaps 20,000 London civilians killed across the capital.

SIGHTS

the same room as photos of Jimi Hendrix, who lived in the attic, now used as the museum office). The programme of events includes Thursday recitals.

★ FREE Royal Institution & Faraday Museum

21 Albemarle Street, W1S 4BS (7409 2992, www.rigb.org). Green Park tube. **Open** 9am-6pm Mon-Fri. **Admission** free. **No credit cards**. **Map** p416 U4.

The Royal Institution was founded in 1799 for 'diffusing the knowledge... and application of science to the common purposes of life'; from behind its neoclassical façade, it's been at the forefront of London's scientific achievements ever since. In 2008, Sir Terry Farrell completed a £22m rebuild, inside and out, with the brief of improving accessibility and finding ways to lure people inside. The result is a more open frontage, a restaurant, a bar and a café.

The Michael Faraday Laboratory, a complete replica of Faraday's former workspace, is in the basement, alongside a working laboratory in which RI scientists can be observed researching their current projects. Some 1,000 of the RI's 7,000-odd scientific objects are on display, including the world's first electric transformer, a prototype Davy lamp and, from 1858, a print of the first transatlantic telegraph signal. The RI also holds a terrific rolling programme of talks and demonstrations in its lecture theatre, most famously at Christmas. *Photo p125.*

Shepherd Market

Just west of Albemarle Street, **44 Berkeley Square** is one of the original houses in this grand square. Built in the 1740s, it was described by architectural historian Nikolaus Pevsner as 'the finest terrace house of London'. Curzon Street, which runs off the south-west corner of Berkeley Square, was home to MI5, Britain's secret service, from 1945 until the '90s. It's also the northern boundary of **Shepherd Market**, named after a food market set up here by architect Edward Shepherd in the early 18th century and now a curious little enclave in the heart of this exclusive area.

From 1686, this was where the raucous May Fair was held, until it was shut down in the late 18th century due to 'drunkenness, fornication, gaming and lewdness'. You'll still manage the drunkenness easily enough at a couple of good pubs (such as **Ye Grapes**, at 16 Shepherd Market). The cobbler on adjoining White Horse Street ('Don't throw away old shoes, they can be restored!') and the ironmongers on Shepherd Street keep things from becoming too genteel.

PICCADILLY & GREEN PARK

Green Park, Hyde Park Corner or Piccadilly Circus tube.

Burlington Arcade.

Piccadilly's name is derived from the 'picadil', a type of suit collar that was in vogue during the 18th century. The first of the area's main buildings was built by tailor Robert Baker and, indicating the source of his wealth, nicknamed 'Piccadilly Hall'. A stroll through the handful of Regency shopping arcades confirms that the rag trade is still flourishing mere minutes away from Savile Row and Jermyn Street. At the renovated **Burlington Arcade** (*see p253*), the oldest and most famous of these arcades, top-hatted security staff known as 'beadles' ensure there's no singing, whistling or hurrying in the arcade: such uncouth behaviour is prohibited by archaic bylaws. Formerly Burlington House (1665), the **Royal Academy of Arts** (*see p128*) is next door to the arcade's entrance. It hosts several lavish, crowd-pleasing exhibitions each year and has a pleasant courtyard café.

On Piccadilly are further representatives of high-end retail. **Fortnum & Mason** (*see p250*), London's most prestigious food store, was founded in 1707 by a former footman to Queen Anne. Look for the fine clock: a 1964 articulated effort, it features 18th-century effigies of Mr Fortnum and Mr Mason, who

SIGHTS

INSIDE TRACK DEEP WATER

The water feature in the basement of **Grays Antique Market** (*see p125*) is formed from the Tyburn Brook. One of London's buried rivers, it runs underground from Hampstead to Westminster.

INSIDE TRACK
HIGH AND MIGHTY

The towering statue in Hyde Park behind **Apsley House** (*see below*) of a naked Achilles wielding his sword and buckler was given to the Duke of Wellington 'by the women of England' in 1822. Achilles' fig leaf has been removed by curious admirers twice, most recently in 1961.

bow to each other on the hour. The plain church at no.197 is **St James's Piccadilly** (*see below*), where William Blake was baptised.

To the west along Piccadilly, smartly uniformed doormen mark the **Wolseley** (*see p220*), a former car showroom that is now a fine (if tiresomely frequently lauded) restaurant, and the expensive, exclusive **Ritz** (*see p197*). The dull, flat, green expanse just beyond the Ritz is **Green Park**. Work your way along Piccadilly, following the northern edge of Green Park past the queue outside the Hard Rock Café (where the Vault's displays of memorabilia are free to visit and open every day) to the Duke of Wellington's old home, **Apsley House**, opposite **Wellington Arch** (for both, *see below*). This is hectic **Hyde Park Corner**; Buckingham Palace (*see p137*) is just a short walk south-east, while Hyde Park (*see p145*) and the upper-crust enclave of Belgravia (*see p142*) are to the west.

Apsley House
149 Piccadilly, W1J 7NT (7499 5676, www. english-heritage.org.uk). Hyde Park Corner tube. **Open** *Nov-Mar* 11am-4pm Wed-Sun. *Apr-Oct* 11am-5pm Wed-Sun. *Tours* by arrangement. **Admission** £6; £3-£5.10 reductions. *Tours* phone in advance. *Joint ticket with Wellington Arch* £7.40; £3.70-£6.30 reductions; £18.50 family. **Credit** MC, V. **Map** p398 G8.
Called No.1 London because it was the first London building encountered on the road to the city from the village of Kensington, Apsley House was built by Robert Adam in the 1770s. The Duke of Wellington kept it as his London home for 35 years. Although his descendants still live here, several rooms are open to the public, providing a superb feel for the man and his era. Admire the extravagant porcelain dinnerware and plates or ask for a demonstration of the crafty mirrors in the scarlet and gilt picture gallery, where a fine Velázquez and a Correggio hang near Goya's portrait of the Iron Duke after he defeated the French in 1812. This was a last-minute edit: X-rays have revealed that Wellington's head was painted over that of Joseph Bonaparte, Napoleon's brother.
▶ *There's a model of the Battle of Waterloo at the National Army Museum; see p141.*

FREE Royal Academy of Arts
Burlington House, W1J 0BD (7300 8000, www.royalacademy.org.uk). Green Park or Piccadilly Circus tube. **Open** 10am-6pm Mon-Thur, Sat, Sun; 10am-10pm Fri. **Admission** free. *Special exhibitions* vary. **Credit** AmEx, DC, MC, V. **Map** p416 U4.
Britain's first art school was founded in 1768 and moved to the extravagantly Palladian Burlington House a century later, but it's now best known not for education but exhibitions. Ticketed blockbusters are generally held in the Sackler Wing or the main galleries; shows in the John Madejski Fine Rooms are drawn from the RA's holdings, which range from Constable to Hockney, and are free. The Academy's biggest event is the Summer Exhibition, which for more than two centuries has drawn from works entered by the public. There's also a December arts programme, 'Contemporary', programming events, exhibitions and films nearby at 6 Burlington Gardens.

FREE St James's Piccadilly
197 Piccadilly, W1J 9LL (7734 4511, www. st-james-piccadilly.org). Piccadilly Circus tube. **Open** 8am-6.30pm daily. *Evening events* times vary. **Admission** free. **Credit** (concerts only) AmEx, DC, MC, V. **Map** p416 V4.
Consecrated in 1684, St James's is the only church Sir Christopher Wren built on an entirely new site. A calming building with few architectural airs or graces, it was almost destroyed in World War II, but painstakingly reconstructed. Grinling Gibbons's delicate limewood garlanding around the sanctuary survived and is one of the few real frills. Beneath a brand-new tiled roof, the church stages regular classical concerts, provides a home for the William Blake Society and hosts markets in the churchyard: for antiques on Tuesday, and arts and crafts from Wednesday to Saturday. There's also a handy café.

Wellington Arch
Hyde Park Corner, W1J 7JZ (7930 2726, www. english-heritage.org.uk). Hyde Park Corner tube. **Open** *Apr-Oct* 10am-5pm Wed-Sun. *Nov-Mar* 10am-4pm Wed-Sun. **Admission** £3.70; £1.90-£3.10 reductions; free under-5s. *Joint ticket with Apsley House* £7.40; £3.70-£6.30 reductions; £18.50 family. **Credit** AmEx, MC, V. **Map** p398 G8.
Built in the late 1820s to mark Britain's triumph over Napoleonic France, Decimus Burton's Wellington Arch was initially topped by an out-of-proportion equestrian statue of Wellington. However, since 1912 Captain Adrian Jones's 38-ton bronze *Peace Descending on the Quadriga of War* has finished it with a flourish. It has three floors of displays, covering the history of the arch and the Blue Plaques scheme, and great views in winter from the balcony.
▶ *Hyde Park Corner contains one of London's finest war memorials: Charles Sargeant Jagger's moving tribute to the Royal Artillery.*

Westminster & St James's

For members' clubs and members of Parliament.

England is ruled from **Westminster**. The monarchy has been in residence here since the 11th century, when Edward the Confessor moved west from the City, and the government of the day also calls it home. It's a key destination for visitors as well, with the most significant area designated a UNESCO World Heritage Site back in 1987.

For such an important part of London, it's surprisingly spacious. **St James's Park** is one of London's finest parks, **Trafalgar Square** (overlooked by the **National Gallery**) is a tourist hotspot, and the **Mall** offers a properly broad and regal route to Buckingham Palace.

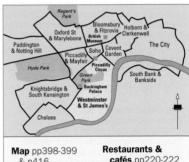

| Map pp398-399 & p416 | Restaurants & cafés pp220-222 |
| Hotels pp198-200 | Pubs & bars p241 |

TRAFALGAR SQUARE

Leicester Square tube or Charing Cross tube/rail.

Laid out in the 1820s by John Nash, Trafalgar Square is the heart of modern London. Tourists come in their thousands to pose for photographs in front of **Nelson's Column**. It was erected in 1840 to honour Vice Admiral Horatio Nelson, who died at the point of victory at the Battle of Trafalgar in 1805. The statue atop the 150-foot Corinthian column is foreshortened to appear in perfect proportion from the ground. The granite fountains were added in 1845; Sir Edwin Landseer's bronze lions joined them in 1867.

Once surrounded on all sides by busy roads, the square was improved markedly by pedestrianisation in 2003 of the North Terrace, right in front of the **National Gallery** (*see right*). The then mayor's ban on feeding pigeons was another positive step. Around the perimeter of the square are three plinths bearing statues of George IV and two Victorian military heroes, Henry Havelock and Sir Charles James Napier. The **fourth plinth** was never filled; since 1999, it's displayed temporary, contemporary art. Sculptor Yinka Shonibare's large-scale model of HMS *Victory*

in a glass bottle will be replaced by one of six nominees for 2012. From spring 2011, at the bottom of the North Terrace steps alongside the fourth plinth, a 6.5m-tall stainless-steel clock will be counting down the time to the London Olympic and Paralympic Games.

Other points of interest around the square include an equestrian statue of Charles I, dating from the 1630s, with a plaque behind it that marks the original site of Edward I's Eleanor Cross, the official centre of London. (A recently renovated Victorian replica of the cross stands outside Charing Cross station, *see p110*.) At the square's north-east corner is the refurbished **St Martin-in-the-Fields** (*see p131*).

★ **FREE** **National Gallery**

Trafalgar Square, WC2N 5DN (7747 2885, www.nationalgallery.org.uk). Leicester Square

INSIDE TRACK OLD SCHOOL

In the north-east corner of Trafalgar Square, you'll find an interesting metal panel that displays the official standard units of imperial measurement.

tube or Charing Cross tube/rail. **Open** 10am-6pm Mon-Thur, Sat, Sun; 10am-9pm Fri. *Tours* 11.30am, 2.30pm daily. **Admission** free. *Special exhibitions* vary. **Credit** (shop) MC, V. **Map** p416 X5.

Founded in 1824 to display 36 paintings, the National Gallery is now one of the world's great repositories for art. There are masterpieces from virtually every European school of art, from austere 13th-century religious paintings to the sensual delights of Caravaggio and Van Gogh.

Furthest to the left of the main entrance, the modern Sainsbury Wing extension contains the gallery's earliest works: Italian masterpieces by masters such as Giotto and Piero della Francesca, as well as the *Wilton Diptych*, the finest medieval English picture in the collection, showing Richard II with the Virgin and Child.

The basement of the Sainsbury Wing is the setting for important temporary exhibitions.

In the West Wing (left of the main entrance) are Italian Renaissance masterpieces by Correggio, Titian and Raphael. Straight ahead on entry, in the North Wing, are 17th-century Dutch, Flemish, Italian and Spanish Old Masters, including works such as Rembrandt's *A Woman Bathing in a Stream* and Caravaggio's *Supper at Emmaus*. Velázquez's *Rokeby Venus* is one of the artist's most famous paintings, a reclining nude asking herself – and us – 'How do we look?' Also in this wing are works by the great landscape artists Claude and Poussin. Turner insisted that his *Dido Building Carthage* and *Sun Rising through Vapour* should hang alongside two Claudes here that particularly inspired him.

On Routie to the Future

The mayor's new take on the classic red London bus.

Ask many Londoners about Routemaster buses, launched in the 1950s, and a faraway look will come into their eyes. They'll talk wistfully about the charm of London's original, open-backed red double-deckers, and they'll praise the convenience of proper bus conductors who accepted coins. The reason for such wistfulness is that these cherished vehicles were ditched in 2005 by former mayor Ken Livingstone, who scrapped the fleet and replaced them with charmless and routinely derided single-decker, 18m-long 'bendy buses'.

When Boris Johnson took over from Ken in 2008, one of his populist commitments was to return the Routemaster to London's streets. In July that year, Johnson launched a competition to design a new, eco-friendly Routemaster, with the aim of reinstating the original's hop-on, hop-off principle. A design was unveiled in spring 2010 (www.london.gov.uk/priorities/transport/new-bus-london, *pictured*) – not looking much like the old Routemasters, it must be said, but you will be able to hop on and off the back. More interestingly, Transport for London promises the new buses will be '15 per cent more fuel efficient than existing hybrid buses, 40 per cent more efficient than conventional diesel double decks and much quieter on the streets'; innovations include a battery that is recharged using energy generated by braking. It is still unclear how the £7.8m design costs will be met by a city already facing brutal transport funding cuts from central government, but Wrightbus's first five prototypes will be in operation by spring 2012.

Until then, experience the joy of the old on two 'heritage routes'. Refurbished buses from the 1960-64 Routemaster fleet run on routes 9 (from Aldwych via the Strand, Trafalgar Square and Piccadilly Circus to the Royal Albert Hall) and 15 (from Trafalgar Square to Tower Hill, with glimpses of the Strand, Fleet Street and St Paul's Cathedral); head to stops B or S in the south-west corner of Trafalgar Square. Buses run every 15 minutes from 9.30am; fares match ordinary buses, but you must buy a ticket before boarding (*see p364*).

In the East Wing (to the right of the main entrance, and most easily reached via the new street-level entrance on Trafalgar Square) are some of the gallery's most popular paintings: works by the French Impressionists and Post-Impressionists, including Monet's *Water-Lilies*, one of Van Gogh's *Sunflowers* and Seurat's *Bathers at Asnières*. Don't miss Renoir's astonishingly lovely *Les Parapluies*.

You shouldn't plan to see everything in one visit, but free guided tours, audio guides and the superb Art Start computer (which allows you to tailor and map your own itinerary of must-sees) help you make the best of your time.

★ FREE National Portrait Gallery

St Martin's Place, WC2H 0HE (7306 0055, www.npg.org.uk). Leicester Square tube or Charing Cross tube/rail. **Open** 10am-6pm Mon-Wed, Sat, Sun; 10am-9pm Thur, Fri. **Admission** free. *Special exhibitions* vary. **Credit** AmEx, MC, V. **Map** p416 X4.

Portraits don't have to be stuffy. The excellent National Portrait Gallery has everything from oil paintings of stiff-backed royals to photographs of soccer stars and gloriously unflattering political caricatures. The portraits of musicians, scientists, artists, philanthropists and celebrities are arranged in chronological order from the top to the bottom of the building.

At the top of the escalator up from the main foyer, on the second floor, are the earliest works, portraits of Tudor and Stuart royals and notables, including Holbein's 'cartoon' of Henry VIII and the 'Ditchley Portrait' of his daughter, Elizabeth I, her pearly slippers placed firmly on a colourful map of England. On the same floor, the 18th-century collection features Georgian writers and artists, with one room devoted to the influential Kit-Cat Club of bewigged Whig (leftish) intellectuals, Congreve and Dryden among them. More famous names include Wren and Swift.

The second floor also shows Regency greats, military men such as Wellington and Nelson, plus Byron, Wordsworth and other Romantics.

The first floor is devoted to the Victorians (Dickens, Brunel, Darwin) and to 20th-century luminaries, such as TS Eliot and Ian McKellen.

► *The second phase of photographic commission* The Road to 2012 *(http://roadto2012.npg.org.uk) will be displayed here in summer 2011.*

FREE St Martin-in-the-Fields

Trafalgar Square, WC2N 4JJ (7766 1122, www.smitf.org). Leicester Square tube or Charing Cross tube/rail. **Open** 8am-7pm Mon-Wed; 8am-9pm Thur-Sat; 11.30am-6pm Sun. *Services* 8am, 1.15pm, 6pm Mon, Tue, Thur, Fri; 8am, 1.15pm, 5.30pm, 6pm Wed; 8am, 10am, 5pm, 6.30pm Sun. *Brass Rubbing Centre* 10am-7pm Mon-Wed; 10am-9pm Thur-Sat; 11am-6pm Sun. **Admission** free. *Brass rubbing* £4.50. **Credit** MC, V. **Map** p416 X4.

There's been a church 'in the fields' between Westminster and the City since the 13th century, but the current one was built in 1726 by James Gibbs, using a fusion of neoclassical and Baroque styles. The parish church for Buckingham Palace (note the royal box to the left of the gallery), St Martin's benefited from a £36m Lottery-funded refurbishment, completed in 2008. The bright interior has been fully restored, with Victorian furbelows removed and the addition of a brilliant altar window that shows the Cross, stylised as if rippling on water. The crypt, its fine café and the London Brass Rubbing Centre have all been modernised. *Photo p133.*

► *For lunchtime and evening concerts, see p317.*

INSIDE TRACK
WHO'S THE BOSS?

Without anyone really noticing, London has become home to the UK's first **Supreme Court**. It was established in 2009 to achieve a complete separation between the United Kingdom's senior judges and the Upper House of Parliament, the separation signified by the Justices moving from their traditional home in the House of Lords across Parliament Square to the early 20th-century neo-Gothic Middlesex Guildhall. The Supreme Court holds permanent and temporary exhibitions in a former cell area downstairs and also has a café selling branded trinkets.

WHITEHALL TO PARLIAMENT SQUARE

Westminster tube or Charing Cross tube/rail.

The offices of the British government are lined along **Whitehall**, itself named after Henry VIII's magnificent palace, which burned to the ground in 1698. Walking south from Trafalgar Square, you pass the old **Admiralty Offices** and **War Office**, the **Ministry of Defence**, the **Foreign Office** and the **Treasury**, as well as the **Banqueting House** (*see p132*), one of the few buildings to survive the blaze. Also here is **Horse Guards**, headquarters of the Household Cavalry, the elite army unit that protects the Queen. The parade ground is to do rather different service during London 2012, as the venue for Beach Volleyball (*see p59*).

Either side of **Downing Street** – home to the prime minister (no.10) and chancellor (no.11), but closed to the public after IRA attacks in the 1980s – are significant war memorials. The millions who died in the service of the nation in World Wars I and II

SIGHTS

are commemorated by Sir Edwin Lutyens's dignified **Cenotaph**, focal point of Remembrance Day (*see p285*), while a separate memorial to the women of World War II, by sculptor John Mills, recalls the seven million women who contributed to the war effort. Just past the Cenotaph and hidden beneath government offices at the St James's Park end of King Charles Street, the claustrophobic **Churchill War Rooms** (*see right*) are where Britain's wartime PM planned his campaigns and delivered his fiery speeches.

The broad sweep of Whitehall is an apt introduction to the monuments of **Parliament Square**. Laid out in 1868, this tiny green space is flanked by the extravagant **Houses of Parliament** (*see right*), the neo-Gothic Middlesex Guildhall (since 2009 the UK's Court; *see p131* **Inside Track**) and the twin, square spires of **Westminster Abbey** (*see p133*). Like a pre-pedestrianised Trafalgar Square, Parliament Square can seem little more than a glorified traffic island, despite all the statues of British politicians (Disraeli, Churchill) and foreign dignitaries (Lincoln, Mandela), but its symbolic value has been brought back into focus in recent years. You'll see the banners and placards of Brian Haw's one-man protest against the wars in Iraq and Afghanistan, which will have been facing Parliament from the east side of the green for a decade this summer, despite a government ban designed specifically to move him on. The 'Democracy Village' tent city was considerably shorter lived: set up in the square by anti-war protestors in May 2010, it was vigorously evicted after only a few months.

Parliament itself simply dazzles. An outrageous neo-Gothic fantasy, the seat of the British government is still formally known as the Palace of Westminster, though the only remaining parts of the medieval palace are **Westminster Hall** and the **Jewel Tower** (*see p133*). At the north end of the palace is the clocktower housing the huge 'Big Ben' bell that gives the tower its popular name (*see right* **Inside Track**); more than seven feet tall, the bell weighs over 13 tons.

Banqueting House

Whitehall, SW1A 2ER (0844 482 7777, www.hrp.org.uk). Westminster tube or Charing Cross tube/rail. **Open** 10am-5pm Mon-Sat. **Admission** £4.80; £4 reductions; free under-16s. **Credit** MC, V. **Map** p399 L8.

This handsome Italianate mansion, which was designed by Inigo Jones and constructed in 1620, was the first true Renaissance building in London. The sole surviving part of the Tudor and Stuart kings' Whitehall Palace, the Banqueting House features a lavish painted ceiling by Rubens, glorifying

James I, 'the wisest fool in Christendom' (*see also p135* **Snapshot**). Regrettably, James's successor, Charles I, did not rule so wisely. After losing the English Civil War to Cromwell's Roundheads, he was executed in front of Banqueting House in 1649 (the event is marked every 31 Jan). Lunchtime concerts are held on the first Monday of every month except August. Call before you visit: the mansion is sometimes closed for corporate functions.

Churchill War Rooms

Clive Steps, King Charles Street, SW1A 2AQ (7930 6961, www.iwm.org.uk). St James's Park or Westminster tube. **Open** 9.30am-6pm daily. **Admission** £14.95; £7.50-£12 reductions; free under-16s. **Credit** MC, V. **Map** p399 K9.

Out of harm's way beneath Whitehall, this cramped and spartan bunker was where Winston Churchill planned the Allied victory in World War II. Open to the public since 1984, the rooms powerfully bring to life the reality of a nation at war. The cabinet rooms were sealed on 16 August 1945, keeping the complex in a state of suspended animation: every pin stuck into the vast charts was placed there in the final days of the conflict. The humble quarters occupied by Churchill and his deputies give a tangible sense of wartime hardship, an effect reinforced by the wailing sirens and wartime speeches on the audio guide (free with admission).

▶ *Along with HMS Belfast (see p80), the Cabinet War Rooms is run by the Imperial War Museum (see p161).*

FREE Houses of Parliament

Parliament Square, SW1A 0AA (7219 4272 Commons information, 7219 3107 Lords information, www.parliament.uk). Westminster tube. **Open** (when in session) *House of Commons Visitors' Gallery* 2.30-10.30pm Mon, Tue; 11.30am-7.30pm Wed; 10.30am-6.30pm Thur; 9.30am-3pm Fri. *House of Lords Visitors' Gallery* 2.30-10.30pm Mon, Tue; 3-10pm Wed; 11am-7.30pm Thur; from 10am Fri. *Tours* summer recess only; see website for details. **Admission** *Visitors' Gallery* free. *Tours* £14; £6-£9 reductions; free under-5s. **Credit** MC, V. **Map** p399 L9.

INSIDE TRACK BIG BEN

As every pedant will tell you, **Big Ben** is not the iconic clocktower of the New Year bongs, but the giant bell they're bonged upon. The template of the bell, which dates to 1858, is around its manufacturer's front door: visit the **Whitechapel Bell Foundry** (*see p154*) on a weekday between 9am and 4.15pm to enter the foyer and see it there.

St Martin-in-the-Fields. *See p131.*

After strict security checks at St Stephen's Gate (the only public access to Parliament), visitors are welcome to observe the debates at the House of Lords and House of Commons. The experience is usually soporific, but an exception is Prime Minister's Question Time at noon on Wednesday, when the incumbent PM fields a barrage of hostile questions from the opposition (and occasionally some of their own rebellious backbenchers) and soft questions from loyal backbenchers eager to present the government in a good light. Tickets must be arranged in advance through your embassy or MP, who can also arrange tours. The best time to visit Parliament is during the summer recess, when the main ceremonial rooms, including Westminster Hall and both Houses, are thrown open to the general public as part of an organised tour (book in advance online).

The first parliamentary session was held in St Stephen's Chapel in 1275, but Westminster only became the permanent seat of Parliament in 1532, when Henry VIII moved to a new des-res in Whitehall. Designed by Charles Barry, the Palace of Westminster is now a wonderful mish-mash of styles, dominated by Gothic buttresses, towers and arches. It looks much older than it is: the Parliament buildings were created in 1860 to replace the original Houses of Parliament, destroyed by fire in 1834. The compound contains 1,000 rooms, 11 courtyards, eight bars and six restaurants, plus a small cafeteria for visitors. Of the original palace, only the Jewel Tower (*see below*) and the ancient Westminster Hall remain.

Jewel Tower
Abingdon Street, SW1P 3JY (7222 2219, www.english-heritage.org.uk). Westminster tube. **Open** *Mar-Oct* 10am-5pm daily. *Nov-Mar* 10am-4pm daily. **Admission** £3.20; £1.60-£2.70 reductions; free under-5s. **Credit** MC, V. **Map** p399 L9.

This easy-to-overlook little stone tower opposite Parliament was built in 1365 to house Edward III's treasure. It is, with Westminster Hall, all that remains of the medieval Palace of Westminster. It contains a small exhibition on Parliament's history. ▶ *Nowadays, the Crown Jewels are on display in the Tower of London; see p97.*

FREE St Margaret's Church
Parliament Square, SW1P 3PA (7654 4840, www.westminster-abbey.org). St James's Park or Westminster tube. **Open** 9.30am-3.30pm Mon-Fri; 9.30am-1.30pm Sat; 2-5pm Sun (times vary due to services). *Services* 11am Sun. **Admission** free. **No credit cards. Map** p399 L9.

Tucked in under the grandeur of Westminster Abbey, this little church was founded in the 12th century; since 1614, it's served as the official church of the House of Commons. The interior features some of the most impressive pre-Reformation stained glass in London. The east window (1509) commemorates the marriage of Henry VIII and Catherine of Aragon; others celebrate Britain's first printer, William Caxton (buried here in 1491), explorer Sir Walter Raleigh (executed in Old Palace Yard in 1618), and writer John Milton (1608-74), who married his second wife here in 1656.

Westminster Abbey
20 Dean's Yard, SW1P 3PA (7222 5152 information, 7654 4900 tours, www.westminster-abbey.org). St James's Park or Westminster tube. **Open** 9.30am-4.30pm Mon, Tue, Thur, Fri;

In Innocents Corner lie the remains of two lads believed to be Edward V and his brother Richard (their bodies were found at the Tower of London), as well as two of James I's children. Poets' Corner is the final resting place of Chaucer, the first to be buried here. Few of the other writers who have stones here are buried in the abbey, but the remains of Dryden, Johnson, Browning and Tennyson are all present. Henry James, TS Eliot and Dylan Thomas have dedications – on the floor, fittingly for Thomas.

In the vaulted area under the former monks' dormitory, one of the abbey's oldest parts, the Abbey Museum celebrated its centenary in 2008. You'll find effigies and waxworks of British monarchs, among them Edward II and Henry VII, wearing the robes they donned in life. The Choir School is the only school in Britain exclusively for the education of boy choristers from eight to 13. Its Christmas services are truly magnificent. The 900-year-old College Garden is one of the oldest cultivated gardens in Britain and a useful place to escape the crowds.

An ongoing refurbishment revealed the restored Cosmati Pavement to the public in spring 2010, but the abbey has ambitious plans to create new visitor facilities and a new gallery – the new refectory should be feeding hungry visitors from late 2011.

MILLBANK

Pimlico or Westminster tube.

Running south from Parliament along the river, Millbank leads eventually to **Tate Britain** (*see p135*), built on the site of an extraordinary pentagonal prison built to hold criminals destined for transportation to Botany Bay. If you're walking south from the Palace of Westminster, look out on the left for **Victoria Tower Gardens**, which contain a statue of suffragette leader Emmeline Pankhurst and the rather colourful Buxton Drinking Fountain, which commemorates the emancipation of slaves. There's also a version of Rodin's sombre *Burghers of Calais*.

On the other side of the road, Dean Stanley Street leads to Smith Square, home to the architecturally striking **St John's Smith Square** (*see p317*), built as a church in grand Baroque style and now a popular venue for classical music. **Lord North Street**, the elegant row of Georgian terraces running north from the square, has long been a favourite address of politicians; note, too, the directions on the wall for wartime bomb shelters.

Across the river from Millbank is **Vauxhall Cross**, the oddly conspicuous HQ of the Secret Intelligence Service (SIS), commonly referred to by its old name MI6. In case any enemies of the state were unaware of its location, the cream and green block appeared as itself in the 1999 James Bond film *The World is Not Enough*.

Westminster Abbey. *See p133.*

9.30am-7pm Wed; 9.30am-4.30pm Sat. *Abbey Museum, Chapter House & College Gardens* 10am-4pm daily. *Tours* phone for details. **Admission** £15; £6-£12 reductions; free under-11s with adult; £30-£36 family. *Abbey Museum* free. *Tours* £3. **Credit** AmEx, MC, V. **Map** p399 K9.

The cultural significance of Westminster Abbey is hard to overstate, but also hard to remember as you're shepherded around, forced to elbow fellow tourists out of the way to read a plaque or see a tomb – get here as early as you can. Edward the Confessor commissioned a church to St Peter on the site of a seventh-century version, but it was only consecrated on 28 December 1065, eight days before he died. William the Conqueror subsequently had himself crowned here on Christmas Day 1066 and, with just two exceptions, every English coronation since has taken place in the abbey.

Many royal, military and cultural notables are interred here. The most haunting memorial is the Grave of the Unknown Warrior, in the nave. Elaborate resting places in side chapels are taken up by the tombs of Elizabeth I and Mary Queen of Scots.

★ **FREE** **Tate Britain**
*Millbank, SW1P 4RG (7887 8888,
www.tate.org.uk). Pimlico tube.* **Open** 10am-6pm
daily; 10am-10pm 1st Fri of mth. *Tours* 11am,
noon, 2pm, 3pm Mon-Fri; noon, 3pm Sat, Sun.
Admission free. *Special exhibitions* vary.
Credit MC, V. **Map** p399 K11.

Tate Modern (*see p76*) gets the attention, but the
original Tate Gallery, founded by sugar magnate Sir
Henry Tate, has a broader brief. Housed in a stately
building on the riverside, Tate Britain is second only
to the National Gallery (*see p129*) when it comes to
British art. The historical collection includes work
by Hogarth, Gainsborough, Reynolds, Constable
(who gets three rooms) and Turner (in the superb
Clore Gallery). Many contemporary works were
shifted to the other Tate when it opened in 2000, but
Stanley Spencer, Lucian Freud and Francis Bacon
are well represented here, and Art Now installations
showcase up-and-coming British artists.

Temporary exhibitions include headline-hungry
blockbusters and the controversy-courting Turner
Prize exhibition (Oct-Jan). The gallery has a good
restaurant and a well-stocked gift shop.

▶ *The handy Tate-to-Tate boat (see p78) zips
along the river to Tate Modern every 40mins.*

VICTORIA

Pimlico tube or Victoria tube/rail.

As you might expect from London's main
backpacker hangout, Victoria is colourful and
chaotic. Victoria rail station is a major hub for
trains to southern seaside resorts and ferry
terminals, while the nearby coach station is
served by buses from all over Europe. Catering
to new arrivals, Belgrave Road provides an
almost unbroken line of cheap and often shabby
B&Bs, hotels and hostels, most set in fading
townhouses. The theatres dotted around
Victoria form a western outpost of the West
End's Theatreland, with a similar programme
of star-vehicle dramas and musicals.

Not to be confused with Westminster Abbey
(*see p133*), **Westminster Cathedral** is the
headquarters of the Roman Catholic church
in England. South and east of Victoria station
are the Georgian terraces of **Pimlico** and
Belgravia. Antiques stores and restaurants
line Pimlico Road; the intriguing independent
shops of Tachbrook Street are worth a look.

North of Victoria Street towards Parliament
Square is **Christchurch Gardens**, burial site
of Thomas ('Colonel') Blood, who stole the
Crown Jewels in 1671. He was apprehended
making his getaway but, amazingly, managed
to talk his way into a full pardon. Also in the
area are **New Scotland Yard**, with its famous
revolving sign, and the art deco headquarters of
London Underground at 55 Broadway.

Public outrage about Jacob Epstein's graphic
nudes on the façade almost led to the
resignation of the managing director in 1929.

FREE **Westminster Cathedral**
*42 Francis Street, SW1P 1QW (7798 9055,
www.westminstercathedral.org.uk). Victoria
tube/rail.* **Open** 7am-6pm Mon-Fri; 8am-6.30pm
Sat; 8am-7pm Sun. *Exhibition* 10am-5pm Mon-Fri;
10am-6pm Sat, Sun. *Bell tower* 9.30am-4.30pm
daily. *Services* 7am, 8am, 10.30am, 12.30pm,
1.05pm, 5.30pm Mon-Fri; 8am, 9am, 10.30am,

Snapshot
Stuart London

Where to see how London lived.

Peter Paul Rubens' painted ceiling in the
Banqueting House (*see p132; pictured*)
is as fine a piece of Stuart propaganda
as you could wish to see, its chubby
cherubs commissioned by Charles I to
celebrate his father James I's rule under
bombastic titles: 'The Union of the
Crowns', 'The Apotheosis of James I',
'The Peaceful Reign of James I'. Inigo
Jones, the building's architect, also built
the **Queen's House** (*see p167*) and **St
Paul's Covent Garden** (*see p109*).

SIGHTS

SIGHTS

Household Cavalry Museum.

12.30pm, 6pm Sat; 8am, 9am, 10.30am, noon, 5.30pm, 7pm Sun. **Admission** free; donations appreciated. *Exhibition* £5; free-£2.50 reductions; £11 family. *Bell tower & exhibition* £8; free-£4 reductions; £17.50 family. **Credit** MC, V. **Map** p398 J10.

With its domes, arches and soaring tower, the most important Catholic church in England looks surprisingly Byzantine. There's a reason: architect John Francis Bentley, who built it between 1895 and 1903, was heavily influenced by the Hagia Sophia in Istanbul. Compared to the candy-cane exterior, the interior is surprisingly restrained (in fact, it's unfinished), but there are still some impressive marble columns and mosaics. Eric Gill's sculptures of the Stations of the Cross (1914-18) were dismissed as 'Babylonian' when they were first installed, but worshippers have come to love them. A new permanent exhibition, 'Treasures of the Cathedral', opened in the upper gallery in 2010 to celebrate the centenary of the cathedral's consecration. It displays an impressive Arts & Crafts coronet, a Tudor chalice, holy relics and Bentley's amazing architectural model of his cathedral, complete with tiny hawks. A lift runs to the top of the 273ft bell tower.

AROUND ST JAMES'S PARK

St James's Park tube.

St James's Park was founded as a deer park for the royal occupants of St James's Palace,

and remodelled by John Nash on the orders of George IV. The central lake is home to various species of wildfowl; pelicans have been kept here since the 17th century, when the Russian ambassador donated several of the bag-jawed birds to Charles II. The pelicans are fed at 3pm daily, though they supplement their diet at other times of the day with the occasional pigeon. The bridge over the lake offers views of **Buckingham Palace** (*see p137*).

Along the north side of the park, the Mall connects Buckingham Palace with **Trafalgar Square** (*see p129*). It looks like a classic processional route, but the Mall was actually laid out as a pitch for Charles II to play 'pallemaille' (an early version of croquet imported from France) after the pitch at Pall Mall became too crowded. On the south side of the park, Wellington Barracks contains the **Guards Museum** (*see p137*) to the east, Horse Guards contains the **Household Cavalry Museum** (*see p137*).

Along the north side of the Mall, **Carlton House Terrace** was the last project completed by John Nash before his death in 1835. Part of the terrace now houses the **ICA** (*see p138*). Just behind this is the **Duke of York column**, commemorating Prince Frederick, Duke of York, who led the British Army against the French. He's the nursery rhyme's 'Grand old Duke of York', who marched his 10,000 men neither up nor down Cassel hill in Flanders.

Buckingham Palace & Royal Mews

The Mall, SW1A 1AA (7766 7300 Palace, 7766 7302 Royal Mews, 7766 7301 Queen's Gallery, www.royalcollection.org.uk). Green Park tube or Victoria tube/rail. **Open** *State Rooms* mid July-Sept 9.45am-6pm (last entry 3.45pm) daily. *Queen's Gallery* 10am-5.30pm daily. *Royal Mews* Mar-July, Oct 11am-4pm Mon-Thur, Sat, Sun; Aug, Sept 10am-5pm daily; Nov-Dec 11am-4pm Mon-Fri. **Admission** *Palace* £17; £9.75-£15.50 reductions; £45 family; free under-5s. *Queen's Gallery* £8.75; £4.50-£7.75 reductions; £22 family; free under-5s. *Royal Mews* £7.75; £5-£7 reductions; £20.50 family; free under-5s. **Credit** AmEx, MC, V. **Map** p398 H9.

Although nearby St James's Palace (*see p138*) remains the official seat of the British court, every monarch since Victoria has used Buckingham Palace as their primary home. Originally known as Buckingham House, the present home of the British royals was constructed as a private house for the Duke of Buckingham in 1703, but George III liked it so much he purchased it for his German bride Charlotte in 1761. George IV decided to occupy the mansion himself after taking the throne in 1820 and John Nash was hired to convert it into a palace befitting a king. Construction was beset with problems, and Nash – whose expensive plans had always been disliked by Parliament – was dismissed in 1830. When Victoria came to the throne in 1837, the building was barely habitable. The job of finishing the palace fell to the reliable but unimaginative Edward Blore ('Blore the Bore'). The neoclassical frontage now in place was the work of Aston Webb in 1913.

As the home of the Queen, the palace is usually closed to visitors, but you can view the interior for a brief period each year while the Windsors are away on their holidays; you'll be able to see the State Rooms, still used to entertain dignitaries and guests of state, and part of the garden. Summer 2010 even saw the introduction of a café – paper cups, sadly, but coloured a pretty blue-green and clearly marked with the palace crest for souvenir-hunters. At any time of year, you can visit the Queen's Gallery to see her personal collection of treasures, including paintings by Rubens and Rembrandt, Sèvres porcelain and the Diamond Diadem crown (familiar from Commonwealth postage stamps). Further along Buckingham Palace Road, the Royal Mews is a grand garage for the royal fleet of Rolls-Royces and home to the splendid royal carriages and the horses, individually named by the Queen, that pull them.

Guards Museum

Wellington Barracks, Birdcage Walk, SW1E 6HQ (7414 3428, www.theguardsmuseum.com). St James's Park tube. **Open** 10am-4pm daily. **Admission** £4; £1-£2 reductions; free under-16s. **Credit** (shop) AmEx, MC, V. **Map** p398 J9.

Just down the road from Horse Guards, this small museum tells the 350-year story of the Foot Guards, using flamboyant uniforms, period paintings, medals and intriguing memorabilia, such as the stuffed body of Jacob the Goose, the Guard's Victorian mascot, who was regrettably run over by a van in barracks. Appropriately, the shop is well stocked with toy soldiers of the British regiments.

▶ *The Guards form up on the parade ground here before the Changing of the Guard; see p279* **Standing on Ceremony**.

Household Cavalry Museum

Horse Guards, Whitehall, SW1A 2AX (7930 3070, www.householdcavalrymuseum.co.uk). Westminster tube or Charing Cross tube/rail. **Open** *Apr-Oct* 10am-6pm daily. *Nov-Mar* 10am-5pm daily. **Admission** £6; £4 reductions; £15 family ticket; free under-5s. **Credit** MC, V. **Map** p399 K8.

Household Cavalry is a fairly workaday name for the military peacocks who make up the Queen's official guard. They get to tell their stories through video diaries at this small but entertaining museum, which also offers the chance to see medals, uniforms and shiny cuirasses (breastplates) up close. You'll also get a peek – and sniff – of the magnificent horses that parade just outside every day: the stables are separated from the main museum by no more than a screen of glass. Interactive displays on the horses have recently been added.

▶ *The parade ground outside the Household Cavalry Museum will host the Beach Volleyball for the London 2012 Games.*

ICA. *See p138.*

SIGHTS

SIGHTS

FREE ICA (Institute of Contemporary Arts)

The Mall, SW1Y 5AH (7930 0493 information, 7930 3647 tickets, www.ica.org.uk). Piccadilly Circus tube or Charing Cross tube/rail. **Open** *Galleries* (during exhibitions) noon-7pm Wed, Fri-Sun; noon-9pm Thur. **Admission** free. **Credit** AmEx, DC, MC, V. **Map** p399 K8.

Founded in 1947 by a collective of poets, artists and critics, the ICA has recently found itself somewhat adrift. The institute moved to the Mall in 1968 and set itself up as a venue for arthouse cinema, performance art, philosophical debates, art-themed club nights and anything else that might challenge convention – but 'convention' is much harder to challenge now, when everyone's doing it. Artistic director Ekow Eshun resigned once threats of immediate closure had been averted, but his successor will face the same challenges. *Photo p137.*

ST JAMES'S

Green Park or Piccadilly Circus tube.

One of London's most refined residential areas, St James's was laid out in the 1660s for royal and aristocratic families, some of whom still live here. It's a rewarding district, a sedate bustle of intriguing mews and grand squares. Bordered by Piccadilly, Haymarket, the Mall and Green Park, the district is centred on **St James's Square**. Just south of the square, **Pall Mall** is lined with exclusive, members-only gentlemen's clubs (in the old-fashioned sense of the word). Polished nameplates reveal such prestigious establishments as the **Institute of Directors** (no.116) and the **Reform Club** (nos.104-105), site of Phileas Fogg's famous bet in *Around the World in Eighty Days*. Around the corner on St James's Street, the **Carlton Club** (no.69) is the official club of the Conservative Party; Lady Thatcher remains the only woman to be granted full membership. Nearby on King Street is **Christie's** (7839 9060, www.christies.com), the world's oldest fine art auctioneers.

At the south end of St James's Street, **St James's Palace** was built for Henry VIII in the 1530s. Extensively remodelled over the

centuries, the red-brick palace is still the official address of the Royal Court, even though every monarch since 1837 has lived at Buckingham Palace. From here, Mary Tudor surrendered Calais and Elizabeth I led the campaign against the Spanish Armada; this is also where Charles I was confined before his 1649 execution. The palace is home to the Princess Royal (the title given to the monarch's eldest daughter, currently Princess Anne); it's closed to the public, but you can attend Sunday services at its historic **Chapel Royal** (1st Sun of mth, Oct-Easter Sunday; 8.30am, 11.15am).

Adjacent to St James's Palace is **Clarence House** (*see below*), former residence of the Queen Mother; a few streets north, delightful **Spencer House** (*see below*) is the ancestral home of the family of the late Princess Diana. Across Marlborough Road lies the pocket-sized **Queen's Chapel**, designed by Inigo Jones in the 1620s for Charles I's Catholic Queen Henrietta Maria, at a time when Catholic places of worship were officially banned. The Queen's Chapel can only be visited for Sunday services (Easter-July; 8.30am, 11.15am).

Clarence House

The Mall, SW1A 1AA (7766 7303, www. royalcollection.org.uk). Green Park tube. **Open** *Aug, Sept* 10am-4pm daily. **Admission** £8.50; £4.50 under-17s; free under-5s. *Tours* pre-booked tickets only. **Credit** AmEx, MC, V. **Map** p398 J8.

Currently the official residence of Prince Charles and the Duchess of Cornwall, this austere royal mansion was built between 1825 and 1827 for Prince William Henry, Duke of Clarence, who stayed on in the house after his coronation as King William IV. Designed by John Nash, the house has been much altered by its many inhabitants, among them the late Queen Mother. Five receiving rooms and the Queen Mother's British art collection usually open to the public in summer, but for advance bookings only.

Spencer House

27 St James's Place, SW1A 1NR (7499 8620, www.spencerhouse.co.uk). Green Park tube. **Open** *Feb-July, Sept-Dec* 10.30am-5.45pm Sun. Last tour 4.45pm. *Gardens* phone or see website for details. **Admission** £9; £7 reductions. Under-10s not allowed. **Credit** MC, V. **Map** p398 J8.

One of the last surviving private residences in St James's, this handsome mansion was designed for John Spencer by John Vardy, but was completed in 1766 by Hellenophile architect James Stuart, which explains the mock Greek flourishes. Lady Georgiana, subject of bodice-ripping film *The Duchess*, lived here, but the Spencers left generations before their most famous scion, Diana, married into the Windsor family. The palatial building has painstakingly restored interiors, now mainly used for corporate entertaining, and a wonderful garden.

Chelsea

Scarlet-coated pensioners and mere traces of the Sixties that swung

Chelsea is where London's wealthy classes play in cultural and geographical isolation. Originally a fishing hamlet, the area was a 'village of palaces' by the 16th century, home to the likes of Henry VIII's ill-fated advisor Sir Thomas More. Artists and poets (Whistler, Carlyle, Wilde) followed from the 1880s, before the fashionistas arrived with the opening of Mary Quant's Bazaar in 1955. Soon after, Chelsea had a raffish reputation and was at the forefront of successive youth culture revolutions. Those days are long gone. Now there are smart shops and street after sleepy street of immaculate terraced housing, but cultural pleasures are few, making the arrival of the **Saatchi Gallery** (*see p140*) especially welcome.

Map p395   **Hotels** p200
Pubs & bars   **Restaurants &**
pp242-244   **cafés** pp222-223

SLOANE SQUARE & THE KING'S ROAD

Sloane Square tube then various buses.

Synonymous with the Swinging Sixties and immortalised by punk, the dissipated phase of the King's Road is now a matter for historians as the street teems with pricey fashion houses and air-conditioned poodle parlours. Yet on a sunny day, it does make a vivid stroll. For one thing, you don't have to take yourself as seriously as the locals. And for another, the area is figuratively rich with historical associations and literally so, with the expensive red-brick houses that slumber down leafy mews and charming, cobbled sidestreets.

At the top (east end) of the King's Road is **Sloane Square**. It's named after Sir Hans Sloane, who provided the land for the Chelsea Physic Garden (*see p141*), invented milk chocolate in the early 18th century and was instrumental in the founding of the British Museum (which was set up to hold his collections when he died). In the middle of the square sits a fountain erected in 1953 (*see p140* **Inside Track**), a gift to the borough from the Royal Academy of Arts (*see p128*). The shaded benches in the middle of the square provide a lovely counterpoint to the looming façades of

Tiffany & Co and the enormous Peter Jones department store, in a 1930s building with excellent views from its top-floor café. A certain edginess is lent to proceedings by the **Royal Court Theatre** (*see p343*), which shocked the nation with its 1956 première of John Osborne's *Look Back in Anger*.

To escape the bustle and fumes, head to the **Duke of York Square**, a pedestrianised enclave of boutiques and restaurants that's presided over by a statue of Sir Hans. In the summer, the cooling fountains attract hordes of children, their parents sitting to watch from the outdoor areas of the cafés or taking advantage of the Saturday food market. The square is also home to the mercilessly modern art of the **Saatchi Gallery** (*see p140*), housed in former military barracks. Around the corner on Chelsea Bridge Road sit more disused army lodgings; the proposed redevelopment of **Chelsea Barracks** became a controversial topic a couple of years back, thanks to the intervention of Prince Charles.

The once-adventurous shops on the King's Road are now a mix of trendier-than-thou fashion houses and high-street chains, but there are a few gems: **John Sandoe** bookshop (*see p257*) represents a glorious past, **Shop at Bluebird** (*see p263*) and London's second branch of **Anthropologie** (*see p262*) suggest

SIGHTS

INSIDE TRACK
FOUNT OF BEAUTY

Sculpted by local man Gilbert Ledward, the **Sloane Square fountain** (*see p139*) depicts Venus; it's an allusion to King Charles II's mistress Nell Gwynne, who lived nearby (hence the King's Road), but it had as its model the mother of actress Greta Scacchi. Scacchi's mother was a member of the Bluebell Girls dance troupe, who travelled the world performing for wide-eyed audiences.

future directions. Wander Cale Street for some pleasing boutiques, or head for the **Chelsea Farmers' Market** on adjoining Sydney Street to find a clutter of artfully distressed rustic sheds housing restaurants and shops selling everything from cigars to garden products. Sydney Street leads to **St Luke's Church**, where Charles Dickens married Catherine Hogarth in 1836.

Towards the western end of the King's Road is **Bluebird**, a dramatic art deco former motor garage housing a café, a restaurant and the hip shop mentioned above. A little further up the road, the **World's End** store (no.430) occupies what was once Vivienne Westwood's notorious leather- and fetishwear boutique Sex; a green-haired Johnny Rotten auditioned for the Sex Pistols here in 1975 by singing along to an Alice Cooper record on the shop's jukebox.

FREE Saatchi Gallery

Duke of York's HQ, off King's Road, SW3 4SQ (7823 2363, www.saatchi-gallery.co.uk). Sloane Square tube. **Open** 10am-6pm daily. **Admission** free. **Credit** (shop) AmEx, MC, V. **Map** p395 F11.

Charles Saatchi's gallery offers 50,000sq ft of space for temporary exhibitions. Given his fame as a promoter in the 1990s of what became known as the Young British Artists – Damien Hirst, Tracey Emin, Gavin Turk, Sarah Lucas et al – it will surprise many that the opening exhibition a few years back was of new Chinese art. More recent shows have continued the international feel. The details of a plan to donate the gallery to the public, as a renamed Museum of Contemporary Art London, by 2012 are being worked out.

CHEYNE WALK & CHELSEA EMBANKMENT

Sloane Square tube then various buses.

Chelsea's riverside has long been noted for its nurseries and gardens. The borough's

horticultural curiosity is still alive, lending a village air that befits a place of retirement for the former British soldiers living in the **Royal Hospital Chelsea** (*see right*). In summer, the Chelsea Pensioners, as they're known, regularly don red coats and tricorn hats when venturing beyond the gates. The Royal Hospital's lovely gardens host the **Chelsea Flower Show** (*see p281*) in May each year. Next door is the **National Army Museum** (*see right*).

West from the river end of Royal Hospital Road is **Cheyne Walk**, less peaceful than it once was due to Embankment traffic. Its river-view benches remain good spots for a sit-down, but the tranquillity of **Chelsea Physic Garden** (*see right*) is the real treat.

Further west on Cheyne Walk, the park benches of **Chelsea Embankment Gardens** face Albert Bridge, where signs still order troops to 'Break step when marching over this bridge'. In the small gardens, you'll find a statue of the great historian Thomas Carlyle – the 'sage of Chelsea', whose home is preserved (*see right* **Carlyle's House**). Nearby, a gold-

Cheyne Walk.

faced statue of Sir Thomas More looks out over the river from the garden of **Chelsea Old Church** (*see below*), where he once sang in the choir and may may well be (partially) buried. Follow Old Church Street north and you'll find the **Chelsea Arts Club** (no.143), founded in 1871 by Whistler.

North of the western extremity of Cheyne Walk are **Brompton Cemetery** (*see p177*) and the home ground of the 2009/10 League champions Chelsea FC, **Stamford Bridge** (*see p336*). Football fans might be interested in the **Chelsea Centenary Museum** (www. chelseafc.com, 10.30am-4.30pm daily except match days; £6, £4 reductions), which contains perhaps the only photograph of Raquel Welch wearing a football kit to be found in any museum in England.

Carlyle's House

24 Cheyne Row, SW3 5HL (7352 7087, www. nationaltrust.org.uk). Sloane Square tube or bus 11, 19, 22, 49, 170, 211, 319. **Open** *Mar-Oct* 11am-5pm Wed-Sun. **Admission** £5.10; £2.60 children; £12.30 family. **Credit** MC, V. **Map** p395 E12.

Thomas Carlyle and his wife Jane moved to this four-storey, Queen Anne house in 1834. The house was inaugurated as a museum in 1896, 15 years after Carlyle's death, offering an intriguing snapshot of Victorian life. The writer's quest for quiet (details of his valiant attempts to soundproof the attic) strikes a chord today: he was plagued by the sound of revelry from Cremorne Pleasure Gardens.

FREE Chelsea Old Church

Old Church Street, SW3 5DQ (7795 1019, www.chelseaoldchurch.org.uk). Sloane Square tube or bus 11, 19, 22, 49, 319. **Open** 2-4pm Tue-Thur; 1.30-5pm Sun. *Services* 8am, 10am, 11am, 12.15pm Sun. *Evensong* 6pm Sun. **Admission** free; donations appreciated. **No credit cards. Map** p395 E12.

Legend has it that the Thomas More Chapel, which remains on the south side, contains More's headless body buried somewhere under the walls (his head, after being spiked on London Bridge, was 'rescued' and buried in a family vault in St Dunstan's church, Canterbury). There's a striking statue of More outside the church. Guides are on hand on Sundays.

★ Chelsea Physic Garden

66 Royal Hospital Road, SW3 4HS (7352 5646, www.chelseaphysicgarden.co.uk). Sloane Square tube or bus 11, 19, 239. **Open** *Apr-Oct* noon-5pm Wed-Fri; noon-6pm Sun. *Tours* times vary; phone to check. **Admission** £8; £5 reductions; free under-5s. *Tours* free. **Credit** (shop) AmEx, MC, V. **Map** p395 F12.

The capacious grounds of this gorgeous botanic garden are filled with healing herbs and vegetables, rare

trees and dye plants. The garden was founded in 1673 by Sir Hans Sloane with the purpose of cultivating and studying plants for medical purposes. The first plant specimens were brought to England and planted here in 1676, with the famous Cedars of Lebanon (the first to be grown in England) arriving a little later. The garden opened to the public in 1893.

▶ *Sloane's specimens are the oldest items in the botany collection of the Natural History Museum; see p143.*

FREE National Army Museum

Royal Hospital Road, SW3 4HT (7730 0717, www.national-army-museum.ac.uk). Sloane Square tube or bus 11, 137, 170. **Open** 10am-5.30pm daily. **Admission** free. **Credit** (shop) AmEx, MC, V. **Map** p395 F12.

More entertaining than its modern exterior suggests, this museum dedicated to the history of the British Army kicks off with 'Redcoats', a gallery that starts at Agincourt in 1415 and ends with the American War of Independence. Upstairs, 'The Road to Waterloo' marches through 20 years of struggle against the French, featuring 70,000 model soldiers. Also on display is the kit of Olympic medal winner Dame Kelly Holmes (an ex-army athlete), while Major Michael 'Bronco' Lane, conqueror of Everest, has donated his frostbitten fingertips.

FREE Royal Hospital Chelsea

Royal Hospital Road, SW3 4SR (7881 5200, www.chelsea-pensioners.org.uk). Sloane Square tube or bus 11, 19, 22, 137, 170, 239. **Open** *Apr-Sept* 10am-noon, 2-4pm Mon-Sat; 2-4pm Sun. *Oct-Mar* 10am-noon, 2-4pm Mon-Sat. **Admission** free. **Credit** MC, V. **Map** p395 F12.

Roughly 350 Chelsea Pensioners (retired soldiers) live in quarters at the Royal Hospital, founded in 1682 by Charles II and designed by Sir Christopher Wren (with later adjustments by Robert Adam and Sir John Soane). Retired soldiers are still eligible to apply for a final posting here if they're over 65 and in receipt of an Army or War Disability Pension for Army Service. The pensioners have their own club room, bowling green and gardens, and get tickets to Chelsea FC home games – the club's home strip for the 2010/11 season added a flash of red at the collar, sleeve and shorts in their honour. The museum, open at the same times as the Hospital, has more about their lives.

INSIDE TRACK ESPIONAGE

Chelsea has long been a popular haunt for spies, real and fictional. KGB agent Kim Philby held meetings at the Markham Arms at 138 King's Road, now a branch of the Abbey bank, and both James Bond and George Smiley were given homes in the area by their respective creators.

Knightsbridge & South Kensington

Nouveaux riches and a wealth of cultural attractions.

A certain type of Londoner goes to **Knightsbridge** to spend, spend, spend. Or, at least, to hang around people who are spend, spend, spending. Many of the key designer labels have major shops in the area, which gets plenty of foot traffic thanks to its world-famous department stores and high-end restaurants. Nearby, **South Kensington**'s footprint is cultural rather than commercial: you'll find three of the world's greatest museums, some extraordinary colleges, a concert hall and a cutting-edge contemporary art gallery.

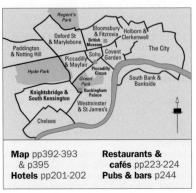

Map pp392-393 & p395	**Restaurants & cafés** pp223-224
Hotels pp201-202	**Pubs & bars** p244

KNIGHTSBRIDGE

Knightsbridge tube.

Knightsbridge in the 11th century was a village celebrated for its taverns, highwaymen and the legend that two knights once fought to the death on the bridge spanning the Westbourne River (later dammed to form Hyde Park's Serpentine lake). In modern Knightsbridge, urban princesses would be too busy unsheathing the credit card to notice such a farrago. Voguish **Harvey Nichols** (*see p253*) holds court at the top of **Sloane Street**, which leads down to Sloane Square. Expensive brands – Gucci, Prada, Chanel – dominate. East of Sloane Street is **Belgravia**, characterised by a cluster of embassies around **Belgrave**

INSIDE TRACK GIDDY-UP!

Watch members of the Household Cavalry emerge from their South Carriage Drive barracks in **Hyde Park** at 10.30am daily (9.30am Sunday). They then ride to Horse Guards Parade for the **Changing of the Guard** (*see p279* **Standing on Ceremony**).

Square. Hidden behind the stucco-clad parades fronting the square are numerous mews, worth exploring for the pubs they conceal, notably the **Nag's Head** (53 Kinnerton Street, 7235 1135).

For many tourists, Knightsbridge means one thing: **Harrods** (*see p253*). From its tan bricks and olive green awning to its green-coated doormen, it's an instantly recognisable retail legend. Further along is the imposing **Brompton Oratory** (*see below*).

FREE Brompton Oratory

Thurloe Place, Brompton Road, SW7 2RP (7808 0900, www.bromptonoratory.com). South Kensington tube. **Open** 6.30am-8pm daily. **Admission** free; donations appreciated. **No credit cards**. **Map** p395 E10.

The second-biggest Catholic church in the country (after Westminster Cathedral; *see p135*) is formally the Church of the Immaculate Heart of Mary, but almost universally known as the Brompton Oratory. Completed in 1884, it feels older, partly because of the Baroque Italianate style but also because much of the decoration pre-dates the structure: Mazzuoli's 17th-century apostle statues, for example, are from Siena cathedral. The 11am Solemn Mass sung in Latin on Sundays is enchanting, as are Vespers, at 3.30pm; the website has details. During the Cold War, KGB agents used the church as a dead-letter box.

▶ *A new chapel, in honour of the recently beatified Cardinal Newman, was due to be completed in late 2010.*

SOUTH KENSINGTON

Gloucester Road or South Kensington tube.

As far as cultural and academic institutions are concerned, this is the land of plenty. It was Prince Albert who oversaw the inception of its world-class museums, colleges and concert hall, using the profits of the 1851 Great Exhibition; the area was nicknamed 'Albertopolis' in his honour. You'll find the **Natural History Museum** (*see p145*) and the **Victoria & Albert** (*see p145*), **Imperial College**, the **Royal College of Art** and the **Royal College of Music** (Prince Consort Road, 7589 3643; call for details of the musical instrument museum), which forms a unity with the **Royal Albert Hall** (*see p316*), open since 1871 and variously used for boxing, motor shows, marathons, table tennis tournaments, fascist rallies and rock concerts. Opposite is the **Albert Memorial** (*see below*).

⟨FREE⟩ Albert Memorial
Kensington Gardens (7495 0916). South Kensington tube. **Tours** 2pm, 3pm 1st Sun of mth. **Admission** *Tours* £5; £4.50 reductions. **No credit cards. Map** p393 D8.
'I would rather not be made the prominent feature of such a monument,' was Prince Albert's reported response when the subject of his commemoration arose. Hard, then, to imagine what he would have made of this extraordinary thing, unveiled 15 years after his death. Created by Sir George Gilbert Scott, it centres around a gilded Albert holding a catalogue of the 1851 Great Exhibition, guarded on four corners by the continents of Africa, America, Asia and Europe. The pillars are crowned with bronze statues of the sciences, and the frieze at the base depicts major artists, architects and musicians. It's one of London's most dramatic monuments.

★ ⟨FREE⟩ Natural History Museum
Cromwell Road, SW7 5BD (7942 5000, www.nhm.ac.uk). South Kensington tube. **Open** 10am-5.50pm daily. **Admission** free; charges apply for special exhibitions. *Tours* free. **Credit** (shop) MC, V. **Map** p395 D10.
Both a research institution and a fabulous museum, the NHM opened in Alfred Waterhouse's purpose-built, Romanesque palazzo on the Cromwell Road in 1881. Now joined by the splendid Darwin Centre extension, the original building still looks quite magnificent. The pale blue and terracotta façade just about prepares you for the natural wonders within.

Taking up the full length of the vast entrance hall is the cast of a Diplodocus skeleton. A left turn leads into the west wing or Blue Zone, where long queues form to see animatronic dinosaurs – the endlessly popular *T Rex* is back after hip surgery in 2010. A display on biology features an illuminated, man-sized model of a foetus in the womb along with graphic diagrams of how it might have got there.

A right turn from the central hall leads past the 'Creepy Crawlies' exhibition to the Green Zone. Stars include a cross-section through a Giant Sequoia tree and an amazing array of stuffed birds, including the chance to compare the egg of a hummingbird, smaller than a little finger nail, with that of an elephant bird (now extinct), almost football-sized.

SIGHTS

Enchanted Palace at Kensington Palace. *See p146.*

SIGHTS

Profile Science Museum

One of London's greatest museums takes on the world's greatest challenge.

Only marginally less popular with kids than its natural historical neighbour, the **Science Museum** (for listings, *see p145*) is a celebration of the wonders of technology in the service of our daily lives. On the ground floor, the shop – selling wacky toys – is part of the 'Energy Hall', which introduces the museum's collections with impressive 18th-century steam engines. In 'Exploring Space', rocket science and the lunar landings are illustrated by dramatically lit mock-ups and models, before the museum gears up for its core collection in 'Making the Modern World'. Introduced by Puffing Billy, the world's oldest steam locomotive (built in 1815), the gallery also contains Stephenson's Rocket. Also here are the Apollo 10 command module, classic cars and an absorbing collection of everyday technological marvels from 1750 right up to the present.

Upstairs in the main body of the museum, the second floor holds displays on computing, marine engineering and mathematics; the third floor is dedicated to flight, among other things, including the hands-on Launchpad gallery, which features levers, pulleys, explosions and all manner of experiments for children (and their associated grown-ups). On the fifth floor, you'll find an old-fashioned but intriguing display on the science and art of medicine.

Beyond 'Making the Modern World', bathed in an eerie blue light, the three floors of the Wellcome Wing are where the museum makes sure it stays on the cutting edge of science. On the ground floor, 'Antenna'

is a web-savvy look at breaking science stories, displaying video interviews and Q&As with real research scientists alongside the weird new objects they've been working on. Upstairs, the enjoyable and troubling 'Who Am I?' gallery was relaunched in summer 2010. The dozen silver pods that surround brightly lit cases of objects have engaging interactive displays – from a cartoon of ethical dilemmas that introduces you to your dorsolateral prefrontal cortex to a chance to find out what gender your brain is. Compelling objects include a jellyfish that's 'technically immortal', the statistically average British man (he's called Jose, by the way) and a pound of human fat, displayed alongside a gastric band. There's also contemporary art, including installations and Stephen Wiltshire's amazingly detailed drawing, from memory, of the Houses of Parliament.

At the end of 2010, the museum is opening a new permanent gallery on the second floor of the Wellcome Wing. 'Atmosphere: Exploring Climate Science' will look at how the climate works, greenhouse gases and what scientists predict will happen.

THREE TO SEE
There's more brilliant science at the **Wellcome Collection** (*see p105*), the **Royal Institution & Faraday Museum** (*see p127*) and the **Royal Observatory** (*see p167*).

Beyond is the Red Zone. 'Earth's Treasury' is a mine of information on a variety of precious metals, gems and crystals; 'From the Beginning' is a brave attempt to give the expanse of geological time a human perspective. Outside, the delightful Wildlife Garden (Apr-Oct only) showcases a range of British lowland habitats, including a 'Bee Tree', a hollow tree trunk that opens to reveal a busy hive.

Many of the museum's 22 million insect and plant specimens are housed in the new Darwin Centre, where they take up nearly 17 miles of shelving. With its new eight-storey Cocoon, this is also home to the museum's research scientists, who can be watched at work. But a great deal of this amazing institution is hidden from public view, given over to labs and specialised storage.

★ FREE Science Museum

Exhibition Road, SW7 2DD (7942 4000 switchboard, 0870 870 4868 information, www.sciencemuseum.org.uk). South Kensington tube. **Open** 10am-6pm daily. **Admission** free; charges apply for special exhibitions. **Credit** MC, V. **Map** p395 D9.
See p144 **Profile**.

★ FREE Victoria & Albert Museum

Cromwell Road, SW7 2RL (7942 2000, www.vam.ac.uk). South Kensington tube. **Open** 10am-5.45pm Mon-Thur, Sat, Sun; 10am-10pm Fri. *Tours* hourly, 10.30am-3.30pm daily.
Admission free; charges for special exhibitions. **Credit** (shop) MC, V. **Map** p395 E10.
The V&A is one of the world's most magnificent museums, its foundation stone laid on this site by Queen Victoria in her last official public engagement in 1899. It is a superb showcase for applied arts from around the world, appreciably calmer than its tearaway cousins on the other side of Exhibition Road. Some 150 grand galleries on seven floors contain countless pieces of furniture, ceramics, sculpture, paintings, posters, jewellery, metalwork, glass, textiles and dress, spanning several centuries. Items are grouped by theme, origin or age, but any attempt to comprehend the whole collection in a single visit is doomed. For advice, tap the patient staff, who field a formidable combination of leaflets, floorplans, general knowledge and polite concern.

Highlights include the seven Raphael Cartoons painted in 1515 as tapestry designs for the Sistine Chapel; the finest collection of Italian Renaissance sculpture outside Italy; Canova's Three Graces; the Ardabil carpet, the world's oldest and arguably most splendid floor covering, in the Jameel Gallery of Islamic Art; Medici porcelain; and the Luck of Edenhall, a 13th-century glass beaker from Syria. The Fashion galleries run from 18th-century court dress right up to contemporary chiffon numbers; the Architecture gallery has videos, models, plans and descriptions of various styles; and the famous Photography collection holds over 500,000 images.

INSIDE TRACK
STREET RADICAL

Exhibition Road is home to an experiment in urban planning called Shared Space (www.shared-space.org), which removes street furnishings and encourages pedestrians and drivers to come to a mutual understanding with regard to use of road and pavement. The improvements should be completed at the end of 2011.

The V&A's FuturePlan has been a revelation. The completely refurbished Medieval & Renaissance Galleries are stunning, but there are many other eye-catching new or redisplayed exhibits: the Gilbert Collection of silver, gold and gemmed ornaments has arrived from Somerset House (*see p111*); the Ceramics Galleries have been renovated and supplemented with an eye-catching bridge; there's lovely Buddhist sculpture in the Robert HN Ho Family Foundation Galleries; and the new Theatre & Performance Galleries take over where Covent Garden's defunct Theatre Museum left off. By the end of 2010, the 14th- to 17th-century sculpture rooms, just off the central John Madejski Garden, will also have been jazzed up: restored mosaic floors and beautiful stained glass will enhance the statues.

HYDE PARK & KENSINGTON GARDENS

Hyde Park Corner, Knightsbridge, Lancaster Gate or Queensway tube.

At one and a half miles long and about a mile wide, **Hyde Park** (7298 2000, www.royalparks.gov.uk) is one of the largest of London's Royal Parks. The land was appropriated in 1536 from the monks of Westminster Abbey by Henry VIII for hunting deer. Although opened to the public in the early 1600s, the parks were favoured only by the upper echelons of society.

At the end of the 17th century, William III, averse to the dank air of Whitehall Palace, relocated to **Kensington Palace** (*see p146*). A corner of Hyde Park was sectioned off to make grounds for the palace and closed to the public, until King George II opened it on Sundays to those wearing formal dress. Nowadays, **Kensington Gardens** is delineated from Hyde Park only by the line of the Serpentine and the Long Water. Beside the Long Water is a bronze statue of **Peter Pan**, erected in 1912: it was in Kensington Gardens beside the Round Pond eight years earlier that playwright JM Barrie met Jack Llewelyn Davies, the boy who was the inspiration for Peter. The **Diana, Princess of Wales Memorial Playground** (*see p291*)

SIGHTS

is a kids' favourite, as is Kathryn Gustafson's ring-shaped **Princess Diana Memorial Fountain**. Near the fountain, Simon Gudgeon's giant bird *Isis* was in 2009 the first sculpture added to the park for half a century. There are changing exhibitions of contemporary art at the **Serpentine Gallery** (*see right*).

The **Serpentine** itself is London's oldest boating lake. Home to ducks, coots, swans, tufty-headed grebes and, every summer, gently perspiring dads rowing their children about, the Serpentine will be a great setting for the Triathlon and Marathon Swimming during the 2012 Games (*see p59*). The lake is at the bottom of **Hyde Park**, which isn't especially beautiful, but is of historic interest. It was a hotspot for mass demonstrations in the 19th century and remains so today; a march protesting against war in Iraq in 2003 was the largest in British history. The legalisation of public assembly in the park led to the establishment of **Speakers' Corner** in 1872 (close to Marble Arch tube), where political and religious ranters – sane and otherwise – still have the floor. Marx, Lenin, Orwell and the Pankhursts all spoke here.

The park perimeter is popular with skaters, as well as with bike- and horse-riders (for the riding school, *see p338*). If you're exploring on foot and the vast expanses defeat you, look out for the **Liberty Drives** (May-Oct). Driven by volunteers, these electric buggies pick up groups of sightseers and ferry them around; there's no fare, but offer a donation if you can.

Enchanted Palace at Kensington Palace

Kensington Gardens, W8 4PX (0844 482 7777 information, 0844 482 7799 reservations, www.hrp.org.uk). High Street Kensington tube or Queensway tube. **Open** *Mar-Oct* 10am-6pm daily. *Nov-Feb* 10am-5pm daily. **Admission** £12.50; £6.25-£11 reductions; £34 family; free under-5s. **Credit** MC, V. **Map** p392 B8.

Sir Christopher Wren extended this Jacobean mansion to palatial proportions on the instructions of William III. Until June 2012, the palace is undergoing renovations. During this period, the 'Enchanted Palace' show is bringing different rooms of the State Apartments to life with stories from the palace's history. This 'animated exhibition' combines live performance, courtesy of Wildworks theatre company, with high-fashion installations. You'll hear ghostly arguments from long-dead princesses, encounter the 'wild boy' who was kept here as a pet, and enter a 'whirling ballroom'. *Photo p143*.

★ FREE Serpentine Gallery

Kensington Gardens, nr Albert Memorial, W2 3XA (7402 6075, www.serpentinegallery.org). Lancaster Gate or South Kensington tube. **Open** 10am-6pm daily. **Admission** free; donations appreciated. **Credit** (shop) AmEx, MC, V. **Map** p393 D8.

The secluded location south-west of the Long Water and Serpentine makes this small and airy former tea house an attractive destination for lovers of contemporary art. The rolling two-monthly programme of temporary exhibitions features up-to-the-minute artists. Every spring, a renowned architect, who's never before built in the UK, is commissioned to build a new pavilion. It then opens to the public, running a hip programme of cultural events from June to September. There's a tiny but rarely less than tempting bookshop as well.

SIGHTS

Snapshot
Victorian London

Where to see how London lived.

The legacy of Queen Victoria's reign is everywhere in London, even in buildings that preceded the Victorians: the likes of **St Paul's Cathedral** (*see p87*) and the **Houses of Parliament** (*see p132*) received 19th-century alterations to make them look more 'historic' and less plain. St Paul's, for example, gained amazing giltwork and mosaics. But South Kensington's three palatial museums and the **Albert Memorial** (*see p143*) must be the finest testaments to the self-confidence and ingenuity of the Victorians, with the coloured brickwork and extravagant detailing of the **Natural History Museum** (*see p143*) almost as arresting as the exhibits within.

Natural History Museum.

North London

A wooded park, an unstoppable market and lots of artistic souls.

The list of famous residents gives an idea of the scope of north London: from Amy Winehouse to Karl Marx and John Keats, a huge variety of people have been drawn to its mix of pretty, sleepy retreats and buzzing, creative party zones. First stop for most is **Camden Town**, with its markets, indie pubs and alternative vibe, but there's fun to be found in the squares of **Islington** and among the grown-up bohemians of **Stoke Newington** and fashionable **Dalston**. To the north, **Hampstead** and **Highgate** offer genteel village life.

| **Map** p404 | **Hotels** pp202-204 |
| **Pubs & bars** pp244-245 | **Restaurants & cafés** pp225-228 |

CAMDEN

Camden Town or Chalk Farm tube.

Despite the pressures of gentrification, Camden refuses to leave behind its grungy history as the cradle of British rock music. Against a backdrop of social deprivation in Thatcher's Britain, venues such as the Electric Ballroom and Dingwalls provided a platform for musical rebels. By the 1990s, the Creation label was based in nearby Primrose Hill (*see p149*), unleashing My Bloody Valentine and the Jesus & Mary Chain on the world, before making it big with Oasis. The Gallaghers were often seen trading insults with Blur at the **Good Mixer** (30 Inverness Street, 7916 7929). The music still plays at Camden icon the **Roundhouse** (*see p321*) and at **Koko** (*see p320*).

Before the Victorian expansion of London, Camden was a watering stop on the highway to Hampstead (*see p149*), with two notorious taverns – the Mother Black Cap and Mother Red Cap (now the **World's End** pub, opposite the tube) – frequented by highwaymen and brigands. After the gaps were filled in with terraced houses, the borough became a magnet for Irish and Greek railway workers, many of them working in the engine turning-house that is now the Roundhouse. The squalor of the area had a powerful negative influence on the young Charles Dickens, who lived briefly on Bayham Street; a blue plaque commemorates his stay. From the 1960s, things started to pick up for

Camden, helped by an influx of students, lured by low rents and the growing arts scene that nurtured punk, then indie, then Britpop – and now any number of short-lived indie-electro and alt-folk hybrids.

Much of Camden still has a rough quality – dealers and junkies loiter around Camden Town tube station – but the hardcore rebellion of the rock 'n' roll years has been replaced by a more laid-back carnival vibe, as goths, indie kids, emos and the last punks vie for attention. Tourists travel here in their thousands for the sprawling mayhem of **Camden Market** (*see p148*), which stretches north from the tube along boutique-lined Camden High Street and Chalk Farm Road. A dozen different countercultures depend on the market for thigh-length Frankenstein boots, studded collars and leather jackets emblazoned with the mispunctuated mantra 'Punks not Dead'.

There are unmistakeable signs of a move upmarket: the summer 2010 opening of **Shaka Zulu** (Stables Market, Chalk Farm Road, 3376 9911, www.shaka-zulu.com), a hugely over-the-top Zulu-themed bar-restaurant, right beneath **Gilgamesh** (7482 5757, www.gilgameshbar. com), a hugely over-the-top Sumerian-themed bar-restaurant, may point to the future. Drop in to **Proud** (*see p330*) if you want to reset your cultural compass.

Cutting through the market is **Regent's Canal**, which opened in 1820 to provide a link between east and west London for horse-drawn narrowboats loaded with coal. Today, the canal

SIGHTS

Camden Lock.

is used by the jolly tour-boats of the London Waterbus Company (7482 2550, www.london waterbus.com) and Walker's Quay (7485 4433, www.walkersquay.com), which run between Camden Lock and **Little Venice** in summer and on winter weekends. Locals use the canal towpath as a convenient walking route west to Regent's Park and **ZSL London Zoo** (see p121), or east to Islington (see p152).

Camden's one avowed 'sight' is west of Camden Town – the excellent **Jewish Museum** (see right) – but it's still a good bit of town for gigs. As well as Koko and the Roundhouse, there are plenty of pub stages where this year's hopefuls try to get spotted: try the **Barfly** (see p323), **Underworld** (see p325) and the **Dublin Castle** (94 Parkway, NW1 7AN, 7485 1773), where Madness and, later, Blur were launched. The **Jazz Café** (see p324) and the **Blues Kitchen** (see p323) offer a different vibe.

Camden Market

Camden Lock Camden Lock Place, off Chalk Farm Road, NW1 8AF (www.camdenlock market.com). **Open** 10am-6pm daily. Note: there are fewer stalls Mon-Fri.
Camden Lock Village east of Chalk Farm Road, NW1 (www.camdenlock.net). **Open** 10am-8.30pm daily.

**INSIDE TRACK
CROWD CONTROL**

Camden Market's crowds can be awful at the weekends – unfortunately, this is also the best time to visit. After you're done shopping, slip out sideways on to the canal and stroll five minutes to sedate **Primrose Hill** (see p149), the perfect place to recuperate and assess your purchases.

Camden Market Camden High Street, at Buck Street, NW1 (www.camdenmarkets.org). **Open** 9.30am-5.30pm daily.
Inverness Street Market Inverness Street, NW1 (www.camdenlock.net). **Open** 8.30am-5pm daily.
Stables Market off Chalk Farm Road, opposite Hartland Road, NW1 8AH (7485 5511, www. stablesmarket.com). **Open** 10.30am-6pm Mon-Fri (reduced stalls); 10am-6pm Sat, Sun.
All Camden Town or Chalk Farm tube.
Map p404 Y2.

Camden Market actually refers to the microcosm of markets that make up the northern Camden Town area. The Camden Market, née Buck Street Market, is the place for neon sunglasses and pseudo-witty slogan garments. Almost next door, and perennially threatened by proposed tube station expansions, is the listed building the Electric Ballroom, which sells vinyl and CDs on weekends and is also a music venue. The Inverness Street Market opposite sells similar garb to the Camden Market as well as a diminishing supply of fruit and vegetables. North, next to the railway bridge, you'll find crafts, clothes, trinkets and small curiosities with a Japanese pop culture influence at Camden Lock and Camden Lock Village, the latter having opened after major fire damage in spring 2009. Just north is the Stables Market where you'll find some good vintage clothes shops. Finally, the Horse Hospital area (which once cared for horses injured while pulling barges) is good for second-hand clothing, food stands and designer furniture. Here, too, is Cyberdog, with probably London's wackiest-looking sales assistants – perfect if you've pink dreadlocks, Buffalos and piercings and need some 'rave toys' or day-glo clubware.

Jewish Museum

Raymond Burton House, 129-131 Albert Street, NW1 7NB (7284 7384, www.jewishmuseum. org.uk). Camden Town tube. **Open** 10am-5pm Mon-Wed, Sun; 10am-9pm Thur; 10am-2pm Fri. **Admission** £7; £3-£6 reductions; free under-5s. **Credit** MC, V. **Map** p404 Y3.

Reopened in 2010, this expanded museum is a brilliant exploration of Jewish life in Britain since 1066. Access is free to the downstairs café, located beside an ancient ritual bath, and the shop you enter past. There is an entry fee for the galleries upstairs, but they're well worth the money, combining fun interactives – you can wield the iron in a tailor's sweatshop, sniff chicken soup, pose for a wedding photo or take part in some Yiddish theatre – with serious history. There's a powerful Holocaust section, using the testimony of a single survivor, Leon Greenman, to bring tight focus to the unimaginable horror of it all. Opposite, a beautiful room of religious artefacts, including a 17th-century synagogue ark and centrepiece chandelier of Hanukkah lamps, does an elegant job of introducing Jewish ritual.

Around Camden

Primrose Hill, to the west of Camden, is just as attractive as the actors and pop stars who frequent the gastropubs and quaint cafés along **Regent's Park Road** and **Gloucester Avenue**. On sunny Sunday mornings, there's no better spot to read the papers than the pavement tables in front of Ukrainian café **Trojka** (101 Regent's Park Road, 7483 3765). Other favourite hangouts on Regent's Park Road include the long-established **Primrose Pâtisserie** (no.136, 7722 7848) and upmarket Greek bistro **Lemonia** (no.89, 7586 7454). For a gastropub feed, head to Gloucester Avenue: both the **Engineer** (no.65, 7722 0950) and **Lansdowne** (no.90, 7483 0409) are here. On a clear day, the walk up the hill is a delight.

ST JOHN'S WOOD

St John's Wood or Swiss Cottage tube.

The woodland that gives St John's Wood its name was part of the great Middlesex Forest, before the land was claimed by the Knights of St John of Jerusalem. Areas of forest were cleared for private villas in the mid 19th century, and

uncharacteristically sensitive redevelopment during the 1950s left the area smart and eminently desirable: even a modest semi can cost £2 million. The expensive tastes of locals are reflected in the posh boutiques along the High Street. The main tourist attraction is **Lord's** cricket ground (*see below*), but a steady stream of music fans pay tribute to the Beatles by crossing the zebra crossing in front of **Abbey Road Studios** (3 Abbey Road). The studio, founded in 1931 by Sir Edward Elgar, is still used to record albums and film scores, including the *Lord of the Rings*.

Lord's Tour & MCC Museum

St John's Wood Road, NW8 8QN (7616 8595, www.lords.org). St John's Wood tube. **Open** *Tours* phone or see website for details. **Admission** £14; £8 reductions; free under-5s; £37 family. **Credit** AmEx, MC, V.
Lord's is more than just a famous cricket ground. As the headquarters of the Marylebone Cricket Club (MCC), it is official guardian of the rules – and self-appointed guardian of the elusive 'spirit' – of cricket. As well as staging Test matches and internationals, the ground is home to the Middlesex County Cricket Club (MCCC). Visitors can take an organised tour round the futuristic, pod-like NatWest Media Centre and the august, portrait-bedecked Long Room. Highlights of the museum include the tiny urn containing the Ashes (this coveted trophy never leaves Lord's, no matter how many times the Australians win it) and memorabilia celebrating the achievements of such legends of the game as WG Grace.
▶ *During the 2012 Games, the Archery competition will take place here; see p59.*

HAMPSTEAD

Hampstead tube, or Gospel Oak or Hampstead Heath rail.

It may have been absorbed into London during the city's great Victorian expansion, but hilltop Hampstead still feels like a Home Counties'

SIGHTS

Hampstead Heath. *See p150.*

village. It has long been a favoured roost for literary and artistic types: Keats and Constable lived here in the 19th century, and sculptors Barbara Hepworth and Henry Moore took up residence in the 1930s. However, the area is now popular with City workers, who are among the only people able to afford what is some of London's priciest property.

The undisputed highlight of the district is **Hampstead Heath** (*photo p149*), the relatively vast and in places wonderfully overgrown tract of countryside between Hampstead village and Highgate that is said to have inspired CS Lewis's Narnia. The heath covers 791 acres of woodland, playing fields, swimming ponds and meadows of tall grass that attract picnickers and couples in search of privacy. It will feel even more delightfully rural if the City of London Corporation's 'aspiration' to graze sheep on the heath as a flock of organic lawnmowers comes to fruition.

The south end of the heath is where you'll find dinky Hampstead village, all genteel shops and cafés, restaurants and lovely pubs such as the **Holly Bush** (*see p245*). While you're there, tour the gorgeous sunken gardens and antique collection at **Fenton House** (*see right*) or gaze at the stars from the **Hampstead Scientific Society Observatory** (Lower Terrace, 8346 1056, www.hampsteadscience.ac.uk/astro), open on clear Friday and Saturday evenings and Sunday lunchtimes from mid September to mid April. A stroll along nearby Judges Walk reveals a line of horse chestnuts and limes virtually unchanged since they appeared in a Constable painting in 1820. Constable was buried nearby at **St John-at-Hampstead Church** (7794 5808), as was the comedian Peter Cook. At the top of Hampstead, North End Way divides the main heath from the wooded West Heath, one of London's oldest gay cruising areas (but perfectly family-friendly by day). Just off North End Way is Hampstead's best-kept secret, the secluded and charmingly overgrown **Hill Garden & Pergola** (open 8.30am-dusk daily), which was built by Lord Leverhulme using soil from the excavation of the Northern line's tunnels.

East of Hampstead tube, a maze of postcard-pretty residential streets shelters **Burgh House** (New End Square, 7431 0144, www.burghhouse.org.uk), a Queen Anne house with a small local history museum and gallery. Also in the area are **2 Willow Road** (*see p151*), architect Ernö Goldfinger's self-designed 1930s residence, and **40 Well Walk**, Constable's home for the last ten years of his life. Downhill towards Hampstead Heath Overground station is **Keats House** (*see p151*). Further west, and marginally closer to Finchley Road tube, is the **Freud Museum** (*see right*), while the innovative

SIGHTS

Camden Passage. See p152.

contemporary art exhibitions of **Camden Arts Centre** (*see p304*) are almost opposite Finchley Road & Frognal Overground station.

Fenton House

3 Hampstead Grove, NW3 6RT (7435 3471, www.nationaltrust.org.uk). Hampstead tube.
Open *Mar* 2-5pm Sat, Sun. *Apr-Oct* 2-5pm Wed-Fri; 11am-5pm Sat, Sun. **Admission** *House & gardens* £6; £3 reductions; free under-5s; £15 family. *Gardens* £1. *Joint ticket with 2 Willow Road* £9. **Credit** MC, V.
Set in a gorgeous garden, with a 300-year-old apple orchard, this manor house is notable for its 17th- and 18th-century harpsichords, virginals and spinets, which are still played at lunchtime and evening concerts (phone for details). Also on display are European and China porcelain, Chippendale furniture and some artful 17th-century needlework.

Freud Museum

20 Maresfield Gardens, NW3 5SX (7435 2002, www.freud.org.uk). Finchley Road tube. **Open** noon-5pm Wed-Sun. **Admission** £6; £3-£4.50 reductions; free under-12s. **Credit** AmEx, MC, V.
Driven from Vienna by the Nazis, Sigmund Freud lived in this quiet suburban house in north London with his wife Martha and daughter Anna until his death in 1939. Now a museum with temporary exhibitions, the house displays Freud's antiques, art and therapy tools, including his famous couch. The building has two blue plaques, one for Sigmund and another for Anna, a pioneer in child psychiatry.

Keats House

*Keats Grove, NW3 2RR (7332 3868, www.cityof
london.gov.uk/keatshousehampstead). Hampstead
tube, Hampstead Heath rail or bus 24, 46, 168.*
Open *Apr-Oct* 1-5pm Tue-Sun. *Nov-Mar* 1-5pm
Fri-Sun. **Admission** £5; £3 reductions; free
under-16s. **Credit** MC, V.

Reopened after refurbishment in 2009, Keats House
was the Romantic poet's last British home before
tuberculosis forced him to Italy and death at the age
of only 25. A leaflet guides you through each room,
starting from the rear, as well as providing context
for Keats's life and that of his less famous friend and
patron, Charles Brown. The 2009 renovation has
ensured the decorative scheme is entirely accurate,
down to the pale pink walls of Keats's humble bedroom. The garden, in which he wrote 'Ode to a
Nightingale', is particularly pleasant.
▶ *For the regular poetry readings and other
events held here, check the website.*

★ FREE Kenwood House/
Iveagh Bequest

*Hampstead Lane, NW3 7JR (8348 1286,
www.english-heritage.org.uk). Hampstead tube, or
Golders Green tube then bus 210.* **Open** 11.30am-
4pm daily. **Admission** free. *Tours* (for groups
by appointment only) £5-£7. **Credit** MC, V.

Set in lovely grounds at the top of Hampstead Heath,
Kenwood House is every inch the country manor
house. Built in 1616, the mansion was remodelled in
the 18th century for William Murray, who made the
pivotal court ruling in 1772 that made it illegal to
own slaves in England. The house was purchased
by brewing magnate Edward Guinness, who was
kind enough to donate his art collection to the nation
in 1927. Highlights include Vermeer's *The Guitar
Player*, a panoramic view of old London Bridge by
Claude de Jongh (1630), Gainsborough's *Countess
Howe*, and one of Rembrandt's finest self-portraits
(dating to c1663).

2 Willow Road

*2 Willow Road, NW3 1TH (7435 6166,
www.nationaltrust.org.uk). Hampstead tube or
Hampstead Heath rail.* **Open** *Mar-Oct* 11am-5pm
Wed-Sun. *Tours* 11am, noon, 1pm, 2pm Wed-Sun.
Admission £6; £3 children; free under-5s; £15
family. *Joint ticket with Fenton House* £9. **No
credit cards.**

INSIDE TRACK
WATER WALKING

If you fancy a walk, the **Regent's Canal**
towpath runs all the way east from south
of Angel tube past Hackney's trendily boho
Broadway Market and the Olympic Park
(*see p53*) as far as the Thames.

A surprising addition to the National Trust's collection of historic houses, this small modernist building
was designed by Hungarian-born architect Ernö
Goldfinger. The house was made to be flexible, with
ingenious movable partitions and folding doors.
Home to the architect and his wife until their deaths,
it contains a fine, idiosyncratic collection of art by the
likes of Max Ernst and Henry Moore. Goldfinger also
designed Notting Hill's Trellick Tower (*see p123*).

HIGHGATE

Archway or Highgate tube.

Taking its name from the tollgate that once
stood on the High Street, Highgate is inexorably
linked with London's medieval mayor, Richard
'Dick' Whittington. As the story goes, the
disheartened Whittington fled the City as
far as Highgate Hill, but turned back when
he heard the Bow Bells peal out 'Turn again,
Whittington, thrice Mayor of London'. Today,
the area is best known for the atmospheric
grounds of **Highgate Cemetery** (*see below*).
Adjoining the cemetery is pretty **Waterlow
Park**, created by low-cost housing pioneer Sir
Sydney Waterlow in 1889, with ponds, a mini-
aviary, tennis courts and a cute garden café in
16th-century **Lauderdale House** (8348 8716,
www.lauderdalehouse.co.uk), former home of
Charles II's mistress, Nell Gwynn. North of
Highgate tube, shady **Highgate Woods** are
preserved as a conservation area, with a nature
trail, adventure playground and a café that
hosts live jazz during the summer.

★ Highgate Cemetery

*Swains Lane, N6 6PJ (8340 1834, www.
highgate-cemetery.org). Archway tube.* **Open** *East
Cemetery* Mar-Oct 10am-5pm Mon-Fri; 11am-5pm
Sat, Sun; Nov-Mar 10am-3.30pm Mon-Fri; 11am-
3.30pm Sat, Sun. *West Cemetery* by tour only.
Admission £3. *Tours* £7. **No credit cards.**

The final resting place of some very famous
Londoners, Highgate Cemetery is a wonderfully
overgrown maze of ivy-cloaked Victorian tombs and
time-shattered urns. Visitors are free to wander
through the East Cemetery, with its memorials to
Karl Marx, George Eliot and Douglas Adams, but
the most atmospheric part of the cemetery is the
foliage-shrouded West Cemetery, laid out in 1839.
Only accessible on an organised tour (book ahead,
dress respectfully and arrive 30mins early), the
shady paths wind past gloomy catacombs, grand
Victorian pharaonic tombs, and the graves of notables such as poet Christina Rossetti, scientist
Michael Faraday and poisoned Russian dissident
Alexander Litvinenko.
▶ *The cemetery closes during burials, so call
ahead before you visit. Note that children under
eight are not allowed in the West Cemetery.*

SIGHTS

SIGHTS

ISLINGTON

Angel tube or Highbury & Islington tube/rail.

Islington started life as a small country village beside one of Henry VIII's expansive hunting reserves. It soon became an important livestock market supplying the Smithfield meat yards, before being enveloped into Greater London. The 19th century brought industrial development along the Regent's Canal and later industrial decay, but locals kept up their spirits at the local music halls, launchpads for such working-class heroes as Marie Lloyd, George Formby and Norman Wisdom. From the 1960s, there was a massive influx of arts and media types, who gentrified the Georgian squares and Victorian terraces and opened cafés, restaurants and boutiques around Upper Street and Essex Road. It is now a suburban bower of the *Guardian*-reading middle classes.

Close to the station on Upper Street, the popular **Camden Passage** antiques market (*see p274; photo p150*) bustles with browsing activity on Wednesdays and Saturdays. The music halls have long gone, but local residents take advantage instead of the offerings at the **Screen on the Green** (*see p300* **Everyman & Screen Cinemas**), the **Almeida** theatre (*see p346*) and **King's Head** pub-theatre (*see p348*).

East of Angel, Regency-era **Canonbury Square** was once home to George Orwell (no.27) and Evelyn Waugh (no.17A). One of the handsome townhouses now contains the **Estorick Collection of Modern Italian Art** (*see right*). Just beyond the end of Upper Street is **Highbury Fields**, where 200,000 Londoners fled in 1666 to escape the Great Fire. The surrounding district is best known

Estorick Collection of Modern Italian Art

as the home of Arsenal Football Club, who abandoned the charming Highbury Stadium in 2006 for the gleaming 60,000-seater behemoth that is the **Emirates Stadium** (*see p336*). Fans can either tour the ground or just check out the memorabilia at the **Arsenal Museum** (7619 5000, www.arsenal.com).

★ Estorick Collection of Modern Italian Art

39A Canonbury Square, N1 2AN (7704 9522, www.estorickcollection.com). Highbury & Islington tube/rail or bus 271. **Open** 11am-6pm Wed, Fri, Sat; 11am-8pm Thur; noon-5pm Sun. **Admission** £5; £3.50 reductions; free under-16s, students. **Credit** AmEx, MC, V.

Originally owned by American political scientist and writer Eric Estorick, this is a wonderful depository of early 20th-century Italian art. It is one of the world's foremost collections of futurism, Italy's brash and confrontational contribution to international modernism. The four galleries are full of movement, machines and colour, while the temporary exhibits meet the futurist commitment to fascism full on. There is also a shop and café.

DALSTON & STOKE NEWINGTON

Dalston Kingsland, Dalston Junction, Rectory Road, Stamford Hill or Stoke Newington rail.

Although scruffy, Dalston scores points for the vibrant African-flavoured market on Ridley Road, and the Turkish *ocakbaşı* (grill restaurants) along Stoke Newington Road, including excellent **Mangal II** (no.4, 7254 7888). Low property prices attracted a growing contingent of student types, who congregate at the appealingly urban **Dalston Jazz Bar** (4 Bradbury Street, 7254 9728) and the brilliant **Vortex Jazz Club** (*see p326*).

Neighbouring **Stoke Newington** is the richer cousin of Dalston and poorer cousin of Islington, home to a disproportionate number of journalists, TV news presenters and lesbians. At weekends, pretty **Clissold Park** (7923 3660) is overrun with picnickers, mums pushing prams and twentysomethings practising capoeira and slacklining.

Most visitors head to Stoke Newington for bijou **Church Street**. This curvy road is lined with second-hand bookshops, cute boutiques and kids' stores, and superior cafés and restaurants – Keralan vegetarian restaurant **Rasa** (no.55, 7249 0344) is probably the best of them. Another local highlight is **Abney Park Cemetery** (7275 7557, www.abney-park.org.uk), a wonderfully wild, overgrown Victorian boneyard that's also a nature reserve, with rare butterflies and bats.

East London

Home of the 2012 Games and a million clubs, shops and galleries.

The planners of London 2012 chose well. For years, east London has been on the cultural cutting edge. Read the style mags, and it's hard to believe how recently the East End was notorious for its slums, petty gangsters and rack-renting landlords. It was also cursed with the smelliest and most unpleasant of London's industries.

How things change. East London now has three of London's most vital areas. Alongside the City, **Spitalfields** and **Brick Lane** are tourist must-visits, with markets, boutiques, restaurants and – as they shade into **Shoreditch** – art-student trendy nightlife. **Docklands** now rivals the City as a centre for blue-chip media companies and banks and **Stratford** is the key gateway to the burgeoning Olympic Park (*see pp53-59*).

| **Map** p401 & p403 | **Hotels** pp204-205 |
| **Pubs & bars** pp245-248 | **Restaurants &** **cafés** pp228-232 |

SPITALFIELDS

Aldgate East tube/Liverpool Street tube/rail.

Approach this area from Liverpool Street Station, up Brushfield Street, and you'll know you're on the right track when the magnificent spike spire of **Christ Church Spitalfields** (*see right*) comes into sight. The area's other signature sight, **Spitalfields Market** (*see p255*), has emerged from redevelopment and the market stalls have moved back underneath the vaulted Victorian roof of the original building.

Outside, along Brushfield Street, the shops might look as if they're from Dickens's day, but most are recent inventions: the charming grocery shop **A Gold** (no.42, 7247 2487) was lovingly restored in the noughties; the owners of the **Market Coffee House** (nos.50-52, 7247 4110) put reclaimed wood panelling and creaky furniture into an empty shell; and the deli **Verde & Co** (no.40, 7247 1924) was opened by its owner, author Jeanette Winterson, inspired by the local food shops she found in – whisper it – France. It's a nice enough stroll, but for another perspective on Spitalfields head a few streets south on a Sunday to find the salt-of-the-earth **Petticoat Lane Market**, hawking knickers and cheap electronics around Middlesex Street. At the foot of Goulston Street, **Tubby Isaacs** seafood stall has sold whelks and cockles since 1919.

A block north of Spitalfields Market is **Dennis Severs' House** (*see p154*), while across from the market, on the east side of Commercial Street and in the shadow of Christ Church, the **Ten Bells** (84 Commercial Street, 7366 1721) is where one of Jack the Ripper's prostitute victims drank her last gin. On the next corner, Sandra Esqulant's **Golden Heart** pub (no.110, 7247 2158) has hosted every Young British Artist of note, ever since the day Gilbert & George decided to pop in on their new local. The streets between here and Brick Lane to the east are dourly impressive, lined with tall, shuttered Huguenot houses; **19 Princelet Street** (www.19princeletstreet. org.uk) is open to the public a few times a year. This unrestored 18th-century house was home first to French silk merchants and later Polish Jews who built a synagogue in the garden.

FREE Christ Church Spitalfields
Commercial Street, E1 6QE (7859 3035, www. christchurchspitalfields.org). Liverpool Street tube/rail or Shoreditch High Street rail. **Open** 11am-4pm Tue; 1-4pm Sun. **Admission** free. **No credit cards. Map** p401 S5.

Whitechapel Gallery.

SIGHTS

Built in 1729 by architect Nicholas Hawksmoor, this splendid church has in recent years been restored to its original state (tasteless alterations had followed a 19th-century lightning strike). Most tourists get no further than cowering before the wonderfully overbearing spire, but the revived interior is impressive, its pristine whiteness in marked contrast to its architect's dark reputation. The formidable 1735 Richard Bridge organ is almost as old as the church. Regular concerts are held here, often from the resident Gabrieli Consort & Players.

★ Dennis Severs' House

18 Folgate Street, E1 6BX (7247 4013, www. dennissevershouse.co.uk). Liverpool Street tube/ rail or Shoreditch High Street rail. **Open** noon-4pm Sun; noon-2pm Mon following 1st & 3rd Sun of mth; times vary Mon evenings. **Admission** £8 Sun; £5 noon-2pm Mon; £12 Mon evenings. **Credit** V. **Map** p401 R5.

The ten rooms of this original Huguenot house have been decked out to recreate snapshots of life in Spitalfields between 1724 and 1914. A tour through the compelling 'still-life drama', as American creator Dennis Severs dubbed it, takes you through the cellar, kitchen, dining room, smoking room and upstairs to the bedrooms. With hearth and candles burning, smells lingering and objects scattered apparently haphazardly, it feels as though the inhabitants had deserted the rooms only moments before.

BRICK LANE

Aldgate East tube.

Join the crowds flowing east from Spitalfields Market along Hanbury Street during the weekend, and the direction you turn at the end determines which Brick Lane you see. Turn right and you'll know you're in 'Banglatown', the name adopted by the ward back in 2002: until you hit the bland modern offices beside the kitsch Banglatown arch, it's almost all Bangladeshi cafés, curry houses, grocery stores, money transfer services and sari shops – plus the **Pride of Spitalfields** (3 Heneage Street, 7247 8933), an old-style East End boozer serving ale to all-comers.

Despite the street's global reputation for Indian food (there's even a Brick Lane restaurant in Manhattan), most of the food on offer is disappointing. For a few nearby exceptions to the rule, *see p231* **Inside Track**. Alternatively, opt for Bengali sweets from the **Madhubon Sweet Centre** at no.42.

Between Fournier Street and Princelet Street, **Jamme Masjid Mosque** is a key symbol of Brick Lane's hybridity. It began as a Huguenot chapel, became a synagogue and was converted, in 1976, into a mosque – in other words, immigrant communities have been layering their experiences on this street at least since 1572, when the St Bartholomew's Day Massacre forced many French Huguenots into exile.

The newest layer is gentrification. On Sunday, there's the lively street market, complemented by the trendier UpMarket – superior, clothes-wise, to Spitalfields market – and Backyard Market (for arts and crafts), both held in the **Old Truman Brewery** (nos.91-95). Pedestrianised Dray Walk is crowded every day. It's full of hip independent businesses like **Rootmaster** (www.root-master.co.uk), a vegetarian café in an old red double-decker bus. Heading north on Brick Lane, you'll find the **Vibe Bar** (7377 2899, www.vibe-bar.co.uk) and shops such as second-hand clothes store **Rokit** (nos.101 & 107, 7375 3864, 7247 3777). Further north, Cheshire Street is good for vintage fashion, too – the cavernous **Beyond Retro** (*see p264*) is the stand-out.

WHITECHAPEL

Aldgate East or Whitechapel tube.

Not one of the prettier London thoroughfares, busy but anonymous Whitechapel Road sets the tone for this area. One bright spot is **Whitechapel Art Gallery** (*see p155*), west from the foot of Brick Lane, while a little to the east, the **Whitechapel Bell Foundry** (nos.32

& 34, 7247 2599, www.whitechapelbellfoundry.
co.uk) continues to manufacture bells, as it has
since 1570. It famously produced Philadelphia's
Liberty Bell and Big Ben. To join one of the
fascinating Saturday tours you'll have to
reserve a place (usually well in advance).

At Whitechapel's foremost place of worship,
it isn't bells but a muezzin that summons
the faithful each Friday: the **East London
Mosque**, founded elsewhere in 1910 and
now the focal point for the largest Muslim
community in Britain, can accommodate 10,000
worshippers. Behind is Fieldgate Street and the
dark mass of **Tower House**, a former doss
house whose 700 rooms have, inevitably, been
redeveloped into flats. This 'sought after
converted warehouse building' was a rather
dismal – but decidedly cheaper – proposition
when Joseph Stalin and George Orwell
(researching his book *Down and Out in Paris
and London*) kipped here for pennies. The
red-brick alleys give a flavour of Victorian
Whitechapel, but this street has also been
home to the cheap seekh kebabs of **Tayyabs**
(*see p230*) for more than three decades.

East again is the Royal London Hospital and,
in a small crypt on Newark Street, the **Royal
London Hospital Archives & Museum**
(7377 7608, closed Mon, Sat and Sun). Inside
are reproduction letters from Jack the Ripper
(including the notorious missive 'From Hell',
delivered with an enclosed portion of human
kidney) and information on Joseph Merrick, the
'Elephant Man', so named for his congenital
deformities. Rescued by surgeon Sir Frederick
Treves, Merrick was given his own room in the
Royal London Hospital.

Behind the hospital is the brand new, high-
tech **Centre of the Cell** (64 Turner Street,
7882 2562, www.centreofthecell.org), which
gives visitors a lively, interactive insight into
cell biology in a purpose-built pod, suspended
over labs investigating cancer and tuberculosis.

★ FREE **Whitechapel Gallery**
*80-82 Whitechapel High Street, E1 7QX (7522
7888, www.whitechapelgallery.org). Aldgate East
tube.* **Open** 11am-6pm Tue, Wed, Fri-Sun; 11am-
9pm Thur. **Admission** free. *Temporary exhibitions*
vary. **Credit** (shop) MC, V. **Map** p403 S6.
This East End stalwart reopened in 2009, following
a major redesign that saw the Grade II-listed building expand into the similarly historic former library
next door – rather brilliantly, the architects left the
two buildings stylistically distinct rather than trying to smooth out their differences. As well as nearly
tripling its available exhibition space, the
Whitechapel gave itself a research centre and
archives room, as well as a proper restaurant (*see
p231*) and café. It looks set to improve a stellar reputation as a contemporary art pioneer built on shows

of Picasso – *Guernica* was shown here in 1939 –
Jackson Pollock, Mark Rothko and Frida Kahlo.
With no permanent collection, there's a rolling pro-
gramme of temporary shows.

SHOREDITCH & HOXTON

Old Street tube/rail.

The story is familiar: impecunious artists
moved into an area of derelict warehouses
in the 1980s, taking advantage of cheap rent,
and quickly turned the triangle formed by
Old Street, Shoreditch High Street and Great
Eastern Street into the place to be. These days,
most of the artists have moved further east, as
City workers happy to pay serious money for
street cred have driven rents through the roof.
Yet this small patch of real estate clings on
to some of its reputation as the city's most
exciting arts and clubbing centre.

Nightlife permeates the whole area, with
centres on Curtain Road, the lower end of
Kingsland Road and around Hoxton Square.
Nostalgists have to pencil in a visit to Old
Street's **333** club (7739 5949, www.333mother.
com) – no longer cutting edge, but a kind of
visually unremarkable landmark – but the final
eviction in 2010 of squatters from scuzzy club
the Foundry (84-86 Great Eastern Street) to
make way for a luxury hotel may be a sign
of things to come. Redchurch Street is a more
hopeful emblem of the new East End (*see p270*
Style Street), with its independent boutiques.

Apart from Hoxton Square galleries
(**White Cube**, *see p304*, is still here) and
Rivington Place (*see p156*), the area's sole
bona fide tourist attraction is the exquisite
Geffrye Museum (*see below*), a short walk
north up Kingsland Road. The surrounding
area is dense with good, cheap Vietnamese
restaurants (try **Sông Quê**; *see p230*).

★ FREE **Geffrye Museum**
*136 Kingsland Road, E2 8EA (7739 9893,
www.geffrye-museum.org.uk). Hoxton rail.* **Open**
10am-5pm Tue-Sat; noon-5pm Sun. *Almshouse*

SIGHTS

**INSIDE TRACK
TRENDY SPOTTING**

If you want to do some serious people-
watching, head to **Broadway Market**
(*see p159*) after midday on a Saturday.
Grab a coffee and watch the east London
hipsterati conga their way around the
gourmet food stalls and surrounding
boutiques. Shocking hair and frightfully
ambitious outfits abound.

tours 1st Sat, 1st & 3rd Wed of mth. **Admission** free; donations appreciated. *Almshouse tours* £2; free under-16s. **Credit** (shop) MC, V. **Map** p401 R3.

Housed in a set of 18th-century almshouses, the Geffrye Museum offers a vivid physical history of the English interior. Displaying original furniture, paintings, textiles and decorative arts, the museum recreates a sequence of typical middle-class living rooms from 1600 to the present. It's an oddly interesting way to take in domestic history, with any number of intriguing details to catch your eye – from a bell jar of stuffed birds to a particular decorative flourish on a chair. There's an airy restaurant overlooking the lovely gardens, which include a walled plot for herbs and a chronological series in different historical styles.

FREE Rivington Place

Rivington Place, EC2A 3BA (7729 9616, www.rivingtonplace.org). Old Street tube/rail or Shoreditch High Street rail. **Open** 11am-6pm Tue, Wed, Fri; 11am-9pm Thur; noon-6pm Sat. **Admission** free. **Credit** (shop) MC, V. **Map** p401 R4.

Designed by David Adjaye and one of Shoreditch's more exciting recent additions, this was London's first new-built public gallery since the opening of the Hayward (*see p75*) in 1968. The programme champions culturally diverse visual arts. Two project spaces provide a platform for British and international work, and there's a ground-floor café.

BETHNAL GREEN

Bethnal Green tube/rail/Cambridge Heath rail/Mile End tube.

Once a suburb of spacious townhouses, by the mid 19th century Bethnal Green was one of the city's poorest neighbourhoods. As in neighbouring Hoxton, a recent upturn in fortunes has in part been occasioned by Bethnal Green's adoption as home by a new generation of artists. The long-standing **Maureen Paley** gallery (*see p306*) remains the key venue, but the new Bethnal Green is typified by places such as **Herald Street** (*see p306*), just down the road, and the arrival of the ambitious **Town Hall Hotel** (*see p204*) and **Viajante** restaurant (*see p231*). Take a seat at **E Pellicci** (*see p230*), the exemplary traditional London caff, for a taste of the old Bethnal Green.

The **V&A Museum of Childhood** (*see right*) is close to Bethnal Green tube station, but the area's other main attraction is a bit of a walk away. Nonetheless, a visit to the weekly **Columbia Road flower market** (*see p255*) is a lovely way to fritter away a Sunday morning. A microcosmic retail community

has grown up around the market: **Treacle** (nos.110-112, 7729 0538) for groovy crockery and cup cakes; **Angela Flanders** (no.96, 7739 7555) for perfume; **Marcos & Trump** (no.146, 7739 9008) for vintage fashion.

FREE Ragged School Museum

46-50 Copperfield Road, E3 4RR (8980 6405, www.raggedschoolmuseum.org.uk). Mile End tube. **Open** 10am-5pm Wed, Thur; 2-5pm 1st Sun of mth. *Tours* by arrangement; phone for details. **Admission** free; donations appreciated. **No credit cards**.

Ragged schools were an early experiment in public education: they provided tuition, food and clothes for destitute children. This one was the largest in London, and Dr Barnardo himself taught here. It's now a sweet local museum that contains complete mock-ups of a ragged classroom and Edwardian kitchen, with displays on vanished local history. The events programme is increasingly lively.

★ FREE V&A Museum of Childhood

Cambridge Heath Road, E2 9PA (8983 5235, www.museumofchildhood.org.uk). Bethnal Green tube/rail or Cambridge Heath rail. **Open** 10am-5.45pm daily. **Admission** free; donations appreciated. **Credit** MC, V.

Home to one of the world's finest collections of children's toys, dolls' houses, games and costumes, the Museum of Childhood shines brighter than ever after extensive refurbishment, which has given it an impressive entrance. Part of the Victoria & Albert Museum (*see p145*), the museum has been amassing childhood-related objects since 1872 and continues to do so, with *Incredibles* figures complementing bonkers 1970s puppets, Barbie Dolls and Victorian praxinoscopes. The museum has lots of hands-on stuff for kids dotted about the many cases of historic artefacts. Regular exhibitions are held upstairs, while the café in the centre of the main hall helps to revive flagging grown-ups.

DOCKLANDS

London's docks were fundamental to the prosperity of the British Empire. Between 1802 and 1921, ten separate docks were built between Tower Bridge in the west and Woolwich in the east. These employed tens of thousands of people. Yet by the 1960s, the shipping industry was changing irrevocably. The new 'container' system of cargo demanded larger, deep-draught ships, as a result of which the work moved out to Tilbury, from where lorries would ship the containers into the city. By 1980, the London docks had closed.

The London Docklands Development Corporation (LDDC), founded in 1981, spent £790 million of public money on redevelopment during the following decade, only for a country-

Sounds of the Sea

London's only lighthouse marks the start of the Lee Valley.

Where the River Lee flows into the Thames, almost directly opposite the white, deflated balloon of the O2 Arena (*see p320*), **Trinity Buoy Wharf** (64 Orchard Place, E14 0JW, www.trinitybuoywharf.com) is pure incongruity. Built in the early 1800s – just as London's docks were entering their period of global dominance – it was a depot and repair yard for shipping buoys, as well as a maintenance dock for lightships. And it was here, in the 1860s, that James Douglass – designer 20 years later of the amazing fourth Eddystone Light – built London's only lighthouse.

The Experimental Lighthouse was used for training lighthouse keepers and trialling new light technology, but now it's literally a work of art. Open to the public every weekend from 11am to 4pm (5pm in summer), the lighthouse is the magnificent setting for a 'sound art' composition by Jem Finer, a founder member of Irish punk-folksters the Pogues. *Longplayer* (http://longplayer.org) is a piece of music that started playing on 1 January 2000 as part of the Dome's millennium exhibition. Performed on gongs and Tibetan singing bowls, this meditative piece is designed not to repeat itself during a continuous performance lasting exactly 1,000 years. It's a soothing soundtrack for the vast Thames, as seen through the astragal bars of the lighthouse's lantern room.

Longplayer isn't the only artistic project here: in September 2010, Marcus Vergette installed a *Time & Tide Bell*, one of a dozen he is slowly placing around the country, each of which is rung by tidal movements. The wharf is also home to a lightship, interesting historical information boards and the brightly coloured Container City, offices and studios built from recycled ship containers by Urban Space Management (also behind the Olympic Park's View Tube; *see p160*).

Take it all in over pastrami and rye in the genuine 1940s diner car Fatboy's Diner (7987 4334, www.fatboysdiner.co.uk, open 10am-5pm Tue-Sun), shipped here from the States, or cakes at the Driftwood Café (8am-3pm Mon-Fri). The wharf is ten minutes' walk from East India DLR, round a small bird reserve where terns nest in summer; otherwise, get the 277 bus for Leamouth from near Mile End tube.

SIGHTS

SIGHTS

wide property slump in the early 1990s to leave the shiny new high-rise offices and luxury flats unoccupied. Nowadays, though, as a financial hub, Docklands is a booming rival to the City of London, with an estimated 90,000 workers commuting to the area each day. For visitors, regular **Thames Clippers** (0870 781 5049, www.thamesclippers.com) boat connections with central London and the **Docklands Light Railway** (DLR) make the area easily accessible.

Just a few stops from where the DLR starts at Bank station is Shadwell, south of which is **Wapping**. In 1598, John Stowe described Wapping High Street as 'a filthy strait passage, with alleys of small tenements or cottages, inhabited by sailors' 'victuallers'. This can still just about be imagined as you walk along it now, flanked by tall Victorian warehouses. The historic **Town of Ramsgate** pub (no.62, 7481 8000), dating to 1545, helps. Here 'hanging judge' George Jeffreys was captured in 1688, trying to escape to Europe in disguise as a woman. Privateer Captain William Kidd was executed in 1701 at Execution Dock, near Wapping New Stairs; the bodies of pirates were hanged from a gibbet until seven tides had washed over them. Further east, the **Prospect of Whitby** (57 Wapping Wall, 7481 1095) dates from 1520 and has counted Samuel Pepys and Charles Dickens among its regulars. It has good riverside terraces and a fine pewter bar counter. Opposite sits a rather more modern 'victualler': **Wapping Food** (*see p231*) occupies an ivy-clad Victorian hydraulic power station.

East of here are the **Isle of Dogs** and Canary Wharf. The origin of the name 'Isle of Dogs' remains uncertain, but the first recorded use is on a map of 1588; one theory claims Henry VIII kept his hunting dogs here. In the 19th century, a huge system of docks and locks transformed what had been just drained marshland; in fact, the West India Docks cut right across the peninsula, so the Isle of Dogs did eventually become true to its name.

Almost all the interest for visitors is to be found in the vicinity of Cesar Pelli's dramatic **One Canada Square**, the country's tallest habitable building since 1991 – it is likely to lose this record to the Shard (*see p79*) by 2012. The only slightly shorter HSBC and Citigroup towers joined it in the noughties, and clones are springing up thick and fast. Shopping options are limited to the mall beneath the towers (www.mycanarywharf.com), but you'll find a soothing if slightly too crisp Japanese garden beside Canary Wharf tube station. Across a floating bridge over the dock to the north, there's the brilliant **Museum of London Docklands** (*see p159*).

It's also well worth hopping on the DLR and heading south to **Island Gardens** station at the tip of the Isle of Dogs. From narrow Island Gardens park, there's a famous Greenwich view – and the entrance to the Victorian pedestrian tunnel. Nearby to the north, at **Mudchute Park & Farm** (Pier Street, 7515 5901, www. mudchute.org; *see also p288* **Mudchute Kitchen**), a complete farmyard of animals ruminate in front of the skyscrapers.

Further east, the Lee River empties into the Thames at **Bow Creek** (*see p157* **Sounds of the Sea**), for which your best stop is East India DLR. If you followed the Lee north, you'd eventually find yourself at the Olympic Park. A couple more stops give you access to London's grandest docks – Royal Victoria, Royal Albert and King George V – as well as the **ExCeL** conference centre, a major venue for events in the London 2012 Olympic and Paralympic Games (*see p59*). Wilkinson Eyre's £30m 'sustainability centre' is due to open here in early 2012. A footbridge from ExCeL, high above Royal Victoria Dock, takes you to the beautiful **Thames Barrier Park** (www. thamesbarrierpark.org.uk). Opened in 2001, this was London's first new park in half a century. It has a lush sunken garden of waggly hedges and offers perhaps the best views from land of the Thames Barrier (*see p168*). If you don't fancy walking, enter the park from Pontoon Dock DLR.

Museum of London Docklands.

Unless you're checking in at **London City Airport** (*see p362*), keep on the DLR as far as King George V to get a free ferry (every 15mins daily, 8853 9400) that chugs pedestrians and cars across the river, or stay in your carriage as the DLR passes under the river all the way to its final stop at Woolwich Arsenal (*see p168*).

★ Museum of London Docklands

No.1 Warehouse, West India Quay, Hertsmere Road, E14 4AL (7001 9844, www.museumin docklands.org.uk). Canary Wharf tube or West India Quay DLR. **Open** 10am-6pm daily. **Admission** free. **Credit** MC, V.

Housed in a 19th-century warehouse (itself a Grade I-listed building), this huge museum explores the complex history of London's docklands and the river over two millennia. Displays spreading over three storeys take you from the arrival of the Romans all the way to the docks' 1980s closure and the area's subsequent redevelopment. The Docklands at War section is very moving, while a haunting new permanent exhibition sheds light on the dark side of London's rise as a centre for finance and commerce, exploring the city's heavy involvement in the transatlantic slave trade. You can also walk through full-scale mock-ups of a quayside and a dingy riverfront alley. Temporary exhibitions are frequently set up on the ground floor, where you'll also find a café and a docks-themed play area for kids. Just like its elder brother, the Museum of London (*see p84* **Profile**), the MoLD has a great programme of screenings and special events.

HACKNEY

London Fields or Hackney Central rail.

The opening of the Overground line in 2010 leaves even bus-averse visitors few excuses to ignore this part of London. It has few blockbuster sights, but is a good example of lived-in London. Its centre is the refurbished but struggling **Hackney Empire** (291 Mare Street, 8985 2424, www.hackneyempire.co.uk), a century-old theatre. It's located beside the art deco town hall and the fine little **Hackney Museum** (1 Reading Lane, 8356 3500, www.hackney.gov.uk/cm-museum.htm). To the east is historic **Sutton House** (*see right*).

The area of London Fields, to the west of Hackney, demonstrates the borough's ongoing gentrification. Once a lacklustre fruit and veg market, **Broadway Market** is now brimming with young urbanites and trendy young families. As well as the food and vintage garb market on Saturdays, there are wonderful shops (**Artwords**, *see p256*; **Black Truffle**, *see p266*) and a fine pub – the **Dove** (nos.24-28, 7275 7617, www.belgianbars.com), with its immense selection of Belgian beers. The old days

are respectably represented by **F Cooke** (no.9, 7254 6458), a pie and mash place that's been here since the early 1900s.

Voted London's favourite park by readers of *Time Out* magazine, **Victoria Park** is southeast of central Hackney. Opened in 1845 to give the impoverished working classes access to green space, it is a sprawling, 290-acre oasis that is both formal and funky. Designed by Sir James Pennethorne, a pupil of John Nash, its elegant landscaping (complete with rose garden and waterfowl lake) is reminiscent of Nash's masterpiece, Regent's Park (*see p120*). But the classicism is softened by a casual East End vibe, including a cool waterfront café and numerous summer musical festivals.

The paths along the Hertford Union Canal and Regent's Canal, on the southern edges of the park, briefly resemble rural Oxfordshire – all leafy branches hanging over the water and picturesque locks – before Hackney's concrete and graffiti reassert their dominance. Across the motorway at the eastern end of the park, **Hackney Wick** is a mess of post-industrial buildings, several of which have been taken over by artists, and a fine local café-restaurant: **Hackney Pearl** (*see p229*).

Sutton House

2-4 Homerton High Street, E9 6JQ (8986 2264, www.nationaltrust.org.uk). Bethnal Green tube then bus 254, 106, D6, or Hackney Central rail. **Open** 12.30-4.30pm Thur-Sun. *Café, gallery & shop* noon-4.30pm Thur-Sun. *Tours* phone for details; free tours on 1st Sun of mth. **Admission** £2.80; 70p 5-16s; £6.30 family; free under-5s, National Trust members. **Credit** MC, V.

Built in 1535 for Henry VIII's first secretary of state, Sir Ralph Sadleir, this red-brick Tudor mansion is east London's oldest home. Now beautifully restored in authentic original decor, with a real Tudor kitchen to boot, it makes no secret of its history of neglect: even some 1980s squatter graffiti has been preserved. The house closes for January each year.

LEE VALLEY

Bromley-by-Bow tube or Stratford tube/DLR/rail.

The atmospheric **Lea Valley Walk** is 50 miles of waterside path that link the Thames, at Bow Creek (*see p157* **Sounds of the Sea**), to the river's source near Luton; for more information, see www.leavalleywalk.org.uk. Get off the tube at Bromley-by-Bow and, once you're past the thundering roads and gasworks that surround it, **Three Mills Island** (*see p160*) is a delight. The Lee River (also known as the Lea at different points along its length) wriggles north-west from here, and following it provides a magical glimpse of hidden London, a mixture of bucolic greenery, bleak forgotten warehouses, moody marshland and posh new-build flats.

Most exciting of all, about 15 minutes walk north of Three Mills, you'll get superb, close-up views of the **Olympic Park** (*see p53*), with the Aquatics Centre and Olympic Stadium right in front of you. There are information boards all around the **View Tube** (*see right*).

A bit further up the river, at pretty **Old Ford Lock**, the Lea splits again into the straighter, artificial Lea Navigation and the windier river proper. If you turn left (west) off the Lea Navigation, by crossing the bridge just past the Olympic Stadium, you can get on to the towpath of the mile-long Hertford Union Canal. A pedestrian bridge, still in sight of the stadium, takes you on to **Fish Island**, an industrial park with the terrific **Counter Café** (4A Roach Road, www.thecountercafe.co.uk) and **Forman's** salmon smokery, restaurant (*see p229*) and art gallery. Keep on the towpath and you'll cut past graffiti artists, a garden centre and a colony of bohemians living on canal boats, eventually running alongside leafy Victoria Park (*see p159*) before joining up with Regent's Canal, which can take you through Hackney, Islington and Little Venice (about eight miles in total).

If you stay on the Lea Navigation north, the path heads along **Hackney Marshes**, passing the Olympic Park's Energy Centre, Handball Arena (*see p57*) and the International Broadcast Centre/Main Press Centre.

Before you reach the busy Lea Bridge Road at the Princess of Wales (146 Lea Bridge Road, 8533 3463), there's a scruffy but enchanting walled-off **nature reserve** with large blocks of granite in it: the 'Nature's Throne' sculpture by Paula Haughney. Turn east on to the Lea Bridge Road itself, towards Walthamstow (*see right*), and you'll pass the WaterWorks Nature Reserve (Lammas Road, 8988 7566, open 8am-8pm or dusk daily), a touchingly odd combination of golf course and birdwatching hides. Both reserves were part of the Middlesex Filter Beds, which were built to purify water during a cholera epidemic.

As the path meanders north, it alternates between urban grit (soap factories), natural beauty (Tottenham Marshes is dotted with wild flowers) and, far to the north, historical splendour (Waltham Abbey, a fine Norman church). A few miles north of the abbey, in the stretch towards Broxbourne, the sluices of the **Lee Valley White Water Centre** (*see p64*) are already up and running.

Three Mills Island

Three Mill Lane, E3 3DU (8980 4626, www. housemill.org.uk). Bromley-by-Bow tube. **Tours** *May-Oct* 1-4pm Sun. **Admission** £3; £1.50 reductions; free under-16s. **No credit cards.**

This pretty island in the River Lea takes its name from the three mills that, until the 18th century, ground flour and gunpowder here. The House Mill, built in 1776, is the oldest and largest tidal mill in Britain and, though out of service, it is occasionally opened to the public. The island has pleasant walks that can feel surprisingly rural. There's also a small café and, to puncture the idyll, one of the other mills is a TV studio.

View Tube

The Greenway, Marshgate Lane, E15 2PJ (www.theviewtube.co.uk). Pudding Mill Lane DLR. **Open** 9am-5pm daily. **Admission** free.
Made out of recycled shipping containers painted a vivid yellow-green, the View Tube feels like it's in touching distance of the Olympic Stadium (*see p53*), with the Aquatics Centre (*see p56*) to the right. Information boards help you figure out what's where, as well as giving loads of interesting information about the site and its development. There's good coffee at the Container Café (*see p229*).

WALTHAMSTOW

Walthamstow Central tube/rail.

Discussions about the future of **Walthamstow Stadium** greyhound track, sold to developers back in 2008, grumble on, but for visitors the spotlight is firmly on this area's other asset: quaint **Walthamstow Village**, just a few minutes' walk east of the tube station, with ancient St Mary's Church and the neat little **Vestry House Museum** (Vestry Road, 8496 4391, www.walthamforest.gov.uk; closed Mon, Tue), which contains one of the first motor cars and has a fine garden for picnics. Further north, near the junction of Hoe Street and Forest Road, is peaceful Lloyd Park; the grand Georgian house at its entrance is home to the **William Morris Gallery** (*see below*) – the Arts and Crafts pioneer was a Walthamstow boy.

FREE **William Morris Gallery**

Lloyd Park, Forest Road, E17 4PP (8496 4390, www.walthamforest.gov.uk/william-morris). Walthamstow Central tube/rail or bus 34, 97, 215, 275. **Open** 10am-5pm Wed-Sun. *Tours* phone for details. **Admission** free; donations appreciated. **Credit** (shop) MC, V.
Artist, socialist and source of flowery wallpaper, William Morris lived here between 1848 and 1856. There are plenty of designs in fabric, stained glass and ceramic on show, produced by Morris and his acolytes. The gallery – in 2010 awarded a £1.5m grant for improvements from the Heritage Lottery Fund – features the medieval-style helmet and sword the designer used as props for some of his murals, but there are also plenty of humble domestic objects: his coffee cup, for instance.

South-east London

A World Heritage Site and several unjustly overlooked attractions.

Beyond the world-famous sights of Greenwich, south-east London used to be ignored by many tourists – largely because the absence of the Underground in this part of the city made it seem remote from the centre. Then the London Overground made the journey from trendy east London to Rotherhithe, Forest Hill and Crystal Palace simple. The wonderful **Horniman Museum** (*see p163*) and the sweet little **Brunel** (*see p164*) and **Crystal Palace** (*see p163*) museums are key beneficiaries of this new transport link.

| Map p402 & p405 | Pubs & bars p248 |
| Hotels p205 | Restaurants & cafés p232 |

In any case, the area's transport difficulties are relative. The most visited neighbourhood is still, deservedly, **Greenwich** (*see p164*), an area that rivals even South Kensington for historic cultural destinations. It's easily reached on the DLR from Bank. The superb **Imperial War Museum** (*see below*) always had a nearby tube station. And, in fact, the rest of south-east London benefits from an extensive bus and rail network: if you're prepared to use it, such delights as the **Dulwich Picture Gallery** (*see p163*) are yours to enjoy.

SIGHTS

KENNINGTON & THE ELEPHANT

Kennington tube or Elephant & Castle tube/rail.

Even back in the 17th century, the **Elephant & Castle** (named, perhaps, after the ivory-dealing Cutlers Company, or maybe after Charles I's once-intended, the Infanta of Castille) was a busy place. In the early 20th century, it was a tram terminus and south London's West End, before losing its looks to World War II bombs and a grisly 1960s makeover. Regeneration of this ugly corner of town has been promised for nearly a decade without ever looking like it might happen, but then the most visible part of a £1.5bn, 170-acre redevelopment project appeared: the new Strata residential skyscraper (www.stratalondon.com) isn't much loved, but it is instantly recognisable – look for a black-and-white building shaped like a beard-trimmer, with three giant wind turbines set into the roof.

Behind the **Imperial War Museum** (*see right*), Kennington Road leads through an area once blighted by factory stink – young resident

Charlie Chaplin's abiding memory. Today, the area's smarter houses are favoured by second-home politicians and lawyers requiring easy access to the city. For many, Kennington means cricket, especially in the beery atmosphere of a Test match at the **Brit Oval** (*see p335*).

★ FREE Imperial War Museum

Lambeth Road, Elephant & Castle, SE1 6HZ (7416 5320, www.iwm.org.uk). Lambeth North tube or Elephant & Castle tube/rail. **Open** 10am-6pm daily. **Admission** free. *Special exhibitions* prices vary. **Credit** MC, V. **Map** p402 N10.
Antique guns, tanks, aircraft and artillery are parked in the main hall of this imposing edifice, built in 1814 as a lunatic asylum (the Bethlehem Royal Hospital, aka Bedlam). After the inmates were moved out in 1930, the central block became the war museum, only to be damaged by World War II air raids. Today, the museum gives the history of armed conflict, especially involving Britain and the Commonwealth, from World War I to today.

Moving on from the more gung-ho exhibits on the ground floor, there are extensive galleries devoted to the two World Wars. The museum's tone darkens as you ascend. On the third floor, the Holocaust Exhibition (not recommended for under-14s) traces the history of European anti-Semitism and its nadir in the concentration camps. Upstairs, Crimes Against Humanity (unsuitable for under-16s) is a minimalist space in which a film exploring contemporary genocide and ethnic violence rolls relentlessly.

There is also the world's largest collection of Victoria Crosses (displayed from autumn 2010) and excellent, long-running temporary exhibitions that are suitable for children: 'Outbreak 1939', looking at ordinary lives as Britain declares war, runs to 6 Sept 2011, while 'Children's War', exploring the Home Front from a child's viewpoint using letters, recordings and a reconstructed 1940s house, will be here until 29 Feb 2012.

CAMBERWELL & PECKHAM

Denmark Hill or Peckham Rye rail.

The Camberwell Beauty butterfly is unlikely to again be found in the area where it was first identified, but there is a lively art scene, centring on the **Camberwell College of Arts** and the **South London Gallery** (*see p165* **Artistic Revival**).

East of here, **Peckham** is still unfairly associated with teenage gangs and dodgy traders, but regeneration schemes continue to spruce up the streets. Rye Lane looks like old Peckham; Will Alsop's award-winning and frankly odd-looking **Peckham Library**, in an area now known as **Peckham Square**, represents the new. Due south on Rye Lane is **Peckham Rye**, where poet-visionary William Blake saw his angels; it's now a prettily laid-out park with well-kept gardens – the 1908 Japanese Garden, restored in 2005, is lovely. Keep walking south from Peckham Rye (or take a P4 or P12 bus) to enjoy views over London and Kent from **Honor Oak** and **One Tree Hill**, where Elizabeth I picnicked with Richard Bukeley of Beaumaris in 1602.

DULWICH & CRYSTAL PALACE

Crystal Palace, East Dulwich, Herne Hill, North Dulwich or West Dulwich rail.

Dulwich is a little piece of rural England that fiercely guards its bucolic prosperity. Tasteful fingerposts offer directions: perhaps towards the attractive park (once a duelling spot), the historic boys' public school or the **Dulwich Picture Gallery** (*see right*). It's a pleasant, brisk half-hour's walk from the gallery across the Dulwich Park and up Lordship Lane to the **Horniman Museum** (*see right*) in Forest Hill.

East and west of Dulwich sit **East Dulwich** and **Herne Hill**, the latter home to an exquisite

Horniman Museum.

art deco lido in Brockwell Park. The two areas represent the middle(-class) way: not as expensive or charismatic as Dulwich, but less challenging than the relentless pace of Brixton.

Crystal Palace is named in honour of Joseph Paxton's famous structure, built for the Great Exhibition in Hyde Park in 1851, moved here three years later and destroyed by fire in 1936. **Crystal Palace Park** contains arches and the sphinx from the Exhibition's Egyptian-themed display; the Dinosaur Park, a lake ringed by Benjamin Waterhouse-Hawkins's life-sized (and decidedly inaccurate) dinosaur statues; and the **National Sports Centre** (see *p335*). The **Crystal Palace Museum** (Anerley Hill, SE19 2BA, 8676 0700, www.crystalpalace museum.org.uk), opened by volunteers each weekend, has an 'exhibition of the Exhibition'.

★ Dulwich Picture Gallery
Gallery Road, Dulwich, SE21 7AD (8693 5254, www.dulwichpicturegallery.org.uk). North Dulwich or West Dulwich rail. **Open** 10am-5pm Tue-Fri; 11am-5pm Sat, Sun. **Admission** £5; free-£4 reductions. **Credit** MC, V.

Lending weight to the idea that the best things come in small packages, this bijou gallery was designed by Sir John Soane in 1811 as the first purpose-built gallery in the UK. It's a beautiful space that shows off Soane's ingenuity with lighting effects, especially in the quiet mausoleum at the heart of the building where the gallery's founders rest. The gallery displays a small but outstanding collection of work by Old Masters, offering a fine introduction to the Baroque era through works by Rembrandt, Rubens, Poussin and Gainsborough. It also has some brilliant temporary exhibitions. For the beginning of the 2011 bicentenary, Peter Randall-Page's *Walking the Dog* sculpture of brain-like, striated boulders was installed, and a new entrance and shop unveiled.
▶ *For Sir John Soane's Museum, an equally curious and compelling attraction, see p99.*

★ FREE Horniman Museum
100 London Road, Forest Hill, SE23 3PQ (8699 1872, www.horniman.ac.uk). Forest Hill rail or bus 363, 122, 176, 185, P4, P13. **Open** 10.30am-5.30pm daily. **Admission** free; donations appreciated. *Temporary exhibitions prices vary.* **Credit** MC, V.

South-east London's premier free family attraction, the Horniman was once the home of tea trader Frederick J Horniman, it's an eccentric-looking art nouveau building (check out the clocktower, which starts as a circle and ends as a square), with a main entrance that gives out on to extensive gardens.

The oldest section is the Natural History gallery, dominated by an ancient walrus (mistakenly over-stuffed by Victorian taxidermists) and now ringed by glass cabinets containing pickled animals, stuffed birds and insect models. Other galleries include the

Nature Base, African Worlds and the Centenary Gallery, which focuses on world cultures. Downstairs, the Music Gallery contains hundreds of instruments: their sounds can be unleashed via touch-screen tables, while hardier instruments (flip-flop drums, thumb pianos) can be bashed with impunity.

The most popular part of the museum is its showpiece Aquarium, where a series of tanks and rock-pools cover seven distinct aquatic ecosystems. There are mesmerising moon jellyfish, strangely large British seahorses, starfish, tropical fish and creatures from the mangroves. It forms a key part of the Evolution 2010 project, which is bringing together the natural history collection, aquarium and gardens to explore biodiversity and the story of how life has evolved on earth.

ROTHERHITHE
Rotherhithe tube.

Once a shipbuilding village and, in the 17th and 18th centuries, a centre for London's whaling trade, the ghostly locale of Rotherhithe has long since seen its docks filled in. Go back in time at the **Brunel Museum** (see *p164*) or the mariners' church of **St Mary's Rotherhithe** (St Mary Church Street, SE16 4JE, www.stmary rotherhithe.org), which contains maritime oddities; among them is a communion table and bishop's chair made from timber salvaged from the HMS *Temeraire*, immortalised by Turner (the painting is in the National Gallery; see *p129*). Captain Christopher Jones was buried here in 1622; his ship, the *Mayflower*, set sail from Rotherhithe in 1620. A waterside pub of the same name marks the spot from which the pilgrims are said to have embarked on their journey.

Rotherhithe's road tunnel takes cars across to Limehouse. At the mouth of the tunnel stands the **Norwegian Church & Seaman's Mission**, one of a number of Scandinavian churches in the area. There's also a Finnish church – with a sauna – at 33 Albion Street (7237 1261). Across Jamaica Road, **Southwark Park** has a gallery (7237 1230, www.cafegalleryprojects.com), an old bandstand, a lake and playgrounds.

SIGHTS

Brunel Museum

Brunel Engine House, Railway Avenue, SE16 4LF (7231 3840, www.brunel-museum.org.uk). Rotherhithe rail. **Open** 10am-5pm daily. *Tours* by appointment only. **Admission** £2; £1 reductions; £5 family; free under-5s. **No credit cards.**

This little museum occupies the engine house where the father-and-son team of Sir Marc and Isambard Kingdom Brunel worked to create the world's first tunnel beneath a navigable river. The story of their achievement is told most entertainingly during guided tours; see the website for details. There's a decent little shop, a café and outdoor space should you wish to picnic.

▶ *If you visit the museum using the Overground line from north of the river, you'll actually travel under the Thames through the master engineers' tunnel, still in perfect working order.*

GREENWICH

Cutty Sark for Maritime Greenwich DLR.

Riverside Greenwich is an irresistible mixture of maritime, royal and horological history, a combination that's earned it recognition as a UNESCO World Heritage Site. The permanent attractions are gathered around **Greenwich Park**, a handsome space with great views, which will provide a grand setting for the London 2012 Equestrian events (*see p60*).

Royalty has stalked the area since 1300, when Edward I stayed here. Henry VIII was born in Greenwich Palace; the palace was built on land that later contained Wren's Royal Naval Hospital, now the **Old Royal Naval College** (*see p166*). The College is now a very handy

first port-of-call. Its Pepys Building not only contains the **Greenwich Tourist Information Centre** (0870 608 2000, www.greenwich.gov.uk), but is also the home of a new exhibition that provides a great overview of Greenwich's numerous attractions. A short walk away, shoppers swarm to **Greenwich Market**, still involved in battles over a controversial redevelopment.

If you keep the river to your left, you reach the Thames-lapped **Trafalgar Tavern** (6 Park Row, 8858 2909), haunt of Thackeray and Dickens, and the **Cutty Sark Tavern** (4-6 Ballast Quay, 8858 3146), which dates to 1695. Near the DLR stop is Greenwich Pier; every 15 minutes (peak times), the popular and speedy **Thames Clipper** boats (0870 781 5049, www.thamesclippers.com) shuttle passengers to and from central London.

The pier from which the Thames Clipper service departs is beside the tarp-covered **Cutty Sark**, built in 1869 and the fastest ever sailing tea clipper in its heyday. In 2007, a conservation project was halted when the boat was devastated by fire, apparently caused by a vacuum cleaner overheating. The restored vessel will be shipshape, 90 per cent original and, for the first time, raised ten feet above curious visitors by the end of 2011; before then, www.cuttysark.org.uk has details of progress. The domed structure by the river is the entrance to a Victorian **pedestrian tunnel** that emerges on the far side of the Thames in Island Gardens (*see p158*).

From the riverside, it's a ten-minute walk (or shorter shuttle-bus trip) up the steep slopes of Greenwich Park to the **Royal Observatory** (*see p167*). The building looks even more

Greenwich Park.

SIGHTS

Artistic Revival

Forget about the East End – Camberwell is a real artistic heartland.

At first glance, Camberwell's blend of run-down Georgian buildings, ugly tower blocks and traffic-choked roads appears less than artful. However, its built-up environs have been fertile ground for a flourishing cultural scene that dates back to Victorian times but found new life in the 21st century.

In 1891, William Rossiter opened the pioneering South London Fine Art Gallery. A century later, renamed the **South London Gallery** (for listings, *see p306*), it found new renown as the first exhibitor of *Everyone I Have Ever Slept With 1963-1995*, Tracey Emin's infamous tent. A beacon for Brit Art during the 1990s, the gallery remains one of London's leading contemporary art venues. Its new £1.8m extension, which swallowed up the three-storey Victorian townhouse next door in order to add a new café, two extra exhibition spaces and a resident artist's flat, should keep it on the cutting edge.

Next door sits the **Camberwell College of Arts** (45-65 Peckham Road, 7514 6302, www.camberwell.arts.ac.uk), where the likes of Pink Floyd's Syd Barrett and film director Mike Leigh once studied. Like the South London Gallery, it's been expanding. In 2010, Peckham Square welcomed the college's **Peckham Space** (7514 2299, www.peckhamspace.com), a new

contemporary art venue that has added to the good programme of free public exhibitions and events staged at the college's Camberwell Space. Outside the college, its students continue to colonise Camberwell bars such as the **Sun & Doves** (61-63 Coldharbour Lane, 7733 1525, www.sunanddoves.co.uk) and the **Bear** (296A Camberwell New Road, 7274 7037, www.thebear-freehouse.co.uk).

The modern-day scene isn't limited to the visual arts: the railway arches are vital spaces for clubbing and other diversions. Under Loughborough Junction station, **Arch 468** (Unit 4, 209A Coldharbour Lane, 07973 302908, www.arch468.com) stages work by emerging playwrights and theatre companies, with regular free rehearsed readings of new pieces. The more established **Blue Elephant** theatre (*see p296*) continues to present a vibrant programme of new writing, classic plays, physical theatre and dance. And talent of all kinds goes into the melting pot each June for the **Camberwell Arts Festival** (www.camberwellarts.org.uk). Previous years have seen Queer Tango sessions and tea dances, while a 'stumble-on-and-hit-upon' orchestra got to play instruments built out of junk. In Camberwell, it seems, getting creative is unavoidable.

stunning at night, when the bright green Meridian Line Laser illuminates the path of the Prime Meridian across the London sky.

The riverside Thames Path leads past rusting piers and boarded-up factories to the **Greenwich Peninsula**, dominated by the **O2 Arena**. Designed by the Richard Rogers Partnership as the Millennium Dome, this once-maligned structure's fortunes have improved considerably since its change of use. Alongside the concerts and sporting events in the huge arena (*see p320*) and movies in the cineplex, attractions include restaurants, big exhibitions and the glossy, permanent **British Music Experience** (*see below*). The Dome is also a key London 2012 venue (*see p60* **North Greenwich Arena**), with planning permission being sought for a cable car that would connect the east flank of the peninsula with Royal Victoria Dock on the north bank of the Thames, for easy access to ExCeL (*see p59*).

It's all something of a contrast with the **Greenwich Peninsula Ecology Park**

(*see p290*), and with the nearby riverside walks that afford broad, flat, bracing views and works of art; you could hardly miss *Slice of Reality*, a rusting ship cut in half by Richard Wilson, and Antony Gormley's 100ft-tall *Quantum Cloud*.

To the south is grassy, upmarket **Blackheath**. Smart Georgian homes and a few stately pubs surround a heath on which some of the world's earliest sports clubs started; among them is the Royal Blackheath Golf Club, said to be the oldest golf club in the world. The heath hosted the week-long Climate Camp of 3,000 anti-capitalist and environmental protesters in August 2009, a conscious echo of Blackheath's long history of radical protest that runs back to the Peasants' Revolt in 1381.

British Music Experience

O2 Bubble, Millennium Way, SE10 0BB (8463 2000, www.britishmusicexperience.com). North Greenwich tube. **Open** 10am-7.30pm daily. **Admission** £15; £12 reductions; £40 family; free under-5s. **Credit** AmEx, MC, V.

Royal Obsevatory & Planetarium.

SIGHTS

The memorabilia on show on the top floor of the O2 Arena (*see p320*) includes David Bowie's Ziggy Stardust costume and Noel Gallagher's Union Jack guitar. The main focus, though, is on interactive exhibits: downloading archive music, trying your hand at guitar tutorials and so on. Workshops, lectures and concerts are also part of the experience.

★ FREE Discover Greenwich & the Old Royal Naval College

2 Cutty Sark Gardens, SE10 9LW (8269 4799, www.oldroyalnavalcollege.org.uk). Cutty Sark DLR or Greenwich DLR/rail. **Open** 10am-5pm daily. *Tours* by arrangement. **Admission** free. **Credit** (shop) MC, V. **Map** p405 X1.

In March 2010, the Pepys Building (the block of the Naval College nearest to the *Cutty Sark*, the pier and Cutty Sark DLR) reopened as the excellent Discover Greenwich. It's full of focused, informative exhibits on architecture and building techniques of the surrounding buildings, the life of Greenwich pensioners, Tudor royalty and so forth, delivered with a real sense of fun: while grown-ups read about coade stone or scagliola (popular fake stone building materials), for example, the nippers can build their own chapel with soft bricks or try on a knight's helmet. There's also a well-stocked shop and Tourist Information Centre (*see p374*).

Designed by Wren in 1694, with Hawksmoor and Vanbrugh helping to complete the project, the Old Royal Naval College is a superb collection of buildings. It was originally a hospital for the relief and support of seamen and their dependants, with pensioners living here from 1705 to 1869, when the complex became the Royal Naval College. The Navy left in 1998, and the neoclassical buildings now house part of the University of Greenwich and Trinity College of Music. The public are allowed into the impressive rococo chapel, where there are free organ recitals, and Painted Hall, a tribute to William and Mary that took Sir James Thornhill 19 years to complete. Nelson lay in state in the Painted Hall for three days in 1806, before being taken to St Paul's Cathedral for his funeral.

There's a lively events programme in the grounds, ranging from comedy shows (*see p293* **Our Own Edinburgh?**) and early music (*see p316* **Festivals**) to weekend appearances from historic figures – costumed actors – ranging from Pepys and Sir James to the 'pirate queen' Grace O'Malley and Joe Brown, veteran of the Battle of Trafalgar.

▶ *Attached to Discover Greenwich, the Old Brewery is an ace bar-restaurant; see p232.*

Fan Museum

12 Crooms Hill, SE10 8ER (8305 1441, www.fan-museum.org). Cutty Sark DLR or Greenwich DLR/rail. **Open** 11am-5pm Tue-Sat; noon-5pm Sun. **Admission** £4; free-£3 reductions; £10 family; free under-7s. **Credit** MC, V. **Map** p405 X2.

The world's most important collection of hand-held fans is displayed in a pair of restored Georgian townhouses. There are about 3,500 fans, including some beauties in the Hélène Alexander collection, but not all are on display at any one time. For details of the regular fan-making workshops and temporary exhibitions, check the website.

★ FREE National Maritime Museum

Romney Road, SE10 9NF (8858 4422, 8312 6565 information, www.nmm.ac.uk). Cutty Sark DLR or Greenwich DLR/rail. **Open** 10am-5pm daily. *Tours* phone for details. **Admission** free; donations appreciated. **Credit** (shop) MC, V. **Map** p405 X2.

The world's largest maritime museum contains a huge store of creatively organised maritime art, cartography, models and regalia. Ground-level galleries include Explorers, which covers great sea expeditions back to medieval times, and Maritime London, which concentrates on the city as a port and currently contains Nelson's uniform, complete with fatal bullet-hole; it will move to the new Sammy Ofer Wing on completion in 2013. Upstairs are Your Ocean, which reveals our dependence on the health of the world's oceans. Level two holds the interactives: the Bridge has a ship simulator, and All Hands lets children load cargo, and you can even try your hand as a ship's gunner. The Ship of War is the museum's collection of models; Oceans of Discovery commemorates the history of world exploration; and the Atlantic World gallery looks at the relationship between Britain, Africa and the Americas.

▶ *From the museum a colonnaded walkway leads to the Queen's House. Up the hill in the park, the Observatory and Planetarium are also part of the museum. For all three, see below.*

FREE Queen's House

Romney Road, SE10 9NF (8312 6565, www. nmm.ac.uk). Cutty Sark DLR or Greenwich DLR/ rail. **Open** 10am-5pm daily. *Tours* noon, 2.30pm daily. **Admission** free; occasional charge for temporary exhibitions. *Tours* free. **Credit** (over £5) MC, V. **Map** p405 X2.

The art collection of the National Maritime Museum (*see left*) is displayed in what was formerly the summer villa of Charles I's queen, Henrietta Maria. Completed in 1638 by Inigo Jones, the house has an interior as impressive as the paintings on the walls. As well as the stunning 1635 marble floor, look for Britain's first centrally unsupported spiral stair, and the fine painted woodwork and ceilings. The collection includes portraits of famous maritime figures and works by Hogarth and Gainsborough, as well as some wartime art from the 20th century and a room of amazing pictures of exotic tropical islands painted during Captain Cook's explorations.

▶ *Other buildings by Inigo Jones include Banqueting House (see p132) and St Paul's Covent Garden (see p109).*

Ranger's House

Chesterfield Walk, SE10 8QX (8853 0035, www.english-heritage.org.uk). Blackheath rail, Cutty Sark DLR or bus 53. **Open** Apr-Sept 11am-5pm Sun. *Tours* 11.30am, 2.30pm Mon-Wed. *Oct-Dec* group bookings only. **Admission** £6; £2.80-£5.10 reductions; free under-5s. **Credit** MC, V. **Map** p405 Y4.

The house of the 'Ranger of Greenwich Park' (a post that was held by George III's niece, Princess Sophia Matilda, from 1815) now contains the collection of treasure – medieval and Renaissance art, jewellery, bronzes, tapestries, furniture, porcelain, paintings – amassed by Julius Wernher, a German who made his considerable fortune trading in South African diamonds. His booty is displayed through a dozen lovely rooms in this red-brick Georgian villa, the back garden of which is the fragrant Greenwich Park rose collection.

★ FREE Royal Observatory & Planetarium

Greenwich Park, SE10 9NF (8312 6565, www. rog.nmm.ac.uk). Cutty Sark DLR or Greenwich DLR/rail. **Open** 10am-5pm daily. *Tours* phone for details. **Admission** *Observatory* free. *Planetarium* £6.50; £4.50 reductions; £17.50 family. **Credit** MC, V. **Map** p405 Y3.

SIGHTS

Firepower. *See p168.*

The northern section of this two-halved attraction chronicles Greenwich's horological connection. Flamsteed House, the observatory that was built in 1675 on the orders of Charles II, contains the apartments of Sir John Flamsteed and other Astronomers Royal, as well as the instruments that have been used in timekeeping since the 14th century. An onion dome houses the country's largest (28-inch) refracting telescope – it was completed in 1893.

The south site houses the Astronomy Centre, home to the Peter Harrison Planetarium and Weller Astronomy Galleries. The 120-seater planetarium's architecture cleverly reflects its astrological position: the semi-submerged cone tilts at 51.5 degrees, the latitude of Greenwich, pointing to the north star, and its reflective disc is aligned with the celestial equator. Daily and weekend shows include 'Black Holes: The Other Side of Infinity' and 'Starlife', a show describing the birth and death of stars.

▶ *In the courtyard of Flamsteed House is the Prime Meridian Line, star of a billion snaps of happy tourists with a foot in each hemisphere.*

WOOLWICH ARSENAL & THE THAMES BARRIER

Woolwich Arsenal DLR/rail or Woolwich Dockyard rail.

Established by the Tudors as the country's main source of munitions, **Woolwich Arsenal** stretched 32 miles along the river by World War I, with its own internal railway system. Much of the land was sold off during the 1960s, but the main section has been preserved and is now home to **Firepower** (*see right*). To the south, **The Royal Artillery Barracks** has the longest Georgian façade in the country. It will host the Shooting for the London 2012 Games (*see p60*). The river is spanned by an architectural triumph that is the Barracks' modern equal: the **Thames Barrier** (*see right*).

INSIDE TRACK BUILDING THE BARRIER

According to a 2005 systems study by Charles Wallace (www.tinyurl.com/thames barrier) keeping the shiny pods of the **Thames Barrier** (*see right*) waterproof required unusually specialised skills: 'When it came to the sheeting of the roofs to the piers... on one side a right-handed plumber could do the job normally, but the other side could only be done by a left-handed plumber, or a right-handed plumber working upside down. Fortunately it appears that enough left-handed plumbers were recruited.'

This is a grim bit of London, but regeneration has begun to arrive in the form of an extension of the DLR from King George V station under the river to Woolwich Arsenal. More charismatic, though, is the ramshackle **Woolwich Ferry** (8853 9400), diesel-driven boats that take pedestrians (for free) and cars across the river every ten minutes daily. A final river-crossing method in this bridge-free part of town is the **Woolwich Foot Tunnel**, whose sinister and shabby appearance should be corrected by refurbishment in March 2011.

Firepower

Royal Arsenal, Woolwich, SE18 6ST (8855 7755, www.firepower.org.uk). Woolwich Arsenal DLR/rail. **Open** 10.30am-5pm Wed-Sun. **Admission** £5; £2.50-£4.50 reductions; free under-5s; £12 family. **Credit** MC, V.

Occupying a series of converted arsenal buildings beside the river, Firepower bristles with preserved artillery pieces, some of them centuries old. An introductory presentation in the Breech Cinema tells the story of the Royal Artillery and leads on to 'Field of Fire', where four screens relay archive film and documentary footage of desert and jungle warfare. Smoke fills the air, searchlights pick out the ordnance that surrounds you and exploding bombs shake the floor. Across the courtyard, another building contains a huge collection of trophy guns and the Cold War gallery, focused on the 'monster bits' (tanks and guns used from 1945 to the present). Army-obsessed kids can get shouted at by real soldiers when they take part in drill call; the website has details of this and other attractions. The on-site café is becomes a bistro in the evening. *Photo p167.*

Thames Barrier Information & Learning Centre

1 Unity Way, Woolwich, SE18 5NJ (8305 4188, www.environment-agency.gov.uk/thamesbarrier). Charlton rail, or North Greenwich tube then bus 472. **Open** Apr-Sept 10.30am-4.30pm daily. Oct-Mar 11am-3.30pm daily. **Admission** £3.50; £2-£3 reductions; free under-5s. **Credit** MC, V.

This adjustable dam has been variously called a triumph of modern engineering and the eighth wonder of the world. The shiny silver fins, lined up across Woolwich Reach, are indeed an impressive sight. Built in 1982 at a cost of £535m, they've already saved London from flooding some 80 times. The barrier is regularly in action for maintenance purposes; check the website for a current timetable.

To learn more, pay £3.50 for a look around the recently refurbished learning centre, where you'll find an account of the 1953 flood that led to the barrier's construction, as well as displays on wildlife in the Thames and how a flood would affect London. There's a pleasant café with picnic benches.

▶ *Some of the best Barrier views are from north of the river in Thames Barrier Park; see p158.*

South-west London

Deprivation, gentrification and the poshest of the posh.

Towards the Surrey border, south-west London starts to feel like a collection of villages rather than a single sprawling metropolis. In **Richmond**, **Barnes** and **Wimbledon**, pretty Georgian houses overlook quaint greens and expansive commons where the blessed clichés of Englishness – tea-drinking, cricket – still hold sway. The rich and royal took advantage of the area's leafy proximity to the central city a long time ago, with visitors able to enjoy their legacy in the form of world-class tourist attractions: **Kew Gardens** (*see p172*), **Hampton Court Palace** (*see p173*) and **Richmond Park** (*see p172*).

| Hotels p206 | Restaurants & |
| Pubs & bars p348 | cafés pp232-233 |

Industrialisation and urban creep soon took over the fields. **Stockwell** and **Brixton** are now just like their south-east London neighbours: diverse, busy and vibrant, despite creeping gentrification.

Between them and the posh suburbs, **Wandsworth** and **Clapham** are a vision of the likely gentrified future: herds of young professionals picnic on the fine commons at weekends, fill the bars and restaurants, and fall asleep on Egyptian cotton sheets dreaming of an apartment beside the river in **Battersea**.

SIGHTS

VAUXHALL, STOCKWELL & BRIXTON

Stockwell tube, or Brixton or Vauxhall tube/rail.

The area now known as Vauxhall was, in the 13th century, home to a big house owned by one Falkes de Bréauté, a soldier rewarded for carrying out King John's dirtier military deeds. Over time, Falkes' Hall became Fox Hall and finally Vauxhall. Vauxhall's heyday was in the 18th century when the infamous Pleasure Gardens, built back in 1661, reached the height of their popularity. As described in William Thackeray's *Vanity Fair*, the wealthy mingled here with the not-so-wealthy, getting into all kinds of trouble on 'lovers' walks'.

The Gardens closed in 1859 and the area became reasonably respectable – all that remains is Spring Garden, behind popular gay haunt the Royal Vauxhall Tavern (aka **RVT**; *see p310*). For a glimpse of old Vauxhall head to lovely, leafy **Bonnington Square**. Down on the river is the cream and emerald ziggurat

designed by Terry Farrell for the Secret Intelligence Service. On the other side of the approach to Vauxhall Bridge, glitzy apartment complex **St George's Wharf** has justifiably been nicknamed the 'five ugly sisters'.

At the top end of the South Lambeth Road, **Little Portugal** – a cluster of Portuguese cafés, shops and tapas bars – is an enticing oasis. At the other end, **Stockwell** is prime commuter territory, with little to lure visitors except some charming Victorian streets: Albert Square, Durand Gardens, Stockwell Park Crescent and Hackford Road – no.87 was briefly home to Van Gogh.

South of Stockwell is **Brixton**, a lively hub of clubs and music. The town centre has been enjoying significant redevelopment, with Windrush Square completed at the end of Coldharbour Lane in 2010 (*see also p170* **Inside Track**). The square's name is significant: HMS *Windrush* was the boat that brought West Indian immigrants from Jamaica in 1948. They were hardly welcomed, but managed to make Brixton a thriving community. As late as the 1980s, tensions were still strong, as the Clash song 'Guns of Brixton' famously illustrates. The rage of the persecuted black community, still finding themselves isolated and under suspicion decades after arriving, is better expressed by dub poet Linton Kwesi Johnson – try 'Sonny's Lettah (Anti-Sus Poem)' for starters. The riots of 1981 and 1985 around Railton Road and Coldharbour Lane left the district scarred for years.

Now, most visitors come to Brixton for its big, chaotic street **market**. The two covered arcades date to the 1920s and '30s and come – with Market Row – Grade II-listed in 2010. The district's main roads are modern and filled with chain stores, but there's also some attractive architecture – check out the **Ritzy Cinema** (Brixton Oval, Coldharbour Lane, 0871 704 2065, www.picturehouses.co.uk), dating to 1911. Brixton's best-known street, **Electric Avenue**, got its name when, in 1880, it became one of the first shopping streets to get electric lights.

Minutes from Brixton's hectic centre, **Brockwell Park** (Brixton Water Lane, www.brockwellpark.com) is one of London's most underrated green spaces. Landscaped in the early 19th century for a wealthy glass maker, the park contains his Georgian country house – now a café – an open-air swimming pool, bowling green, walled rose garden and miniature railway. Each July, there's an enjoyable traditional country fair.

BATTERSEA

Battersea Park or Clapham Junction rail.

Battersea started life as an island in the Thames, but it was reclaimed when the surrounding marshes were drained. Huguenots settled here from the 16th century and, prior to the Industrial Revolution, the area was mostly farmland. The river is dominated by Sir Giles Gilbert Scott's magnificent four-chimneyed **Battersea Power Station** (www.battersea powerstation.org.uk), which can be seen close up from all trains leaving Victoria station. Images of this iconic building have graced album covers (notably Pink Floyd's *Animals*) and films (among them Ian McKellen's *Richard III* and Michael Radford's *1984*), and its instantly recognisable silhouette pops up repeatedly as you move around the capital. Work started on what was to become the largest brick-built structure in Europe in 1929, and the power station was in operation through to the early 1980s. Too impressive to be destroyed, its future continues to be the subject of intense public debate – in the meanwhile, it's carved out a niche as a venue for circus spectaculars and extreme sports festivals.

Overlooking the river a little further west, **Battersea Park** (www.batterseapark.org) has beautiful lakes (one with a fine Barbara Hepworth sculpture) and gardens. Much of the park was relandscaped in 2004 according to the original 19th-century plans, albeit with some modern additions left in place: the Russell Page Garden, designed for the 1951 Festival of Britain; a Peace Pagoda, built by a Buddhist sect in 1985 to commemorate Hiroshima Day; a petting zoo (7924 5826; *see p289*); and an art gallery (the Pumphouse, 7350 0523, www.wandsworth.gov.uk/gallery). The park extends to the Thames; from the wide and lovely riverside walk you can see both the elaborate **Albert Bridge** and the simpler **Battersea Bridge**, rebuilt between 1886 and 1890 by sewer engineer Joseph Bazalgette.

West of the bridges, you'll find the beautiful church of **St Mary's Battersea** (Battersea Church Road); this was where poet William Blake was married and Benedict Arnold, who contrived to fight on both sides during the American War of Independence, is buried. From here, JMW Turner used to paint the river.

CLAPHAM & WANDSWORTH

Clapham Common tube, or Wandsworth Common or Wandsworth Town rail.

In the 18th and 19th centuries, **Clapham** was colonised by the wealthy upper classes and social reformers, notably abolitionist William Wilberforce's Clapham Sect. But the coming of the railways meant that the posh folk upped sticks, and from 1900 the area fell into decline. Nowadays, it is once again one of the capital's more desirable addresses. **Clapham Common** provides an oasis of peace amid busy traffic, with Holy Trinity Church, which dates from 1776, at its perimeter. From Clapham Common station, turn north into the **Pavement** – it leads to the pubs and shops of Clapham Old Town. Alternatively, head south to the smart shops and cafés of **Abbeville Road**. The area to the west of the common is known as 'Nappy Valley', because of the many young middle-class families who reside there. If you can fight your way between baby carriages, head for **Northcote Road** – especially on weekends, when a lovely little market sets up.

PUTNEY & BARNES

East Putney or Putney Bridge tube, or Barnes or Putney rail.

If you want proof of an area's well-to-do credentials, count the rowing clubs: **Putney** has a couple of dozen. **Putney Bridge** is partly responsible, as its buttresses made it difficult for large boats to continue upstream, creating a stretch of water conducive to rowing. The **Oxford & Cambridge Boat Race** (*see p280*) has started in Putney since 1845. The river has good paths in either direction; heading west along the Putney side of the river will take you past the **WWT Wetland Centre** (*see below*), which lies alongside Barnes Common. The main road across the expanse, Queen's Ride, humpbacks over the railway line below. It was here, on 16 September 1977, that singer Gloria Jones's Mini drove off the road, killing her passenger (and boyfriend) T-Rex singer Marc Bolan. The slim trunk of the sycamore hit by the car is covered with notes, poems and declarations of love; steps lead to a bronze bust.

★ WWT Wetland Centre
Queen Elizabeth's Walk, Barnes, SW13 9WT (8409 4400, www.wwt.org.uk). Hammersmith tube then bus 283, Barnes rail or bus 33, 72, 209. **Open** *Mar-Oct* 9.30am-6pm daily. *Nov-Feb* 9.30am-5pm daily. **Admission** £9.95; £5.50-£7.40 reductions; £27.75 family; free under-4s. **Credit** MC, V.

Reclaimed from industrial reservoirs a decade ago, the 43-acre Wildfowl & Wetlands Trust Wetland Centre is four miles from central London, but feels a world away. Quiet ponds, rushes, rustling reeds and wildflower gardens all teem with bird life – some 150 species – as well as the now very rare water vole. Naturalists ponder its 27,000 trees and 300,000 aquatic plants and swoon over 300 varieties of butterfly, 20 types of dragonfly and four species of bat (now sleeping in a stylish new house designed by Turner Prize-winning artist Jeremy Deller). You can explore water-recycling initiatives in the new RBC Rain Garden or check out the new interactive section: pilot a submerged camera around a pond, learn about the life-cycle of a dragonfly or make waves in a digital pool. Traditionalists needn't be scared – plain old pairs of binoculars can be hired.

KEW & RICHMOND

Kew Gardens or Richmond tube/rail, or Kew Bridge rail.

Much of Kew has a rarified air, with leafy streets that lead you into a quaint world of teashops, tiny bookstores and gift shops, a sweet village green, ancient pubs and pleasant riverpaths. Kew's big appeal is its vast and glorious **Royal Botanic Gardens** (*see p172*), but the **National Archives** – formerly the Public Records Office – are housed here too, a repository for everything from the Domesday Book to recently released government

Brixton Market.

SIGHTS

documents. The place is always full of people researching their family trees. Overlooking the gardens, **Watermans Arts Centre** (40 High Street, 8232 1010, www.watermans.org.uk) contains a gallery, cinema and theatre focusing on Brit-Asian and South Asian arts.

Originally known as the Shene, the wealthy area of **Richmond**, about 15 minutes' walk west down Kew Road, has been linked with royalty for centuries: Edward III had a palace here in the 1300s and Henry VII loved the area so much that in 1501 he built another (naming it Richmond after his favourite earldom); this was where Elizabeth I spent her last summers. Ultimately, the whole neighbourhood took the palace's name, although the building itself is long gone – pretty much all that's left is a small gateway on **Richmond Green**. On the east side of the green, medieval alleys (such as Brewer's Lane) replete with ancient pubs lead to the traffic-choked high street. The **Church of St Mary Magdalene**, on Paradise Road, blends architectural styles from 1507 to 1904.

A short walk away in Richmond's Old Town Hall, you'll find the small **Museum of Richmond** (Whittaker Avenue, 8332 1141, www.museumofrichmond.com, closed Mon & Sun). Nearby, the riverside promenade is eminently strollable and dotted with pubs; the **White Cross** (Water Lane, 8940 6844), which has been here since 1835, has a special 'entrance at high tide' – the river floods regularly. The 13 arches of **Richmond Bridge** date from 1774 – this is the oldest surviving crossing over the Thames and offers fine sweeping views.

Richmond Park is the largest of the Royal Parks, occupying some 2,500 acres. There are hundreds of red and fallow deer roaming free across it – presumably much happier without having to listen out for the 'View halloo!' of one of Henry VIII's hunting parties. Within the park's bounds is the Palladian splendour of White Lodge and Pembroke Lodge, childhood home to philosopher Bertrand Russell but now a café. *See also right* **Inside Track**.

★ Royal Botanic Gardens (Kew Gardens)

Kew, Richmond, Surrey TW9 3AB (8332 5655, www.kew.org). Kew Gardens tube/rail, Kew Bridge rail or riverboat to Kew Pier. **Open** *Apr-Aug* 9.30am-6.30pm Mon-Fri; 9.30am-7.30pm Sat, Sun. *Sept, Oct* 9.30am-6pm daily. *Late Oct-early Feb* 9.30am-4.15pm daily. *Early Feb-Mar* 9.30am-5.30pm daily. **Admission** £13.50; £11.50 reductions; free under-17s. **Credit** AmEx, MC, V. Kew's lush, landscaped beauty represents the pinnacle of our national gardening obsession. From the early 1700s until 1840, when the gardens were given to the nation, these were the grounds for two fine royal residences – the White House and Richmond

Ham House.

Lodge. Early resident Queen Caroline, wife of George II, was very fond of exotic plants brought back by voyaging botanists. In 1759, the renowned 'Capability' Brown was employed by George III to improve on the work of his predecessors here, William Kent and Charles Bridgeman. Thus began the shape of the extraordinary garden that today attracts hundreds of thousands of visitors each year.

Covering half a square mile, Kew feels surprisingly big – pick up a map at the ticket office and follow the handy signs. Head straight for the 19th-century greenhouses, filled to the roof with plants – some of which have been here as long as the huge glass structures themselves. The sultry Palm House holds tropical plants: palms, bamboo, tamarind, mango and fig trees, not to mention fragrant hibiscus and frangipani. The Temperate House features *Pendiculata sanderina*, the Holy Grail for orchid hunters, with petals some 3ft long.

Also worth seeking out are the Princess of Wales Conservatory, divided into ten climate zones; the Marine Display, downstairs from the Palm House (it isn't always open, but when it is you can see the seahorses); the lovely, quiet indoor pond of the Waterlily House (closed in winter); and the Victorian botanical drawings of the fabulous Marianne North Gallery. The Xstrata Treetop Walkway has been a hugely popular addition to the gardens, allowing you to walk in the leaf canopy 60ft up.

▶ *Britain's smallest royal palace is also within the gardens: Kew Palace (www.hrp.org.uk/KewPalace; £5, free-£4.50 reductions) dates all the way back to the 18th century.*

WIMBLEDON

Wimbledon tube/rail.

Beyond the world-famous tennis tournament, **Wimbledon** is little but a wealthy and genteel suburb. Turn left out of the station on to the uninspiring Broadway, and you'll wonder why you bothered. So turn right instead, climbing a steep hill lined with huge houses. At the top is **Wimbledon Village**, a trendy little enclave of posh shops, eateries and some decent pubs.

From here you can hardly miss **Wimbledon Common**, a huge, wild, partly wooded park, criss-crossed by paths and horse tracks. The windmill (Windmill Road, 8947 2825, www. wimbledonwindmillmuseum.org.uk) provides an eccentric touch: Baden-Powell wrote *Scouting for Boys* (1910) here; it's now home to a tearoom and hands-on milling museum.

East of the common lies **Wimbledon Park**, with its boating lake, and the **All England Lawn Tennis Club** and **Wimbledon Lawn Tennis Museum** (*see below*). Two other attractions are worth seeking out – Grade II-listed **Cannizaro Park** (www.cannizaropark. org.uk) is lovely, as is the **Buddhapadipa Temple** (14 Calonne Road, Wimbledon Parkside, 8946 1357, www.buddhapadipa.org). When it was built in the early 1980s, this was the only Thai temple in Europe. The Shrine Room contains a golden statue of Buddha, a copy of the Buddhasihing that is on show in Bangkok's National Museum.

Wimbledon Lawn Tennis Museum

Museum Building, All England Lawn Tennis Club, Church Road, SW19 5AE (8946 6131, www.wimbledon.org/museum). Southfields tube or bus 493. **Open** 10am-5pm daily; ticket holders only during championships. **Admission** (incl tour) £18; £13-£15.75 reductions; free under-5s. **Credit** MC, V.
Highlights at this popular museum on the history of tennis include a 200° cinema screen that allows you to find out what it's like to play on Centre Court and a re-creation of a 1980s men's dressing room, complete with a 'ghost' of John McEnroe. Visitors can also enjoy a behind-the-scenes tour.
▶ *Wimbledon will be hosting the London 2012 Tennis competition; see p63.*

FURTHER SOUTH-WEST

Richmond tube/rail, or Hampton Court or St Margaret's rail.

If the water level allows, follow the river from Richmond west. You could stop at **Petersham**, home to the **Petersham Nurseries** with its garden café (Church Lane, off Petersham Road,

8605 3627, www.petershamnurseries.com), or take in a grand country mansion, perhaps **Ham House** (*see below*) or **Marble Hill House**, with the **Orleans House Gallery** (for both, *see p174*) right next door.

The river runs on past **Twickenham**, home to rugby's **Twickenham Stadium** (*see p174*), to the curious Gothic 'castle' **Strawberry Hill** (*see p174*). Several miles further along the Thames, the river passes beside the magnificent **Hampton Court Palace** (*see below*). Few visitors will want to walk this far, of course – instead take a train from Waterloo or, for that extra fillip of adventure, a boat.

Ham House

Ham Street, Richmond, Surrey TW10 7RS (8940 1950, www.nationaltrust.org.uk/ham house). Richmond tube/rail then bus 371. **Open** *Gardens* Jan, Nov, Dec 11am-4pm Mon-Sun; Feb-Oct 11am-5pm Mon-Sun. *House* Feb, Mar 11.30am-3.30pm Mon-Thur, Sat, Sun; Apr-Oct 12am-4pm Mon-Thur, Sat, Sun; Nov 11.30am-3pm Mon, Tue, Sat, Sun. **Admission** prices vary; check website for details. **Credit** MC, V.
Built in 1610 for one of James I's courtiers, Thomas Vavasour, this lavish red-brick mansion is full of period furnishings, rococo mirrors and ornate tapestries. Detailing is exquisite, down to a table in the dairy with sculpted cows' legs. The restored formal grounds also attract attention: there's a lovely trellised Cherry Garden and some lavender parterres. The tearoom in the old orangery turns out historic dishes (lavender syllabub, for instance) using ingredients from the Kitchen Gardens.
▶ *Between February and October (weekends only for the winter months), a ferry crosses the river to Marble Hill House; see p174.*

★ Hampton Court Palace

East Molesey, Surrey KT8 9AU (0844 482 7777, www.hrp.org.uk). Hampton Court rail, or riverboat from Westminster or Richmond to Hampton Court Pier (Apr-Oct). **Open** *Palace* Apr-Oct 10am-6pm

---

INSIDE TRACK
MAGNIFICENT VISTA

From the top of **Richmond Hill**, the view of lush meadowland, munching cows and meandering river has remained relatively unchanged since the 1700s. England's only view protected by its own Act of Parliament, it has been immortalised by artists including Turner and Reynolds. On a clear day you can see, Hampton Court Palace (*see above*) and even St Paul's Cathedral (*see p87*), more than 12 miles in the distance.

daily; Nov-Mar 10am-4.30pm daily. *Park* dawn-dusk daily. **Admission** *Palace, courtyard, cloister & maze* £14; £7-£11.50 reductions; £38 family; free under-5s. *Maze only* £3.50; £2.50 reductions. *Gardens only* Apr-Oct £4.60; £4 reductions; Nov-Mar free. **Credit** AmEx, MC, V.

It may be a half-hour train ride from central London, but this spectacular palace, once owned by Henry VIII, is well worth the trek. It was built in 1514 by Cardinal Wolsey, the high-flying Lord Chancellor, but Henry liked it so much he seized it for himself in 1528. For the next 200 years it was a focal point of English history: Elizabeth I was imprisoned in a tower by her jealous and fearful elder sister Mary I; Shakespeare gave his first performance to James I in 1604; and, after the Civil War, Oliver Cromwell was so besotted by the building he ditched his puritanical principles and moved in to enjoy its luxuries.

Centuries later, the rosy walls of the palace still dazzle. Its vast size can be daunting, so it's a good idea to take advantage of the guided tours. If you do decide to go it alone, start with Henry VIII's State Apartments, which include the Great Hall, noted for its beautiful stained-glass windows and elaborate religious tapestries; in the Haunted Gallery, the ghost of Catherine Howard – Henry's fifth wife, executed for adultery in 1542 – can reputedly be heard shrieking. The King's Apartments, added in 1689 by Wren, are notable for a splendid mural of Alexander the Great, painted by Antonio Verrio. The Queen's Apartments and Georgian Rooms feature similarly elaborate paintings, chandeliers and tapestries. The Tudor Kitchens are great fun, with their giant cauldrons, fake pies and blood-spattered walls.

More spectacular sights await outside, where the exquisitely landscaped gardens contain superb topiary, peaceful Thames views, a reconstruction of a 16th-century heraldic garden and the famous Hampton Court maze. In summer, there's a music festival and a flower show that rivals the more famous one at Chelsea; every winter, an ice-skating rink is installed.

Marble Hill House

Richmond Road, Twickenham, Middx TW1 2NL (8892 5115, www.english-heritage.org.uk). Richmond tube/rail, St Margaret's rail or bus 33, 90, 490, H22, R70. **Open** *Apr-Oct* 10am-2pm Sat; 10am-5pm Sun; group visits Mon-Fri by request. *Nov-Mar* by request. **Admission** £5; £2.50-£4.30 reductions; free under-5s; £12.50 family. **Credit** MC, V.

King George II spared no expense to win the favour of his mistress, Henrietta Howard. Not only did he build this perfect Palladian house (1724) for his lover, he almost dragged Britain into a war while doing so: by using Honduran mahogany to construct the grand staircase, he managed to spark off a major diplomatic row with Spain. Frankly, it was worth it. Picnickers are welcome to the grounds, as are sporty types (there are tennis, putting and cricket facilities).

▶ *A programme of concerts keeps things busy in the summer, and ferries regularly cross the Thames to Ham House; see p173.*

FREE Orleans House Gallery

Riverside, Twickenham, Middx TW1 3DJ (8831 6000, www.richmond.gov.uk/orleans_house_gallery). Richmond tube then bus 33, 490, H22, R68, R70, or St Margaret's or Twickenham rail. **Open** *Apr-Sept* 1-5.30pm Tue-Sat; 2-5.30pm Sun. *Oct-Mar* 1-4.30pm Tue-Sat; 2-4.30pm Sun. **Admission** free. **Credit** MC, V.

Secluded in pretty gardens, this Grade I-listed riverside house was constructed in 1710 for James Johnson, Secretary of State for Scotland. It was later named after the Duke of Orleans, Louis-Philippe, who lived in exile here from 1800 until 1817. Though partially demolished in 1926, the building retains James Gibbs's neoclassical Octagon Room. There are also regularly changing temporary exhibitions here and in the nearby Stables Gallery.

▶ *The new café (Karmarama, open Wed-Sun) is a welcome addition, offering good coffee and snacks.*

Strawberry Hill

268 Waldegrave Road, Twickenham, Middx TW1 4ST (8744 3124, www.strawberryhill house.org.uk). Richmond tube then bus R68, or Strawberry Hill rail. **Open** *Apr-Oct* noon-4.30pm Mon, Tue, Wed, Sat, Sun. **Admission** £8; £7 reductions; free under-5s; £20 family (2+3). **Credit** MC, V.

Antiquarian and novelist Horace Walpole, who created the Gothic novel with his book *The Castle of Otranto*, was laying the groundwork for the Gothic Revival of Victorian times as early as the 18th century. This 'little Gothic castle' reopened to the public in autumn 2010 after a £9m restoration. Pre-booked tickets, timed at 20min intervals, will allow you to explore the crepuscular nooks and crannies of Walpole's 'play-thing house'.

World Rugby Museum/ Twickenham Stadium

Twickenham Rugby Stadium, Rugby Road, Twickenham, Middx TW1 1DZ (8892 8877, www.rfu.com). Hounslow East tube then bus 281, or Twickenham rail. **Open** *Museum* 10am-5pm Tue-Sat; 11am-5pm Sun. *Tours* 10.30am, noon, 1.30pm, 3pm Tue-Sat; 1pm, 3pm Sun. **Admission** £14; £8 reductions; £40 family. **Credit** AmEx, MC, V.

The impressive Twickenham Stadium is the home of English rugby union. Tickets for international matches are extremely hard to come by, but the Museum of Rugby is also on the site to provide some measure of compensation. Guided tours take in the England dressing room, the players' tunnel and the Royal Box. Memorabilia (a jersey from 1871, the Calcutta Cup) charts the game's development from the late 19th century, and there's a scrum machine.

West London

Where recent immigration meets old money.

It's fitting that west London still has a distinct air of aristocash. This was, after all, the first of the city's frontiers to be developed, just outside the City of Westminster and out of the way of the westerly smog-carrying winds. Even today, the elegant Georgian townhouses of **Holland Park** and **Kensington** have retained their high status.

Unlike London's north, east and south, where the posher neighbourhoods are tucked away in more remote, leafier suburbs, the smartest parts of the west – chiefly Fulham, Kensington and Notting Hill – are conveniently central, while the working-class districts of **Southall** and **Wembley**, now the first stop for those who've arrived in the country via Heathrow, are further out.

Map p394	**Hotels** pp206-207
Pubs & bars p249	**Restaurants &**
	cafés pp233-234

SIGHTS

KENSINGTON & HOLLAND PARK

High Street Kensington or Holland Park tube.

There are more millionaires per square mile in this corner of London than in any other part of Europe, a hangover from the days when Kensington was a semi-rural retreat for aristocrats. Just off **Kensington High Street**, one of London's smarter mainstream shopping stretches, an array of handsome squares are lined with grand 19th-century houses, many of which still serve as single-family homes. The houses here are not as ostentatiously grand as they are in, say, Belgravia, but nor is the wealth worn as lightly and subtly it is in many corners of Mayfair. You're always aware that you're around money.

Linking with Notting Hill (*see p123*) to the north, **Kensington Church Street** has many antiques shops selling furniture so fine you would probably never dare use it. **St Mary Abbots** (7937 6032, www.st maryabbotschurch.org), at the junction of Church Street and High Street, is a wonderful Victorian neo-Gothic church, built on the site of the 12th-century original by Sir George Gilbert Scott between 1869 and 1872. Past worshippers have included Isaac Newton and William

Wilberforce. As well as beautiful stained-glass windows, it has London's tallest spire (278 feet).

Across the road is a striking art deco building, once the department store Barkers but now taken over by Texan organic food giant **Whole Foods Market** (nos.63-97, 7368 4500, www.wholefoodsmarket.co.uk). South down Derry Street, past the entrance to the **Roof Gardens** – a restaurant and private members' club, which boasts flamingos and a stream, 100 feet above central London – is Kensington Square, which has one of London's highest concentrations of blue plaques. The writer William Thackeray lived at no.16 and

---

**INSIDE TRACK
TRAINS, TAXIS AND BUSES**

Transport boffins and fans of design classics: the **London Transport Museum** (*see p109*) opens its Acton depot to visitors on a few weekends a year. The warehouse contains over 370,000 objects that wouldn't fit into the Covent Garden museum, including vehicles – a 1950s Routemaster bus prototype among them – and vintage posters and uniforms. See www.ltmuseum.co.uk for details.

---

the painter Edward Burne-Jones at no.41; at no.18, John Stuart Mill's maid made her bid for 'man from Porlock' status by using Carlyle's sole manuscript of *The French Revolution* to start the fire. The houses, though much altered, date from the development of the square in 1685, and – hard to believe now – were surrounded by fields until 1840.

Further to the west is one of London's finest green spaces: **Holland Park**. Along its eastern edge, Holland Walk is one of the most pleasant paths in central London, but the heart of the park is the Jacobean **Holland House**. Left derelict after World War II, it was bought by the London County Council in 1952; the east wing now houses the city's best-sited youth hostel (*see p208*). In summer, open-air theatre and opera are staged on the front terrace. Three lovely formal gardens are laid out near the house. A little further west, the Japanese-style Kyoto Garden has huge koi carp and a bridge at the foot of a waterfall. Elsewhere, rabbits hop about and peacocks stroll around with the confidence due to such supremely beautiful creatures. To the south of the park are another two historic houses: **Linley Sambourne House** and, reopened after extensive refurbishment in spring 2010, **Leighton House** (for both, *see below*).

Leighton House.

★ Leighton House

12 Holland Park Road, W14 8LZ (7602 3316, www.rbkc.gov.uk). High Street Kensington tube. **Open** 10am-5.30pm Mon, Wed-Sun. *Tours* 3pm Wed (other times by appointment only). **Admission** £5; free-£1 reductions. **Credit** MC, V. **Map** p394 A9.

Behind its sternly Victorian red-brick façade, Leighton House has received a £1.6m refurbishment. In the 1860s, artist Frederic Leighton commissioned a showpiece house, which he filled with classical treasures from all over the world, as well as his own works and those of his contemporaries. Every inch of his house is decorated in high style: magnificent downstairs reception rooms designed for lavish entertaining; a dramatic staircase leading to a light-filled studio that takes up most of the first floor; and, above all, the 'Arab Hall', which showcases Leighton's huge collection of 16th-century Middle Eastern tiles. The only private space in the whole house is a tiny single bedroom.

Linley Sambourne House

18 Stafford Terrace, W8 7BH (7938 1295 information, 7602 3316 tours, www.rbkc.gov.uk/linleysambournehouse). High Street Kensington tube. **Open** *mid Sept-mid June* by appointment only Wed, Sat, Sun. **Tours** £6; £1-£4 reductions. **Credit** MC, V. **Map** p394 A9.

The home of cartoonist Edward Linley Sambourne was built in the 1870s and has almost all of its orig-

inal fittings and furniture. Tours must be booked in advance; they last 90mins, with weekend tours led by an actor in period costume.

▶ *If you enjoy the re-enactment tours here, note that something similar is offered at Benjamin Franklin House; see p110.*

EARL'S COURT & FULHAM

Earl's Court, Fulham Broadway or West Brompton tube.

Earl's Court sells itself short, grammatically speaking, since it was once the site of the courthouse of two earls: both the Earl of Warwick and the Earl of Holland. The 1860s saw Earl's Court move from rural hamlet to investment opportunity as the Metropolitan Railway arrived. Some 20 years later it was already much as we see it today, bar the fast food joints. The terraces of grand old houses are mostly subdivided into bedsits and cheap hotels; today, the transient population tends to be Eastern European or South American.

In 1937, the **Earls Court Exhibition Centre** was built, and in its day it was the largest reinforced concrete building in Europe – a phrase that truly makes the heart sing. The centre hosts a year-round calendar of events, from trade shows to pop concerts (Pink Floyd built and tore down *The Wall* here), and will host the London 2012 Volleyball (*see p59*). The Exhibition Centre is close to the diverting little **Metropolitan Police Museum** (ground floor, Empress State Building, Empress Approach, Lillie Road, SW6 1TR, 7161 1234, www.met.police.uk; open 10am-4pm Mon-Fri). Two minutes south down Warwick Road is a tiny venue, with an impressive pedigree: the **Troubadour** (263-267 Old Brompton Road, 7370 1434, www.troubadour.co.uk), a 1950s coffeehouse with a downstairs club that hosted Jimi Hendrix, Joni Mitchell, Bob Dylan and Paul Simon in the 1960s. While it's no longer at the cutting edge, it still delivers a full programme of music, poetry and comedy.

Heading west along Warwick Road you come to the gates of **Brompton Cemetery**. It's full of magnificent monuments to the famous and infamous, including suffragette Emmeline Pankhurst and, his grave marked by a lion, boxer 'Gentleman' John Jackson – 'Gentleman' John taught Lord Byron to box. The peace and quiet of the cemetery are regularly disturbed at its southern end by neighbouring **Stamford Bridge**, home of Chelsea FC. **Craven Cottage** (for both, *see p336*), the home of west London's other Premiership team, Fulham FC, is west of here, at the northern end of the park that surrounds **Fulham Palace** (*see right*).

FREE **Fulham Palace & Museum**
Bishop's Avenue, off Fulham Palace Road, SW6 6EA (7736 3233, www.fulhampalace.org). Putney Bridge tube or bus 14, 74, 220, 414, 430. **Open** *Museum & gallery* 1-4pm Mon-Wed, Sat, Sun. *Gardens* dawn-dusk daily. *Tours* 2pm 2nd & 4th Sun of mth. **Admission** free; under-16s must be accompanied by an adult. *Tours* £5; free under-16s. **No credit cards.**

Fulham Palace was the episcopal retreat of the Bishops of London. The present building was built in Tudor times, with later significant Georgian and Victorian additions. It would be more accurate to call it a manor house than a palace, but it gives a fine glimpse into the changing lifestyles and architecture of nearly 500 years, from the Tudor hall to the splendid Victorian chapel; try out the echo in the courtyard. There's also access to a glorious stretch of riverside walk. Best of all, these delights still seem largely undiscovered by the majority of Londoners.
▶ *The Drawing Room Café has outdoor tables looking out over an expansive lawn.*

SHEPHERD'S BUSH

Goldhawk Road or Shepherd's Bush Market tube, or Shepherd's Bush tube/rail.

Shepherd's Bush was once west London's impoverished backwater, the setting for junkyard sitcom *Steptoe & Son*. Now, a couple of decades after house prices started going through the roof, there's visible evidence of gentrification. **Queens Park Rangers** (*see p336*), the underperforming local football team, has benefited from a huge cash injection from three of the world's richest businessmen, while Shepherd's Bush got a similar boost from the gargantuan **Westfield London** shopping mall (*see p255*). The **Bush** theatre (*see p346*) stages excellent leftfield drama, while **Bush Hall** (*see p323*), a beautifully restored former snooker hall, and the **O2 Shepherd's Bush Empire** (*see p320*), an old BBC theatre, have become essential destinations on the music scene. The bar at the **K West** hotel (Richmond Way, W14 0AX, 8008 6600, www.k-west.co.uk) is a good place if you're interested in spotting trendy young American bands after they've played the Empire.

BBC Television Centre
TV Centre, Wood Lane, W12 7RJ (0370 603 0304, www.bbc.co.uk/tours). White City or Wood Lane tube. **Open** by appointment only Mon-Sat. **Admission** £9.95; £7.50-£8.95 reductions; £30 family. No under-9s. **Credit** MC, V.

Half a mile north of Shepherd's Bush Green is the BBC TV Centre where, if you book in advance, you can catch a fascinating tour around the temple of British televisual history. Tours include visits to the

SIGHTS

news desk, the TV studios and the Weather Centre, though children and *Doctor Who* fans might be most excited about the TARDIS on display.

▶ *Fancy being part of a BBC television show audience? Apply for free tickets at www.bbc.co.uk/ showsandtours/tickets/ or by phone on 0370 901 1227 (9am-6pm Mon-Fri).*

HAMMERSMITH

Hammersmith tube.

Dominated by the grey concrete of its flyover, the centre of Hammersmith, **Hammersmith Broadway**, was once a grotty bus garage. It's now a shiny new shopping mall. Make it over the road and you'll find the **HMV Hammersmith Apollo** (*see p319*). Opened in 1932 as the Gaumont Palace, it entered rock legend as the Hammersmith Odeon, hosting pivotal gigs by such bands as the Beatles, Motörhead and Public Enemy.

Hammersmith Bridge, the city's oldest suspension bridge, is a green and gold hymn to the strength of Victorian ironwork. There's a lovely walk west along the Thames Path from here that takes in a clutch of historic pubs including the **Blue Anchor** (13 Lower Mall, W6 9DJ, 8748 5774); head in the opposite direction for cultural happenings at the **Riverside Studios** (*see p301*).

CHISWICK

Turnham Green tube or Chiswick rail.

Once a sleepy, semi-rural suburb, Chiswick is now one of London's swankiest postcodes, its residents including broadcasters, directors, actors, advertising bods and a smattering of rock 'n' roll royalty. In recent years, **Chiswick High Road**, its main thoroughfare, has developed a gastronomic reputation, with dozens of high-end eateries.

Chiswick also has a surprising number of sightseeing attractions. **Chiswick Mall** is a beautiful residential path that runs alongside the river from Hammersmith, and includes **Kelmscott House** (26 Upper Mall, 8741 3735, www.morrissociety.org), once home to pioneering socialist William Morris but now a private house that opens to the public 2-5pm on Thursdays and Saturdays. From here, it's a short walk to **Fuller's Brewery** and **Hogarth's House**, while the **Kew Bridge Steam Museum** and the **Musical Museum** are only a bus ride away; for all, *see right*. It's possible to return to the river path after visiting **Chiswick House** (*see right*), and the wonderful Royal Botanic Gardens at Kew (*see p172*) are just over the bridge. Further upstream is **Syon House**

(*see p179*), with enough attractions to fill most of a day – among them the Tropical Forest animal sanctuary (8847 4730, www. tropicalforest.co.uk, £5.50-£6.50).

Chiswick House
Burlington Lane, W4 2RP (8995 0508, www.chgt.org.uk). Hammersmith tube then bus 190, or Chiswick rail. **Open** *Apr-Oct* 10am-5pm Mon-Wed, Sun. **Admission** £5; £2.50-£4.30 reductions; free under-5s. **Credit** MC, V.

Richard Boyle, third Earl of Burlington, designed this lovely Palladian villa in 1725 as a place to entertain the artistic and philosophical luminaries of his day. The Chiswick House & Gardens Trust has been restoring the gardens to Burlington's original design, with much now reopened to the public. The restoration will be helped by details from the newly acquired painting *A View of Chiswick House from the South-west* by Dutch landscape artist Pieter Andreas Rysbrack (c1685-1748).

▶ *There's a good new café here (8995 6356, www.chiswickhousecafe.co.uk).*

Fuller's Brewery
Griffin Brewery, Chiswick Lane South, W4 2QB (8996 2000, www.fullers.co.uk). Turnham Green tube. **Open** *Tours* hourly 11am-3pm Mon-Fri, by appointment only. *Shop* 10am-8pm Mon-Fri. **Admission** (incl tasting session) £10; £7-£8 reductions. **Credit** MC, V.

Fuller Smith & Turner PLC is London's last family-run brewery. Most of this current building dates back to 1845 but there's been a brewery on this site since Elizabethan times. The two-hour tours need to be booked in advance, but – surprise – there is a pub next door if you can't get on a tour.

▶ *London Pride and ESB are the most popular Fuller's brews in London pubs. For more on tasty ale, see p246* **Bigging Up the Beer**.

FREE Hogarth's House
Hogarth Lane, Great West Road, W4 2QN (8994 6757). Turnham Green tube or Chiswick rail. **Open** *Apr-Oct* 1-5pm Tue-Fri; 1-6pm Sat, Sun. *Nov, Dec, Feb, Mar* 1-4pm Tue-Fri; 1-5pm Sat, Sun. **Admission** free; donations appreciated. **No credit cards.**

Due to reopen after refurbishment by early 2011, this was the country retreat of the 18th-century painter, engraver and social commentator William Hogarth. On display are some famous engravings, including *Gin Lane, Marriage à la Mode* and a copy of *Rake's Progress*, as well as biographical information.

★ Kew Bridge Steam Museum
Green Dragon Lane, Kew, Surrey TW8 0EN (8568 4757, www.kbsm.org). Gunnersbury tube/rail or Kew Bridge rail. **Open** 11am-4pm Tue-Sun. **Admission** £9.50; £8.50 reductions; free under-16s. **Credit** MC, V.

Kew Bridge Stream Museum

One of London's most engaging small museums, this impressive old Victorian pumping station is a reminder that steam wasn't just used for powering trains but also for supplying enough water to the citizens of an expanding London. It's now home to an extraordinary collection of different engines. There are lots of hands-on exhibits for kids, a great dressing-up box and even a miniature steam train.

★ Musical Museum
399 High Street, Kew, Surrey TW8 0DU (8560 8108, www.musicalmuseum.co.uk). Kew Bridge rail or bus 65, 237, 267. **Open** 11am-5.30pm (last admission 4.30pm) Tue-Sun. **Admission** £8; £6.50 reductions, accompanied under-16s free. **Credit** MC, V.
Housed in a converted church, this museum contains one of the world's foremost collections of automatic instruments. From tiny Swiss musical boxes to the self-playing Mighty Wurlitzer, the collection has an impressive array of sophisticated pianolas, cranky barrel organs, spooky orchestrions, residence organs and violin players, as well as over 30,000 piano rolls.

Syon House
Syon Park, Brentford, Middx TW8 8JF (8560 0882, www.syonpark.co.uk). Gunnersbury tube/rail then bus 237, 267. **Open** *House* (mid Mar-Oct only) 11am-5pm Wed, Thur, Sun. *Gardens* (all year) 10.30am-dusk daily. *Tours* by arrangement. **Admission** *House & gardens* £9; £4-£8 reductions; £20 family. *Gardens only* £4.50; £2.50-£3.50 reductions; £10 family. *Tours* free. **Credit** MC, V.
The Percys, Dukes of Northumberland, were once known as 'the Kings of the North'. Their old house is on the site of a Bridgettine convent, suppressed by Henry VIII in 1534. The building was converted into a house in 1547 for the Duke of Northumberland, its neoclassical interior created by Robert Adam in 1761; there's an outstanding range of Regency portraits by the likes of Gainsborough. The gardens, by 'Capability' Brown, are enhanced by the splendid Great Conservatory and in winter you can take an evening walk through illuminated woodland.

SOUTHALL
Southall rail.

Immigrants used to enter London via the docks and settle in the East End. Now, though, they come via Heathrow and settle here: thus a huge arc of suburban west London – Hounslow, Hayes, Southall, Harrow, Wembley, Neasden – has become home to Europe's biggest South

---

INSIDE TRACK MOON MAN

Thomas Harriot was the first person to study the moon through a telescope, more than 400 years ago at **Syon House** (*see left*) but, because he never published his findings, Galileo grabbed all the glory. Perhaps Harriot didn't mind too much: he had already sailed to the New World, learnt Algonquin, written the first English-language publication on the Americas, developed a symbolic notation for algebra (still taught in schools) and constucted a binary number system rather like that used in digital devices today.

SIGHTS

Asian population. **Southall** is Britain's best-established immigrant community. From the 1950s onwards, Punjabi Sikhs flocked to the area to work at the Wolf Rubber Factory and in London Transport; the area soon developed a thriving Asian infrastructure of restaurants, shops and wholesalers that attracted Hindus, Muslims, Tamils, Indian Christians and, more recently, Somalis and Afghans. Take a 607 bus from Shepherd's Bush or a Great Western train from Paddington and, on arrival in Southall, you'll think you're in downtown Delhi – all pounding Bollywood hits, sari fabrics, pungent spices and freshly fried samosas.

Southall Broadway is well worth a visit if only to gawp at **Southall Market**, a unique mix of rural India and Cockney London, which until 2007 sold squawking poultry and horses. It still does a brisk trade in general bric-a-brac on Friday and, on Saturday, pretty much everything else. Equally worthy of diversion is the programme of movies at the three-screen **Himalaya Palace** (14 South Road, www.himalayapalacecinema.co.uk), a restored old movie house dedicated to Bollywood epics.

But it's the food that makes Southall really special; for more, *see p231* **Inside Track**. There's even a Punjabi pub, the **Glassy Junction** (97 South Road, 8574 1626): all the trappings of a white working men's club – patterned carpet, keg beer – plus the boon of hot parathas. It's said to be the only pub in the UK that accepts payment in rupees.

A short walk south of Southall railway station, the **Gurdwara Sri Guru Singh Sabha Southall** (Havelock Road, 8574 4311, www.sgsss.org) is the largest Sikh place of worship outside India. Its golden dome is visible from the London Eye in the east and Windsor Castle to the west; it also provides vegetarian food free to all visitors from the *langar*, or communal kitchen. Non-Sikh visitors are welcome but must take off their shoes before entering, and women must wear a headscarf (they're provided, should you not have one to hand). Enthroned within is the Guru Granth Sahib, the Sikh scripture and supreme spiritual authority of Sikhism.

To the north, **Wembley** is home to a secular religion: British football has its home and heart at **Wembley Stadium** (*see p335*), stunningly redeveloped by Lord Foster. The distinctive arch has become a welcome sign of home-coming for Londoners driving back to the city from the West Country. The stadium will be hosting the Football for the London 2012 Games (*see p63*), while the nearby **Wembley Arena** (*see p321*) will be the venue for the Badminton and Rhythmic Gymnastics (*see p63*).

The neighbouring suburb of Neasden has its own claim to British Asian fame: the **Shri Swaminarayan Mandir** (105-119 Brentfield Road, 8965 2651, www.mandir.org), the largest Hindu temple outside India to have been built using traditional methods. To this end, nearly 5,000 tons of stone and marble were shipped out to India, where craftsmen carved it into the intricate designs that make up the temple. Then the temple was shipped, piece by piece, to England, where it was assembled on site. The shining marble temple stands incongruously close to one of IKEA's giant blue boxes.

Shri Swaminarayan Mandir.

Consume

Columbia Road Market. *See p255*.

Hotels

Prices are high and openings many in the run-up to London 2012.

In certain respects, the excitement of London 2012 is being most keenly felt in the hotel industry. There are so many new openings planned for 2012, already under way or open, it's sometimes hard to keep up. Even previously unfancied parts of east London are beginning to gain swanky and characterful boutique properties and new budget hotels (*see p203* **The New East**).

The excitement isn't confined to the east. In the West End, the reopening of the **Savoy** (*see p191*) in October 2010 might be the biggest event, but the appearance of the new **St John Hotel** (*see p189* **Come and St John the Fun**) – a fabulous company and a fabulous location just off Leicester Square – might be more significant.

It seems likely there will be splashy openings this year across all price ranges. Around the time this guide hits the shelves, the **W Leicester Square**, the **City Inn Tower of London** and the masculine new sibling of the Dorchester (*see p197*), **45 Park Lane**, are all due to open. The **Zetter** (*see p186*) is to open new bedrooms in a townhouse just across the square from the original. The much-delayed redevelopment of the Grade I-listed frontage of St Pancras station into the **Renaissance Marriott St Pancras** may finally reach completion this year. The hotshot New York hotelier André Balazs is said to be developing a property in London, and Kit Kemp's exemplary Firmdale Group is already at work on a new luxury hotel in Soho's Ham Yard.

Room prices remain high across London. Significantly, **Dean Street Townhouse** (*see p191*), its slightly younger sibling **Shoreditch Rooms** (*see p205*) and **St John** (*see p192*) chose to offer 'tiny' or 'post-supper' rooms – their smallest or otherwise less-appealing rooms at lower-than-you-might-fear rates. The popularity of hip new B&Bs (**Rough Luxe**, *see p188*; **40 Winks**, *see p205*) and no-frills hotel concepts (*see p206* **Inside Track**) speaks to the same need.

STAYING IN LONDON

Hotels in this chapter are classified by the average price of a double room. You can expect to pay more than £300 a night for hotels in the **Deluxe** category, £200-£300 for **Expensive** hotels, £100-£200 for **Moderate** properties and under £100 a night for hotels listed as **Budget**.

The rates we've listed are only for guidance. The variation within these room rates, top to bottom and over the course of the year, can be huge. As a rule, book as far ahead as possible, and always try hotels' own websites first: many offer special online deals throughout the year.

If you can't book ahead, websites such as **www.alpharooms.com**, **www.hotels.com**, **www.expedia.co.uk**, **www.london-discount-hotel.com** and the like may offer keen rates for short-notice bookings, assuming the property in question isn't already fully booked. In addition, the obliging staff at **Visit London** (1 Lower Regent Street, 0870 156 6366,

> ❶ Red numbers given in this chapter correspond to the location of each hotel on the street maps. See pp392-416.

www.visitlondon.com) can look for a room within your selected price range and neighbourhood for free.

In general, the geography of London gives some guidance as to the price and type of lodging you're likely to find in a particular part of town. Many of the city's swankier hotels are found in Mayfair (W1), for example, whereas Bloomsbury (WC1) is good for mid-priced hotels and B&Bs. If you're looking for a cheap hotel, try Ebury Street in Victoria (SW1) or Gower Street in Bloomsbury (WC1), as well as Earl's Court (SW5), Bayswater (W2), Paddington (W2) and South Kensington (SW7).

Room rates in this chapter include VAT (sales tax, added at the current rate of 17.5% but due to rise to 20% in early 2011). Be aware that not all hotels include VAT in the rates they quote – always check before committing to the price. And watch out for added extras (*see p191* **Inside Track**). We've listed the prices of some extras in this chapter, but again, always check before signing up.

At the end of each review, we've listed a selection of services offered by each hotel: restaurants and bars, internet access, spas and the like. The hotel may offer additional services, too: call the hotel or check its website if you're after something specific and unusual. If you're bringing a car to the city (not recommended), always check with the hotel before you arrive: few central hotels offer parking, and those that do tend to charge the earth for it.

In addition to the standard services, note that hotel concierges can often help with additional services: theatre tickets, dinner reservations, babysitters and so on. We've also tried to indicate which hotels offer rooms adapted for disabled customers, but it's always best to confirm the precise facilities with each place before you travel. **Tourism for All** (0845 124 9971, www.tourismforall.org.uk) has details of wheelchair-accessible places.

THE SOUTH BANK & BANKSIDE
Moderate

Bermondsey Square Hotel
Bermondsey Square, Tower Bridge Road, SE1 3UN (0870 111 2525, www.bespokehotels.com). Borough tube or London Bridge tube/rail. **Rates** £109-£199 double. **Rooms** 80. **Credit** AmEx, MC, V. **Map** p403 Q10 ❶

This is a deliberately kitsch new-build on a newly developed square. Suites are named after the heroines of psychedelic rock classics (Lucy, Lily and so on), there are classic discs on the walls, and you can kick your heels from the suspended Bubble Chair at reception. But, although occupants of the Lucy suite

get a multi-person jacuzzi (with a great terrace view), and anyone can get sex toys from reception, the real draw isn't the gimmicks – it's well-designed rooms for competitive prices. The Brit food restaurant-bar is a bit hit-or-miss, but the hotel's pretty staff are happy and helpful.

Bar/café. Conference facilities. Internet: wireless (free). Restaurant. TV.

Park Plaza County Hall
1 Addington Street, SE1 7RY (7021 1800, www.parkplaza.com). Waterloo tube/rail. **Rates** £120-£200 double. **Rooms** 398. **Credit** MC, V. **Map** p399 M9 ❷

Park Plaza County Hall is an enthusiastically – if somewhat haphazardly – run new-build. Each room has its own kitchenette with microwave and sink, and room sizes aren't bad across the price range (the floor-to-ceiling windows help them feel bigger). There's a handsomely vertiginous atrium, enabling you to peer down into the central restaurant from the frustratingly infrequent glass lifts, and the ground-floor bar is buzzy with business types after work. The gargantuan Park Plaza Westminster Bridge (200 Westminster Bridge Road, SE1 7UT) has now opened nearby, at the southern end of Westminster Bridge. It's London's largest new-build hotel for four decades.

Bars/cafés (2). Concierge. Conference facilities. Disabled-adapted rooms. Gym. Internet: wireless (free). Parking: £15/day. Restaurant. Room service. Spa facilities. TV: pay movies.

CONSUME

Threadneedles. *See p185.*

CONSUME

Rough Luxe. *See p188*.

Premier Inn London County Hall

County Hall, Belvedere Road, SE1 7PB (0870 238 3300, www.premierinn.com). Waterloo tube/rail. **Rates** £111-£150 double. **Rooms** 314. **Credit** AmEx, DC, MC, V. **Map** p399 M8 ❸

Its position right by the London Eye, the Thames, Westminster Bridge and Waterloo Station is a gift for out-of-towners on a bargain weekend break. Extra points are garnered for its friendly and efficient staff, making this newly refurbished branch of the Premier Travel chain the acceptable face of budget convenience. Check-in is quick and pleasant; rooms are spacious, clean and warm with comfortable beds and decent bathrooms with very good showers. Breakfast, a buffet-style affair in a comfortable dining room, is extra but provides ballast for a day of sightseeing/shopping, or indeed meetings. But given the daily cost of the Wi-Fi, you're better off leaving the work at home.

Bars/café. Disabled-adapted rooms. Internet: wireless (£10/day). Restaurant. TV.

THE CITY

Deluxe

Andaz Liverpool Street

40 Liverpool Street, EC2M 7QN (7961 1234, www.london.liverpoolstreet.andaz.com). Liverpool Street tube/rail. **Rates** £240-£300 double. **Rooms** 267. **Credit** AmEx, DC, MC, V. **Map** p403 R6 ❹

A faded railway hotel until its £70m Conran overhaul in 2000, the red-brick Great Eastern became in 2007 the first of Hyatt's new Andaz portfolio. The new approach means out with gimmicky menus, closet-sized minibars and even the lobby reception desk, and in with down-to-earth, well-informed service and eco-friendliness. The bedrooms still wear style-mag uniform – Eames chairs, Frette linens – but free services (local calls, wireless internet, healthy minibar) and savvy efforts to connect with the vibey local area are appreciated: witness the Summer Garden, temporarily installed at the base of the atrium as a place to lounge over cocktails or enjoy the Designer Jumble Sale, and entertainment in the hotel's wonderfully gothic Freemasons' Temple.

Bars/cafés (5). Business centre. Concierge. Disabled-adapted rooms. Gym. Internet: wireless & high-speed (free). Restaurants (5). Room service. Smoking rooms. TV.

Expensive

Threadneedles

5 Threadneedle Street, EC2R 8AY (7657 8080, www.theetoncollection.com). Bank tube/DLR. **Rates** £225-£525 double. **Rooms** 69. **Credit** AmEx, MC, V. **Map** p403 Q6 ❺

Threadneedles boldly slots some contemporary style into a fusty old dame of a building, formerly the grand Victorian HQ of the Midland Bank, bang next to the Bank of England and the Royal Exchange. The etched glass-domed rotunda of the lobby soars on columns over an artful array of designer furniture and shelving that looks like the dreamchild of some powerful graphics software – it's a calm space, but a stunning one. The bedrooms are individual, coherent and soothing examples of City-boy chic, in muted beige and textured tones, with limestone bathrooms and odd views of local landmarks: St Paul's, Tower 42 and the Lloyds building. It's all well run and well thought out. *Photo p183.*

Bar/café. Concierge. Disabled-adapted rooms. Internet: wireless (free). Restaurant. Room service. TV: pay movies.

Moderate

Apex London Wall

7-9 Copthall Avenue, EC2R 7NJ (7562 3030, www.apexhotels.co.uk). Bank tube or Moorgate tube/rail. **Rates** £130-£311 double. **Rooms** 89. **Credit** AmEx, MC, V. **Map** p403 Q6 ❻

The mini-chain's newest London hotel shares the virtues of its predecessor (Apex City of London, 1 Seething Lane, 7702 2020). The service is obliging, the rooms are crisply designed with all mod cons, and there are comforting details – rubber duck in the impressive bathrooms, free jelly beans, free local calls and internet, kettle and iron provided. The City of London branch has the better location for tourists, a short walk from the Tower of London, but this one – tucked in among offices – is handier for business. From the suites, a terrace peers over commercial buildings, but the view from the restaurant – of the flamboyantly sculpted frieze on a business institute – is rather pleasing.

Bar/café. Disabled-adapted rooms. Gym. Internet: wireless (free). Restaurant. Room service. TV.

HOLBORN & CLERKENWELL

Expensive

Malmaison

Charterhouse Square, EC1M 6AH (7012 3700, www.malmaison.com). Barbican tube. **Rates** £235 double. **Rooms** 97. **Credit** AmEx, DC, MC, V. **Map** p400 O5 ❼

Malmaison is deliciously located, looking out on a lovely cobbled square on the edge of the square mile, near the bars, clubs and better restaurants of the East End. This being design-conscious Clerkenwell, it's no surprise that the decor throughout makes a cool statement (note the Veuve Cliquot ice buckets built into the love seats at reception). The rooms overlooking the square are the pick of the bunch, with the best of the views and morning sunshine that pours through large sash windows on to big, white firm beds. Gripes? The muted, business-friendly decor in the rooms is a bit of a let-down after

CONSUME

**INSIDE TRACK
UPSTAIRS, DOWNSTAIRS**

Thanks to Britain's class system, it's easy to find the biggest rooms in almost every renovated townhouse hotel. The rule is simple: servants' quarters were at the top of the house, so those rooms have lower ceilings than the rooms for the family. Opt for the first floor if possible.

---

the dark and sultry foyer. There's lovely, smiley service downstairs in the lovely basement brasserie, and the first half-hour of internet usage is free.
Bars/cafés (2). Disabled-adapted rooms. Gym. Internet: wireless (£10/day). Parking: £20/day. Restaurant. Room service. TV.

★ Rookery

12 Peter's Lane, Cowcross Street, EC1M 6DS (7336 0931, www.rookeryhotel.com). Farringdon tube/rail. **Rates** *£253 double.* **Rooms** 33. **Credit** AmEx, DC, MC, V. **Map** p400 O5 ❽
Sister hotel to Hazlitt's (*see p191*), the Rookery has long been something of a celebrity hideaway deep in Clerkenwell. Its front door is satisfyingly hard to find, especially when the streets around are teeming with Fabric (*see p329*) devotees; the front rooms can be noisy on these nights, but the place is otherwise as creakily calm as a country manor house. Once inside, guests enjoy an atmospheric warren of rooms, each individually decorated in the style of a Georgian townhouse: huge clawfoot baths, elegant four-posters, brass shower fittings. There's an honesty bar in the bright and airy drawing room at the back, which opens on to a sweet little patio. The ground-floor suite has its own hallway, a cosy boudoir and a subterranean bathroom. Topping it all is the huge split-level Rook's Nest suite, which has views of St Paul's Cathedral (*see p87*).
Bar/café. Concierge. Internet: wireless (free). Room service. TV: DVD.

★ Zetter

86-88 Clerkenwell Road, EC1M 5RJ (7324 4444, www.thezetter.com). Farringdon tube/rail. **Rates** *£180-£423 double.* **Rooms** 59. **Credit** AmEx, MC, V. **Map** p400 O4 ❾
Zetter is a fun, laid-back, modern hotel with some interesting design notes. There's a refreshing lack of attitude and a forward-looking approach, with friendly staff and firm eco-credentials (such as occupancy detection systems in the bedrooms, which switch the lights off when you're not in). The rooms, stacked up on five galleried storeys around an impressive atrium, look into an intimate and recently refreshed bar area. They are smoothly functional, but cosied up with choice home comforts like hot-water bottles and old Penguin paperbacks, as well as

having walk-in showers with Elemis smellies. The arrival in 2010 of the superlative Bistrot Bruno Loubet (*see p212*) and plans to open Zetter Townhouse in a historic building just across the square in early 2011 should widen the place's appeal.
Bar/café. Concierge. Conference facilities. Disabled-adapted rooms. Internet: wireless (free). Restaurant. Room service. TV: DVD.

Moderate

★ Fox & Anchor

115 Charterhouse Street, EC1M 6AA (0845 347 0100, www.foxandanchor.com). Barbican tube or Farringdon tube/rail. **Rates** *£112-£280 double.* **Rooms** 6. **Credit** AmEx, DC, MC, V. **Map** p400 ❿
Check in at the handsome attached boozer (*see p236*) and you'll be pointed to the separate front entrance, with its lovely floor mosaic, and a handful of well-appointed, atmospheric and surprisingly luxurious rooms. Each of them is different, but the high-spec facilities (big flatscreen TV, clawfoot bath and drench shower) and quirky attention to detail (bottles of ale in the minibar, the 'Nursing hangover' signs to hang out for privacy) are common throughout. Expect some clanking noise in the early mornings, but proximity to the historic Smithfield meat market also means you get a feisty fry-up in the morning in the pub.
Bar/café. Internet: high-speed (free). Restaurant. TV: DVD.

BLOOMSBURY & FITZROVIA
Deluxe

★ Charlotte Street Hotel

15-17 Charlotte Street, W1T 1RJ (7806 2000, www.firmdale.com). Goodge Street or Tottenham Court Road tube. **Rates** *£230-£255 double.* **Rooms** 52. **Credit** AmEx, DC, MC, V. **Map** p397 K5 ⓫
Now a fine exponent of Kit Kemp's much imitated fusion of flowery English and avant-garde, this gorgeous hotel was once a dental hospital. Public rooms have genuine Bloomsbury Set paintings, by the likes of Duncan Grant and Vanessa Bell, while bedrooms mix English understatement with bold flourishes: soft beiges and greys spiced up with plaid-floral combinations. The huge, comfortable beds and trademark polished granite and oak bathrooms are suitably indulgent, and some rooms have unbelievably high ceilings. The Oscar restaurant and bar are classy and busy with a smart crowd of media and ad people. On Sundays, combine a three-course set meal with a classic film screened in the mini-cinema.
Bar/café. Concierge. Disabled-adapted rooms. Gym. Internet: wireless & high-speed (£20/day). Restaurant. Room service. Smoking rooms. TV: DVD.

Sanderson

50 Berners Street, W1T 3NG (7300 1400,
www.morganshotelgroup.com). Oxford Circus
tube. **Rates** £235-£470 double. **Rooms** 150.
Credit AmEx, DC, MC, V. **Map** p416 V1 **12**
No designer flash in the pan, the Sanderson remains
a statement hotel, a Schrager/Starck creation that
takes clinical chic in the bedrooms to new heights.
Colour is generally conspicuous by its absence from
many of the rooms. The design throughout is all
flowing white net drapes, gleaming glass cabinets
and retractable screens. The residents-only Purple
Bar sports a button-backed purple leather ceiling
and fabulous cocktails; in particular, try the Vesper.
The 'billiard room' has a purple-topped pool table,
surrounded by strange tribal adaptations of classic
dining room furniture.
Bars/cafés (2). Business centre. Concierge.
Disabled-adapted rooms. Gym. Internet: wireless
& high-speed (£10/day). Parking: £45/day.
Restaurant. Room service. Spa facilities. TV: DVD.

Expensive

Myhotel Bloomsbury (11-13 Bayley Street,
WC1B 3HD, 7667 6000, www.myhotels.co.uk) is
a grown-up, urban brother to Myhotel Chelsea
(*see p200*), giving the trademark Asian touches
a masculine, minimalist twist.

Sanderson.

Academy Hotel

21 Gower Street, WC1E 6HG (7631 4115,
www.theetoncollection.com). Goodge Street tube.
Rates £230-£345 double. **Rooms** 49. **Credit**
AmEx, DC, MC, V. **Map** p397 K5 **13**
One of a family of seven glamorous hotels in the Eton
Collection – *see p185* Threadneedles and *p202*
Academy for its other London establishments – the
Academy goes for the country intellectual look to suit
Bloomsbury's studious yet decadent history. It's
made up of five Georgian townhouses, and provides
in all its rooms a tranquil generosity of space that's
echoed in the Georgian squares sitting serenely
between the arterial traffic rush of Gower Street and
Tottenham Court Road. There's a restrained country-
house style in the summery florals and checks and a
breath of sophistication in the handsome, more
plainly furnished suites. The library and conservatory open on to fragrant walled gardens where drinks
and breakfast are served in summer.
Bar/café. Internet: wireless & high-speed
(£15/day). Restaurant. Room service. TV.

Moderate

Harlingford Hotel

61-63 Cartwright Gardens, WC1H 9EL (7387
1551, www.harlingfordhotel.com). Russell Square
tube or Euston tube/rail. **Rates** £112-£120
double. **Rooms** 40. **Credit** AmEx, MC, V.
Map p397 L4 **14**
An affordable hotel with bundles of charm in the
heart of Bloomsbury, the perkily styled Harlingford
has light airy rooms with evident boutique aspirations. The decor is lifted from understated sleek to
quirky with the help of vibrant colour splashes from
coloured glass bathroom fittings and mosaic tiles –
a gentle refurb has sought to bring in something of
a Scandinavian feel. The crescent it's set in has a
lovely and leafy private garden where you can lob
a tennis ball about or just dream under the trees on
a summer's night.
Internet: wireless (free). TV.

Morgan

24 Bloomsbury Street, WC1B 3QJ (7636 3735,
www.morganhotel.co.uk). Tottenham Court Road
tube. **Rates** £115 double. **Rooms** 21. **Credit**
MC, V. **Map** p397 K5 **15**
This brilliantly located, comfortable budget hotel in
Bloomsbury looks better than it has for a while after
some recent renovations. The rooms have ditched
their previous floral decorations in favour of neutrals. The rooms are well equipped and all are geared
up for the electronic age with wireless, voicemail,
flatscreen tellies with freeview and air-conditioning.
A good, slap-up English breakfast is served in a
good-looking room with wood panelling, London
prints and blue and white china plates. The spacious
flats are excellent value.
Internet: wireless (free). TV.

CONSUME

Rough Luxe

1 Birkenhead Street, WC1H 8BA (7837 5338, www.roughluxe.co.uk). King's Cross tube/rail. **Rates** £177-£285 double. **Rooms** 9. **Credit** AmEx, MC, V. **Map** p397 L3

The latest in hotel design chic is – in the owners' words – Rough Luxe. In a bit of King's Cross that's choked with ratty B&Bs and cheap chains, this Grade II-listed property has walls artfully distressed, torn wallpaper, signature works of art, old-fashioned TVs that barely work and even retains the sign for the hotel that preceded Rough Luxe: 'Number One Hotel'. Each room has free wireless internet, but otherwise have totally different characters: there's the one with the free-standing copper tub, the one with the rose motif and so on. The set-up is flexible too: rooms with shared bathrooms can be combined for group bookings, and the owners are more than happy to chat over a bottle of wine in the back courtyard where a great breakfast is served. *Internet: wireless (free).*

Budget

Clink78

78 King's Cross Road, WC1X 9QG (7183 9400, www.clinkhostels.com). King's Cross tube/rail. **Rates** £40-£50 double; £9-£10 bed. **Beds** 717. **Credit** MC, V. **Map** p397 M3

Located in a listed courthouse, the Clink set the bar high for party-style hosteldom when it opened a few years back. There was the setting: the hostel retains the superb original wood-panelled lobby and courtroom where the Clash once stood before the beak. Then there's the urban chic ethos that permeates the

whole enterprise, from the streamlined red reception counter to the Japanese-style 'pod' beds. By the time this guide hits the shelves, a thorough redesign of the public areas and licensed bar downstairs should give things a new rock 'n' roll fillip, with street-art decor and more comfortable furniture to enhance the place's good-time vibe. Clink261 – a rebrand of the nearby Ashlee House, which has had its public areas pepped up in 2010 – might be a better choice for older and calmer hostellers.

Bar/café. Internet: shared terminal (£3/hr). TV. **Other locations** Clink261, 261-265 Gray's Inn Road, Bloomsbury, WC1X 8QT (7833 9400, www.clinkhostels.co.uk).

Jenkins Hotel

45 Cartwright Gardens, WC1H 9EH (7387 2067, www.jenkinshotel.demon.co.uk). Russell Square tube or Euston tube/rail. **Rates** £95 double. **Rooms** 12. **Credit** MC, V. **Map** p397 K3

This well-to-do Georgian beauty has been a hotel since the 1920s. It still has an atmospheric, antique air, although the rooms have mod cons enough – TVs, mini-fridges, tea and coffee. Its looks have earned it a role in *Agatha Christie's Poirot*, but it's not chintzy, just quite floral in the bedspread and curtain department. The breakfast room is handsome, with snowy cotton tablecloths and Windsor chairs. *Internet: wireless (free). TV.*

YHA London Central

104 Bolsover Street, Fitzrovia, W1W 5NU (0845 371 9154, www.yha.org.uk). Great Portland Street tube. **Rates** from £20 adult. **Beds** 294. **Credit** MC, V. **Map** p396 J5

Covent Garden Hotel.

CONSUME

Come and St John the Fun

The hipsters are salivating over pioneer restaurant St John's first hotel.

St John restaurant (*see p213*) has led a revolution in modern British cooking, with chef Fergus Henderson's (*pictured, right*) concept of 'nose-to-tail eating' – bringing back to the table simple preparations of flavour-packed cuts of meat that had fallen out of favour – now so familiar in London it hardly seems surprising any more. Eyebrows were raised, however, at the announcement that a **St John Hotel** (*see p192*) was opening in the heart of the West End in November 2010. There were happy smiles, too, when co-owner Trevor Gulliver (*pictured, left*) explained it would be 'that rare thing – a hotel where people would actually want to eat'. To which end, the first floor, ground floor and basement are given over to a bar and restaurant; above them, there are 15 rooms and a three-bedroom rooftop suite – the bathroom's round window looks west to Big Ben. On premises well known to a previous generation of Soho theatre-diners – the site used to be Manzi's 'famous seafood restaurant' – the decor is in keeping with the white, masculine, minimalist style of the original Smithfield restaurant, itself converted from a derelict smokehouse.

St John's approach to the hotel trade isn't entirely unprecedented. The template of carefully designed but thoroughly simple rooms that was set by the Soho House hotels (**Dean Street Townhouse**, *see p191*; **Shoreditch Rooms**, *see p205*; **High Road House**, *see p206*) can perhaps be seen in St John Hotel's offhand self-descriptions: 'Mini Grand, Urban Hut' or, in relation to the cheapest 'Post-Supper Rooms', 'These smaller guest rooms remove the need for a taxi home after supper.'

But no one is forgetting that the St John Hotel can add catering credentials to its clubbily jocular take on a room for the night: the bar is confident enough to list just three cocktails (Dry Martini, Negroni, Dr Henderson) and the restaurant serves breakfast, elevenses, lunch, a 'Little Bun Moment' at teatime, and supper, brilliantly, until 2am. St John's foray into hotels may not be another revolution, but it will surely be a massive success.

CONSUME

The Youth Hostel Association's newest hostel is one of its best – as well as being one of the best hostels in London. The friendly and well-informed receptionists are stationed at a counter to the left of the entrance, in a substantial café-bar area. The basement contains a well-equipped kitchen and washing areas; above it, five floors of clean, neatly designed rooms, many en suite. Residents have 24hr access (by individual key cards) and the location is quiet but an easy walk from most of central London.
Bar/café. Internet: wireless (free). TV.

COVENT GARDEN & THE STRAND

Deluxe

★ **Covent Garden Hotel**
10 Monmouth Street, WC2H 9LF (7806 1000, www.firmdale.com). Covent Garden or Leicester Square tube. **Rates** £290-£395 double. **Rooms** 58. **Credit** AmEx, MC, V. **Map** p416 X2 ❷⓿

The location and tucked-away screening room of this Firmdale hotel ensure it continues to attract starry customers, with anyone needing a bit of privacy able to retreat upstairs to the lovely panelled private library and drawing room. In the guestrooms, Kit Kemp's distinctive style mixes pinstriped wallpaper, pristine white quilts, floral upholstery with bold, contemporary elements; each room is unique, but each has the Kemp trademark upholstered mannequin and granite and oak bathroom. On the ground floor, the 1920s Paris-style Brasserie Max and its retro zinc bar retain their buzz – outdoor tables give a perfect viewpoint on Covent Garden boutique life in summer.
Bar/café. Concierge. Gym. Internet: wireless & high-speed (£20/day). Parking: £37/day. Restaurant. Room service. Smoking rooms. TV: DVD.

One Aldwych
1 Aldwych, WC2B 4RH (7300 1000, www.onealdwych.com). Covent Garden or

Montagu Place. *See p192.*

Temple tube, or Charing Cross tube/rail. **Rates** £235-£395 double. **Rooms** 105. **Credit** AmEx, DC, MC, V. **Map** p416 Z3 ㉑

You only have to push through the front door and enter the breathtaking Lobby Bar to know that you're in for a treat. Despite the building's weighty history – the 1907 building was once the offices of the *Morning Post* – One Aldwych is a thoroughly modern place, with Frette linen, bathroom mini-TVs and an environmentally friendly loo-flushing system. Flowers and fruit are replenished daily and a card with the next day's weather forecast appears at turndown. The location is perfect for the West End theatres and has become a popular with attendees of London Fashion Week (*see p283*), particularly since many of the events are now held nearby in Somerset House. The three round corner suites are very romantic, and a cosy screening room, excellent spa and a downstairs swimming pool where soothing opera is played may dissuade you from ever stepping outside.

Bar/café. Concierge. Disabled-adapted rooms. Gym. Internet: wireless (free), high-speed

(£15.50/day). Parking: £45/day. Pool: indoor. Restaurants (2). Room service. Spa facilities. TV: DVD & pay movies.

St Martins Lane Hotel

45 St Martin's Lane, WC2N 4HX (7300 5500, www.morganshotelgroup.com). Leicester Square tube or Charing Cross tube/rail. **Rates** £230-£450 double. **Rooms** 204. **Credit** AmEx, DC, MC, V. **Map** p416 X4 ㉒

When it opened a decade ago, the St Martins was the toast of the town. The flamboyant, theatrical lobby was constantly buzzing, and guests giggled like schoolgirls at Philippe Starck's playful decor. The Starck objects – such as the giant chess pieces and gold tooth stools in the lobby – remain, but the space, part of the Morgans Hotel Group, lacks the impact of its heyday. There's still much to be impressed by: the all-white bedrooms have comfortable minimalism down to a T, with floor-to-ceiling windows, gadgetry secreted in sculptural cabinets and sleek limestone bathrooms with toiletries from the spa at sister property Sanderson (*see p187*).

Bar/café. Business centre. Concierge. Disabled-adapted rooms. Gym. Internet: high-speed (£10/day). Parking: £45/day. Restaurant. Room service. TV: DVD & pay movies.

★ Savoy
Strand, WC2R 0EU (7836 4343, www.fairmont.com). Covent Garden or Embankment tube, or Charing Cross tube/rail. **Rates** £435-£1,550 double. **Rooms** 268. **Credit** AmEx, DC, MC, V. **Map** p416 Z4 ㉓

The superluxe, Grade II-listed Savoy reopened after more than £100m of renovations in October 2010 – the numerous delays testimony to the difficulty of bringing a listed building, loved by generations of visitors for its discreet mix of Edwardian neo-classical and art deco, up to scratch as a modern luxury hotel. Built in 1889 to put up theatregoers from Richard D'Oyly Carte's Gilbert & Sullivan shows, the Savoy is the hotel from which Monet painted the Thames, where Vivien Leigh met Laurence Olivier, where Londoners learned to love the martini. The famous cul-de-sac at the front entrance now has a garden of new topiary and centrepiece Lalique crystal fountain, but the welcome begins before you arrive with a phone call to ascertain your particular requirements. There's a new tearoom with glass-roofed conservatory; the leather counter of the new Beaufort champagne bar is set on a stage that once hosted big bands for dinner dances; and the Savoy Grill is again under the control of Gordon Ramsay's company. Traditionalists can relax: the American Bar remains unchanged.
Bars (3). Concierge. Disabled-adapted rooms. Gym. Internet (dataport/wireless). Pool (indoor). Restaurants (3). Room service. Spa facilities. TV (pay movies/DVD).

SOHO & LEICESTER SQUARE
Deluxe

Soho Hotel
4 Richmond Mews, W1D 3DH (7559 3000, www.firmdale.com). Tottenham Court Road tube. **Rates** £290-£460 double. **Rooms** 91. **Credit** AmEx, DC, MC, V. **Map** p416 W2 ㉔

You'd hardly know you were in the heart of Soho once you're inside Firmdale's edgiest hotel: the place is wonderfully quiet, with what was once a car park now feeling like a converted loft building. The big bedrooms exhibit a contemporary edge, with modern furniture, industrial-style windows and nicely planned mod cons (digital radios as well as flatscreen TVs), although they're also classically Kit Kemp with bold stripes, traditional florals, plump sofas, over-sized bedheads and upholstered tailor's dummies. The quiet drawing room and other public spaces feature groovy colours – shocking pinks, acid greens – while Refuel, the loungey bar and restaurant, has an open kitchen and, yes, a car-themed mural.

Bar/café. Concierge. Gym. Internet: wireless & high-speed (£20/day). Parking: £44/day. Restaurant. Room service. Smoking rooms. Spa facilities. TV: DVD.

Expensive

★ Dean Street Townhouse & Dining Room
69-71 Dean Street, W1D 3SE (7434 1775, www.sohohouse.com). Leicester Square or Piccadilly Circus tube. **Rates** £90-£370 double. **Rooms** 39. **Credit** AmEx, MC, V. **Map** p416 W3 ㉕

This Grade II-listed, 1730s townhouse has been converted into another winning enterprise from the people behind Soho House members' club, **Shoreditch Rooms** (*see p205*) and **High Road House** (*see p206*). To one side of a buzzy ground-floor restaurant are four floors of bedrooms that run from full-size rooms with early Georgian panelling and reclaimed oak floors to half-panelled 'Tiny' rooms that are barely bigger than their double beds – but can be had from the website for as little as £95. The atmosphere is gentleman's club cosy (there are cookies in a cute silver Treats container in each room), but modern types also get rainforest showers, 24hr room service, Roberts DAB radios, free wireless internet and big flatscreen TVs. Even the calm little library room behind reception manages to be both low-key and luxurious.
Bar/café. Disabled-adapted rooms. Internet: wireless (free). Restaurant. Room service. TV: DVD.

★ Hazlitt's
6 Frith Street, W1D 3JA (7434 1771, www.hazlittshotel.com). Tottenham Court Road tube. **Rates** £169-£259 double. **Rooms** 30. **Credit** AmEx, DC, MC, V. **Map** p416 W2 ㉖

Four Georgian townhouses comprise this absolutely charming place, named after William Hazlitt, the spirited 18th-century essayist who died here in abject poverty. With flamboyance and staggering attention to detail the rooms evoke the Georgian era, all heavy fabrics, fireplaces, free-standing tubs and exquisitely carved half-testers, yet modern luxuries – air-conditioning, TVs in antique cupboards and triple-glazed windows – have been subtly attended to as well. It gets creakier and more crooked the

> ### INSIDE TRACK
> ### BUYER BEWARE!
> Many high-end hotels charge extra for services that some travellers assume will be free, most commonly internet access and breakfast. Always check in advance if you're blowing the budget for a treat.

CONSUME

higher you go, culminating in enchanting garret single rooms with rooftop views. Of seven new bedrooms, the main suite is a real knock-out: split-level, with a huge eagle spouting water into the raised bedroom bath and a rooftop terrace with sliding roof, it's a joyous extravaganza. Entertainingly, from the back alley outside, the extension has been made to look like 1700s shopfronts.

Bar/café. Concierge. Conference facilities. Internet: wireless & high-speed (free). Room service. Smoking rooms. TV: DVD.

★ St John Hotel

1 Leicester Street, off Leicester Square, WC2H 7BL (7251 0848, www.stjohnhotellondon.com). Leicester Square or Piccadilly Circus tube. **Rates** from £200 double. **Rooms** 16. **Credit** AmEx, DC, MC, V. **Map** p416 W4 ㉗

When one of London's finest restaurants decides to move into the hotel trade, it's well worth taking notice. *See p189* **Come and St John the Fun**.

Bar. Concierge. Disabled-adapted room. Internet: broadband, high-speed. Restaurant. Room service. TV: DVD/movies.

OXFORD STREET & MARYLEBONE

Expensive

Cumberland

Great Cumberland Place, off Oxford Street, W1H 7DL (0871 376 9014, www.guoman.com). Marble Arch tube. **Rates** £160-£363 double. **Rooms** 1,019. **Credit** AmEx, DC, MC, V. **Map** p393 F6 ㉘

Perfectly located by Marble Arch tube (turn the right way and you're there in seconds), the Cumberland is a bit of a monster: in addition to the 900 rooms in the main block, there are another 119 in an annexe down the road. The echoing, rather chaotic lobby has some dramatic modern art and sculptures, as well as an impressive but somewhat severe waterfall. The rooms are minimalist, with acid-etched headboards, neatly modern bathrooms and plasma TVs – nicely designed, but rather small. The hotel's excellent dining room is the exclusive Rhodes W1, but there are also a bar-brasserie and boisterous, trash-industrial style, late-night DJ bar. Weekend breakfasts can feel like feeding the 5,000.

Bars/cafés (3). Concierge. Gym. Internet: wireless & high-speed (£15/day). Restaurants (3). Room service. TV: pay movies.

Montagu Place

2 Montagu Place, W1H 2ER (7467 2777, www.montagu-place.co.uk). Baker Street tube. **Rates** £200-£260 double. **Rooms** 16. **Credit** AmEx, DC, MC, V. **Map** p396 G5 ㉙

A small, fashionable townhouse hotel, Montagu Place fills a couple of Grade II-listed Georgian residences with sharply appointed rooms graded according to size. The big ones are entitled Swanky, and have king-size beds and big bathrooms – some have narrow front terraces. More modest in size, the Comfy category has queen-size beds and, being at the back of the building, no street views. All rooms have a cool and trendy look, with cafetières and ground coffee instead of Nescafé sachets, as well as flatscreen TVs (DVD players are available from reception). The decision to combine bar and reception desk (situated at the back of the house) means you can get a drink at any time and retire to the graciously modern lounge. Service is at once sharp and very obliging. *Photos p190.*

Bar/café. Internet: wireless & high-speed (free). Room service. TV: DVD.

Moderate

Sumner

54 Upper Berkeley Street, W1H 7QR (7723 2244, www.thesumner.com). Marble Arch tube. **Rates** (incl breakfast) £150-£200 double. **Rooms** 19. **Credit** AmEx, DC, MC, V. **Map** p393 F6 ㉚

The Sumner's cool, deluxe looks have earned it many fans, not least in the hospitality industry – the hotel won gold in Visit London's Best Small Hotel Awards in 2008, and had already scooped best London B&B of the Year from the AA. You won't be at all surprised when you get here: from the soft dove and slatey greys of the lounge and halls you move up to glossily spacious accommodation with brilliant walk-in showers. The breakfast room feels soft and sunny, with a lovely, delicate buttercup motif and vibrant Arne Jacobsen chairs to cheer you on your way to the museums, but the stylishly moody front sitting room is also a cosy gem.

Concierge. Internet: wireless (free). TV.

22 York Street

22 York Street, W1U 6PX (7224 2990, www.22yorkstreet.co.uk). Baker Street tube. **Rates** £100-£120 double. **Rooms** 10. **Credit** AmEx, MC, V. **Map** p396 G5 ㉛

Bohemian French chic – white furniture, palest pink lime-washed walls, mellow wooden floors, subtly faded textiles and arresting *objets d'époque* – makes this delightfully unpretentious bed and breakfast in the heart of Marylebone a sight to behold. It doesn't announce itself from the outside, so you feel as if you've been invited to stay in someone's arty home, especially when you're drinking good coffee at the gorgeous curved table that dominates the breakfast room-cum-kitchen. Guests are also given free rein with the hot beverages in a lounge full of knick-knacks upstairs, while a cluttered smaller room downstairs has an internet station for those without wireless. All rooms are a decent size and have en suite baths, a rarity at this price and in this part of town, but some are rather eccentrically arranged.

Bar/café. Internet: wireless (free). TV.

Stylotel. *See p195.*

PADDINGTON & NOTTING HILL
Deluxe

Hempel
31-35 Craven Hill Gardens, W2 3EA (7298 9000, www.the-hempel.co.uk). Lancaster Gate or Queensway tube or Paddington tube/rail. **Rates** £179-£599 double. **Rooms** 50. **Credit** AmEx, DC, MC, V. **Map** p392 C6 ⓮

Since the mid 1990s, the serried white stucco façades of Craven Hill Gardens, a quiet backwater square in Bayswater, have concealed a dramatic alternative universe dreamed up by Anouska Hempel. The vision still works. Though no longer under her ownership, this boutique hotel started a minimalist design revolution. H is the logo and clinical the look: the coffee tables sunk into the polished stone floor of the lobby; the empty expanses of magnolia paint on the walls; the green plastic turf in the 'Zen-like' garden. The rooms are all different, but defiantly black and white, and minimal to the point of barely furnished. The upstairs restaurant serves a menu of European and Japanese fish dishes.
Bar/café. Concierge. Disabled-adapted rooms. Internet: wireless (free). Restaurant. Room service. TV: DVD & pay movies.

Expensive

Portobello Hotel
22 Stanley Gardens, W11 2NG (7727 2777, www.portobellohotel.com). Holland Park or Notting Hill Gate tube. **Rates** (incl breakfast) £220-£350 double. **Rooms** 21. **Credit** AmEx, MC, V. **Map** p404 Y5 ⓭

The Portobello is a hotel with approaching half a century of celebrity status, having hosted the likes of Johnny Depp, Kate Moss and Alice Cooper, who used his tub to house a boa constrictor. It remains a pleasingly unpretentious place, with a more civilised demeanour than its legend might suggest. There is now a lift to help rockers who are feeling their age up the five floors, but there's still a 24hr guest-only bar downstairs for those who don't yet feel past it. The rooms are themed – the superb basement Japanese Water Garden, for example, has an elaborate spa bath, its own private grotto and a small private garden – but all are stylishly equipped with a large fan, tall house plants and round-the-clock room service.
Bar/café. Internet: wireless (free). Restaurant. Room service. TV.

Moderate

Guesthouse West
163-165 Westbourne Grove, W11 2RS (7792 9800, www.guesthousewest.com). Notting Hill Gate tube. **Rates** (incl continental breakfast) £140-£195 double. **Rooms** 20. **Credit** AmEx, MC, V. **Map** p404 Z4 ⓮

CONSUME

By doing away with any stuffy formality – and the vagaries of room service (a list of local restaurants and takeaways is provided in lieu) – this modish little number is an affordable treat. It's blessed with affable staff and an owner with an artistic bent. His connections with art galleries in Spain and London furnish the delightfully retro lobby bar's changing exhibitions, and there's added interest in the summer of a flowery terrace out front where you can sit and preen for the Notting Hill set. Food is served in the downstairs bar (it's only licensed to serve booze to outsiders until 11pm, but has a 24hr licence for guests). The minimalist bedrooms – with new queen-sized beds – have enough extras to keep hip young things happy: wireless internet, flatscreen TVs, Molton Brown toiletries.
Bar/café. Concierge. Disabled-adapted rooms. Internet: wireless (free). Restaurant. TV: DVD & pay movies.

Hotel Indigo London Paddington

16 London Street, W2 1HL (7706 4444, www.ichotelsgroup.com). Paddington tube/rail. **Rates** £169-£250 double. **Rooms** 64. **Credit** AmEx, DC, MC, V. **Map** p393 D6 ㉟

The first of four boutique properties planned for London from the people behind Crowne Plaza and Holiday Inn has a relaxed all-day bar-restaurant, sharp-witted and friendly staff, and rooms with all mod cons (excellent walk-in showers rather than baths) – the smaller and cheaper attic rooms have most character. The decor is a bit try-hard: a clinical white foyer gives on to acid-bright striped carpets and wardrobe interiors that are an assault by psychedelic swirl. Photographs of Paddington past and ingenious ceiling strips of sky show how less could have been more. A second Hotel Indigo (142 Minories, EC3N 1LS, 7265 1014) opened in 2010 on the eastern edge of the City.
Bar/café. Disabled-adapted rooms. Internet: wireless (free). Restaurant. Room service. TV: pay movies.

New Linden

59 Leinster Square, W2 4PS (7221 4321, www.newlinden.co.uk). Bayswater tube. **Rates** £95-£149 double. **Rooms** 50. **Credit** AmEx, MC, V. **Map** p392 B6 ㊱

Modern, modish and moderately priced – that's the Mayflower Group for you. This is its Bayswater baby; it chooses to call the area 'trendy Notting Hill' on the website, but that's stretching the bounds of London geography a little far. It looks very cool, however, and it is a fantastically comfortable place to stay. The lobby and lounge are slick and glamorous – there's a beautiful teak arch in the lounge and the rooms are creamily low key with some vibrant, twirly eastern influences. Some of the larger family rooms retain their elaborate period pillars and cornicing. The bathrooms are a symphony in marble; the walk-in showers have deluge heads. There's a pleasant little patio, upstairs at the back, for morning coffee and evening drinks.
Concierge. Internet: wireless (free). TV.

Vancouver Studios

30 Prince's Square, W2 4NJ (7243 1270, www.vancouverstudios.co.uk). Bayswater or Queensway tube. **Rates** £120-£155 double. **Rooms** 48. **Credit** AmEx, DC, MC, V. **Map** p392 B6 ㊲

Step into the hall or comfortably furnished sitting room of this imposing townhouse and it feels like the gracious home of a slightly dotty uncle, with decor in the public spaces comprising colonial swords and historic prints. The studio or apartment accommodation is more modern in tone. Each room has its own style – from cool contemporary lines to a softer, more homely feel – and all are well equipped with kitchen appliances so that guests can do a bit of self-catering, should they wish. Zeus the cat lords it over the building and can show you into the pretty garden with its fountain and heady scent of jasmine – a shady stunner.
Internet: wireless (free). TV: DVD.

Budget

Garden Court Hotel

30-31 Kensington Gardens Square, W2 4BG (7229 2553, www.gardencourthotel.co.uk). Bayswater or Queensway tube. **Rates** (incl breakfast) £78-£119 double. **Rooms** 32. **Credit** MC, V. **Map** p392 B6 ㊳

Once people have discovered the Garden Court, they tend to keep coming back, says Edward Connolly, owner-manager of this long-established hotel, with quiet pride. There aren't many places this close to Hyde Park and Portobello Market that give such excellent value for money and impeccable service. The rooms in this grand Victorian terrace have a bright, modern look and plenty of space, and the lounge, with its wood floor, leather-covered furniture, sprightly floral wallpaper and elegant mantelpiece is a lovely place to linger. As the name suggests, there's a small walled garden, lushly planted, and laden guests might be cheered by the presence of a lift.
Internet: wireless (free). TV.

THE BEST HIGH-CLASS HOTELS

Charlotte Street Hotel
Charming, beautiful, relaxed. *See p186.*

Claridge's
The definition of luxury. *See p196.*

Hazlitt's
For eccentric period drama. *See p191.*

CONSUME

Haymarket Hotel. *See p197.*

Pavilion

34-36 Sussex Gardens, W2 1UL (7262 0905, www.pavilionhoteluk.com). Edgware Road tube, or Marylebone or Paddington tube/rail. **Rates** £85-£100 double. **Rooms** 29. **Credit** MC, V. **Map** p393 E5 ③

A hotel that describes itself as 'fashion rock 'n' roll' is never going to be staid, but Danny and Noshi Karne's Pavilion is quite mind-bogglingly excessive. The rooms have attention-grabbing names, such as 'Enter the Dragon' (Chinese themed), 'Flower Power' (blooming flowery) and 'Cosmic Girl' (way out there, man) and are frequently used for fashion shoots: the website has an impressive list of celebrities who have rocked up here over the years. Bizarre and voluptuous choice of decor notwithstanding, this crazy hotel represents excellent value and has the usual amenities. You might be disappointed if you want cool contemporary elegance and poncey toiletries – the Pavilion's much more fun than that. *Internet: wireless (free). Parking: £10/day. Room service. TV: DVD.*

Stylotel

160-162 Sussex Gardens, W2 1UD (7723 1026, www.stylotel.com). Edgware Road tube, or Marylebone or Paddington tube/rail. **Rates** £90 double. **Rooms** 39. **Credit** AmEx, MC, V. **Map** p393 E6 ⑩

Partly due to the young manager's enthusiasm, it's hard not to like this place. It's a retro-futurist dream: metal floors and panelling, lots of royal blue (the hall walls, the padded headboards) and pod bathrooms. But the real deal at Stylotel is its bargain studio and apartment (respectively, £120-£150 and £150-£200, breakfast £6 extra), around the corner above a pub. Designed – like the rest of the hotel – by the owner's son, they suggest he's calmed down with age. Here's real minimalist chic: sleek brushed steel or white glass wall panels, simply styled contemporary furniture upholstered in black or white. *Photos p193. Concierge. Internet: wireless (£2/hr). Parking: £12/day. Smoking rooms. TV.*

26 Hillgate Place

26 Hillgate Place, W8 7ST (7727 7717, www.26 hillgateplace.co.uk). Notting Hill Gate tube. **Rates** £80-£105 double. **Rooms** 2. **No credit cards. Map** p404 Y6 ④

Artist Hilary Dunne has furnished her B&B with paintings of glossy-skinned, doe-eyed women inspired by her travels in the West Indies, as well as the spoils from her former life as a textiles importer. The ground-floor room with its large en suite bathroom contains some of the Caribbean collection; the smaller, more colourful second room, with shared bathroom, is bright with wall hangings and cushions from India. The overall effect is of a much-loved, warm and lived-in family home. Breakfast is taken in a busy little space next to the galley kitchen, with French windows opening on to a tiny, ivy-clad courtyard. A slightly larger patio upstairs, home to Hilary's extensive plant collection, looks out over the gardens of Hillgate Place. *Internet: wireless (free). TV.*

PICCADILLY CIRCUS & MAYFAIR

Deluxe

Brown's

Albemarle Street, W1S 4BP (7493 6020, www. roccofortecollection.com). Green Park tube. **Rates** *£327-£587 double.* **Rooms** 117. **Credit** AmEx, DC, MC, V. **Map** p416 U4 ⓐ

Brown's was opened in 1837 by James Brown, butler to Romantic poet, hedonist and freedom-fighter Lord Byron. The first British telephone call was made from here in 1876, five years after Napoleon III and Empress Eugenie took refuge in one of the considerable suites after fleeing the Third Republic. Ethiopian Emperor Haile Selassie and Rudyard Kipling were also guests. The bedrooms are all large and extremely comfortable, furnished with original art, collections of books and, in the suites, fireplaces; the elegant, classic British hotel restaurant, the Albemarle (*see p219*), gives a nod to modernity with a series of contemporary British artworks, including pieces by the likes of Tracey Emin, but the public spaces of the hotel thrum with history. Non-residents can visit: try the £37 afternoon tea in the English Tea Room or sip a cocktail in the classily masculine Donovan Bar.

Bar/café. Business centre. Concierge. Disabled-adapted rooms. Gym. Internet: wireless (free), high-speed (£15/day). Restaurant. Room service. Spa facilities. TV: pay movies.

★ Claridge's

55 Brook Street, W1K 4HR (7629 8860, www.claridges.co.uk). Bond Street tube. **Rates** *£289-£690 double.* **Rooms** 202. **Credit** AmEx, DC, MC, V. **Map** p396 H6 ⓐ

Claridge's is sheer class and pure atmosphere, with its signature art deco redesign still simply dazzling. Photographs of Churchill and sundry royals grace the grand foyer, as does an absurdly over-the-top Dale Chihuly chandelier. Without departing too far from the traditional, Claridge's bars and restaurant are actively fashionable – Gordon Ramsay is the in-house restaurateur, and the A-listers can gather for champers and sashimi in the bar. The rooms divide evenly between deco and Victorian style, with period touches such as deco toilet flushes in the swanky marble bathrooms. Bedside panels control the mod-con facilities at the touch of a button. If money's no object, opt for a David Linley suite, done out in gorgeous duck-egg blue and white, or lilac and silver. *Bars/cafés (2). Business centre. Concierge. Disabled-adapted rooms. Gym. Internet: wireless (free). Restaurants (2). Room service. Smoking rooms. Spa facilities. TV: DVD & pay movies.*

★ Connaught

Carlos Place, W1K 2AL (7499 7070, www.the-connaught.co.uk). Bond Street tube. **Rates** £490-£650 double. **Rooms** 119. **Credit** AmEx, DC, MC, V. **Map** p398 H7 ⓐ

This isn't the only hotel in London to provide butlers, but there can't be many that offer 'a secured

Lux Pod. *See p202.*

CONSUME

gun cabinet room' for hunting season. This is traditional British hospitality for those who love 23-carat gold leaf trimmings and stern portraits in the halls, but all mod cons in their room, down to flatscreens in the en suite. Too lazy to polish your own shoes? The butlers are trained in shoe care by the expert cobblers at John Lobb. Both of the bars – gentleman's club cosy Coburg and cruiseship deco Connaught (*see p241*) – and the Hélène Darroze restaurant are very impressive. In the new wing, which doubled the number of guestrooms, there's a swanky spa and 60sq m swimming pool.
Bars/cafés (2). Concierge. Disabled-adapted rooms. Gym. Internet: wireless (free). Pool: indoor. Restaurants (2). Room service. Smoking rooms. Spa facilities. TV: DVD.

★ Dorchester
53 Park Lane, W1K 1QA (7629 8888, www.the dorchester.com). Hyde Park Corner tube. **Rates** £280-£600 double. **Rooms** 250. **Credit** AmEx, DC, MC, V. **Map** p398 G7 ⑮
A Park Lane fixture since 1931, the Dorchester's interior may be thoroughly, opulently classical, but the hotel is cutting edge in attitude, providing an unrivalled level of personal service. With the grandest lobby in town, amazing views of Hyde Park, state-of-the-art mod cons and a magnificently refurbished (to the tune of £3.2m) spa, it's small wonder the hotel continues to welcome movie stars (its lineage stretches from Elizabeth Taylor to Tom Cruise) and political leaders (Eisenhower planned the D-Day landings here). You're not likely to be eating out, either: the Dorchester employs 90 full-time chefs at the Grill Room, Alain Ducasse and the wonderfully atmospheric China Tang. There's even an angelic tearoom in the new spa: the Spatisserie. The Dorchester is due to open an entirely new hotel, 45 Park Lane (www.45parklane.com), early in 2011 in the former Playboy club premises, almost opposite the entrance to its predecessor.
Bar/café. Concierge. Disabled-adapted rooms. Gym. Internet: wireless & high-speed (£19.50/ day). Parking: £50/day. Restaurants (5). Room service. Smoking rooms. Spa facilities. TV: DVD & pay movies.

★ Haymarket Hotel
1 Suffolk Place, SW1Y 4BP (7470 4000, www. firmdale.com). Piccadilly Circus tube. **Rates** £250-£330 double. **Rooms** 50. **Credit** AmEx, DC, MC, V. **Map** p416 W5 ⑯
A terrific addition to Kit Kemp's Firmdale portfolio, this block-size building (a private townhouse within the hotel can be rented) was designed by John Nash, the architect of Regency London. The public spaces are a delight, with Kemp's trademark combination of contemporary arty surprises (a giant light-bulb affair over the library's chessboard, a gothic little paper-cut of layered skulls above the tray of free afternoon canapés) and impossible-to-leave, bright, plump, flo-

ral sofas. Wow-factors include the surprisingly bling basement swimming pool and bar (shiny sofas, twinkly roof) and the couldn't-be-more central location. Rooms are generously sized (as are bathrooms), individually decorated and discreetly stuffed with facilities, and there's plenty of attention from the switched-on staff. The street-side bar and restaurant are top-notch, the breakfast exquisite. *Photos p195.*
Bar/café. Concierge. Disabled-adapted rooms. Gym. Internet: wireless (£20/day). Pool: indoor. Restaurant. Room service. Smoking rooms. Spa facilities. TV: DVD.

Metropolitan
19 Old Park Lane, W1K 1LB (7447 1000, www.metropolitan.como.bz). Hyde Park Corner tube. **Rates** £229-£425 double. **Rooms** 150. **Credit** AmEx, DC, MC, V. **Map** p398 H8 ⑰
The flashier little sister of the Halkin (*see p201*) the Metropolitan may have had its fashion heyday in the 1990s, but it still retains a buzzy, relaxed sense of cool. The Met bar and Nobu restaurant continue to attract celebrities and models, bands like Kings of Leon still rock up, and many mere mortals drop by to rubberneck. The hotel itself is bright and uncluttered. The rooms are a little clinical and appear ever-so-slightly dated, but pear-wood furnishings, super-soft mattresses and suede throws keep things very comfortable, and the Shambhala spa toiletries in the bathrooms are a cut above the usual chuck-away fodder. As well as annual replacement of the carpets and a rolling programme that refurbishes one room each year, £3.5m has recently been spent upgrading the bathrooms. The hotel's greatest asset, however, is the prime location, overlooking a corner of Hyde Park.
Bar/café. Business centre. Concierge. Gym. Internet: wireless, high-speed & shared terminal (free). Parking: £40/day. Restaurant. Room service. Smoking rooms. Spa facilities. TV: DVD & pay movies.

Ritz
150 Piccadilly, W1J 9BR (7493 8181, www. theritzlondon.com). Green Park tube. **Rates** £586-£646 double. **Room** 136. **Credit** AmEx, DC, MC, V. **Map** p398 J8 ⑱

CONSUME

If you like the idea of a world where jeans and trainers are banned and jackets must be worn by gentlemen when dining (the requirement is waived for breakfast), the Ritz is for you. Founded by hotelier extraordinaire César Ritz, the hotel is deluxe *in excelsis*. The show-stopper is the ridiculously ornate, vaulted Long Gallery, an orgy of chandeliers, rococo mirrors and marble columns, but all the high-ceilinged, Louis XVI-style bedrooms have been painstakingly renovated to their former glory in restrained pastel colours. Amid the old-world luxury, mod cons include free wireless in most rooms, large TVs and a gym. An elegant afternoon tea in the Palm Court (book ahead) is the way in for interlopers. *Bar/café. Concierge. Gym. Internet: high-speed (£26/day); wireless (£26/day). Restaurant. Room service. Smoking rooms. Spa facilities. TV: DVD.*

Expensive

No.5 Maddox Street
5 Maddox Street, W1S 2QD (7647 0200, www.living-rooms.co.uk). Oxford Circus tube. **Rates** £270-£410 double. **Rooms** 12. **Credit** AmEx, DC, MC, V. **Map** p416 U2 ⓭
This bolthole just off Regent Street is perfect for visiting film directors looking to be accommodated in a chic apartment at a reasonable long-term rate. Here they can shut the closet brown front door, climb the stairs and flop into a home from home with all contemporary cons, including new flatscreen TVs. The East-meets-West decor is classic 1990s minimalist, but very bright and clean after a gentle refurbishment. Each apartment has a fully equipped kitchen, but room service will shop for you as well as providing usual hotel amenities. There's no bar, but breakfasts and snacks are served, and there's a Thai restaurant (Patara) on the ground floor. *Concierge. Internet: wireless & high-speed (£15/day, £60/wk). Room service. TV: DVD.*

WESTMINSTER & ST JAMES'S
Deluxe

Royal Horseguards
2 Whitehall Court, SW1A 2EJ (0871 376 9033, www.guoman.com). Embankment tube or Charing Cross tube/rail. **Rates** £360-£400. **Rooms** 281. **Credit** AmEx, MC, V. **Map** p399 L8 ⓮
The Royal Horseguards occupies a French château discreetly located off Whitehall. The building was designed by Alfred 'Natural History Museum' Waterhouse for the National Liberal Club in 1887, and club founder, William Gladstone, great reformer that he was, probably would have approved of the recent refurb of the interior by the Guoman group. It's immaculately clean, 'classic but modern' in style, with welcoming staff. The bedrooms have useful dressing tables, iPod docks and wonderfully com-

fortable Hypnos beds, and bathrooms come with flatscreen TV and Elemis products. The buffet-style breakfasts are ordinary, but from the upper floors the river views of County Hall and the London Eye – whisper it – rival those of the Savoy (*see p191*). *Bars/cafés (2). Business centre. Concierge. Disabled-adapted rooms. Gym. Internet: wireless (free). Restaurant. Room service. TV.*

Expensive

City Inn Westminster
30 John Islip Street, SW1P 4DD (7630 1000, www.cityinn.com). Pimlico tube. **Rates** £99-£344. **Rooms** 460. **Credit** AmEx, DC, MC, V. **Map** p399 K10 ⓯
There's nothing flashy about this new-build hotel, but it is well run, neatly designed and obliging: the rooms have all the added extras you'd want (CD/DVD library, broadband, iMac that doubles as a flatscreen TV) and the floor-to-ceiling windows mean that river-facing suites on the 12th and 13th floors have superb night views – when the businessmen go home for the weekend you might grab one for £125. With half an eye on near-neighbour Tate Britain (*see p135*), the owners have collaborated with the Chelsea College of Art to provide changing art through the lobbies and meeting rooms; outside the unconvincing City Café, you can sit on a Ron Arad chair. A new City Inn is due to open near the Tower of London in spring 2011. *Bars/cafés (2). Business centre. Concierge. Disabled-adapted rooms. Gym. Internet: wireless (free). Parking: £30/day. Restaurant. Room service. Smoking rooms. TV: DVD & pay movies.*

Trafalgar
2 Spring Gardens, Trafalgar Square, SW1A 2TS (7870 2900, www.thetrafalgar.com). Charing Cross tube/rail. **Rates** £235-£294 double. **Rooms** 129. **Credit** AmEx, DC, MC, V. **Map** p416 X5 ⓰
The Trafalgar is part of the Hilton chain of hotels, but you'd hardly notice. The mood is young and dynamic at the chain's first 'concept' hotel, for all that it's housed in the imposing edifice that was once headquarters of Cunard (this was where the *Titanic*

INSIDE TRACK ONE OF A KIND

If you want to stay in an 18th-century Spitalfields weaver's house or a Georgian property in Smithfields (next door to where John Betjeman, poet and architectural preservationist, used to live), visit the **Landmark Trust** website (www.landmarktrust.org.uk). The Trust has been restoring notable old buildings as holiday lets since 1965.

40 Winks. See p205.

was conceived). To the right of the open reception is the Rockwell Bar, boisterous at night, although thick walls should prevent sound leaking up to the rooms; breakfast downstairs is accompanied by gentler music, sometimes played live. It's the none-more-central location, however, that's the hotel's biggest draw – the handful of corner suites look directly into the square (prices reflect location). Those without their own view can always avail themselves of the little rooftop bar, which is now open to the public. *Bars/cafés (2). Business centre. Concierge. Disabled-adapted rooms. Gym. Internet: wireless & high-speed (£15/day). Restaurant. Room service. Smoking rooms. TV: DVD & pay movies.*

Moderate

B+B Belgravia
64-66 Ebury Street, SW1W 9QD (7259 8570, www.bb-belgravia.com). Victoria tube/rail. **Rates** (incl breakfast) £125 double. **Rooms** 17. **Credit** AmEx, MC, V. **Map** p398 H10 ⑬
How do you make a lounge full of white and black contemporary furnishings seem cosy and welcoming? Hard to achieve, but the owners have succeeded at B+B Belgravia, which takes the B&B experience to a new level. It's fresh and sophisticated without being hard-edged: there's nothing here that will make the fastidiously design-conscious wince (leather sofa, arty felt cushions, modern fireplace), but nor is it overly precious. A gleaming espresso machine provides 24/7 caffeine, and there's a large but somewhat dark garden to sit out in at the rear.

Disabled-adapted rooms. Internet: wireless (free). TV.

Windermere Hotel
142-144 Warwick Way, SW1V 4JE (7834 5163, www.windermere-hotel.co.uk). Victoria tube/rail. **Rates** (incl breakfast) £119-£144 double. **Rooms** 20. **Credit** AmEx, MC, V. **Map** p398 H11 ㊌
Heading the procession of small hotels that are strung out along Warwick Way, the Windermere is a comfortable, traditionally decked-out London hotel with, thankfully, no aspirations to boutique status. The decor may be showing its age a bit in the hall, but you'll receive a warm welcome and excellent service – there are over a dozen staff for just 20 rooms. There's a cosy basement restaurant-bar, where the breakfasts are top-notch.
Bar/café. Internet: wireless (free). Restaurant. Room service. TV.

Budget

Morgan House
120 Ebury Street, SW1W 9QQ (7730 2384, www.morganhouse.co.uk). Pimlico tube or Victoria tube/rail. **Rates** (incl breakfast) £78-£98 double. **Rooms** 11. **Credit** AmEx, MC, V. **Map** p398 G10 ㊌
The Morgan has the understated charm of the old family home of a posh but unpretentious English friend: a pleasing mix of nice old wooden or traditional iron beds, pretty floral curtains and coverlets

in subtle hues, the odd chandelier or big gilt mirror over original mantelpieces, and padded wicker chairs and sinks in every bedroom. The bedrooms have also benefited from a refurbishment and have better bathrooms and new carpets. Though there's no guest lounge, guests can sit in the little patio garden, and for Belgravia, the prices are a steal. *Internet: wireless (free). TV.*

CHELSEA
Expensive

Myhotel Chelsea
35 Ixworth Place, SW3 3QX (7225 7500, www.myhotels.com). South Kensington tube. **Rates** £148-£290 double. **Rooms** 45. **Credit** AmEx, DC, MC, V. **Map** p395 E11 ⑤⑥
The Chelsea Myhotel feels a world away from its sleekly modern Bloomsbury sister (*see p187*). The Sloane Square branch has an aesthetic that is softer and decidedly more English – with a floral sofa and plate of scones in the lobby, and white wicker headboards, velvet cushions and Bee Kind toiletries in the guestrooms. These feminine touches contrast nicely with the mini-chain's feng shui touches, its Eastern-inspired treatment room, and its sleek aquarium. The modernised country farmhouse feel of the bar-restaurant works better for breakfast than it does for a boozy cocktail, but the central library, that is done out conservatory style, is simply wonderful. Just pick up a book, sink into one of the ample comfy chairs and listen to the tinkling water feature or your own choice of CD.
Bar/café. Business centre. Concierge. Disabled-adapted rooms. Gym. Internet: wireless & high-speed (free). Restaurant. Room service. Spa facilities. TV: DVD.
Other locations 11-13 Bayley Street, Bloomsbury, WC1B 3HD (7667 6000).

San Domenico House
29-31 Draycott Place, SW3 2SH (7581 5757, www.sandomenicohouse.com). Sloane Square tube. **Rates** £235-£360 double. **Rooms** 15. **Credit** AmEx, MC, V. **Map** p395 F11 ⑤⑦
Along a quiet terrace of late 19th-century red-stone buildings just off Sloane Square, San Domenico owes much of its tasteful, historic look to previous owner Sue Rogers, the interior designer who transformed this former private residence into a boutique hotel masterpiece. Each of the four categories of guestroom, including the split-level gallery suites, feature original furnishings or antiques. Royal portraits, Victorian mirrors and Empire-era travelling cases are complemented by fabrics of similar style and taste, offset by contemporary touches to bathrooms. The spacious bedrooms enjoy wide-angle views of London, some from little balconies. Breakfasts are taken up to guests or laid out in the room downstairs, while main meals may be taken in the sumptuous coffee room by the lobby.
Bar/café. Internet: wireless (free). Restaurant. Room service. TV.

CONSUME

Hoxton Hotel. *See p205.*

KNIGHTSBRIDGE & SOUTH KENSINGTON
Deluxe

Blakes
33 Roland Gardens, SW7 3PF (7370 6701, www.blakeshotels.com). South Kensington tube.
Rates £265-£375 double. **Rooms** 48. **Credit** AmEx, DC, MC, V. **Map** p395 D11 ⓾
As original as when Anouska Hempel opened it in 1983 – the scent of oranges and the twittering of a pair of lovebirds fill the dark, oriental lobby – Blakes and its maximalist decor have stood the test of time, a living casebook for interior design students. Each room is in a different style, with influences from Italy, India, Turkey and China. Exotic antiques picked up on the designer's travels – intricately carved beds, Chinese birdcages, ancient trunks – are set off by sweeping drapery and piles of plump cushions. Downstairs, the Eastern-influenced restaurant caters for a celebrity clientele enticed by the hotel's discreet, residential location.
Bar/café. Business centre. Concierge. Internet: wireless & high-speed (£12/day). Parking: £40/day. Restaurant. Room service. TV: DVD & pay movies.

Gore
190 Queen's Gate, SW7 5EX (7584 6601, www.gorehotel.com). South Kensington tube.
Rates £180-£440 double. **Rooms** 50. **Credit** AmEx, MC, V. **Map** p395 D9 ⓾
This fin-de-siècle period piece was founded by descendants of Captain Cook in two grand Victorian townhouses. The lobby and staircase are close hung with old paintings, and the bedrooms all have fantastic 19th-century carved oak beds, sumptuous drapes and shelves of old books. The suites are spectacular: the Tudor Room has a huge stone-faced fireplace and a minstrels' gallery, while tragedy queens should plump for the Venus room and Judy Garland's old bed (and replica ruby slippers). Bistrot 190 provides a casually elegant setting for great breakfasts, while the warm, wood-panelled 190 bar (*see p244*) is a charming setting for cocktails.
Bar/café. Concierge. Internet: wireless & high-speed (£20/24hrs). Restaurant. Room service. TV.

Halkin
Halkin Street, SW1X 7DJ (7333 1000, www.halkin.como.bz). Hyde Park Corner tube.
Rates £450 double. **Rooms** 41. **Credit** AmEx, DC, MC, V. **Map** p398 G9 ⓾
Set up by Singaporean fashion mogul Christina Ong (who also owns the Metropolitan; *see p197*), the Halkin marries Eastern charm, style and food with a central and quiet location in Knightsbridge. The rooms, all located off black curved, almost trompe l'oeil wooden corridors, are comfortable and full of Asian artefacts and clever gadgetry (a touch-screen bedside panel controls everything from the air-con to the 'do not disturb' sign on the door). Bathrooms are well equipped and heavy on the marble, and come stocked with a range of products from Ong's Shambhala spa. The Michelin-starred Thai restaurant Nahm (*see p224*), a gastronomic sensation, is on the ground floor.
Bar/café. Concierge. Disabled-adapted rooms. Gym. Internet: wireless & high-speed (free). Parking: £45/day. Restaurant. Room service. TV: DVD & pay movies.

★ Lanesborough
1 Lanesborough Place, SW1X 7TA (7259 5599, www.lanesborough.com). Hyde Park Corner tube.
Rates £475-£675 double. **Rooms** 95. **Credit** AmEx, DC, MC, V. **Map** p398 G8 ⓾
Considered one of London's more historic luxury hotels, the Lanesborough was in fact redeveloped – impressively – only in 1991. Occupying an 1820s Greek Revival building designed as a hospital by William Wilkins (the man behind the National Gallery; *see p129*), its luxurious guestrooms are traditionally decorated with thick fabrics, antique furniture and lavish Carrera-marble bathrooms. Electronic keypads control everything from the air-conditioning to the superb 24hr room service at the touch of a button. As luxury hotels go, the Lanesborough's rates are unusually inclusive: high-speed internet access, movies and calls within the EU and to the USA are complimentary, as are personalised business cards stating your residence. The Library Bar is excellent.
Bar/café. Business centre. Concierge. Disabled-adapted rooms. Gym. Internet: wireless & high-speed (free). Parking: £40/day. Restaurant. Room service. Spa facilities. TV: DVD & pay movies.

Milestone Hotel & Apartments
1-2 Kensington Court, W8 5DL (7917 1000, www.milestonehotel.com). High Street Kensington tube. **Rates** £280-£322 double. **Rooms** 57. **Credit** AmEx, DC, MC, V. **Map** p392 C8 ⓾
Wealthy American visitors make annual pilgrimages here, their arrival greeted by the comforting, gravel tones of their regular concierge, as English as roast beef, and the glass of sherry in the room. Yet amid old-school luxury (butlers on 24hr call) thrives inventive modernity (the resistance pool in the spa). Rooms overlooking Kensington Gardens feature the inspired decor of South African owner Beatrice Tillman: the Safari suite contains tent-like draperies and leopard-print upholstery; the Tudor Suite has an elaborate inglenook fireplace, minstrels' gallery and a pouffe concealing a pop-up TV.
Bar/café. Business centre. Concierge. Disabled-adapted rooms. Gym. Internet: wireless & high-speed (free). Pool: indoor. Restaurant. Room service. Smoking rooms. Spa facilities. TV: DVD & pay movies.

CONSUME

Expensive

★ Number Sixteen

16 Sumner Place, SW7 3EG (7589 5232,
www.firmdale.com). South Kensington tube.
Rates £205-£280 double. **Rooms** 42. **Credit**
AmEx, DC, MC, V. **Map** p395 D10 ❻❸

This may be Kit Kemp's most affordable hotel but
there's no slacking in style – witness the fresh flowers and origami-ed birdbook decorations in the comfy
drawing room. Bedrooms are generously sized,
bright and very light, and carry the Kemp trademark mix of bold and traditional. The whole place
has an appealing freshness about it, enhanced by a
delicious, large back garden with its central water
feature. By the time you finish breakfast in the city.
Bar/café. Concierge. Internet: wireless & high-
speed (£20/day). Parking: £45/day. Room service.
TV: DVD.

Moderate

Aster House

3 Sumner Place, SW7 3EE (7581 5888,
www.asterhouse.com). South Kensington tube.
Rates (incl breakfast) £135-£225 double.
Rooms 13. **Credit** MC, V. **Map** p395 D11 ❻❹

This swish archetypal white-terraced South
Kensington street is a great setting for a hotel. The
Aster has become an award-winner through attention to detail (like impeccable housekeeping, the
mobile phone guests can borrow, and the introduction of wireless internet and flatscreen TVs) and the
warmth of its managers, Leona and Simon Tan. It's
all low-key, comfortably soothing creams with
touches of dusty rose and muted green. Star of the
show is the plant-filled conservatory that serves as
a breakfast room and guest lounge – star, that is,
after Ollie and Cordelia, the resident ducks.
Internet: wireless & high-speed (free). TV.

★ Lux Pod

38 Gloucester Road, SW7 4QT (7460 3171,
www.theluxpod.com). Gloucester Road tube.
Rates (min three-night stay) £107 double.
Rooms 1. **No credit cards. Map** p394 C9 ❻❺

This marvellously eccentric little hideaway is the
pride and joy of its owner, Judith Abraham, with
many of the features purpose-designed. Little is the
operative word: it's a tiny space that ingeniously
packs in a bathroom, slide-top kitchenette and lounge,
with the comfy bed high up above the bathroom and
accessible only by ladder. All is shiny and modern,
and the room is packed with gadgets (iPod dock with
fine speakers, flatscreen TV, funky cooker hobs and
lighting arrangements, electronic curtains) and high-
style details (leather flooring, hip chairs). The tight
space is ideal for one, a little fiddly to get round for
two, but terrific fun for any design fan. *Photo p196.*
Internet: wireless (free). TV: DVD.

Vicarage Hotel

10 Vicarage Gate, W8 4AG (7229 4030,
www.londonvicaragehotel.com). High Street
Kensington or Notting Hill Gate tube. **Rates**
(incl breakfast) £95-£125 double. **Rooms** 17.
Credit AmEx, MC, V. **Map** p392 B8 ❻❻

Scores of devotees return regularly to this tall
Victorian townhouse, which has a great location,
tucked in a quiet leafy square just off High Street
Ken, hard by Kensington Gardens. It's a comfortable,
resolutely old-fashioned establishment – and that's
what the punters come for. The refurbished entrance
hall is wonderfully grand, with red and gold striped
wallpaper, a huge gilt mirror and chandelier. A
sweeping staircase ascends from there to an assortment of good-sized rooms, furnished in pale florals
and nice old pieces of furniture.
Internet: wireless (free). TV.

NORTH LONDON

Expensive

York & Albany

127-129 Parkway, Camden, NW1 7PS (7387
5700, www.gordonramsay.com). Camden Town
tube. **Rates** £175-£575 double. **Rooms** 9.
Credit AmEx, DC, MC, V. **Map** p404 X3 ❻❼

Overcommitment to TV and transatlantic enterprises might have knocked a little gloss off Gordon
Ramsay's restaurants, but his only hotel is still
going strong. Housed in a grand John Nash building
that was designed as a coaching house but spent the
recent past as a pub, it consists of a restaurant (split
over two levels), bar and delicatessen downstairs;
above them a selection of nine rooms, handsomely
designed by Russell Sage in mellow shades. The
decor is an effective mix of ancient and modern,
sturdy and quietly charismatic furniture married to
modern technology; if you're lucky, you'll have views
of Regent's Park from your bedroom window.
Bar/café. Disabled-adapted rooms. Internet:
wireless (free). Restaurant. Room service.
TV: DVD.

Moderate

Colonnade

2 Warrington Crescent, Little Venice, W9
1ER (7286 1052, www.theetoncollection.com/
colonnade). Warwick Avenue tube. **Rates** £140-
£215 double. **Rooms** 43. **Credit** AmEx, MC, V.
Map p392 C4 ❻❽

Housed in an imposingly sited white mansion, the
Colonnade has been lushly done up in interior-
designer traditional – lots of swagged curtains, deep
opulent colours, luxurious fabrics and careful
arrangements of smoothly upholstered furniture.
Some of the larger high-ceilinged rooms have had
mezzanine floors added. Guests breakfast in a subterranean tapas bar. The bar is beneath a front-of-

CONSUME

The New East

Hotels are boldly going where few have gone before.

For several years, east London seemed to be the province only of boutique hotel pioneers – the four-year-old budget-chic **Hoxton Hotel** (*see p205*), the two-year-old **Boundary** (*see p204*) – and a scattering of budget and, especially around Docklands and the fringes of the City, business chains. But London 2012 seems to be having a rather stimulating effect on creative accommodation in the area.

In 2010 alone, we've seen the arrival of the **Shoreditch Rooms** (*see p205*), which is still in striking distance of the City, and the **Town Hall Hotel & Apartments** (*see p204*), which at first glance isn't in striking distance of much apart from pound shops. In fact, the latter might prove a savvier venture than it seems. The kind of urban culture-vultures who will appreciate its remodelling of a 1909 town hall might well also enjoy exploring the contemporary art galleries on Vyner Street (*see p307* **Wilkinson Gallery**), the craft and homeware shops on Columbia Road Market (*see p255*) at the weekends and the V&A Museum of Childhood (*see p156*), and the area's commercial potential is underlined by the planned redevelopment of the FymFyg Bar comedy club, the other side of Bethnal Green tube station from the Town Hall, as a Travelodge.

Around the Olympic Park (*see p53*) itself, planning permission is being sought for several new hotels. At the luxury end of the market, the Manhattan Loft Corporation has proposed a seven-floor, 150-room hotel, beneath many more floors of apartments, just north-east of Stratford International station. The new Westfield Stratford City mall is developing a project that will include a 188-room Holiday Inn

Shoreditch Rooms.

and 162 Staybridge serviced apartments, which would be built in addition to a 267-room Premier Inn.

Of course, the shift in geographical emphasis from west to east isn't all being driven by London 2012. In Shoreditch, squatters were eventually evicted from arty nightclub the Foundry in 2010, so the site can make way for an 18-storey art'otel, while in central Greenwich the focus of redevelopment will be the Greenwich Market Hotel – both of these hotels are due to open in 2013.

Town Hall Hotel & Apartments.

hotel terrace that makes a good spot for lingering with a glass of wine on warm evenings.
Bar/café. Internet: wireless (free). Parking: £20/day. Restaurant. Room service. TV.

Rose & Crown

199 Stoke Newington Church Street, N16 9ES (7923 3337, www.roseandcrownn16.co.uk). Bus 73. **Rates** (incl breakfast) £120-£175 double. **Rooms** 6. **Credit** AmEx, MC, V.

The Rose has always been popular as a pub, but now a separate entrance leads to a contemporary B&B. Landscape gardener Will, who with Diane runs the place, transformed three floors to create individually and tastefully styled guestrooms (drench showers, quality smellies and furnishings), a breakfast room and a sun-catching roof terrace with a large table, a couple of loungers, a patio heater and a view across to central London from the illuminated glow of 13th-century St Mary's Church alongside. Pricier rooms feature a stand-alone bathtub, and the suite by the breakfast room is vast. Truman Brewery touches from yesteryear remain: the pub sign lettering, a finely carved pre-war stair rail and the Mystery Arrow games machine.
Internet: wireless (free). TV.

Budget

Hampstead Village Guesthouse

2 Kemplay Road, Hampstead, NW3 1SY (7435 8679, www.hampsteadguesthouse.com). Hampstead tube or Hampstead Heath rail. **Rates** £80-£95 double. **Rooms** 9. **Credit** AmEx, MC, V.

Owner Annemarie van der Meer loves to point out all the quirky space-saving surprises as she shows you round her wonderful and idiosyncratic bed and breakfast: here's the folding sink, there's the bed that pops out of an antique wardrobe... The special atmosphere at this double-fronted Victorian house, set on a quiet Hampstead street, means that guests return year after year. Each room is uniquely decorated with eclectic furnishings – like the French steel bathtub in one room – and there's a self-contained studio with its own kitchen. All guests may make use of a range of home comforts, from hot-water bottles to mobile phones, as well as a laptop to borrow. Breakfast (£7) may be taken in the garden that surrounds this lovely property on all four sides.
Internet: wireless (free). Parking: £10/day. TV.

66 Camden Square

66 Camden Square, Camden, NW1 9XD (7485 4622, rodgerdavis@btinternet.com). Camden Town tube or Camden Road rail. **Rates** (incl continental breakfast) £100 double. **Rooms** 2. **No credit cards. Map** p404 Z1 ⓺⓽

A world away from the dreary Eurobustle of Camden Market, lovely 66 Camden Square isn't actually on Camden Square – it's on Murray Street, behind 1

Camden Square, an easy no.29 bus hop to town. A radical design by co-owner/architect Rodger Davis allows natural light to flood through the open-plan interior. Breakfast, taken in the expansive living room or on the terrace, is overseen by Rodger's hospitable other half Sue and a colourful parrot by the name of Peckham. The two guestrooms (one double, one single) are upstairs, convivial and comfortable. Neither is en suite, and the owners are keen to point out that they wouldn't have strangers sharing the bathroom. Rates are simple: £50 per person per night, £5 supplement for one-nighters, maximum stay one week. For pedestrians and cyclists, a newly opened path will get you to St Pancras International in 15 minutes.
Internet: wireless (free). TV.

EAST LONDON

For details on the many ways in which accommodation is changing in this part of London, *see p203* **The New East**.

Expensive

Boundary

2-4 Boundary Street, Shoreditch, E2 7DD (7729 1051, www.theboundary.co.uk). Liverpool Street tube/rail or Shoreditch High Street rail. **Rates** £140-£230 double. **Rooms** 17. **Credit** AmEx, DC, MC, V. **Map** p401 R4 ⓻⓪

Design mogul Sir Terence Conran's Boundary Project warehouse conversion was a labour of love. Its restaurants – which include Albion (*see p228*), one of the best openings of 2009, a downstairs fine-dining establishment and a rooftop bar – are high-quality but relaxed, and all 17 bedrooms are beautifully designed. Each has a wet room and handmade bed, but are otherwise individually furnished with classic furniture and original art. The five split-level suites range in style from the bright and sea-salt fresh Beach to a new take on Victoriana by Polly Dickens, while the remaining rooms (the slightly larger corner rooms have windows along both external walls) are themed by design style: Mies van der Rohe, Eames, Shaker. There's also a charming Heath Robinson room, decorated with the cartoonist's sketches of hilariously complex machines. Opt for a Boundary Room on a Sunday night and you can enjoy all this cool elegance for just £140.
Bar/café. Concierge. Disabled-adapted rooms. Internet: wireless (free). Restaurant. Room service. TV: DVD.

Town Hall Hotel

Patriot Square, Bethnal Green, E2 9NF (7871 0460, www.townhallhotel.com). Bethnal Green tube. **Rates** £260-£320 double. **Rooms** 98. **Credit** AmEx, MC, V.

In 2010, a grand, Grade II-listed, early 20th-century town hall was transformed into a classy modern aparthotel – despite its location between a council

estate and a scruffy row of shops. The decor is minimal, retaining many features (walnut panelling and marble for the interior, Portland stone outside, stained glass and fire hoses on old brass reels scattered about) that would be familiar to the bureaucrats who used to toil here, but jazzed up with contemporary art and a patterned aluminium 'veil' that covers the new floor at the top of the building. The pale-toned, spacious apartments are well equipped for self-catering, but hotel luxuries such as free wireless internet and TV/DVD players are also in place. The De Montfort Suite is the size of most houses, stretching over three floors, with a living room as big as a council chamber, and the attached restaurant, Viajante (see p231), is one of the hottest in town. Under a conservatory roof, there's a narrow basement swimming pool with sparkly tiles. *Photos p203.*
Bar/café. Business centre. Concierge. Disabled-adapted rooms. Gym. Internet: wireless (free). Restaurant. Room service. Pool (1, indoor). TV: DVD.

Moderate

40 Winks

109 Mile End Road, Stepney, E1 4UJ (7790 0259, 07973 653944, www.40winks.org). Stepney Green tube. **Rates** £130 double. **Rooms** 2. **No credit cards.**
Opposite a housing estate and cheap Somali diners, the family home of an interior designer has become the B&B of choice for movie stars and fashion movers. The 'micro-boutique hotel' looks extraordinary (kitchen frescoes, a music room with Beatles drumkit, a lion's head tap in the bath), but each stay is made individual by owner David Carter's commitment to his guests, making them feel they're staying with a fabulous friend rather than just renting a room. Too late to book? Intriguing soirées such as Bedtime Stories (for which everyone must wear pyjamas) open the house to a wider audience. It's flamboyant, fashionable and very cool. *Photos p199.*
Internet: wireless (free). Parking: free.

Hoxton Hotel

81 Great Eastern Street, Shoreditch, EC2A 3HU (7550 1000, www.hoxtonhotels.com). Old Street tube/rail. **Rates** (incl breakfast) £59-£199 double. **Rooms** 208. **Credit** AmEx, MC, V. **Map** p401 Q4 ⑩
Famous for its low rates (including some publicity-garnering £1-a-night rooms), the Hoxton deserves credit for many other things. First, there's the hip Shoreditch location – hip enough for Soho House to have taken over the downstairs bar-brasserie a couple of years ago. Then there are the great design values (the foyer is a sort of postmodern country lodge, complete with stag's head). Finally, the rooms are well thought out, if mostly rather small, with lots of nice touches – free milk in the fridges, a cold snack for breakfast, free wireless internet. Nowadays, there

are even three individually designed suites. The downside? The hotel's popularity. If you don't book well in advance and plan to visit during the week rather than at the weekend, you could pay as much as at one of the big chains. *Photos p200.*
Bar/café. Business centre. Disabled-adapted rooms. Internet: wireless (free). Restaurant. Room service. TV: pay movies.

★ Shoreditch Rooms

Ebor Street, Shoreditch, E1 6AW (7739 5040, www.shoreditchhouse.com). Shoreditch High Street rail. **Rates** £75-£215 double. **Rooms** 26. **Credit** AmEx, MC, V. **Map** p401 S4 ⑫
The most recent hotel opening from Soho House members' club (see also p191 **Dean Street Townhouse**; p206 **High Road House**) might even be the best, perfectly catching the local atmosphere with its unfussy, slightly retro design. The rooms feel a bit like urban beach huts, with pastel-coloured tongue-and-groove, shutters and swing doors to the en suite showers. They feel fresh, bright and comfortable, even though they're furnished with little more than a bed, an old-fashioned phone and DAB radio, and a big, solid dresser (minibar, hairdryer and treats within, flatscreen TV on top). Guests get access to the fine eating, drinking and fitness facilities (yes, a gym, but more importantly an excellent rooftop pool) in the members' club next door. Everything's put together with a light touch, from the 'Borrow Me' bookshelf by the lifts (jelly beans, umbrellas, boardgames and sex toys) to the room nomenclature: Tiny (from just £75), Small and Small+ (with little rooftop balconies and loungers from which to survey the grey horizon). *Photo p203.*
Bar/café. Conference facilities. Disabled-adapted room. Gym. Internet: wireless (free). Restaurant (2). Pool: outdoor. TV.

SOUTH-EAST LONDON
Moderate

Church Street Hotel

29-33 Camberwell Church Street, Camberwell, SE5 8TR (7703 5984, www.churchstreet hotel.com). Denmark Hill rail or bus 36, 436. **Rates** (incl breakfast) £120-£170 double. **Rooms** 31. **Credit** AmEx, MC, V.
Craftsman José Raido is behind this attractive and original family-run hotel, near Camberwell Green. Funky bathroom tiles in the bright, high-ceilinged bedrooms, for example, come from Guadalajara, and are thus a perfect match for Mexicana such as imported film posters, while the bed frames were forged by José himself. The colours are as vivid as a Mexican sunset. Bathroom products are organic, as are the pastries and cereals served for breakfast in an icon-filled dining room that also operates as a 24hr honesty bar. You pay only £90 for a double

CONSUME

with shared bathroom, which is a real bargain, and the hotel tapas restaurant, Angels & Gypsies, has been a big hit locally since opening in 2009.
Bar/café. Internet: wireless (free). Restaurant. TV.

SOUTH-WEST LONDON
Expensive

★ Bingham
61-63 Petersham Road, Richmond, Surrey, TW10 6UT (8940 0902, www.thebingham. co.uk). Richmond tube/rail. **Rates** £190-£285 double. **Rooms** 15. **Credit** AmEx, DC, MC, V.
Quality boutique hotel, destination restaurant (under Shay Cooper's award-winning supervision) and sun-filled cocktail bar in one, the Bingham makes excellent use of its superb riverside location by Richmond Bridge. Six of its individually styled and high-ceilinged rooms overlook the Thames; all of them are named after a poet, in honour of the Bingham's artistic past (lesbian aunt-and-niece couple Katherine Harris Bradley and Edith Emma Cooper lived here in the 1890s, regularly hosting members of the Aesthetic Movement while they were in residence). Each room accommodates an ample bathtub and shower, art deco touches to the furnishings and irresistibly fluffy duck-and-goose

---

INSIDE TRACK NO FRILLS

Chain hotels aren't covered in this chapter, unless they're new, especially well located (**Premier Inn London County Hall**; *see p185*) or otherwise unusually praiseworthy. This is simply because the internal logic of chain hotels is that one should be as similar as possible to another, with reliability one major virtue – and price the other. You can find double rooms for around £100 at **Holiday Inn** and **Holiday Inn Express** (www.ichotelsgroup. com), **Ibis** (www.ibishotel.com) and **Travelodge** (www.travelodge.co.uk).

A relatively new development has been the 'no frills' approach – very low rates, with nothing inessential included. Airline-offshoot **EasyHotel** (www.easyhotel.com) was the first, but it now has a challenger: the first British hotel from **Tune** (www. tunehotels.com) is located not far inland from the South Bank, across the river from the Houses of Parliament. Rooms are usually around £50 a night.

If you've got an awkward departure time from Gatwick or Heathrow, consider the neat and funky 'pod' rooms at a **Yotel** (www.yotel.com). A four-hour stay will cost £45.

---

feather duvets. Run by the Trinder family for the last 25 years, the Bingham manages to feel both grand and boutique. A treat.
Bar/café. Internet: wireless (free). Parking: £10/day. Restaurant. Room service. TV: DVD.

WEST LONDON
Moderate

Base2Stay
25 Courtfield Gardens, Earl's Court, SW5 0PG (7244 2255, www.base2stay.com). Earl's Court tube. **Rates** £117-£135 double. **Rooms** 67. **Credit** AmEx, MC, V. **Map** p394 B10 🅰
Base2Stay looks good, with its modernist limestone and taupe tones, and keeps prices low by removing inessentials: no bar, no restaurant. Instead, there's the increasingly popular solution of a 'kitchenette' (microwave, sink, silent mini-fridge, kettle), but here with all details carefully attended to (not just token cutlery, but sufficient kitchenware with corkscrew and can opener, and guidance about where to shop). The rooms, en suite (with power showers) and air-conditioned, are as carefully thought out, with desks, modem points and flatscreens, but the single/bunkbed rooms are small. Discount vouchers for nearby chain eateries are supplied by the friendly duo on 24hr reception duty.
Disabled-adapted rooms. Internet: wireless (free). Parking: £30/day. TV: pay movies.

★ Garret
Troubadour, 263-267 Old Brompton Road, Earl's Court, SW5 9JA (7370 1434, www. troubadour.co.uk). West Brompton tube/rail. **Rates** £165 double. **Rooms** 1. **Credit** AmEx, MC, V. **Map** p394 B11 🅰
This idiosyncratic attic apartment is an absolute treat. High above the Troubadour (*see p177*), a 1960s counter-culture café that still hosts poetry and music events, it's unjustly named: yes, the rooms are in the attic and have charming pitched roofs, but there are acres of space for two – and even enough for a small family, if the kids sleep on the pull-out sofa in the lounge-kitchen. The huge, high main bed lies under a skylight and there's a writing desk, but any thought of poetic torment is banished by the well-executed Arts & Crafts decor and fully equipped kitchen area, right down to the cafetière and wines.
Bar/café. Internet: wireless (free). Room service. TV: DVD.

High Road House
162 Chiswick High Road, Chiswick, W4 1PR (8742 1717, www.highroadhouse.co.uk). Turnham Green tube. **Rates** £145-£165 double. **Rooms** 14. **Credit** AmEx, MC, V.
This west London outpost of Nick Jones's ever-fashionable Soho House stable (*see also p191* **Dean Street Townhouse**; *p205* **Shoreditch Rooms**)

Rockwell.

Rockwell

*181-183 Cromwell Road, Earl's Court, SW5 0SF
(7244 2000, www.therockwell.com). Earl's Court
tube.* **Rates** £160-£200 double. **Rooms** 40.
Credit AmEx, MC, V. **Map** p394 B10 ⑦⑥
The Rockwell aims for relaxed contemporary elegance – and succeeds magnificently. The listed
premises mean there are no identikit rooms here:
they're all different sizes and individually designed,
but share gleaming woods and muted glowing
colours alongside more sober creams and neutrals.
Among the rooms, pleasing eccentricities include a
pair of central single rooms with skylights, and basement garden rooms that have tiny patios, complete
with garden furniture, looking up at the ground-level
bridge that leads on to the garden terrace proper
from the handsome bar-restaurant. Each room has
a power shower, Starck fittings and bespoke cabinets in the bathrooms, and triple-glazing ensures
you never notice the noisy road just outside.
*Bar/café. Concierge. Internet: high-speed (free).
Restaurant. TV: pay movies.*

Twenty Nevern Square

*20 Nevern Square, Earl's Court, SW5 9PD
(7565 9555, www.twentynevernsquare.co.uk).
Earl's Court tube.* **Rates** (incl breakfast) £90-
£150 double. **Rooms** 25. **Credit** AmEx, MC, V.
Map p394 A11 ⑦⑦
Only the less-than-posh location of this immaculate
boutique hotel keeps the rates reasonable. Tucked
away in a private garden square, it feels far from its
locale. The modern-colonial style was created by its
well-travelled owner, who personally sourced many
of the exotic and antique furnishings (as well as
those in sister hotel the Mayflower; *see p207*). In the
sleek marble bathrooms, toiletries are tidied away
in decorative caskets, but the beds are the real stars:
from elaborately carved four-posters to Egyptian
sleigh styles, all with luxurious mattresses. The
vaguely Far Eastern feel extends into the lounge and
the airy conservatory, with its dark wicker furniture.
*Bar/café. Internet: wireless & high-speed (free).
Parking: £25/day. Room service. TV: DVD.*

features guestrooms designed by Ilse Crawford, and
a members' bar and restaurant above the buzzing
ground-floor brasserie. Serving a modern British
menu, this has a retro sophisticated-Parisian-bistro-
meets-Bloomsbury feel and, as you might expect, the
food and service are excellent. Guestrooms are
soothing, unadorned, white Shaker Modern with little fizzes of colour (and little hidden treats), the bathrooms well stocked with Cowshed products.
*Bars/cafés (2). Disabled-adapted rooms. Internet:
wireless (free). Restaurants (2). Room service.
TV: DVD & pay movies.*

★ Mayflower Hotel

*26-28 Trebovir Road, Earl's Court, SW5 9NJ
(7370 0991, www.mayflower-group.co.uk). Earl's
Court tube.* **Rates** (incl continental breakfast)
£99-£115 double. **Rooms** 46. **Credit** AmEx,
MC, V. **Map** p394 B11 ⑦⑥
After fighting on the frontlines of the Earl's Court
budget-hotel style revolution, the Mayflower's taken
the struggle to other parts of London (New Linden;
see p194). But this is where the lushly contemporary
house style evolved, proving affordability can be
opulently chic. Cream walls and sleek dark woods
are an understated background for richly coloured
fabrics and intricate wooden architectural fragments
sourced from Asia, like the lobby's imposing Jaipuri
arch. The facilities too are well up to scratch, featuring marble bathrooms, Egyptian cotton sheets and
CD players in the rooms.
Internet: wireless (free). Parking: £25/day. TV.

APARTMENT RENTAL

The companies listed below specialise in
holiday lets. Typical daily rates on a reasonably
central property run to around £70-£90 for
a studio or one-bed apartment to £100 or
thereabouts for a two-bed place. However, as
with any style of accommodation in London,
if you've money to burn, then the sky's the
limit. Note that many of these firms operate
minimum-stay requirements, which means
that apartment rental is only an option if you're
planning a relatively protracted visit to the city.

Respected all-rounders with properties
around the city include **Holiday Serviced
Apartments** (0845 060 4477, www.holiday

CONSUME

apartments.co.uk) and **Palace Court Holiday Apartments** (7727 3467, www.palacecourt. co.uk). **London Holiday Accommodation** (7265 0882, www.londonholiday.co.uk) offers half a dozen decent-priced self-catering options in the West End and on the South Bank. For serviced apartments, try the South Bank or Earl's Court 'campuses' run by **Think Apartments** (0845 602 9437, www.think-apartments.com). **Accommodation Outlet** (7287 4244, www.outlet4holidays.com) is a recommended lesbian and gay agency that has some excellent properties across London in general and in Soho in particular.

CAMPING & CARAVANNING

If putting yourself at the mercy of English weather in a far-flung suburban field doesn't put you off, the rather transport links into central London might do the job instead. Still, you can't really beat the prices.

Crystal Palace Caravan Club *Crystal Palace Parade, Crystal Palace, SE19 1UF (8778 7155). Crystal Palace rail or bus 3.* **Open** *Mar-Sept 9am-6pm daily. Oct-Jan 9.30am-5.30pm Mon-Sun.* **Rates** *Caravan £5-£8. Tent £5-£15.* **Credit** MC, V.

Lee Valley Campsite *Sewardstone Road, Chingford, E4 7RA (8529 5689, www.leevalley park.org.uk). Walthamstow Central tube/rail then bus 215.* **Open** *Jan, Mar-Dec 8am-9pm daily.* **Rates** £7.40; £3.30 under-16s; free under-2s. **Credit** MC, V.

STAYING WITH THE LOCALS

Several agencies can arrange for individuals and families to stay in Londoners' homes. Prices for a stay are around £20-£85 for a single and £45-£105 for a double, including breakfast, and depending on the location and degree of comfort. Agencies include **At Home in London** (8748 1943, www.athomeinlondon.co.uk), **Host & Guest Service** (7385 9922, www.host-guest.co.uk), **London Bed & Breakfast Agency** (7586 2768, www.londonbb.com) and **London Homestead Services** (7286 5115, www.lhslondon.co.uk). You can usually expect for there to be a minimum length of stay.

UNIVERSITY RESIDENCES

During vacations, much of London's dedicated student accommodation is available to visitors. Central locations can make these a bargain.

International Students House *229 Great Portland Street, Marylebone, W1W 5PN (7631 8300, www.ish.org.uk). Great Portland Street*

tube. **Open** *Reception 7.45am-10.30pm Mon-Fri, 8am-10.30pm Sat, Sun.* **Rates** £12-£21 (per person) dormitory; £34 single; £53 twin. **No credit cards**. **Map** p396 H4 ⑦⑧

King's College Conference & Vacation Bureau *Strand Bridge House, 138-142 Strand, Covent Garden, WC2R 1HH (7848 1700, www.kcl.ac.uk/kcvb). Temple tube.* **Rates** £20-£40 single; £54-£59 twin. **No credit cards**. **Map** p416 Z3 ⑦⑨

LSE *Bankside House, 24 Sumner Street, Holborn, SE1 9JA (7107 5773, www.lsevacations.co.uk). London Bridge tube.* **Rates** £33-£55 single; £57-£75 twin/double. **Credit** MC, V. **Map** p402 O8 ⑧⓪
The London School of Economics has vacation rentals across town, but Bankside House (tucked just behind Tate Modern) is the best located.

YOUTH HOSTELS

For Youth Hostel Assocation venues, you can get extra reductions on the rates detailed below if you're a member of the IYHF (International Youth Hostel Federation): you'll pay £3 less a night. Joining costs only £15.95 (£9.95 for under-25s), and can be done on arrival or through www.yha.org.uk prior to departure. All under-18s receive a 25 per cent discount, in any case. YHA hostel beds are arranged either in dormitories or in twin rooms. Our favourite hostels are reviewed (**YHA London Central**, *see p188*; **Clink78**, *see p188*), but those listed below are all handily located across town.

Earl's Court *38 Bolton Gardens, Earl's Court, SW5 0AQ (7373 7083, www.yha.org.uk). Earl's Court tube.* **Open** 24hrs daily. **Rates** £18-£74. **No credit cards**. **Map** p394 B11 ⑧①

Holland Park *Holland Walk, South Kensington, W8 7QU (7937 0748, www.yha.org.uk). High Street Kensington tube.* **Open** 24hrs daily. **Rates** £18-£60. **No credit cards**. **Map** p392 A8 ⑧②

Meininger *Baden-Powell House, 65-67 Queen's Gate, South Kensington, SW7 5JS (7590 6910, www.meininger-hostels.com). Gloucester Road or South Kensington tube.* **Rates** £15-£40. **Credit** MC, V. **Map** p395 D10 ⑧③

Oxford Street *14 Noel Street, Soho, W1F 8GJ (7734 1618, www.yha.org.uk). Oxford Circus tube.* **Open** 24hrs daily. *Reception 7am-11pm daily.* **Rates** £22-£70. **Credit** MC, V. **Map** p416 V2 ⑧④

St Pancras *79-81 Euston Road, King's Cross, NW1 2QE (7388 9998, www.yha.org.uk). King's Cross tube/rail.* **Open** 24hrs daily. **Rates** £15-£69. **Credit** MC, V. **Map** p397 L3 ⑧⑤

St Paul's *36 Carter Lane, the City, EC4V 5AB (7236 4965, www.yha.org.uk). St Paul's tube or Blackfriars rail.* **Open** 24hrs daily. **Rates** £19-£50. **Credit** MC, V. **Map** p402 O6 ⑧⑥

CONSUME

Restaurants & Cafés

Delicious food from every nation – even England.

It took a decade or more, but British cuisine has moved from being a national embarrassment to the most obvious choice for every hotel menu. Put it down to the **St John** (*see p213*) effect. Fergus Henderson's pioneering restaurant, which is still superb, made unloved ingredients and simple preparations fashionable. He initially inspired worthy successors, from **Great Queen Street** (*see p215*) to **Hereford Road** (*see p224*), but there are also an increasing number of Brit-by-numbers places to avoid. In the same way, the **Eagle** (*see p212*) unwittingly spawned a multitude of two-a-penny gastropubs that do its legacy no favours at all. In this chapter, we'll guide you to the best of both types of venue.

While you're here, be sure also to take advantage of the culinary riches London's many immigrants have brought here. Fine Bangladeshi, Moroccan, Lebanese, Turkish and Vietnamese restaurants are listed here, as are top-notch exponents of the cuisines of France, Italy, Japan, Spain, China and Thailand.

There are old-school options too: fish and chips, a classic café (**E Pellicci**; *see p230*) and even **M Manze** (*see p210*), the city's finest old pie and mash shop.

CONSUME

ESSENTIAL INFORMATION

Try to book a table in advance. At many places, booking is vital; at a select few restaurants, you may need to book far in advance. Smoking is banned in all restaurants and cafés. Tipping is standard practice: ten to 15 per cent is usual. Many restaurants add this charge as standard to bills; some do so but still present the credit card slip as 'open', cheekily encouraging the customer to tip twice. Always check the bill.

We've listed a range of meal prices for each place. However, restaurants often change their menus, so treat these prices only as guidelines. Budget venues are marked **£**. For good places to eat with children, *see pp288-289*.

THE SOUTH BANK & BANKSIDE

Borough Market (*see p268*), full of stalls selling all kinds of wonderful food, is a superb forage for gourmet snackers. **Tate Modern**

Café: **Level 2** (*see p288*) is great for those with children, as are the neighbouring outposts of **Wagamama** and **Giraffe** (*see p288*) under the Royal Festival Hall.

Anchor & Hope

36 The Cut, SE1 8LP (7928 9898). Southwark tube or Waterloo tube/rail. **Open** 5-11pm Mon; noon-11pm Tue-Sat; 12.30-5pm Sun. *Meals served* 6-10.30pm Mon; noon-2.30pm, 6-10.30pm Tue-Sat; 2pm sitting Sun. **Main courses** £11.80-£22. **Credit** MC, V. **Map** p402 N8 ❶ **Gastropub**
The most common complaint about this relaxed Waterloo gastropub is the no-booking policy. Those who end up having to wait at the bar can salivate over the seasonal British menu on the blackboard, but choose carefully: despite good sourcing, not all dishes are equally successful. Arbroath smokie is a good bet if it's available; other dishes might include cold roast beef and dripping on toast. There's a single sitting on Sundays.

About the reviews
This chapter is compiled from Time Out's annual guide to London's Best Restaurants *(£11.99), available from www.timeout.com.*

❶ Blue numbers given here correspond to the location of each restaurant and café on the street maps. *See pp392-416.*

CONSUME

Baltic

74 Blackfriars Road, SE1 8HA (7928 1111,
www.balticrestaurant.co.uk). Southwark tube.
Open noon-3pm, 5.30-11.15pm Mon-Sat; noon-
10.30pm Sun. **Main courses** £10.50-£17. **Credit**
AmEx, MC, V. **Map** p402 N8 ❷ **Eastern**
European
This stylish spot remains the brightest star on
London's east European restaurant scene. The menu
combines the best of east European cuisine – from
Georgian-style lamb with aubergines to Romanian
sour cream *mamaliga* (polenta) – with a light, modern European twist. Great cocktails, a wide choice
of vodkas, an eclectic wine list and friendly service
add to the appeal. In the high-ceilinged restaurant,
gaze up at hundreds of shards of golden amber in
the stunning chandelier.

Canteen

Royal Festival Hall, Belvedere Road, SE1
8XX (0845 686 1122, www.canteen.co.uk).
Embankment tube or Waterloo tube/rail. **Open**
8am-11pm Mon-Fri; 9am-11pm Sat, Sun. **Main**
courses £8.50-£14.50. **Credit** AmEx, MC, V.
Map p399 M8 ❸ **British**
Furnished with utilitarian tables and booths, this
branch of Canteen is tucked into the back of the
Royal Festival Hall (*see p317* **Southbank Centre**).
No surprise, then, that it's often busy. Dishes range
from a bacon sandwich and afternoon jam scones to
full roasts. Classic breakfasts (eggs benedict, welsh
rarebit) are served all day, joined by the likes of
macaroni cheese or sausage and mash from lunchtime.
Other locations 2 Crispin Place, off Brushfield
Street, Spitalfields, E1 6DW; Park Pavilion, 40
Canada Square, Docklands, E14 5FW; 55 Baker
Street, Marylebone, W1U 8EW.

Magdalen

152 Tooley Street, SE1 2TU (7403 1342,
www.magdalenrestaurant.co.uk). London Bridge
tube/rail. **Open** noon-2.30pm, 6.30-10pm Mon-Fri;

THE BEST CLASSIC BRITISH

Albion
Conran comes up trumps again. *See p228.*

Fish Central
Our favourite fish 'n' chip shop in London.
See p211.

Hereford Road
The best of the new breed of modern
British restaurants. *See p224.*

St John
A pioneer that's still setting the standard.
See p213.

6.30-10pm Sat. **Main courses** £13.50-£20. **Set**
lunch £15.50 2 courses, £18.50 3 courses. **Credit**
AmEx, MC, V. **Map** p403 Q8 ❹ **British**
Magdalen makes the most of fairly unprepossessing
surroundings. A la carte prices are just about reasonable (£17.50 for flavoursome Middle White belly
with veg and good gravy, £16.50 for a beautifully
presented fish stew), but portions aren't huge; opt
instead for the set lunch, a steal at £15.50 for two
courses or £18.50 for three. Poached rhubarb with
shortbread and crème anglaise is the pick of the puddings, and there's a tempting collection of British
cheeses. Staff are young, friendly and efficient.

£ M Manze

87 Tower Bridge Road, SE1 4TW (7407 2985,
www.manze.co.uk). Bus 1, 42, 188. **Open** 11am-
2pm Mon; 10.30am-2pm Tue-Thur; 10am-2.15pm
Fri; 10am-2.45pm Sat. **Main courses** £2.75-
£5.20. **No credit cards. Map** p403 Q10 ❺ **Pie**
& mash
Manze's is the finest remaining purveyor of the dirt-
cheap traditional foodstuff of London's working
classes. It's the oldest pie shop in town, established
in 1902, with tiles, marble-topped tables and worn
wood benches. Orders are simple: minced beef pies
or, for braver souls, stewed eels with mashed potato
and liquor (a thin parsley sauce).

Roast

Floral Hall, Borough Market, Stoney Street, SE1
1TL (7940 1300, www.roast-restaurant.com).
London Bridge tube/rail. **Open** 7-11am, noon-
3pm, 5.30-11pm Mon-Fri; 8-11.30am, noon-4pm,
6-11pm Sat; 11.30am-6pm Sun. **Main courses**
£14.50-£24.50. **Credit** AmEx, MC, V. **Map** p402
P8 ❻ **British**
A big airy restaurant by Borough Market, Roast
gets crammed on market days, but staff cope
admirably. The restaurant menu (there's a much
cheaper bar menu from 3pm) offers the best of
British cuisine. Cold poached Devon sea trout with
wild garlic salad cream is typical, with Neal's Yard
cheeses and trad desserts for afters. Add to this an
impressive drinks list, including a fine roster of teas,
and you have a great all-rounder.

Tapas Brindisa

18-20 Southwark Street, SE1 1TJ (7357 8880,
www.brindisa.com). London Bridge tube/rail.
Open 11am-11pm Mon-Sat. **Tapas** £3.20-£22.
Credit AmEx, MC, V. **Map** p402 P8 ❼ **Spanish**
Top-quality ingredients have always been the key
at Brindisa, but its genius lies in the ability to assemble them into eminently tempting tapas. The set-up
is equally simple: a bar area at one end dotted with
high tables, and a close-packed, concrete-floored dining room at the other. Both are generally thronged.
Behind the bar is a hatch into the kitchen, from
which chefs in immaculate whites produce a succession of delicious and deceptively simple dishes.

Roast.

Other locations 7-9 Exhibition Road, South Kensington, SW7 2HE; 46 Broadwick Street, Soho, W1F 7AF.

Zucca

184 Bermondsey Street, SE1 3TQ (7378 6809, www.zuccalondon.com). London Bridge tube/rail or Bermondsey tube. **Open** noon-3pm, 6.30-10pm Tue-Sat; noon-3pm Sun. **Main courses** £8.50-£13.95. **Credit** MC, V. **Map** p403 Q9 ❽ **Italian**

If only more restaurants had Zucca's approach: good food at great prices, served by interested staff with a genuine regard for diners. It sounds so simple, yet it's pretty rare. The modern Italian menu is part-nered by an all-Italian wine list, and the staff are happy to help or enlarge upon both. The restaurant is open-plan, with the kitchen completely exposed to view, and the decor runs to shiny white surfaces with occasional splashes of intense orange.

THE CITY

In several parts, the City remains a working-hours kind of place, with venues shut in the evenings and at weekends. Pretty much everywhere is busiest for weekday lunches.

Bodean's

16 Byward Street, EC3R 5BA (7488 3883, www.bodeansbbq.com). Tower Hill tube. **Open** noon-3pm, 6-10pm Mon-Fri; 6-10pm Sat. **Main courses** £8-£16. **Credit** AmEx, MC, V. **Map** p403 R7 ❾ **American**

Bodean's has five branches: Soho, Fulham, Clapham and, very handy for the Tower of London (*see p97*),

here. The schtick remains unchanged at each of them: Kansas City barbecue, with a small informal upstairs and bigger, smarter downstairs with US sport on TV. The food is decent, generous and very, very meaty – bring an appetite.

Other locations throughout the city.

£ Fish Central

149-155 Central Street, EC1V 8AP (7253 4970). Old Street tube/rail or bus 55. **Open** 11am-2.30pm Mon-Sat; 5-10.30pm Mon-Thur; 5-11pm Fri, Sat. **Main courses** £7.95-£12.95. **Credit** MC, V. **Map** p400 P3 ❿ **Fish & chips**

A large photograph on the wall shows Fish Central as it was pre-makeover: just your everyday chippy. Today, it's quite a lively, trendy set-up. The specials board contains the likes of warm squid salad, but tradition-seekers won't be disappointed. Good chips and mushy peas, decent wines and a welcome choice of tap beers make this a fine local.

Restaurant at St Paul's

St Paul's Cathedral, St Paul's Churchyard, EC4M 8AD (7248 2469, www.restaurant atstpauls.co.uk). St Paul's tube. **Open** noon-4.30pm daily. **Set lunch** £20 2 courses, £24 3 courses. **Credit** MC, V. **Map** p402 O6 ⓫ **British**

This is a really rather dull moniker for a handsome, light-filled space in the crypt of the great cathedral, with very sensuous and textural decor; it's perfect for a restaurant, a little surprising beneath a place of worship. Seasonality and provenance are the focus of the menu, and the excellent food reveals a deft pair of hands in the kitchen. We've enjoyed the likes of summery asparagus and poached Gressingham duck egg, treacle-cured salmon with watercress, Trigger Farm barnsley chop and porto-bello mushroom wellington.

▶ *The restaurant is closed in the evening, but there are some good alternatives in Paternoster Square: try the Paternoster Chop House (Warwick Court, EC4M 7DX, 7029 9400, www.paternosterchophouse.com) or the spacious Corney & Barrow wine bar.*

Sweetings

39 Queen Victoria Street, EC4N 4SA (7248 3062). Mansion House tube. **Open** 11.30am-3pm Mon-Fri. **Main courses** £12-£27.50. **Credit** AmEx, MC, V. **Map** p402 P6 ⓬ **Fish & seafood**

No-nonsense British food served in a quintessen-tially English setting. Diners at the communal tables at the rear can survey walls hung with old cartoons, photos and cricket mementos. Specials might include gull's eggs and smoked salmon pâté while the 'bill of fare' proffers traditional dishes. Sweetings opens only for lunch, takes no bookings, and is full soon after noon, so order a silver pewter mug of Guinness and enjoy the wait.

CONSUME

HOLBORN & CLERKENWELL

Home to pioneers of the two huge trends in contemporary London food – modern British at **St John** (*see p213*), the gastropub at the **Eagle** (*see right*) – this scrubby bit of nowhere much is the location of a surprising proportion of London's best eating options.

★ Bistrot Bruno Loubet

St John's Square, 86-88 Clerkenwell Road, EC1M 5RJ (7324 4455, www.thezetter.com). Farringdon tube/rail. **Open** 7-10.30am, noon-2.30pm, 6-10.30pm Mon-Fri; 7.30-11am, noon-3pm, 6-10.30pm Sat; 7.30-11am, noon-3pm, 6-10pm Sun. **Main courses** £15-£18.50. **Credit** AmEx, MC, V. **Map** p400 O4 ⑬ **French**

Bruno Loubet has completely reinvigorated the restaurant at the Zetter hotel (*see p186*). The menu is short, but reads like a dream: beetroot ravioli, fried breadcrumbs and sage with rocket salad; soused mackerel, watercress salad and buckwheat bread with prawn butter; quail with spinach and egg yolk raviolo; braised beef with mango and herb salad. The room is fairly plain, with quirky touches (including a waiters' station made from refashioned furniture, and retro lamps). Tables are squeezed into the slightly awkward space, but huge windows look straight into St John's Square and there's a buzz of happy diners. A restaurant with a real wow factor.

£ Caravan

11-13 Exmouth Market, EC1R 4QD (7833 8115, www.caravanonexmouth.co.uk). Farringdon tube/rail. **Open** 8am-10.30pm Mon-Fri; 10am-10.30pm Sat; 10am-4pm Sun. **Main courses** £4.50-£15. **Credit** AmEx, MC, V. **Map** p400 N4 ⑭ **International**

Caravan has slotted easily into the Exmouth Market dining scene. The casual vibe and industrial-funky design – rough wooden tables, white pipework, light fittings made from old-fashioned cow-milking bottles – are part of the appeal, but it's the food that's the draw. Expect a parade of unusual, international tastes: peanut butter and blue cheese wontons, salt beef fritters with green beans. Young staff zip between tables, but are never too rushed to smile.

Le Comptoir Gascon

61-63 Charterhouse Street, EC1M 6HJ (7608 0851, www.comptoirgascon.com). Farringdon tube/rail. **Open** noon-2pm, 7-10pm Tue, Wed; noon-2pm, 7-10.30pm Thur, Fri; 10.30am-2.30pm, 7-10pm Sat. **Main courses** £7.50-£13.50. **Credit** AmEx, MC, V. **Map** p400 O5 ⑮ **French**

The bistro offshoot of Club Gascon is a deservedly popular spot. A small, convivial brick-lined room that doubles as a deli, it offers the over-30s refuge on a street lined with raucous bars. Even more importantly, the food is great and nicely priced.

Splendid, taste-packed mains of grilled lamb and beef onglet are excellent; sides are worth the extra, especially mighty french fries cooked in duck fat. Try the own-made ice-creams for dessert.
▶ *The smarter, similarly excellent Club Gascon (57 West Smithfield, EC1A 9DS, 7796 0600, www.clubgascon.com) is across the meat market.*

Eagle

159 Farringdon Road, EC1R 3AL (7837 1353). Farringdon tube/rail. **Open** noon-11pm Mon-Sat; noon-5pm Sun. *Meals served* 12.30-3pm, 6.30-10.30pm Mon-Fri; 12.30-3.30pm, 6.30-10.30pm Sat; 12.30-3.30pm Sun. **Main courses** £5-£17. **Credit** MC, V. **Map** p400 N4 ⑯ **Gastropub**

Widely credited with being the first gastropub (it opened in 1991), the Eagle is still recognisably a pub with quality food: noisy, often crowded (you'll usually be sharing a table), with no-frills service. The room is dominated by a giant open range at which T-shirted cooks toss earthy grills in theatrical bursts of flame. The kitchen takes up one half of the long bar, with the hearty Med-influenced menu chalked up above it. A short wine list is available by glass or bottle; there are also real ales on tap.

Hix Oyster & Chop House

36-37 Greenhill Rents, off Cowcross Street, EC1M 6BN (7017 1930, www.hixoysterandchophouse.co.uk). Farringdon tube/rail. **Open** noon-

Bistro Bruno Loubet.

3pm, 5.30-11pm Mon-Fri; 5.30-11pm Sat; noon-9pm Sun. **Main courses** £10.75-£34.50. **Credit** AmEx, MC, V. **Map** p400 O5 **⓱ British**
Although the name tells diners what to expect, there's more to Mark Hix's place than chops and oysters: free-range Goosnargh chicken with wild garlic sauce (for two), for example. But oysters (such as Helford natives or Colchester rocks), chops and steaks feature prominently; accordingly, most diners are male. Puddings are nicely retro, but usually with an imaginative modern twist.
▶ *The superb Hix (66-70 Brewer Street, W1F 9UP, 7292 3518, www.hixsoho.co.uk) opened in Soho, with Mark's Bar (see p240) downstairs.*

★ Modern Pantry
47-48 St John's Square, EC1V 4JJ (7250 0833, www.themodernpantry.co.uk). Farringdon tube/rail. **Open** *Café* 8am-11pm Mon-Fri; 9am-11pm Sat; 10am-10pm Sun. *Restaurant* noon-3pm, 6-10.30pm Tue-Fri; 6-11pm Sat. **Main courses** £13.50-£22.50. **Credit** (both) AmEx, MC, V. **Map** p400 O4 **⓲ International**
A culinary three-parter spread across two Georgian townhouses, the Modern Pantry feels savvy and of the moment. The venue is fashionable without being annoying, and service is spot on. Both pantry (takeaway) and café (informal) are at street level; upstairs are adjoining dining rooms (still reasonably informal). Each of Anna Hansen's dishes is a complex fusion of all kinds of fine ingredients, in such multiplicity it seems they could never work together – and yet they never seem to fail. The weekend brunch is popular, so be sure to book. *See p226* **Eating Out.**

Moro
34-36 Exmouth Market, EC1R 4QE (7833 8336, www.moro.co.uk). Farringdon tube/rail or bus 19, 38, 341. **Open** 12.30-10.30pm Mon-Sat. **Main courses** £14.50-£20. **Tapas** £3.50-£14.50. **Credit** AmEx, DC, MC, V. **Map** p400 N4 **⓳ North African**
A meal that excites the senses is a rarity, but Sam and Sam Clarke's Moro often manages to produce just that. For a restaurant with a big reputation, its decor is unpretentious, the centrepiece being a simple view of the kitchen's big wood-fired oven. You can enjoy tapas at the bar or sit down for a more leisurely wander through the Moorish menu, with inspiration from Egypt to Portugal, Spain to the Lebanon. The drinks list is a point of pride: almost all the wines, sherries and cava come from the Iberian peninsula.
▶ *Next door, Morita (no.32, EC1R 4QE, 7278 7007, closed Mon, Sun) is a superb new tapas bar, opened by the Clarkes in autumn 2010.*

★ St John
26 St John Street, EC1M 4AY (7251 0848, www.stjohnrestaurant.com). Barbican tube or Farringdon tube/rail. **Open** noon-3pm, 6-11pm

---

THE BEST BARGAINS

Arbutus
Fine haute cuisine in Soho. *See p216.*

Hummus Bros
Simple, easy, filling. *See p217.*

Lantana
Café culture comes alive. *See p214.*

Mon-Fri; 6-11pm Sat; 1-3pm Sun. **Main courses** £13.50-£22.50. **Credit** AmEx, DC, MC, V. **Map** p400 O5 **⓴ British**
Chef-patron Fergus Henderson opened the daddy of new-wave British restaurants in the shell of a Smithfield smokehouse in 1995, and hasn't looked back since. The focus is on seasonal and unusual British produce, simply cooked. Although it's a world-famous restaurant, it's completely unstuffy: staff are approachable as well as highly competent and the French wine list won't frighten anyone. While prices aren't low, they're not excessive for the quality; if you are a bit strapped for cash, having a snack in the airy bar is even cheaper.
▶ *St John has ventured into the hotel trade; see p189* **Come and St John the Fun.**

BLOOMSBURY & FITZROVIA

Just next door to Benito's Hat, classy **Salt Yard** (*see p217* **Dehesa**) provides superb Spanish-Italian tapas.

£ Benito's Hat
56 Goodge Street, W1T 4NB (7637 3732, www.benitos-hat.com). Goodge Street tube. **Open** 11.30am-10pm Mon-Wed, Sun; 11.30am-11pm Thur-Sat. **Main courses** £5-£6. **Credit** MC, V. **Map** p396 J5 **㉑ Mexican**
Tex-Mex eateries are currently ten a peso in London, but the Benito's Hat production line serves some of the best burritos in town. Try the slow-cooked pork, wrapped in a soft, floury tortilla along with fiery salsa brava (made several times daily) and black beans authentically flavoured with avocado leaves. If you're having a drink, the margaritas are suitably merciless. The counter, facing the entrance, serves lots of takeaways, but there tables on the pavement, window perches and proper seating in the rear.
Other locations 19 New Row, Covent Garden, WC2N 4LA (7240 5815).

Camino
3 Varnishers Yard, Regents Quarter, N1 9FD (7841 7331, www.camino.uk.com). King's Cross tube/rail. **Open** *Restaurant* 8-11.30am, noon-3pm, 6.30-11pm Mon-Fri; 9am-4pm, 7-11pm Sat; 8-11.30am, noon-4pm Sun. *Bar*

CONSUME

CONSUME

noon-4pm, 4.30-11pm Sat, Sun. **Main courses** £10.50-£23. **Credit** AmEx, MC, V. **Map** p397 L3 ㉒ **Tapas**

Camino's cavernous premises contain sleek bar and restaurant areas, and, outside, a courtyard where drinkers sip iced Cruzcampo and nibble plump, golden-crumbed croquetas. The tapas list, dotted with regional specialities, can be eaten anywhere, but the full menu of classic Iberian fare with some modern European forays has to be eaten in the restaurant, where the self-consciously modern, stripped-down aesthetic is softened by muted candlelight and the hum of conversation.

▶ *Camino's new Bar Pepito serves a superb selection of sherries just across the courtyard.*

★ Giaconda Dining Room

9 Denmark Street, WC2H 8LS (7240 3334, www.giacondadining.com). Tottenham Court Road tube. **Open** noon-2.15pm, 6-9.15pm Mon-Fri. **Main courses** £12-£14. **Credit** AmEx, MC, V. **Map** p416 X2 ㉓ **Modern European**

Giaconda is a thoroughly likeable restaurant. The decor is nothing special and the room is a bit cramped, but the food served is what most people want to eat most of the time: the Australian owners describe it as French-ish with a bit of Spain and Italy, but there are also big-flavoured grills, fish of the day and any number of intriguing assemblages (chorizo, chicken liver, trotters and tripe, for instance). *See also p226* **Eating In**.

Hakkasan

8 Hanway Place, W1T 1HD (7927 7000, www.hakkasan.com). Tottenham Court Road tube. **Open** *Restaurant* noon-3pm, 6-11pm Mon-Wed; noon-3pm, 6pm-midnight Thur, Fri; noon-4pm, 6pm-midnight Sat; noon-4pm, 6-11pm Sun. *Bar* noon-12.30am Mon-Wed; noon-1.30am Thur-Sat; noon-midnight Sun. **Main courses** £9.50-£58. *Dim sum* £3-£20. **Credit** AmEx, MC, V. **Map** p416 W1 ㉔ **Chinese**

Creator Alan Yau sold this esteemed restaurant to an Abu Dhabi-based company a few years back, but the changes it's made are minimal. Why mess with brilliance? It's hard not to be enamoured by the sultry enclave of chinoiserie that is this underground restaurant, where sleek staff glide out of the shadows carrying all manner of elegantly presented modern Chinese fare. To dine on dim sum here is a pleasure, the sweet scallop *siu mai* with glistening flying-fish roe a highlight.

▶ *On a budget? Visit at lunchtime to enjoy the Hakkasan experience for much less.*

★ £ Lantana

13 Charlotte Place, W1T 1SN (7637 3347, www.lantanacafe.co.uk). Goodge Street tube. **Open** 8am-3pm Mon-Wed; 8am-3pm, 5-9pm Thur, Fri; 9am-3pm Sat, Sun. **Main courses** £4.50-£10.50. **Credit** MC, V. **Map** p396 J5 ㉕ **Café**

This cheerful but busy Aussie café won *Time Out*'s Best New Café award in 2009. It's open for breakfast through to lunch (dinner at the end of the week). Sweetcorn fritters with crispy bacon or smoked salmon with lime aïoli is one highlight, the delicious banana bread another. The combination of Monmouth beans and a La Marzocco espresso machine ensures flawless coffee every time.

Paramount

32nd floor, Centre Point, 101-103 New Oxford Street, WC1A 1DD (7420 2900, www.paramount. uk.net). Tottenham Court Road tube. **Open** 8-10am, noon-3pm, 6-11pm Mon-Fri; 10am-3pm, 6-11pm Sat. **Main courses** £14.50-£25.50. **Credit** AmEx, MC, V. **Map** p416 X1 ㉖ **Modern European**

A private members' club opened on the 32nd floor of the landmark Centre Point building – almost exactly a month after the 2008 recession began in earnest. So, in 2010, owners Pierre and Kathleen Condou hired an excellent chef and opened it as a smart restaurant. The handsome Tom Dixon-designed interior is upstaged by the superb view, but Colin Layfield's menu manages to hold its own, with carefully constructed dishes that appeal to the eye and the tongue. The attached bar is open only to members or diners.

▶ *If dinner prices are too vertiginous, check out the surprisingly reasonable breakfast menu.*

COVENT GARDEN

The newer branch of **Benito's Hat** (*see p213*) is just off the market square.

£ Abeno Too

17-18 Great Newport Street, WC2H 7JE (7379 1160, www.abeno.co.uk). Leicester Square tube. **Open** noon-11pm Mon-Sat; noon-10.30pm Sun. **Main courses** £9-£24. **Credit** MC, V. **Map** p416 X3 ㉗ **Japanese**

The tables and counter at Abeno Too are all fitted with hot plates for cooking the *okonomiyaki* (pancakes with nuggets of vegetables, seafood, pork and other titbits added to a disc of noodles) that are the speciality of this small chain. The lovely staff cook the pancakes to order, right in front of you: hearty,

---

THE BEST TREAT EATS

Bistrot Bruno Loubet
Pure dining delight. *See p212.*

Paramount
For dinner with a view. *See above.*

Wolseley
Drop-dead glamour. *See p220.*

Paramount.

comforting stuff it is too. If *okonomiyaki* doesn't suit your mood, choose from *katsu* curries, sashimi, salads, rice and noodle dishes and *teppanyaki*. A third branch is promised for Hampstead.
Other locations 47 Museum Street, Bloomsbury, WC1A 1LY (7405 3211).

£ Dishoom
12 Upper St Martin's Lane, WC2H 9FB (7420 9320, www.dishoom.com). Covent Garden or Leicester Square tube. **Open** 8am-11pm Mon-Fri; 10am-11pm Sat; 10am-10pm Sun. **Main courses** £1.90-£9.20. **Credit** AmEx, MC, V. **Map** p416 X3 ㉘ **Pan-Indian**
Dishoom has got the look of a Mumbai 'Irani' café (cheap, cosmopolitan eateries set up by Persian immigrants in the 1900s) spot on. Solid oak panels, antique mirrors and ceiling fans say 'retro grandeur'; a web of black cables for the pendant lights say 'contemporary and fun'. A fascinating display of old magazine covers, nostalgic adverts and fading photos of Indian families adorns the walls. Parts of the menu are familiar street snacks (a terrific *pau bhaji*), but chocolate fondant, classy cocktails and intriguing lassi flavours move things upmarket.

£ Food for Thought
31 Neal Street, WC2H 9PR (7836 9072). Covent Garden tube. **Open** noon-8.30pm Mon-Sat; noon-5pm Sun. **Main courses** £4.70-£7.80. **No credit cards. Map** p416 Y2 ㉙ **Vegetarian café**
Taking the stairs to this old basement café, where sharing tables is the norm, is like making a steady descent to the 1970s. Of its type, the food is excellent, fresh and with big, well-considered flavours. Prices are persuasive, but service can be sloppy.

★ Great Queen Street
32 Great Queen Street, WC2B 5AA (7242 0622). Covent Garden or Holborn tube. **Open** *Restaurant* noon-2.30pm, 6-10.30pm Mon-Sat;

noon-3pm Sun. *Bar* 5-11.30pm Tue-Sat. **Main courses** £10.80-£22. **Credit** MC, V. **Map** p416 Z2 ㉚ **British**
The staff at this casual eaterie are a helpful young bunch. The ex-pub premises have been tarted up, but not too much, and the food is direct and robust; expect the likes of hare with noodles. Other plus points: desserts are taken seriously, and wines come in glass, carafe and bottle sizes. In the basement, drinks and snacks are served. Pretty much the ideal local, set right in the centre of town. As you'd expect, booking is essential – but later drop-ins can sometimes be accommodated.

£ Rock & Sole Plaice
47 Endell Street, WC2H 9AJ (7836 3785). Covent Garden tube. **Open** 11.30am-10.30pm Mon-Sat; noon-9.30pm Sun. **Main courses** £9-£12. **Credit** MC, V. **Map** p416 Y2 ㉛ **Fish & chips**
Exactly when the Rock & Sole Plaice (or its predecessor) started battering fish is in dispute; some say 1871, others maintain that it opened just after World War II. Either way, this small corner chippy near Drury Lane continues to thrive. West End theatre posters line the interior, but, on warmer days, you'll do best to try to squeeze on to one of the inevitably busy roadside tables.

£ Scoop
40 Shorts Gardens, WC2H 9AB (7240 7086, www.scoopgelato.com). Covent Garden tube. **Open** 11am-9pm daily. Times may vary, phone to check. **Ice-cream** £2.50/scoop. **Credit** AmEx, MC, V. **Map** p416 Y2 ㉜ **Ice-cream**
The peak-time queues are testament to the quality of the ice-creams, even the dairy-free health versions, at this Italian artisan's shop. Flavours include ricotta and fig, and a very superior Piedmont hazelnut type. **Other locations** 53 Brewer Street, Soho, W1F 9UJ (7494 3082).

CONSUME

★ J Sheekey

28-34 St Martin's Court, Leicester Square,
WC2N 4AL (7240 2565, www.j-sheekey.co.uk).
Leicester Square tube. **Open** noon-3pm, 5.30pm-
midnight Mon-Sat; noon-3.30pm, 6-11pm
Sun. **Main courses** £13.50-£39.50. **Credit**
AmEx, DC, MC, V. **Map** p416 X4 ❸
Fish & seafood

Unlike many of London's period-piece restaurants
(which this certainly is, having been chartered in the
mid 19th century), Sheekey's buzzes with fashionable folk and famous faces. And it seldom turns out
a dud from a menu that runs from sparklingly simple seafood platters to dishes that are interesting
without being elaborate. You'll pay for the privilege
of dining here, and booking ahead is essential, but
the rewards are worth both expense and effort.

▶ *Next door, the J Sheekey Oyster Bar (nos.33-*
34, WC2N 4AL) serves a similar menu but to
customers sitting casually at the counter, and
with an expanded choice of oysters.

£ Wahaca

66 Chandos Place, WC2N 4HG (7240 1883,
www.wahaca.co.uk). Covent Garden or Leicester
Square tube. **Open** noon-11pm Mon-Sat; noon-
10.30pm Sun. **Main courses** £3.25-£9.95.
Credit AmEx, MC, V. **Map** p416 Y4 ❹
Mexican

Wahaca has many points in its favour: a central location, colourful and casually fashionable decor, a
trendy Mexican menu and pretty comfortable prices.
It's run by celebrity chef of sorts: Thomasina Miers,
a former winner of BBC's *MasterChef*, appears frequently on TV and in the recipe press. The kitchen's
aim is to marry locally sourced ingredients with
Mexican-inspired recipes: a laudable aim, but some
substitutions are better than others.

Other locations Southern Terrace, Westfield
Shopping Centre, Shepherd's Bush, W12 7GF
(8749 4517); Park Pavilion, 40 Canada Square,
Docklands, E14 5FW (7516 9145).

SOHO & CHINATOWN

Chinatown stalwarts such as **Mr Kong**
(21 Lisle Street, 7437 7341) and **Wong Kei**
(41-43 Wardour Street, 7437 8408) still ply
their reliable Anglo-Cantonese trade, but
there's more gastronomic excitement offered
by the newer likes of **Barshu** (*see p217*) or, on
Ganton Street a little to the west, **Cha Cha
Moon** (*see p217*). Cheaper, non-Chinese cheap
eats are also served on Ganton Street at the
Diner (nos.16-18, 7287 8962, www.thediner
soho.com) and **Mother Mash** (no.26, 7494
9644, www.mothermash.co.uk). On Brewer
Street in central Soho, try top-class luxury
dining at **Hix** (*see p212* **Hix Oyster &
Chop House**) or the excellent ice-cream
at the new branch of **Scoop** (*see p215*).

Wahaca.

★ Arbutus

63-64 Frith Street, W1D 3JW (7734 4545,
www.arbutusrestaurant.co.uk). Tottenham Court
Road tube. **Open** noon-2.30pm, 5-11pm Mon-Sat;
noon-3pm, 5.30-10.30pm Sun. **Main courses**
£14-£19.95. **Credit** AmEx, MC, V. **Map** p416
W2 ❸ Modern European

Providing very fine cooking at very fair prices isn't
an easy trick, but Anthony Demetre makes it look
easy. Although it's not cheap to eat à la carte, the set
lunch (three courses £16.95) and 'pre-theatre' dinner
(three courses £18.95) are famously good value. The
restaurant pioneered 250ml carafes for sampling the
wines from the well-edited list; try a carafe of
macabeo with a juicy, herby mullet with gnocchi,
spinach and clams.

▶ *Sister restaurant Wild Honey (12 St George*
Street, W1S 2FB, 7758 9160, www.wildhoney
restaurant.co.uk) is great value for lunch.

Barshu

*28 Frith Street, W1D 5LF (7287 6688, www.
bar-shu.co.uk). Leicester Square or Tottenham
Court Road tube.* **Open** noon-11pm Mon-Thur,
Sun; noon-11.30pm Fri, Sat. **Main courses**
£8.90-£28.90. **Credit** AmEx, MC, V. **Map**
p416 W3 ➌ Chinese

Since opening in 2006, Barshu has done much to
popularise Sichuan cuisine in London. Its owners
now run two other restaurants nearby, but the cooking continues to thrill and it is still an exceedingly
charming venue, its decor modelled on that of an old
Beijing teahouse. A dive into the large menu with
its helpful illustrations reveals a number of 'blood
and guts' dishes: the likes of crunchy ribbons of jellyfish with a dark vinegar sauce and sesame oil.
▶ *For more unusual (and cheap) Chinese food in
Soho, try Barshu's siblings Ba Shan (24 Romilly
Street, W1D 5AH, 7287 3266) and Baozi Inn
(25 Newport Court, WC2H 7JS, 7287 6877).*

Bocca di Lupo

*12 Archer Street, W1D 7BB (7734 2223,
www.boccadilupo.com). Piccadilly Circus tube.*
Open 12.30-3pm, 5.30-11pm Mon-Sat; noon-4pm
Sun. **Main courses** £8.50-£22. **Credit** AmEx,
MC, V. **Map** p416 W3 ➐ Italian

This busy, informal Italian has a lively open kitchen
and tapas-style menu of regional specialities. Select
one small dish from several different categories of
the menu (raw and cured, fried, pastas and risottos,
soups and stews, roasts, and so on) and you should
enjoy a fairly balanced meal; for those who prefer
not to share, large portions of each dish are also
offered. *See also p226* Eating In.
▶ *The same team runs the fine gelateria Gelupo,
down the road at no.7 (7287 5555).*

£ Cha Cha Moon

*15-21 Ganton Street, W1F 9BN (7297 9800,
www.chachamoon.com). Oxford Circus tube.*
Open 11.30am-11pm Mon-Thur; 11.30am-
11.30pm Fri, Sat; 11.30am-10.30pm Sun. **Main
courses** £5.50-£8. **Credit** AmEx, MC, V. **Map**
p416 U3 ➌ Chinese

Like Wagamama before it, Alan Yau's Cha Cha
Moon offers fast food of mixed Asian inspiration at
low prices, served on long cafeteria-style tables in a
sleek room. The main focus is on excellent noodle
dishes, hailing from Hong Kong, Shanghai and elsewhere in China, clocking in at a bit over £5 each.

★ **Dehesa**

*25 Ganton Street, W1F 9BP (7494 4170).
Oxford Circus tube.* **Open** noon-11pm Mon-Sat;
noon-5pm Sun. **Tapas** £3.50-£7.25. **Credit**
AmEx, MC, V. **Map** p416 U3 ➌ Spanish/
Italian tapas

After running a no-reservations policy for a while,
this informal yet sophisticated spot now takes bookings, which makes it easier to enjoy its Spanish-

Italian tapas. The black-footed Ibérico pig (the place
is named after its woodland home) appears in nutty-
flavoured ham and other charcuterie, but local sourcing comes to the fore in tapas such as confit of Old
Spot pork belly with cannellini beans. Staff are
bright, well informed and efficient.
▶ *North of Oxford Street in Fitzrovia, Salt Yard
is another excellent choice for tapas (54 Goodge
Street, W1T 4NA, 7637 0657).*

★ **£ Hummus Bros**

*88 Wardour Street, W1F 0TH (7734 1311,
www.hbros.co.uk). Oxford Circus or Tottenham
Court Road tube.* **Open** noon-10pm Mon-Wed,
Sun; noon-11pm Thur-Sat. **Main courses** £2.80-
£5.80. **Credit** AmEx, MC, V. **Map** p416 W3 ➍
Café

The simple and hugely successful formula at this
café/takeaway is to serve houmous as a base for a
selection of toppings, which you scoop up with excellent, pillowy pitta bread that's toasted while you
wait. That's it. There's are two or three sweet things
for pudding, plus some hot and cold drinks, but the
key attraction is quick, tasty, nutritious, filling and
great value food, whether you eat in or take away.
Other locations 37-63 Southampton Row,
Bloomsbury, WC1B 4DA (7404 7079); 128
Cheapside, the City, EC2V 6BT (7726 8011).

£ Maison Bertaux

*28 Greek Street, W1D 5DQ (7437 6007).
Leicester Square tube.* **Open** 8.30am-11pm Mon-
Sat; 8.30am-7.30pm Sun. **Main courses** £1.50-
£4.50. **No credit cards.** **Map** p416 X3 ➍ Café
Oozing arty, bohemian charm, this café dates back
to 1871 when Soho was London's little piece of the
Continent. Battered old bentwood tables and chairs
add to the feeling of being in a pâtisserie in rural
France, albeit one with a bit of additional camp Soho
flamboyance. The provisions (cream cakes, greasy
pastries, pots of tea) are really beside the point.

★ **£ Princi**

*135 Wardour Street, W1F 0UF (7478 8888,
www.princi.co.uk). Leicester Square or Tottenham
Court Road tube.* **Open** 7am-midnight Mon-Sat;
9am-11pm Sun. **Main courses** £5-£8.50. **Credit**
AmEx, MC, V. **Map** p416 W3 ➍ Bakery-café

INSIDE TRACK CHINATOWN

For atmosphere, drop in for a 'bubble tea'
(sweet, icy, full of balls of jelly and slurped
up with a straw) at late-night fave **HK Diner**
(22 Wardour Street, 7434 9544). If you
need to eat especially late, Cantonese
old-stager the **New Mayflower** (68-70
Shaftesbury Avenue, 7734 9207) is
open nightly until 4am.

Asian-cuisine supremo Alan Yau teamed up with a prestigious Italian bakery chain for this popular venture. The premises consist of a vast L-shaped granite counter and communal seating, a stylish variation on his much-copied Wagamama noodle bar concept. As well as cakes, tiramisu and pastries, there's a vast range of savoury dishes. The big slices of pizza have a springy base, the margherita variety pungent with fresh thyme; caprese salad comes with creamy balls of buffalo mozzarella and big slices of beef tomato. Princi can get hectic, but it's a solid option for inexpensive snacks.

Yauatcha

15 Broadwick Street, W1F 0DL (7494 8888). Piccadilly Circus or Tottenham Court Road tube. **Open** noon-11.45pm Mon-Sat; noon-10.30pm Sun. **Dim sum** £3-£12. **Credit** AmEx, MC, V. **Map** p416 V2 ⓭ **Dim sum/tearoom**

Serving dim sum day and night over two floors, Yauatcha happily cocks a snook at traditionalists who believe the treats to 'touch the heart' (the meaning of *dim sum*) should never be served past 5pm. Much is made of the unusually good (and lengthy) tea list, and the choice of dim sum dishes is extended with congee, noodles and some intriguing stir-fries. The place's popularity with Soho creatives shows no sign of easing.

OXFORD STREET & MARYLEBONE

★ L'Autre Pied

5-7 Blandford Street, W1U 3DB (7486 9696, www.lautrepied.co.uk). Baker Street tube. **Open** noon-2.30pm, 6-10.30pm Mon-Sat; noon-3pm,

6.30-9.30pm Sun. **Main courses** £21.50-£27.95. **Credit** AmEx, MC, V. **Map** p396 G5 ⓮ **Modern European**

For a far less eye-watering outlay than a meal at older sibling Pied à Terre, L'Autre Pied offers nuanced cooking in handsome rooms. With a light touch and subtle use of herbs, chef Marcus Eaves doesn't stint on the dairy, as demonstrated by an intensely creamy mushroom and leek risotto. Despite the trappings of somewhere that takes food very seriously, L'Autre Pied is accessible and relaxing. The kitchen doesn't put a foot wrong.

★ £ Busaba Eathai

8-13 Bird Street, W1U 1BU (7518 8080). Bond Street tube. **Open** noon-11pm Mon-Thur; noon-11.30pm Fri, Sat; noon-10pm Sun. **Main courses** £5.50-£10.90. **Credit** AmEx, MC, V. **Map** p396 G6 ⓯ **Thai**

All the branches of this handsome Thai fast food canteen are excellent and busy, but this one is superbly located for Oxford Street shoppers. The interior combines shared tables and bench seats with a touch of dark-toned oriental mystique, and the dishes are always intriguing, as you'd expect of a menu developed by David Thompson of the exemplary Thai fine-dining resto Nahm (*see p224*). **Other locations** throughout the city.

Fairuz

3 Blandford Street, W1U 3DA (7486 8108, www.fairuz.uk.com). Baker Street or Bond Street tube. **Open** noon-11.30pm Mon-Sat; noon-11pm Sun. **Main courses** £12-£19.95. *Set meze* £19.95. **Cover** £1.50. **Credit** AmEx, MC, V. **Map** p396 G5 ⓰ **Middle Eastern**

Momo. *See p220.*

The combination of Lebanese food, neighbourhood-taverna surroundings and West End location has proved enduringly popular for this longstanding Marylebone favourite. Its collection of meze – smooth houmous, zingy *fuul moukala* (green broad beans with olive oil, lemon and coriander), tabouleh, spinach *fatayer* – is brilliantly executed.

£ La Fromagerie
2-6 Moxon Street, W1U 4EW (7935 0341, www.lafromagerie.co.uk). Baker Street or Bond Street tube. **Open** 8am-7.30pm Mon-Fri; 9am-7pm Sat; 10am-6pm Sun. **Main courses** £6-£15. **Credit** AmEx, MC, V. **Map** p396 G5 ❹ Café
There aren't many cafés in London where Herefordshire snails cooked in garlic butter make the menu, but Patricia Michelson's high-end deli/café has always ploughed its own, very stylish, culinary furrow, and its communal tables are often packed with devotees. The basic menu, which includes a classy ploughman's lunch, is supplemented by a separate breakfast offer (own-made baked beans, granola with posh French yoghurt) and a 'kitchen menu' from 12.30pm.

£ Golden Hind
73 Marylebone Lane, W1U 2PN (7486 3644). Bond Street tube. **Open** noon-3pm, 6-10pm Mon-Fri; 6-10pm Sat. **Main courses** £5-£10.70. **Credit** AmEx, MC, V. **Map** p396 G5 ❹
Fish & chips
The Golden Hind's walls are lined with old black and white photos and a blackboard listing the names of owners back as far as 1914. The current Hellenic ownership is reflected in a menu that places mixed Greek pickles and deep-fried feta alongside standard starters such as fish cakes. Try for a seat on the ground floor so you can gawp at the stunning art deco fryer (sadly, no longer used). Staff are jovial and service is quick.

PICCADILLY CIRCUS & MAYFAIR

Lunch at **Wild Honey** (*see p216* **Arbutus**), the sister establishment to Anthony Demetre's Arbutus restaurant, is a great option for an affordable treat.

Albemarle
Brown's, 33-34 Albemarle Street, W1S 4BP (7493 6020, www.thealbemarlerestaurant.com). Green Park tube. **Open** noon-6.10.30pm Mon-Sat; 12.30-3pm, 7-10.30pm Sun. **Main courses** £14.50-£32.50. **Credit** AmEx, DC, MC, V. **Map** p416 U4 ❹ British
The modern art-strewn dining room at Brown's (*see p196*) is much more enticing than most hotel restaurants. A blend of period and modern furnishings, comfortable chairs and charming staff makes for a

relaxed and enjoyable meal – even before you get to the excitement of the menu. Seasonal British ingredients are used throughout. Vegetarians get their own menu, and there's a great-value set meal – on Sunday, this includes the roast.

★ Bentley's Oyster Bar & Grill
11-15 Swallow Street, W1B 4DG (7734 4756, www.bentleysoysterbarandgrill.co.uk). Piccadilly Circus tube. **Open** *Oyster Bar* noon-midnight Mon-Sat; noon-10pm Sun. *Restaurant* noon-3pm, 6-11pm Mon-Fri; 6-11pm Sat. **Main courses** *Oyster Bar* £8.75-£36. *Restaurant* £18.95-£38. **Credit** AmEx, MC, V. **Map** p416 V4 ❺
Fish & seafood
There's something timeless about Richard Corrigan's restoration of this classic oyster house. World War I was raging when Bentley's first opened, but the suited gents who flock here today enjoy their seafood with the same gusto as their great-grandfathers before them. While the first-floor dining rooms are more sedate and well mannered, the downstairs oyster bar is where the action is.
▶ *Corrigan also runs the estimable Corrigan's Mayfair (28 Upper Grosvenor Street, W1K 7EH, 7499 9943).*

Chisou
4 Princes Street, W1B 2LE (7629 3931, www.chisou.co.uk). Oxford Circus tube. **Open** noon-2.30pm, 6-10.15pm Mon-Sat. **Main courses** £12-£23.50. **Credit** AmEx, MC, V. **Map** p416 T2 ❺ Japanese
Chisou looks quiet enough from the outside; inside, though, this modestly fashionable restaurant hums with purposeful activity. Friendly waitresses keep things moving at the blonde-wood tables, while to the rear is a fun sushi bar. Salted belly pork, and the pure *ume cha* (rice in a light hot broth with pickled plum) are highlights, and there's a serious saké and shochu list. Next door is Chisou's excellent noodle and *donburi* bar.

★ Hibiscus
29 Maddox Street, W1S 2PA (7629 2999, www.hibiscusrestaurant.co.uk). Oxford Circus tube. **Open** noon-2.30pm, 6.30-10pm Tue-Fri; 6-10pm Sat. **Set meals** £29.50-£75 3 courses; £95 tasting menu. **Credit** AmEx, MC, V. **Map** p416 U3 ❺ Haute cuisine
Tables in this simple Mayfair dining room are arranged around a large central workstation topped with an extravagant floral display. The crowd is well heeled and rather businesslike, even when their intentions are social. Many stick with the set lunch (as usual, far cheaper than the equivalent dinner menu), on which you might find the moussaka of Elwy Valley mutton with feta and anchovy jus that has become something of a signature dish for Hibiscus. For dessert, try clafoutis with almonds and an unusually rich pistachio ice-cream.

CONSUME

CONSUME

Momo
25 Heddon Street, W1B 4BH (7434 4040,
www.momoresto.com). Piccadilly Circus tube.
Open noon-2.30pm, 6.30-11.30pm Mon-Sat; 6.30-
11pm Sun. **Main courses** £13-£15. **Credit**
AmEx, DC, MC, V. **Map** p416 U3 **③** **North
African**
The ornate Momo, opened in 1997, made Algerian-
born international restaurateur Mourad Mazouz's
reputation. Carved screens, tasselled cushions, brass
lanterns and low tables transport diners to Morocco's
most fashionable imaginary club. Tables are tightly
packed, adding to a lively mood; come during the day
for a more serene vibe. The alfresco terrace evokes
riad-cool and offers shisha pipes; downstairs is Mô
Café (mint tea, wraps, meze) and Bazaar (books, CDs,
furniture), plus the luxurious Kemia bar. The menu
ranges from harira and chicken tagine with preserved lemons and olives or an inventive *briouat* of
cheese, mint and potatoes with quince marmalade to,
well, rump of lamb with jerusalem artichoke purée,
garlic and rosemary jus. *Photo p218.*

Parlour
1st floor, Fortnum & Mason, 181 Piccadilly,
W1A 1ER (7734 8040, www.fortnumandmason.
co.uk). Green Park or Piccadilly Circus tube.
Open 10am-7.30pm Mon-Sat; noon-4.30pm Sun.
Ice-cream £6-£10. **Credit** AmEx, MC, V. **Map**
p416 V5 **④** **Ice-cream**
David Collins' quirky design for this café is all ice-
cream and chocolate tones, with retro kitchenette
seating. It's a great place to meet friends, though
prices are high. The best option is an ice-cream
'flight': you'll get three scoops of your choice, served
with wonderfully silky Amedei dark- or milk-choco-
late sauce for £10.

Sketch: The Parlour
9 Conduit Street, W1S 2XJ (0870 777 4488,
www.sketch.uk.com). Oxford Circus tube. **Open**
8am-9pm Mon-Fri; 10am-9pm Sat. *Tea served* 3-
6.30pm Mon-Sat. **Main courses** £4-£8.50. *Set
tea* £9.50-£24. **Credit** AmEx, MC, V. **Map** p416
U3 **⑤** **Café**
Of the three parts of Pierre Gagnaire's legendarily
expensive Sketch, which also includes destination
dining at the Gallery and the Lecture Room's haute-
beyond-haute cuisine, Parlour appeals the most for
its tongue-in-cheek sexiness. Saucy nudes illustrate
the chairs, and the chandelier appears to be covered
with pairs of red fishnet tights. Gagnaire's menu
includes simple hearty dishes and quirky high-
concept creations, such as the club sandwich with
red and green bread and a layer of stencilled jelly on
top; it's mostly air-dried ham with tiny flecks of
grapefruit. Absolutely delicious.

£ Tibits
12-14 Heddon Street, W1B 4DA (7758 4110,
www.tibits.ch). Oxford Circus tube. **Open** 9am-
10.30pm Mon-Wed; 9am-midnight Thur-Sat;
10am-10.30pm Sun. **Buffet** £2/100g. **Credit** MC,
V. **Map** p416 U3 **⑥** **Vegetarian café**
Designers Guild fabrics in raspberry and lime contrast with a black ceiling and smart wicker chairs at
this modern take on the buffet restaurant. Part of a
small Swiss chain, Tibits may be vegetarian but it's
not puritanical. Fill your plate from the salads and
hot dishes in the central 'boat' and take it to the
counter for weighing. There are organic Freedom
lagers on tap, plus a handful of wines, and coffees.

★ Wolseley
160 Piccadilly, W1J 9EB (7499 6996,
www.thewolseley.com). Green Park tube. **Open**
7am-midnight Mon-Fri; 8am-midnight Sat; 8am-
11pm Sun. *Tea served* 3-6.30pm Mon-Fri, Sun;
3.30-5.30pm Sat. **Main courses** £6.75-£28.75.
Set tea £9.75-£21. **Cover** £2. **Credit** AmEx, DC,
MC, V. **Map** p416 U5 **⑦** **Brasserie**
An interpretation of the grand cafés of continental
Europe, the Wolseley serves breakfast, lunch, tea
and dinner to a smart set of Londoners and visitors
in its opulent dining room. Huge bronze doors open
up to an art deco dining room, while an entrance
table displays a selection of the day's choices. No one
comes here just for the food, but breakfast at the
Wolseley is a failsafe treat. Attention to detail from
beginning to end suggests the place is under no
threat of losing its iconic status.

WESTMINSTER & ST JAMES'S

Cinnamon Club
*Old Westminster Library, 30-32 Great Smith
Street, SW1P 3BU (7222 2555, www.cinnamon
club.com). St James's Park or Westminster tube.*
Open 7.30-9.30am, noon-2.30pm, 7.30-9.30pm
Mon-Fri; noon-2.30pm, 7.30-9.30pm Sat. **Main
courses** £11-£29. **Credit** AmEx, DC, MC, V.
Map p399 K9 **⑧** **Indian**
Aiming to create a complete Indian fine-dining expe-
rience, Cinnamon Club provides cocktails, fine
wines, tasting menus, breakfasts (Indian, Anglo-
Indian, British), private dining rooms and all atten-
dant flummery in an impressive, wood-lined space.
Executive chef Vivek Singh devises innovative
dishes; even the well-priced set meal (£20 for two
courses) is invitingly out of the ordinary.
Other locations Cinnamon Kitchen, 9
Devonshire Square, the City, EC2M 4WY (7626
5000, www.cinnamonkitchen.co.uk).

Inn the Park
St James's Park, SW1A 2BJ (7451 9999,
www.innthepark.com). St James's Park tube.
Open 8-11am, noon-3pm, 6-9pm Mon-Fri; 9-
11am, noon-4pm, 6-9pm Sat, Sun. *Tea served* 3-
5pm Mon-Fri; 4-5pm Sat, Sun. **Main courses**
£10.50-£8.50. **Credit** AmEx, MC, V. **Map** p399
K8 **⑨** **British**

Prime Locations

Is the happy marriage of dining and sightseeing starting to show strain?

Not long ago, London's big galleries and museums fed only the soul, their cafés and restaurants little more than an afterthought. Then Oliver Peyton took it upon himself to up the ante. Following his opening in 2004 of the interesting but not entirely successful **Inn the Park** (*see p220*), almost within sight of Buckingham Palace alongside the waterfowl lake in St James's Park, Peyton launched the **National Dining Rooms** (*see p222*) at the National Gallery in 2006, quickly followed by the convivial, later-opening **National Café**. The Dining Rooms wasn't merely a cut above most establishments of its type, it immediately became a destination in its own right – no matter the quality of the Impressionist paintings just along the corridor. Suddenly Peyton seemed to be opening a restaurant as often as the rest of us would open a newspaper: the Wallace Collection, the ICA, the Wellcome Collection, St Pancras International and the British Library all got full-scale restaurants or a Peyton & Byrne bakery-café, with its distinctive Scotch eggs, big sausage rolls and fist-sized fairy cakes.

The honchos couldn't fail to recognise the footfall potential of brushing up their catering. Benugo, a company named in honour of founders Ben and Hugo Warner, opened a couple of popular bar-restaurants in BFI Southbank, the **Serpentine Bar & Kitchen** (*see p223* **Lido Restaurant Hyde Park**) in Hyde Park, and the London Wall Bar & Kitchen at the entrance to the Museum of London. The relaunched Saatchi Gallery hit gold with its vivacious brasserie **Gallery Mess** (*see p222*), and even St Paul's Cathedral won acclaim for its **Restaurant at St Paul's** (*see p211*).

But there are signs of trouble in this perfect marriage of fine food and high culture. Peyton's openings since the National Dining Rooms have failed to garner the same unequivocal praise, and the prices begin to feel a bit high, while the tendency of every significant destination in London to launch carbon-copy 'sophisticated' bar-restaurants feels a little weary. Tom Aikens may be the one to feel the backlash: despite our love of the original **Tom's Kitchen** (*see p222*) in Chelsea and a wonderful Thames-side location, we found Tom's Terrace at Somerset House a 'lacklustre and overpriced experience' in summer 2010 – £17.50 for a grilled steak sandwich? The views are splendid from Waterloo Bridge, right next door, for the few quid it costs to buy a supermarket sarnie.

CONSUME

Inn the Park.

It's all about the location at this beautifully appointed and designed café-restaurant. The seasonal British cooking isn't always up to expectations, especially given the prices, but there is plenty on the plus side: staff are lovely, and the setting (overlooking the duck lake, with trees all around and the London Eye in the distance) is really wonderful.

▶ *In 2004, Inn the Park was the first Oliver Peyton restaurant to open in a major London sight. For details, see p221* **Prime Locations**.

National Dining Rooms

Sainsbury Wing, National Gallery, Trafalgar Square, WC2N 5DN (7747 2525, www.the nationaldiningrooms.co.uk). Charing Cross tube/ rail. **Open** *Bakery* 10am-5.30pm Mon-Thur, Sat, Sun; 10am-8.30pm Fri. *Restaurant* noon-3.15pm Mon-Thur, Sat, Sun; noon-3.15pm, 5-7pm Fri. **Main courses** *Bakery* £8-£12. *Restaurant* £22 2 courses; £25 3 courses. **Credit** AmEx, MC, V. **Map** p416 X4 ⑩ **British**
Oliver Peyton's restaurant in the Sainsbury Wing of the National Gallery (*see p129*) offers far better food than the unpleasant fare museum diners have become accustomed to, albeit at a price: oak-smoked Cornish duck, pea shoots with quince jelly and a val fries, perhaps, followed by wild wood pigeon with currant and beetroot glaze. The few window seats have prized views over Trafalgar Square, and the bakery side of the operation ably fulfils the cakes-and-a-cuppa role of the familiar museum café. *See also p221* **Prime Locations**.

Saké No Hana

23 St James's Street, SW1A 1HA (7925 8988). Green Park tube. **Open** noon-3pm, 6-11.30pm Mon-Sat. **Main courses** £4-£40. **Credit** AmEx, MC, V. **Map** p398 J8 ⑪ **Japanese**
The food presentation at Alan Yau's upmarket venture is unmistakably high-end, as are the smart staff's black uniforms and architect Kengo Kuma's cool tatami and cedar design. Sashimi and sushi account for much of the menu, but pricier cooked dishes such as miso Chilean sea bass in houba leaf make menu-perusing more interesting. The saké and shochu list is substantial.

CHELSEA

The **Cadogan Arms** (*see p242*) is a great pub, but – run by the Martin brothers – it's also a superb place to eat. If you fancy fish and chips, check out the new **Geales** (*see p224*).

Chelsea Brasserie

7-12 Sloane Square, SW1W 8EG (7881 5999, www.chelsea-brasserie.co.uk). Sloane Square tube. **Open** 11.30am-3.30pm, 6-10.30pm Mon-Sat; 11am-4pm Sun. **Main courses** £13-£21.50. **Set** *dinner* (6-7.30pm) £19.75 2 courses. **Credit** MC, V. **Map** p398 G10 ⑫

Prices are higher than the brasserie norm, but this polished establishment is no run-of-the-mill local. Service is impeccable, and the decor, while not cutting edge, is a handsome backdrop for a clientele of well-heeled tourists and SW1 locals. The cooking is good, sometimes very good – as in a main of pan-fried calf's liver with caramelised shallots, smoked bacon and sage jus, with creamy mash. As befits a proper brasserie, the bar can provide anything from fresh juices to a bloody mary.

Gallery Mess

Saatchi Gallery, Duke of York's HQ, King's Road, SW3 4LY (7730 8135, www.saatchi-gallery.co. uk). Sloane Square tube. **Open** 10am-9.30pm Mon-Sat; 10am-7pm Sun. **Main courses** £9-£12. **Credit** AmEx, MC, V. **Map** p395 F11 ⑬ **Brasserie**
The Saatchi Gallery (*see p140*) welcomed this fabulous brasserie shortly after opening. You can sit inside surrounded by modern art, but the grounds outside – littered with portable tables until 6pm, if the weather's fair – can be a more attractive option in summer. There's a simple breakfast menu of pastries, eggs and toast or fry-up served until 11.30am, then lunch and dinner take over, with the expected salads, pastas and burgers joined by more ambitious daily specials: perhaps steamed salmon served in a yellow 'curry' broth or saddle of lamb drizzled with a zig-zag of yoghurt. Of the desserts, knickerbocker glory is a triumph.

★ Tom's Kitchen

27 Cale Street, SW3 3QP (7349 0202, www. tomskitchen.co.uk). Sloane Square or South Kensington tube. **Open** 8-11am, noon-3pm, 6-11pm Mon-Fri; 10am-4pm, 6-11pm Sat, Sun. **Main courses** £14.50-£29.50. **Credit** AmEx, MC, V. **Map** p395 E11 ⑭ **Brasserie**
White-tiled walls, vast expanses of marble and a busy open kitchen ensure Tom Aikens' place sounds full even when it isn't – for weekend lunches it can often be packed. The big draw here is the pancake: well over an inch thick and almost as big as the serving plate, it's categorically London's best, filled with

---

THE BEST LATE EATS

Brick Lane Beigel Bake
The post-club, pre-bed refuelling classic.
See p229.

Hakkasan
For a bit of moody sophistication when the Chinatown lates (*see p217* **Inside Track**) just won't do the trick. *See p214.*

Princi
Italian bakery snacks in Soho. *See p217.*

blueberries and drizzled with maple syrup. Lunch and dinner menus make the most of the wood-smoked oven, spit-roast and grill. Expect hearty, big-tasting comfort food.

▶ *For similar food and prices that match the superb river views, try Tom's Kitchen & Terrace at Somerset House; see p221* **Prime Locations.**

KNIGHTSBRIDGE & SOUTH KENSINGTON

Amaya
19 Motcomb Street, 15 Halkin Arcade, SW1X 8JT (7823 1166, www.amaya.biz). Knightsbridge tube. **Open** 12.30-2.15pm, 6.30-11.30pm Mon-Sat; 12.45-2.45pm, 6.30-10.30pm Sun. **Main courses** £8.50-£25. **Credit** AmEx, DC, MC, V. **Map** p398 G9 🌐 **Indian**
Slinky by night, when its black leather seating, modish chandeliers and soundtrack of cool beats attract smooching couples, Amaya is light and breezy by day. From the open kitchen, black-aproned chefs display consummate skill at the tawa griddle, the tandoor oven and at the house-speciality charcoal grill.

★ Bar Boulud
Mandarin Oriental Hyde Park, 66 Knightsbridge, SW1X 7LA (7201 3899, www.barboulud.com). Knightsbridge tube. **Open** noon-2.30pm, 5.30-10.30pm daily. **Main courses** £12.50-£23. **Set meals** £20 3 courses. **Credit** AmEx, MC, V. **Map** p393 F8 🌐 **Brasserie**
The UK's top chef, Heston Blumenthal, had yet to instal his liquid nitrogen canisters and flamethrowers at the Mandarin Oriental as we went to press, but the posh hotel's new basement brasserie was already a hit. Daniel Boulud, a French chef rated one of the best restaurateurs in New York, has brought over some Big Apple style and French polish. The menu points to Lyon, the heart of French gastronomy, with amazing charcuterie and refined country classics, and to New York with three types of burger. The *île flottante* was a masterpiece; the service well informed, well mannered and utterly professional.

£ Lido Restaurant Hyde Park
The Serpentine, Hyde Park, W2 2UH (7706 7098, www.lidohydepark.co.uk). Hyde Park Corner or Marble Arch tube. **Open** *Jan, Feb, Nov, Dec* 8am-4pm daily. *Mar, Oct* 8am-5pm daily. *Apr* 8am-6pm daily. *May* 8am-7.30pm daily. *June* 8am-8pm daily. *July, Aug* 8am-9pm daily. *Sept* 8am-7pm daily. **Main courses** £6.50-£10. **Credit** MC, V. **Map** p393 E8 🌐 **Café**
A year-round haven with a menu ranging from summery calamari to warming slow-cooked shoulder of lamb with creamed flageolet – and plenty of outdoor seating. The mace-flavoured brown shrimp salad with soft-boiled egg is a delight. Children's plates include pizzettas, fish fingers and home-made orange jelly. A jolly choice of wines starts at £3.95

Min Jiang.

per glass; speciality beers include Theakston Old Peculier and London's own Meantime pale ale, and the cocktail list features tempting breakfast options.
▶ *At the eastern end of the lake, the Serpentine Bar & Kitchen (7706 8114, www.serpentine barandkitchen.com) also has great lakeside tables.*

Madsen
20 Old Brompton Road, SW7 3DL (7225 2772, www.madsenrestaurant.com). South Kensington tube. **Open** noon-10pm Mon, Sun; noon-11pm Tue-Thur; noon-midnight Fri, Sat. **Main courses** £11.50-£17.50. **Credit** MC, V. **Map** p395 D10 🌐 **Scandinavian**
Danes might feel frustrated that this chic, serene and very friendly café-cum-restaurant doesn't reflect the excitement surrounding Copenhagen's food scene, but the straightforward home cooking on offer – chicken breast fillet with horseradish cream sauce and roast root vegetables, *stegt rødspætte* (pan-fried plaice with melted butter and carrots) is pleasing. Skip the brief, international wine list in favour of the wonderful speciality Danish beers from Ærø. See also p226 **Eating In.**

Min Jiang
Royal Garden Hotel, 2-4 Kensington High Street, W8 4PT (7361 1988, www.minjiang. co.uk). High Street Kensington tube. **Open** noon-3pm, 6-10.30pm daily. **Main courses** £10-£48. **Credit** AmEx, MC, V. **Map** p392 B8 🌐 **Chinese**
Located on the tenth floor of the hotel, Min Jiang has fabulous views over Kensington Gardens (*see p145*) and beyond. Much money has been spent on ensuring the interior is suitably swish, with lattice screens and faux-Ming pottery, but the food is also pretty

good. Invest in an authentic Beijing duck: you'll get a chance to admire the carving skills of the chef at your table – a sure-fire hit with first-timers.

Nahm
Halkin, Halkin Street, SW1X 7DJ (7333 1234, www.nahm.como.bz). Hyde Park Corner tube. **Open** noon-2.30pm, 7-10.45pm Mon-Fri; 7-10.45pm Sat; 7-9.45pm Sun. **Main courses** £9.50-£19.50. **Credit** AmEx, DC, MC, V. **Map** p398 G9 ⓲ Thai

Done out in gold and bronze tones, the elegant dining room at the Halkin (*see p201*) feels opulent yet unfussy. Tables for two look out over a manicured garden, and the opportunity to share rare dishes of startling flavour combinations from Australian-born David Thompson's kitchen always makes for a memorable meal. He seeks to interpret historic Thai cooking, yet flashes of inspiration bring the dishes firmly into the modern era: for example, a chicken and banana-flower salad unusually, but successfully, includes samphire and palourdes clams. Presentation is exquisite.

Racine
239 Brompton Road, SW3 2EP (7584 4477). Knightsbridge or South Kensington tube, or bus 14, 74. **Open** noon-3pm, 6-10.30pm Mon-Fri; noon-3.30pm, 6-10.30pm Sat; noon-3.30pm, 6-10pm Sun. **Main courses** £12.50-£20.75. **Credit** AmEx, MC, V. **Map** p395 E10 ⓲ French

Heavy curtains inside the door allow diners to make a grand entrance into Racine's warm, vibrant 1930s retro atmosphere. The clientele seems to have become less varied in recent times, feeling more male and moneyed than before, but there's still plenty to enjoy from the menu: try a starter such as garlic and saffron mousse with mussels, or, for dessert, a clafoutis with morello cherries in kirsch.

★ Zuma
5 Raphael Street, SW7 1DL (7584 1010, www.zumarestaurant.com). Knightsbridge tube. **Open** *Restaurant* noon-2.30pm, 6-11pm Mon-Fri; 12.30-3.15pm, 6-11pm Sat; 12.30-3.15pm, 6-10.30pm Sun. *Bar* noon-11pm Mon-Fri; 12.30-11pm Sat; 12.30-10.30pm Sun. **Main courses** £14.80-£70. **Credit** AmEx, DC, MC, V. **Map** p395 F9 ⓲ Japanese

Zuma has established itself as a must-go destination for every rich visitor to London. The stylishly displayed bottles, skilful lighting and slickly presented sushi and robata bars still impress, and kitchen standards are as high as ever. Two things stand out: the quality of raw ingredients, and the imaginative flavour combinations, such as ginger, lime and coriander on the *tataki* (seared raw beef).

▶ *For fine cocktails, head to sister establishment Shochu Lounge (see p238), downstairs from the Roka restaurant.*

PADDINGTON & NOTTING HILL

Assaggi
1st floor, 39 Chepstow Place, W2 4TS (7792 5501). Bayswater, Notting Hill Gate or Queensway tube. **Open** 12.30-2.30pm, 7.30-11pm Mon-Fri; 1-2.20pm, 7.30-11pm Sat. **Main courses** £18-£24. **Credit** MC, V. **Map** p404 Z5 ⓲ Italian

This Notting Hill icon fills the first floor of a Georgian house above the Chepstow pub. The dining room has a mere dozen tables, so it's clamorous when full – as it usually is. The effusive greeting and uncompromising menu, both entirely in Italian, that once gave an exciting sense of place, now come across as a bit clichéd, but Assaggi remains delightful for Saturday lunch. Although pricey, the Sardinian food and wine here are better value than at London's other fashionable Italian restaurants.

★ Le Café Anglais
8 Porchester Gardens, W2 4DB (7221 1415, www.lecafeanglais.co.uk). Bayswater tube. **Open** noon-3.30pm, 6.30-11pm Mon-Thur; noon-3.30pm, 6.30-11.30pm Fri; noon-3.30pm, 6.30-11.30pm Sat; noon-3.30pm, 6.30-10.15pm Sun. **Main courses** £8-£27.50. **Cover** £1.80. **Credit** AmEx, MC, V. **Map** p392 B6 ⓲ Modern European

Chef-proprietor Rowley Leigh's fine restaurant opened to great acclaim and remains very popular – an all-day café/oyster bar was a welcome addition in 2010. Despite its location in Whiteleys shopping centre, the big, art deco-style room is glamorous, with floor-to-ceiling leaded windows on one side, and the open kitchen, rotisserie and bar opposite. It's a see-and-be-seen place with a menu perfect for grazers.

Geales
2 Farmer Street, W8 7SN (7727 7528, www.geales.com). Notting Hill Gate tube. **Open** 6-10.30pm Mon; noon-2.30pm, 6-10.30pm Tue-Fri; noon-10.30pm Sat; noon-9.30pm Sun. **Main courses** £8-£29.50. **Credit** AmEx, MC, V. **Map** p404 Z6 ⓲ Fish & seafood

Don't come here looking for exotic species or fancy cooking: Geales is all about good, classic dishes, served in simple but smart premises. The chef's only glance beyond these shores is towards the Continent, with steamed mussels and a tomatoey fish soup. Otherwise it's oysters, smoked salmon, prawn cocktail and firm, white fish in faultlessly crisp batter. Puddings confirm the place's fine British pedigree. **Other locations** 1 Cale Street, Chelsea, SW3 3QT (7965 0555).

★ Hereford Road
3 Hereford Road, W2 4AB (7727 1144, www.herefordroad.org). Bayswater tube. **Open** noon-3pm, 6-10.30pm Mon-Fri; noon-3.30pm, 6-10.30pm Sat; noon-4pm, 6-10pm Sun. **Main courses** £9.50-£14.50. **Credit** AmEx, MC, V. **Map** p404 Z5 ⓲ British

Hereford Road has the assurance of somewhere that's been around much longer than its actual three years of operation. It's an easy place in which to relax, with a mixed crowd and a happy buzz. Starters include the likes of (undyed) smoked haddock with white beans and leeks, while mains might feature mallard with braised chicory and lentils.

£ Kiasu

48 Queensway, W2 3RY (7727 8810). Bayswater or Queensway tube. **Open** noon-11pm daily. **Main courses** £6.90-£8. **Credit** (minimum £10) MC, V. **Map** p392 C6 ⑦ **Malaysian**
This former winner of *Time Out*'s Best Cheap Eats award has had its ups and downs in terms of quality, but lately seems to be on the ascendant again. The casual, modern decor can put a smile on your face with its quirky touches, and the best of the dishes – among them a stellar version of *char kway teow* (wok-fried flat noodles) – keep a fine balance between sweet and salty, moist and al dente.

Ledbury

127 Ledbury Road, W11 2AQ (7792 9090, www.theledbury.com). Westbourne Park tube. **Open** noon-2.30pm, 6.30-10.30pm Mon-Sat; noon-3pm, 7-10pm Sun. **Set meals** £19.50-£60. **Credit** AmEx, MC, V. **Map** p404 Y4 ⑱ **French**
The cheeriness that defines a midweek lunch in this residential backwater is testament to the reputation of Brett Graham's cooking. The imaginative, meticulous dishes are never overwrought, the sourcing is impeccable and the drinks list is exceptional. The comfort and noise-level, service and food seamlessly knit together to produce unruffled pleasure.

Chin Chin Laboratorists. *See p226.*

£ Taqueria

139-143 Westbourne Grove, W11 2RS (7229 4734, www.taqueria.co.uk). Notting Hill Gate tube. **Open** noon-11pm Mon-Thur, Sun; noon-11.30pm Fri; noon-10.30pm Sat. **Main courses** £5.50-£8.50. **Credit** MC, V. **Map** p404 Z4 ⑲ **Mexican**
Pop-art prints of iconic Mexican insurrectionist Emiliano Zapata adorn the walls of this classy cantina. The food isn't exactly revolutionary – classic Mexican street food of tacos, tortas and tostadas, for the most part – but the standard is sound, and Taqueria's traditional Mexican hot chocolate is every bit as spicy and frothy as it should be.
► *Nearby Garcia (246 Portobello Road, 7221 6119, W11 1LL, www.cafegarcia.co.uk) is an excellent traditional Spanish café.*

NORTH LONDON

As one of London's foremost nightlife areas, Camden also has plenty of good venues for drinking – whether civilised gastropubs (**Crown & Goose**; *see p244*) or boisterous clubs (**Proud**; *see p330*).

CONSUME

Eating In...

Our pick of the best winter dining.

Bocca di Lupo
See p217.
Jacob Kenedy's welcoming Italian restaurant is a brightly lit, cosy eaterie when the streets of Soho get bleak in bad weather. Try meaty specials, such as own-made pork and foie gras sausages with *farro*, or a warming stew.

Dishoom
See p215.
Sometimes nothing so warms the cockles of the heart as dreaming you're a thousand miles away – and several degrees warmer. This convincing rendering of a characteristic Mumbai café does the job perfectly.

Giaconda Dining Room
See p214.
At Giaconda you can rely on getting bold, meaty flavours that will delight but not overwhelm. For cold winter nights, tuck into the likes of braised tripe with chorizo, butter beans and paprika, or a trad duck confit with Lyonnaise potatoes.

Madsen
See p223.
If it's chilly but you still want to be outside, think native. What would the Scandinavians do? Madsen's pavement tables have no patio heaters, but the restaurant provides thick, soft blankets to keep you cosy while tucking into Nordic specialities and Danish beer.

Dishoom.

£ Chin Chin Laboratorists
49-50 Camden Lock Place, Camden, NW1 8AF (www.chinchinlabs.com). Camden Town tube. **Open** 11am-6pm Wed, Thur, Sun; 11am-7pm Fri, Sat. **No credit cards**. **Map** p404 X2 ⑳ Ice-cream
The 'laboratorists' are husband-and-wife duo Ahrash Akbari-Kalhur and Nyisha Weber. In their ice-cream parlour, which looks like a mad scientist's lab, they use liquid nitrogen to make ice-cream on demand. Gimmicky? Of course, but Chin Chin Laboratorists is run without pretension and is a whole lot of fun. And its ice-cream, frozen so fast no coarse ice-crystals can form, is wonderfully smooth. The practical application of science has never been cooler or tastier. *Photos p225.*

Haché
24 Inverness Street, Camden, NW1 7HJ (7485 9100, www.hacheburgers.com). Camden Town tube. **Open** noon-10.30pm Mon-Sat; noon-10pm Sun. **Main courses** £6.95-£12.95. **Credit** AmEx, MC, V. **Map** p404 Y2 ㉛ Burgers
There's a wide choice of gourmet burgers on the menu at Haché, ranging from duck and venison to a welcome vegetarian selection. But the place also excels at top-notch basic burgers, such as steak au naturel and lamb au naturel – portions are large and the meat first-rate, and sides of frites, potato wedges or salad shouldn't disappoint.
Other locations 329 Fulham Road, Chelsea, SW10 9QL (7823 3515).

Horseshoe
28 Heath Street, Hampstead, NW3 6TE (7431 7206). Hampstead tube. **Open** 10am-11pm Mon-Thur; 10am-midnight Fri, Sat; 10am-10.30pm Sun. **Main courses** £8-£15. **Credit** AmEx, MC, V. **Gastropub**
The kitchen at this gastropub cooks with real flair and, pleasingly, the pub has stayed true to its ancestry by serving excellent beer. It brews its own ales downstairs, but the homebrew is supplemented by a great range of bottled options and a pretty decent winelist. Service can be a bit too laid-back, but if you're happy to chill, the Horseshoe makes a relaxing stop for the likes of refreshing artichoke, tomato, basil and ragstone cheese salad, juicy Blythburgh pork fillet with celery and walnuts, or Heveningham Hall lamb loin with white beans in marjoram pesto.

Manna
4 Erskine Road, Chalk Farm, NW3 3AJ (7722 8028, www.manna-veg.com). Chalk Farm tube or bus 31, 168. **Open** 6.30-10.30pm Tue-Fri; noon-3pm Sat, Sun. **Main courses** £10-£18. **Credit** MC, V. **Map** p404 W2 ㉜ Vegetarian
Going strong after upwards of 40 years, Manna appears to have settled into more mature makeover of a few years back. The dining space consists of a

CONSUME

tiny conservatory and a cosy, curtained snug for more intimate encounters. The menu picks and chooses from around the world, with the popular chef's salad (beetroot, avocado, balsamic-marinated onions, pumpkin seeds and protein from a selection of halloumi, feta or crispy tofu) always a feature.

Market

43 Parkway, Camden, NW1 7PN (7267 9700, www.marketrestaurant.co.uk). Camden Town tube. **Open** noon-2.30pm, 6-10.30pm Mon-Sat; 1-3.30pm Sun. **Main courses** £9-£14. **Credit** AmEx, DC, MC, V. **Map** p404 Y2 ⊕ **British**
Parkway doesn't have a reputation as a foodie destination, so hats off to Market for succeeding on this very tricky Camden thoroughfare. Behind an unassuming black frontage, a wide demographic of groups, couples, families and lone diners lap up the good-value, broadly British fare, with occasional European flourishes (gazpacho, say, or gnocchi with peas, broad beans and ragstone cheese). Service is brisk, but comes with a smile.

Marquess Tavern

32 Canonbury Street, Islington, N1 2TB (7354 2975, www.themarquesstavern.co.uk). Highbury & Islington tube/rail or Essex Road rail. **Open** 5-11pm Mon-Thur; 4pm-midnight Fri; noon-midnight Sat; noon-10.30pm Sun. **Main courses** £12-£17. **Credit** AmEx, MC, V. **Gastropub**
A former winner of *Time Out*'s Gastropub of the Year award and several other prizes, the Marquess Tavern has survived a change of ownership with nary a stumble. The blackboard of beef fore-rib sizes and prices is still here, so too the engaging beer list and the sky-lit rear dining room with its stark white walls and chandelier (out front is a pubbier bar with a few popular roadside tables). Staff are charming.

★ Ottolenghi

287 Upper Street, Islington, N1 2TZ (7288 1454, www.ottolenghi.co.uk). Angel tube or Highbury & Islington tube/rail. **Open** 8am-10pm Mon-Wed; 8am-10.30pm Thur-Sat; 9am-7pm Sun. **Main courses** £8-£10. **Credit** AmEx, MC, V. **Map** p400 O1 ⊕ **Bakery-café**
Ottolenghi is more than an inviting bakery. Behind the pastries piled in the window is a comparatively prim deli counter with lush salads, available day and evening, eat-in or take away. This is a brilliant and stylish daytime café, but people book well in advance for dinner too – the inventive fusion menu (currently only available at this branch) is fabulous. **Other locations** 1 Holland Street, Kensington, W8 4NA (7937 0003); 63 Ledbury Road, Notting Hill, W11 2AD (7727 1121); 13 Motcomb Street, Belgravia, SW1X 8LB (7823 2707).

£ S&M Café

4-6 Essex Road, Islington, N1 8LN (7359 5361, www.sandmcafe.co.uk). Angel tube.

...and Eating Out

Our pick of the best summer dining.

Boundary Project

*See p228 **Albion**.*
Terence Conran's three-tiered Shoreditch eaterie not only comprises the laid-back Albion café, which has great pavement tables, but a chic rooftop bar-restaurant where summer evening barbecues are perfect for watching the sun set over the fabulous ugliness of London's hippest quarter.

Chin Chin Laboratorists

See left.
When you're too hot, you think of ice-cream, right? Well, here you get to watch the stuff being made, complete with theatrical dry-ice, right in front of your eyes. Don't worry: you get to eat it too.

Lido Restaurant Hyde Park

See p223.
Us working stiffs look at visitors sprawled on the grass in the Royal Parks with bitter envy – when summer gets humid, they seem to be the only places in town that stay cool. The Lido sits alongside a whole lake of coolness, complete with quacking ducks and splashing boats. Better than a desk fan, any day.

Modern Pantry

See p213.
Anna Hansen's genre-bending cuisine style, featuring gems such as sugar-cured prawn omelette with smoky *sambal*, is just made to be enjoyed in the sun – and her restaurant's outdoor tables are the perfect place to enjoy her Antipodean flair.

Chin Chin Laboratorists.

CONSUME

Open 7.30am-11pm daily. **Main courses** £5.25-£9.95. **Credit** AmEx, MC, V. **Map** p400 O1 ⑤ **Café**
Preserved by S&M founder Kevin Finch, the decor of the former Alfredo's is a mix of periods, with panelling covering a probable multitude of building sins, blue Formica tables and tiny red leather chairs. It's cramped, but jovial, a worthy revival of the greasy spoon that starred in *Quadrophenia*. All-day breakfasts are as popular as the titular sausage and mash. **Other locations** throughout the city.

EAST LONDON

Spitalfields, Shoreditch and Hoxton are key nightlife districts and well furnished with bars; *see pp245-248*. The curry restaurants of Brick Lane rarely live up to their reputation, however; *see p231* **Inside Track**.

★ £ **Albion**
2-4 Boundary Street, Shoreditch, E2 7DD (7729 1051, www.albioncaff.co.uk). Shoreditch High

---

Front Row Seats

Great dining with impeccable views of the Olympic Park.

Forman's

If you want a close-up view of the Olympic Park (*see p53*) as it steadily approaches completion by summer 2011, the lovely waterways that surround the site make for an outstanding stroll. But how about studying proceedings over a cup of tea or a glass of fine wine.

Made out of recycled metal shipping containers and painted a vivid yellow-green, the View Tube (www.theviewtube.co.uk) has been placed on a ridge a short walk from Pudding Mill Lane DLR to provide the best possible vantage on the Olympic Park. It also has terrific catering, courtesy of the ground-floor **Container Café** (for listings, *see p229*). Furnished with blue stools that echo the angular London 2012 logo, it has floor-to-ceiling windows through which to watch the action, but spare a glance for the short blackboard list of hot eats (bacon

baguette and relish, pie, soup of the day) and drinks (coffee is made from Square Mile beans). Further temptations rest on the counter: chocolate brownies, cookies, appealingly overstuffed savoury croissants.

There's a posh option too. Walk north to where the Lee Navigation joins the Hereford Union canal, and cross the two bridges to Fish Island. Here you can enjoy London-cure smoked salmon, which **Forman's** (for listings, *see p229*) invented and has been manufacturing in the East End since 1905. The firm's original factory closed to make way for the Olympic Park, but the café-bar and restaurant at these new premises have a superb view (*pictured*) and food to match. In addition to the salmon, served with buckwheat blinis, other seasonal British produce on offer includes Hampshire buffalo mozzarella and smoked eel.

CONSUME

Street rail. **Open** 8am-midnight daily. **Main courses** £8-£10. **Credit** AmEx, MC, V. **Map** p401 R4 ⑯ **Café**
Almost every new London restaurant seems to be mining the vein of nostalgia for traditional British cuisine these days, but few have pulled it off as well as Terence Conran's stand-out 'caff', *Time Out's* Best New Cheap Eats for 2009. You get platters of cupcakes and doorstop-thick slices of battenberg, baked on-site, and mains such as toad in the hole or devilled kidneys. The English breakfast is superb, coming with buttery scrambled eggs and juicy mushrooms. *See also p227* **Eating Out**.
▶ *For the hotel upstairs, see p204* **Boundary**.

★ £ Brick Lane Beigel Bake
159 Brick Lane, E1 6SB (7729 0616). Liverpool Street tube/rail or bus 8. **Main courses** £1.95-£5.95. **No credit cards.** **Map** p401 S4 ⑰ **Jewish**
This charismatic little East End institution rolls out perfect bagels (egg, cream cheese, salt beef), superb bread and moreish cakes. Even at 3am, fresh-baked goods are pulled from the ovens at the back; no wonder the queue for bagels trails out the door when the innumerable local bars and clubs begin to close.

£ Container Café
View Tube, the Greenway, Marshgate Lane, E15 2PJ (07702 125081, www.theviewtube.co.uk). Pudding Mill Lane DLR. **Open** 9am-4.30pm daily. **Main courses** £3-£6.50. **No credit cards.** **Café**
Right opposite the Olympic Stadium, this is a perfect location from which to watch the Olympic Park develop (*see left* **Front Row Seats**).

★ Eyre Brothers
70 Leonard Street, Shoreditch, EC2A 4QX (7613 5346, www.eyrebrothers.co.uk). Old Street tube/rail. **Open** noon-2.45pm, 6.30-10.45pm Mon-Fri; 7-11pm Sat. **Main courses** £15-£27.50. **Credit** AmEx, DC, MC, V. **Map** p401 Q4 ⑱ **International**
This long, attractive room is extremely popular with City gents and the media crowd. Robert and David Eyre have taken the food of the Iberian peninsula into their heart and soul, and reproduce it in a form that's true to its rustic roots yet sophisticated enough to compete with top-level French or Italian cooking. The tapas are sensational.

Gun
27 Coldharbour, Isle of Dogs, E14 9NS (7515 5222, www.thegundocklands.com). Canary Wharf tube/DLR or Blackwall DLR. **Open** 11am-midnight Mon-Fri; 11.30am-midnight Sat; 11.30am-11pm Sun. **Main courses** £11.50-£23. **Credit** AmEx, MC, V. **Gastropub**
The Gun is a little off the beaten track, but it remains a favourite: for its watery views, its sophisticated

informality and the fact that, on balance, it's still the best place to eat in Docklands. Sink into one of the deep sofas for pub grub such as home-made fish finger sandwiches, sausage rolls or the pint o' prawns that seemed chosen from the start to underline the 'pub' in gastropub.

Hackney Pearl
11 Prince Edward Road, Hackney Wick, E9 5LX (8510 3605, www.thehackneypearl.com). Hackney Wick rail. **Open** 10am-11pm Tue-Sun. **Main courses** £9.50-£14.50. **Credit** MC, V. **Café-bar**
Very sure of itself, Hackney Pearl perfectly fits the brief for a friendly neighbourhood hangout, with the owners having made something special out of not very much. Two former shop units in a post-industrial enclave between Victoria Park and the Lea Navigation have been enlivened by furniture that seems to have been salvaged from a groovy thrift shop – colourful rugs, Formica tables and old dressers. The compact menu lists simple but imaginative food, with an eastern European slant. A worthy winner of our Best New Café award in 2010.

Forman's Restaurant
Stour Road, Fish Island, E3 2NH (8525 2365, www.formans.co.uk/restaurant). Pudding Mill Lane DLR or Hackney Wick rail. **Open** *Restaurant* 7-11pm Thur, Fri; 9am-noon, 7-11pm Sat; noon-4pm Sun. *Gallery Bar* 5-9pm Thur, Fri; noon-5pm Sat, Sun. **Main courses** £13-£21.50. **Credit** MC, V. **British**
Come here to enjoy a truly local speciality in a truly amazing setting: London-cure smoked salmon, scoffed in plain view of the Olympic Park (*see left* **Front Row Seats**).

Luxe
109 Commercial Street, Spitalfields, E1 6BG (7101 1751, www.theluxe.co.uk). Liverpool Street tube/rail or Shoreditch High Street rail. **Open** 8am-11.30pm Mon-Sat; 9.30am-10pm Sun. **Main courses** £13-£15. **Credit** AmEx, MC, V. **Map** p401 S5 ⑲ **Modern European**
This restaurant in Spitalfields' Grade II-listed Old Flower Market building provides a different eating and drinking experience on each floor. The centrepiece is a premium-priced first-floor dining room with a show kitchen – white marble bar cut out and filled with logs – and deft combinations of ingredients (Japanese glazed mackerel with pickled cucumber and sesame, for example). The bustling ground-floor café-bar and its charming rear terrace are great for breakfast or a casual lunch, while the basement bar and music venue is dark and moody.

£ Needoo Grill
87 New Road, Whitechapel, E1 1HH (7247 0648, www.needoogrill.co.uk). Whitechapel tube. **Open** 11.30am-11.30pm daily. **Main courses** £6-£20. **Credit** AmEx, MC, V. **Pakistani**

CONSUME

Princess of Shoreditch.

Needoo Grill, with its boisterous mix of young families and groups of friends, has the vibe of a community meeting place. It offers meaty Pakistani-Punjabi staples but also earthy vegetarian dishes, made with care. Past the grill near the entrance, the decor of the main seating area is as big and bold as the cooking. Sparkly black granite tiles, red leatherette banquettes and plasma screens contrast with the functional wipe-clean tables, paper napkins and metal water pitchers.

★ £ E Pellicci

332 Bethnal Green Road, Bethnal Green, E2 0AG (7739 4873). Bethnal Green tube/rail or bus 8. **Open** 7am-4pm Mon-Sat. **Main courses** £5-£6. **No credit cards.** Café

This hive of humanity, a family business to the core, has been trading since 1900. It's an aesthetic delight: the art deco wood-panelled interior holds Grade II-listed status. The menu features sandwiches, rolls and ciabattas; big breakfasts; steak pies and lasagnes; and boarding-school classic desserts. Although it's been trading for 110 years, the prices remain firmly rooted in the old East End.

Pizza East

56 Shoreditch High Street, Shoreditch, E1 6JJ (7729 1888, www.pizzaeast.com). Shoreditch High Street rail. **Open** noon-11pm Mon-Wed, Sun; noon-midnight Thur; noon-1am Fri, Sat. **Main courses** £7-£19. **Credit** AmEx, MC, V. **Map** p401 R4 ⑨⓪ Pizza

This Soho House-owned newcomer is located in the capacious Tea Building, a few doors along from the swish Shoreditch House hotel rooms (*see p205*). There's an Italian-American slant to the pizzas, such as a New England speciality clam pizza that comes garnished with cherry tomatoes, garlic and pecorino. The vibe is cool, but friendly and relaxed, with beams and concrete indicating its industrial past.
▶ *Downstairs in the lower basement, Concrete serves up food, booze and varied club nights until midnight (1am or 2am at weekends).*

Princess of Shoreditch

76-79 Paul Street, EC2A 4NE (7729 9270, www.theprincessofshoreditch.com). Old Street tube/rail or bus 55. **Open** noon-11pm daily. **Main courses** £10.50-£16.50. **Credit** AmEx, MC, V. **Map** p401 Q4 ⑨⓵ Gastropub

The Princess has new owners, but the gentle refurb wisely didn't monkey about with the historic decor – the place was built in 1742. It is indeed a princess among gastropubs, somewhere you'll feel equally comfortable scoffing or quaffing (local cask ales, a respectable list of wines by the glass, bottle and carafe, bloody marys), a combination of attributes that won it our award for Best Gastropub in 2010.

£ Sông Quê

134 Kingsland Road, Shoreditch, E2 8DY (7613 3222). Hoxton rail. **Open** noon-3pm, 5.30-11pm Mon-Sat; 12.30-11pm Sun. **Main courses** £4.50-£6.20. **Credit** MC, V. **Map** p401 R3 ⑨⓶ Vietnamese

North-east London retains its monopoly on the capital's most authentic Vietnamese restaurants, several of which cluster on this street. Sông Quê, which was the key pioneer, remains the benchmark for all of them. It's an efficient, canteen-like operation to which diners of all types are attracted – be prepared to share tables at busy times, and ready to taste the fresh herby kick of proper Viet soups and noodles.

£ Tayyabs

83 Fieldgate Street, Whitechapel, E1 1JU (7247 9543, www.tayyabs.co.uk). Aldgate East or Whitechapel tube. **Open** noon-11.30pm daily. **Main courses** £6-£10. **Credit** AmEx, MC, V. Pakistani

Behind the green frontage of a former pub, Tayyabs is a bright, modern Pakistani café that bucks up this down-at-heel backstreet. Droves of City suits are attracted for lunch, along with students and locals. The upbeat mood is accentuated by Bollywood beats, a crimson, ochre and mustard colour scheme and the bustle from an open-view kitchen.

Les Trois Garçons

1 Club Row, Shoreditch, E1 6JX (7613 1924, www.lestroisgarcons.com). Shoreditch High Street rail. **Open** 6-10.30pm Mon-Thur; 6-11pm Fri, Sat. **Set dinner** £39.50 2 courses, £45.50 3 courses. **Credit** AmEx, DC, MC, V. **Map** p401 S4 **③**
French

Behind the sober façade of another converted pub, Les Trois Garçons is a paean to decorative excess. Crystal chandeliers hang from the ceiling, while stuffed animals perch on the bar or crane from the walls, swathed in costume jewellery. On the food menu, rich, classical French cuisine is tempered with modern British influences, along with simple but impeccably sourced ingredients. Excellent service has helped make this a fiercely popular venue.

Viajante

Patriot Square, Bethnal Green, E2 9NF (7871 0461, www.viajante.co.uk). Bethnal Green tube/rail or Cambridge Heath rail. **Open** noon-2pm, 7-9.30pm daily. **Set lunch** £24-£40 3 courses. **Set dinner** £60-£90 6 courses. **Credit** AmEx, MC, V. **Pan-Asian & fusion**

The lofty dining room of Viajante is unpretentious and relaxed, its smooth wood and icy blue fabrics complemented by a rotation of big band tunes and lounge music. The open kitchen provides the real entertainment, however, as chef Nuno Mendes and his handful of chefs (each armed with tweezers) put the finishing touches to the dishes. The humble, ebullient Mendes serves several dishes himself, but all the staff are charming and clued-up. A meal here doesn't come cheap, but it's a fun ride through extraordinary combinations of flavour and texture – Mendes's time cooking at El Bulli has clearly informed his playful, joyful approach to food.
▶ *If you like the restaurant, there's a hotel attached: Town Hall Hotel, see p204.*

Wapping Food

Wapping Hydraulic Power Station, Wapping Wall, E1W 3ST (7680 2080, www.thewapping project.com). Wapping rail or Shadwell rail/DLR. **Open** noon-3.30pm, 6.30-11pm Mon-Fri; 10.30am-4pm, 7-11pm Sat; 10.30am-4pm Sun. **Main courses** £11-£22. **Credit** AmEx, MC, V. **Modern European**

This red-brick Victorian pumping station has been minimally converted into a restaurant, striking performance space and contemporary art gallery, the disused industrial engines left to slumber beside the tables in the high-ceilinged main chamber. The satisfying cooking includes the likes of Brecon lamb on a bed of sprouting broccoli, or roast pork with baked polenta, spring greens and pear chutney, perhaps finished with a sorbet of elderflowers plucked from the garden outside. The all-Australian wine list is fabulous, with plenty available by the glass.
▶ *In good weather, pop upstairs to see the pretty rooftop lily pond.*

Whitechapel Gallery Dining Room

Whitechapel Gallery, 77-82 Whitechapel High Street, E1 7QX (7522 7888, www.whitechapel gallery.org/dine). Aldgate East tube. **Open** noon-2.30pm Tue, Sun; noon-2.30pm, 5.30-11pm Wed-Sat. **Main courses** £13.75-£18. **Credit** AmEx, MC, V. **Map** p403 S6 **③** **Modern European**

In an attractive former library, with ceiling-height windows and tall mirrors to bring in much-needed light, this is a small but vibrant art gallery restaurant. Chef Michael Paul makes skilful use of interesting produce (lemon verbena, wild garlic, Kentish sparkling wine in a bellini). The seasonal menu emphasises provenance and might include rump of Romney Marsh lamb, or Gloucester Old Spot pork terrine with gala apple salad. Cheerful staff and customers who range from East End arty to posh arty create a pleasant atmosphere.
▶ *For the equally impressive gallery, see p155.*

Yi-Ban

London Regatta Centre, Dockside Road, E16 2QT (7473 6699, www.yi-ban.co.uk). Royal Albert DLR. **Open** noon-11pm Mon-Sat; 11am-10.30pm Sun. **Main courses** £4-£30. **Credit** AmEx, MC, V. **Chinese**

INSIDE TRACK
CURRY IN FAVOUR?

Brick Lane (*see p154*) is a terrific part of town, but the widely fêted Indian food served at its countless popular restaurants is nothing special. Only a few caffs near the south end of the street – **Ruchi** (303 Whitechapel Road, E1 1BY, 7247 6666), for example – offer proper Bangladeshi dishes. Instead, try the ever-popular **Tayyabs** (*see p230*) or the less well-known **Needoo Grill** (*see p229*).

In truth, curry pilgrims are better off in Wembley (*see p234* **Sakonis**) or Southall, where the likes of **Brilliant** (72-76 Western Road, 8574 1928, UB2 5DZ, www.brilliantrestaurant.com) serve superb East African Punjabi food. The best kebabs and yoghurt-based snacks can be had at the **New Asian Tandoori Centre** (114-118 The Green, UB2 4BQ, 8574 2597).

There is now some decent, cheap Indian food in the West End too: in addition to **Dishoom** (*see p215*), you could drop in on **Imli** in Soho (167-169 Wardour Street, W1F 8WR, 7287 4243, www.imli.co.uk) or the often-crowded Covent Garden **Masala Zone** (48 Floral Street, WC2E 9DA, 7379 0101, www.masalazone.com; *see also p234*).

CONSUME

CONSUME

Yi-Ban is one of the few places in London where the food is as good as the view. Granted, it's a view of London City Airport, but that has its own charm. The long, spacious room takes cues from hotel dining areas and Chinese wedding banquets – gold lamé in particular makes an amusing appearance – but the food doesn't have to follow crispy duck and sweet-and-sour pork clichés. Experiment instead with the daytime dim sum, west lake soup or Cantonese-style crispy roast pork belly. The staff are a charming bunch, serving the terrific food with style and efficiency. The restaurant is very handy for ExCeL (*see p59*) too.

SOUTH-EAST LONDON

Amid the over-styled bistros and high-street chain restaurants, Greenwich is the stand-out eateries. **Inside**, the **Old Brewery** (for both, *see below*) and some solid boozers (*see p248*) are pretty much it.

Inside

19 Greenwich South Street, Greenwich, SE10 8NW (8265 5060, www.insiderestaurant.co.uk). Greenwich rail/DLR. **Open** noon-2.30pm, 6.30-11pm Tue-Fri; 6.30-11pm Sat; noon-3pm Sun. **Main courses** £12.95-£18.95. **Credit** AmEx, MC, V. **Map** p405 W3 ⑨⑤ **Modern European**
There are too few neighbourhood restaurants in south-east London that tantalise you with fresh flavours, however often or seldom you dine there. With proficient, unobtrusive service, a smart little interior and reasonable prices, Inside manages to do this, with careful and imaginative sourcing matched by lively combinations of ingredients: roasted cod, Spanish paprika, white bean and chorizo cassoulet with steamed leeks and tomato coulis was a recent hit. Desserts are good enough to convert even the usually pudding-averse.

Old Brewery

Pepys Building, Old Royal Naval College, Greenwich, SE10 9LW (3327 1280, www.old brewerygreenwich.com). Cutty Sark DLR. **Open** 10am-10.30pm daily. **Main courses** £6-£17.50. **Credit** MC, V. **Map** p405 X1 ⑨⑥ **British**

INSIDE TRACK EAT TURKISH

From Dalston Kingsland station north to Stoke Newington Church Street is the Turkish and Kurdish heart of Hackney: both **19 Numara Bos Cirrik** (34 Stoke Newington Road, N16 7XJ, 7249 0400) and **Mangal Ocakbaşı** (10 Arcola Street, E8 2DJ, 7275 8981, www.mangal1.com) serve superb grilled meats, marinated and cooked to perfection.

By day, the Old Brewery is a café; by night, a restaurant. There's a small bar, with tables outside in a large walled courtyard – a lovely spot in which to test the 50-strong beer list – but most of the action is in the vast, high-ceilinged main space, beneath a wave-like structure of empty bottles and a wall of shiny copper vats – handsome enough to net our award for Best Design in 2010. The short menu highlights provenance and seasonality, with matching beers suggested for each dish.

£ Pavilion Tea House

Greenwich Park, Blackheath Gate, SE10 8QY (8858 9695, www.companyofcooks.com). Blackheath rail or Greenwich rail/DLR. **Open** 9am-5.30pm Mon-Fri; 9am-6pm Sat, Sun. **Main courses** £4.95-£6.60. **Credit** MC, V. **Map** p405 Y3. ⑤⑦ **Café**
Diagonally opposite the Royal Observatory (*see p167*), set in its own pretty, fenced-in grounds, the Pavilion Tea House provides a convivial cake-and-a-break for weary parents. If you're stuck for breakfast or a proper hot meal, it also punches above its weight, and the salads, snacks and sandwiches are all a notch above average.

SOUTH-WEST LONDON

Chez Bruce

2 Bellevue Road, Wandsworth, SW17 7EG (8672 0114, www.chezbruce.co.uk). Wandsworth Common rail. **Open** noon-2pm, 6.30-10pm Mon-Thur; noon-2pm, 6.30-10.30pm Fri; noon-3pm, 6.30-10.30pm Sat; noon-3pm, 7-9pm Sun. **Set meals** £25.50-£40 3 courses. **Credit** AmEx, DC, MC, V. **French**
Chez Bruce is still the destination of choice for fine dining in south London, although it has developed a softer, less minimalist feel over the years; indeed, it was closed for another refurb and slight expansion as we went to press. Some things don't change, though, and the wine list remains a gorgeous (and gorgeously priced) parade through the world's best bottles. The brief menu – first-rate French food with brief forays into Spain and Italy – changes slightly through the week and seasonally.
▶ *If you're in Kew, try Bruce's sister restaurant Glasshouse (14 Station Parade, TW9 3PZ, 8940 6777, www.glasshouserestaurant.co.uk).*

Côte

8 High Street, Wimbledon, SW19 5DX (8947 7100, www.cote-restaurants.co.uk). Wimbledon tube/rail. **Open** 8am-11pm Sat; 9am-10.30pm Sun. **Main courses** £8.75-£17. **Credit** AmEx, MC, V. **French**
Côte has ambitions to be a bistro version of Pizza Express. There are already several across London, but this one in Wimbledon was the first, setting the tone with its smart, glossy interior, with polished dark wood and moody grey paintwork. The food is

Old Brewery.

predictable (steak-frites, moules) but decently done and friendly in price. The wine, champagne, beer, cider and aperitifs are all French.
Other locations throughout the city.

Earl Spencer
260-262 Merton Road, SW18 5JL (8870 9244, www.theearlspencer.co.uk). Southfields tube. **Open** 11am-11pm Mon-Thur; 11am-midnight Fri, Sat; noon-10.30pm Sun. **Main courses** £8.50-£14. **Credit** AmEx, MC, V. **Gastropub**
The Earl Spencer was a gastropub pioneer and has continued on the same path, with a short, chalkboard menu, scrubbed wooden tables, good ales and friendly, laid-back staff. The Earl is a popular local pitstop (the seats in the front garden are at a premium come summer), keeping regulars happy with salt beef sandwiches or big bowls of Thai-spiced mussels.

★ £ Franco Manca
4 Market Row, Electric Lane, Brixton, SW9 8LD (7738 3021, www.francomanca.co.uk). Brixton tube/rail. **Open** noon-5pm Mon-Sat. **Main courses** £4-£6. **Credit** MC, V. **Pizza**

Inside one of the arches on Brixton Market (*see p170*), with a dining area that mixes indoor and outdoor seating, Franco Manca has been showered with acclaim. The menu is precise (just six pizzas) and cheap, but the pizzas are among London's best: key to their success are the sourdough bases, thin and flavoursome. The organic lemonade is almost as unmissable. A delight.
Other locations 144 Chiswick High Road, Chiswick, W4 1PU (8747 4822).

WEST LONDON

Clarke's
124 Kensington Church Street, Kensington, W8 4BH (7221 9225, www.sallyclarke.com). Notting Hill Gate tube. **Open** 12.30-2pm, 6.30-10pm Mon-Fri; noon-2pm, 6.30-10pm Sat; noon-2pm Sun. **Main courses** £9.50-£22. **Set dinner** £39.50 3 courses. **Credit** AmEx, DC, MC, V. **Map** p404 Z6 ❾ **Modern European**
Chef-proprietor Sally Clarke has been espousing the 'seasonal and local' ethic since the mid 1980s. The food at this stylishly low-key restaurant shows

influences from western Europe, executed with a deft hand, and the wine list has some very good bottles. Don't miss the breads, for which the deli next door (& Clarke's) is justly famed.

★ Gate

51 Queen Caroline Street, Hammersmith, W6 9QL (8748 6932, www.thegate.tv). Hammersmith tube. **Open** noon-2.45pm, 6-10.45pm Mon-Fri; 6-10.45pm Sat. **Main courses** £10.50-£13.75. **Credit** AmEx, MC, V. **Vegetarian**
Having celebrated its 20th birthday, west London's most prominent vegetarian restaurant continues to impress with its innovative dishes and atmospheric, high-ceilinged dining room. The mood is casual and pleasantly noisy with the clatter of cutlery and the chatter of bourgeois meat-avoiders. Dishes can often feature a bewildering number of flavours from around the world. Desserts are equally tempting.

Harwood Arms

Corner of Walham Grove & Farm Lane, Fulham, SW6 1QP (7386 1847, www.harwoodarms.com). Fulham Broadway tube. **Open** 5.30-11pm Mon; noon-11pm Tue-Thur; noon-midnight Fri, Sat; noon-11pm Sun. **Main courses** £14-£16. **Credit** AmEx, MC, V. **Map** p394 A13 ❺❾ **Gastropub**
Snagging a table has become far more difficult since a Michelin star was awarded to this terrific gastropub – a source of frustration, surely, for the locals who saw it as a neighbourhood watering hole that happened to serve brilliant food. The posh-country feel is created via rustic design details: hessian napkins, linen bags in place of a bread basket, slabs of wood for presentation. Service is smart-shirted, but laid-back and friendly.

£ Masala Zone

147 Earl's Court Road, Earl's Court, SW5 9RQ (7373 0220, www.masalazone.com). Earl's Court tube. **Open** 12.30-3pm, 5.30-11pm Mon-Fri; 12.30-11pm Sat; 12.30-10.30pm Sun. **Main courses** £10-£15. **Credit** MC, V. **Map** p394 B10 ❿❿❿ **Indian**
Branches of this smart, clever chain are popping up faster than mustard seeds in a hot pan of ghee. Each outlet is decorated with a different theme – this branch has striking work by tribal artists. The mood is both vibrant and relaxed – as cheering to single-tons having a thali for supper, as it is to family groups and couples. Good food at good prices. **Other locations** throughout the city.

Mesopotamia

115 Wembley Park Drive, Wembley, Middx HA9 8HG (8453 5555, www.mesopotamia.ltd.uk). Wembley Park tube. **Open** 5.30pm-midnight Mon-Sat. **Main courses** £8-£15.50. **Credit** AmEx, DC, MC, V. **Iraqi**
Outside is traffic-clogged Wembley; inside is Middle Eastern romance. Under a ceiling of billowing silk,

Mesopotamia's long, dimly lit interior is decorated with an intricately carved dresser, a wall frieze of Babylonian beasts and palms in relief, and dark, metallic light fittings. It's an enchanting spot, helped along by kindly service (although proceedings can slow during busy spells). The menu encompasses various meze starters followed by mains of kebabs or stews, and special set dinners are served before events at Wembley Stadium (*see p335*).

Mohsen

152 Warwick Road, Earl's Court, W14 8PS (7602 9888). Earl's Court tube or Kensington (Olympia) tube/rail. **Open** noon-midnight daily. **Main courses** £12-£15. Unlicensed. Corkage no charge. **No credit cards. Map** p394 A10 ❿❿❶ **Iranian**
It is consistency, not evolution, that has kept this place among our favourite Iranian restaurants for so long. Some of its Kensington contemporaries have meddled with their formula – diluting their all-Iranian staff, employing belly dancers and catering to hordes of late-night kebab-seekers – but Mohsen has retained the family atmosphere that remains its biggest draw. Expect little in the way of frills (there are plastic laminated menus and dog-eared travel posters), but the welcome from Mrs Mohsen is warm, and the food – *mirza ghasemi* (baked aubergine dip with eggs and onions), perhaps London's finest *ghorm-e sabzi* (lamb stew with greens and kidney beans) – excellent.

River Café

Thames Wharf, Rainville Road, Hammersmith, W6 9HA (7386 4200, www.rivercafe.co.uk). Hammersmith tube. **Open** 12.30-5pm, 7-9.30pm Mon-Sat; 12.30-5pm Sun. **Main courses** £12.50-£40. **Credit** AmEx, DC, MC, V. **Italian**
Despite the death in 2010 of co-founder Rose Gray, the River Café continues on its tranquil way. Inside is all cool, calming blues, white and steel with the occasional splash of bright yellow; outside is a pretty little herb and vegetable garden in which guests can sup during good weather. Staff are young, friendly and dressed just a little more fashionably than the core Fulham and Kensington customer base. The food is simple, usually brilliantly so, but costly.

£ Sakonis

129 Ealing Road, Wembley, Middx HA0 4BP (8903 9601, www.sakonis.co.uk). Alperton tube. **Open** noon-10pm daily. **Main courses** £2-£7.99. **Credit** MC, V. **Gujarati vegetarian**
A mainstay of the Ealing Road Indian dining scene, Sakonis attracts hordes of shoppers at the weekend. It's a sizeable, utilitarian café with tiled walls, melamine tableware and easy-wipe tables. At the front is a snack counter, a well-liked source of take-aways, while to the rear is a buffet popular with South Asian families. We particularly rate the street food – crisp onion bhajis and crunchy *bhel pooris*.

Pubs & Bars

The grape, the grain and the swizzle stick – London loves them all.

Every visitor to London has a perfect mind's-eye vision of the traditional pub – polished brass, etched mirrors, panelling, a row of wood-handled beer pumps and a portly waistcoated publican usually feature. Such places do exist, and we've listed our favourites in the following chapter, but Londoners thrive on variety. They've also become far more discerning over the years: a flat pint of nitrokeg beer and warm glass of white plonk are unlikely to be met with approval.

It's far from a static scene. The last decade has seen a vast increase in the availability and popularity both of real ale (*see p246* **Bigging Up the Beer**) and top-class cocktails (**69 Colebrooke Row**, *see p245*; **Purl**, *see p240*). Gourmets will be delighted to see the gastropub revolution continues to yield benefits across the board, with good-quality pub grub far easier to find than it was even five years ago. Wine bars have also been making a quiet comeback: not those suburban faux-sophisticated numbers from the 1980s, but places that serve rare biodynamic wines (**Terroirs**, *see p238*) or use wine dispensers to ensure every glass reaches you in perfect shape (**Kensington Wine Rooms**, *see p240*).

THE SOUTH BANK & BANKSIDE

If top-quality beer is your priority, there's a superb range at the tiny **Rake** (14A Winchester Walk, SE1 9AG, 7407 0557; closed Sun), in Borough Market, and the new branch of **Draft House** (206-208 Tower Bridge Road, SE1 2UP, 7378 9995, www.drafthouse.co.uk; *see p248*), at the south side of Tower Bridge.

★ Gladstone Arms
64 Lant Street, SE1 1QN (7407 3962). Borough tube. **Open** noon-11pm Mon-Thur; noon-midnight Fri, Sat; noon-10.30pm Sun. *Food served* noon-10pm daily. **Credit** MC, V. **Map** p402 P9 ❶
While the Victorian prime minister still glares into the massive mural on the outer wall, inside is now funky, freaky and candlelit. Gigs (blues, folk, acoustic, five nights a week) take place at one end of a cosy space; opposite, a bar dispenses ales and

❶ Green numbers given in this chapter correspond to the location of each pub or bar on the street maps. *See pp392-416.*

lagers. Pies provide sustenance. Retro touches include an old-fashioned 'On Air' studio sign and a communist-style railway clock.

Skylon
Royal Festival Hall, Belvedere Road, SE1 8XX (7654 7800, www.danddlondon.com). Waterloo tube/rail. **Open** 11am-midnight daily. *Food served* noon-10.30pm Mon-Wed, Sun; noon-11.30pm Thur-Sun. **Credit** AmEx, MC, V. **Map** p399 M8 ❷
There can't be many better views than this in town. Sit at the cocktail bar (between the two restaurant areas), and gaze at trains trundling out of Charing Cross, cars and buses whizzing across Waterloo Bridge, and boats and cruisers pootling along the Thames. In spite of its aircraft-hangar proportions, it feels intimate. Drinks include ten bellinis, a large range of liqueurs and a list of classics (manhattans, sidecars, negronis), all at a price. *Photo p236.*

Wine Wharf
Stoney Street, SE1 9AD (7940 8335, www.winewharf.co.uk). London Bridge tube/rail. **Open** 4-11.30pm Mon-Wed; noon-11.30pm Thur-Sat. *Food served* 5.30-10pm Mon-Wed; noon-3pm, 5.30-10pm Thur-Sat. **Credit** AmEx, DC, MC, V. **Map** p402 P8 ❸

Part of the Vinopolis complex, Wine Wharf inhabits two storeys of a reclaimed Victorian warehouse, all exposed brickwork and high-ceilinged industrial chic. You could drink very well indeed here: the 250-bin list stretches to 1953 d'Yquem and some very serious prestige cuvée champagnes. But with nearly half the wines available by the glass, there's a great opportunity to experiment.
Other locations Brew Wharf, Stoney Street, SE1 9AD (7378 6601, www.brewwharf.com).

THE CITY

Artillery Arms

102 Bunhill Row, EC1Y 8ND (7253 4683). Moorgate or Old Street tube/rail. **Open** noon-11pm Mon-Sat; noon-10.30pm Sun. *Food served* noon-9pm Mon-Thur; noon-4pm Fri. **Credit** AmEx, MC, V. **Map** p400 P4 ④

Close to the Barbican and opposite Bunhill Fields (for both, *see p89*), this small tucked-away pub has an agreeably local feel, as post-work City folk mix easily with neighbourhood stalwarts at the sturdy, immovable bar. It has a slightly austere feel, but is an easy place to lose track of an evening, aided by the predictably fine Fuller's beers: easygoing Chiswick, toothsome London Pride and potent ESB.

Vertigo 42

Tower 42, 25 Old Broad Street, EC2N 1HQ (7877 7842, www.vertigo42.co.uk). Bank tube/DLR or Liverpool Street tube/rail. **Open** noon-3pm, 5-11pm Mon-Fri; 5-11pm Sat. *Food served* noon-2.15pm, 5-9.30pm Mon-Fri; 5-9.30pm Sat. **Credit** AmEx, DC, MC, V. **Map** p403 Q6 ⑤

Stretching across the City, the views from this 42nd-floor bar are breathtaking. So, too, are the prices (house wine, £8 a glass). Food is more down to earth: options include wild mushroom tart with artichoke salad, and seared peppered tuna steak. Seating is arranged so everyone can enjoy the 360° panorama, but with the opening of Paramount (*see p214*) and a rooftop bar promised for Heron Tower (*see p93*), Vertigo has some competition for the high-life.
▶ *You must book ahead, promise a minimum £10 spend and undergo airport-style security.*

HOLBORN & CLERKENWELL

Clerkenwell has a compelling claim to being the birthplace of the now ubiquitous gastropub: the **Eagle** (*see p212*) kicked things off. Other food pioneers that provide great drinking are **St John** (*see p213*) and **Cellar Gascon** (59 West Smithfield, EC1A 9DS, 7600 7561, www.cellar gascon.com; *see p212* **Le Comptoir Gascon**).

Café Kick

43 Exmouth Market, EC1R 4QL (7837 8077, www.cafekick.co.uk). Angel tube or Farringdon tube/rail. **Open** noon-11pm Mon-Thur; noon-

midnight Fri, Sat; 1-10.30pm Sun. *Food served* noon-3pm, 6-10pm Mon-Thur; noon-3pm, 6-11pm Sun. **Credit** AmEx, MC, V. **Map** p400 N4 ⑥

Clerkenwell's most likeable bar is this table-football themed gem. The soccer paraphernalia is authentic, retro-cool and mainly Latin (you'll find a Zenit St Petersburg scarf amid the St Etienne and Lusitanian gear); bar staff, beers and bites give the impression you could be in Lisbon. A modest open kitchen ('we don't microwave or deep-fry') dishes out tapas, sandwiches and charcuterie platters.
Other locations Bar Kick, 127 Shoreditch High Street, Shoreditch, E1 6JE (7739 8700).

★ Fox & Anchor

115 Charterhouse Street, EC1M 6AA (7250 1300, www.foxandanchor.com). Barbican tube or Farringdon tube/rail. **Open** 7am-11pm Mon-Thur; 7am-1am Fri; 8.30am-1am Sat; 8.30am-10pm Sun. *Food served* 7am-11am, noon-9.45pm Mon-Fri; 8.30am-11am, noon-9.45pm Sat; 8.30am-11am, noon-4pm, 6-9pm Sun. **Credit** AmEx, MC, V. **Map** p400 O5 ⑦

Pristine mosaic tiling and etched glass scream 'sensitive refurbishment' at this Smithfield treasure. The dark wood bar is lined with pewter tankards; to the back is the Fox's Den, a series of intimate rooms used for both drinking and dining. Local sourcing is a priority and a pleasure: in addition to the own-label ale, cask beers might include Red Poll and Old Growler from Suffolk's fine Nethergate brewery. There are plenty more delights among the bottles.

Skylon. *See p235.*

★ Seven Stars
53 Carey Street, WC2A 2JB (7242 8521).
Chancery Lane or Holborn tube. **Open** 11am-
11pm Mon-Fri; noon-11pm Sat; noon-10.30pm
Sun. *Food served* noon-10pm Mon-Fri; 1-10pm
Sat; 1-9pm Sun. **Credit** AmEx, MC, V. **Map**
p397 M6 ❽
Barristers bring their clients to this lovely little pub
for champagne after winning a case at the nearby
Royal Courts of Justice. In a glass display case sits
a copy of *Home from the Inn Contented*, a cookbook
by landlady Roxy Beaujolais; it's a sign that the simple pub food advertised on the blackboard (herring
with potato salad, say) will be a cut above the norm.
Real ales and fairly priced wines by the glass are the
tipples of choice.

Three Kings of Clerkenwell
7 Clerkenwell Close, EC1R 0DY (7253 0483).
Farringdon tube/rail. **Open** noon-11pm Mon-Fri;
7-11pm Sat. *Food served* noon-3pm, 6.30-10pm
Mon-Fri. **No credit cards. Map** p400 N4 ❾
Rhinoceros heads, Egyptian felines and photos of
Dennis Bergkamp provide the decorative backdrop
against which a regular bunch of discerning bohos
glug Scrumpy Jack, Beck's Vier, Old Speckled Hen
or London Pride, and tap the well-worn tables to the
Cramps and other gems from an outstanding jukebox that is crammed with fabulous old platters.

Vinoteca
7 St John Street, EC1M 4AA (7253 8786,
www.vinoteca.co.uk). Farringdon tube/rail. **Open**
noon-11pm Mon-Sat. *Food served* noon-2.45pm,
5.450-10pm Mon-Fri; noon-4pm, 5.45-10pm Sat.
Credit MC, V. **Map** p400 O5 ❿
Inspired in name and approach by the Italian *enoteca*
(a blend of off-licence and wine bar, with snacks
thrown in), Vinoteca is more of a serious gastropub
in spirit. But even if you're not in the mood for much
more than a plate of bread and olive oil, it's worth
heading here for the impressive 200-bottle wine list,
of which 25 are available by the glass. Bonus: all
wines are available to take away at retail price.

BLOOMSBURY & FITZROVIA

For sheer style, try the wow-factor bar at
Hakkasan (*see p214*). In King's Cross,
Camino (*see p213*) added a dedicated sherry
bar called Pepito, while the **Big Chill House**
(*see p330*) is great for boozy music fans.

★ All Star Lanes
Victoria House, Bloomsbury Place, WC1B 4DA
(7025 2676, www.allstarlanes.co.uk). Holborn
tube. **Open** 5-11.30pm Mon-Wed; 5pm-midnight
Thur; noon-2am Fri, Sat; noon-11pm Sun. *Food*
served 5-10.30pm Mon-Thur; noon-10.30pm Thur-
Sun. *Bowling* £7.75-£8.75/person per game.
Credit AmEx, MC, V. **Map** p397 L5 ⓫

> THE BEST PUB INTERIORS

Fox & Anchor
A Smithfield Market mainstay, beautifully
reconstructed. *See left.*

Lamb
Peer through old-fashioned 'snob screens'
to order your pint. *See below.*

Princess Louise
A stunning gin-palace-turned-boozer,
all dark wood and mirrors. *See p238.*

Of Bloomsbury's two subterranean bowling dens,
this is the one with aspirations. Walk past the lanes
and smart, diner-style seating, and you'll find yourself in a comfortable, subdued side bar with chilled
glasses, classy red furnishings, an unusual mix of
bottled lagers (try Anchor Steam) and some impressive cocktails. There's an American menu and, at
weekends, a range of DJs. **Other locations** Whiteleys, 6 Porchester
Gardens, Bayswater, W2 4DB (7313 8363);
Old Truman Brewery, 91 Brick Lane, E1 6QL
(7426 9200).
► *Nearby, Bloomsbury Bowling Lanes (Bedford*
Way, 7183 1979, WC1H 9EU, www.bloomsbury
bowling.com) offers a pints-and-worn-carpets take
on the game – and private karaoke booths.

Bradley's Spanish Bar
42-44 Hanway Street, W1T 1UT (7636 0359).
Tottenham Court Road tube. **Open** noon-11pm
Mon-Sat; noon-10pm Sun. **Credit** MC, V. **Map**
p416 W1 ⓬
There's something of the Barcelona dive bar about
the place, and San Miguel or Cruzcampo on draught,
but Bradley's isn't really very Spanish. A hotch-
potch of local workers, shoppers and foreign
exchange students fill the cramped two-floor space,
or enrage taxi drivers by spilling on to the narrow
street, unperturbed by the routinely unpleasant toilets. After all, there's a good jukebox and good
atmosphere – what more could anyone want?

Lamb
94 Lamb's Conduit Street, WC1N 3LZ (7405
0713). Holborn or Russell Square tube. **Open**
noon-11.30pm Mon-Wed; noon-12.30am Thur-Sat;
noon-10.30pm Sun. *Food* noon-9pm daily. **Credit**
AmEx, MC, V. **Map** p397 M4 ⓭
The standard range of Young's beers is dispensed
from a central horseshoe bar in this 280-year-old
pub, around which are ringed original etched-glass
snob screens, used to prevent Victorian gentlemen
from being seen when liaising with 'women of dubi-
ous distinction'. A sunken back area gives access to
a convenient square of summer patio.

CONSUME

CONSUME

Long Bar

Sanderson, 50 Berners Street, W1T 3NG (7300 1400, www.sandersonlondon.com). Oxford Circus or Goodge Street tube. **Open** 11am-midnight Mon-Wed; 11am-1am Thur-Sat; noon-10.30pm Sun. *Food served* noon-11.30pm Mon-Wed; noon-12.30pm Thur-Sat; 1-10pm Sun. **Credit** AmEx, DC, MC, V. **Map** p396 J5 ⓮

Its early noughties celeb-infested glory days may now only be a faded memory, but the Long Bar still has plenty of easy glamour. The long bar in question is a thin onyx affair, though despite its length, nabbing one of the eyeball-backed stools is an unlikely prospect. A better bet is the lovely courtyard, where table service, candlelight and watery features make a much nicer setting for the fine cocktails. Bar snacks are priced high.

Shochu Lounge

Basement, Roka, 37 Charlotte Street, W1T 1RR (7580 9666, www.shochulounge.com). Goodge Street or Tottenham Court Road tube. **Open** 5pm-midnight Mon, Sat; noon-midnight Tue-Fri; 6pm-midnight Sun. *Food served* 5.30-11.30pm Mon, Sat; noon-3.30pm, 5.30-11.30pm Tue-Fri; 6-10.30pm Sun. **Credit** AmEx, DC, MC, V. **Map** p396 J5 ⓯

Beneath landmark Japanese restaurant Roka, the chic Shochu Lounge offers drinks based on the vodka-like distilled spirit of the same name. Shochu is often overlooked for its better-known and more widespread counterpart, saké, but it's here used in healthy tonics, in cocktails, and sold by the 50ml measure. With a 13.5% service charge, drinks run to around £10. The full Roka menu is available if you're hungry.

INSIDE TRACK
DRINK IN HISTORY

In the vicinity of the City are some London's most impressive historic pubs. Some, like the **Jerusalem Tavern** (55 Britton Street, EC1M 5UQ, 7490 4281, www.stpetersbrewery.co.uk), on the site of a former coffee house, and **Ye Old Mitre** (1 Ely Court, Ely Place side of 8 Hatton Garden, EC1N 6SJ, 7405 4751), charmingly hidden between two streets, are great boozers in their own right. The **Black Friar** (174 Queen Victoria Street, EC4V 4EG, 7236 5474) may not be London's best pub, but it has an absolutely superb Arts and Crafts interior. The **Cittie of York** (22 High Holborn, WC1V 6BN, 7242 7670) is another pub to gladden the eye – so long as you push past the dull front room into the massive banqueting hall of a back room.

COVENT GARDEN
& THE STRAND

★ Gordon's

47 Villiers Street, Strand, WC2N 6NE (7930 1408, www.gordonswinebar.com). Embankment tube or Charing Cross tube/rail. **Open** 11am-11pm Mon-Sat; noon-10pm Sun. *Food served* noon-10pm Mon-Sat; noon-9pm Sun. **Credit** AmEx, MC, V. **Map** p416 Y5 ⓰

Gordon's was established in its present form in 1890, but the atmospheric exposed brickwork and flickering candlelight make this basement feel older still. Although this is the definitive old-school wine bar, it gets packed with a young and lively crowd, half of whom seem to be on first dates. The wine list is surprisingly modern; still, in such surroundings, it seems a shame not to drink the fortified wines, drawn directly from casks behind the bar.

Lamb & Flag

33 Rose Street, WC2E 9EB (7497 9504). Covent Garden tube. **Open** 11am-11pm Mon-Thur; 11am-11.30pm Fri, Sat; noon-10.30pm Sun. *Food served* noon-3pm Mon-Fri; noon-4.30pm Sat, Sun. **Credit** MC, V. **Map** p416 Y3 ⓱

This dog-leg alleyway used to be a pit of prostitution and bare-knuckle bashes, the latter hosted at this historic, low-ceilinged tavern back when it was called the Bucket of Blood; poet John Dryden was beaten up here in 1679. Space is always at a premium, hence the pavement cluster on summer evenings. Two centuries of mounted cuttings and caricatures amplify the sense of character.

▶ *If it's too busy, try the Benelux-themed beer-café Lowlander (36 Drury Lane, WC2B 5RR, 7379 7446, www.lowlander.com).*

Princess Louise

208-209 High Holborn, WC1V 7BW (7405 8816). Holborn tube. **Open** 11.30am-11pm Mon-Fri; noon-11pm Sat; noon-10.30pm Sun. *Food served* noon-2.30pm, 6-8.30pm Mon-Thur; noon-2.30pm Fri. **Credit** AmEx, MC, V. **Map** p416 Z1 ⓲

With half-a-dozen ornately carved, sumptuously tiled bar areas under one high, stucco ceiling, the Princess Louise is a classic example of the Victorian public house in which drinking was segregated according to class. Today, it's an across-the-board Sam Smith's pub, prices starting at an egalitarian £1.99 for a pint of bitter. Sandwiches, baguettes and pub food satisfy hungrier diners, who are also accommodated in the upstairs bar (mealtimes only).

★ Terroirs

5 William IV Street, WC2N 4DW (7036 0660, www.terroirswinebar.com). Charing Cross tube/rail. **Open/food served** 11am-10pm Mon-Fri; 11am-4pm Sat. **Credit** AmEx, MC, V. **Map** p416 Y4 ⓳

Dog & Duck

Now extending over two floors, Terroirs is a superb and very popular wine bar that specialises in the new generation of organic and biodynamic, sulphur-, sugar- or acid-free wines. The list is only slightly shorter than the Bible, with tasting notes that are honest to a fault – a wine like a hedgehog? All in all, a place for oenophiliac adventure. The line-up of Calvados and Armagnac bottles is impressive and the food terrific: a tapas-style selection of French bar snacks, charcuterie and seafood.
▶ *The downstairs is a bit of an awkward space, so stay upstairs if you can.*

SOHO & LEICESTER SQUARE

Soho is a focus for gay nightlife; *see pp309-314.*

Dog & Duck
18 Bateman Street, W1D 3AJ (7494 0697). Tottenham Court Road tube. **Open** 10am-11pm Mon-Thur; 10am-11.30pm Fri, Sat; noon-10.30pm Sun. *Food served* 10am-10pm Mon-Sat; noon-9pm Sun. **Credit** AmEx, MC, V. **Map** p416 W2 ⑳
This Soho landmark is known for its literary heritage, vintage interior (etched mirrors, carved mahogany) and ever-changing ale selection, ranging from the familiar likes of London Pride to altogether rarer beers from the Newman Brewery. Sausages are another feature. The George Orwell room upstairs, where the writer once celebrated a book launch, offers more room; downstairs, punters spill out on to the pavement.

★ French House
49 Dean Street, W1D 5BG (7437 2799, www.frenchhousesoho.com). Leicester Square or Piccadilly Circus tube. **Open** noon-11pm Mon-Sat; noon-10.30pm Sun. *Food served* noon-3pm, 5.30-11pm Mon-Sat. **Credit** AmEx, DC, MC, V. **Map** p416 W3 ㉑
Through the door of this venerable Gallic establishment have passed many titanic drinkers of the pre-

and post-war era, the Bacons and the Behans. The venue's French heritage also enticed De Gaulle to run a Resistance operation from upstairs – it's now, incongruously, a tiny Venetian-style restaurant. De Gaulle's image survives behind the bar, where beer is served in half-pints and litre bottles of Breton cider are still plonked on the famed back alcove table.
▶ *The little upstairs restaurant, Polpetto (7734 1969, www.polpetto.co.uk), is the first off-shoot of the popular Polpo – and every bit as crammed.*

★ LAB
12 Old Compton Street, W1D 4TQ (7437 7820, www.lab-townhouse.com). Leicester Square or Tottenham Court Road tube. **Open** 4pm-midnight Mon-Sat; 4-10.30pm Sun. *Food served* 6-11pm Mon-Sat; 6-10.30pm Sun. **Credit** MC, V. **Map** p416 X2 ㉒
Newer spots have overtaken the '70s-meets-'90s decor, but few can match the sheer enthusiasm and knowledge of the staff at the London Academy of Bartending. Cocktails are king here, and many original combinations are mixed using LAB's own infusions and syrups (chorizo tequila, anyone?). Pull up a chair and let one of the ultra-helpful mixologists guide you through the menu. The unashamed party vibe means this place fills up early.

Lucky Voice
52 Poland Street, W1F 7LR (7439 3660, www.luckyvoice.co.uk). Oxford Circus tube. **Open/food served** 5.30pm-1am Mon-Thur; 3pm-1am Fri, Sat; 3-10.30pm Sun. **Credit** AmEx, MC, V. **Map** p416 V2 ㉓
There are nine rooms at this karaoke venue, each of them with space for between four and 12 singers; some come with props such as hats, wigs and inflatable electric guitars. A drinks menu includes cocktails (£7), saké and spirits, brought to your room when you press the 'thirsty' button; food is limited to pizzas and snacks. The perfect place to discover your inner Susan Boyle.

Mark's Bar.

Other locations 173-174 Upper Street, Islington, N1 1RG (7354 6280).

★ Mark's Bar

66-70 Brewer Street, W1F 9UP (7292 3518, www.hixsoho.co.uk). Piccadilly Circus tube. **Open/food served** noon-12.30am Mon-Sat; 11am-11pm Sun. **Credit** AmEx, MC, V. **Map** p416 V3 ㉔

In the basement under Mark Hix's fine Soho restaurant, this is a sort-of subterranean speakeasy without the smugness. There's a low zinc bar, retro rugs and comfy Chesterfields slouched next to a bar billiards table. Service is flawless and the drinks menu crafted by an all-star cocktail dream-team, led by Nick Strangeway. The 150-strong wine list might be expected in a restaurant bar, but it's rare to find such an enlightened beer menu. You have to order some food (it's part of the licence requirement), but that's no hardship: it includes the entire à la carte menu from upstairs and lovely bar snacks.

★ Milk & Honey

61 Poland Street, W1F 7NU (7292 9949, www.mlkhny.com). Oxford Circus tube. **Open** *Non-members* 6-11pm Mon-Sat (2hrs max, last admission 9pm). **Credit** AmEx, DC, MC, V. **Map** p416 V2 ㉕

You could walk past the inconspicuous door of this semi-mythical, dimly lit Soho speakeasy every day and never know it was here, and that's probably just how they like it. It's members-only most of the time, but mere mortals can book a table until 11pm, although even then you're not likely to get a table later on in the week. While the place may not be at its best earlier in the evening, what it then lacks in atmosphere it more than makes up for with its outstanding cocktails.

OXFORD STREET & MARYLEBONE

Artesian

Langham Hotel, 1C Portland Place, W1B 1JA (7636 1000, www.artesian-bar.co.uk). Oxford Circus tube. **Open/food served** 4pm-midnight Mon-Fri; noon-midnight Sat, Sun. **Credit** AmEx, DC, MC, V. **Map** p396 H5 ㉖

David Collins' redesign of the historic Langham hotel artfully blends Victorian decadence with modern detail. Rum is a passion: the impressive drinks menu offers more than 60, from a £9 Gosling's Black Seal to a £300 Havana Club Maximo. There's also a clever 'cocktail grazing menu', which allows you to work your way through the extensive selection with less impact on both wallet and sobriety.

★ Purl

50 Blandford Street, W1U 7HX (7935 0835, www.purl-london.com). Bond Street tube. **Open** 5pm-11.30pm Mon-Thur; 5pm-midnight Fri, Sat. **Credit** AmEx, MC, V. **Map** p396 G5 ㉗

This new cocktail bar has a speakeasy/Prohibition feel. There's even a (working) retro phone booth. The four young chaps behind it claim inspiration from the golden age of bartending. Accordingly, a lot of effort goes into each drink: for Mr Hyde's Fixer Upper (£9), a Smoking Gun hand-held food smoker pipes applewood smoke into a flask of rum, cola reduction and orange bitters. The flask is then sealed with candlewax before being served with a silver goblet.

PADDINGTON & NOTTING HILL

Kensington Wine Rooms

127-129 Kensington Church Street, W8 7LP (7727 8142, www.greatwinesbytheglass.com).

Notting Hill Gate tube. **Open** noon-midnight daily. *Food served* noon-11pm daily. **Credit** MC, V. **Map** p404 Z6 ㉓

With about 100 varieties, the wine list here isn't the longest in the capital, but the mix of lesser-known Old World styles and contemporary New World wines is exceptionally well chosen. Bottles can be taken away, but it's really all about the 40 wines by the glass, dispensed from five Enomatic machines in the cosy front room. The dining room is usually filled with well-to-do locals.

★ Lonsdale

44-48 Lonsdale Road, W11 2DE (7727 4080, www.thelonsdale.co.uk). Ladbroke Grove or Notting Hill Gate tube. **Open** 6pm-midnight Mon-Thur; 6pm-1am Fri, Sat; 6-11.30pm Sun. *Food served* 6-10.30pm daily. **Credit** AmEx, MC, V. **Map** p404 Y4 ㉙

It's been the best part of a decade since he mixed drinks here, but bartender Dick Bradsell's influence is still felt in the outstanding modern cocktails: try the elderflower fizz (elderflower cordial, lemon juice and champagne). Comprising a sun-catching front terrace, a long bar counter and a wide, candlelit seating area at the back, the Lonsdale treats cocktail history with reverence; drinks invented in London between 1914 and 1934 are a specialist subject.

Portobello Star

171 Portobello Road, W11 2DY (7229 8016, http://portobellostar.co.uk). Ladbroke Grove or Notting Hill Gate tube. **Open** 11am-11pm Mon-Thur; 11am-12.30am Fri; 10am-12.30am Sat; 11am-11.30pm Sun. **Credit** MC, V. **Map** p404 X4 ㉚

This 'cocktail tavern' deftly blends discerning bar and traditional boozer. The bountifully stocked bar is manned by friendly staff thoroughly educated in the art of adult refreshment; 'Drink less but better' is the mantra of leading mixologist Jake Burger. His impeccable, approachable directory of discerning drinks is the last word on sophisticated intoxication. If you want to mix drinking with music, there are DJs on Friday and Saturday nights.

THE BEST COCKTAIL BARS

LAB
The London Academy of Bartending is perfect for a big night out. *See p239.*

Purl
Elaborate confections at surprisingly reasonable prices. *See left.*

69 Colebrooke Row
Invention in Islington courtesy of star bartender Tony Conigliaro. *See p245.*

PICCADILLY CIRCUS & MAYFAIR

★ Connaught Bar

Connaught, Carlos Place, W1K 2AL (7499 7070, www.the-connaught.co.uk). Bond Street tube. **Open** 4pm-1am Mon-Sat. **Credit** AmEx, DC, MC, V. **Map** p398 H7 ㉛

The main bar of the swish Connaught hotel (*see p196*) is grown-up, darkly elegant and reminiscent of a cruise liner, with unobtrusive lighting and a deco feel. The expensive drinks and the service have a lot to live up to in the surroundings, but they do so. The Connaught martini is worth ordering for the tableside theatre alone and the staff are faultless – slightly formal, but never standoffish.

▶ *Across the lobby, the hotel's cosy and discreet Coburg Bar is both smart and unpretentious.*

Galvin at Windows

London Hilton, Park Lane, W1K 1BE (7208 4021, www.galvinatwindows.com). Green Park or Hyde Park Corner tube. **Open** 11am-1am Mon-Wed; 11am-3am Thur, Fri; 3pm-3am Sat; 11am-10.30pm Sun. *Food served* 6pm-12.30am Mon-Wed; 6pm-2.30am Thur-Sat; 6-10pm Sun. **Credit** AmEx, DC, MC, V. **Map** p398 G8 ㉜

There's suddenly no shortage of rooftop venues in London – Vertigo (*see p236*) and Paramount (*see p214*) will be joined by a cluster in the City over the next few years – but the location of Windows is still superb. It offers remarkable panoramic views from the 28th floor of the Park Lane Hilton. Add a sleek interior that mixes art deco glamour with a hint of 1970s petrodollar kitsch, and you can't go wrong. The wine and cocktails don't come cheap, but the drinks are assembled with care, and the service is attentive without being obsequious.

Only Running Footman

5 Charles Street, W1J 5DF (7499 2988, www.therunningfootman.biz). Green Park tube. **Open** 7.30am-11pm daily. *Food served* 7.30am-10.30pm daily. **Credit** AmEx, MC, V. **Map** p398 H7 ㉝

Despite a dramatic recent refurbishment, this place still looks as if it's been here forever. On the ground floor, jolly chaps prop up the mahogany bar, enjoying three decent ales and an extensive menu. A fine full English breakfast is served for only £8.50, a fraction of what you'd pay in nearby Claridge's. On the first floor, there's a quieter, formal dining room.

WESTMINSTER & ST JAMES'S

Albannach

66 Trafalgar Square, WC2N 5DS (7930 0066, www.albannach.co.uk). Charing Cross tube/rail. **Open** noon-1am Mon-Sat. *Food served* noon-11pm Mon-Sat. **Credit** AmEx, DC, MC, V. **Map** p416 X5 ㉞

CONSUME

Cadogan Arms.

drinking single malts from a terrific range. That said, the outstanding wine list is surprisingly affordable, with house selections starting at under £20. Additional appeal comes from live jazz (six nights a week) and a heated cigar terrace.

Other locations Boisdale of Bishopsgate, Swedeland Court, 202 Bishopsgate, the City, EC2M 4NR (7283 1763).

★ Dukes Bar

35 St James's Place, SW1A 1NY (7491 4840, www.dukeshotel.co.uk). Green Park tube. **Open** 2pm-midnight Mon-Thur, Sun; noon-midnight Fri, Sat. **Credit** AmEx, DC, MC, V. **Map** p398 J8 ❸⑥
This titchy bar looks like an upper-class Georgian sitting room. The martinis are among the best in London and priced accordingly. Sipping one amid the polite murmur of the very adult clientele, while munching on complimentary nuts and Puglian olives, is a soothing experience. Alternatives include nearly a dozen good wines by the glass.

St Stephen's Tavern

10 Bridge Street, SW1A 2JR (7925 2286). Westminster tube. **Open** 10am-11.30pm Mon-Sat; 10.30am-11pm Sun. *Food served* noon-10pm daily. **Credit** MC, V. **Map** p399 L9 ❸⑦
Done out with dark woods, etched mirrors and Arts and Crafts-style wallpaper, this is a lovely old pub. The food is reasonably priced and the ales are excellent, but drinks can be expensive. Opposite Big Ben, its location is terrific, yet it's neither too touristy nor too busy. If the downstairs bars are full, head upstairs and look for a seat on the mezzanine.
▶ *Its nearest rival is the Red Lion (48 Parliament Street, SW1A 2NH, 7930 5826), by tradition the politicians' favourite and certainly clad in plenty of handsome wood.*

1707

Fortnum & Mason, 181 Piccadilly, W1A 1ER (7734 8040, www.fortnumandmason.com). Piccadilly Circus tube. **Open** noon-10pm Mon-Sat. *Food served* noon-9.30pm Mon-Sat. **Credit** AmEx, MC, V. **Map** p416 V5 ❸⑧
Although it's named after the year in which Fortnum & Mason was founded, 1707 looks firmly towards the future. Unpolished wooden slats line the walls, and the lines are clean and modern, but the star is the wine and champagne list; you can drink any of the wines sold within the wine department if you're willing to pay £10 corkage on the retail price. By comparison, food is a bit of an afterthought.
▶ *For Fortnum & Mason itself, see p250.*

CHELSEA

★ Cadogan Arms

298 King's Road, SW3 5UG (7352 6500, www.thecadoganarmschelsea.com). Sloane Square tube. **Open** 11am-11pm Mon-Sat; 11am-10.30pm

Right on Trafalgar Square, Albannach (as opposed to 'sassanach') specialises in Scotch whiskies and cocktails thereof. A map in the menu details the origins of these Highland and Island malts, the pages brimming with 17-year-old Glengoynes, 12-year-old Cragganmore and 29-year-old Auchentoshan. That said, kilted staff, illuminated reindeer and too many loud office groups detract from the quality on offer.

Boisdale of Belgravia

13-15 Eccleston Street, SW1W 9LX (7730 6922, www.boisdale.co.uk). Victoria tube/rail. **Open/ food served** noon-1am Mon-Fri; 6pm-1am Sat. **Admission** £4.50 before 10pm, then £12. **Credit** AmEx, DC, MC, V. **Map** p398 H10 ❸⑤
There's nowhere quite like this posh, Scottish-themed enterprise, and that includes its sister branch in the City. If you're here to drink, you'll be

In the Mix

Cocktail maestro Tony Conigliaro gets a place to call his own.

Tony Conigliaro started out in the bar trade 15 years ago, working with, among others, the brother of his current business partner, Camille Hobby-Limon. After time spent at the likes of Isola and Shochu Lounge (*see p238*), Conigliaro and Hobby-Limon opened **69 Colebrooke Row** (*see p245*), a tiny, quietly handsome establishment (book ahead if you can) serving unusual, flavourful cocktails. We spoke to the cocktail-meister.

Time Out (TO): Our reviewer dubbed 69 Colebrooke Row 'the El Bulli of booze' in our first review. Would you agree?
Tony Conigliaro (TC): I think that might be an exaggeration, but it's a big compliment. What they've been doing there [chef Ferran Adrià's 'molecular gastronomy'] is a 28-year project. We're using modern methods and modern ideas, but they're not necessarily that obvious. Our dry martinis, for example, have an essence of dry, which is basically a distillation of polyphenols, tannins and grape seeds. It doesn't have a flavour, but it does have an effect: it slightly dries out your tongue as you're drinking your martini. It's not whizz-bang fireworks.

TO: Have drinkers lagged behind foodies, then, or bartenders behind chefs?
TC: I think the history is different. Food goes back centuries. The history of cocktails only goes back 200 years.

TO: What is it about cocktails that first appealed to you?
TC: I really like all the different aspects of them. It's not just about the drinks: it's about being a host, making a venue, about the history of drinks.

TO: What drew you to this quiet Islington sidestreet?
TC: It was more the venue that sold it for us. Camille knew I wanted to open a very small, Tokyo-style bar just off the beaten track. Our references are more 1950s film noir than anything else. It also had a garret-style room upstairs, which has become a kind of workshop where we work on new ideas.

TO: Are you proudest of any one particular creation?
TC: I like whatever I'm working on, pushing things forward. Right now, we're working on a Somerset sour for the autumn. It's basically Somerset cider brandy made sour, but we've created a diorama around it, adding cider; for garnish, there's a little apple that floats up and down inside the drink, a reference to the apple-bobbing at Halloween. The garnish is infused with the scent of hay using a vacuum cooker.

TO: What do you find most rewarding about the work?
TC: Customers coming back!

CONSUME

CONSUME

Sun. *Food served* noon-3.30pm, 6-10.30pm Mon-Fri; noon-10.30pm Sat; noon-9pm Sun. **Credit** AmEx, DC, MC, V. **Map** p395 E12 ❸
In 2009, this 19th-century Chelsea pub was given a major rebuild by its new owners, the Martin brothers. It now has a countrified look, complete with stuffed animals and fly-fishing displays, and remains a proper boozer, with top-quality real ales, notwithstanding the snug and smoothly run dining area, where great food is on offer.
▶ *On Sloane Square, the Martin brothers' Botanist (no.7, 7730 0077) provides a similar mix of fine booze and hearty food.*

Tini
87-89 Walton Street, SW3 2HP (7589 8558, www.tinibar.com). Knightsbridge or South Kensington tube. **Open** 6pm-midnight Mon-Thur; 6pm-1am Fri, Sat; 6pm-12.30am Sun. **No credit cards. Map** p395 E10 ❹
Located around the point where the noblesse of Knightsbridge gives way to swanky Chelsea, Tini is a cocktail lounge hangout for haves and have-yachts, proper posh and a bit ridiculous. Serviced by genteel Gianfrancos in suits and spread under low ceilings, it's laced with traces of pink neon and fancy fleshiness courtesy of an Italian-leaning drinks list and Pirelli calendars from yesteryear.

KNIGHTSBRIDGE & SOUTH KENSINGTON

Anglesea Arms
15 Selwood Terrace, SW7 3QG (7373 7960, www.capitalpubcompany.com). South Kensington tube. **Open** 11am-11pm Mon-Sat; noon-10.30pm Sun. *Food served* noon-3pm, 6.30-10pm Mon-Fri; noon-5pm, 6-10pm Sat; noon-5pm, 6-9.30pm Sun. **Credit** AmEx, MC, V. **Map** p395 D11 ❹
Formerly the local of both Charles Dickens and DH Lawrence, this old boozer is packed tight on summer evenings, the front terrace and main bar filled with professional blokes chugging ale, and their

female equivalents putting bottles of Sancerre on expenses. But the Anglesea has always had more aura than the average South Kensington hostelry; perhaps it's the link with the Great Train Robbery, reputedly planned here.

Blue Bar
Berkeley, Wilton Place, SW1X 7RL (7235 6000, www.the-berkeley.co.uk). Hyde Park Corner tube. **Open** 4pm-1am Mon-Sat; 4-11pm Sun. **Credit** AmEx, DC, MC, V. **Map** p398 G9 ❹
It isn't just a caprice: this David Collins-designed bar really lives up to its name. The sky-blue bespoke armchairs, the deep-blue ornate plasterwork and the navy-blue leather-bound menus combine with discreet lighting to striking effect. It's more a see-and-be-seen place than somewhere to kick back, but don't let the celeb-heavy reputation put you off: staff treat everyone like royalty, and the cocktails are a masterclass in sophistication.

190 Queensgate
Gore Hotel, 190 Queensgate, SW7 5EX (7584 6601, www.gorehotel.co.uk). Gloucester Road or South Kensington tube. **Open** noon-1.30am daily. **Credit** AmEx, MC, V. **Map** p395 D9 ❹
In a library atmosphere of dark wood and low lighting, this bar at the Gore (*see p201*) provides varied, classy cocktails – including 20 flavoured mojitos – to a varied, classy clientele. Beaumont des Crayères is the bubbly of choice; wines and beers display a Spanish touch. The Iberian management could do far better than the desultory tapas on offer, but the service is top-notch.

NORTH LONDON

The **Lock Tavern** and **Proud** (for both, *see p330*) are excellent Camden DJ bars, while the **Blues Tavern** (*see p323*) and scuzzy indie-den the **Dublin Castle** (94 Parkway, NW1 7AN, 7485 1773) supply live music. In Islington, the boisterous **King's Head** (*see p348*) is as good a pub as it is a theatre, and the **Marquess** (*see p227*) is an excellent gastropub. For own-brewed ales, try the **Horseshoe** (*see p226*) in Hampstead.

Crown & Goose
100 Arlington Road, Camden, NW1 7HP (7485 8008, www.crownandgoose.co.uk). Camden Town tube. **Open** noon-midnight Mon-Thur, Sun; noon-2am Fri, Sat. **Credit** MC, V. **Map** p404 Y3 ❹
Its popularity breeds contempt among some people, but the C&G remains a near-perfect local: far enough off the beaten track to elude the hordes and packed with Victorian charm, from the scrubbed furniture to the antique portraits and gilt-framed mirrors on its pea-green walls. Small and cosy, never more so than when evening comes and staff draw blinds, the Crown also turns out simple but superb pub food.

Driver

2-4 Wharfdale Road, King's Cross, N1 9RY (7278 8827, www.driverlondon.co.uk). King's Cross tube/rail. **Open** noon-midnight Mon-Fri; 5pm-midnight Sat; noon-6pm Sun. **No credit cards.** **Map** p397 M2 ⓯

Spread over five floors, with decor alternating from urban to intricate, this soaring yet svelte Swiss army knife of a venue encompasses a pub-style restaurant, a small roof terrace, a members' bar, a lounge and a dining room that, later, transforms *Bugsy Malone*-style into a dancefloor with decks. The Driver has given a green-fingered salute to convention by planting its garden vertically on the outside wall.

★ Holly Bush

22 Holly Mount, Hampstead, NW3 6SG (7435 2892). Hampstead tube or Hampstead Heath rail. **Open** noon-11pm Mon-Sat; noon-10.30pm Sun. *Food served* noon-3pm, 6-10pm Mon-Fri; noon-5pm, 6-10pm Sat, Sun. **Credit** (over £10) MC, V.

As the trend for gutting old pubs claims yet more Hampstead boozers, this place's cachet increases. Located on a quiet hilltop backstreet, it was built as a house in the 1790s and used as the Assembly Rooms in the 1800s, before becoming a pub in 1928. A higgledy-piggledy air remains, with three low-ceilinged bar areas and one bar counter at which are poured decent pints. Sound food and a good choice of wines by the glass are further draws.

★ 69 Colebrooke Row

69 Colebrooke Row, Islington, N1 8AA (07540 528593, www.69colebrookerow.com). Angel tube. **Open** 5pm-midnight Mon-Wed; 5pm-1am Thur; 5pm-2am Fri, Sat. **Credit** AmEx, MC, V. **Map** p400 O2 ⓰

See p243 **In the Mix**.

★ Wenlock Arms

26 Wenlock Road, Hoxton, N1 7TA (7608 3406, www.wenlock-arms.co.uk). Old Street tube/rail. **Open** noon-midnight Mon-Thur, Sun; noon-1am Fri, Sat. *Food served* noon-9pm daily. **No credit cards.** **Map** p400 P3 ⓱

Peek through the door of this traditional boozer and you'll immediately see its raison d'être: real ales, around eight of them at one time. The scruffy decor is a perfect match for the down-at-heel location, but there's a real community feel to the place: how many Islington pubs have cricket and football teams, or offer up free triangle sandwiches on a Sunday night as an impromptu jazz session unfolds in the corner? More formal jazz gigs take place on Friday and Saturday nights, and there's a quiz each Thursday.

EAST LONDON

Late-night **Charlie Wright's International Bar** (*see p326*) is as much about drinking as it is about music; there's music, food and booze at

Holly Bush.

Concrete, beneath **Pizza East** (*see p230*). In Shoreditch, for the thriving gay scene, *see pp308-314*; for nightclubs, *see pp331-332*.

★ Callooh Callay
65 Rivington Street, Shoreditch, EC2A 3AY (7739 4781). Old Street tube/rail or Shoreditch High Street rail. **Open** 5-11pm Mon-Thur, Sun; 5.30pm-1am Fri; 6pm-1am Sat. **Credit** MC, V. **Map** p401 R4 ❹
Only a pair of intertwined Cs divulges Callooh Callay's location. Inside, it's warm and whimsical; the neo-Victorian decor is as eclectic as 'Jabberwocky',

the poem by Lewis Carroll from which the bar gets its name. A laid-back lounge, a mirrored bar and loos tiled in old cassettes lie behind an oak Narnia wardrobe. Stake out seats here to people-watch: lots of vintage fabrics and fixed-gear cyclists.

Carpenter's Arms
73 Cheshire Street, Brick Lane, E2 6EG (7739 6342, www.carpentersarmsfreehouse.com). Shoreditch High Street rail. **Open** 4-11.30pm Mon; noon-11.30pm Tue-Thur, Sun; noon-12.30am Fri, Sat. *Food served* 5-10pm Mon; 1-10pm Tue-Sun. **Credit** MC, V. **Map** p401 S4 ❹

Bigging Up the Beer

Is the huge variety and complexity of beer finally getting the respect it deserves?

At Time Out, we've long been fans of 'real ale'. Ale was first called 'real' in the 1970s by CAMRA, the campaign launched to save traditional beers from a rising tide of processed, keg stuff. Crucially, real ale matures and is managed in its barrel or cask (hence it is also known as 'cask ale' or 'cask-conditioned ale'). Stored in the cool pub cellar, it's served fresh on site, by hand pump, not electric tap. It's a living entity: the beer drinker's equivalent of farmhouse cheese, as flavoursome and various as good wine. Most Londoners, however, prefer fizzy, processed lager or 'nitrokeg' ale, both of which are more easily kept by the publican but are the taste equivalent of wine from a box.

Perhaps the tide is starting to turn against the fizzy rubbish. The first London brewery festival – featuring nearly a dozen city brewers, from Fullers to Kernel – was held in September 2010 (www.london brewers.org). One participant, the Meantime Brewery, last year opened a superb new flagship bar-restaurant called the **Old Brewery** (*see p232*). A long-term pioneer of interesting beer in the capital, Meantime is dedicating its new micro-brewery to the research and revival of the kind of beers that would have been drunk in the Old Royal Naval College hundreds of years ago.

Following the success of the **Rake** (*see p235*) in trying to appeal to a wider public than the clichéd bearded beer nerd, a new generation of what we might call 'beer-cafés' is starting to appear. **Draft House** (*see p248*) is a prime example of the type, its venues feeling more like a bar than a pub, despite the rows of shiny pumps. Its offer of beers in third of a pint measures

makes exploring the breadth of its list easy.

Those who prefer to sup top-quality pints in a traditional environment needn't go home disappointed: the **Jerusalem Tavern** and **Ye Olde Mitre** (*see p238* **Inside Track**) serve great beer in properly atmospheric surroundings. Planning a picnic? **Drink of Fulham** (349 Fulham Palace Road, SW6 6TB, 7610 6795, www.drinkoffulham.com) is a small shop that sells a changing array of 600 beers. There are even a few tables outside on a terrace, should you be too impatient to try out your purchases.

Old Brewery.

At one time, this cosy boozer took centre stage in East End gangsterland. It was bought by the Kray twins in 1967 for their dear old mum, and it was here that Ronnie tanked up on dutch courage before murdering Jack 'the Hat' McVitie. Today, Hoxtonites, fashionistas, the odd ironic moustache and a few ambitious hats fill the snug space. The drinks selection is great, and the cut-above food (boards of cheese, Sunday roasts) isn't sold at stupid prices.

Commercial Tavern

142 Commercial Street, Spitalfields, E1 6NU (7247 1888). Liverpool Street tube/rail or Shoreditch High Street rail. **Open** 5-11pm Mon-Fri; noon-11pm Sat; noon-10.30pm Sun. **Credit** AmEx, MC, V. **Map** p401 R5 (50)

The inspired chaos of retro-eccentric decor and warm, inclusive atmosphere make this landmark flat-iron corner pub very likeable. It seems to have escaped the attentions of the necking-it-after-work masses, perhaps because of the absence of wall-to-wall lager pumps in favour of some proper real ale. The bar is made up of colourful art deco tiles, and there's a distinct decorative playfulness throughout; it's a great example of how a historic pub can be lit up with new life.

► *Just down the street, the fabulous, every-busy Golden Heart (no.110, E1 6LZ, 7247 2158) is a famous nursery for East End artists.*

Grapes

76 Narrow Street, Limehouse, E14 8BP (7987 4396). Westferry DLR. **Open** noon-3pm, 5.30-11pm Mon-Wed; noon-11pm Thur-Sat; noon-10.30pm Sun. *Food served* noon-2.30pm, 7-9.30pm Mon-Sat; noon-3.30pm Sun. **Credit** AmEx, MC, V.

If you're trying to evoke the feel of the Thames docks before their Disneyfication into Docklands, these narrow, ivy-covered and etched-glass 1720 riverside premises are a good place to start: the downstairs is all wood panels and nautical jetsam; the upstairs plainer, but it's easier to find seats for Sunday lunch. It's a fairly blokey pub: expect good ales and a half-dozen wines of each colour by glass and bottle, plus jugs of kir royale or strawberry fizz for summer and port for winter. There's a tiny terrace too.

► *Nearby, Gordon Ramsay's Narrow (44 Narrow Street, E14 8DQ, 7592 7950, www.gordonramsay.com) does great bar snacks.*

★ Green & Red

51 Bethnal Green Road, Shoreditch, E1 6LA (7749 9670, www.greenred.co.uk). Liverpool Street tube/rail or Shoreditch High Street rail. **Open** 5.30pm-midnight Mon-Thur; 5.30pm-2am Fri, Sat; 5.30-10.30pm Sun. *Food served* 6-10.30pm Mon-Thur, Sun; 6-11pm Fri, Sat. **Credit** AmEx, MC, V. **Map** p401 S4 (51)

Named after the green and red of the Mexican flag, G&R attracts people going to the nearby Rich Mix

Commercial Tavern.

cineplex and couples happy to pick at plates of meatballs or octopus ceviche upstairs. There's also some serious drinking to be done, for which we suggest repairing downstairs to the late-night basement bar and its welcomingly slouchy sofas. Young professionals neck Negra Modelo lager and smoke on the titchy front terrace, but specialist tequilas and tequila cocktails are the real joy.

Loungelover

1 Whitby Street, Shoreditch, E1 6JU (7012 1234, www.loungelover.co.uk). Liverpool Street tube/rail or Shoreditch High Street rail. **Open** 6pm-midnight Mon-Thur, Sun; 5.30pm-1am Fri; 6pm-1am Sat. *Food served* 6-11.30pm Mon-Thur, Sun; 7pm-midnight Fri, Sat. **Credit** AmEx, DC, MC, V. **Map** p401 S4 (52)

This louche cocktail lounge parades low-lit decadence in its decor, a mish-mash of baroque, kitsch and exotic with distressed wooden armoires, vintage palm-frond chandeliers, a stuffed hippo's head and tea lights set on elegant, glass-topped tables. It may all be a little pretentious, but the staff are helpful; if you're looking for somewhere that will impress, the place can hardly be bettered. Cocktails involved deft mixes; food includes sushi and hot Japanese snacks.
▶ *The same folks are behind the nearby Les Trois Garçons restaurant; see p231.*

SOUTH-EAST LONDON

Dartmouth Arms
7 Dartmouth Road, Forest Hill, SE23 3HN (8488 3117, www.thedartmoutharms.com). Forest Hill rail or bus 122, 176, 185. **Open** noon-11pm Mon-Sat; noon-10.30pm Sun. *Food served* noon-3.30pm, 6.30-10pm Mon-Fri; noon-10pm Sat; noon-9pm Sun. **Credit** MC, V.
This gastropub is ideally located for the Horniman Museum (*see p163*). The front bar is now a well-aired, sepia-tinted space perfect for relaxing with the papers or the free Wi-Fi; there's also an adjoining 'snug bar' (the red walls of which boast exhibitions by local artists) and a rear dining room. Cocktails are just £5.50-£6.25, and there's a long wine list, but beers are limited: Brakspear and Bombardier, Staropramen and Kronenbourg.

Gipsy Moth
60 Greenwich Church Street, Greenwich, SE10 9BL (8858 0786, www.thegipsymothgreenwich. co.uk). Cutty Sark DLR. **Open** noon-11pm Mon-Thur; noon-midnight Fri, Sat; noon-10.30pm Sun. *Food served* noon-10pm Mon-Fri; noon-10pm Sat; noon-9.30pm Sun. **Credit** AmEx, MC, V. **Map** p405 W2 ⑤
The split-level garden and roomy interior at this moderately funky pub are ideal for a sit-down after roaming around Greenwich. The pub offers an impressive number of beers (Früli, Budvar, Paulaner and at least six others), well-priced wines and pretty decent food, from full breakfasts through bar snacks (olives, pistachios, pork crackling) to solid mains such as pork sausage and sage mash.
▶ *In good weather, the riverside seats of Cutty Sark Tavern (4-6 Ballast Quay, SE10 9PD, 8858 3146, www.cuttysarktavern.co.uk) are popular.*

Greenwich Union
56 Royal Hill, Greenwich, SE10 8RT (8692 6258, www.greenwichunion.com). Greenwich rail/DLR. **Open** noon-11pm Mon-Fri; 11am-11pm Sat; 11.30am-10.30pm Sun. *Food served* noon-10pm Mon-Fri; 11am-10pm Sat; 11am-9pm Sun. **Credit** MC, V. **Map** p405 W3 ⑤④
Decorated with framed covers of the *Picture Post*, this tidy operation is the spiritual home of Alistair Hook's mission to bring his Meantime Brewery's

German-style beers to the British public. Six tap options complement a couple of dozen bottled international beers, and food runs from a humble bacon butty to chargrilled steaks. Coffee, tea and a small front terrace make it a decent option for non-drinking visitors to Greenwich's many attractions.
▶ *Near the Thames – and on the premises of the Old Royal Naval College – the Old Brewery (see p232) is Meantime's flagship bar-restaurant.*

SOUTH-WEST LONDON

Also worth a look here are the **Dogstar** (*see p332*) on Brixton's Coldharbour Lane, and the scruffy but likeable **Windmill** (*see p325*).

Draft House
94 Northcote Road, Battersea, SW11 6QW (7924 1814, www.drafthouse.co.uk). Clapham South tube or Clapham Junction rail. **Open** 11am-11pm Mon-Fri; 10am-11pm Sat; 10am-11.30pm Sun. *Food served* 11am-10pm Mon-Sat; 10am-9pm Sun. **Credit** AmEx, MC, V.
This attractive beer bistro is clad in wood, warmed by candlelight and brightened with pop art and green furniture. The curved bar sports 17 shiny draught fonts and there are three-dozen bottles in the fridge. Served in third, half and full pints, the beers range across Europe and as far as the craft breweries of the United States, while ale-friendly tucker includes ham hock salad and a succulent Roquefort burger.
Other locations 206-208 Tower Bridge Road, the City, SE1 2UP (7378 9995); 74-76 Battersea Bridge Road, Battersea, SW11 3AG (7228 6482).
▶ *The bar also offers tours of the Sambrook's Brewery in nearby Battersea.*

Effra
38A Kellet Road, Brixton, SW2 1EB (7274 4180). Brixton tube/rail. **Open** noon-11pm Mon-Thur; noon-midnight Fri; 10am-midnight Sat; 10am-10.30pm Sun. *Food served* noon-10pm Mon-Fri; 11am-10pm Sat; 11am-9.30pm Sun. **No credit cards**.
This old-school pub has more of an Afro-Caribbean community feel than many Brixton watering holes. The daily changing menu offers the likes of seaweed callaloo and jerk pork, and palm fronds tower over drinkers in the cosy patio garden. One look at the fading Victorian splendour of the gold-corniced ceiling and pretty domed glass lamps, and it's no wonder locals pack the place out each night.

Lost Angel
339 Battersea Park Road, Battersea, SW11 4LF (7622 2112, www.lostangel.co.uk). Battersea Park rail. **Open** noon-11pm Tue, Wed; noon-1am Thur; noon-2am Fri, Sat; noon-11pm Sun. *Food served* noon-10pm Mon-Thur; noon-10.30pm Fri, Sat; noon-9pm Sun. **Credit** AmEx, MC, V.

You might not expect to find a bar as likeable as this along such a sorry-looking stretch of the Battersea Park Road. The range of drinks covers most bases: the three ales may include Wandle from nearby Sambrook's Brewery, while the cocktail list is split between classics, reinventions and shouldn't-work-but-do corruptions. They're all served within an eye-catching interior that falls pleasingly between corner pub and modish bar (trombones on the ceiling, white phone box). The kitchen offers poshed-up bar food and entertainment runs from DJs to quiz nights.

▶ *Not far away, the same owners run the award-winning Lost Society (697 Wandsworth Road, SW8 3JF, 7652 6526, www.lostsociety.co.uk).*

★ White Horse

1-3 Parsons Green, Parsons Green, SW6 4UL (7736 2115, www.whitehorsesw6.com). Parsons Green tube. **Open** 9.30am-11.30pm Mon-Wed, Sun; 9.30am-midnight Thur-Sat. *Food served* 10am-10.30pm daily. **Credit** AmEx, MC, V.
Only a lack of ceiling fans stops the main bar of this renowned hostelry from feeling like something from the days of the Raj. The Victorian ceilings are airily high, and wide windows with wooden venetian blinds let in plenty of light. Chesterfield-style sofas surround huge tables, though the umbrella-covered pavement tables are most coveted. Expect plenty of turned-up collars, rugby shirts and pashminas, although the mix of customers is wider than you might imagine. There are usually six to eight hand-pumped ales alongside the 135 bottled beers.

WEST LONDON

Botanist on the Green

3-5 Kew Green, Kew, Surrey TW9 3AA (8948 4838, www.thebotanistkew.com). Kew Gardens tube/rail or bus 65, 391. **Open** noon-11pm Mon-Thur; noon-midnight Fri, Sat; noon-10.30pm Sun. *Food served* noon-3pm, 6-10pm Mon-Fri; noon-10pm Sat; noon-9pm Sun. **Credit** AmEx, MC, V.
The name is a nod to its floral neighbour, the Royal Botanic Gardens (*see p172*); certainly, this pub's position on the corner of Kew Green makes it a perfect place for a relaxing pint after a mooch around the gardens. The space has cosy nooks – one with a fabulous double-sided fireplace – and raised areas that give it a more intimate feel.

Ladbroke Arms

54 Ladbroke Road, Holland Park, W11 3NW (7727 6648, www.capitalpubcompany.com). Holland Park tube. **Open** 11.30am-11pm Mon-Sat; noon-10.30pm Sun. *Food served* noon-2.30pm, 7-9.30pm Mon-Fri; 12.30-2.45pm, 7-9.30pm Sat, Sun. **Credit** AmEx, MC, V. **Map** p404 Y6 ⊕
The Ladbroke caters to moneyed fortysomethings sinking Sancerre on the front terrace and to ale aficionados after a pint of Sharp's Cornish Coaster. The decor in the light main bar is noteworthy, with an original 1920s poster for Fap'Anis on one side and a pre-war French ad for olive oil on the other. A back room fills with middle-aged chatter, while a narrow corridor behind provides peace for bookreaders.

CONSUME

White Horse.

Shops & Services

Innovative boutiques, classic department stores and shiny new malls.

In its celebration of both tradition and cutting-edge style, the revamp of department store **Liberty** (*see p253*) captured everything that's great about the capital's shopping scene. For each fashion-forward new opening and pop-up store in the city – east London's **Redchurch Street** (*see p270* **Style Street**) has been particularly lively over the past year – you'll find a classic independent that's still going strong after centuries (take a bow, umbrella specialists **James Smith & Sons**; *see p271*).

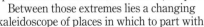

Between those extremes lies a changing kaleidoscope of places in which to part with your cash: multicultural street markets, deluxe department stores, flashy food shops and, of course, chain-store flagships. You'll also find some of the best places in Europe to buy books, records and second-hand clothes. Despite credit crunches and chopped-up bank cards, London is one of the world's most exciting, exhaustive and exhausting retail centres.

SHOPPING IN LONDON

The listings in this chapter concentrate on British brands and shops that are not only unique to the city, but also relatively central. For the key shopping areas around London, *see right* **Where to Shop**.

Most goods – with the notable exceptions of books, food and children's clothes – are subject to value added tax (VAT), which is almost always included in the prices advertised by shops. VAT was levied at 17.5 per cent in 2010, but is due to rise to 20 per cent in early 2011. Some shops operate a scheme allowing visitors from outside the European Union to claim back VAT when leaving the country; for details, *see p372*. Central London shops stay open late (until 7pm or 8pm) one night a week – it's Thursday in the West End, and Wednesday in Chelsea and Knightsbridge.

General

DEPARTMENT STORES

High-street favourite for undies, sandwiches and ready meals, **Marks & Spencer** (www.marksandspencer.co.uk) also offers several reliable fashion ranges, including its designer Autograph collection for men and women, and the younger, trend-led Per Una line and Limited Collection.

Fortnum & Mason

181 Piccadilly, St James's, W1A 1ER (7734 8040, www.fortnumandmason.co.uk). Green Park or Piccadilly Circus tube. **Open** 10am-8pm Mon-Sat; noon-6pm Sun. **Credit** AmEx, DC, MC, V. **Map** p416 V4.

Revamped in 2007, to coincide with its 300th anniversary, Fortnum & Mason is one of London's most inspiring department stores. A sweeping spiral staircase soars through the four-storey building, while light floods down from a central glass dome. The iconic eau de nil blue and gold colour scheme with flashes of rose pink abound on both the store design and the packaging of the fabulous ground-floor treats, such as the chocolates, biscuits, teas and preserves. The five restaurants, all redesigned by David Collins (of Wolseley fame), are equally impressive. A food hall in the basement has a huge range of fresh produce and more wines than ever before; beehives installed on top of the building in 2008 mean that Fortnum's Bees honey is as local as it gets. The shop is redolent of a time when luxury meant the highest degree of comfort rather than ostentation, but that's not to say it's beyond the means of a modest budget. The famous hampers start from £35 for the Tea at Four Hamper, going up to £500.

CONSUME

Where to Shop

London's best shopping neighbourhoods in brief.

COVENT GARDEN & SOHO
The famous former flower market is choked with chains and crowds, but **Neal Street** and the streets radiating off **Seven Dials** rule for trainers and streetwear. Another urbanwear hotspot is Soho's **Carnaby Street**, which has traded tacky tourist shops for hip chains and independents. **Berwick Street** is still hanging on to some record shops, while **Charing Cross Road** and **Cecil Court** are prime browsing territory for bookish types.

OXFORD STREET & MARYLEBONE
London's commercial backbone, **Oxford Street** heaves with department stores and big chains, which spill over on to elegant **Regent Street**. In contrast, **Marylebone** has a villagey atmosphere and small shops that sell everything from designer jewellery to artisan cheeses. Venture further north to **Church Street** for antiques.

NOTTING HILL
Best known for its antiques market on **Portobello Road**, Notting Hill also has an impressive cache of posh boutiques around the intersection of **Westbourne Grove** and **Ledbury Road** – a laid-back alternative to the West End and Chelsea. The area is also good for rare vinyl and vintage clothes.

MAYFAIR & ST JAMES'S
The traditional home of tailors (**Savile Row**) and shirtmakers (**Jermyn Street**), this patch also retains venerable specialist hatters, cobblers and perfumers. **Bond Street** glitters with jewellers and designer stores, while the reinvigorated **Mount Street** is now the place for niche upmarket labels.

CHELSEA & KNIGHTSBRIDGE
King's Road is pretty bland these days, but punctuated with some interesting shops. Designer salons line **Sloane Street** and mix with chains on **Knightsbridge**, which is anchored by deluxe department stores.

KENSINGTON
Once a hub of hip fashion, **Kensington High Street** has surrendered to the chains, but it's still worth exploring the backstreets leading up to Notting Hill Gate. Rarefied antiques shops gather on **Kensington Church Street**. In South Ken, **Brompton**

Cross has glossy contemporary furniture showrooms and designer boutiques.

EAST LONDON
East London is great for quirkier shops and some of the city's best markets; head there on a Sunday for **Columbia Road** (*pictured*) and Spitalfields markets. Head for **Brick Lane** and its offshoots, especially up-and-coming Redchurch Street, for clothing, accessories and home goods that have been made or adapted by idiosyncratic young designers, and heaps of vintage fashion. **Shoreditch** and **Hoxton** have hip boutiques, furniture stores and bookshops, while Hackney's **Broadway Market** hosts a Saturday farmers' market as well as a clutch of cool indie stores.

NORTH LONDON
The grungy markets of **Camden** are best left to the under-25s, but nearby **Primrose Hill** has an exquisite selection of small shops selling, among other things, quirky lingerie and vintage clothes. Antiques dealers are thinning out on Islington's **Camden Passage**, but there's a growing number of other indies, including gourmet chocolatier Paul A Young and new lifestyle boutique Smug.

CONSUME

Profile Selfridges

The Edwardian superstore that's always been on the cutting edge.

Selfridges (for listings, *see right*) celebrated its 100th anniversary in 2009 with a big party and Centenary Exhibition, but it has hardly sat on its laurels since: the vastly ambitious Selfridges Shoe Galleries (bigger, the store claims, than Tate Modern's Turbine Hall, displaying some 4,000 pairs of shoes and hosting exclusive designer 'apartments' for the likes of Chanel, Fendi and Dior) was, in autumn 2010, only the latest innovation. Selfridges remains the best department store for fashion, with store-wide themed events, concession boutiques and collections from the hottest new brands. It stocks a winning combination of new talent, edgy labels, smarter high-street labels, mid- and high-end brands. There are even useful floor plans that make navigating the store easy-peasy.

This London institution was founded by an American: Wisconsin-born Henry Gordon Selfridge. 'Mile-a-Minute Harry' was a wealthy 49-year-old before he even set foot in London, but selling still brought out his youthful exuberance. An early advocate of shopping as a fun experience, Selfridge was also a believer in slogans: he didn't coin the phrase 'The customer is always right', but he made heavy use of it in his advertisements.

When Mile-a-Minute's £400,000 department store opened on 15 March 1909, on the least trendy part of Oxford Street, it was a sensation. The architecture was beautiful and Selfridge was smart enough to secure the phone number 1 for this fledgling enterprise. He was also showman enough to exhibit Louis Blériot's plane (in 1909 it had just become the first aircraft to cross the English Channel) and host the first public demonstrations of television

in 1925. By then, Mile-a-Minute was known as 'the Earl of Oxford Street' – a blue plaque marks his home of the period, on swanky Berkeley Square.

The Great Depression hit Selfridge hard, but he saw no need to restrict his lavish lifestyle – the shop's website winningly blames his misfortunes on a taste for 'reckless gambling and expensive women'. When he died in 1947, he was a pauper.

One can't help thinking Selfridge would have loved the liveliness of the current store. Its recent 3rd Central initiative has all the hippest brands, an evolving mix of contemporary labels such as Ashish, Future Classics and Opening Ceremony, and there's a top-drawer Food Hall. Other concessions cater for the fit – a first-floor Cycle Surgery – and the lovelorn – rose-specialist Beautiful Blooms is on the ground floor. Back in 1918, appropriately enough, Selfridge had titled his book *The Romance of Commerce*.

HISTORIC SHOPPING
These two shops are also Edwardian beauties.

Daunt Books
See p256.
F Flittner
See p272.

CONSUME

Harrods

87-135 Brompton Road, Knightsbridge, SW1X 7XL (7730 1234, www.harrods.com). Knightsbridge tube. **Open** 10am-8pm Mon-Sat; noon-6pm Sun. **Credit** AmEx, DC, MC, V. **Map** p395 F9.

All the glitz and marble can be a bit much, but in the store that boasts of selling everything, it's hard not to leave with at least one thing you'll like. In fact, it even sold itself in 2010: former owner Mohammed Al Fayed received a reported £1.5bn from Qatar Holdings for the place. It's on the fashion floors that Harrods really comes into its own, with a 10,000sq ft Designer Studio on the first floor, featuring well-edited collections from the heavyweights, including a revamped Chanel boutique. There's also an excellent lingerie section, a Louis Vuitton menswear boutique, a luxury pet department and a top-notch sport section. The legendary food halls and restaurants on the ground floor have added a branch of Venetian coffee bar Caffè Florian, and the 5J ham and tapas bar from Spain's oldest Jabugo ham-producing company.
► *Nearby Harvey Nichols (109-125 Knightsbridge, SW1X 7RJ, 7235 5000, www.harveynichols.com) is coasting a little these days, but you'll still find a worthy clutch of unique fashion brands, plus a belle epoque-style champagne bar.*

★ Liberty

Regent Street, Soho, W1B 5AH (7734 1234, www.liberty.co.uk). Oxford Circus tube. **Open** 10am-9pm Mon-Sat; noon-6pm Sun. **Credit** AmEx, DC, MC, V. **Map** p416 U2.

Charmingly idiosyncratic, Liberty is housed in a 1920s mock Tudor structure. The store was given a major revamp in early 2009 (dubbed the 'Liberty Renaissance'), with new lines and the creation of a dedicated scarf room, as well as a frequently changing Bazaar area – referencing the days when the store was famous for offering never-seen-before items from far-flung places. The perfumerie section also goes from strength to strength, with new arrivals including Le Labo, mixed by hand, and fresh and modern scents from Eau d'Italie. Walk in the main entrance on Great Marlborough Street, flanked by Paula Pryke's exuberant floral concession, and you'll find yourself in a room devoted to the store's own label, in the middle of a galleried atrium. Shopping here is about more than just spending money; artful and arresting window displays, exciting new collections and luxe labels make it an experience to savour for its own sake.

Despite being up with the latest fashions, Liberty still respects its dressmaking heritage with an extensive range of cottons in the third-floor haberdashery department. Stationery also pays homage to the traditional, with beautiful Liberty of London notebooks, address books, photo albums and diaries embossed with the art nouveau 'Ianthe' print.

★ Selfridges

400 Oxford Street, Marylebone, W1A 1AB (0800 123 400, www.selfridges.com). Bond Street

or Marble Arch tube. **Open** 9.30am-9pm Mon-Sat; noon-6pm Sun. **Credit** AmEx, DC, MC, V. **Map** p396 G6.

See left **Profile**.

SHOPPING CENTRES & ARCADES

The **Royal Arcades** in the vicinity of Piccadilly are a throwback to shopping past – the Burlington Arcade (*see below*) is both the largest and grandest, but the Piccadilly Arcade, opposite it, and the Royal Arcade, at 28 Old Bond Street, are also worth a visit.

At the opposite end of the shopping centre spectrum is new mall **One New Change** (www.onenewchange.com), due to have opened near St Paul's Cathedral towards the end of 2010; the contemporary structure will house high-street heavyweights such as Topshop, Reiss and Banana Republic.

★ Burlington Arcade

Piccadilly, St James's, W1 (7630 1411, www.burlington-arcade.co.uk). Green Park tube. **Open** 8am-6.30pm Mon-Wed, Fri; 8am-7pm Thur; 9am-6.30pm Sat; 11am-5pm Sun. **No credit cards**. **Map** p408 U4.

In 1819, Lord Cavendish commissioned Britain's very first shopping arcade. Nearly two centuries later, the Burlington is still one of London's most prestigious shopping 'streets', patrolled by 'beadles' decked out in top hats and tailcoats. Highlights include collections of classic watches at David

Liberty.

CONSUME

CONSUME

Spitalfields Market.

Duggan, classic British fragrance house Penhaligon's, British luxury luggage brand Globe-Trotter (*see p266*), and Sermoneta, selling Italian leather gloves in a range of bright colours. High-end food shops come in the form of Luponde Tea and Ladurée; head to the latter for exquisite Parisian macaroons. Burlington also houses a proper shoe-shine boy working with waxes and creams for just £3.50.

Kingly Court
Carnaby Street, opposite Broadwick Street, Soho, W1B 5PW (7333 8118, www.carnaby.co.uk). Oxford Circus tube. **Open** 10am-7pm Mon-Sat; noon-6pm Sun. **No credit cards. Map** p408 U3.
Kingly Court has helped Carnaby Street reclaim some of its 1960s reputation as the heart of swinging London. The three-tiered complex boasts a funky mix of chains and independents – including several good vintage and craft shops – and a branch of Triyoga.

Westfield London
Ariel Way, Shepherd's Bush, W12 7GF (7333 8118, www.uk.westfield.com/london). White City or Wood Lane tube, or Shepherd's Bush tube/rail. **Open** 10am-10pm Mon-Wed, Fri; 10am-10pm Thur; 9am-9pm Sat; noon-6pm Sun. **No credit cards. Map** p408 U3.
Occupying 46 acres and covering nine different postcodes, Westfield London took the crown of Europe's largest city shopping centre when it opened in autumn 2008. The impressive site, which held the 1908 Olympics, cost around £1.6 billion to build, and houses some 265 shops. Popular labels that have never had stand-alone stores in the UK, such as Hollister, have shops here; you'll also find luxury fashion houses Louis Vuitton and Burberry. Highlights from the boutique-like labels include Sienna Miller's Twenty8Twelve, Tabio, Myla lingerie and Cos. Michelin-starred chefs Pascal Aussignac and Vincent Labeyrie can soothe away any shopping-induced stress with their gastronomic creations at Croque Gascon. If they don't manage to tempt your taste buds, then one of the other 50 eateries (including branches of Balans, Square Pie and Wahaca) surely will.

INSIDE TRACK
FOOD AND FASHION

Open only on Sundays, the Old Truman Brewery's **Sunday (Up)Market** (91 Brick Lane, 7770 6100, www.sundayupmarket.co.uk) is a buzzy collection of 140 stalls selling interesting and occasionally edgy fashion from fresh young designers, vintage clothing, art and crafts, and keenly priced jewellery. Food stalls offer everything from cupcakes to yakisoba and dim sum. It's more relaxed, cheaper and all-round hipper than near-neighbour **Spitalfields Market** (*see right*).

▶ *In late 2011, easily in time for the London 2012 Olympic and Paralympic Games, Westfield Stratford City is due to open beside the Olympic Park (see p53). It will take over from Westfield London as Europe's largest urban mall.*

MARKETS

London's street markets are a great place to sample street life while picking up bargains. Below is a selection of the best; for **Camden Market**, *see p148*; for food markets, *see p268*.

Columbia Road Market
Columbia Road, Bethnal Green, E2. Hoxton rail or bus 26, 48, 55. **Open** 8am-2pm Sun. **Map** p401 S3.
On Sunday mornings, this unassuming East End street is transformed into a swathe of fabulous plant life and the air is fragrant with blooms and the shouts of old-school Cockney stallholders (most offering deals for 'a fiver'). But a visit here isn't only about flowers and pot plants: alongside the market is a growing number of shops selling everything from pottery, Mexican glassware and arty prints to cupcakes and perfume; don't miss Ryantown's delicate paper cut-outs at no.126 (7613 1510). Get there early for the pick of the crops, or around 2pm for the bargains; refuel at Jones Dairy (23 Ezra Street, 7739 5372, www.jonesdairy.co.uk). *Photos p256.*

Portobello Road Market
Portobello Road, Notting Hill, W10 (www.portobelloroad.co.uk). Ladbroke Grove or Notting Hill Gate tube. **Open** *General* 8am-6.30pm Mon-Wed, Fri, Sat; 8am-1pm Thur. *Antiques* 4am-4pm Fri, Sat. **No credit cards. Map** p404 Y4.
Best known for antiques and collectibles, this is actually several markets rolled into one: antiques start at the Notting Hill end; further up are food stalls; under the Westway and along the walkway to Ladbroke Grove are emerging designer and vintage clothes on Fridays (usually marginally less busy) and Saturdays (invariably manic). For the excellent vintage buys of Portobello Green Market, *see p122* **Inside Track**.

Spitalfields Market
Commercial Street, between Lamb Street & Brushfield Street, the City, E1 6AA (7247 8556, www.oldspitalfieldsmarket.com). Liverpool Street tube/rail. **Open** *General* 9.30am-5pm Thur, Fri, Sun. *Antiques* 8.30am-4.30pm Thur. *Food* 10am-5pm Fri-Sun. *Fashion* 9.30am-5pm Fri. *Records & books* 10am-4pm 1st & 3rd Fri of mth. **No credit cards. Map** p403 R5.
Redevelopment has seen this East End stalwart combine the refurbished 1887 covered market with a modern shopping precinct. Around the edge of Old Spitalfields Market, enthusiastic stallholders sell grub from around the world. The busiest day is Sunday,

Columbia Road Market. *See p255.*

CONSUME

when nearby Brick Lane Market and Sunday (Up)Market in the Old Truman Brewery (strong on edgy designer and vintage fashion; www.sundayupmarket.co.uk) create a fashion shoot-meets-Bangladeshi-bazaar vibe in the neighbourhood. There's also a new fine food market held three times a week in Crispin Place.

Specialist

BOOKS & MAGAZINES

Central branches of the big book-selling chains include the **Waterstone's** flagship (203-206 Piccadilly, SW1Y 6WW, 7851 2400, www.waterstones.co.uk), which has a fine bar-café and an on-site branch of the Trailfinders travel agency, and the academic bookseller **Blackwell** (100 Charing Cross Road, WC2H 0JG, 7292 5100, www.blackwell.co.uk).

General

★ Daunt Books

83-84 Marylebone High Street, Marylebone, W1U 4QW (7224 2295, www.dauntbooks.co.uk). Baker Street tube. **Open** 9am-7.30pm Mon-Sat; 11am-6pm Sun. **Credit** AmEx, MC, V. **Map** p396 G5.
This beautiful Edwardian shop's elegant three-level back room – complete with oak balconies, viridian-green walls and stained-glass window – houses a much-praised travel section featuring row upon row of guidebooks, maps, language reference, travelogues and related fiction. Travel aside, Daunt is also a first-rate stop for literary fiction, biography, gardening and much more.
Other locations 158-164 Fulham Road, Chelsea, SW10 9PR (7373 4997); 112-114 Holland Park Avenue, Holland Park, W11 4UA (7727 7022); 51 South End Road, Hampstead, NW3 2QB (7794 8206); 193 Haverstock Hill, Belsize Park, NW3 4QL (7794 4006).

Foyles

113-119 Charing Cross Road, Soho, WC2H 0EB (7437 5660, www.foyles.co.uk). Tottenham Court Road tube. **Open** 9.30am-9pm Mon-Sat; noon-6pm Sun. **Credit** AmEx, MC, V. **Map** p416 X2.

Probably the single most impressive independent bookshop in London, Foyles built its reputation on the sheer volume and breadth of its stock: there are 56 specialist subjects covered here, in the flagship store. The music, gay-interest, foreign fiction, law and philosophy sections are especially strong. The shop's five storeys accommodate several concessions, too, including one for Unsworth's antiquarian booksellers and another, on the third floor, for Ray's Jazz (*see p275*). The popular first-floor café hosts readings from the likes of Douglas Coupland and Sebastian Faulks, as well as occasional gigs and other events. In addition to branches in the Southbank Centre (*see p317*) and St Pancras International (*see p106*), a fourth branch has opened in Westfield (*see p255*).

John Sandoe

10 Blacklands Terrace, Chelsea, SW3 2SR (7589 9473, www.johnsandoe.com). Sloane Square tube. **Open** 9.30am-5.30pm Mon, Tue, Thur-Sat; 9.30am-7.30pm Wed; noon-6pm Sun. **Credit** AmEx, DC, MC, V. **Map** p395 F11.

Tucked away on a Chelsea sidestreet, this independent looks just as a bookshop should and, after being in business for over half a century, remains a firm local favourite. The stock is packed to the rafters; of the 25,000 books here, 24,000 are a single copy, so there's serious breadth.

Specialist

Artwords

20-22 Broadway Market, Hackney, E8 4QJ (7923 7507, www.artwords.co.uk). London Fields rail. **Open** 10am-6.30pm Mon-Fri; 10am-6pm Sat; 10.30am-7pm Sun. **Credit** AmEx, MC, V.

Artwords has its finger firmly on the pulse when it comes to contemporary visual arts publications. Stock relating to contemporary fine art dominates, but there are also plenty of architecture, photography, graphic design, fashion, advertising and film titles, plus an excellent range of industry and creative magazines.

Other locations 65A Rivington Street, Shoreditch, EC2A 3QQ (7729 2000).

Books for Cooks

4 Blenheim Crescent, Notting Hill, W11 1NN (7221 1992, www.booksforcooks.com). Ladbroke Grove tube. **Open** 10am-6pm Tue, Wed, Fri, Sat; 10am-5.30pm Thur. **Credit** MC, V. **Map** p404 X4.

Books in this celebrated shop cover hundreds of cuisines, chefs and cookery techniques. Even better, the shop's kitchen-café tests different recipes every day, sold to eager customers from noon.

Stanfords

12-14 Long Acre, Covent Garden, WC2E 9LP (7836 1321, www.stanfords.co.uk). Covent Garden or Leicester Square tube. **Open** 9am-7.30pm Mon, Wed, Fri; 9.30am-7.30pm Tue; 9am-8pm Thur; 10am-8pm Sat; noon-6pm Sun. **Credit** MC, V. **Map** p416 Y3.

Three floors of travel guides, travel literature, maps, language guides, atlases and magazines. The basement houses the full range of British Ordnance Survey maps; you can plan your next trip over Fairtrade coffee in the Natural Café.

Used & antiquarian

Marchpane

16 Cecil Court, Covent Garden, WC2N 4HE (7836 8661, www.marchpane.com). Leicester Square tube. **Open** 11am-6pm Mon-Sat. **Credit** MC, V. **Map** p416 X4.

This specialist in classic children's books is on bookshop passageway Cecil Court (*see below* **Inside Track**), and a perfect fit for its locale. Stock includes titles such as *Winnie-the-Pooh* and *The Wind in the Willows*, but the shop's forte is Lewis Carroll, with a collection of illustrated editions of *Alice's Adventures in Wonderland*. A BBC Dalek and a Scalextric track in the basement add to the nostalgia.

Simon Finch Rare Books

26 Brook Street, Mayfair, W1K 5DQ (7499 0974, www.simonfinch.com). Bond Street or Oxford Circus tube. **Open** 10am-6pm Mon-Fri. **Credit** MC, V. **Map** p396 J6.

This era-spanning, idiosyncratic collection has wonderful surprises, from an original copy of *Last Exit to Brooklyn* to esoterica like *Mushrooms, Russia & History*. Prices start at around £20. *Photos p259.*

Skoob

Unit 66, The Brunswick, Bloomsbury, WC1N 1AE (7278 8760, www.skoob.com). Russell Square tube. **Open** 10.30am-8pm Mon-Sat; 10.30am-6pm Sun. **Credit** MC, V. **Map** p397 L4.

INSIDE TRACK BOOK ALLEY

Bookended by Charing Cross Road and St Martin's Lane, picturesque **Cecil Court** (www.cecilcourt.co.uk) is known for its antiquarian book, map and print dealers. Notable residents include children's specialist **Marchpane** (*see above*), 40-year veteran **David Drummond at Pleasures of Past Times** (no.11, 7836 1142), specialising in theatre and magic, and, recently saved from closure, 100-year-old mystical and spiritual specialist **Watkins** (nos.19 & 21, 7836 2182).

CONSUME

Anthropologie. *See p262*.

A back-to-basics basement beloved of students from the nearby University of London, Skoob showcases some 50,000 titles covering virtually every subject, from philosophy and biography to politics and the occult. Prices are very reasonable.

CHILDREN
Fashion

In addition, try baby superstore **Mamas & Papas** (256-258 Regent Street, W1B 3AF, 0870 850 2845, www.mamasandpapas.co.uk).

Caramel Baby & Child
291 Brompton Road, South Kensington, SW3 2DY (7589 7001, www.caramel-shop.co.uk). South Kensington tube. **Open** 10am-6pm Mon-Sat; noon-5pm Sun. **Credit** AmEx, MC, V. **Map** p395 E10.
Now more than a decade old, Caramel is a great place to head to for tasteful togs for children, from babies to 12-year-olds. The look is relaxed, but the clothes are well finished in modern, muted colour schemes. While the styles have clearly been inspired by the sturdy clothes of the past, they never submit to full-blown nostalgia.
Other locations 77 Ledbury Road, Notting Hill, W11 2AG (7727 0906); 259 Pavilion Road, Chelsea, SW1X 0BP (7730 2564); 82 Hill Rise, Richmond, Middx TW10 6UB (8940 6325).

Their Nibs
214 Kensington Park Road, Notting Hill, W11 1NR (7221 4263, www.theirnibs.com). Ladbroke Grove or Notting Hill Gate tube. **Open** 10am-6pm Mon-Sat; noon-5pm Sun. **Credit** AmEx, MC, V. **Map** p404 Y4.
A visit to this shop is a treat. The vintage-inspired gear encompasses quirky dungarees for crawling babes and demure summer frocks for preening girls; there's also a play corner with a blackboard, books and toys to occupy tinies while older ones browse.

Toys

Their Nibs (*see above*) has a great toy selection, and **Selfridges** (*see p253*) and **Harrods** (*see p253*) have dedicated toy departments. The famous **Hamley's** (188-196 Regent Street, W1B 5BT (0871 704 1977, www.hamleys.com) has all the must-have toys, but is a noisy, potentially stressful experience.

★ Benjamin Pollock's Toyshop
44 The Market, Covent Garden, WC2E 8RF (7379 7866, www.pollocks-coventgarden.co.uk). Covent Garden tube. **Open** 10.30am-6pm Mon-Sat; 11am-4pm Sun. **Credit** AmEx, MC, V. **Map** p416 Z3.
Best known for its toy theatres (from £6.50 for a Miniature Regency Theatre to about £70 for the

Simon Finch Rare Books. *See p257.*

more elaborate models), Pollock's is also superb for traditional toys, such as knitted animals, china tea sets, masks, glove puppets, cards, spinning tops and fortune-telling fish.
▶ *There is another branch of the shop at the associated toy museum; see p106.*

Honeyjam
267 Portobello Road, Notting Hill, W11 1LR (7243 0449, www.honeyjam.co.uk). Ladbroke Grove tube. **Open** 9.30am-5.30pm Mon-Sat; 11am-4pm Sun. **Credit** MC, V. **Map** p404 Y4.
Don't be put off by the hype (the shop is co-owned by former model Jasmine Guinness); Honeyjam is full of fun, slightly nostalgic toys, with a good selection of pocket money-priced trinkets.

Playlounge
19 Beak Street, Soho, W1F 9RP (7287 7073, www.playlounge.co.uk). Oxford Circus or Piccadilly Circus tube. **Open** 11am-7pm Mon-Sat; noon-5pm Sun. **Credit** AmEx, MC, V. **Map** p416 V3.
Compact but full of fun, this groovy little shop has action figures, gadgets, books and comics, e-boy posters, T-shirts and clothes that appeal to kids and

Albam.

adults alike. Those nostalgic for illustrated children's literature shouldn't miss the Dr Seuss PopUps and *Where the Wild Things Are* books.

ELECTRONICS & PHOTOGRAPHY

General

Ask
248 Tottenham Court Road, Fitzrovia, W1T 7QZ (7637 0353, www.askdirect.co.uk). Tottenham Court Road tube. **Open** 10am-7pm Mon-Wed, Fri, Sat; 10am-8pm Thur; noon-6pm Sun. **Credit** AmEx, DC, MC, V. **Map** p397 K5.
Some shops on Tottenham Court Road feel gloomy and claustrophobic, but Ask has four capacious, well-organised floors that give you space to browse. Stock, spanning digital cameras, MP3 players, laptops, hi-fis and TVs, concentrates on the major consumer brands. Prices are competitive.

THE BEST FASHION

Diverse
For the best boutique labels. *See right.*

Dover Street Market
Edgy capsule collections. *See p263.*

Goodhood
Get the boyfriend shopping too. *See right.*

Specialist

Behind its grand façade, the **Apple Store** (235 Regent Street, 7153 9000, www.apple.com) offers all the services you'd expect, including the trademark 'Genius Bar' for technical support. Another – arguably even grander – branch opened in Covent Garden (1-7 The Piazza) in August 2010. Several shops on Tottenham Court Road offer laptop repairs; instead, consider **Einstein Computer Services** (07957 557065, www.einsteinpcs.co.uk), which operates on a call-out basis for £20 per hour. **Adam Phones** (2-3 Dolphin Square, Edensor Road, W4 2ST, 0800 123 000, www.adamphones.com) offers mobile phone handsets for hire at reasonable rates. For film processing, try **Snappy Snaps** (www.snappysnaps.co.uk) and **Jessops** (www.jessops.com); the latter also has a wide range of photography equipment for sale.

Aperture Photographic
44 Museum Street, Bloomsbury, WC1A 1LY (7242 8681, www.apertureuk.com). Holborn or Tottenham Court Road tube. **Open** 11am-7pm Mon-Fri; noon-7pm Sat. **Credit** AmEx, MC, V. **Map** p397 L5.
This camera shop-cum-café has a great atmosphere. The photographic side centres on an excellent selection of new and vintage, manual and autofocus Nikons, Leicas, Canons and Hasselblads, along with a sprinkling of other makes, at reasonable prices. The café is frequented by paparazzi and camera enthusiasts. Staff are happy to answer questions.

FASHION

Multi-label boutiques

The following shops stock garments for both women and men.

★ b store
24A Savile Row, Mayfair, W1S 3PR (7734 6846, www.bstorelondon.com). Oxford Circus tube. **Open** 10.30am-6.30pm Mon-Fri; 10am-6pm Sat. **Credit** AmEx, MC, V. **Map** p416 U3.
A platform for cutting-edge designers in the heartland of traditional tailoring, b store is the place to preview next big things, with pieces from recent fashion graduates sitting alongside established iconoclasts such as Peter Jensen and Opening Ceremony. The eponymous own label, offering stylish basics and shoes, is going from strength to strength.

Browns
23-27 South Molton Street, Mayfair, W1K 5RD (7514 0000, www.brownsfashion.com). Bond Street tube. **Open** 10am-6.30pm Mon-Wed, Fri, Sat; 10am-7pm Thur. **Credit** AmEx, MC, V. **Map** p396 H6.

Margaret Howell. *See p262.*

Among the 100-odd designers jostling for attention in Joan Burstein's five interconnecting shops (menswear is at no.23) are Chloé, Christopher Kane, Marc Jacobs, Balenciaga and Osman Yousefzada, with plenty of fashion exclusives. Browns Focus is younger and more casual; Labels for Less is loaded with last season's leftovers. Browns celebrated its 40th anniversary in 2010.

Other locations 11-12 Hinde Street, Marylebone, W1U 3BE (7514 0056); 6C Sloane Street, Chelsea, SW1X 9LE (7514 0040); Browns Focus, 38-39 South Molton Street, Mayfair, W1K 5RN (7514 0063); Browns Labels for Less, 50 South Molton Street, Mayfair, W1K 5SB (7514 0052).

Diverse

294 Upper Street, Islington, N1 2TU (7359 8877, www.diverseclothing.com). Angel tube. **Open** 10.30am-6.30pm Mon-Wed, Fri, Sat; 10.30am-7.30pm Thur; 11.30am-5.30pm Sun. **Credit** AmEx, DC, MC, V. **Map** p400 O1.
Islington's stalwart boutique Diverse does a fine job of keeping N1's style queens in fashion-forward mode. Despite the cool clobber, chic layout and striking window displays, this is the sort of place where you can still rock up in jeans and scuzzy Converse trainers and not feel uncomfortable trying on next season's See by Chloé.

★ Goodhood

41 Coronet Street, Hoxton, N1 6HD (7729 3600, www.goodhood.co.uk). Old Street tube/rail. **Open** 11am-7pm Mon-Fri; 11am-6.30pm Sat. **Credit** AmEx, MC, V. **Map** p401 R3.

A first stop for East End trendies, Goodhood is owned by streetwear obsessives Kyle and Jo. Japanese independent labels are well represented, while other covetable brands include Australia's Rittenhouse, Norse Projects and Wood Wood.

Single-label boutiques

Albam

23 Beak Street, Soho, W1F 9RS (3157 7000, www.albamclothing.com). Oxford Circus tube. **Open** noon-7pm Mon-Sat; noon-5pm Sun. **Credit** AmEx, MC, V. **Map** p416 V3.
With its refined yet rather manly aesthetic, this rapidly expanding menswear label dresses well-heeled gents, fashion editors and regular guys who like no-nonsense style. The focus is on classic, high-quality design with a subtle retro edge; Steve McQueen is an inspiration.
Other locations 111A Commercial Street, Spitalfields, E1 6BG (7247 6254); 286 Upper Street, Islington, N1 2TZ (7288 0835).

Hurwundeki

98 Commercial Street, Spitalfields, E1 6LZ (7734 1050, www.hurwundeki.com). Liverpool Street tube/rail. **Open** 11am-7.30pm Mon-Fri; 10am-7.30pm Sat, Sun. **Credit** AmEx, MC, V. **Map** p401 S5.
The successful Hurwundeki own-label mixes British and Far Eastern, with an arty twist. Shopping here is an instant passport to east London boho-chic. The idiosyncratic interior – exposed brick, stripped floors, assorted curios – complements the garments.

123 Boutique.

Margaret Howell

*34 Wigmore Street, Marylebone, W1U 2RS
(7009 9009, www.margarethowell.co.uk). Bond
Street tube.* **Open** 10am-6pm Mon-Wed, Fri, Sat;
10am-7pm Thur. **Credit** AmEx, DC, MC, V.
Map p396 H5.

Margaret Howell's wearable clothes are made in
Britain with an old-fashioned attitude to quality.
These principles combine with her elegant designs
to make for the best 'simple' clothes for sale in
London. Her pared-down approach means prices
seem steep, but these are clothes that last and seem
to only get better with time. *Photos p261.*

Preen

*5 Portobello Green, 281 Portobello Road,
Ladbroke Grove, W10 5TZ (8968 1542,
www.preen.eu).* **Open** 11am-6pm Thur, Fri;
10am-6pm Sat. **Credit** AmEx, DC, MC, V.
Map p404 X4.

Preen – the hip British label from Justin Thornton
and Thea Bregazzi – brings imaginative takes to traditional silhouettes. Collections are characterised by
urban, minimalist shapes and interesting splashes
of colour. Look out for a great range of bags and
shoes, plus an accessories range.

YMC

*11 Poland Street, Soho, W1F 8QA (7494 1619,
www.youmustcreate.com). Oxford Circus tube.*
Open 11am-7pm Mon-Sat. **Credit** AmEx, MC, V.
Map p416 V2.

Impeccably designed staples are the forte of this
London label, which opened its first store in 2010.
It's the place to head to for simple vest tops and T-
shirts, stylish macs and duffle coats, tasteful knits
and chino-style trousers, for both men and women.

Concept stores

Concept stores are a growing consumer trend;
defined as shops selling a wide range of
covetable and exclusive items, they provide
a shopping 'experience' rather than just a
marketplace. London's concept stores are
especially strong in the realm of fashion.

Anthropologie

*158 Regent Street, W1B 5SW (7529 9800,
www.anthropologie.co.uk). Piccadilly Circus
tube.* **Open** 10am-7pm Mon-Wed; 10am-8pm
Thur; 10am-7pm Fri, Sat; noon-6pm Sun.
Credit AmEx, MC, V. **Map** p416 U3.

Anthropologie, the romantically inclined elder sister to fellow US brand Urban Outfitters, opened the
doors of its first European store in autumn 2009.
Stock is of a feminine bent, with delicate necklaces
and soft-knit cardies, while the store's signature
large-scale window displays and 1,500sq ft living
wall of plants are worth the trip alone. A second
store opened on the King's Road in spring 2010.
Other locations 131-141 King's Road, Chelsea,
SW3 4PW (7349 3110).

★ Dover Street Market

*17-18 Dover Street, Mayfair, W1S 4LT (7518
0680, www.doverstreetmarket.com). Green
Park tube.* **Open** 11am-6pm Mon-Wed; 11am-
7pm Thur-Sat. **Credit** AmEx, MC, V. **Map**
p398 J7.

Comme des Garçons designer Rei Kawakubo's
ground-breaking six-storey space combines the
edgy energy of London's indoor markets – concrete
floors, tills inside corrugated iron shacks, Portaloo
dressing rooms – with a fine range of rarefied labels.

CONSUME

All 14 of the Comme collections are here, alongside exclusive lines from such designers as Hussein Chalayan and Azzedine Alaïa.

123 Boutique

123 Bethnal Green Road, Bethnal Green, E2 7DG (www.123bethnalgreenroad.co.uk). Shoreditch High Street rail. **Open** noon-7pm Tue, Wed, Fri, Sat; noon-8pm Thur; 11am-6pm Sun. **Credit** AmEx, MC, V. **Map** p401 S4.

This avant-garde, four-storey mini department store opened in 2010 in a Grade II-listed warehouse on the corner of Brick Lane and Bethnal Green Road. The Dover Street Market of the East End isn't packed with big brands, however, but – whisper it – recycled clothing, with fashion labels such as JJ Hudson's NHS that are both cutting edge and sustainable.

Shop at Bluebird

350 King's Road, Chelsea, SW3 5UU (7351 3873, www.theshopatbluebird.com). Sloane Square tube. **Open** 10am-7pm Mon-Sat; noon-6pm Sun. **Credit** AmEx, MC, V. **Map** p395 D12.

Part lifestyle boutique and part design gallery, the Shop at Bluebird offers a shifting showcase of clothing for men, women and children (Emma Cook, Peter Jensen, Marc Jacobs), accessories, furniture, books and gadgets. The shop has a retro feel, with vintage furniture, reupholstered seating and hand-printed fabrics. The menswear range is particularly strong.

High-end designer

Key British designers include **Vivienne Westwood** (44 Conduit Street, W1S 2YL, 7439 1109, www.viviennewestwood.com), **Paul Smith** (Westbourne House, 120 Kensington Park Road, W11 2EP, 7727 3553, www.paulsmith.co.uk), **Alexander McQueen** (4-5 Old Bond Street, W1S 4PD, 7355 0088, www.alexandermcqueen.com) and **Stella McCartney** (30 Bruton Street, W1J 6QR, 7518 3100, www.stellamccartney.com). Louis Vuitton opened its wildly luxurious **Louis Vuitton Maison** flagship (17-20 New Bond Street, W1S 2UE, 7399 3856, www.louisvuitton.com) in 2010.

Discount

Tussle with teens for bargains at cheap-as-chips **Primark** (499-517 Oxford Street, 7495 0420, www.primark.co.uk). Grown-ups might prefer **Browns Labels for Less** (*see p260*).

Burberry Factory Shop

29-31 Chatham Place, Hackney, E9 6LP (8328 4287). Hackney Central rail. **Open** 10am-6pm Mon-Sat; 11am-5pm Sun. **Credit** AmEx, MC, V.

This warehouse space showcases seconds and excess stock reduced by 50% or more. Classic men's macs can be had for around £199 or less.

Paul Smith Sale Shop

23 Avery Row, Mayfair, W1X 9HB (7493 1287, www.paulsmith.co.uk). Bond Street tube. **Open** 10.30am-6.30pm Mon-Wed, Fri, Sat; 10.30am-7pm Thur; 1-5.30pm Sun. **Credit** AmEx, DC, MC, V. **Map** p398 H7.

Samples and previous season's stock at a 30-50% discount. Stock includes clothes for men, women and children, as well as a range of accessories.

High street

The best of the high-street chains are designer-look **Reiss** (Kent House, 14-17 Market Place, Fitzrovia, W1H 7AJ, 7637 9112, www.reiss.co.uk); **Banana Republic** (224 Regent Street, W1B 3BR, 7758 3550, www.bananarepublic.eu) – a newcomer to British shores, which now has a branch on Covent Garden's Long Acre; H&M's upmarket sibling **COS** (222 Regent Street, W1B 5BD, 7478 0400, www.cosstores.com); and **Urban Outfitters** (200 Oxford Street, W1D 1NU, 7907 0815, www.urbanoutfitters.co.uk), with a great range of boutique labels. **Topshop**'s (*see below*) massive, throbbing flagship continues to push the envelope, while branches of US casualwear brand **American Apparel** (www.americanapparel.net) can now be found across the city.

★ Topshop

214 Oxford Street, W1W 8LG (0844 848 7487, www.topshop.com). Oxford Circus tube. **Open** 9am-9pm Mon-Sat; 11.30am-6pm Sun. **Credit** AmEx, DC, MC, V. **Map** p416 U2.

Topshop has been the queen of the British high street for the past decade, and walking into the busy Oxford Street flagship, it's easy to see why. Spanning three huge floors, the place lays claim to being the world's largest fashion shop, and is always buzzing with fashion-forward teens and twentysomethings keen to get their hands on the next big trends. The store covers a huge range of styles and sizes, and includes free personal shoppers, boutique label concessions, capsule collections (from Christopher Kane, Stella McCartney and, most famously, Kate Moss), a Daniel Hersheson Blow Dry Bar (*see p272*), Nails Inc manicures, a café and sweet shop. Topman is also catching up with its big sister, stocking niche menswear labels such as Garbstore and Baracuta, and housing an outpost of indie record store Rough Trade (*see p275*), as well as a trainer boutique and a suit section.
Other locations throughout the city.

Tailors

Chris Kerr

52 Berwick Street, Soho, W1F 8SL (7437 3727, www.eddiekerr.co.uk). Oxford Circus tube. **Open** 8am-5.30pm Mon-Fri; 8.30am-1pm Sat. **Credit** AmEx, MC, V. **Map** p416 V2.

CONSUME

Chris Kerr, son of legendary 1960s tailor Eddie Kerr, is the man to visit if Savile Row's prices or attitude aren't to your liking. The versatile Kerr has no house style; instead, he makes every suit to each client's exact specifications, and those clients include Johnny Depp and David Walliams. A good place to get started with British tailoring.

▶ *For the tailors of Savile Row, see p126.*

Timothy Everest
35 Bruton Place, Mayfair, W1J 6NS (7629 6236, www.timothyeverest.co.uk). Bond Street tube. **Open** 10am-6pm Mon-Fri; 11am-5pm Sat. **Credit** AmEx, MC, V. **Map** p398 H7.
One-time apprentice to the legendary Tommy Nutter, Everest is a star of the latest generation of London tailors. He's well known for his relaxed 21st-century definition of style.

Used & vintage

★ Beyond Retro
112 Cheshire Street, Shoreditch, E2 6EJ (7613 3636, www.beyondretro.com). Shoreditch High Street rail. **Open** 10am-7pm Mon-Wed, Fri, Sat; 10am-8pm Thur; 10am-6pm Sun. **Credit** MC, V. **Map** p403 S4.
This enormous palace of second-hand clothing and accessories is the starting point for many an expert stylist, thrifter or fashion designer on the hunt for bargains and inspiration. The 10,000 items on the warehouse floor include 1950s dresses, cowboy boots and denim hot pants, many under £20. In-store events, such as live bands, add to the lively and supremely east London vibe.
Other locations 58-59 Great Marlborough Street, Soho, W1F 7JY (7434 1406).

Girl Can't Help It
Alfie's Antique Market, 13-25 Church Street, Marylebone, NW8 8DT (7724 8984, www.thegirlcanthelpit.com). Edgware Road tube or Marylebone tube/rail. **Open** 10am-6pm Tue-Sat. **Credit** AmEx, MC, V. **Map** p393 E4.
New Yorker Sparkle Moore and her Dutch partner Jasja Boelhouwer preside over the cache of vintage Hollywood kitsch. For ladies, there are red-carpet gowns and 1950s circle skirts (£100-£350), plus glam accessories. The suave menswear encompasses Hawaiian shirts (from £50).
▶ *For more on Alfie's Antique Market, see p274.*

Rellik
8 Golborne Road, Ladbroke Grove, W10 5NW (8962 0089, www.relliklondon.co.uk). Westbourne Park tube. **Open** 10am-6pm Tue-Sat. **Credit** AmEx, MC, V.
This celeb fave was set up in 2000 by three Portobello market stallholders: Fiona Stuart, Claire Stansfield and Steven Philip. The trio have different

tastes, which means there's a mix of pieces by the likes of Halston, Vivienne Westwood, Bill Gibb, Christian Dior and the ever-popular Ossie Clark.

FASHION ACCESSORIES & SERVICES

Clothing hire

Lipman & Sons
22 Charing Cross Road, Soho, WC2H 0HR (7240 2310, www.lipmanandsons.co.uk). Leicester Square tube. **Open** 9am-6pm Mon-Wed, Fri, Sat; 9am-8pm Thur. **Credit** AmEx, DC, MC, V. **Map** p416 X4.
A reliable, long-serving formalwear specialist.

Cleaning & repairs

British Invisible Mending Service
32 Thayer Street, Marylebone, W1U 2QT (7935 2487, www.invisible-mending.co.uk). Bond Street tube. **Open** 8.30am-5.30pm Mon-Fri; 10am-1pm Sat. **No credit cards**. **Map** p396 G5.
A 24-hour service is offered.

Celebrity Cleaners
9 Greens Court, Soho, W1F 0HJ (7437 5324). Piccadilly Circus tube. **Open** 8.30am-6.30pm Mon-Fri. **No credit cards**. **Map** p416 W3.
Dry-cleaner to West End theatres and the ENO.
Other locations Neville House, 27 Page Street, Pimlico, SW1P 4JJ (7821 1777).

Fifth Avenue Shoe Repairers
41 Goodge Street, Fitzrovia, W1T 2PY (7636 6705). Goodge Street tube. **Open** 8am-6.30pm Mon-Fri; 10am-6pm Sat. **Credit** AmEx, MC, V. **Map** p396 J5.
High-calibre, speedy shoe repairs.

Hats

For bold hats by the king of couture headgear, head to **Philip Treacy** (69 Elizabeth Street, SW1 9PJ, 7730 3992, www.philiptreacy.com).

Bernstock Speirs
234 Brick Lane, Brick Lane, E2 7EB (7739 7385, www.bernstockspeirs.com). Shoreditch High Street rail. **Open** 10am-6pm Tue-Fri; 11am-5pm Sat, Sun. **Credit** AmEx, MC, V.
Paul Bernstock and Thelma Speirs' unconventional hats for men and women have a loyal following, being both wearable and fashion-forward. Past ranges have included collaborations with Peter Jensen and Emma Cook.

Jewellery

There are also some lovely pieces for sale in **Contemporary Applied Arts** (*see p271*).

ec one

*41 Exmouth Market, Clerkenwell, EC1R 4QL
(7713 6185, www.econe.co.uk). Farringdon
tube/rail.* **Open** 10am-6pm Mon-Wed, Fri; 11am-
7pm Thur; 10.30am-6pm Sat. **Credit** MC, V.
Map p400 N4.

Husband-and-wife team Jos and Alison Skeates have
a magpie's eye for good design, which makes for
delightfully varied browsing at this stylish
Clerkenwell shop. Over 50 designers are showcased:
temptingly inexpensive trinkets include colourful
lucite bangles and sweet little heart necklaces.
Among the slightly pricier standouts are Celestine
Soumah's beguilingly simple silver designs.
Other locations 56 Ledbury Road, Notting
Hill, W11 2AJ (7243 8811).

Garrard

*24 Albemarle Street, Mayfair, W1S 4HT (0870
871 8888, www.garrard.com). Bond Street or
Green Park tube.* **Open** 10am-6pm Mon-Fri;
10am-5pm Sat, Sun. **Credit** AmEx, DC, MC, V.
Map p416 U5.

The Crown Jeweller's diamond-studded designs
have appealed to a new generation of bling-seekers
since the brand was modernised by Jade Jagger. It's
now in the hands of London-based jeweller Stephen
Webster, who took over as creative director in 2009.

Kabiri

*18 The Market, The Piazza, Covent Garden,
WC2E 8RB (7240 1055, www.kabiri.co.uk).
Covent Garden tube.* **Open** 10.30am-6.30pm
Mon-Wed; 10.30am-7.30pm Thur; 10.30am-7pm
Fri, Sat; noon-6pm Sun. **Credit** AmEx, MC, V.
Map p416 Y3.

The work of more than 100 jewellery designers,
from emerging talent to established names, is
showcased at Kabiri's flagship in Covent Garden.
Innovation and sophistication are both highly
prized, and the pieces cover a good range of price
categories. Several designers are exclusive to
Kabiri, including K Brunini and Roberto Marroni.
There's a smaller shop on Marylebone High Street,
as well as a concession in Selfridges (*see p253*).
Other locations 37 Marylebone High Street,
Marylebone, W1U 4QE (7224 1808).

Lingerie & underwear

Agent Provocateur is now a glossy
international chain, but the original outpost of
the shop that went on to popularise high-class
kink around the world is still in Soho (6
Broadwick Street, W1F 8HL, 7439 0229,
www.agentprovocateur.com). **Alice & Astrid**
(30 Artesian Road, W2 5DD, 7985 0888,
www.aliceandastrid.com) sells pretty lingerie
and loungewear in light cottons and silks from
its cutesy Notting Hill shop. For a serious
bespoke service, royal corsetière **Rigby &**

Peller (22A Conduit Street, W1S 2XT, 0845 076
5545, www.rigbyandpeller.com) is in Mayfair.
Erotic emporium **Coco de Mer** (*see p271*) also
has a small selection of lingerie.

★ Apartment C

*70 Marylebone High Street, Marylebone,
W1U 5JL (7935 1854, www.apartment-c.com).
Regent's Park tube.* **Open** 10am-6pm Mon-Sat;
noon-5pm Sun. **Credit** AmEx, MC, V. **Map**
p396 G4.

From the boudoir-like fitting rooms to the independent gallery in the basement, Apartment C is
London's most stylish place to buy your smalls.
Bras, briefs, bodies, suspenders and corsets are displayed alongside lounge- and swimwear, and the
long list of designers includes the likes of Damaris
and Stella McCartney.

Myla

*74 Duke of York Square, King's Road, Chelsea,
SW3 4LY (7730 0700, www.myla.com). Sloane
Square tube.* **Open** 10am-6.30pm Mon-Sat; noon-
5pm Sun. **Credit** AmEx, MC, V.

Luxury lingerie brand Myla has acquired a devoted
following. There are now five London stores and various concessions around town, which makes getting
one's hands on the label's stylish, high-quality bras,
knickers, toys and accessories a breeze.

Luggage & bags

Harrods (*see p253*) and **Selfridges** (*see
p253*) have excellent selections of luggage
and bags, while **Mimi** (40 Cheshire Street,
Spitalfields, E2 6EH, 7729 6699, www.mimi
berry.co.uk) sells leather satchels, shoulder
bags in muted tones and cool clutches that
have become the carry-around staples of
the East End fashion-pack.

★ Ally Capellino

*9 Calvert Avenue, Shoreditch, E2 7JP (7613
3073, www.allycapellino.co.uk). Shoreditch High
Street rail.* **Open** *noon-6pm Wed-Fri; 10am-6pm
Sat; 11am-4pm Sun.* **Credit** *AmEx, MC, V.*
Map p401 R4.

This shop stocks the full range of Ally Capellino's
stylishly understated unisex leather and waxed cotton bags, satchels, wallets, purses and laptop cases.
Prices start at around £40 for a cute leather coin
purse, rising from there to over £300 for larger, more
structured models.

Globe-Trotter

*54-55 Burlington Arcade, Mayfair, W1J 0LB
(7529 5950, www.globe-trotterltd.com). Green
Park tube.* **Open** *10am-6pm Mon-Sat.* **Credit**
AmEx, MC, V. **Map** p398 J7.

Globe-Trotter's indestructible steamer-trunk luggage, available here in various sizes and colours,
accompanied the Queen on honeymoon. Iconic
Mackintosh coats share the shop space.
▶ *Looking for luggage that's a solution rather
than an investment? Marks & Spencer (www.
marksandspencer.co.uk) does reliable basics.*

Shoes

Among the best footwear chains are **Office** (57
Neal Street, Covent Garden, WC2H 4NP, 7379
1896, www.office.co.uk), which offers funky
styles for guys and girls at palatable prices.
Kurt Geiger (198 Regent Street, W1B 5TP,
3238 0044, www.kurtgeiger.com) and **Russell
& Bromley** (24-25 New Bond Street, W1S 2PS,
7629 6903, www.russellandbromley.co.uk) both
turn out classy takes on key trends for both
sexes; and **Clarks** (476 Oxford Street, W1C
1LD, 0844 499 9302, www.clarks.co.uk) has
shed its school-shoe image and gone on to be
known as the inventor of Wallabes.

Carnaby Street is a great place for trainers,
with branches of **Size?** (nos.33-34,
www.size.co.uk), **Puma** (nos.52-55,
www.puma.com) and **Vans** (no.47,
www.vans.eu) among the options.

Black Truffle

*4 Broadway Market, Hackney, E8 4QJ (7923
9450, www.blacktruffle.co.uk). London Fields
rail or bus 394.* **Open** *11am-6pm Tue-Sat;
noon-6pm Sun.* **Credit** *AmEx, MC, V.*

This Hackney favourite sells quirky, stylish yet
wearable footwear for women, men and children
from its deceptively large space on the canal end of
Broadway Market. Look out for shoes by Melissa,
Vialis, F Troupe and Falke, knee-high boots by
Alberto Fermani and bags from Ally Capellino and
Matt & Nat.
Other locations 52 Warren Street, Fitzrovia,
W1T 5NJ (7388 4547).

Georgina Goodman

*44 Old Bond Street, Mayfair, W1F 4GD (7493
7673, www.georginagoodman.com). Green Park
tube.* **Open** *10am-6pm Mon-Wed, Fri, Sat;
10am-7pm Thur.* **Credit** *AmEx, DC, MC, V.*
Map p398 H8.

Goodman started her business crafting sculptural,
made-to-measure footwear from a single piece of
untreated vegetan leather; a couture service is still
available at her airy, gallery-like shop. The excellent
ready-to-wear range (from £165 for her popular slippers) has brought Goodman's individualistic
approach to a wider customer base. She is known
for using a dramatic mix of textures and colours,
with snakeskin, satin and patent leather often
appearing. Each shoe bears Goodman's signature
stripe on the bottom, with the stamp 'Made in Love'.

Kate Kanzier

*67-69 Leather Lane, Holborn, EC1N 7TJ (7242
7232, www.katekanzier.com). Chancery Lane tube
or Farringdon tube/rail.* **Open** *8.30am-6.30pm
Mon-Fri; 11am-4pm Sat.* **Credit** *AmEx, MC, V.*
Map p400 N5.

Adored for great-value directional footwear for
women, Kate Kanzier is the place to visit for brogues
(£30), ballerinas (£20), sandles and leather boots in a
huge range of colours. Sexy high-heeled pumps in
patent, suede, leather and animal prints are characterised by vintage designs. Handbags and clutches
are also stocked in the spacious Holborn shop.

Algerian Coffee Stores.

FOOD & DRINK

Bakeries

Konditor & Cook
*22 Cornwall Road, Waterloo, SE1 8TW
(7261 0456, www.konditorandcook.com).
Waterloo tube/rail.* **Open** 7.30am-6.30pm
Mon-Fri; 8.30am-2.30pm Sat. **Credit** AmEx,
MC, V. **Map** p402 N10.
Gerhard Jenne caused a stir when he opened this
bakery on a South Bank sidestreet in 1993, selling
gingerbread people for grown-ups and lavender-
flavoured cakes. Success lay in lively ideas such as
magic cakes that spell the recipient's name in a
series of individually decorated squares. Quality
prepacked salads and sandwiches are also sold. The
brand is now a mini-chain, with several branches.
Other locations throughout the city.

Primrose Bakery
*69 Gloucester Avenue, Primrose Hill, NW1 8LD
(7483 4222, www.primrosebakery.org.uk). Chalk
Farm tube.* **Open** 8.30am-6pm Mon-Sat; 10am-
5.30pm Sun. **Credit** MC, V. **Map** p404 X2.
Catch a serious sugar high from Martha Swift's
pretty, generously sized cupcakes in vanilla, coffee
and lemon flavours. The tiny, retro-styled shop also
sells peanut butter cookies and layer cakes.
Other locations 42 Tavistock Street, Covent
Garden, WC2E 7PB (7836 3638).

Drinks

★ Algerian Coffee Stores
*52 Old Compton Street, Soho, W1V 6PB (7437
2480, www.algcoffee.co.uk).* **Open** 9am-7pm
Mon-Wed; 9am-9pm Thur, Fri; 9am-8pm Sat.
Credit AmEx, DC, MC, V. **Map** p416 W3.
For over 120 years, this unassuming little shop has
been trading over the same wooden counter. The
range of coffees is broad, with house blends sold
alongside single-origin beans, and some serious teas
and brewing hardware are also available.
▶ *Passing? Take away a single or double espresso
for £1, or a cappuccino or a latte for £1.20.*

Berry Bros & Rudd
*3 St James's Street, Mayfair, SW1A 1EG (7396
9600, www.bbr.com). Green Park tube.* **Open**
10am-6pm Mon-Fri; 10am-5pm Sat. **Credit**
AmEx, DC, MC, V. **Map** p398 J8.
Britain's oldest wine merchant has been trading on
the same premises since 1698, and its heritage is
reflected in its panelled sales and tasting rooms.
Burgundy- and claret-lovers will drool at the hundreds of wines, but there are also decent selections
from elsewhere in Europe and the New World. Prices
are generally fair.

Cadenhead's Whisky Shop & Tasting Room
*26 Chiltern Street, Marylebone, W1U 7QF (7935
6999, www.whiskytastingroom.com). Baker Street
tube.* **Open** 10.30am-6.30pm Mon-Sat. **Credit**
DC, MC, V. **Map** p416 Z3.
Cadenhead's is a survivor of a rare breed: the independent whisky bottler. And its shop is one of a
kind, at least in London. Cadenhead's selects barrels
from distilleries all over Scotland and bottles them
without filtration or any other intervention.
▶ *For a wider range of spirits – the widest in
London, according to the staff – try Gerry's (74
Old Compton Street, Soho, W1D 4UW, 7734
4215, www.gerrys.uk.com). It's not far from
Milroy's (3 Greek Street, Soho, W1D 4NX,
7437 2385, www.milroys.co.uk), another
whisky specialist.*

★ Postcard Teas
*9 Dering Street, Mayfair, W1S 1AG (7629 3654,
www.postcardteas.com). Bond Street or Oxford
Circus tube.* **Open** 10.30am-6.30pm Tue-Sat.
Credit AmEx, MC, V. **Map** p396 H6.
The range in Timothy d'Offay's exquisite little shop
is not huge, but it is selected with care: for instance,
some of its Darjeeling teas (£3.50-£9.95/50g) are currently sourced from the Glenburn estate, regarded
as one of the best in the region. There's a central
table for those who want to try a pot; or book in for
one of the tasting sessions held on Saturdays
between 10am and 11am. Tea-ware and accessories
are also sold.

CONSUME

Hope & Greenwood.

CONSUME

General

You'll find supermarkets **Sainsbury's** (www.
sainsburys.co.uk) and **Tesco** (www.tesco.com)
across the city. Superior-quality **Waitrose**
(www.waitrose.com) has central branches on
Marylebone High Street and in Bloomsbury's
Brunswick Centre (www.brunswick.co.uk).

Whole Foods Market
*63-97 Kensington High Street, South Kensington,
W8 5SE (7368 4500, www.wholefoodmarket.com).
High Street Kensington tube.* **Open** 8am-10pm
Mon-Sat; 10am-6pm Sun. **Credit** AmEx, DC,
MC, V.
The London flagship of the American health-food
supermarket chain occupies the handsome deco
department store that was once Barkers. There are
several eateries on the premises.

Markets

The farmers' markets in the capital reflect
Londoners' concern over provenance and green
issues. Two central ones are in Marylebone
(Cramer Street car park, corner of Moxton
Street, off Marylebone High Street, 10am-2pm
Sun) and Notting Hill (behind Waterstone's,
access via Kensington Place, W8, 9am-1pm Sat).
For a fashion show and farmers' market in one,
head to Hackney's **Broadway Market** on
Saturday. Contact **London Farmers'
Markets** (7833 0338, www.lfm.org.uk).

★ Borough Market
*Southwark Street, Borough, SE1 (7407 1002,
www.boroughmarket.org.uk). London Bridge
tube/rail.* **Open** 11am-5pm Thur; noon-6pm Fri;
8am-5pm Sat. **No credit cards. Map** p402 P8.
The food hound's favourite market occupies a
sprawling site near London Bridge. Gourmet goodies run the gamut, from Flour Power City Bakery's
organic loaves and brownies to chorizo and rocket
rolls from Spanish specialist Brindisa, plus rare-
breed meats, fruit and veg, cakes and all manner of
preserves, oils and teas; head out hungry to take
advantage of the numerous free samples. The market is now open on Thursdays, when it tends to be
quieter than at always-mobbed Saturdays. A rail
viaduct planned for above the space is still going
ahead, despite a campaign against it, but a recent
plan for the market to expand into the adjacent
Jubilee Market area means that space shouldn't be
lost (even if some Grade II-listed structures are). The
new area will be reserved for 'raw food' specialists.

Specialist

Daylesford Organic
*44B Pimlico Road, Belgravia, SW1W 8LJ (7881
8060, www.daylesfordorganic.com). Sloane
Square tube.* **Open** 8am-8pm Mon-Sat; 10am-4pm
Sun. **Credit** AmEx, MC, V. **Map** p398 G11.
This offshoot of Lady Carole Bamford's Cotswold-
based farm shop is set over three floors, and includes
a café. Goods include ready-made dishes, staples such
as pulses, pastas, cakes and breads, and cheeses.

Hope & Greenwood

1 Russell Street, Covent Garden, WC2B 5JD
(7240 3314, www.hopeandgreenwood.co.uk).
Covent Garden tube. **Open** 11am-7.30pm Mon-
Wed; 11am-8pm Thur, Fri; 10.30am-7.30pm
Sat; 11.30am-5.30pm Sun. **Credit** MC, V.
Map p416 Z3.

The central branch of this Victorian-style sweetshop
is always packed with customers searching for a
sweet brand of nostalgia. It's the perfect place to find
the sweets, sherbets, chews and chocolates that were
once the focus of a proper British childhood. Tall
glass jars filled with a wish list of suckable pleasures
line the back wall, delicate plates of chocolates are
displayed on the counter, and various gift sets fill
the rest of the shop. A 400g glass jar of lemon bon-
bons will set you back £7.99; alternatively, you can
just pop in for a sugar pig, a Curly Wurly or a packet
of sherbet Dip Dabs.
Other locations 20 Northcross Road, East
Dulwich, SE22 9EU (8613 1777).

Lina Stores

18 Brewer Street, Soho, W1F 0SH (7437 6482).
Open 8am-6.30pm Mon-Fri; 8am-5.30pm Sat.
Credit AmEx, MC, V. **Map** p416 W3.

Behind the 1950s green ceramic Soho frontage and
crowded windows is an iconic family-run Italian deli
that's been in business for over half a century.
Besides dried pastas, there's a deli counter chock-
full of cured meats, hams, salamis, olives, pesto,
cheeses, marinated artichokes and fresh pastas. Lina
is also one of the best places to come to buy truffles
when they are in season.

★ Neal's Yard Dairy

17 Shorts Gardens, Covent Garden, WC2H
9UP (7240 5700, www.nealsyarddairy.co.uk).
Covent Garden tube. **Open** 11am-7pm Mon-
Thur; 10am-7pm Fri, Sat. **Credit** MC, V.
Map p416 Y2.

Neal's Yard buys from small farms and creameries
and matures the cheeses in its own cellars until
they're ready to sell in peak condition. Names such
as Stinking Bishop and Lincolnshire Poacher are as
evocative as the aromas in the shop. It's best to walk
in and ask what's good today: you'll be given tasters
by the well-trained staff. There's a shop in Borough
Market too (6 Park Street, SE1 9AB, 7367 0799).
▶ *In Marylebone, there are more great cheeses at*
La Fromagerie (see p219).

Paul A Young Fine Chocolates

33 Camden Passage, Islington, N1 8EA
(7424 5750, www.payoung.net). Angel tube.
Open 11am-6pm Wed, Thur, Sat; 11am-7pm
Fri; noon-5pm Sun. **Credit** AmEx, MC, V.
Map p400 O2.

A gorgeous boutique with almost everything –
chocolates, cakes, ice-cream – made in the downstairs
kitchen and finished in front of customers. Young is
a respected pâtissier as well as a chocolatier and has
an astute chef's palate for flavour combinations: the
white chocolate with rose masala is divine, as are the
salted caramels.
▶ *England's oldest chocolatier, Prestat (14*
Princes Arcade, St James's, SW1Y 6DS, 0800
021 3023, www.prestat.co.uk) offers unusual and
traditional flavours in brightly coloured gift boxes.

Lina Stores.

CONSUME

Style Street

Redchurch Street is leading the way with its funky independent shops.

London's fashion- and experience-led shopping scene has been thriving over the past couple of years, with exciting new independents, concept stores and pop-up shops appearing all over town. One shabby Shoreditch cut-through has undergone a particularly dramatic transformation, now finding itself at the centre of London cool. Redchurch Street's location in the midst of the hipster East End, surrounded by Bethnal Green Road, Shoreditch High Street, Calvert Avenue and Club Row, made it ripe for fashion-focused gentrification and it is now a strong contender for the capital's best shopping street.

Vintage homewares specialist **Caravan** (no.3, 7033 3532, www.caravanstyle.com), which relocated from Spitalfields Market in 2009, led the charge. Selling an assortment of homely oddities, such as vintage cushions, retro desk lamps and plastic birds that tweet, it's a first-port-of-call for stylists. This end of the street then saw a flurry of openings. One of our favourites is **Aesop** (no.5A, 7613 3793, www.aesop-europe. com), the botanical beauty shop from the Aussie luxury skincare brand. The geranium leaf body balm is an exquisitely scented, paraben-free treat. There's also a really lovely new fashion boutique at no.7: **Sunspel** (www.sunspel.com). The first retail outlet of the classic British menswear-makers, it specialises in quality underwear, T-shirts and polo shirts.

For goods that are equally English, but edible rather than sartorial, head to **Albion** (*see p228*), the café-shop that's part of Terence Conran's Boundary Project (*see p204*), on the corner of Redchurch and Boundary streets. You'll find a wealth of home-grown brands in the shop, from HP Sauce to Daylesford Organic via Neal's Yard. The buzz surrounding Redchurch Street was intensified by the hullabaloo that greeted Boundary and nearby members' club Shoreditch House (*see p205*), which houses an open-to-all branch of the **Cowshed** spa (7749 4531; *see p273*). A little further up Boundary Street,

new womenswear boutique **11 Boundary** (no.11, 7033 0330, www.11boundary.com) sells floaty bits from Wildfox and tailoring from Twenty8Twelve.

Further up Redchurch Street, there are more exciting new shops. **Hostem** (nos.41-43, 7739 9733, www.hostem.co.uk) is a darkly lit menswear shop with a well-edited selection from the likes of Philip Lim. Decadent **Maison Trois Garçons** (no.45, 7613 1924, www.lestroisgarcons.com) deals in interiors. **The Painted Lady** (no.65, 7729 2154), a cute hair salon and nail bar, specialises in vintage-style up-dos and offers great-value manicures. There's even a grungy thrift shop, **Sick** (no.105, 7033 2961), run by the founders of cult 1980s label Boy, which specialises in 1990s, for want of a better word, vintage.

Two of the highest-profile arrivals are capacious British concept store **Aubin & Wills** (nos.64-66), where you can buy men's, women's and homeware lines in a sort of grown-up collegiate style reminiscent of Abercrombie & Fitch, as well as catching a film in the small luxury cinema or some art in the gallery, and the large new premises of the much-loved Cheshire Street homeware shop **Labour & Wait** (*see p274*).

After this style overload, you may need some light refreshment. Head to the **Owl & the Pussycat** (no.34, 7613 3628) for a proper pint of bitter. Despite a recent revamp, this is still a proper boozer, one of the few reminders of this happening street's former self.

GIFTS & SOUVENIRS

★ Coco de Mer

23 Monmouth Street, Covent Garden, WC2H 9DD (7836 8882, www.coco-de-mer.com). Covent Garden tube. **Open** 11am-7pm Mon-Wed, Fri, Sat; 11am-8pm Thur; noon-6pm Sun. **Credit** AmEx, MC, V. **Map** p416 Y2.

London's most glamorous erotic emporium sells a variety of tasteful books, toys and lingerie, from glass dildos that double as objets d'art to a Marie Antoinette costume of crotchless culottes and corset. Trying on items can be fun as well: the peepshow-style velvet changing rooms allow your lover to peer through and watch you undress from a 'confession box' next door.

Contemporary Applied Arts

2 Percy Street, Fitzrovia, W1T 1DD (7436 2344, www.caa.org.uk). Goodge Street or Tottenham Court Road tube. **Open** 10am-6pm Mon-Sat. **Credit** AmEx, MC, V. **Map** p397 K5.

This airy gallery, run by a charitable arts organisation, represents more than 300 makers. The work embraces the functional – jewellery, tableware, textiles – but also includes unique, purely decorative pieces. The ground floor hosts exhibitions by individual artists, or themed by craft; in the basement shop, you'll find pieces for all pockets. Glass is always exceptional here.

James Smith & Sons

53 New Oxford Street, Holborn, WC1A 1BL (7836 4731, www.james-smith.co.uk). Holborn or Tottenham Court Road tube. **Open** 9.30am-5.15pm Mon-Fri; 10am-5.15pm Sat. **Credit** AmEx, MC, V. **Map** p416 Y1.

More than 175 years after it was established, this charming shop, with Victorian fittings still intact, is holding its own in the niche market of umbrellas and walking sticks. The stock here isn't the throwaway type of brolly that breaks at the first sign of bad weather. Lovingly crafted 'brellas, such as a classic City umbrella with a Malacca Cane handle at £120, are built to last. A repair service is also offered.

London 2012 Shop

Unit 2A, St Pancras International, Pancras Road, King's Cross, NW1 2QP (7837 8558, http://shop.london2012.com). King's Cross tube/rail. **Open** 7.30am-9pm Mon-Sat; 9am-7pm Sun. **Credit** V. **Map** p397 L3.

If you want to browse for Games merchandise in person rather than online, drop in at the dedicated shop. You'll find everything from collectable pin badges, mugs and die-cast models of cabs or double-decker buses to Stella McCartney-designed sportswear and cuddly Wenlock and Mandeville mascot toys. **Other locations** John Lewis (fifth floor), 300 Oxford Street, W1A 1EX (7629 7711, www.johnlewis.com).

★ Shelf

40 Cheshire Street, Brick Lane, E2 6EH (7739 9444, www.helpyourshelf.co.uk). Shoreditch High Street rail. **Open** 1-6pm Fri, Sat; 11am-6pm Sun. **Credit** MC, V. **Map** p401 S4.

Artist Katy Hackney and costume designer Jane Petrie's gift shop-cum-gallery is a great place to pick up unique presents, such as Prague-based sculptor Pravoslav Rada's enigmatic ceramics, or one of the limited-edition screenprint collaborations with east London artist Rob Ryan. The Moomin Valley storage jars and mugs are especially desirable.

Smug

13 Camden Passage, Islington, N1 8EA (7354 0253, www.ifeelsmug.com). Angel tube. **Open** 11am-6pm Wed, Fri, Sat; noon-7pm Thur; noon-5pm Sun. **Credit** AmEx, MC, V. **Map** p400 O2.

Graphic designer Lizzie Evans has decked out this cute new lifestyle boutique with all her favourite things. With its rainbow kitchen accessories, Lisa Stickley wash bags, vintage-inspired soft toys and 1950s and '60s furniture, you can see why she might be proud of it. Retro brooches, notebooks and Casio watches complete the picture.

HEALTH & BEAUTY

Complementary medicine

Hale Clinic

7 Park Crescent, Marylebone, W1B 1PF (7631 0156, www.haleclinic.com). Great Portland Street or Regent's Park tube. **Open** 9am-9pm Mon-Fri; 9am-5pm Sat. **Credit** MC, V. **Map** p396 H4.

Around 100 practitioners are affiliated to the Hale Clinic, which was founded with the aim of integrating complementary and conventional medicine and opened by the Prince of Wales in 1988. The treatment list is an A-Z of alternative therapies, while the shop stocks supplements, skincare products and books.

Hairdressers & barbers

If the options listed below are out of your range, try a branch of **Mr Topper's** (7631 3233; £7 men, £20 women).

THE BEST
TALKING-POINT SOUVENIRS

Coco de Mer
A bit of London sauce. *See above.*

London 2012 Shop
All your Games memorabilia. *See left.*

Smug
Retro-tinged homewares. *See above.*

Daniel Hersheson

*45 Conduit Street, Mayfair, W1F 2YN
(7434 1747, www.danielhersheson.com).
Oxford Circus tube.* **Open** 9am-6pm Mon-Wed,
Sat; 9am-8pm Thur, Fri. **Credit** AmEx, MC, V.
Map p416 U3.

Despite its location in the heart of upmarket Mayfair,
this modern two-storey salon isn't at all snooty, with
a staff of very talented cutters and colourists. Prices
start at £55 (£40 for men), though you'll pay £300 for
a cut with Daniel (£150 for men). There's also a menu
of therapies; the swish Harvey Nichols (*see p253*)
branch has a dedicated spa. Hersheson's Blow Dry
Bars are located at Topshop (*see p263*; 7927 7888 to
book), Westfield London (*see p255*; 8743 0868) and
One New Change, which opens in the City in late 2010.

★ F Flittner

*86 Moorgate, the City, EC2M 6SE (7606 4750,
www.fflittner.com). Moorgate tube/rail.* **Open**
8am-6pm Mon-Wed, Fri; 8am-6.30pm Thur.
Credit AmEx, MC, V. **Map** p403 Q6.

In business since 1904, Flittner seems not to have
noticed that the 21st century has begun. Hidden
behind beautifully frosted doors (marked 'Saloon') is
a simple, handsome room, done out with an array of
classic barber's furniture that's older than your gran.
Within these hushed yet welcoming confines, up to
six black coat-clad barbers deliver straightforward
haircuts (dry cuts £16-£17.50, wet cuts £23-£26) and
shaves with skill and dignity.

▶ *For a modern take on the art of the wet shave,
try Murdock (340 Old Street, Shoreditch, EC1V
9DS, 7729 2288, www.murdocklondon.com).*

Tommy Guns

*65 Beak Street, Soho, W1F 9SN (7439 0777,
www.tommyguns.com). Oxford Circus or Picadilly
Circus tube.* **Open** 10am-8pm Mon-Fri; 10am-
6pm Sat. **Credit** AmEx, MC, V.

Now over a decade old, and with new branches on
Brewer Street and all the way over in New York City,
Tommy Guns remains a very cool prospect indeed.
This original Soho space, complete with retro fit-
tings, is filled with youthful colourists and cutters
and there's a friendly, relaxed buzz to the place most
days. Men's cuts start from £39, and women's cuts
can be had from £49.
Other locations 49 Charlotte Road, Shoreditch,
EC2A 3QT (7739 2244); 65 Brewer Street, Soho,
W1F 9TQ (7287 0011).

Opticians

Dollond & Aitchison (www.danda.co.uk) and
Specsavers (www.specsavers.com) are chains
with branches on most high streets.

Cutler & Gross

*16 Knightsbridge Green, Knightsbridge, SW1X
7QL (7581 2250, www.cutlerandgross.com).*
Knightsbridge tube. **Open** 9.30am-7pm Mon-
Sat; noon-4pm Sun. **Credit** AmEx, MC, V.
Map p395 F9.

C&G celebrated its 40th anniversary in 2009, and its
stock of handmade frames is still at the cutting edge
of optical style. Stock runs from Andy Warhol-
inspired glasses to naturally light buffalo-horn
frames, and recent collaborations have included
frames with trend-leaders Comme des Garçons.
Vintage eyewear from the likes of Ray-Ban and
Courrèges is at the sister shop down the road.
Other locations 7 Knightsbridge Green,
Knightsbridge, SW1X 7QL (7590 9995).

▶ *For cool vintage frames and sunglasses,
check out the Klasik stall (www.klasik.org) at
Old Spitalfields Market (see p255) every Sunday.*

Pharmacies

National chain **Boots** (www.boots.com) has
branches across the city, offering dispensing
pharmacies and photo processing. The store
on Piccadilly Circus (44-46 Regent Street, W1B
5RA, 7734 6126) is open until midnight (except
Sunday, when it closes at 6pm).

DR Harris

*29 St James's Street, St James's, SW1A 1HB
(7930 3915, www.drharris.co.uk). Green Park or
Piccadilly Circus tube.* **Open** 8.30am-6pm Mon-
Fri; 9.30am-5pm Sat. **Credit** AmEx, MC, V.
Map p398 J8.

Founded in 1790, this venerable chemist has a royal
warrant. Wood-and-glass cabinets are filled with
bottles, jars and old-fashioned shaving brushes and
manicure kits. The smartly packaged own-brand
products such as the bright blue Crystal Eye Gel
have a cult following.

Shops

Eco pioneer **Neal's Yard Remedies** (15 Neal's
Yard, Covent Garden, WC2H 9DP, 7379 7222,
www.nealsyardremedies.com) has several
central London branches, offering organic
products and a herbal dispensary. Beauty chain
Space NK (8-10 Broadwick Street, Soho, W1F
8HW, 7734 3734, www.spacenk.com) has also
expanded in recent years, and is a great source
of niche skincare and make-up brands.

Liz Earle Naturally Active Skincare

*38-39 Duke of York Square, Chelsea, SW3 4LY
(7730 9191, www.lizearle.com). Sloane Square
tube.* **Open** 10am-7pm Mon, Wed-Sat; 10.30am-
7pm Tue; 11am-5pm Sun. **Credit** AmEx, MC, V.
Map p395 F11.

The London flagship of Liz Earle's botanical skincare
range is housed in a large, fresh space in Chelsea's
Duke of York Square, and stocks the full range of
streamlined products based on a regime of cleansing,

CONSUME

Labour & Wait. *See p274.*

toning and moisturising. Highlights include the Instant Boost Skin Tonic (£11.50 for 200ml) and Superskin Moisturiser. 'Minis' and essentials packs are a great introduction (£13 for a starter kit).

▶ *Niche Aussie skincare brand Aesop (www.aesop-europe.com) now has three standalone London boutiques, on Mayfair's Mount Street, Westbourne Grove and, since summer 2010, east London's Redchurch Street (see p270* **Style Street***).*

Lost in Beauty

117 Regent's Park Road, Primrose Hill, NW1 8UR (7586 4411, www.lostinbeauty.com). Chalk Farm tube. **Open** 10am-7pm Mon-Fri; 10am-6pm Sat; 11am-5pm Sun. **Credit** AmEx, MC, V. **Map** p404 W2.

Kitted out with vintage shop fittings, this chic, vintage-inspired boutique stocks a well-edited array of beauty brands, including Phyto, Environ, Caudalie, Dr Hauschka, Shu Uemura, REN, Butter London and cult cosmetics brand Becca.

Miller Harris

21 Bruton Street, Mayfair, W1J 6QD (7629 7750, www.millerharris.com). Bond Street or Green Park tube. **Open** 10am-6pm Mon-Sat. **Credit** AmEx, MC, V. **Map** p398 H7.

Grasse-trained British perfumer Lyn Harris's distinctive, long-lasting scents, in their lovely decorative packaging, are made with natural extracts and oils. Noix de Tubéreuse, a lighter and more palatable tuberose scent than many on the market, is a perennial favourite, while Fleurs de Bois evokes a traditional English garden. Prices aren't cheap – between £64 and £110 for 100ml – but you'll be paying for top-quality ingredients.

Other locations 14 Needham Road, Notting Hill, W11 2RP (7221 1545); 14 Monmouth Street, Covent Garden, WC2H 9HB (7836 9378).

Spas & salons

Many of London's luxury hotels – including the **Sanderson** (*see p187*) and the **Dorchester** (*see p197*) – make their excellent spa facilities available to the public.

Cowshed

119 Portland Road, Notting Hill, W11 4LN (7078 1944, www.cowshedclarendoncross.com). Holland Park tube. **Open** 9am-8pm Mon-Fri; 9am-7pm Sat; 10am-5pm Sun. **Credit** AmEx, MC, V. **Map** p404 X6.

The London outpost of Babington House's Cowshed does its country cousin proud. The chic, white ground floor is buzzy, with a tiny café area on one side, and a manicure/pedicure section on the other. For facials, massages and waxing head downstairs. **Other locations** 31 Fouberts Place, Soho, W11 7QG (7534 0870); Ebor Street, Bethnal Green, E1 6AW (7749 4531).

Elemis Day Spa

2-3 Lancashire Court, Mayfair, W1S 1EX (7499 4995, www.elemis.com). Bond Street tube. **Open** 9am-9pm Mon-Sat; 10am-6pm Sun. **Credit** AmEx, MC, V. **Map** p396 H6.

This leading British spa brand's exotic, unisex retreat is tucked away down a cobbled lane off Bond Street. The elegantly ethnic treatment rooms are a lovely setting in which to relax and enjoy a spot of pampering, from wraps to facials.

CONSUME

Run & Become. *See p276.*

HOUSE & HOME
Antiques & second-hand

Although boutiques have encroached on their territory, there are still some quirky dealers on Islington's **Camden Passage** (off Upper Street, 7359 0190, www.camdenpassage antiques.com); try the Pierrepont Arcade. Marylebone's **Church Street** is now a major area for vintage homewares, and host to Alfie's Antique Market (*see below*), but **Portobello Road** (*see p255*) remains the biggest, best-known market for antiques. For a less hectic experience, **Anthropologie** (*see p262*) has a lovely range of vintage-inspired homewares.

Alfie's Antique Market
13-25 Church Street, Marylebone, NW8 8DT (7723 6066, www.alfiesantiques.com). Edgware Road tube or Marylebone tube/rail. **Open** 10am-6pm Tue-Sat. **No credit cards. Map** p393 E4.
Alfie's hosts more than 100 dealers in vintage furniture and fashion, art, accessories, books, maps and the like. Check out Dodo Posters for '20s and '30s ads.

Ben Southgate
4 The Courtyard, Ezra Street, Bethnal Green, E2 7RH (07905 960792, www.bsouthgate.co.uk). Hoxton or Shoreditch High Street rail. **Open** 9am-3pm Sun. **Credit** MC, V.
Ben Southgate spent over a decade as a furniture restorer before opening this stylish grown-up boys'

paradise among the blooms of Columbia Road. Stock includes clubby 1930s and '40s leather armchairs, enamel lampshades, polished medical cabinets, vintage board games and 1950s football tables. It's a lovely spot for a Sunday browse after the market.

Core One
Gas Works, 2 Michael Road, Fulham, SW6 2AD (7823 3900). Sloane Square tube then bus 11, 19, 22, 319, 211. **Open** 10am-6pm Mon-Fri; 11am-4pm Sat. **No credit cards.**
A group of antiques and 20th-century dealers has colonised this industrial building in Fulham, including Dean Antiques (7610 6997, www.deanantiques. co.uk) for dramatic pieces, and De Parma (7736 3384, www.deparma.com) for elegant mid-century design.

Grays Antique Market & Grays in the Mews
58 Davies Street, W1K 5LP & 1-7 Davies Mews, Mayfair, W1K 5AB (7629 7034, www.grays antiques.com). Bond Street tube. **Open** 10.30am-6.30pm Mon-Wed, Fri, Sat; 10.30am-7.30pm Thur; noon-5pm Sun. **No credit cards. Map** p396 H6.
More than 200 dealers in this smart covered market sell everything from antique furniture and rare books to vintage fashion and jewellery.

General

Habitat (121 Regent Street, W1B 4TB, 0844 499 1134, www.habitat.co.uk) is a good source of affordable modern design.

Conran Shop
Michelin House, 81 Fulham Road, Fulham, SW3 6RD (7589 7401, www.conran.co.uk). South Kensington tube. **Open** 10am-6pm Mon, Tue, Fri; 10am-7pm Wed, Thur; 10am-6.30pm Sat; noon-6pm Sun. **Credit** MC, V. **Map** p395 E10.
Sir Terence Conran's flagship store in the Fulham Road's beautiful 1909 Michelin Building showcases furniture and design for every room in the house as well as the garden; as well as design classics, such as the Eames Dar chair, there are plenty of portable accessories, gadgets, books, stationery and toiletries that make great gifts or souvenirs.
Other locations 55 Marylebone High Street, Marylebone, W1U 5HS (7723 2223).

Labour & Wait
18 Cheshire Street, off Brick Lane, Spitalfields, E2 6EH (7729 6253, www.labourandwait.co.uk). Shoreditch High Street rail. **Open** 11am-5pm Wed, Fri; 1-5pm Sat; 10am-5pm Sun. **Credit** MC, V. **Map** p401 S4.
This much-celebrated shop pays homage to timeless, unfaddy domestic goods that combine beauty with utility: think Victorian pantry crossed with 1950s kitchen. The quintessentially British homewares include traditional feather dusters;

enamel soap dishes, lampshades and kitchenware; sturdy canvas bags; and tins of twine. Labour & Wait also has a space at concept store Dover Street Market (*see p263*), and opened a large new shop on east London's ultra-hip Redchurch Street (*see p270* **Style Street**) in August 2010. *Photo p273.*

MUSIC & ENTERTAINMENT
CDs, records & DVDs

Oxford Street's last music megastore, **HMV** (www.hmv.co.uk), offers a comprehensive line-up of CDs and DVDs, plus some vinyl. Serious browsers, however, head south into Soho, where indie record stores are still clinging on around Berwick and D'Arblay streets.

Flashback
50 Essex Road, Islington, N1 8LR (7354 9356, www.flashback.co.uk). Angel tube then bus 38, 56, 73, 341. **Open** 10am-7pm Mon-Sat; 11.30am-6pm Sun. **Credit** AmEx, MC, V. **Map** p400 O1.
Stock is scrupulously organised at this second-hand treasure trove. The ground floor is dedicated to CDs, while the basement is vinyl-only: an ever-expanding jazz collection jostles for space alongside soul, hip hop and a carpal tunnel-compressing selection of library sounds. A range of rarities is pinned in plastic sleeves to the walls.

Honest Jon's
278 Portobello Road, Notting Hill, W10 5TE (8969 9822, www.honestjons.com). Ladbroke Grove tube. **Open** 10am-6pm Mon-Sat; 11am-5pm Sun. **Credit** AmEx, MC, V. **Map** p404 X4.
Honest Jon's found its way to Notting Hill in 1979, where it was reportedly the first place in London to employ a Rastafarian. The owner helped James Lavelle set up Mo'Wax records. You'll find jazz, hip hop, soul, broken beat, reggae and Brazilian music on the shelves.

Pure Groove Records
6-7 West Smithfield, Clerkenwell, EC1A 9JX (7778 9278, www.puregroove.co.uk). Farringdon tube/rail. **Open** noon-7pm Mon-Fri. **Credit** MC, V. **Map** p400 O5.
Pure Groove is a stylish, multimedia collection of vinyl, poster art and CD gems covering all things indie, alternative and cutting edge in guitar and electronic music. The rear, housing T-shirts, cotton bags and posters, doubles as a stage for the regular live-band sets and film screenings.
▶ *Up Farringdon Road, Brill (27 Exmouth Market, EC1R 4QL, 7833 9757) is a small CD shop-cum-café with a fine curated selection.*

Ray's Jazz at Foyles
Foyles Bookshop, 113-119 Charing Cross Road, Soho, WC2H 0EB (7440 3205, www.foyles.co.

uk). Tottenham Court Road tube. **Open** 9.30am-9pm Mon-Sat; 11.30am-6pm Sun. **Credit** AmEx, MC, V. **Map** p416 X2.
London's least beardy jazz shop is to be found on the third floor of Foyles bookshop (*see p257*). The predominantly CD-based stock contains a good selection of blues, avant-garde, gospel, folk and world, but modern jazz is the main draw.

★ Rough Trade East
Dray Walk, Old Truman Brewery, 91 Brick Lane, Spitalfields, E1 6QL (7392 7788, www.rough trade.com). Liverpool Street tube/rail. **Open** 8am-9pm Mon-Thur; 8am-8pm Fri, Sat; 11am-7pm Sun. **Credit** AmEx, DC, MC, V. **Map** p401 S5.
Celebrating its 35th birthday in 2011, this infamous temple to indie music has never looked more upbeat, its new-found impetus provided by the 2007 opening of Rough Trade East. The 5,000sq ft record store, café and gig space offers a dizzying range of vinyl and CDs, spanning punk, indie, dub, soul, electronica and more. With 16 listening posts and a stage for live sets, this is close to musical nirvana.
Other locations 130 Talbot Road, Notting Hill, W11 1JA (7229 8541).

Musical instruments

Site of the legendary recording studio Regent Sounds in the 1960s, **Denmark Street**, off Charing Cross Road, is now a hub for music shops, especially if you're looking for a new, second-hand or rare vintage guitar.

Chappell of Bond Street
152-160 Wardour Street, Soho, W1F 8YA (7432 4400, www.chappellofbondstreet.co.uk). Tottenham Court Road tube. **Open** 9.30am-6pm Mon-Fri; 10am-5.30pm Sat. **Credit** AmEx, MC, V. **Map** p416 V2.

INSIDE TRACK
INDEPENDENT SPIRIT

London's indie shopping scene has been getting better and better over the past few years. Despite the tough economic climate, there were lots of exciting openings in 2010, and specialist old faves continue to attract new customers. For the most interesting finds, head off the main thoroughfares and discover the city's more hidden streets and alleyways. Bloomsbury's **Lamb's Conduit Street**, Hackney's **Broadway Market**, Islington's **Camden Passage** and **Redchurch Street** in Shoreditch (*see p270* **Style Street**) all excel in their selection of boutiques and specialist independent shops.

It's retained its old name, but Chappell recently moved from Bond Street (its home for nearly 200 years) to this amazing three-storey musical temple. This is the leading Yamaha stockist in the UK, and the collection of sheet music (classical, pop and jazz) is reputedly the largest in Europe.

SPORTS & FITNESS

Harrods (*see p253*) has a good fitness department. Bike chains **Evans Cycles** (www.evanscycles.com) and **Cycle Surgery** (www.cyclesurgery.com) each have a number of branches across the city. For the best places to find fashion trainers, *see p266*.

Decathlon
Canada Water Retail Park, Surrey Quays Road, Rotherhithe, SE16 2XU (7394 2000, www.decathlon.co.uk). Canada Water tube. **Open** 9am-9pm Mon-Fri; 9am-7pm Sat; 11am-5pm Sun. **Credit** MC, V.
The warehouse-sized London branch of this French chain offers London's biggest single collection of sports equipment. You'll find a vast array of reasonably priced equipment and clothing for all mainstream racket and ball sports as well as swimming, running, surfing, fishing, skiing and more.

Run & Become
42 Palmer Street, Victoria, SW1H 0PH (7222 1314, www.runandbecome.com). St James's Park tube. **Open** 9am-6pm Mon-Wed, Fri, Sat; 9am-8pm Thur. **Credit** MC, V. **Map** p398 J9.

Tokyo Fixed.

The experienced staff here, most of them enthusiastic runners, are determined to find the right pair of shoes for your particular physique and running style. The full gamut of running kit, from clothing to speed monitors, is also available. *Photo p274.*

Tokyo Fixed
4 Peter Street, Soho, W1F 0AD (7734 1885, www.tokyofixedgear.com). Piccadilly Circus tube. **Open** 11am-8pm daily. **Credit** MC, V. **Map** p416 W3.
The fixed-wheel cycling scene has seen an explosion in popularity and, in response, bike nuts Tokyo Fixed have moved from merely importing keirin frames from Japan to opening their own two-storey shop in Soho. Here you'll find all things fixed-wheel, including frames, wheels, books, mags and bags – everything you need to look Shoreditch trendy.

TICKETS

For London performances, whether musical, theatrical or in some other cultural orbit, it's worth booking ahead – surprisingly obscure acts sell out, and high-profile gigs and sporting events can do so in seconds. It's almost always cheaper to bypass ticket agents and go direct to the box office: agents charge booking fees that often top 20 per cent. If you have to use an agent, booking agencies include **Ticketmaster** (0870 277 4321, www.ticketmaster.co.uk), **Stargreen** (7734 8932, www.stargreen.com), **Ticketweb** (0844 477 1000, www.ticketweb. co.uk), **See Tickets** (0870 264 3333, www.see tickets.com) and **Keith Prowse** (0870 840 1111, www.keithprowse.com). However, there are several ways to save money on tickets. For specific tips on where to get tickets (and how to keep the cost down) for the theatre, *see p342*; for gigs and concerts, *see p315 and p319*.

TRAVELLERS' NEEDS

Independent travel specialist **Trailfinders** (European travel 0845 050 5945, worldwide flights 0845 058 5858, www.trailfinders.com) has several branches in the capital, including in the Piccadilly Waterstone's (nos.203-206, SW1Y 6WW, 7851 2400, www.waterstones.co.uk).

Excess Baggage Company
4 Hannah Close, Great Central Way, Wembley, Middx NW10 0UX (0800 783 1085, www. excess-baggage.com). **Credit** AmEx, MC, V.
Ships goods to over 300 countries and territories worldwide, including the USA, Canada, Australia, New Zealand and South Africa, from a single suitcase to complete household removal. Prices are reasonable and include cartons and other packing materials. There are branches in the city's main rail stations, as well as Heathrow and Gatwick airports.

CONSUME

Arts & Entertainment

Dex. *See p332.*

Calendar

Wherever and whenever – the lowdown on what's going on.

Forget about British reserve. There's nothing many Londoners like more than finding a crowd and making fools of themselves. Festivals and events play ever more elaborate variations on the age-old themes of parading and dancing, nowadays with ever-larger sprinklings of arts and culture. Weather plays a part in the timing, with a concentration of things to do in the hotter months, but the city's calendar is pretty busy for most of the year.

As the London 2012 Games draw closer, more and more associated cultural and sporting events are planned: for a selection, *see p67*; for regular sporting events through the year, *see p333*. As well as merry-making opportunities listed in this chapter, a series of boxes through the book details events specifically dedicated to dance (*see p296*), film (*see p301*), art (*see p306*), music (*see p316, p321 and p324*), theatre (*see p345*) and gay culture (*see p312*).

The weekly *Time Out London* magazine, in print and online (www.timeout. com/london), is a great source of information. If you're planning your trip around a particular event, always be sure to confirm the details in advance – events can be cancelled and dates may change with little notice.

ARTS & ENTERTAINMENT

ALL YEAR ROUND

For the **Changing of the Guard**, *see p279* **Standing on Ceremony**.

Ceremony of the Keys
Tower of London, Tower Hill, the City, EC3N 4AB (0844 482 7777, www.hrp.org.uk). Tower Hill tube/Tower Gateway DLR. **Date** 9.30pm daily (advance bookings only). **Map** p403 R7.
Join the Yeoman Warders after-hours at the Tower of London as they ritually lock the fortress's entrances in this 700-year-old ceremony. You enter the Tower at 9.30pm and it's all over just after 10pm, but places are hotly sought after – apply at least two months in advance; full details are on the website.

Gun Salutes
Green Park, Mayfair & St James's, W1, & Tower of London, the City, EC3. **Dates** 6 Feb (Accession Day); 21 Apr & 14 June (Queen's birthdays); 2 June (Coronation Day); 10 June (Duke of Edinburgh's birthday); 15 June (Trooping the Colour); State Opening of Parliament (*see p285*); 12 Nov (Lord Mayor's Show); 13 Nov (Remembrance Sunday); also for state visits. **Map** p398 H8.

There are gun salutes on many state occasions – see the list of dates given above for a breakdown. A cavalry charge features in the 41-gun salutes mounted by the Kings Troop Royal Horse Artillery in Hyde Park at noon (it takes place opposite the Dorchester Hotel; *see p197*), whereas, on the other side of town, the Honourable Artillery Company ditches the ponies and piles on the firepower with its 62-gun salutes (1pm at the Tower of London). If the dates happen to fall on a Sunday, the salute is held on Monday.

JANUARY-MARCH

This is a good time of year for dance events, among them **Resolution!** at the Place; *see p296* **Festivals**. For the **London Lesbian & Gay Film Festival**, *see p301*.

★ London International Mime Festival
7637 5661, www.mimefest.co.uk. **Date** 15-30 Jan.
This long-running festival aims to explode any prejudices you may have against mime and its related theatrical forms. Expect innovative and visually stunning theatre from across the globe.

Joseph Grimaldi Memorial Service

Holy Trinity Church, Beechwood Road, Dalston,
E8 3DY (www.clowns-international.co.uk).
Dalston Kingsland rail. **Date** 7 Feb.
Join hundreds of motley-clad 'Joeys' for their annual service commemorating the legendary British clown, Joseph Grimaldi (1778-1837).

★ Chinese New Year Festival

Around Gerrard Street, Chinatown, W1,
Leicester Square, WC2, & Trafalgar Square,
WC2 (7851 6686, www.chinatownchinese.co.uk).
Leicester Square or Piccadilly Circus tube. **Date**
6 Feb. **Map** p416 W3.
Launch the Year of the, er, Rabbit in style at celebrations that engulf Chinatown and Leicester Square. Dragon dancers writhe alongside a host of impressive acts in the grand parade to Trafalgar Square, while the restaurants of Chinatown get even more packed than usual.
▶ *For sights around Chinatown, see p115.*

Pancake Day Races

Great Spitalfields *Dray Walk, off Brick Lane,*
E1 6QL (7375 0441, www.alternativearts.co.uk).
Liverpool Street tube/rail.
Poulters Annual *Guildhall Yard, the City,*
EC2P 2EJ (www.poulters.org.uk). Bank tube/
DLR or Moorgate tube/rail.
Both Date 8 Feb.

Shrove Tuesday brings out charity pancake racers. Don a silly costume and join the Great Spitalfields Pancake Race (register in advance) or watch City livery companies race in full regalia at the event organised by the Worshipful Company of Poulters.

Who Do You Think You Are? Live

Olympia, Hammersmith Road, Kensington,
W14 8UX (www.whodoyouthinkyouarelive.co.uk).
Kensington Olympia tube/rail. **Date** 25-27 Feb.
A spin-off from the hugely successful BBC TV series that keeps Brits glued to the box watching weepy celebs uncover their ancestry, this enormous family history event could help you trace yours.

★ Kew Spring Festival

For listings, *see p172* **Royal Botanic Gardens**.
Date early Mar-Apr.
Kew Gardens is at its most beautiful in spring, with five million flowers carpeting the grounds.

National Science & Engineering Week

0870 770 7101, www.britishscienceassociation.
org/nsew. **Date** 11-20 Mar.
From the weirdly wacky to the profound, this annual series of events engages the public in celebrating science, engineering and technology.

St Patrick's Day Parade & Festival

7983 4100, www.london.gov.uk. **Date** 17 Mar.

Standing on Ceremony

London is a past master when it comes to parades and ceremonials.

On alternate days from 10.45am (www. royal.gov.uk/RoyalEventsandCeremonies/ ChangingtheGuard/Overview.aspx has the details), one of the five Foot Guards regiments lines up in scarlet coats and tall bearskin hats in the forecourt of Wellington Barracks; at exactly 11.27am, the soldiers start to march to **Buckingham Palace** (*see p137*), joined by their regimental band, to relieve the sentries there in a 45-minute ceremony for the **Changing of the Guard**.

Not far away, at **Horse Guards Parade** in Whitehall, the Household Cavalry mount the guard daily at 11am (10am on Sunday). Although this ceremony isn't as famous as the one at Buckingham Palace, it's more visitor-friendly: the crowds aren't as thick as they are at the palace, and spectators aren't held far back from the action by railings. After the old and new guard have stared each other out in the centre of the parade ground, you can nip through to the Whitehall side to catch the departing old guard perform their hilarious dismount

choreography, a synchronised, firm slap of approbation to the neck of each horse before the gloved troopers all swing off.

As well as these near-daily ceremonies, London sees other, less frequent parades on a far grander scale. The most famous is **Trooping the Colour**, staged to mark the Queen's official birthday on 13 June (her real one's in April). At 10.45am, the Queen rides in a carriage from Buckingham Palace to Horse Guards Parade to watch the soldiers, before heading back to Buckingham Palace for a midday RAF flypast and the impressive gun salute from Green Park.

Also at Horse Guards, on 3-4 June, a pageant of military music and precision marching begins at 7pm when the Queen (or another royal) takes the salute of the 300-strong drummers, pipers and musicians of the Massed Bands of the Household Division. This is known as **Beating the Retreat** (7414 2271, tickets 7839 5323).

INSIDE TRACK
TRAFALGAR SQUARE

Among ex-mayor Ken Livingstone's most popular initiatives was pedestrianising the north side of Trafalgar Square, and then programming almost weekly events in it. Even under budget-slashing Boris, expect all kinds of entertainment here – music, film, theatre, dance – and usually for free. For details, check www.london.gov.uk/trafalgarsquare.

Join the London Irish out in force for this huge annual parade through central London followed by toe-tapping tunes in Trafalgar Square.

Oxford & Cambridge Boat Race
River Thames, from Putney to Mortlake (www.theboatrace.org). Putney Bridge tube, or Barnes Bridge, Mortlake or Putney rail.
Date 26 Mar.
Blue-clad Oxbridge students race each other in a pair of rowing eights, watched by tens of millions worldwide. Experience the excitement from the riverbank (along with 250,000 other fans) for the 157th instalment of the historic race.

APRIL-JUNE

Early summer is terrific for outdoor events. There's excellent alfresco theatre at the **Greenwich & Docklands International Festival** and, on the South Bank, **Watch This**

Space (for both, *see p345* **Festivals**). Fans of sport can go racing (**Royal Ascot**, the **Epsom Derby**), queue for **Wimbledon** tickets or watch a football playoff; for all, *see pp333-335*. For classical music at the **City of London Festival** and the **Hampton Court Palace Festival**, *see p316* **Festivals**; for rockier fare at the **Camden Crawl**, the **Wireless Festival** and the **Somerset House Summer Series**, *see p321* **Festivals**.

Shakespeare's Birthday
For listings, *see p76* **Shakespeare's Globe**.
Date wknd closest to 23 Apr.
To celebrate the Bard's birthday, the Globe Theatre throws open its doors for a series of events.

★ Virgin London Marathon
Greenwich Park to the Mall via the Isle of Dogs, Victoria Embankment & St James's Park (7902 0200, www.london-marathon.co.uk). Blackheath & Maze Hill rail (start), or Charing Cross tube/rail (end). **Date** 17 Apr.
One of the world's elite long-distance races, the London Marathon is also one of the world's largest fundraising events – nearly 80% of participants run for charity, so zany costumes abound among the 35,000 starters. If you haven't already applied to run, you're too late: just go along to watch.

Covent Garden May Fayre
& Puppet Festival
Garden of St Paul's Covent Garden, Bedford Street, Covent Garden, WC2E 9ED (7375 0441, www.alternativearts.co.uk). Covent Garden tube. **Date** 8 May. **Map** p416 Y4.

Chelsea Flower Show.

All-day puppet mayhem (10.30am-5.30pm) devoted to celebrating Mr Punch at the scene of his first recorded sighting in England in 1662. Mr P takes to the church's pulpit at 11.30am.

Chelsea Flower Show

Royal Hospital, Royal Hospital Road, Chelsea, SW3 4SR (www.rhs.org.uk). Sloane Square tube. **Date** 24-28 May. **Map** p395 F12.
Elbow past the crowds to admire perfect blooms, or get ideas for your own plot. The first two days are reserved for Royal Horticultural Society members and tickets for the open days are hard to come by. The show closes at 5.30pm on the final day, with display plants being sold off from around 4.30pm.

Coin Street Festival

Bernie Spain Gardens (next to Oxo Tower Wharf), South Bank, SE1 9PH (7021 1600, www.coinstreet.org). Southwark tube or Waterloo tube/rail. **Date** June-Aug. **Map** p402 N8.
Celebrating London's cultural diversity, this free, summer-long Thames-side festival features a series of music-focused events, usually involving a few guest musicians or theatre groups from across the world, as well as local talent. Food stalls too.

Open Garden Squares Weekend

www.opensquares.org. **Date** 11-12 June.
Secret – and merely exclusive – gardens are thrown open to the public. You can visit roof gardens, prison gardens and children-only gardens, as well as a changing selection of those tempting oases railed off in the middle of the city's finest squares. Some charge an entrance fee.

Exhibition Road Music Day

Exhibition Road, South Kensington, SW7 (www.exhibitionroad.com). South Kensington tube. **Date** last wknd of June. **Map** p395 D9.
London's counterpart to France's midsummer Fête de la Musique ranges through institutions that border Exhibition Road and spills into Hyde Park. With Imperial College and the Ismaili Centre among the participants, you can expect anything from experimental music to Sufi chants.

JULY-SEPTEMBER

Summer sees some of the most important music festivals of the year – namely, the **BBC Sir Henry Wood Promenade Concerts** (more commonly, the Proms), the **Lovebox Weekender**, the **English Heritage Picnic Concerts** at Kenwood House and the teenager-friendly **Underage** festival (for all, *see p316 and p321* **Festivals**) – as well as the city's major gay event, **Pride London** (*see p312* **Festivals**). There are also two cutting-edge dance events, the **Place Prize** and **Dance Umbrella** (for both, *see p296* **Festivals**).

Notting Hill Carnival. *See p282.*

ARTS & ENTERTAINMENT

Mayor of London's Skyride.

London Literature Festival
Southbank Centre, Belvedere Road, SE1 8XX (0844 847 9939, www.londonlitfest.com). Waterloo tube/rail. **Date** 1st 2wks of July. **Map** p399 M8.
Now in its fourth year, the London Literature Festival combines superstar writers with stars from other fields: architects, comedians, sculptors and cultural theorists examining anything from queer literature to migration.

★ Chap Olympiad
www.thechap.net. **Date** 2nd wknd of July.
English eccentrics are in full cry at this annual event mounted by the *Chap* magazine, which starts with the lighting of the Olympic Pipe. 'Sports' include cucumber sandwich discus and hop, skip and G&T. Check the venue closer to the time: it has been held in Bloomsbury for the last few years.

Broadwalk Ballroom
Regent's Park, Marylebone, NW1 (www.dance alfresco.org). Regent's Park tube. **Date** 2 wknds in Aug. **Map** p396 G3.
Regent's Park's Broadwalk is transformed into a dancefloor over two weekends in July and August, with dancing from 2pm to 6pm. Ballroom is held on Saturdays and tango on Sundays, with lessons for novices at 1pm.

Carnival del Pueblo
Various locations from City Hall to Burgess Park (www.carnavaldelpueblo.co.uk). Elephant & Castle tube/rail. **Date** 1st wknd of Aug.
This vibrant outdoor parade and festival is more than just a loud-and-proud day out for South

American Londoners: it attracts people from all walks of life (as many as 60,000, most years) looking to inject a little Latin spirit into the weekend.

Great British Beer Festival
Earls Court Exhibition Centre, Warwick Road, SW5 9TA (01727 867201, www.camra.org.uk). Earl's Court tube. **Date** 2-6 Aug. **Map** p394 A11.
Real ale is the star at this huge event devoted to British brews, including cider and perry (a pear cider). Foreign beers and lagers get a look-in at what's been called 'the biggest pub in the world'.

London Mela
Gunnersbury Park, Ealing, W3 (7387 1203, www.londonmela.org). Acton Town or South Ealing tube. **Date** early-mid Aug.
Thousands flock to west London for this exuberant celebration of Asian culture, dubbed the Asian Glastonbury. You'll find urban, classical and experimental music, circus, dance, visual arts, comedy, children's events, and great food.

★ Notting Hill Carnival
Notting Hill, W10, W11 (7727 0072, www. thenottinghillcarnival.com). Ladbroke Grove, Notting Hill Gate or Westbourne Park tube. **Date** 28-29 Aug. **Map** p404 Z4.
Two million people stream in to Notting Hill to Europe's largest street party, full of the smells, colours and music of the Caribbean. Massive mobile sound systems dominate the streets with whatever bass-heavy party music is currently hip, but there's plenty of tradition from the West Indies too: calypso music and a spectacular costumed parade. *Photos p281.*
▶ *For sightseeing in Notting Hill, see p123.*

Great River Race
River Thames, from Ham House, Richmond, Surrey TW10, to Island Gardens, Isle of Dogs, E14 (8398 9057, www.greatriverrace.co.uk). **Date** 11 Sept.
The alternative Boat Race (*see p280*) is much more fun, with an exotic array of around 300 traditional rowing boats from across the globe racing the 22 miles from Richmond to Greenwich. Hungerford Bridge, the Millennium Bridge and Tower Bridge all provide good viewpoints.

Mayor's Thames Festival
Between Westminster Bridge & Tower Bridge (7928 8998, www.thamesfestival.org). Waterloo tube/rail or Blackfriars rail. **Date** 10-11 Sept. **Map** p402 N7.
A giant party along the Thames, this is the largest free arts festival in London. It's a spectacular and family-friendly mix of carnival, pyrotechnics, art installations, river events and live music alongside craft and food stalls. The highlight is the last-night lantern procession and firework finale – Blackfriars Bridge provided a stunning viewpoint last year.

Great Gorilla Run.

ARTS & ENTERTAINMENT

London Fashion Week

Somerset House, the Strand, WC2R 1LA (7759 1999, www.londonfashionweek.co.uk). Charing Cross tube/rail or Embankment tube. **Date** Sept.
The biannual showcase (it returns each February) embellishes London's reputation for cutting-edge street style and sartorial innovation. Until recently, it was considered the least significant of the big four trade shows, behind New York, Milan and Paris. Not any more. Its 25th anniversary was celebrated in 2009 with a new principal venue (Somerset House; *see p111*) and renewed energy.

Mayor of London's Skyride

www.goskyride.com. **Date** early Sept.
Each year since 2007, this cycling festival has encouraged around 50,000 people to don branded fluorescent vests and ride a traffic-free route from Buckingham Palace to the Tower of London, as well as any number of subsidiary routes. Enjoy music, car-less roads and the chance to meet sports stars on the way.
▶ *For the new Barclays Cycle Hire scheme, see p339* **Cycle City**.

★ Open-City London

3006 7008, http://open-city.org.uk.
Date 3rd wknd of Sept.
Londoners' favourite opportunity to snoop round other people's property: more than 500 palaces, private homes, corporate skyscrapers, pumping stations and bomb-proof bunkers, many of which are normally closed to the public. Along with the building openings, there's a programme of debates on architecture, plus the 20-mile London Night Hike.
▶ *For more on architecture, see pp34-40.*

Great Gorilla Run

Mincing Lane, the City, EC3 (7916 4974, www.greatgorillas.org/london). Monument or Tower Hill tube, or Fenchurch Street rail. **Date** 24 or 25 Sept. **Map** p403 R7.
Go ape with a 600-strong pack of gorilla-suited runners, who take on a 7km course through the City in aid of gorilla conservation. As we go to press, the date for 2011 was not yet confirmed.

Pearly Kings & Queens Harvest Festival

St Martin-in-the-Fields, Trafalgar Square, Westminster, WC2N 4JJ (7766 1100, www. pearlysociety.co.uk). Leicester Square tube or Charing Cross tube/rail. **Date** late Sept/ early Oct. **Map** p416 Y4.
London's Pearly Kings and Queens assemble for their annual thanksgiving service dressed in spangly (and colossally heavy) Smother Suits covered in hundreds of pearl buttons. These sensational outfits evolved from Victorian costermongers' love of decorating their clothes with buttons, and remain a cherished Cockney tradition.

INSIDE TRACK STAY OUT LATE

Most of the city's blockbuster museums and galleries combine late-opening with a monthly one-off evening event (usually with films, DJs or live music, and always a cash bar). For details of the current programme, see www.lates.org.

Kids' Stuff

How to keep the little 'uns entertained.

Many of London's best family-friendly festivals are held in summer. One of the best is **Watch This Space** (www.nationaltheatre.org.uk/wts), which makes the **Royal National Theatre**'s Theatre Square the jolliest piece of astroturf to be found in town.

Held in Hackney's Victoria Park in early August, the **Underage Festival** (www.underagefestivals.com) was launched a few years ago as the world's first music festival aimed at under-17s. In the last couple of years, it's attracted around 7,000 teens, donning free T-shirts and grooving to the likes of Patrick Wolf, Ladyhawke and the Horrors. And now, even babies are getting into the groove, thanks to organisations such as **Baby Loves Disco** (www.babylovesdisco.co.uk) and **Planet Angel** (www.planetangel.net). All of them run regular club nights and days for cutting-edge or cutting-teeth customers and their parents.

Also in summer, **Kids Week** (www.officiallondontheatre.co.uk) livens up London's Theatreland for a fortnight, during which five- to 16-year-olds can see West End shows for free, if accompanied by a full-paying adult.

The cosy **Children's Book Week** (www.booktrust.org.uk) in early October gets libraries, schools and celebrated children's authors involved in encouraging children to read. In November, the **Children's Film Festival** (www.londonchildrenfilm.org.uk) offers a week of screenings at the **Barbican** (*see p342*; it includes the First Light Young Juries scheme, in which children aged from seven to 16 are invited to be film critics.

In the first week of February, **National Storytelling Week** (www.sfs.org.uk) presents events for tellers and listeners of all ages all across town. In the dog days of winter, there's nothing better than curling up with your thumb in your mouth to listen to a good yarn, well told. Also in February, the **Imagine** children's literature festival at the **Southbank Centre** (www.southbankcentre.co.uk) includes storytelling, comedy, workshops and all sorts of other frolics across the site. Children as young as five can have great fun here.

OCTOBER-DECEMBER

Along with the launch of the Turner Prize, the **Frieze Art Fair** and **Zoo** (for both, *see p306* **Festivals**) are huge art events. The **London Film Festival** (*see p301* **Festivals**) takes place in October, and this is also the season for the **London Jazz Festival** (*see p324* **Festivals**) and the winter instalment of the **Spitalfields Festival** (*see p316* **Festivals**).

Story of London
www.london.gov.uk/storyoflondon.
Date early Oct.
The Mayor of London's extravaganza staggers towards its third instalment. A celebration of the past, present and future of the capital, it has suffered from a lack of focus and poor publicity. But choose carefully from a fortnight's worth of loosely themed events and you'll come up with some real gems.

Big Draw
8351 1719, www.campaignfordrawing.org.
Date 1-31 Oct.
Engage with your inner artist at the Big Draw, a nationwide frenzy of drawing using anything from pencils to vapour trails. The British Library's Big Picture Party brings out heavy art hitters.

Diwali
Trafalgar Square, Westminster, WC2 (7983 4100, www.london.gov.uk). Charing Cross tube/rail. **Date** 26 Oct. **Map** p416 X5.
A vibrant celebration of the annual Festival of Light by London's Hindu, Jain and Sikh communities. There are fireworks, food, music and dancing.

London to Brighton Veteran Car Run
Serpentine Road, Hyde Park, W2 2UH (01327 856024, www.lbvcr.com). Hyde Park Corner tube. **Date** 1st Sun of Nov. **Map** p393 E8.
The London to Brighton is not so much a race as a sedate procession southwards by around 500 pre-1905 cars. The first pair trundles off at sunrise (7am-8.30am), but you can catch them a little later crossing Westminster Bridge or view them in lovingly polished repose on a closed-off Regent's Street the day before the event (11am-3pm).

Bonfire Night
Date 5 Nov & around.
Diwali pyrotechnics segue seamlessly into Britain's best-loved excuse for setting off fireworks: the celebration of Guy Fawkes' failure to blow up the Houses of Parliament in 1605. Try Battersea Park, Alexandra Palace or Victoria Park for fireworks, or pre-book a late ride on the London Eye (*see p71*).

ARTS & ENTERTAINMENT

★ Lord Mayor's Show

Through the City (7332 3456, www.lordmayors show.org). **Date** 12 Nov.

This big show marks the traditional presentation of the new Lord Mayor for approval by the monarch's justices. The Lord Mayor leaves Mansion House in a fabulous gold coach at 11am, along with a colourful procession of floats and marchers, heading to the Royal Courts of Justice (*see p83*). There he makes his vows, and is back home easily in time for afternoon tea. At 5pm, there's a fireworks display from a Thames barge.

▶ *The Lord Mayor is a City officer, elected each year by the livery companies and with no real power outside the City of London; don't confuse him with the Mayor of London, Boris Johnson.*

Remembrance Sunday Ceremony

Cenotaph, Whitehall, Westminster, SW1. Charing Cross tube/rail. **Date** 13 Nov. **Map** p399 L8.

Held on the Sunday nearest to 11 November – the day World War I ended – this solemn commemoration honours those who died fighting in the World Wars and later conflicts. The Queen, the Prime Minister and other dignitaries lay poppy wreaths at the Cenotaph (*see p132*). A two-minute silence at 11am is followed by a service of remembrance.

State Opening of Parliament

Palace of Westminster, Westminster, SW1A 0PW (7219 4272, www.parliament.uk). Westminster tube. **Date** Nov. **Map** p399 L9.

Pomp and ceremony attend the Queen's official reopening of Parliament after its summer recess. She arrives and departs in the state coach, accompanied by troopers of the Household Cavalry.

Christmas Celebrations

Covent Garden (0870 780 5001, www.covent gardenlondonuk.com); Bond Street (www.bond streetassociation.com); St Christopher's Place (7493 3294, www.stchristophersplace.com); Marylebone High Street (7580 3163, www. marylebonevillage.com); Trafalgar Square (7983 4100, www.london.gov.uk). **Date** Nov-Dec.

Of the big stores, Fortnum & Mason (*see p250*) still creates enchantingly old-fashioned Christmas windows, and Harvey Nichols (*see p253*) usually produces show-stopping displays. Otherwise, though, skip the commercialised lights on Oxford and Regent's streets and head, instead, for smaller shopping areas such as St Christopher's Place, Bond Street, Marylebone High Street and Covent Garden. It's traditional to sing carols beneath a giant Christmas tree in Trafalgar Square (*see p129*) – an annual gift from Norway in gratitude for Britain's support during World War II – but you can also join in a mammoth singalong at the Royal Albert Hall (*see p316*) or an evocative carol service at one of London's historic churches. Londoners have also taken to outdoor ice-skating in a big way; *see p338*.

New Year's Eve Celebrations

Date 31 Dec.

The focus of London's public celebrations has officially moved from overcrowded Trafalgar Square (though it's still sure to be packed) to the full-on fireworks display launched from the London Eye and rafts on the Thames. The best view is from nearby bridges, but you'll have to get there early. Otherwise, overpriced festivities in clubs, hotels and restaurants take place across the capital. Those with stamina can take in the New Year's Day Parade the next day.

ARTS & ENTERTAINMENT

Diwali.

Children

Castles, museum interactives and good old-fashioned running about.

With so many museums, parks and farms clamouring for their attention, kids are unlikely to get bored in London. Many key attractions, such as the **Natural History Museum** (*see p143*) and the **Science Museum** (*see p144* **Profile**), are free; many of those that aren't, such as the **Tower of London** (*see p97*), give you a lot of fun for your entry fee.

Over-stimulation is more likely to be a problem: bustle the kids around too many landmarks and you do risk sulks and tantrums, especially if there's a half-hour journey back to your hotel.

For children's festivals, *see p284* **Kids' Stuff**. For weekly event listings, check the Around Town pages in *Time Out* magazine. For useful tips, visit the Mayor's site at www.london.gov.uk/young-london.

WHERE TO GO
South Bank & Bankside (pp70-80)

There's so much to see and do here for children – just tell them to watch out for joggers and cyclists. The expensive end is around **London Eye** (*see p71*), **London Aquarium** (*see p73*) and **London Film Museum** (*see p71*). Moving east, visit the **Southbank Centre** (*see p73 and p317*) to see what's happening in the Royal Festival Hall foyer: free shows and workshops take place for holidays and weekends. Next, the **National Theatre** (*see p342*) offers free entertainment during summer.

Keep going along the riverbank, past Gabriel's Wharf, a riverside cluster of shops and restaurants. Until redevelopment of Blackfriars station is complete in 2012, you have to head briefly inland to get to **Tate Modern** (*see p76*) at the foot of the Millennium Bridge. Tate Modern has gallery trails and books to browse in the Family Zone, as well as events in the Bloomberg Learning Zone on Level Five. (There's a boat service from here to **Tate Britain**, *see p135*.)

Once you've emerged, pick up the Bankside Walk, ducking under the southern end of Southwark Bridge. Walk down cobbly Clink Street towards the **Golden Hinde** (*see p76*) and **Southwark Cathedral** (*see p79*), having passed the **Clink Prison Museum** (*see p76*), a cheaper alternative to the **London Dungeon** and **London Bridge Experience** (for both,

see p79). From Tooley Street, march through Hays Galleria to regain the riverside path, which takes you to the warship museum **HMS Belfast** (*see p80*) and on, past the dancing fountains, to **City Hall** and **Tower Bridge** (*see p97*).

The City (pp81-97)

It seems pricey, but the **Tower of London** (*see p97*) is a top day out for all ages. If it is free stuff you're after, though, the **Museum of London** (*see p84* **Profile**) is superb, with lots of family events during the school holidays, and creative workshops and storytelling sessions happening all year. There are also activity sheets to guide children through the expanded permanent exhibitions. Nearby, the **Bank of England Museum** (*see p92*) is a surprising hit with bullion-obsessed youth, who can try to lift a gold bar.

THE BEST LONDON LESSONS

For history
Tower of London. See p97.

For geography
Prime Meridian Line. See p168.

For English literature
Shakespeare's Globe. See p76.

Bloomsbury (pp101-105)

Children are captivated by the mummies at the **British Museum** (*see p102*). However, the size of the collection can make it overwhelming, so children may prefer a short, sharp Eye Opener family tour to an unstructured wander. Events and workshops are often held; there are free backpacks for kids, filled with puzzles and games, as well as various trails. For weekends and school holidays, the Ford Centre for Young Visitors provides a picnic-style eating area.

Central London's best playground for children, **Coram's Fields** (*see p291*), is close, and the **Foundling Museum** (*see p104*) next door well worth a visit. The **Cartoon Museum** (*see p102*) holds children's workshops and family fun days every second Saturday of the month.

The other side of Tottenham Court Road in Fitzrovia, **Pollock's Toy Museum** (*see p106*) is a nostalgia trip best suited to parents. Kids will appreciate the shop, however, with its range of pop-up theatres, traditional wooden and handcrafted toys.

Covent Garden & the Strand (pp107-111)

London Transport Museum (*see p109*) is a joyful place with buses, trains and taxis that children can climb on. It has a programme of school-holiday events. For freestyle fun, the acts pulling in crowds in front of **St Paul's Covent Garden** (*see p109*) are worth watching. On the south side of the Strand, **Somerset House** (*see p111*) allows kids to play outside among the fountains in summer and skate on the winter ice rink. There are also regular art workshops.

Trafalgar Square (pp129-131)

London's central square (www.london.gov.uk/ trafalgarsquare) has been a free playground for children since time immemorial – those lions beg to be clambered on. Festivals take place most weekends. Even if all is quiet in the square, the **National Gallery** (*see p129*) has paper trails and audio tours, as well as regular kids' and teens' workshops and storytelling sessions for under-fives. For three- to 12-year-olds, the **National Portrait Gallery** (*see p131*) runs Family Faces art workshops and storytelling sessions once a month, as well as a range of weekend and holiday events.

Just nearby, the refurbished church of **St Martin-in-the-Fields** (*see p131*) has London's only brass-rubbing centre, an absorbing activity beloved by tweenies, as well as a fine café that does plenty of the type of food that goes down well with children.

South Kensington (pp143-145)

Top of any Grand Day Out itinerary is this cultural goldmine. The **Science Museum** (*see p144* **Profile**) offers plenty of excitement, with six play zones for all ages, from the Garden in the basement for under-sixes to the relaunched Launchpad upstairs, where children can try some 50 experiments. Dinosaur fans won't rest until they've visited the **Natural History Museum** (*see p143*), but there's far more to this monster museum than prehistoric lizards. Though natural Beasts may capture your attention, the real Beauty is the **Victoria & Albert Museum** (*see p145*). Its free weekend and school holiday drop-in family events (featuring trails, activity-based backpacks, and interactive workshops) provide great ways of focusing on the collection. Educational resources are available in the Sackler Centre studios and the Theatre & Performance Galleries. (Its sister gallery, Bethnal Green's **V&A Museum of Childhood**, *see p156*, has an excellent programme of events for children.)

Greenwich (pp164-168)

Magical Greenwich provides a lovely day out away from the mayhem of the West End. Arrive by boat to appreciate its riverside charms, then

London Transport Museum.

ARTS & ENTERTAINMENT

Mudchute Kitchen.

take time to get the latest on the restorations to the **Cutty Sark** (due for completion in 2011) and to explore the excellent new **Discover Greenwich** (*see p166*). Then head to the very child-friendly **National Maritime Museum** (*see p166*). From here it's a pleasant leg-stretch in the Royal Park for views from the very top of the hill, crowned by the spectacular **Royal Observatory & Planetarium** (*see p167*). When the stars come out, keep an eye out for the luminous green Meridian Line that cuts across the sky towards the city.

EATING & DRINKING

Of the venues listed in the Restaurants & Cafés chapter, **Inn the Park** (*see p220*) and **Masala Zone** (*see p234*) are particularly child-friendly.

Frizzante@Hackney City Farm

1A Goldsmith's Row, Hackney, E2 8QA (7739 2266, www.frizzanteltd.co.uk). Hoxton rail. **Open** 10am-4pm Tue-Sun. **Main courses** £14-£17. **Credit** AmEx, DC, MC, V.
A family-friendly farmhouse kitchen in the heart of Hackney. Once you've trotted around visiting pigs, poultry and sheep, you can settle down to eat their relatives (or stick to vegetarian options). The oil-cloth-covered tables heave with families tucking into healthy nosh, including farm breakfasts.

Giraffe

Riverside Level 1, Royal Festival Hall, Belvedere Road, Waterloo, SE1 8XX (7928 2004, www.giraffe.net). Embankment tube or Waterloo tube/rail. **Open** 8am-11pm Mon-Fri; 9am-11pm Sat; 9am-10.30pm Sun. **Main courses** £7.95-£14.95. **Set meal** (5-7pm Mon-Fri) £7.95 2 courses. **Credit** AmEx, MC, V. **Map** p399 M8.
This popular branch of the global mini-chain pulls families in with balloons and babycinos. Burgers are juicy and the brunch menu lists favourites such as pancakes and eggs and bacon. The kids' lunchtime

deal (noon-3pm) includes a drink and dessert for £4.95. There are several branches all over the city.
► *If nothing on the menu appeals, branches of the excellent noodle bar Wagamama and pizzeria Strada are right next door.*

Mudchute Kitchen

Mudchute Park & Farm, Pier Street, Isle of Dogs, Docklands, E14 3HP (7515 5901, www.mudchute.org). Mudchute DLR. **Open** 9am-5pm Tue-Sun. **Main courses** £4.50-£8.50. **Credit** MC, V.
A farm fenced in by skyscrapers is an amusing place for anyone to eat lunch, but Mudchute is ideal for families. You can eat at farmhouse kitchen tables in the courtyard, while your babies roll around on a big futon or in the toy corner, or in the spacious interior. A new chef took over in 2010, producing the likes of lentil and chard soup or slow-roast pork belly with chicory and sweet potato mash – to be followed, of course, by superb cakes.

Rainforest Café

20 Shaftesbury Avenue, Piccadilly, W1D 7EU (7434 3111, www.therainforestcafe.co.uk). Piccadilly Circus tube. **Open** noon-10pm Mon-Thur; noon-8pm Fri; 11.30am-8pm Sat; 11.30am-10pm Sun. **Main courses** £12.95-£18.90. **Credit** AmEx, DC, MC, V. **Map** p416 W4.
The themed restaurant is designed to thrill children with animatronic wildlife, cascading waterfalls and jungle sound-effects. The menu has lots of family-friendly fare, from 'paradise pizza' and 'Bamba's bangers' to a host of amusing dishes for grown-ups. The children's menu costs £11.95 for two courses.

★ Tate Modern Café: Level 2

Tate Modern, Sumner Street, Waterloo, SE1 9TG (7401 5014, www.tate.org.uk). St Paul's tube or Blackfriars rail. **Open** 10am-5.30pm Mon-Thur, Sun; 10am-9.30pm Fri; 10am-7.30pm Sat. **Main courses** £9.95-£10.50. **Credit** AmEx, MC, V. **Map** p402 O7.

In addition to views from the windows framing the busy Thames, there are literacy and art activities on the junior menu, handed out with a pot of crayons. Children can choose haddock fingers with chips, pasta bolognese with parmesan or a ham and cheese bake with foccacia, finished off with ice-cream or a fruit salad, for £5.10; a free kids' main is offered when an adult orders a regular main. There is also a range of half-price dishes from the adult menu.

TGI Friday's
6 Bedford Street, Covent Garden, WC2E 9HZ (7379 0585, www.tgifridays.co.uk). Covent Garden tube or Charing Cross tube/rail. **Open** noon-11.30pm Mon-Sat; noon-11pm Sun. **Main courses** £8.95-£17. **Credit** AmEx, MC, V. **Map** p416 Y4.
The cheery staff, handing out balloons and crayons, are on a mission to make children welcome. The food veers towards barbecues, Tex-Mex dishes, burgers and chips. The children's menu has all the fried regulars, but also pasta dishes and fruity sundaes for pudding – or dirt and worm pie for chocolate fiends.

That Place on the Corner
1-3 Green Lanes, Stoke Newington, N16 9BS (7704 0079, www.thatplaceonthecorner.co.uk). Canonbury rail then bus 73, 141, 341. **Open** 10.30am-6pm Mon-Thur; 10.30am-8pm Fri; 10.30am-2.30pm Sat, Sun. **Main courses** £4.85-£8.25. **Credit** MC, V.
London's only child-friendly café that won't let in unaccompanied grown-ups. There's a library, puppet theatre and dressing-up corner, as well as baking, dance and music classes. The menu sticks to the trusted pasta/panini/big breakfast formula, with brasserie staples like fish cakes.

ENTERTAINMENT
City farms & zoos

There's always something new at **ZSL London Zoo** (*see p121; photo p290*); the interactive Animal Adventure children's zoo is one recent addition. The admission charge seems high, but there's loads to do. Easier on the budget is the adorable **Battersea Park Children's Zoo** (www.batterseaparkzoo. co.uk), where ring-tailed lemurs, giant rabbits, inquisitive meerkats, playful otters and kune kune pigs are among the inhabitants.

City farms all over London charge nothing to get in. Try **Freightliners City Farm** (www.freightlinersfarm.org.uk) and **Kentish Town City Farm** (www.aapi.co.uk/cityfarm) or, in the east, **Mudchute City Farm** (www. mudchute.org) and **Hackney City Farm** (www.hackneycityfarm.co.uk), both of which have terrific cafés (for both, *see opposite*).

Puppets

★ **Little Angel Theatre**
14 Dagmar Passage, off Cross Street, Islington, N1 2DN (7226 1787, www.littleangeltheatre.com).

Meet the Mascots

Let us introduce you to London 2012's sport-crazy cheerleaders.

There's more to the official London 2012 mascots than meets the eye, or at least the ear. The name of Wenlock – the orange and silver one with a little 'W' above its eye – is inspired by Much Wenlock, the Shropshire town where the 'Olympian Games' that so enthused De Coubertin still take place (*see pp47-51* **Olympic City**). Mandeville – blue and silver, with an 'M' – is named after Stoke Mandeville, the birthplace of the Paralympic Games (*see p51* **Birth of the Paralympic Games**).

The story of their creation, written by the acclaimed children's author Michael Morpurgo (you can see the story, animated beautifully at www.london2012.com/mascots), tells how they were crafted in Sheffield from two drops of British steel, the last ones left after the girders that hold up the Olympic Stadium were finished. They then came to life, full of a can-do enthusiasm for getting involved with Olympic and Paralympic sports. Just as well, really: they've got a busy programme of school events, festivals and opening weekends to get through over the coming months.

Angel tube or Highbury & Islington tube/rail.
Open *Box office* 10am-6pm Mon-Fri; 9am-4pm
Sat, Sun. **Tickets** £5-£12.50. **Credit** MC, V.
Map p400 O1.
Established by John Wright in 1961, London's only
permanent puppet theatre stages diverse produc-
tions, devised here or by visiting companies. All
aspects of puppetry are covered, with themes, styles
and stories drawn from an broad array of traditions.
There's a Saturday Puppet Club and a Puppet
Academy. Shows are often for fives and above.

Puppet Theatre Barge
*Opposite 35 Blomfield Road, Little Venice, W9
2PF (07836 202745 summer, 7249 6876 winter,
www.puppetbarge.com). Warwick Avenue tube.*
Open *Box office* 10am-6pm daily. **Tickets** £10;
£8.50 reductions. **Credit** AmEx, MC, V.
This intimate waterborne stage is the setting for quality puppet shows that put a modern twist on traditional tales. The barge is here between October and
July; shows are held at 3pm on Saturday and Sunday,
daily during school holidays. The barge also holds
performances in Richmond and central London.

Science & nature

FREE Camley Street Natural Park
*12 Camley Street, King's Cross, N1C 4PW (7833
2311, www.wildlondon.org.uk). King's Cross tube/
rail.* **Open** 10am-5pm daily. **Admission** free.
No credit cards. Map p397 L2.
A small green oasis on the site of a former coal yard,
right at the heart of renovated King's Cross. London
Wildlife Trust's flagship reserve hosts pond-dipping
and nature-watching for children; its wood-cabin
visitor centre is used by the Wildlife Watch Club.

FREE Greenwich Peninsula Ecology Park
*Thames Path, John Harrison Way, Greenwich,
SE10 0QZ (8293 1904, www.urbanecology.
org.uk). North Greenwich tube or bus 108, 161,
422, 472, 486.* **Open** 10am-5pm (or dusk) Wed-
Sun. **Admission** free. **No credit cards.**
This wetland haven is a pleasant riverside walk
from the O2 Arena (*see p320*). Family fun days, and
summer play activities, such as bat-box making and
den building, are part of a busy calendar of events.

ZSL London Zoo. *See p289.*

ARTS & ENTERTAINMENT

INSIDE TRACK ON THE BUS

Tours too expensive? An economical way of doing London as a family is by bus, since everyone under the age of 20 currently travels free (over-11s do need different types of ID; *see p363*). Good routes for sightseeing are the 7, 8, 11 and 12 (all double-deckers). For a riverside route, take the RV1 (Tower Hill to South Bank). Routemasters 9 and 15 are Heritage Routes (for details, *see p130* **On Routie to the Future**).

Theatre

Half Moon Young People's Theatre

43 White Horse Road, Limehouse, E1 0ND (7709 8900, www.halfmoon.org.uk). Limehouse DLR/rail. **Open** *Box office* Apr-Oct 10am-6pm Mon-Fri; 10am-5pm Sat. **Tickets** £6. **Credit** MC, V.

The Half Moon's inclusive policy places particular emphasis on engaging those often excluded by ethnicity and disabilities. Two studios provide a calendar of performances for children from just a few months old, and kids can join one of the seven youth theatre groups (for five- to 17-year-olds).

Unicorn Theatre

147 Tooley Street, Bankside, SE1 2HZ (7645 0560, www.unicorntheatre.com). London Bridge tube/rail. **Open** *Box office* 9.30am-6pm Mon-Fri; 10am-6pm Sat; noon-5pm Sun. **Tickets** £10-£18; £7-£12 reductions. **Credit** MC, V. **Map** p403 Q8.

This light, bright building near Tower Bridge, with its huge white unicorn in the foyer has two performance spaces. Its small ensemble company of actors performs in all Unicorn shows and focuses on an outreach programme for local children.

Theme parks

Three theme parks are within easy reach of London, heading out west (see map p351). **Legoland** (Winkfield Road, Windsor, Berks SL4 4AY, 0870 504 0404, www.legoland.co.uk) is always a hit with youngsters, with rides including the wet 'n' wild Viking's River Splash, and the extraordinary Miniland London, made of 13 million Lego bricks. **Thorpe Park** (Staines Road, Chertsey, Surrey KT16 8PN, 0871 663 1673, www.thorpepark.com) has the fastest rollercoaster in Europe, called Stealth, and the terrifying horror-movie ride, Saw; it's best for older kids and teens. And **Chessington World of Adventures** (Leatherhead Road, Chessington, Surrey KT9 2NE, 0871 663 4477, www.chessington.com) is a gentler option. This theme park, open since the 1930s, is partly a zoo, and children can pay to be zoo keeper for a day.

Always call or check the websites for opening times, which vary throughout the year. Only Thorpe Park is open all year; the others close in November until February or March. All cost about £30-£35 per adult, with different pricing schemes for families. Arrive early in the morning to avoid the worst queues, and note that height and health restrictions apply on some rides.

SPACES TO PLAY

London's parks are lovely. **Hyde Park** (*see p145*) and **St James's Park** (*see p136*) are very central, but it isn't much further to **Regent's Park** (*see p120*), and even **Hampstead Heath** (*see p150*) is easily reached on public transport.

FREE Coram's Fields

93 Guilford Street, Bloomsbury, WC1N 1DN (7837 6138, www.coramsfields.org). Russell Square tube. **Open** *Apr-Sept* 9am-7pm daily. *Oct-Mar* 9am-dusk daily. **Admission** free (adults only admitted if accompanied by child under 16). **No credit cards**. **Map** p397 L4.

No adult can enter Coram's Fields without a child. The historic site dates to 1747, when Thomas Coram established the Foundling Hospital, but only opened as a park in 1936. It has sandpits, a paddling pool, a football pitch and a zip wire.

▶ *For the museum now located in the Foundling Hospital, see p104.*

★ FREE Diana, Princess of Wales Memorial Playground

Near Black Lion Gate, Broad Walk, Kensington Gardens, South Kensington, W8 2UH (7298 2141, www.royalparks.gov.uk). Bayswater or Queensway tube. **Open** *Summer* 10am-6.45pm daily. *Winter* 10am-dusk daily. **Admission** free; adults only admitted if accompanied by under-12s. **No credit cards**. **Map** p393 E8.

Bring buckets and spades, if you can, to this superb playground: the huge, central pirate ship is moored in a sea of sand. Other attractions include a tepee camp and a treehouse encampment, and excellent provision is made for children with special needs.

Discover

1 Bridge Terrace, Stratford, E15 4BG (8536 5555, www.discover.org.uk). Stratford tube/rail/DLR. **Open** 10am-5pm Tue-Fri; 11am-5pm Sat, Sun. *School holidays* 10am-5pm Mon-Fri; 11am-5pm Sat, Sun. **Admission** £4.50. **Credit** MC, V.

The UK's first creative learning centre for children is committed to promoting cultural diversity and providing learning opportunites for socially and economically disadvantaged children. The interactive Pirates Ahoy! exhibition allows kids to find hidden treasure, explore secret caves and scrub the decks.

Comedy

Laugh in all the right places.

London is the best city in Britain, and one of the best in the world, for comedy. New talents are constantly arriving in town, hoping for their own BBC show or – failing that – work writing for one of the capital's innumerable production companies. The result is around 250 gigs a week, ranging from open-mic nights in pubs all the way up to arena tours, and a weight of competition that ensures the comedians here stay at the top of their game.

Where to begin? Probably at the purpose-built **Comedy Store**, fail-safe home of alternative laughs and a must for anyone into stand-up. Don't stop there. Explore the whole variety of the London scene: dingy pubs and clubs where skills are honed; arenas and theatres for the finished acts.

London's comedy scene is always lively, but does get a bit quieter during the mass comedy-industry exodus to Edinburgh every August. For weekly line-ups, check *Time Out* magazine and www.timeout.com.

CENTRAL

Amused Moose Soho
Moonlighting, 17 Greek Street, Soho, W1D 4DR (7287 3727, www.amusedmoose.com). Leicester Square or Tottenham Court Road tube. **Shows** *Oct-Mar 8.30pm Sat.* **Admission** *£9-£12.50.* **Credit** MC, V. **Map** p416 W2.
Hils Jago's rosters are always strong, with names such as Bill Bailey and Eddie Izzard continuing to justify the club's multi-award-winning status. Jago has a lot of special guests who can't be named – in other words, really top names trying out new material – and runs the Amused Moose Laugh Offs; finalists have included Jimmy Carr and Simon Amstell.
Other locations Walkabout's DownUnder Bar, 11 Henrietta Street, Covent Garden, WC2E 8PS (7287 3727); Comedy Cellar at the Washington, 50 England's Lane, NW3 4UE (7287 3727).

Comedy Camp
Barcode, 3-4 Archer Street, Soho, W1D 7AP (tickets 0844 477 1000, www.comedycamp.co.uk). Leicester Square or Piccadilly Circus tube. **Shows** *8.30pm Tue.* **Admission** *£10 (incl £2 members' fee).* **Credit** MC, V. **Map** p416 W3.
This intimate, straight-friendly gay club is one of the best nights out anywhere in town. The audiences are always up for a big evening, and resident host and promoter Simon Happily only books fabulous acts.

★ Comedy Store
1A Oxendon Street, Soho, SW1Y 4EE (0844 847 1728, www.thecomedystore.co.uk). Leicester Square or Piccadilly Circus tube. **Shows** *phone for details Mon; 8-10.30pm Tue-Thur, Sun; 8pm & midnight Fri, Sat.* **Admission** *£14-£20.* **Credit** AmEx, MC, V. **Map** p416 W4.
Alternative line-ups at this, the daddy of British comedy clubs, helped launch esteemed jokers such as Alexei Sayle, Dawn French and Paul Merton on to the national stage. The legendary gong show, in which would-be stand-ups are given only as much time on stage as the audience will allow, is on the last Monday of the month.

Funny Side of Covent Garden
The George, 213 the Strand, WC2R 1AP (0844 478 0404, www.thefunnyside.info). Covent Garden tube or Leicester Square tube. **Shows** *8pm Fri, Sat.* **Admission** *£12.50.* **Credit** AmEx, MC, V. **Map** p399 M6.
This is an enjoyable club upstairs in a mock Tudor pub, but calling it 'Covent Garden' is a bit of a stretch, geographically speaking – it's on the fringes of the City near the Royal Courts of Justice (*see p83*). Well-known comedians such as Felix Dexter, Tiernan Douieb, Meryl O'Rourke and Phil Kay have all performed here.
Other locations the Spectator (downstairs), 6 Little Britain, the City, EC1A 7BX; the Alexandra

ARTS & ENTERTAINMENT

(upstairs), 14 Clapham Common South Side, Clapham, SW4 7AA; the Black Heart (upstairs), 3 Greenland Place, Camden, NW1 0AP.

Just the Tonic
Leicester Square Theatre, 6 Leicester Place, Leicester Square, Soho, WC2H 7BX (0844 847 2475, www.justthetonic.com). Leicester Square tube. **Shows** 9.45pm Fri, Sat. **Admission** £15. **Credit** AmEx, MC, V. **Map** p416 X4.
Darrell Martin's London outpost of the acclaimed Nottingham comedy fixture never fails to deliver a cracking night of top-flight comics.
▶ *Leicester Square Theatre (www.leicestersquare theatre.com) programmes more comedy: names in the main house, rising stars in the basement.*

Lowdown at the Albany
240 Great Portland Street, Marylebone, W1W 5QU (7387 5706, www.lowdownatthealbany. com). Great Portland Street tube. **Shows** times vary. **Admission** £6-£10. **No credit cards.** **Map** p396 H4.
This rough-around-the-edges basement venue is a simple set-up that hosts stand-up, sketch shows and the odd play. It's great for Edinburgh previews.

★ Soho Theatre
For listings, *see p348.*
The Soho Theatre is one of the best places to see comics break out of their normal club sets to perform more substantial solo shows. There's always a good mix of home-grown and international talent.

Our Own Edinburgh?

The Greenwich Comedy Festival brings the laughs to south-east London.

Over a long weekend in early September, the lawns of the **Old Royal Naval College** (*see p166*) and **Up the Creek** (*see p294*) play host to London's biggest and best comedy festival, with a big top, smaller pavilions and a temporary bar pitching up against one of the most beautiful backdrops in the city – the Thames on one side, Wren's serenely beautiful colonnades on the other. Add light shows, jugglers, dance troupes, stilt-walkers, clowns and musicians and the **Greenwich Comedy Festival** (www. greenwichcomedyfestival.co.uk) might rub the August smugness off Edinburgh's face.

Even in its first year, the festival had sufficient pulling power to be able to feature headline names such as Russell Howard, Jo Brand and Ardal O'Hanlon. By 2010, the roster included Bill Bailey (*Black Books, Never Mind the Buzzcocks*), the British debut of Tom Green (*Freddy Got Fingered, Road Trip*), three-time Perrier Award nominee Reginald D Hunter and the continuing resurrection of alt-comedy hero Stewart Lee. Performances in the big top and Up the Creek are ticketed, but pop down with a picnic and you can enjoy plenty of events on the college lawns for nothing.

ARTS & ENTERTAINMENT

Greenwich Comedy Festival.

NORTH LONDON

Downstairs at the King's Head
*2 Crouch End Hill, Crouch End, N8 8AA
(8340 1028, www.downstairsatthekings
head.com). Finsbury Park tube/rail then W7
bus.* **Shows** 8pm Thur-Sun. **Admission**
£4-£9. **No credit cards.**
Founded in what seems like the comedic pre-history
of 1981, this venue is still run with huge enthusiasm
by immensely knowledgeable promoter Pete
Grahame. It's an easy going, comfortable place
where comedians can experiment and play around
with complete freedom. It's popular with comics
wanting to do warm-up shows for TV and tours.

★ Hen & Chickens
*109 St Paul's Road, Highbury Corner, Islington,
N1 2NA (7704 2001, www.henandchickens.com).
Highbury & Islington tube/rail.* **Shows** times
vary **Admission** £7-£10. **No credit cards.**
This dinky, black-box theatre above a cosy
Victorian corner pub is well known as the place to
see great solo shows, especially those warming up
for a tour. Acts have included Jenny Eclair, Frankie
Boyle, Rhona Cameron and Jimmy Carr.

EAST LONDON

Comedy Café
*66-68 Rivington Street, Shoreditch, EC2A 3AY
(7739 5706, www.comedycafe.co.uk). Liverpool
Street or Old Street tube/rail.* **Shows** 9pm Wed,
Thur, Sat; 8pm Fri. **Admission** £8-£15; free
Wed. **Credit** MC, V. **Map** p401 R4.
The Comedy Café is another purpose-built club set
up by a comedian. Noel Faulkner, who worked on
trawlers and was wanted by the FBI in his time, now
mainly keeps to the back room but, with the emphasis on inviting bills and satisfied punters, his influence can still be felt. The atmosphere is fun and food
is an integral part of the experience.

Theatre Royal Stratford East
For listings, *see p348.*
A gem of a comedy night is held here every Monday
at 8pm, and it's free. The gig, which takes place in
the long bar upstairs, has great line-ups, especially
considering you're not paying a penny.

SOUTH LONDON

Banana Cabaret
*The Bedford Arms, 77 Bedford Hill, Balham,
SW12 9HD (8682 8940, www.bananacabaret.
co.uk). Balham tube/rail.* **Shows** 9pm Fri, Sat.
Admission £4-£16. **Credit** MC, V.
Satisfaction is pretty much guaranteed every Friday
and Saturday at this exciting, long-running club in
the big roundhouse setting of the Bedford Arms pub.
A safe bet for a good night out.

Highlight Clapham Junction
*The Rise, 49 Lavender Gardens, Clapham,
SW11 1DJ (0844 844 0044, www.thehighlight.
co.uk). Clapham Junction rail.* **Shows** 8pm Fri;
7pm Sat. **Admission** from £15. **Credit** MC, V.
A management buy-out of Jongleurs (*see below*) created Highlight. The unashamedly business-like
approach that characterised Jongleurs hasn't
changed very much: expect big names performing
in sets of three to boozed-up stag and hen parties.
Raucous fun, then, but not one for the connoisseur.
Other locations 11 East Yard, Camden, NW1
8AB (7428 5929).

Up the Creek
*302 Creek Road, Greenwich, SE10 9SW
(8858 4581, www.up-the-creek.com). Greenwich
DLR/rail.* **Shows** 9pm Fri; 8.30pm Sat, Sun.
Admission £10, £6 reductions Fri; £15, £12
reductions Sat; £6, £4 reductions Sun. **Credit**
MC, V. **Map** p405 W2.
Set up by the late and legendary Malcolm Hardee
('To say that he has no shame is to drastically exag-
gerate the amount of shame he has,' quipped one
critic), this purpose-built club has been around since
the 1990s, and is still one of the best places to see
live comedy. It's renowned for its lively, bearpit
atmosphere, but there's a more chilled feel to the
'Sunday Special Club' (www.sundayspecial.co.uk).

WEST LONDON

Headliners
*George IV, 185 Chiswick High Road,
Chiswick, W4 2DR (8566 4067, www.
headlinerscomedy.com). Turnham Green tube.*
Shows 9pm Fri, Sat. **Admission** £12.
No credit cards.
West London isn't blessed with many good comedy
nights, but Headliners does what it can to redress
the balance from its purpose-designed warehouse
tucked behind the pub. The experienced Simon
Randall, who also ran Ha Bloody Ha, is at the helm.

Jongleurs
*Rutland Grove, Hammersmith, W6 9DJ (0870
011 1960, www.jongleurs.com). Hammersmith
tube.* **Shows** 8.30pm Sat. **Admission** £17.
Credit MC, V.
Started in 1983 by Maria Kempinska with a £300
bank loan, the Jongleurs brand was soon one of the
biggest players in the British comedy industry. Its
subsequent owner, Regent Inns, went bust in 2009:
the Jongleurs venues became Highlight (*see above*)
and the name reverted to Kempinska, who opened
these two venues in 2010. Covent Garden is the main
one, but west London was really in need of this one.
Expect three acts a night of big-name crowd-
pleasers, playing to rowdy fans.
Other locations 61-65 Great Queen Street,
Covent Garden, WC2B 5BZ.

Dance

London dance doesn't stand still.

The strength of London's traditions in dance sometimes leave the capital lagging behind the innovations elsewhere in Europe, but there's still a lot of ambition and inventiveness here. Many local choreographers feed off the unbridled creativity for which London is renowned in the other arts, or feed into the vibrant cross-cultural pollinations that are part and parcel of life in the city. Even the 80-year-old **Royal Ballet** (*see below*) is now producing groundbreaking new work, thanks to resident choreographer Wayne McGregor.

There are also plenty of chances to get moving yourself. Look out, especially, for the city's tea dances and old-time balls, their popularity in part inspired by the success of TV series *Strictly Come Dancing*. For information on upcoming events and classes, pick up *Time Out* magazine or see www.timeout.com/london/dance.

DANCE COMPANIES

There are two long-established classical dance companies. The **Royal Ballet**, founded in 1931 and resident at the Royal Opera House (*see p296*), is a company of global stature, whose 100 or so dancers include such global guest stars as Carlos Acosta. The only slightly less prestigious **English National Ballet** is a touring company, founded in 1950, that performs most often at the Coliseum (*see p317*) and, for the regular *Swan Lake* 'in the round', at the Royal Albert Hall (*see p316*). Its principals include British dancer Begoña Cao and the Cuban Yat-Sen Chang.

Although the **Rambert Dance Company** (www.rambert.org.uk) has been around since before World War II, a regular turnover of great dancers and new works keeps the troupe fresh, and its programmes of contemporary dance are always accessible. Another popular name is **Matthew Bourne** (www.new-adventures.net), who reimagines classic tales (from *Swan Lake* to *Edward Scissorhands*) with great sets and plenty of humour. On a smaller scale, the **New Art Club** (www.newartclub.org) are a duo whose work lies between contemporary dance, theatre and stand-up. The career of **Michael Clark** (www.michaelclarkcompany.com) has

had its controversial moments, but he's now reconciled his classical roots and punk spirit.

Many London choreographers absorb cross-cultural influences. **Shobana Jeyasingh** (www.shobanajeyasingh.co.uk), **Akram Khan** (www.akramkhancompany.net) and Nina Rajarani's **Srishti** (www.srishti.co.uk) all work to varying degrees with South Asian dance, while Zimbabwean **Bawren Tavaziva** (www.tavazivadance.com) is one of several figures adding African dance to the melting pot.

MAJOR VENUES

Barbican Centre

For listings, see p315.

Conceived in the 1960s and completed in 1982, the Barbican attracts and nurtures experimental dance,

---

About the author
Lyndsey Winship *is the dance editor of* Time Out *magazine.*

INSIDE TRACK
WHITE LODGE MUSEUM

Serious balletomanes should pay a visit to the small **White Lodge Museum** (White Lodge, Richmond Park, Surrey TW10 5HR, 8392 8440, www.royal-ballet-school.org.uk), at the home of the Royal Ballet School in the wilds of Richmond Park. Opening hours are limited, though, and advance booking is essential.

especially in the perfectly intimate Pit Theatre. The year-round Barbican International Theatre Events series (BITE; www.barbican.org.uk/theatre) offers plenty of noteworthy dance performances.

★ Place

17 Duke's Road, Bloomsbury, WC1H 9PY (7121 1100, www.theplace.org.uk). Euston tube/rail. **Box office** noon-6pm Mon-Sat; noon-8pm on performance days. **Tickets** £6-£17. **Credit** MC, V. **Map** p399 K3.

For genuinely emerging dance, look to the Place. The theatre is behind the Place Prize for choreography, which rewards the best in British contemporary dance as well as regular seasons of new work such as the biennial Resolution! (short works; Jan/Feb) and Spring Loaded (Apr/May).

★ Royal Opera House

For listings, see p319.

Festivals Dance

What not to miss this year.

Dance Umbrella (Oct-Nov, www.dance umbrella.co.uk) has been the daddy of London dance festivals for more than 30 years, always staging a stimulating mix of local and international artists, established names and brand new talent across a number of London venues.

Although it's a relative newcomer to the festival calendar, Spring Dance (Mar-Apr, www.sadlerswells.com) is a big hitter, bringing major companies to the 2,400-seater Coliseum (*see p317*). The line-up for 2010 features the Ballet Nacional de Cuba, among others. At the other end of the scale, the Place's biennial **Resolution!** festival (Jan-Feb, www.theplace.org.uk) presents young choreographers, many of whom are presenting their first works. Also at the Place, also biennial, the **Place Prize** (Sept, www.theplaceprize.com) sees established choreographers competing against unknowns for big money.

Other festivals take a niche: the four-day, Thames-side **London International Tango Festival** (Sept, http://rivertango.co.uk), the **Flamenco Festival** (Feb, www.sadlerswells.com) and hip hop weekend **Breakin' Convention** (May, www.sadlerswells.com). If you'd rather take part, the **Big Dance** (July, www.bigdance2010.com) offers classes, workshops and performances in everything from disco to folk dance.

For the full ballet experience, nothing beats the Royal Opera House, home of the Royal Ballet. The current incarnation of the building is an appropriately grand space in which to see the likes of Carlos Acosta. Tours of the building sometimes take in a ballet rehearsal. There's edgier fare in the Linbury Studio Theatre and the Clore Studio Upstairs.

★ Sadler's Wells

Rosebery Avenue, Finsbury, EC1R 4TN (0844 412 4300, www.sadlerswells.com). Angel tube. **Box office** *In person* 9am-8.30pm Mon-Sat. *By phone* 24hrs daily. **Tickets** £10-£60. **Credit** AmEx, MC, V. **Map** p402 N3.

Purpose-built in 1998 on the site of a 17th-century theatre of the same name, this dazzling complex is home to impressive local and international performances. The smaller Lilian Baylis Studio offers smaller-scale new works and works-in-progress, and the Peacock Theatre (on Portugal Street in Holborn) operates as a satellite venue.

Siobhan Davies Dance Studios

85 St George's Road, Southwark, SE1 6ER (7091 9650, www.siobhandavies.com). Elephant & Castle tube/rail. **Box office** 9am-9pm Mon-Fri; 10am-2pm Sat, Sun. **Tickets** £3-£18. **Credit** MC, V. **Map** p402 N10.

This award-winning studio was designed in consultation with dancers, ensuring it met their needs. As well as being home to Davies's own company, the studio hosts talks and performances at the more experimental end of the scale. The performance programme is sporadic: check details before setting out.

Southbank Centre

For listings, see p317.

The refurbishment of the Royal Festival Hall (RFH) has led to a revival in the dance programme of the cluster of venues collectively known as the Southbank Centre: the mammoth RFH, the medium-sized Queen Elizabeth Hall, the intimate Purcell Room and the riverside terrace. Nicky Molloy has had a couple of years to settle into her role as the head of dance here, so you can expect more progressive programming, often mixing dance and theatre.

OTHER VENUES

Blue Elephant

59A Bethwin Road, Camberwell, SE5 0XT (7701 0100, 0844 477 1000 tickets, www.blue elephanttheatre.co.uk). Oval tube. **Box office** *In person* 1hr before performance. *By phone* 24hrs. **Tickets** £7-£12.50; free under-26s. **No credit cards.**

Hidden away in the wilds of south London, the Blue Elephant Theatre is a little off the beaten path. However, its accessible programme of quality contemporary dance, which runs alongside theatre and other performance, is worth seeking out.

Greenwich Dance Agency

*Borough Hall, Royal Hill, Greenwich, SE10 8RE
(8293 9741, www.greenwichdance.org.uk).
Greenwich DLR/rail.* **Open** *Box office* 9.30am-
9pm Mon-Thur; 9.30am-5.30pm Fri; 10am-3pm
Sat. **Tickets** £7-£15. **Credit** MC, V. **Map**
p405 W3.

Home to resident artist Temujin Gill, of the Temujin
Dance Company, and Noel Wallace, who made
history as the English National Ballet's first black
dancer, this art deco venue in Greenwich hosts entertaining classes and workshops, as well as the surely
unique GDA cabaret, which delivers dance performances in short bursts among punters who are
happily tucking into full table-service meals.

Laban Centre

*Creekside, Deptford, SE8 3DZ (8691 8600
information, 8469 9500 tickets, www.laban.org).
Deptford DLR or Greenwich DLR/rail.* **Open**
10am-8pm Mon-Sat. **Tickets** £6-£15. **Credit**
MC, V.

The home of Transitions Dance Company, this beautiful independent conservatoire for dance training
was founded by Rudolf Laban (1879-1958), creator
of a unique and enduring discipline for movement.
Designed by Herzog & de Meuron of Tate Modern
fame, the premises include a 300-seat auditorium.
▶ *Also in Deptford, the Albany (Douglas Way,
SE8 4AG, 8692 4446, www.thealbany.org.uk)
specialises in hip hop theatre.*

Dramatic Dancing

London is beginning to expand the boundaries of the art.

The blurring of the boundaries separating
dance from performance art and physical
theatre is nothing new: the late Pina Bausch
made Tanztheater famous back in the
1980s, for instance. However, Britain has
traditionally preferred its dance based on
technique, athleticism and musical moves
to the more conceptual European approach
– until now. Companies such as Belgium's
Les Ballets C de la B have made an impact
in London both on artists and on audiences,
who are opening up to boundary-blurring
work that often doesn't contain much of
what you'd call 'dance' at all.

Physical theatre has been presented
in the UK for years by groups such as the
politically pointed **DV8** (www.dv8.co.uk)
and the witty **Protein Dance** (www.protein
dance.co.uk), and by choreographers such
as **Jasmin Vardimon** (www.jasminvardimon.
com), who combines quirky characters with
explosive physicality. Young names to look
out for include **Maresa von Stockert** (www.
tilted.org.uk), **Lost Dog** (www.lostdogdance.
co.uk) and **MIKS** (www.miks.org.uk).

Even the big venues have started to
get in on the act: Nicky Molloy at the
Southbank Centre (*see left*) has been
keen to introduce boundary-bothering
European approaches into her programming
from the start; the **English National Opera**
(*see p317*) was to collaborate with theatre
group Complicité's Simon McBurney at the
end of 2010; and **Sadler's Wells** (*see left*)
has transferred collaborative work from
fringe theatres.

'Because theatre is such an important
part of our culture, we have a history that
sometimes weighs us down a little,' says

Alistair Spalding, the artistic director of
Sadler's Wells. 'I think it's important to
stop thinking in that way, that dance has
got to be separate. We definitely don't want
to be stuck in a dance ghetto.'

The Lilian Baylis Studio, the theatre's
smaller space, has been repositioned as a
home for more experimental work. 'Some
of these artists have hardly ever been
represented in London and they're quite
well known in the rest of Europe, so we're
playing a bit of catch-up,' says Spalding.
Hopefully, it shouldn't take too long to
get up to speed.

Protein Dance.

Film

An increasingly commercial scene, with some superb independents.

It isn't until you stroll round London that you realise how often the city itself has played a starring role in films, with both its iconic sights (rampaging mummies at the British Museum) and characterful neighbourhoods (a floppy-haired bookseller in Notting Hill) giving visitors a visual preview of the capital. There's a lively and varied culture of screenings too. Giant picture palaces hosting red-carpet premières attended by A-list actors? Check out the **Odeon Leicester Square** (*see p299*). Cheap-as-chips repertory cinema? The **Prince Charles** (*see p300*) is right around the corner. Refurbished art deco gems? Try the gorgeous, historic **Phoenix** (*see p300*). A world-class film festival? Happens every autumn. Outdoor screenings in remarkable settings, ciné clubs, film seasons devoted to every genre and national cinema under the sun? Yes, yes and yes. Get some popcorn and sit yourself down.

WHERE TO GO

While Leicester Square has the biggest first-run cinemas and stages most of the big-budget premières, it also has the biggest prices. By contrast, the independents provide a cheaper and often more enjoyable night out, and they often show films that wouldn't come within a million miles of a red carpet.

Among the rep cinemas, the British Film Institute's flagship venue gets top billing. **BFI Southbank** (*see p300*) screens seasons exploring and celebrating various genres of cinema and TV. After the BFI, London's best repertory cinema is found at the **Riverside Studios** (*see p301*), where you'll find special seasons and film events. Despite the loss of two of the three screens at the **Barbican** (*see right*), it's always worth checking out the self-explanatory Directorspective strand.

Unexpected venues for film-viewing include the big museums and galleries. The **British Museum** (*see p102*), **National Gallery** (*see p129*), **Imperial War Museum** (*see p161*) and **Tate Modern** (*see p76*) all have regular screenings themed to their temporary exhibitions, the **Museum of London** (*see p84 Profile*) screens a classic London film each month, and even **St Paul's Cathedral** (*see p87*) has carved out a niche for silent movies with live organ soundtracks. Several luxury hotels open their screening rooms to the public; those at the **Soho Hotel** (*see p191*) and **One Aldwych** (*see p189*) are favourites.

Outdoor summertime screens have popped up across the capital. The most glamorous is the **Somerset House Summer Screen** (www.somersethouse.org.uk/film), for which recent blockbusters and old classics are run in a magnificent Georgian courtyard, and Park Nights at the **Serpentine Gallery** (*see p146*), where you can watch films in the annual temporary, starchitect-built pavilion. Fans of memorabilia can check out the enjoyable **London Film Museum** (*see p71*), but the latest trend is to mix cinema with other forms of entertainment, from DJs to pub quizzes, themed fancy dress to secret locations (*see p300* **Inside Track**).

The lowdown

Consult *Time Out* magazine's weekly listings or visit www.timeout.com/film for full details of what's on and performance times; note that the programmes change on a Friday. Films released in the UK are classified under the following categories: **U** – suitable for all ages; **PG** – open to all, parental guidance is advised; **12A** – under-12s only admitted with an over-18; **15** – no one under 15 is admitted; **18** – no one under 18 is admitted.

FIRST-RUN CINEMAS
Central London

Barbican
*Silk Street, the City, EC2Y 8DS (7638 8891,
www.barbican.org.uk). Barbican tube or
Moorgate tube/rail.* **Tickets** £10.50; £6.50-£8.50
reductions; £6.50 Mon. **Screens** 1. **Credit**
AmEx, MC, V. **Map** p400 P5.
The closure of tiny Screens 2 and 3 at the huge
concrete art centre (*see p89*) in 2010 has meant a single screen now shows the Barbican's excellent film
programme – no matter, the raked seats always
made Screen 1 the best of the three. Expect new
releases of quality world and independent films and
an inventive range of seasons, such as the Bad Film
Club and, for surveys of the likes of Werner Herzog
and Jacques Tati, the Directorspective strand.

Curzon Cinemas
Chelsea *206 King's Road, SW3 5XP (0871 703
3990). Sloane Square then bus 11, 19, 22, 319.*
Screens 1. **Map** p395 E12.
Mayfair *38 Curzon Street, W1J 7TY (0871 703
3989). Green Park or Hyde Park Corner tube.*
Screens 2. **Map** p398 H8.
Soho *99 Shaftesbury Avenue, W1D 5DY (0871
703 3988). Leicester Square tube.* **Screens** 3.
Map p416 X3.
All *www.curzoncinemas.com.* **Tickets** £7-£12;
£5-£9 reductions. **Credit** MC, V.

Screen on the Green. *See p300.*

Expect a superb range of shorts, rarities, double-bills
and seasons alongside new international releases
across the small Curzon chain. There's 1970s splendour in Mayfair (it's sometimes used for premières)
and comfort in Chelsea, which is perfect for a
Sunday screening after a King's Road brunch. But
the coolest of the bunch is the Soho outpost, which
has a buzzing café and a decent basement bar.

★ ICA Cinema
*Nash House, the Mall, SW1Y 5AH (7930 0493,
7930 3647 tickets, www.ica.org.uk). Charing
Cross tube/rail.* **Tickets** £7-£9; £8 reductions.
Screens 2. **Credit** MC, V. **Map** p399 K8.
London's small contemporary arts centre (*see p138*)
has met its brief not only by screening an eclectic
range of cinema, but by distributing some of the
most noteworthy films of recent years – we wait to
see whether recession-led redundancies blunt its
ambition. Serious types discuss in the ICA Café.

Odeon Leicester Square
*Leicester Square, WC2H 7LQ (0871 224 4007,
www.odeon.co.uk). Leicester Square tube.*
Tickets vary; check website for details.
Screens 6. **Credit** AmEx, MC, V. **Map** p416 X4.
You'll often find the red carpets and crush barriers
up outside this art deco gem – it's the city's leading
site for star-studded premières. If you're lucky, you
might catch one of the sporadic silent film screenings, with accompaniment on a 1937 Compton organ
that really does come up through the floor.
Otherwise, it's big-volume mainstream hits.

Outer London

Electric Cinema
*191 Portobello Road, Notting Hill, W11 2ED
(7908 9696, www.electriccinema.co.uk). Ladbroke
Grove or Notting Hill Gate tube.* **Tickets** £12.50-
£14.50; £7.50-£10 Mon. **Screens** 1. **Credit**
AmEx, MC, V. **Map** p404 X4.
The Electric has gone from past-it fleapit to luscious
luxury destination with leather seats and sofas, foot-
stools and a bar inside the auditorium. It also has a
fashionable brasserie next door.

ARTS & ENTERTAINMENT

INSIDE TRACK FILM CLUBBING

The desire to show films anywhere but in the buildings dedicated to that purpose has almost reached saturation point, but for real filmic flair, seek out **Secret Cinema**. The organisers keep their film, venue and theme completely secret until the day before the event, giving their punters just 24 hours to plan costumes, get to whatever crazy location has been selected and discover themselves in the middle of the film itself – *Aliens* and *Bugsy Malone* are among the many movies that have had the Secret Cinema total immersion treatment. Register at www.secretcinema.org and await news.

Everyman & Screen Cinemas

Everyman *5 Hollybush Vale, Hampstead, NW3 6TX. Hampstead tube.* **Tickets** £12-£16; £7.50 reductions. **Screens** 2.
Screen on the Green *83 Upper Street, Islington, N1 0NP. Angel tube.* **Tickets** £10-£12.50; £7.50 reductions. **Screens** 2. **Map** p400 O2.
Both *0871 906 9060, www.everymancinema.com.* **Credit** MC, V.
London's most elegant cinema, the Everyman has a glamorous bar and two-seaters (£30) in its 'screening lounges', complete with foot stools and wine coolers. Everyman now also owns three former Screen cinemas, of which the Islington's Screen on the Green is the best – carefully refurbished in late 2009, it lost seats to make space for the more comfortable kind, gained an auditorium bar and a stage for live events, but kept its lovely exterior neon sign. *Photo p299.*

★ Phoenix

52 High Road, East Finchley, N2 9PJ (8444 6789, www.phoenixcinema.co.uk). East Finchley tube. **Tickets** £6-£9; £6 reductions. **Screens** 1. **Credit** MC, V.
Built in 1910 and revamped in the 1930s, the Grade II-listed Phoenix reopened in autumn 2010, restored to its copper and gold, art deco glory, at a cost of £1.1m. It has real old-fashioned glamour, and is London's oldest cinema to have remained in continuous operation. Owned by a charitable trust enjoying strong community support, it runs a varied programme including live theatre and opera transmissions, and now has a café-bar on the premises.

Rio Cinema

107 Kingsland High Street, Dalston, E8 2PB (7241 9410, www.riocinema.org.uk). Dalston Kingsland rail. **Tickets** £8.50; £6.50 reductions. **Screens** 1. **Credit** AmEx, MC, V.
Another great deco survivor, restored to its original sleek lines, the Rio is east London's finest independent. Alongside mainstream releases, the Rio is well known for its Turkish and Kurdish film festivals, catering to strong local communities.

Vue Westfield London

Westfield London, Shepherd's Bush, W12 7GF (0871 224 0240, www.myvue.com). White City or Wood Lane tube, or Shepherd's Bush tube/rail. **Tickets** check website for details. **Screens** 14. **Credit** MC, V.
This Vue multiplex was a great addition to the vast shopping centre (*see p255*). All the screens are digital, with five 3D-ready and two 18m by 10m whoppers. The main rooms are functional black boxes with good sightlines, but you can also fork out for over-18s 'Scene' screens: you get reclining chairs and access to a private bar and a cloakroom. **Other locations** throughout the city.

REPERTORY CINEMAS

Several first-run cinemas also offer rep-style fare – check *Time Out* magazine for locations.

★ BFI Southbank

South Bank, SE1 8XT (7928 3535, 7928 3232 tickets, www.bfi.org.uk). Embankment tube or Waterloo tube/rail. **Tickets** £9; £5-£6.25 reductions; £5 Tue. **Screens** 4. **Credit** AmEx, MC, V. **Map** p399 M8.
Back in 2007, the expanded, former National Film Theatre gained a new name, a destination bar-restaurant (from museum-caterers Benugo) and the superb Mediatheque. Since then the deathlessly popular promenade-facing café-bar has also been improved by Benugo, but the BFI's success is still built on its core function: providing thought-provoking seasons that give film-hungry locals the chance to enjoy rare and significant British and foreign films.
▶ *Mediatheque gives you free access to the BFI's huge film and documentary archive.*

Ciné Lumière

Institut Français, 17 Queensberry Place, South Kensington, SW7 2DT (7073 1350, www.institut-francais.org.uk). South Kensington tube. **Tickets** £7-£9; £5-£7 reductions; £7 Mon. **Screens** 1. **Credit** MC, V. **Map** p395 D10.
Ciné Lumière reopened in early 2009 with more comfortable seating and a refreshed art deco interior. No longer screening French films only (there are still, however, regular French previews and classics), the Lumière is a standard-bearer for world cinema in the capital, hosting several country-themed festivals.

Prince Charles

7 Leicester Place, off Leicester Square, WC2H 7BY (0870 811 2559, www.princecharles cinema.com). Leicester Square tube. **Tickets** £5.50-£10; £1.50-£6 reductions. **Screens** 2. **Credit** MC, V. **Map** p416 X3.

Central and cheap, the Prince Charles is just up an alley from the pricey Leicester Square monsters, but even films on the new screen are a relative bargain. Perfect for catching up on still-fresh films you missed first time round, it is renowned for riotous singalong screenings and in 2010 began to carve out a new niche for marathon screenings: the entire six-series run of *Lost*, for example, or every *Star Trek* movie in sequence.

★ Riverside Studios
Crisp Road, Hammersmith, W6 9RL (8237 1111, www.riversidestudios.co.uk). Hammersmith tube. **Tickets** £7.50; £6.50 reductions. **Screens** 1. **Credit** MC, V.
The Riverside offers a superb programme of films: regular double-bills slot between special seasons, many of them spotlighting Eastern European cinema (there were films from Georgia in autumn 2010) or hard-hitting documentaries. The café-bar and riverside terrace are usually packed with a voluble mix of film- and theatregoers.

IMAX

BFI IMAX
1 Charlie Chaplin Walk, South Bank, SE1 8XR (0870 787 2525, www.bfi.org.uk/imax). Waterloo tube/rail. **Tickets** £14-£16; £9.75-£12 reductions. **Screens** 1. **Credit** AmEx, MC, V. **Map** p399 M8.
London's biggest screen mixes made-for-IMAX fare and scenery-heavy documentaries with mainstream blockbusters, such as *Avatar*, shown either very big – or very big and in disorienting 3D.
▶ *Science Museum has an IMAX too; see p144.*

Festivals Film

What not to miss this year.

There's a film festival in the capital pretty much any given week, but the **London Film Festival** (www.bfi.org.uk/lff, Oct) is far and away the most prestigious. Nearly 200 new British and international features are screened, mainly at the BFI Southbank and Leicester Square's Vue West End. It's preceded by the delightfully leftfield **Raindance Festival** (www.raindance.co.uk), which offers independent features and a terrific shorts programme.

The **London Lesbian & Gay Film Festival** (7928 3232, www.bfi.org.uk/llgff, late Mar) is the UK's third largest film festival, preceded in the month by **Birds Eye View** (www.birds-eye-view.co.uk), a highly rated celebration of women filmmakers. Also in spring, the **Human Rights Watch International Film Festival** (7713 1995, www.hrw.org/iff, mid-late Mar) aims to put a human face on threats to individual freedom and dignity, while the **East End Film Festival** (www.eastendfilmfestival. com, late Apr) explores cinema's great potential to cross cultural boundaries, reserving a special place for films starring London – 2010's screening of Hitchcock's *The Lodger* in Spitalfields Market with a live soundtrack was great.

Several festivals screen the output of a particular foreign territory. Among them are the Polish Cultural Institute's **Kinoteka** (www.kinoteka.org.uk, Mar); the wonderful **Mosaïques** festival (Ciné Lumière, June); and the **Discovering Latin America Film Festival** (www.discoveringlatinamerica.com,

BFI 53rd London Film Festival Awards.

Nov), for films, documentaries and shorts that rarely get distribution, and the **Latin American Film Festival** (www.latinamericanfilmfestival.com, Nov), which showcases some of the latest commercial features.

Short films are featured at the **London Short Film Festival** (www.shortfilms.org.uk) in the new year. In July, the **Rushes Soho Shorts** festival (www.sohoshorts.com) features everything from film concepts to music promos, while August's **London International Animation Festival** (www. liaf.org.uk) screens 300 or more animated shorts from around the globe. Last but by no means least, the **Portobello Film Festival** (www.portobellofilmfestival.com, early Sept) offers an eclectic programme of screenings that are free of charge to members of the public.

ARTS & ENTERTAINMENT

Galleries

Its heart is in the east, but London's art scene thrives all over town.

London's galleries seem to have made reasonably serene progress through the recession, with contemporary art still a very lively component of the city's cultural mix. The most interesting developments have been in the non-profit sector, with **Raven Row** (*see p306*) leading the way in Spitalfields and the **Showroom** (*see p304*) bringing its nurturing presence to Marylebone, having been an East End stalwart for decades. The 'outsider art' at the **Museum of Everything** (*see p304*) has been another refreshing addition to the scene.

ARTS & ENTERTAINMENT

FINE ART

For weekly listings, check *Time Out* magazine and www.timeout.com, or the free *New Exhibitions of Contemporary Art*, available at most galleries and www.newexhibitions.com.

Central London

Mayfair's reputation as prime art hunting territory has been challenged recently by the rejuvenated Fitzrovia, where **Pilar Corrias**, **Stuart Shave/Modern Art** and the **David Roberts Foundation** are near neighbours.

INSIDE TRACK
MAJOR COLLECTIONS

Alison Jacques Gallery
16-18 Berners Street, Fitzrovia, W1T 3LN (7631 4720, www.alisonjacquesgallery.com). Goodge Street or Oxford Circus tube. **Open** 10am-6pm Tue-Sat, or by appointment. **No credit cards**. **Map** p396 J5.
Jacques shows emerging and established names such as Ian Kiaer and André Butzer, plus works from the estates of Robert Mapplethorpe and Hannah Wilke.

Bloomberg Space
50 Finsbury Square, the City, EC2A 1HD (7330 7959, www.bloombergspace.com). Moorgate tube/rail. **Open** 11am-6pm Mon-Sat. **No credit cards**. **Map** p401 Q5.
Instead of simply leasing or buying art for its European HQ, Bloomberg dedicates a space within its London building to an ongoing exhibition programme of contemporary and commissioned art. 'Comma', the latest incarnation, is a lively schedule of new commissions by artists who are given the opportunity to experiment and expand their practice.

★ Gagosian
6-24 Britannia Street, King's Cross, WC1X 9JD (7841 9960, www.gagosian.com). King's Cross tube/rail. **Open** 10am-6pm Tue-Sat. **No credit cards**. **Map** p397 M3.
Visitors flock to this vast space, part of US super-dealer Larry Gagosian's expanding empire, to see big names such as Cy Twombly, Jeff Koons and Howard Hodgkin, plus a second tier of fashionable US and European artists including Mark Grotjahn and 2009 Turner Prize nominee Richard Wright. **Other locations** 17-19 Davies Street, Mayfair, W1K 3DE (7493 3020).

David Roberts Foundation

*111 Great Titchfield Street, Fitzrovia, W1W 6RY
(7637 0868, www.davidrobertsartfoundation.com).
Warren Street tube.* **Open** 10am-6pm Tue-Fri;
11am-4pm Sat. **No credit cards. Map** p397 M3.
David Roberts is the latest in a line of collectors to
start a charitable foundation and open premises in
which to show their acquisitions. The programme
is a mix of solo presentations and group shows
organised by invited curators.

Haunch of Venison

*6 Burlington Gardens, Mayfair, W1S 3ET (7495
5050, www.haunchofvenison.com). Piccadilly
Circus tube.* **Open** 10am-6pm Mon-Fri; 10am-
5pm Sat. **Credit** AmEx, MC, V. **Map** p416 U4.
Now owned by auction house Christie's, the Haunch
has moved to palatial premises behind the Royal
Academy of Arts (*see p128*), where it mounts shows
by major names (Turner Prize winners Keith Tyson
and Richard Long), mid-career artists (Diana Thater,
Zarina Bhimji) and emerging talent (Jitish Kallat).

★ Hauser & Wirth London

*23 Savile Row, Mayfair, W1S 2ET (7287 2300,
www.hauserwirth.com). Piccadilly Circus tube.*
Open 10am-6pm Tue-Sat. **No credit cards.**
Map p416 U5.
This Swiss-owned gallery opened in 2003 in a for-
mer bank, with intact basement vaults, but has
moved its flagship to a swanky new Savile Row
space. H&W represents big name artists including
Louise Bourgeois, international names such as Anri
Sala, and home-grown talents such as Martin Creed.
Other locations 196A Piccadilly, Mayfair, W1J
9DY (7287 2300)*;* Hauser & Wirth Colnaghi, 15
Old Bond Street, Mayfair, W1S 4AX (7287 2300).

Jerwood Space

*171 Union Street, Borough, SE1 0LN (7654 0171,
www.jerwoodspace.co.uk). Borough or Southwark
tube.* **Open** 10am-5pm Mon-Fri; 11am-3pm Sat,
Sun. **No credit cards. Map** p402 O8.
Part of a larger set-up of theatre and dance spaces
(and a great café), the Jerwood had an erratic visual
arts presence until recently. Now various awards are
grouped under the banner Jerwood Visual Arts: in
spring, Jerwood Contemporary Painters, summer's
Jerwood Contemporary Makers and the Jerwood
Drawing Prize each autumn.

Lisson

*52-54 Bell Street, Marylebone, NW1 5DA
(7724 2739, www.lissongallery.com). Edgware
Road tube.* **Open** 10am-6pm Mon-Fri; 11am-5pm
Sat. **No credit cards. Map** p393 E5.
Founded in 1967 by Nicholas Logsdail, the Lisson
continues to be a superb platform for major interna-
tional names such as Marina Abramovic and Dan
Graham, not forgetting the trio of British sculptors
that grew up with the gallery: Anish Kapoor, Tony
Cragg and Richard Wentworth.
Other locations 29 Bell Street, Marylebone,
NW1 5BY (7535 7350).

Pilar Corrias

*54 Eastcastle Street, Fitzrovia, W1W 8EF
(7323 7000, www.pilarcorrias.com). Oxford
Circus tube.* **Open** 10am-6pm Mon-Fri; 11am-
6pm Sat. **No credit cards. Map** p416 V1.
Formerly a director at the Lisson and Haunch of
Venison (for both, *see above*), Corrias opened this Rem
Koolhaas-designed gallery in 2008 with a giant aluminium Christmas tree by Philippe Parreno. Other
artists include Charles Avery and Shahzia Sikander.

Gagosian.

★ Sadie Coles HQ

*69 South Audley Street, Piccadilly, W1K 2QZ
(7493 8611, www.sadiecoles.com). Oxford Circus
or Piccadilly Circus tube.* **Open** 10am-6pm Tue-
Sat. **No credit cards. Map** p416 U3.

Coles represents some of the hippest artists from
both sides of the Atlantic: her programme includes
work by Raymond Pettibon, Matthew Barney and
Andrea Zittel. After leaving her original HQ in
Heddon Street (first opened in 1997), she added a second space in New Burlington Place, which opened
in late 2010 with a show by Swiss bad-boy installation artist Urs Fischer.

Other locations Sadie Coles, 4 New Burlington
Place, Mayfair, W1S 2HS (7493 8611).

Showroom

*63 Penfold Street, Marylebone, NW8 8PQ
(7724 4300, www.theshowroom.org). Edgware
Road tube.* **Open** noon-6pm Wed-Sat. **No credit
cards. Map** p393 E4.

In 2009, 25 years after its inception, the Showroom
moved into these new premises. Its mission remains
the same: to support artists at pivotal stages of their
careers, often by offering them debut solo shows.
The actual works range across all forms of contemporary art practice.

Sprüth Magers London

*7A Grafton Street, Mayfair, W1S 4EJ (7408
1613, www.spruethmagers.com). Green Park
tube.* **Open** 10am-6pm Tue-Sat. **No credit
cards. Map** p398 H7.

Fischli & Weiss, Cindy Sherman, John Baldessari
and Robert Morris are just a few of the major-league
international artists that have shown in this handsome gallery housed in an 18th-century building just
off Old Bond Street.

Stuart Shave/Modern Art

*23-25 Eastcastle Street, Fitzrovia, W1W 8DF
(7299 7950, www.modernart.net). Oxford Circus
tube.* **Open** 11am-6pm Tue-Sat. **No credit
cards. Map** p416 V1.

This always on-trend gallery shows the likes of
Jonathan Meese, Matthew Monahan, Eva Rothschild
and Barry McGee, as well as group shows including
artists such as Katy Moran.

INSIDE TRACK THURSDAYS

Many smaller galleries close during the
early part of the week, so focus visits on
a Thursday, the most popular day for
private views. **Time Out First Thursdays**
sees hundreds of East End galleries stay
open late on the first Thursday of every
month, with many holding special events.
For details, see www.firstthursdays.co.uk.

★ White Cube

*25-26 Mason's Yard, St James's, SW1Y 6BU
(7930 5373, www.whitecube.com). Green Park
tube.* **Open** 10am-6pm Tue-Sat. **Credit** AmEx,
MC, V. **Map** p416 V5.

Jay Jopling's famous gallery reasserted its West End
presence with the opening of this purpose-built
5,000sq ft space, which maintained his familiar
warehouse aesthetic. White Cube Hoxton Square
still runs an excellent programme of shows by the
gallery's expanding stable, but this larger space
mostly focuses on A-list Brits, such as Tracey Emin,
Jake and Dinos Chapman, and Antony Gormley.

Other locations 48 Hoxton Square, Shoreditch,
N1 6PB (7930 5373).

North London

★ Camden Arts Centre

*Arkwright Road, Finchley, NW3 6DG (7472
5500, www.camdenartscentre.org). Finchley
Road tube or Finchley Road & Frognal rail.*
Open 10am-6pm Tue, Thur-Sun; 10am-9pm
Wed. **Credit** MC, V.

Under the directorship of Jenni Lomax, Camden Arts
Centre has eclipsed larger venues. The annual artist-
curated shows – by, among others, Tacita Dean –
have been among the most memorable in recent history. The Centre also hosts a comprehensive programme of talks, events and workshops and boasts
a good bookshop and a great café, which opens on
to a surprisingly tranquil garden.

★ Museum of Everything

*Corner of Regent's Park Road & Sharpleshall
Street, Primrose Hill, NW1 (www.museumof
everything.com). Chalk Farm tube.* **Open** 11am-
6pm Wed-Sun. **No credit cards. Map** p404 W2.

Re-emerging after a successful opening in 2009 and
an itinerant series of exhibitions since then (Tate
Modern, then Turin… you know, all local venues),
this quirky former dairy hidden in leafy Primrose
Hill houses a changing display of naïve, outsider and
folk art. Taking its core from the collection of film-
maker James Brett it has also featured a display of
Peter Blake's trinkets and curios, as well as Mr
Potter's Museum of Curiosities, which contains the
bizarre work of this amateur Victorian taxidermist.

Parasol Unit

*14 Wharf Road, Islington, N1 7RW (7490 7373,
www.parasol-unit.org). Angel tube or Old Street
tube/rail.* **Open** 10am-6pm Tue-Sat; noon-5pm
Sun. **No credit cards. Map** p400 P3.

This former warehouse (adjacent to Victoria Miro) has
been beautifully converted by architect Claudio
Silverstrin into exhibition spaces on two floors and a
reading area. It shows work by emerging and major-
league figures, often international (Tabaimo from
Japan, Finnish film artist Eija-Liisa Ahtila and
Parisian-Algerian Adel Abdessemed have all shown).

Museum of Everything.

ARTS & ENTERTAINMENT

★ Victoria Miro

*14 & 16 Wharf Road, Islington, N1 7RW
(7336 8109, www.victoria-miro.com). Angel
tube or Old Street tube/rail.* **Open** 10am-6pm
Tue-Sat. **Credit** MC, V. **Map** p400 P3.
A visit to this canalside, Victorian former furniture
factory rarely disappoints. High-calibre artists on
show include Chris Ofili, Peter Doig and Doug
Aitken. The gallery expanded into no.14 a few years
ago, enlarging the space to allow it to show special
projects such as Grayson Perry's massive 'The
Walthamstow Tapestry'.

★ Zabludowicz Collection

*176 Prince of Wales Road, Chalk Farm, NW5
3PT (7428 8940, www.zabludowiczcollection.
com). Chalk Farm tube or Kentish Town West
rail.* **Open** noon-6pm Thur-Sun. **Credit** MC, V.
Map p404 W1.
Launched in September 2007 as Project Space 176,
this former Methodist chapel – a remarkable neoclassical building that makes a superb setting for
art exhibitions – holds three shows a year, enabling
artists to create experimental new work and curators to build exhibitions around the Collection's
global emerging art in all media.

East London

Hoxton Square, **Cambridge Heath Road**
and **Vyner Street** are all good places to start
an exploration of east London's galleries, but
it's worth planning your visit carefully (*see left*
Inside Track). For grass-roots alternatives,
head further east to **Hackney Wick**, where
you'll find a cluster of studios and galleries,
generally ad hoc, showing new art in former

industrial buildings almost in the shadow of the
Olympic Park. **Elevator** (www.elevatorgallery.
co.uk) is one of the longer established ones.

Approach

*1st floor, 47 Approach Road, Bethnal Green,
E2 9LY (8983 3878, www.theapproach.co.uk).
Bethnal Green tube or Cambridge Heath rail.*
Open noon-6pm Wed-Sun. **No credit cards.**
Occupying an elegant former pub function room, the
Approach has a reputation for showing both emerg-
ing artists and more established names such as John
Stezaker, Rezi van Lankveld and Germaine Kruip.
The downstairs pub has great real ales.

Calvert 22

*22 Calvert Avenue, Shoreditch, E2 7JP (7613
2141, www.calvert22.org). Shoreditch High Street
rail.* **Open** 10am-6pm Wed-Sat; 11am-5pm Sun.
No credit cards. **Map** p401 R4.
London's first not-for-profit foundation specialising
in art from Russia and Central and Eastern Europe.
Founded by Russian art collector and economist
Nonna Materkova, the gallery presents five curated
exhibitions a year.

Chisenhale Gallery

*64 Chisenhale Road, Bow, E3 5QZ (8981 4518,
www.chisenhale.org.uk). Bethnal Green or bus 8,
277, D6.* **Open** 1-6pm Wed-Sun. **No credit
cards**. **Map** p401 R4.
The Chisenhale commissions up to five shows a year
by emerging artists. Famous works such as Rachel
Whiteread's *Ghost*, the concrete cast of a house, and
Cornelia Parker's exploded shed *Cold Dark Matter*
were Chisenhale commissions. They cover everything from sculpture to sound installations.

Flowers

82 Kingsland Road, Hoxton, E2 8DP (7920 7777, www.flowerseast.com). Hoxton rail. **Open** 10am-6pm Tue-Sat. **Credit** AmEx, MC, V. **Map** p401 E3.

Flowers East might not garner the press attention of some of its neighbours, but it's an admired East End institution. It represents more than 50 artists, including Patrick Hughes, Derek Hirst and Nicola Hicks. The main gallery also houses Flowers Graphics; and there's a smaller West End space. **Other locations** 21 Cork Street, Mayfair, W1S 3LZ (7439 7766).

Herald Street

2 Herald Street, Bethnal Green, E2 6JT (7168 2566, www.heraldst.com). Bethnal Green tube/ rail. **Open** 11am-6pm Tue-Fri; noon-6pm Sat, Sun. **No credit cards**. **Map** p401 R4.

Herald Street shows fashionable young things such as Oliver Payne and Nick Relph, as well as work by a slightly older generation. In 2010, the gallery even imported the Armory Show NYC. You might find anything here from genre-crossing sculpture to an exhibition of sparky drawings.

★ Matt's Gallery

42-44 Copperfield Road, Mile End, E3 4RR (8983 1771, www.mattsgallery.org). Mile End tube. **Open** noon-6pm Wed-Sun; or by appointment. **No credit cards**. **Map** p401 R4.

Few galleries in town are as well respected as Matt's, named after founder/director Robin Klassnik's dog. Since 1979, Klassnik has supported artists in their often ambitious ideas for projects. Richard Wilson's sump oil installation *20:50* (now in the Saatchi Gallery; *see p140*) and Mike Nelson's *Coral Reef* were both Matt's commissions.

★ Maureen Paley

21 Herald Street, Bethnal Green, E2 6JT (7729 4112, www.maureenpaley.com). Bethnal Green tube/rail. **Open** 11am-6pm Wed-Sun; or by appointment. **No credit cards**. **Map** p401 R4.

Maureen Paley opened her East End gallery long before the area became the art hive it is today. The gallery represents high-profile artists such as Turner Prize winners Wolfgang Tillmans and Gillian Wearing, plus Kaye Donachie and sculptor Rebecca Warren.

MOT International

54 Regents Studios, 8 Andrew's Road, Hackney, E8 4QN (7923 9561, www.motinternational.org). Bethnal Green tube or Cambridge Heath rail. **Open** 11am-6pm Wed-Sun; or by appointment. **No credit cards**. **Map** p401 R4.

Successfully making the transition from artist-run space to commercial enterprise, Chris Hammond's gallery shows rapidly emerging names including Amanda Beech, Clunie Reid and Simon Bedwell, in a fifth-floor space overlooking Regent's Canal.

★ Raven Row

56 Artillery Lane, Spitalfields, E1 7LS (7377 4300, www.ravenrow.org). Liverpool Street tube/rail. **Open** 11am-6pm Wed-Sun. **No credit cards**. **Map** p401 R5.

Occupying two stunning 18th-century buildings, Raven Row opened in 2009 with a survey of proto-Pop artist Ray Richardson, and quickly set itself up as the non-profit space to watch. The beautifully restored rooms have been used for cracking shows by David Hullfish Bailey and Nils Norman, and a reappraisal of Eduardo Paolozzi's work for *Ambit* magazine. There's also a residency programme, with flats upstairs for the artists and curators.

Festivals Art & Design

What not to miss this year.

The main event is the **Frieze Art Fair** (mid Oct, www.friezeartfair.com), which sees over 150 of the world's best galleries descend on Regent's Park for four days of trading and schmoozing. Many other smaller fairs occupy the same time-frame, including newcomer **Sunday** (www.sunday-fair.com), featuring younger galleries, and **Multiplied** (www.multipliedartfair.com), which caters for limited editions and prints.

Spring sees **COLLECT** (6-9 May, www.craftscouncil.org.uk), a contemporary applied arts fair at the Saatchi Gallery (*see p140*). The stunts and serious-minded discussions of the biennial **London Festival of Architecture** (www.lfa2010.org) won't

return until summer 2012, but the week-long **London Design Festival** (mid Sept, www.londondesignfestival.com) will be happening in 2011: it's a monster annual celebration of architecture and design.

May and June see London's many art schools present their degree shows. Among the best are the two shows staged by the **Royal College of Art** (www.rca.ac.uk): the first devoted to painting and photography (late May-early June), the second dedicated to design (late June-early July). Over at the Old Truman Brewery, just off Brick Lane, **Free Range** (www.free-range.org.uk) is an eight-week degree show bonanza in June and July, which features dozens of colleges.

▶ *Raven Row is one of a growing cadre of non-profit venues; others include Calvert 22 (see p305), the Parasol Unit (see p304) and the Zabludowicz Collection (see p305).*

Vilma Gold
6 Minerva Street, Bethnal Green, E2 9EH (7729 9888, www.vilmagold.com). Bethnal Green tube or Cambridge Heath rail. **Open** 11am-6pm Wed-Sun. **No credit cards. Map** p401 R4.
No longer the new kid on the block, Vilma Gold still attracts the cognoscenti who come for such fashionable fare as the neo-expressionist paintings of Sophie von Hellermann and the anti-heroic assemblages of Brian Griffiths, as well as work by international newcomers such as London-based sculptor Alexandre da Cunha.

Wilkinson Gallery
50-58 Vyner Street, Bethnal Green, E2 9DQ (8980 2662, www.wilkinsongallery.com). Bethnal Green tube or Cambridge Heath rail. **Open** 11am-6pm Wed-Sat; noon-6pm Sun; or by appointment. **No credit cards. Map** p401 R4.
Anthony and Amanda Wilkinson's gallery, the first purpose-built gallery in E2, dominates Vyner Street and has an international reputation for showing high-calibre artists including the German painters Thoralf Knobloch and Matthias Weischer. Quirkier fare can be found in the first-floor project space.

South London

Corvi-Mora/Greengrassi
1A Kempsford Road, Kennington, SE11 4NU (Corvi-Mora 7840 9111, Greengrassi 7840 9101, www.corvi-mora.com, www.greengrassi. com). Kennington tube. **Open** 11am-6pm Tue-Sat. **No credit cards.**
These two galleries share a building that comprises a warehouse space on the ground floor and a smaller gallery upstairs. Greengrassi's artists include painters Lisa Yuskavage and Tomma Abts. Jim Isermann, Tomoaki Suzuki and Dee Ferris are part of Corvi-Mora's eclectic stable.

South London Gallery
65 Peckham Road, Peckham, SE5 8UH (7703 9799, www.southlondongallery.org). Oval tube then bus 436, or Elephant & Castle tube/rail then bus 12, 171. **Open** 11am-6pm Tue, Thur-Sun; 11am-9pm Sun. **Credit** MC, V.
See p165 **Artistic Revival.**

ARCHITECTURE & DESIGN

Architectural Association
36 Bedford Square, Fitzrovia, WC1B 3ES (7887 4000, www.aaschool.net). Tottenham Court Road tube. **Open** 10am-7pm Mon-Fri; 10am-5pm Sat. **Credit** MC, V. **Map** p397 K5.

INSIDE TRACK BUILT TO LAST

New London Architecture (26 Store Street, WC1E 7BT, 7636 4044, www.new londonarchitecture.org) combines excellent temporary exhibitions on all aspects of public design and architecture, from cycle parking to pod hotels, with an impressive 40ft-wide model of London with all the new buildings for which planning has been granted shown on it.

Talks, events, exhibitions: three good reasons for visiting these elegant premises. If that isn't enough, the café and a smart little bookshop should clinch the deal. During the summer months, the gallery shows work by students graduating from the AA School in a display that often spills into the square.

Royal Institute of British Architects
66 Portland Place, Marylebone, W1B 1AD (7307 3888, 7631 0467 café, www.architecture.com). Great Portland Street tube. **Open** 10am-5pm Mon-Sat. **Café** 8am-3pm Mon-Fri. **Credit** MC, V. **Map** p396 H5.
Temporary exhibitions such as the annual Housing Design Awards are held in RIBA's appropriately handsome, Grade II-listed, 1930s deco headquarters, which houses a bookshop, a first-floor café and one of the finest architectural libraries in the world. RIBA also hosts compelling lectures.

PHOTOGRAPHY

Michael Hoppen Gallery
3 Jubilee Place, Chelsea, SW3 3TD (7352 4499, www.michaelhoppengallery.com). Sloane Square tube. **Open** 10.30am-6pm Mon-Fri; 10.30am-5pm Sat; or by appointment. **Credit** MC, V. **Map** p395 E11.
This three-storey space shows a mixture of classic vintage photography by the likes of William Klein and Garry Winogrand, and contemporary work, including Japanese photographer Nobuyoshi Araki.

★ Photographers' Gallery
16-18 Ramillies Street, Soho, W1A 1AU (0845 262 1618, www.photonet.org.uk). Oxford Circus tube. **Open** 11am-6pm Tue, Wed, Sat; 11am-8pm Thur, Fri; noon-6pm Sun. **Credit** AmEx, DC, MC, V. **Map** p416 U2.
Home of the annual £30,000 Deutsche Börse International Photography Prize, this is London's largest gallery devoted to the art of the camera, hosting great shows and related events. In late 2008, it moved, along with its café and shop, to this transitionary space. It is being completely redeveloped through to late 2011, but will continue to programme pop-up shows and events around the Soho area.

Gay & Lesbian

Where the out go out.

Sydney's got the sun, New York City and San Francisco have the history and Rio's got the bodies, but – despite some grumbling among spoilt locals – London's got the buzz. Whatever your taste in music, from thunderous indie to thumping disco, you'll find a gay club that specialises in it, on a nightlife scene that runs around the clock and throughout the week. Add in an array of cabaret nights and literary salons, a handful of cafés and restaurants, a major gay and lesbian film festival and the ever-popular annual Pride celebration, and there should be something to keep you busy.

THE GAY SCENE IN LONDON

Roughly speaking, London's gay scene is split into three distinct zones: **Soho**, **Vauxhall** and **east London**. Each of these three districts has its own character: in a nutshell, Soho is the most mainstream, Vauxhall is the most decadent and east London is the most outré.

Centred on Old Compton Street, the Soho scene continues to attract the crowds. Luvvies take in a singalong at the **Green Carnation**, fit freaks work out at **Sweatbox** and everyone else mills around the plethora of gay-slanted bars and cafés. And just down the road, close to Charing Cross station, sits the legendary **Heaven**, home to **G-A-Y**. If your dream has always been to see Madonna or Kylie in a club, here's your chance – the list of singers who've done live PAs here reads like a *Who's Who* of squeal-tastic gay pop icons.

Down south, Vauxhall is more hedonistic. You could arrive in London on a Friday evening and dance non-stop here for an entire weekend before flying out of town again. But it's not all

about going wild: venues such as the **RVT** and the Eagle (home to the superb **Horse Meat Disco**) draw loyal local followings.

The most alternative and creative of the capital's queer scenes is in east London. In the likes of the **George & Dragon** and the **Dalston Superstore**, you'll be rubbing shoulders with fashion and music's movers and shakers, but some club nights in Vauxhall can get raunchy. The monthly **Hard On** (www.hardonclub.co.uk) is the top pick on the calendar for lovers of fetish and leather.

For lesbians, clubby **Candy Bar** (*see p310*) is the key venue. For bars, **Green** (*see p313*) and Monday or Wednesday at **Retro** (*see p314*) are good choices. **First Out** (*see right*) café is jammed with gals, and the women-only **Glass Bar**, having survived threats of closure, is back in vogue. New stand-alone nights pop up all the time, but Duckie and Bar Wotever at **RVT** (*see p310*), Bird Club at the **Bethnal Green Working Men's Club** (*see p331*), exclusive Code at **Green Carnation** (*see p313*), Ruby Tuesdays at **Ku** (*see p310*) and Twat Boutique

Keen to cut to the chase? **Chariots** (*see p314*) is the sauna chain of choice, although **Vault 139** (*see p314*) and **Pleasuredrome** (Arch 124, Alaska Street, Waterloo, SE1 8XE, 7633 9194, www.pleasuredrome.com) also have their followers. Most regular bars don't have backrooms,

INSIDE TRACK ONE, TWO... KU

In 2010, a new satellite **Ku** (*see p310*) opened around the corner in Frith Street. Owned by Gary Henshawe, who kickstarted the gay Soho scene back in the early 1990s, it has three storeys, with a loungey area on top. Afternoon tea is served from noon to five – very civilised.

at **Dalston Superstore** (*see p313*) are recommended. Over the last decade, **100% Babe** in the basement at the Roxy (3-5 Rathbone Place, Fitzrovia, W1P 1DA, 7636 1598, www.theroxy.co.uk) has become an institution. Happening every Sunday night before a bank holiday, expect popular house music, feel-good floorfillers and a party mood.

Craving queer culture that's a little more cerebral? Try out London's new breed of queer salons, essentially literary or cultural get-togethers – events from the **House of Homosexual Culture** (on Facebook), **Tart Women's Salon** (www.tartsalon.co.uk/home.php) and **Polari** (www.myspace.com/polarigaysalon) are all recommended.

RESTAURANTS & CAFES

More or less every café and restaurant in London welcomes gay custom. Certainly nowhere in or around Soho will so much as bat an eyelid at you and your other half having a romantic dinner; **J Sheekey** (*see p216*), the **Wolseley** (*see p220*) and **Arbutus** (*see p216*) have particularly enthusiastic gay followings. For thirtysomething lesbians, there are fun cocktail evenings amid the mom-and-pop Italian vintage decor of **Star at Night** (22 Great Chapel Street, Soho, W1F 8FR, 7494 2488, www.thestaratnight.com, open 6-11.30pm Tue-Sat) – by day, it's just an old greasy spoon.

Balans
60 Old Compton Street, Soho, W1D 4UG (7439 2183, www.balans.co.uk). Leicester Square or Piccadilly Circus tube. **Open** 8am-5am Mon-Thur; 8am-6am Fri, Sat; 8am-1am Sun. **Admission** £2.50 after midnight Mon-Sat. **Credit** AmEx, MC, V. **Map** p416 W3.
The gay café-restaurant of choice for many years, Balans is all about location, location, location (plus hot waiters, decent food and ridiculous opening hours). Situated across from Compton's bar and next door to Clone Zone, it's the beating heart of the Soho scene. The nearby Balans Café (no.34) serves a shorter version of the menu. Both are open almost all night and are good for a post-club bite. **Other locations** throughout the city.

First Out
52 St Giles High Street, Covent Garden, WC2H 8LH (7240 8042, www.firstoutcafebar.com). Tottenham Court Road tube. **Open** 9am-11pm Mon-Sat; 10am-10.30pm Sun. **Credit** MC, V. **Map** p416 X1.
This was London's first homosexual café when it opened back in 1986. It still packs in a crowd, mostly of lesbians these days. A busy noticeboard, friendly service and yummy vegetarian food give the place a community feel that's unusual in the West End, and the cocktails and beer makes it a convivial meeting place for pre-club drinks.

NIGHTCLUBS

London's club scene is particularly subject to change: venues close, nights end and new soirées start. Check *Time Out* magazine or www.timeout.com for details on what's on when you're here. In particular, look for one-off nights from **Bastard Batty Bass** (www.battybass.com)

Candy Bar. *See p310.*

and **Trailer Trash** (www.clubtrailertrash.com). For arty cabaret, check out **Bethnal Green Working Men's Club** (*see p331*).

If you want to stay up all night and all day, head to Vauxhall. At **Fire** (South Lambeth Road, SW8 1UQ, www.fireclub.co.uk), nights such as Gravity, Later and Orange keep dancers furnished with funky house from Friday morning through until Tuesday. Other clubs in the area include **Union** and **Area**, on the Albert Embankment (no.66 and nos.67-68).

★ Candy Bar

4 Carlisle Street, Soho, W1D 3BJ (7287 5041, www.candybarsoho.com). Tottenham Court Road tube. **Open** 4-11.30pm Mon-Thur; 2pm-2am Fri, Sat; 5-11pm Sun. **Admission** free; £4 after 9pm Fri, Sat. **Credit** MC, V. **Map** p416 W2.

Opened in 1996, the Candy Bar was London's first full-time drinking den for lesbians. It made a splash with its location – in Soho, the heart of boystown – and entertainment: female strippers and lapdances for lesbians. There is still stripping on the first Friday and third Saturday of the month – but you can do your own dancing in the basement (DJs spin everything from house and R&B to electro and old school). The crowd varies from lipstick lesbian to butch, from student to professional. The three-storey bar is being refurbished, with an upstairs cocktail lounge and kitchen on the cards. *Photo p309.*

Club Kali

Dome, 1 Dartmouth Park Hill, Tufnell Park, N19 5QQ (7272 8153, www.clubkali.com). Tufnell Park tube. **Open** 10pm-3am 3rd Fri of mth. **Admission** £8; £5 reductions. **No credit cards.**

The world's largest LGBT Asian dance club offers Bollywood, bhangra, Arabic tunes, R&B and dance classics spun by DJs Ritu, Riz & Qurra.

Exilio Latin Dance Club

Guy's Bar, Boland House, St Thomas Street, Bankside, SE1 9RT (07931 374391, www.exilio. co.uk). London Bridge tube/rail. **Open** 9.30pm-2.30pm every other Sat. **Admission** £5 before 11pm; £8 after 11pm. **No credit cards. Map** p399 M6.

This is London's principal queer Latino spot, with girls and guys getting together for merengue, salsa, cumbia and reggaeton.

Heaven

Underneath the Arches, Villiers Street, Covent Garden, WC2N 6NG (7930 2020, www.heaven-london.com). Embankment tube or Charing Cross tube/rail. **Open** hrs vary. **Admission** prices vary. **No credit cards. Map** p416 Y5.

London's most famous gay club is a bit like *Les Misérables* – it's camp, it's full of history and tourists love it. Popcorn (Mon) has long been a good bet, but it's really all about G-A-Y (Thur-Sat). For years,

divas with an album to flog (Madonna, Kylie, Girls Aloud) have turned up to play here at the weekend.

★ Horse Meat Disco

Eagle London, 349 Kennington Lane, Vauxhall, SE11 5QY (7793 0903, www.horsemeatdisco. co.uk). Vauxhall tube/rail. **Open** 8pm-3am Sun. **Admission** £6. **No credit cards.**

Not your average gay club. Skinny Soho boys and fashionistas rub shoulders with scally lads and bears in a traditional old boozer. The hip soundtrack is an inspired mix of Studio 54, New York punk and new wave. As one *Time Out* critic put it: 'if you ever wished you could hang out in a club like the one in *Beyond the Valley of the Dolls* or *Scarface*, you'll love Horse Meat Disco'. Special events include the 'Vauxhall is Gurning' Vogue Ball. A must.

▶ *When Horse Meat isn't in residence, the Eagle is a hub for those wishing to try a bit of leather without a strict dress code.*

★ Ku

30 Lisle Street, Chinatown, WC2H 7BA (7437 4303, www.ku-bar.co.uk). Leicester Square tube. **Open** *Bar* noon-11.30pm daily. *Club* 10pm-3am daily. **Credit** MC, V. **Map** p416 X3.

Voted London's best central gay bar by the readers of *Boyz* and *Pink Paper*, Ku must be doing something right. Formerly known as West Central, it has morphed from a mediocre space into a popular bar and club that offers everything from film nights to comedy. The sheer variety of club nights (held in the basement) is impressive, from Sandra D's Ruby Tuesdays for lesbians to the poptastic O-Zone on Fridays, hosted by veteran drag DJ Dusty O.

▶ *The nearest rival to G-A-Y Bar (see p313), Ku is the first gay venue you reach after Leicester Square tube, so it gets a lot of passing trade.*

Popstarz

The Den, 18 West Central Street, Covent Garden, WC1A 1JJ (7240 1864, www.popstarz.org). Holborn or Tottenham Court Road tube. **Open** 10pm-4am Fri. **Admission** free before 11pm, then £5-£8. **Credit** MC, V. **Map** p416 Y1.

What G-A-Y is to cheese, Popstarz is to indie. It's studenty, drunken, attitude-free and popular – so popular, in fact, that the club has spawned imitators from New York to Paris. There are also occasional PAs from in-demand acts.

★ RVT

Royal Vauxhall Tavern, 372 Kennington Lane, Vauxhall, SE11 5HY (7820 1222, www.rvt.org. uk). Vauxhall tube/rail. **Open** 7pm-midnight Mon, Wed, Thur; 6pm-midnight Tue; 7pm-2am Fri; 9pm-2am Sat; 2pm-midnight Sun. **Admission** £5-£7. **Credit** MC, V.

This pub-turned-legendary-gay-venue, a much-loved stalwart on the scene for years, operates an anything-goes booking policy. The most famous fixture is

ARTS & ENTERTAINMENT

Get the Look

How to dress for Dalston.

Dalston Superstore. *See p313.*

ARTS & ENTERTAINMENT

At some of the cooler clubs on the gay scene – Sunday's Wet Yourself at **Fabric** (*see p329*), Hannah Holland's forward-thinking **Bastard Batty Bass** (www.batty bass.com), anything at **Dalston Superstore** (*see p313*) or its surrounding nexus of hip, DIY ethos clubs – you can expect to see mind-blowing outfits. Fashion students show up having spent a week perfecting their David Bowie make-up, models wear 'something they found at Beyond Retro' (*see p264*), and impossibly hip-looking kids rock looks they invented earlier that night.

However, the presence on the scene of such style mavens doesn't mean you need to bring a whole suitcase just for clubbing. For a city as wound-up as London, nightlife fashions are surprisingly relaxed, with a focus on individuality and DIY. The ultimate fashion faux pas is turning up in a 'look' ripped off from a shop-window mannequin or – worse – Kate Moss. Turn up in head-to-toe Topshop and people will cringe. But turn up in your mother's stonewashed jeans, customised and patched by you, and people will (discreetly) take notes.

The first thing to remember is that most venues are hot. If you leave a coat with a cloakroom, put your coat-check ticket in your purse or wallet and not in your pocket, where it will get damp, fall apart and leave you stuck at the club until everyone has left so you can claim the last remaining jacket.

Skinny jeans on boys and girls still reign supreme, from black to acid stonewash via faded grunge, travel-unfriendly white and good ol' blue. Couple them with a vest or cool T-shirt. Boys? Not too baggy (this isn't Brooklyn). Girls? Draped off a shoulder, accessorised with a chain-strap handbag.

The 1980s are still an influence, but the cool kids have been working the early 1990s of late: from music to plenty of gold bling, dressed head-to-toe in black. Don't even think about nu-rave gear, best described as what would happen if someone shut their eyes, rifled through the trends from '85 to '95 and put them all on at once.

For girls, heels that work with jeans work just as well with a dress (and the dress works just as well with flats). Comfortable ballerina pumps or Converse are reliable options. For boys, trainers ('80s Nike Airs, perhaps) or a pair of brogues (for snappy dressers) should go down well. Add colour-rimmed sunglasses and some oversized jewellery from the market.

Make-up won't take up much space. In fact, swing by MAC at the airport and get them to suggest a makeover: bright red Lady Courage lipstick, perhaps; gold over outer eyelid and upper cheekbone; or, simply, plenty of kohl. And finally, pack some gel for that directional haircut, spiky, flat-top or geeky side parting.

Ultimately, confidence is key. No one here really knows what to wear or how to wear it. But there are no excuses for failing to own that dancefloor.

Saturday's queer performance night Duckie (www.duckie.co.uk), with Amy Lamé hosting performances at midnight that range from strip cabaret to porn puppets; Sunday's Dame Edna Experience drag show, from 5pm, is also essential, drawing quasi-religious devotees. The aim is always to please the crowd of regulars, reliably vocal with their feedback. Punters verge on the bear, but the main dress code is 'no attitude'. The monthly Kimono Krush night packs in arty bears and bearded trannies.

Work!

Hidden, 100 Tinworth Street, Vauxhall, SE11 5EQ (7820 6613, www.heaven-london.com). Vauxhall tube/rail. **Open** 11pm-4am Wed. **Admission** £6; £1-£3 reductions or with flyer before 12.30am. **Credit** (bar) MC, V. **Map** p399 L11.

Patrick Lilley's new night has brought a touch of urban music to Vauxhall. Hosted by Fredi Dimanche and the vision of loveliness that is Le Gateau Chocolat, Work! offers music to suit (almost) all tastes. DJs including Big John, Jeffrey Hinton, Biggy C, Freddie Thomas and Tuomo Fox play the best in pop, funky bashment and old school.

XXL

The Arches, 51-53 Southwark Street, Borough, SE1 1RU (7403 4001, www.xxl-london.com). London Bridge tube/rail. **Open** 10pm-3am Wed; 10pm-6am Sat. **Admission** £3-£12. **No credit cards**. **Map** p402 P8.

The world's biggest club for bears and their friends, XXL is nirvana for chubbier, hairier and blokier gay men and their twinky admirers. True to its name, the venue is bigger than average, with two dancefloors, two bars and even an outdoor beer garden.

PUBS & BARS

Unless otherwise stated, the pubs and bars listed here are open to both gay men and lesbians. The bar at **Ku** (*see p310*) is another good option if you're in the West End.

Barcode Vauxhall

Arch 69, Goding Street, Vauxhall, SE11 4AD (7582 4180, www.bar-code.co.uk). Vauxhall tube. **Open** 4pm-1am Mon-Wed; 4pm-2am Thur; 4pm-5am Fri; 4pm-7am Sat; 5pm-1am Sun. **Admission** £4 after 10pm Fri, Sat. **Credit** MC, V.

Prior to the arrival of BCV, Vauxhall was mostly for clubbing, with pre-dance drinks to be enjoyed anywhere-else-but. Now those pre-dancing punters are joined by folks just after a drink at this massive, lavish venue, which attracts a blokey-ish crowd despite its shiny surfaces.

▶ *BCV's forerunner Barcode, off Shaftesbury Avenue, hosts the mostly gay and thoroughly excellent Comedy Camp night; see p292.*

Box

32-34 Monmouth Street, Covent Garden, WC2H 9HA (7240 5828, www.boxbar.com). Leicester Square tube. **Open** noon-11pm Mon-Thur; noon-midnight Fri, Sat; noon-10.30pm Sun. **Credit** MC, V. **Map** p416 X2.

Muscle boys and theatre luvvies adore this place, set near the historic Seven Dials monument, a popular perching point for Sunday afternoon drinkers.

▶ *Box is just opposite Dress Circle, a music shop specialising in Broadway and West End musicals. Just so you know.*

Festivals Gay & Lesbian

Key dates in the queer year.

Pride London (www.pridelondon.org, *pictured*) remains popular each June, perhaps more for the street party in a traffic-free Soho than for the long-standing parade from Oxford Street to Victoria Embankment – these days, it seems to be as much about the corporate quest for the pink pound than making a political point. A two-week cultural festival precedes the big day. **Soho Pride** (www.sohopride.net) sees the same West End streets overrun in late summer. In Regent's Park, **Black Pride** (www.ukblackpride.org.uk), a queer alternative to the Notting Hill Carnival (*see p282*) – which still, sadly, has zero gay presence – continues to grow every year. In spring, there's the annual **London Lesbian & Gay Film Festival** (*see p301*

Festivals), with an emphasis on edgier fare in the wake of *Brokeback Mountain*. Also worth checking out is July's **London Literature Festival** (*see p282*), which often hosts gay-oriented readings and talks.

★ Dalston Superstore
117 Kingland High Street, Dalston, E8 2PB
(7254 2273). Dalston Kingsland rail. **Open**
noon-2am Mon-Fri; 11am-2am Sat, Sun. **Credit**
AmEx, MC, V.
The opening of this gay arts space-cum-bar a couple of years back cemented Dalston's status as the
final frontier of the East End's gay scene. Come during the day for the café grub, Wi-Fi and art exhibitions on the walls; at night, you can expect queues
for an impressive roster of guest DJs spinning anything from garage to pop. *Photo p311.*

Freedom Bar
66 Wardour Street, Soho, W1F OTA (7734 0071,
www.freedombarsoho.com). Leicester Square or
Piccadilly Circus tube. **Open** 4pm-3am Mon-Fri;
2pm-3am Sat; 2-11pm Sun. **Admission** £5 after
10pm Fri, Sat. **Credit** MC, V. **Map** p416 W3.
A glitzy cocktail lounge and DJ bar, spread over two
floors. The glam ground-floor bar attracts a fashion-
conscious crowd, who sip cocktail among chandeliers, zebra-print banquettes and Venetian mirrors.
A few 'strays' and dolled-up gal pals add colour. The
large basement club and performance space hosts
weekday cabaret and gets busy with the gay party
crowd over the weekend.
▶ *In winter, the cosy alcoves of nearby retro-*
styled basement bar Friendly Society (no.79, 7434
3804) are great for cocktails and first dates.

G-A-Y Bar
30 Old Compton Street, Soho, W1D 4UR
(7494 2756, www.g-a-y.co.uk). Leicester Square
or Tottenham Court Road tube. **Open** noon-
midnight daily. **Credit** MC, V. **Map** p416 W3.
The G-A-Y night at Heaven (*see p310*) gets the
celebrity cameos, but this popular bar is still a shrine
to queer pop idols, with nightly drinks promos every
time they play a video from the current diva du jour.
There's also a women's bar in the basement, called
(delightfully) Girls Go Down – popular with flirty,
student lesbians, loathed by most older women.
▶ *G-A-Y bar's plush late-night sibling, G-A-Y*
Late, is round the corner on 5 Goslett Yard.

George & Dragon
2 Hackney Road, Bethnal Green, E2 7NS (7012
1100). Old Street tube/rail or Shoreditch High
Street rail. **Open** 6pm-midnight daily. **Credit**
MC, V. **Map** p401 S3.
The trendy location of this mini-pub ensures a
stylish and up-for-it clientele, while the decor (a wall-
mounted horse's head, creepy puppets, random
garbage) keeps the vibe fun. The music here – pop,
indie and accessible electronica – is often delivered
with a healthy sense of humour. Gay pub or not, this
is one of London's best boozers.
▶ *Just up the road is another east London gay*
institution: rough-round-the-edges watering hole
the Joiners Arms (116-118 Hackney Road).

Shadow Lounge. *See p314.*

Green
74 Upper Street, Islington, N1 0NY (7226 8895).
Angel tube. **Open** 5pm-midnight Mon-Wed; 5pm-
1am Thur; noon-2am Fri, Sat; noon-midnight Sun.
Credit MC, V. **Map** p400 O2.
For lesbians in fashionable Islington, the choice of
gay bars has always been limited. Then along came
the Green, with its Soho swagger: plush decor, cocktails and a sophisticated crowd. Refurbished, it now
boasts a contemporary aesthetic that still manages
to feel warm and cosy, with plenty of sofa seating.
It's narrow and can get congested on weekends –
when there are DJs – but you might just bump into
a pretty girl; around 20% of the crowd comprises
women, most of them older, local professionals.

Green Carnation
4-5 Greek Street, Soho, W1D 4DB (8123 4267,
www.greencarnationsoho.co.uk). Tottenham
Court Road tube. **Open** 4pm-12.30am Mon; 4pm-
12.30am Sun. **Admission** £5 after 11pm Mon-
Sat. **Credit** AmEx, MC, V. **Map** p416 W2.
The Green Carnation had a major refit a couple of
years back, to spectacular effect. Head upstairs for
cocktails in posh surroundings, with chandeliers
and piano music to heighten the senses and raise the
tone. There's a bar and a dancefloor downstairs. It's
a haven for West End Wendies, always on hand to
belt out a minor Sondheim in the wee hours.

Hoist
Arches 47B & 47C, South Lambeth Road,
Vauxhall, SW8 1RH (7735 9972, www.the
hoist.co.uk). Vauxhall tube/rail. **Open** 9pm-2am

ARTS & ENTERTAINMENT

Wed; 8pm-midnight 3rd Thur of mth; 10pm-3am Fri; 10pm-4am Sat; 2-8pm, 10pm-2am Sun. **Admission** £6 Fri, Sun; £6-£10 Sat; varies Thur. **No credit cards.**

One of two genuine leather bars in town, this club sits under the arches and makes the most of its underground and industrial setting. The Sunday afternoon event SBN (Stark Bollock Naked) gives you the tone; leather, uniforms, rubber, skinhead or boots are the dress code. Strictly no trainers.

KW4

77 Hampstead High Street, Hampstead, NW3 1RE (7435 5747, www.kingwilliamhampstead. co.uk). Hampstead tube or Hampstead Heath rail. **Open** 11am-11pm Mon-Thur; 11am-midnight Fri-Sun. **Credit** AmEx, MC, V.

The perfect evening ending (or beginning) to time spent on the heath, this fabulous old local – the King William IV, or King Willy to those with longer memories – attracts a very Hampstead crowd (read: well-off and ready for fun). On summer weekends, the cute little beer garden tends to fill up with a mix of gay and straight punters keen to put down their shopping bags. The pub is more popular with lesbians in summer too, as a stop-off after a dip in the heath's women's bathing pond.

Retro Bar

2 George Court, off the Strand, Covent Garden, WC2N 6HH (7839 8760). Charing Cross tube/rail. **Open** noon-11pm Mon-Fri; 2-11pm Sat; 5-10.30pm Sun. **Credit** AmEx, MC, V. **Map** p416 Y4.

Iggy Pop and Kate Bush are on the walls of this bar of the Popstarz ilk (*see p310*), where nights are dedicated to indie rock and Eurovision hits. The crowd here is mixed in every sense: gay/straight, gay/lesbian and scene queen/true eccentric. Quiz nights are popular, and the bar on occasion lets punters be the DJ – bring your iPod.

Shadow Lounge

5 Brewer Street, Soho, W1F 0RF (7287 7988, www.theshadowlounge.co.uk). Leicester Square

---

INSIDE TRACK CAB LORE

'**Vauxhall** has a big one-way system,' says Angela, a taxi driver for three years. 'After a club, make your way to the bridge, on the south side of the railway, for a ride to the northern side of the river. You'll catch cabs that have gone south and are coming back.' If you're in **Soho**, says Peter, another cabbie, 'Try and get on to Shaftesbury Avenue, Charing Cross Road or Oxford Street. The Soho sidestreets become very congested at night so not many drivers go there.'

---

or Piccadilly Circus tube. **Open** 10pm-3am Mon-Sat. **Admission** £5 after 11pm Mon-Thur; £10 after 11pm Fri, Sat. **Credit** AmEx, MC, V. **Map** p416 W3.

For celebrity sightings, suits, cuties and fancy boots, this is your West End venue. Expect a hefty cover charge and a queue on the weekends, but there's often a sublime atmosphere inside. *Photo p313.*

Yard

57 Rupert Street, Soho, W1V 7BJ (7437 2652, www.yardbar.co.uk). Piccadilly Circus tube. **Open** 4-11pm Mon-Thur; 11am-11.30pm Fri, Sat; 4-10.30pm Sun. **Credit** AmEx, MC, V. **Map** p416 W3.

Come for the courtyard in summer, stay for the Loft Bar in winter. This unpretentious bar offers a great open-air courtyard in a central location, attracting pretty boys, blokes and lesbians in equal measure.

► *A similar crowd can be found at Rupert Street (no.50), particularly popular with professional chaps after work or pre-partying at the weekends.*

SEX CLUBS & SAUNAS

Chariots

1 Fairchild Street, Shoreditch, EC2A 3NS (7247 5333, www.gaysauna.co.uk). Liverpool Street tube/rail or Shoreditch High Street rail. **Open** noon-9am daily. **Admission** £15; £13 reductions. **Credit** AmEx, MC, V. **Map** p401 R4.

Chariots is a sauna chain with outlets all over town. The original is this one in Shoreditch, the biggest and busiest, although not necessarily the best. That accolade probably goes to the one on the Albert Embankment at Vauxhall (nos.63-64, 7247 5333). The Waterloo branch (101 Lower Marsh, 7401 8484) has the biggest sauna in the UK.

Other locations throughout the city.

★ Sweatbox

Ramillies House, 1-2 Ramillies Street, Soho, W1F 7LN (3214 6014, www.sweatboxsoho.com). Oxford Circus tube. **Open** noon-2am Mon-Thur, Sun; noon-7am Fri, Sat. **Admission** £20 day pass; £15 spa only; £10 under-25s. **Credit** MC, V. **Map** p416 U2.

Sweatbox Soho looks more like a nightclub than a typical gym, with the sleek design offset by friendly staff. Though small, the space is well laid out, with a multigym and a free weights room. Qualified masseurs offer treatments. If that doesn't do the trick, there's a sauna downstairs.

Vault 139

139B-143 Whitfield Street, Fitzrovia, W1T 5EN (7388 5500, www.vault139.com). Warren Street tube. **Open** 4pm-1am Mon-Sat; 1pm-1am Sun. **No credit cards. Map** p396 J4.

Hidden away on a quiet back street, Vault 139 is London's most central cruise bar – and it's classy too, with plush sofas, TV screens and a DJ booth.

Music

London's music scene is lively, lovable and full of variety.

The current crop of London-based musicians seems to be unusually open-minded. There are classical nights in rock clubs and electronica gigs in classical auditoriums. Street-wise dubstep producers rub shoulders with free-jazz hippies. Grime artists rap with indie rockers, and classical conductors check out the nightclubs with drum 'n' bass DJs. There are few cities that can rival London's music scene for diversity and choice, with the city continuing to exert a magnetic pull on the world's top musicians in all genres. But as well as this prevailing mix-and-match aesthetic, passionate purists remain. With scenes fiercely dedicated to everything from cosy folk music to grubbily low-brow indie, the capital can service any musical fancy. Check *Time Out* magazine or www.timeout.com to get the weekly picture.

ARTS & ENTERTAINMENT

Classical & Opera

London's classical scene has never looked or sounded more current, with the **Southbank Centre** (*see p317*), the **Barbican Centre** (*see right*) and **Kings Place** (*see p316*) all working with strong programmes, and youthful music directors such as Edward Gardner at the **English National Opera** (*see p317*) keen to retain a spirit of adventure.

Tickets & information

Tickets for most classical and opera events are available direct from the venues, online or by phone. Always book ahead. Several venues, such as the Barbican and the Southbank Centre, operate standby schemes, offering unsold tickets at cut-rate prices just before the show.

CLASSICAL VENUES

In addition to the major venues below, you can hear what tomorrow's classical music might sound like at the city's music schools, which stage regular concerts by pupils and visiting professionals. Check the websites of the **Royal Academy of Music** (7873 7300, www.ram.ac.uk), the **Royal College of Music** (7589 3643, www.rcm.ac.uk), the **Guildhall School of Music & Drama** (7628 2571, www.gsmd.ac.uk) and **Trinity College of Music** (8305 4444, www.tcm.ac.uk).

★ Barbican Centre

Silk Street, the City, EC2Y 8DS (7638 4141 information, 7638 8891 tickets, www.barbican. org.uk). Barbican tube or Moorgate tube/rail. **Box office** 9am-8pm Mon-Sat; 11am-8pm Sun. **Tickets** £7-£32. **Credit** AmEx, MC, V. **Map** p400 P5.

Europe's largest multi-arts centre is easier to navigate than ever after a renovation. And the programming remains rich: alongside the London Symphony Orchestra, guided by principal conductor Valery Gergiev, and the BBC Symphony Orchestra, under Jiří Bělohlávek, the Great Performers series presents recitals from major musicians, and there's a laudable amount of contemporary classical music.

Cadogan Hall

5 Sloane Terrace, off Sloane Street, Chelsea, SW1X 9DQ (7730 4500, www.cadoganhall.com).

INSIDE TRACK
LISZT FOR LUNCH

London's classical music students are responsible for many of the fine lunchtime concerts that are held on many weekdays at historic churches around the City. Admission is usually free or by small donation only; there's a monthly guide published online at **www.cityevents.co.uk**.

Sloane Square tube. **Box office** 10am-8pm Mon-Sat. **Tickets** £10-£39. **Credit** MC, V. **Map** p398 G10.

Jazz groups and rock bands have been attracted by the acoustics in this renovated former Christian Science church. However, the programming at the austere yet comfortable 900-seat hall is dominated by classical music. The Royal Philharmonic Orchestra are resident; other orchestras also perform, and there's regular chamber music (including lunchtime concerts during the Proms).

★ Kings Place

90 York Way, King's Cross, N1 9AG (0844 264 0321, www.kingsplace.co.uk). King's Cross tube/rail. **Box office** noon-8pm Mon-Sat; noon-7pm Sun (performance days only). **Tickets** £6.50-£34.50. **Credit** MC, V. **Map** p397 L2. *See p318* **Profile**.

LSO St Luke's

161 Old Street, the City, EC1V 9NG (7490 3939 information, 7638 8891 tickets, www.lso.co.uk/lsostlukes). Old Street tube/rail. **Box office** 9am-8pm Mon-Sat; 11am-8pm Sun. **Tickets** free-£32. **Credit** AmEx, MC, V. **Map** p400 P4.

This Grade I-listed church, built by Nicholas Hawksmoor in the 18th century, was beautifully converted into a performance and rehearsal space by the LSO several years ago. The orchestra occasionally welcomes the public for open rehearsals

(book ahead); the more formal side of the programme takes in global sounds and some pop alongside classical music, including lunchtime concerts every Thursday that are broadcast on BBC Radio 3.

▶ *Hawksmoor also designed Christ Church Spitalfields; see p153.*

Royal Albert Hall

Kensington Gore, South Kensington, SW7 2AP (7589 3203 information, 7589 8212 tickets, www.royalalberthall.com). South Kensington tube or bus 9, 10, 52, 452. **Box office** 9am-9pm daily. **Tickets** £4-£275. **Credit** AmEx, MC, V. **Map** p395 D9.

In constant use since opening in 1871, the Royal Albert Hall continues to host a wide array of events throughout the year. The classical side of the programming is dominated by the Proms, which runs every night for two months each summer (*see below*) and sees a wide array of orchestras and other ensembles battling rising temperatures and a far-from-ideal acoustic. Otherwise, rock and pop dominates.

St James's Piccadilly

197 Piccadilly, Piccadilly, W1J 9LL (7381 0441, www.st-james-piccadilly.org). Piccadilly Circus tube. **Box office** 10am-6.30pm Mon-Sat. **Tickets** free-£25. **No credit cards. Map** p416 V4.

This community-spirited Wren church holds free lunchtime recitals (Mon, Wed, Fri at 1.10pm) and offers regular evening concerts in a variety of fields.

Festivals Classical

What not to miss this year.

The **Proms** – officially, the BBC Sir Henry Wood Promenade Concerts (0845 401 5040, www.bbc.co.uk/proms) – overshadow all other classical music festivals in the city. Held between mid July and mid September at the Royal Albert Hall (*see above*), with a few supplementary events at other venues, the season includes around 70 concerts, covering everything from early music recitals to orchestral world premières. You can buy tickets in advance, but many prefer to queue on the day for £5 'promenade' tickets, which allow entry to the standing-room stalls or the gallery at the very top of the auditorium.

Held in June and July, the **City of London Festival** (7583 3585, www.colf.org) presents a wide array of concerts in a variety of genres, with an emphasis on classical music and jazz. Many concerts are held in unusual venues (historic churches, handsome courtrooms, the halls of the

ancient livery companies); there's always a strong programme of free events. Close by, the **Spitalfields Festival** (www.spitalfields festival.org.uk) stages two short series of concerts every June and December.

The height of summer sees concerts held in the grounds of various palaces and stately homes: the **English Heritage Picnic Concerts** at Kenwood House (www.picnic concerts.com; *see p151*) are excellent fun. Another brilliant annual alfresco event is **Opera Holland Park** (0845 230 9769, www.operahollandpark.com), which sees a canopied theatre host a season of opera.

There are sparser pickings in winter, but in mid November the **Greenwich International Early Music Festival** (www.earlymusicfestival.com) takes place in the lovely setting of the Old Royal Naval College (*see p166*). As well as concerts, exhibitors display all manner of outlandish instruments, such as sackbutts, crumhorns and hurdy-gurdies.

St John's, Smith Square

Smith Square, Westminster, SW1P 3HA (7222 1061, www.sjss.org.uk). Westminster tube. **Box office** 10am-5pm Mon-Fri. **Tickets** £10-£50. **Credit** MC, V. **Map** p399 K10.

This curiously shaped 18th-century church – it is said the four-turret design was the result of Queen Anne's demand that architect Thomas Archer make it look like a footstool that she had kicked over – hosts concerts more or less nightly. Down in the crypt are two bars for interval drinks and the Smith Square Bar & Restaurant.

St Martin-in-the-Fields

Trafalgar Square, Westminster, WC2N 4JJ (7766 1100, www.stmartin-in-the-fields.org). Charing Cross tube/rail. **Box office** *In person* 8am-5pm Mon, Tue; 8am-8pm Wed-Sat. *By phone* 10am-5pm Mon-Sat. **Tickets** £7-£28. **Credit** MC, V. **Map** p416 X4.

This church is one of the capital's most amiable, populist venues, hosting performances of Bach, Mozart and Vivaldi by candlelight, jazz in the crypt's café and lunchtime recitals (Mon, Tue, Fri) from young musicians, many of them students at the city's music colleges. The interior has been beautifully restored.
▶ *For more on the church, see p131.*

★ Southbank Centre

Belvedere Road, South Bank, SE1 8XX (7960 4200 information, 0844 875 0073 tickets, www.southbankcentre.co.uk). Embankment tube or Waterloo tube/rail. **Box office** *In person* 10am-8pm. *By phone* 9am-8pm. **Tickets** £7-£75. **Credit** AmEx, MC, V. **Map** p399 M8.

A £90m renovation has improved the Royal Festival Hall, externally and acoustically. There are three main halls here: the Royal Festival Hall, which holds nearly 3,000 seats and counts the Philharmonia and the Orchestra of the Age of Enlightenment as residents; the Queen Elizabeth Hall, which has room for around 900 concertgoers; and the 365-capacity Purcell Room, about one-third the size of the QEH and the scene for regular recitals. Programming is rich in variety; the same is true of the foyer stage, which hosts hundreds of free concerts every year.

★ Wigmore Hall

36 Wigmore Street, Marylebone, W1U 2BP (7935 2141, www.wigmore-hall.org.uk). Bond Street tube. **Box office** *In person* 10am-8.30pm daily. *By phone* 10am-7pm daily. **Tickets** £5-£75. **Credit** AmEx, DC, MC, V. **Map** p396 G6.

Built in 1901 as the display hall for Bechstein Pianos, this world-renowned, 550-seat concert venue has perfect acoustics for the 400 concerts that take place each year. Music from the classical and romantic periods are mainstays, usually performed by major classical stars, but under artistic director John Gilhooly there has been a broadening in the remit: more baroque, a young composer-in-residence (Luke

Royal Opera, Royal Opera House.
See p319.

Bedford) and increased (mostly unamplified) jazz, including late-night gigs. Monday-lunchtime recitals are broadcast live on BBC Radio 3.

OPERA VENUES

In addition to the two big venues below, look out for occasional concert performances at **Cadogan Hall** (*see p315*), summer's **Opera Holland Park** (*see left* **Festivals**) and sporadic appearances by **English Touring Opera** (www.englishtouringopera.org.uk).

English National Opera, Coliseum

St Martin's Lane, Covent Garden, WC2N 4ES (0871 911 0200 tickets, www.eno.org). Leicester Square tube or Charing Cross tube/rail. **Box office** *In person* 10am-6pm Mon-Sat. *By phone* 24hrs daily. **Tickets** £17-£93. **Credit** MC, V. **Map** p416 X4.

Built as a music hall in 1904, the home of the English National Opera (ENO) is in fine condition following a renovation in 2004. And after a shaky period several years ago, ENO itself is in solid shape under the youthful stewardship of music director Edward Gardner, with the last few years having offered some fascinating collaborations (such as with physical theatre troupe Complicité) and rare contemporary works (a flamboyant version of Ligeti's *Le Grand Macabre*). All works are in English, and prices are generally cheaper than at the Royal Opera.

ARTS & ENTERTAINMENT

Profile Kings Place

Hear it all of London's musical enthusiasms in one place.

Scruffy and neglected, the streets around King's Cross Station have rarely had much to recommend them. However, things are changing, and fast. The renovation of St Pancras station (*see p106*) and the opening of the new Eurostar terminal have coincided with plenty of other new developments in and around the area, of which the most impressive is tucked away up York Way.

Aware that office blocks are an 'unfriendly building type', property developer Peter Millican wanted **Kings Place** (for listings, *see p316*) to be different from the norm. The building, designed by the architectural firm of Dixon Jones, is tidily integrated with the adjacent canal basin. Above the airy lobby, the top seven floors of the building are given over to offices; the *Guardian* newspaper is the most high-profile resident. There's a gallery, a restaurant and a café on the ground floor. But the real appeal lies in the basement, where you'll find one of the city's most exciting music venues.

With just over 400 seats, the main hall is a beauty, dominated by wood carved from a single, 500-year-old Black Forest oak tree and ringed by invisible rubber pads that kill unwanted ambient noise. Whether for amplified jazz or small-scale chamber music, the sound is always immaculate. There's also a versatile second hall and a number of smaller rooms, given over to workshops, lectures and other special events.

And the programming, overseen by Millican himself, is tremendous. Each week, the selection of concerts takes a different theme: anything from baroque opera to Norwegian jazz, 21st-century classical music to English folk. Some series are built around the London Sinfonietta and the Orchestra of the Age of Enlightenment, the two resident ensembles. These weekly themes are supplemented by other strands (chamber music on Sundays, experimental music on Mondays) and one-offs, as well as the annual Kings Place Festival in September: 100 events in just four days. It's all part of an ethos that dares to be different.

OUTER LIMITS

For an equivalent degree of adventure, on a community scale, head to Dalston for **Café Oto** (*see p326*) and the **Vortex** (*see p326*).

★ Royal Opera, Royal Opera House

Covent Garden, WC2E 9DD (7304 4000, www.roh.org.uk). Covent Garden tube. **Box office** 10am-8pm Mon-Sat. **Tickets** £8-£210. **Credit** AmEx, MC, V. **Map** p416 Z3.

Thanks to a turn-of-the-century refurbishment, the Royal Opera House has once again taken its place among the ranks of the world's great opera houses. Critics sometimes suggest that the programming can be a little spotty, especially so given the famously elevated ticket prices, and not all of chief executive Tony Hall's attempts to win a new audience seem dignified. But there are still many fine productions here, often taking place under the baton of Antonio Pappano, and the modern outlook taken by Hall and his comrades is laudable. Productions take in well-established favourites (Prokofiev, Verdi) and some modern composers (Thomas Adès). *Photo p317.*
▶ *It's not just music at the Opera House. The Royal Ballet is also based here. For more on the famous troupe, see p296.*

Rock, Pop & Roots

The longtime London cliché of indie bands playing in a sticky dive endures, but the capital's rock and pop scene is far from predictable. Close your eyes and stick a pin in *Time Out*'s weekly gig listings, and you might find yourself watching an American country star in a tiny basement, an African group under a railway arch or a torch singer in an ancient church.

Of late, big firms from outside the industry – record retailer HMV, phone company O2 – have been investing in many of the capital's large venues. The results of their involvement have been both welcome (improved sound systems, smarter decor) and undesirable (overpriced bars, edgeless ambience). Regardless of who runs the venues, the range of acts playing in them is as good as it's ever been.

Tickets & information

Your first stop should be *Time Out* magazine, which lists hundreds of gigs every week. Most venues' websites detail future shows. Check ticket availability before setting out: venues large and small can sell out weeks in advance. The main exceptions are pub venues, which sell tickets only on the day. Prices vary wildly: you could pay £150 to see Madonna at the O2 Arena or see a superb singer-songwriter for free. Many venues offer tickets online via their websites, but beware: most online box offices are operated by ticket agencies, which add booking fees that can raise the ticket price by as much as 30 per cent. Try to pay cash in person if possible (*see below*); for details of London's ticket agencies, *see p276*.

> ### INSIDE TRACK FREE GIGS
>
> London's live music scene sometimes offers something for nothing. Regular events include the RoTa, a showcase for the Rough Trade label's indie acts that's held every Saturday between 4pm and 8pm at the **Notting Hill Arts Club** (*see p332*), and the fine programme of after-work concerts staged in the foyer of the Royal Festival Hall at the **Southbank Centre** (*see p317*); for others, see the weekly listings in *Time Out* magazine.

There's often a huge disparity between door times and stage times; the Jazz Café opens at 7pm, for instance, but the gigs often don't start until after 9pm. Some venues run club nights after the gigs, which means the show has to be wrapped up by 10.30pm; but at other venues, the main act won't even start until 11pm. If in doubt, call ahead.

MAJOR VENUES

In addition to the venues below, the **Barbican Centre** (*see p315*), the **Southbank Centre** (*see p317*) and the **Royal Albert Hall** (*see p316*) stage regular gigs.

HMV Forum

9-17 Highgate Road, Kentish Town, NW5 1JY (7428 4099 information, 0844 847 2405 tickets, www.kentishtownforum.com). Kentish Town tube/rail. **Box office** *In person* 4-8pm performance days. *By phone* 24hrs daily. **Tickets** £5-£30. **Credit** MC, V. **Map** p400 N2.

Built as a cinema in 1934, this cramped, 2,000-capacity art deco hall is now co-owned by HMV, part of the music retailer's attempt to shore up its business by diversifying into the increasingly lucrative live market. The high calibre of alt-rock bands who play here (Sonic Youth, Kasabian, White Lies) is a sign of its strong pulling power.
▶ *The time-honoured choice for a pre-gig pint is the nearby Bull & Gate, which also stages gigs.*

HMV Hammersmith Apollo

45 Queen Caroline Street, Hammersmith, W6 9QH (8563 3800 information, 0844 844 4748 tickets, www.hammersmithapollo.net). Hammersmith tube. **Box office** *In person* 4pm-8pm performance days. *By phone* 24hrs daily. **Tickets** £10-£35. **Credit** MC, V.

This 1930s cinema doubles as a 3,600-capacity all-seater theatre (popular with big comedy acts and children's shows) and a 5,000-capacity standing-room-only gig space, hosting shows by major rock bands and others not quite ready for the O2.

Roundhouse.

Avoid standing beneath the sound-muffling overhang downstairs and you may find that this former music hall, formerly the Camden Palace, is among London's finest venues. The 1,500-capacity hall stages weekend club nights and gigs by indie rockers, from the small and cultish to those on the up.

★ O2 Academy Brixton

211 Stockwell Road, Brixton, SW9 9SL (7771 3000 information, 0844 477 2000 tickets, www.o2academybrixton.co.uk). Brixton tube/rail. **Box office** *In person* 2hrs before doors on performance days. *By phone* 24hrs daily. **Tickets** £10-£40. **Credit** AmEx, MC, V.
Brixton is still the preferred venue for metal, indie and alt-rock bands looking to play their triumphant 'Look, ma, we've made it!' headline show. Built in the 1920s, this ex-cinema is the city's most atmospheric big venue. And with its sloping floor, everyone's guaranteed a decent view.

O2 Academy Islington

N1 Centre, 16 Parkfield Street, Islington, N1 0PS (7288 4400 information, 0844 477 2000 tickets, www.o2academyislington.co.uk). Angel tube. **Box office** *In person* noon-4pm Mon-Sat. *By phone* 24hrs daily. **Tickets** £10-£25. **Credit** AmEx, MC, V. **Map** p400 N2.
Located in the heart of a shopping mall, this 800-capacity room was never likely to be London's edgiest venue. Still, as a stepping stone between the pubs of Camden and the city's larger venues, it's a good place to catch fast-rising indie acts and re-formed '80s bands, not least because of the great sound system. The adjacent Bar Academy hosts smaller bands.

★ O2 Arena

Millennium Way, North Greenwich, SE10 0BB (8463 2000 information, 0844 856 0202 tickets, www.theo2.co.uk). North Greenwich tube. **Box office** *In person* noon-7pm daily. *By phone* 24hrs daily. **Tickets** £10-£100. **Credit** AmEx, MC, V.
Since its launch in 2007, this conversion of the former Millennium Dome has been a huge success, taking over from Wembley Arena (*see p321*) and Earls Court as the arena venue of choice. With outstanding sound, unobstructed sightlines and the potential for artists to perform 'in the round', shows from even the world's biggest acts (Britney, Led Zep) don't feel very far away. IndigO2 (*see left*) is on the same site.
▶ *The O2 will be hosting London 2012 Games events as the North Greenwich Arena; see p60.*

O2 Shepherd's Bush Empire

Shepherd's Bush Green, Shepherd's Bush, W12 8TT (8354 3300 information, 0844 477 2000 tickets, www.o2shepherdsbushempire.co.uk). Shepherd's Bush Market tube or Shepherd's Bush tube/rail. **Box office** *In person* 6-8pm performance days. *By phone* 24hrs daily. **Tickets** £8-£40. **Credit** AmEx, MC, V.

IndigO2

For listings, see right **O2 Arena**.
The little brother of the vast O2 Arena (*see right*) is really only little in comparison with the vast expanses of its elder sibling; with a capacity of 2,350 (part-standing room, part-amphitheatre seating, sometimes part-table seating), IndigO2 is impressive in its own right. Its niche roster of MOR acts is dominated by soul, funk, pop-jazz and wearied old pop acts, though it also hosts after-show parties for those headlining the O2.

★ Koko

1A Camden High Street, Camden, NW1 7JE (0870 432 5527 information, 0844 847 2258 tickets, www.koko.uk.com). Mornington Crescent tube. **Box office** *In person* 1-5pm Mon-Fri (performance days only). *By phone* 24hrs daily. **Tickets** £3-£25. **Credit** AmEx, MC, V. **Map** p404 Z3.

INSIDE TRACK
ALWAYS ON CALL

Many of London's venues are open into the small hours, and not all of them have taxi ranks nearby. If you're stuck, text 'CAB' to 60835, and you'll be given numbers for one taxi and two licensed minicab firms in the area.

Festivals Rock, Pop & Roots

What not to miss this year.

Both Camden and Shoreditch are home to a handful of rock and pop 'microfestivals', which are a cross between a pub crawl and a music festival. Buy a ticket (usually a coloured wristband) and you get access to a multitude of gigs in proximate venues over a couple of days. April's two-day **Camden Crawl** (www.thecamdencrawl.com) is the original, presenting a mix of hip indie acts. In May in Shoreditch, look out for the indie-friendly **Stag & Dagger** (www.staganddagger.com, late May) and the multi-arts **Concrete & Glass** (www.concreteandglass.co.uk, May).

As the weather improves, outdoor events take over for the summer. As well as one-off mega gigs, Hyde Park hosts heritage-rock weekender **Hard Rock Calling** (www.hardrockcalling.co.uk) and the poppier, more contemporary **Wireless Festival** (www.wirelessfestival.co.uk) in late June. In July, Victoria Park is home to the leftfield **Field Day** (www.fielddayfestivals. com), the under-18s-only **Underage Festival** (www.underagefestivals.com) and Groove Armada's **Lovebox Weekender** (www.lovebox.net). And Clapham Common lords it over the August Bank Holiday with its **SW4** rave-up (www.southwestfour.com).

There's more mainstream fare for the **Somerset House Summer Series**, during which Somerset House (*see p111*) welcomes an array of big and generally pretty mainstream acts for roughly ten days of open-air shows. Autumn sees Camden host the **BBC Electric Proms** (www.bbc.co.uk/electricproms), with most major events staged at the Roundhouse (*see below*). And in summer, the Southbank Centre (*see p317*) invites a guest artist to curate **Meltdown**, a fortnight of gigs, films and other events. David Bowie, Ornette Coleman, Patti Smith and Richard Thompson are among the previous curators.

Other events are limited to a single genre. The best of them include the Southbank Centre's **London African Music Festival** (7328 9613, www.londonafrican musicfestival.com, Sept); **La Linea** (8693 1042, www.comono.co.uk, early Apr), a fortnight of contemporary Latin American music; and the terrific, ever-changing series of thematic folk and world events at the **Barbican** (*see p315*).

Holding 2,000 standing or 1,300 seated, this former BBC theatre is a fine mid-sized venue. Sightlines are good, the sound is decent (with the exception of the alcove behind the stalls bar and the scarily vertiginous top floor) and the roster of shows is quite varied, with acts at the poppier end of the scale joined by everyone from folkies to grizzled '70s rockers.

★ Roundhouse

Chalk Farm Road, Camden, NW1 8EH (7424 9991 information, 0844 482 8008 tickets, www.roundhouse.org.uk). Chalk Farm tube. **Box office** *In person* 11am-6pm Mon-Sat. **Tickets** £5-£50. **Credit** MC, V. **Map** p404 W1.
The main auditorium's supporting pillars mean there are some poor sightlines, but this one-time railway turntable shed, used for hippie happenings in the 1960s before becoming a famous rock (and punk) venue in the '70s, has been a fine addition to London's music venues since its reopening in 2006. Expect a mix of arty rock gigs, dance performances, theatre and multimedia events.

Scala

275 Pentonville Road, King's Cross, N1 9NL (7833 2022, www.scala-london.co.uk). King's Cross tube/rail. **Box office** 10am-6pm Mon-Fri. **Tickets** £8-£15. **Credit** MC, V. **Map** p397 L3.
Built as a cinema after World War I, the TARDIS-like, multi-floored Scala stages an agreeably broad range of indie, electronica, hip hop and folk, and is a frequent destination for one-off superparties. Its chilly air-con isn't rivalled anywhere in London – but the cheesy ballads of the Ultimate Power night are anything but cool. You can also check out rock, metal and punk at Freedom or the University of Dub.

Wembley Arena

Arena Square, Engineers Way, Wembley, HA9 0DH (8782 5566 information, 0844 815 0815 tickets, www.livenation.co.uk/wembley). Wembley Park tube. **Box office** *In person* 10.30am-9pm performance days; 10.30am-4.30pm non-performance days. *By phone* 24hrs daily.
Tickets £5-£100. **Credit** AmEx, MC, V.
Wembley Arena may have seen its commercial heyday end with the arrival of the O2 (*see p320*). It's hardly anyone's favourite venue, not least because the food and drink could be cheaper and better, but most Londoners have warm memories of at least one Arena megagig, and a £30m refurbishment has improved this 12,500-capacity venue.

ARTS & ENTERTAINMENT

Sounds and Pictures

Ten album covers that show various corners of the capital.

ABBEY ROAD
THE BEATLES (1969)
Abbey Road, NW8
You probably know this one already.

MEATY BEATY BIG AND BOUNCY
THE WHO (1971)
Railway Hotel, Railway Approach, HA3
The cover of this greatest-hits compilation shows seminal mod hangout the Railway Hotel in Harrow. It's now the site of four blocks of flats, each named after a member of the Who.

THE RISE AND FALL OF ZIGGY STARDUST AND THE SPIDERS FROM MARS
DAVID BOWIE (1972)
Heddon Street, W1
The red telephone box was returned to its original location in Heddon Street's recent makeover. The K West sign is long gone.

NEW BOOTS AND PANTIES!!
IAN DURY (1977)
Vauxhall Bridge Road, SW1
The title referred to the only clothes a thrifty Dury wouldn't buy from charity shops. The cover was shot outside a now-defunct clothing store called Axford's; the kid is Baxter Dury, Ian's son.

THIS IS THE MODERN WORLD
THE JAM (1977)
Under the Westway, W10
Behind Paul Weller, Rick Buckler and Bruce Foxton rise the towers of the Silchester West council estate, not far from Latimer Road tube station.

ANIMALS
PINK FLOYD (1977)
Battersea Power Station, east of Chelsea Bridge, SW8
During the photo shoot, the inflatable pig came loose from its moorings and disappeared into the London sky.

PARKLIFE
BLUR (1994)
Walthamstow Stadium, 300 Chingford Road, E4
A visual hymn to the East End. The album was launched at the stadium, with Blur sponsoring a race.

(WHAT'S THE STORY) MORNING GLORY
OASIS (1995)
Berwick Street, W1
The two men passing each other on this Soho street are believed to be Oasis art director Brian Cannon and DJ Sean Rowley.

ORIGINAL PIRATE MATERIAL
THE STREETS (2002)
Kestrel House, City Road, EC1
The photograph was taken in 1995 by German snapper Rut Blees Luxemburg, the same photographer who supplied the cover shot for Bloc Party's *A Weekend in the City*.

BURIAL
BURIAL (2006)
Wandsworth, SW18
William Bevan's dystopian dubstep is coloured by his life in south London. This shot looks down from the sky towards Wandsworth Prison.

▶ *During the London 2012 Olympic Games, Wembley Arena will be hosting the Rhythmic Gymnastics and Badminton.*

CLUB & PUB VENUES

In addition to the venues listed below, a handful of London nightclubs also stage gigs. Try the **Notting Hill Arts Club** (*see p332*), **Madame JoJo's** (*see p329*), **Proud** (*see p330*) and the **ICA** (*see p138*). And it's also worth checking the very varied schedules at the excellent **Café Oto** (*see p326*).

Barfly
49 Chalk Farm Road, Chalk Farm, NW1 8AN (7688 8994 information, 0844 847 2424 tickets, www.barflyclub.com). Chalk Farm tube. **Open** 3pm-2am Mon, Thur; 3pm-1am Tue, Wed; 3pm-3am Fri, Sat; 3pm-midnight Sun. *Shows* from 7.30pm daily. **Admission** £5-£20. **Credit** MC, V. **Map** p404 X1.
As other similarly sized venues open with smarter decor and less conventional booking policies, this 200-capacity venue's star was beginning to fade until our kicking London Sessions moved in over summer 2010. The venue is part of London's indie-rock fabric, a key player in the fusion of indie guitars and electro into an unholy, danceable row.

Bloomsbury Bowling Lanes
Basement, Tavistock Hotel, Bedford Way, Bloomsbury, WC1H 9EU (7183 1979, www.bloomsburybowling.com). Russell Square tube. **Open** 1pm-midnight Mon-Wed, Sun; 1pm-2am Thur; 1pm-3am Fri; noon-3am Sat. **Admission** varies. **Credit** AmEx, MC, V. **Map** p397 K4.
Offering a late-night drink away from Soho, BBL has been putting on live bands and DJs for a while now – and the range of activities make it like a playground for grown-ups. As well as the eight lanes for bowling, there's pool by the hour, table football, karaoke booths and, beside the entrance, a small cinema. Live music and club nights tend to be vintage: try 'We, Like You', 'Work it Versus Livin' Proof' and 1950s rock 'n' roll night 'Rock A Hula'.

★ Borderline
Orange Yard, off Manette Street, Soho, W1D 4JB (0844 847 2465, www.meanfiddler.com). Tottenham Court Road tube. **Open** hrs vary. **Admission** £3-£20. **Credit** AmEx, MC, V. **Map** p416 W2.
A small, sweaty dive bar-slash-juke joint right in the heart of Soho, the Borderline has long been a favoured stop-off for touring American bands of the country and blues varieties, though you'll also find a variety of indie acts and singer-songwriters going through their repertoire here. Be warned, though, that it can get very, very cramped.

Blues Kitchen
111 Camden High Street, Camden, NW1 7JN (7387 5277, www.theblueskitchen.com). Camden Town or Mornington Crescent tube. **Open** noon-midnight Mon-Wed; noon-1am Thur; noon-3am Fri; 11am-3am Sat; 11am-midnight Sun. **Admission** free; £3 after 10pm Fri; £4 after 10pm Sat. **Map** p404 Y3.
Celebrating its first birthday in autumn 2010 with a gig by Seasick Steve, the Blues Kitchen combines credible live music (roots blues, rockabilly and so on) with a rather high-end interior. The food is spicy New Orleans fare and there's a huge range of American bourbon for sippin'. All in all, it makes for a pleasant Sunday afternoon hangout as well as a late-opening gig venue.

★ Bush Hall
310 Uxbridge Road, Shepherd's Bush, W12 7LJ (8222 6955, www.bushhallmusic.co.uk). Shepherd's Bush Market tube. **Open** hrs vary. *Shows* from 7.30pm. **Tickets** £6-£20. **Credit** MC, V.
Over the years, this handsome room has been a dance hall, a soup kitchen and a snooker club. But now, with its original fittings intact, it plays host to big bands performing stripped-down shows, top folk outfits and rising indie rockers.

Corsica Studios
Elephant Road, Elephant & Castle, SE17 1LB (7703 4760, www.corsicastudios.com). Elephant & Castle tube/rail. **Open** hrs vary. **Tickets** £5-£12. **No credit cards. Map** p402 O10.
Corsica Studios is an independent, not-for-profit arts complex whose ethos is to breed creativity and culture. The flexible performance space is increasingly being used as one of London's most adventurous live music venues and clubs, supplementing bands with

---

INSIDE TRACK
AVOID THE FEES

You can avoid the brutal booking fees levied by many major venues by buying your tickets in cash from two box offices. Tickets for shows at the **Borderline** (*see left*), the **HMV Apollo** (*see p319*), the **HMV Forum** (*see p319*), the **Jazz Café** (*see p324*) and the **Relentless Garage** (*see p325*) cost face value if purchased with cash at the Jazz Café's box office (10.30am-5.30pm Mon-Sat). And tickets for the **O2 Academy Brixton** (*see p320*), the **O2 Academy Islington** (*see p320*) and the **O2 Shepherd's Bush Empire** (*see p320*) can be bought for face value at the O2 Academy Islington's box office (noon-4pm Mon-Sat).

ARTS & ENTERTAINMENT

sundry poets, live painters and lunatic projectionists. Main nights here include Baba Yaga's Hut, which showcases a selection of both established and up-and-coming bands, while Club Mofo arrived here in autumn 2010 after the closure of Barden's in Dalston.

Green Note
106 Parkway, Camden, NW1 7AN (7485 9899, www.greennote.co.uk). Camden Town tube. **Open** 7-11pm Wed, Thur, Sun; 7pm-midnight Fri; 6.30pm-midnight Sat. *Shows* 9pm daily. **Tickets** £4-£15. **Credit** MC, V. **Map** p404 X3.
A stone's throw from Regent's Park, this cosy little venue and vegetarian café-bar was a welcome addition to the city's roots circuit back in 2005. Singer-songwriters, folkies and blues musicians make up the majority of the gig roster, with a handful of big names in among the listings.

Hoxton Square Bar & Kitchen
2-4 Hoxton Square, Shoreditch, N1 6NU (7613 0709, www.hoxtonsquarebar.com). Old Street tube/rail or Shoreditch High Street rail. **Open** 11am-midnight Mon; 11am-1am Tue-Thur; 11am-2am Fri, Sat; 11am-12.30am Sun. **Tickets** £5-£12. **Credit** AmEx, MC, V. **Map** p401 R3.
Set in the heart of hipsterland, this 450-capacity venue is more than just a place to be seen: the venue's finger-on-the-pulse line-ups are always cutting edge and fun, with the venue often hosting a band's first London outing. Get there early or be prepared for a long queue.

Festivals Jazz

What not to miss this year.

Showcasing London's thriving jazz scene while simultaneously welcoming an array of big names from abroad, November's excellent **London Jazz Festival** (7324 1880, www.londonjazzfestival.org.uk) covers most bases, from trad to free improv. It's comfortably the biggest jazz festival of the year, though you may also find some interesting events at the all-free, open-air **Ealing Jazz Festival** (8825 6064, www.ealing.gov.uk, July). In late August, the **Hampton Court Palace Beer & Jazz Festival** (www.hamptoncourt beerandjazz.com) presents a rather mainstream selection of jazz-funk and pop-inflected big band jazz in a great setting. For something edgier, look out for occasional showcases organised by the **Loop Collective** (www.loopcollective. org) and the **F-IRE Collective** (www.f-ire. com), which feature some of the best young talents in the country.

★ 100 Club
100 Oxford Street, Soho, W1D 1LL (7636 0933, www.the100club.co.uk). Oxford Circus tube. **Open** *Shows* 7.30pm-midnight Mon; 7.30-11.30pm Tue-Thur; 7.30pm-12.30am Fri; 7.30pm-1am Sat; 7.30-11pm Sun. **Tickets** £6-£20. **Credit** MC, V. **Map** p416 V1.
Perhaps the most adaptable venue in London, this wide, famous, 350-capacity room has long provided a home for trad jazz, pub blues, northern soul and, famously, punk: the venue staged a historic show in 1976 that featured the Sex Pistols, the Clash and the Damned. These days, it offers jazz, indie acts and ageing rockers.
▶ *The 100 Club also hosts the monthly Limelight (http://londonlimelight.co.uk) – concert hall-quality classical music in a relaxed environment.*

Jazz Café
5 Parkway, Camden, NW1 7PG (7688 8899 information, 0844 847 2514 tickets, www.jazzcafe.co.uk). Camden Town tube. **Box office** *In person* 10.30am-5.30pm Mon-Sat. *By phone* 24hrs daily. **Tickets** £10-£30. **Credit** MC, V. **Map** p404 Y2.
While there is some jazz on the schedule, this two-floor club does tend to belie its name by dealing more in soul, R&B and hip hop these days. It's become the first port of call for soon-to-be-huge US acts: Mary J Blige, John Legend and the Roots all played their first European dates here.

★ Lexington
96-98 Pentonville Road, Islington, N1 9JB (7837 5371, www.thelexington.co.uk). Angel tube. **Open** noon-2am Mon-Thur; noon-4am Fri, Sat; noon-midnight Sun. **Tickets** free-£10. **Credit** AmEx, MC, V. **Map** p400 N2.
They've put a lot of thought into things at the Lexington. Downstairs, there's a lounge bar offering a vast array of US beers and bourbons, above-par bar food and a Rough Trade music quiz (every Monday). And upstairs is a 200-capacity venue, with a superb sound system in place for the leftfield indie bands that dominate the programme.

★ Luminaire
311 Kilburn High Road, Kilburn, NW6 7JR (7372 7123, www.theluminaire.co.uk). Kilburn tube or Brondesbury rail. **Open** 7.30pm-midnight Mon-Wed, Sun; 7.30pm-1am Thur; 7.30pm-2am Fri, Sat. **Tickets** £6-£20. **Credit** AmEx, MC, V.
The Luminaire won *Time Out*'s Venue of the Year accolade way back in 2006, but it has remained one of the best music clubs in town. The policy is fantastically broad, taking in just about everything from alt-country hero Howe Gelb to surf guitar maestro Dick Dale and noise-mongers Jesu. The sound system is out of the top drawer, the decor is stylish and the staff are lovely.

93 Feet East

150 Brick Lane, Spitalfields, E1 6QL (7770 6006, www.93feeteast.co.uk). Aldgate East tube. **Open** 5-11pm Mon-Thur; 5pm-1am Fri; noon-1am Sat; noon-10.30pm Sun. *Shows* vary. **Admission** free-£10. **Credit** MC, V. **Map** p401 S5.

With three rooms, a balcony and a wrap-around courtyard that's great for barbecues, 93 Feet East manages by its breadth of programme to overcome its not very late licence. You can expect tech-house DJs, a mix of indie-dance bands and various art-rockers, plus short films and arty happenings.

Relentless Garage

20-22 Highbury Corner, Highbury, N5 1RD (7619 6720 information, 0844 847 1678 tickets, www.thegarage.co.uk). Highbury & Islington tube/rail. **Box office** *By phone* 24hrs daily. **Tickets** £3-£20. **Credit** AmEx, MC, V.

This 650-capacity alt-rock venue reopened in 2009 after three years of impressive refurbishment. It now books an exciting and surprisingly wide-ranging calendar of indie and art-rock gigs, from ancient punk survivors like the Pop Group and Sham 69 to the poppier end of the indie singer-songwriter scale (Fran Healy in the smaller Upstairs, for example).

12 Bar Club

22-23 Denmark Place, Soho, WC2H 8NL (7240 2622, www.12barclub.com). Tottenham Court Road tube. **Open** *Café* 8am-7pm Mon-Sat; noon-7pm Sun. *Bar* 7pm-3am Mon-Sat; 7-12.30am Sun. *Shows* from 7.30pm; nights vary. **Admission** £3-£13. **Credit** MC, V. **Map** p416 X2.

A London treasure, this easy-to-miss hole-in-the-wall venue among the guitar shops of Denmark Street books a grab-bag of low-key stuff, though its tiny size (audience capacity of 100, minuscule stage) dictates a predominance of singer-songwriters.

Underworld

174 Camden High Street, Camden, NW1 0NE (7734 1932, www.theunderworldcamden.co.uk). Camden Town tube. **Box office** *In person* 11am-11pm Mon-Sat; noon-10.30pm Sun. *By phone* 24hrs daily. **Shows** hrs vary. **Admission** £5-£20. **No credit cards.** **Map** p404 Y2.

A dingy maze of pillars and bars below Camden, this subterranean oddity is an essential for metal and hardcore fans who want their ears bludgeoned by bands with names such as the Atomic Bitchwax, Skeletonwitch and Decrepit Birth.

Union Chapel

Compton Terrace, Islington, N1 2XD (7226 1686, www.unionchapel.org.uk). Highbury & Islington tube/rail. **Open** hrs vary. **Tickets** free-£40. **No credit cards.**

This Victorian Gothic church still holds regular services each Sunday, but it's also one of London's most atmospheric gig venues, booking acts such as Judie

Tzuke, bits and bobs of contemporary classical or electronica, even acoustic sets from hoary old rock bands. Look out for its many thematic series, as well as freebie Daylight gigs on Sundays. The acoustic is better suited to smaller line-ups.

★ Windmill

22 Blenheim Gardens, Brixton, SW2 5BZ (8671 0700, www.windmillbrixton.co.uk). Brixton tube/rail. **Open** *Shows* 8-11pm Mon-Thur; 8pm-1am Fri, Sat; 5-11pm Sun. **Admission** free-£10. **Credit** MC, V.

If you can live with the iffy sound and the amusingly taciturn barflies, you might think this pokey little L-shaped pub is one of the city's best venues. Mark it down to the adventurous bookings (punk, country, techno, folk, metal) and cheap admission.

Jazz

The international big hitters keep on visiting London, but these are exciting times too for the city's homespun jazz scene. Inspired by freewheeling attractions at the **Vortex** (*see p326*) and the sporadic, unhinged **Boat-Ting Club** nights (www.boat-ting.co.uk), acts such as Portico Quartet, Led Bib and Kit Downes Trio have won Mercury Prize nominations with recent albums, and the F-IRE and Loop Collectives are busy nurturing boundary-pushing future stars.

Café Oto. *See p326.*

ARTS & ENTERTAINMENT

ARTS & ENTERTAINMENT

In addition to the venues below, the **100 Club** (*see p324*) hosts trad groups, while the **Spice of Life** at Cambridge Circus (6 Moor Street, W1D 5NA, 7437 7013, www.spiceoflife soho.com) has solid mainstream jazz. The **Jazz Café** (*see p324*) lives up to its name from time to time; there's a good deal of very good jazz at the excellent **Kings Place** (*see p316*); and both the **Barbican** (*see p315*) and the **Southbank Centre** (*see p317*) host dozens of big names. For the increasingly excellent **London Jazz Festival**, *see p324* **Festivals**.

Bull's Head
373 Lonsdale Road, Barnes, SW13 9PY (8876 5241, www.thebullshead.com). Barnes Bridge rail. **Open** noon-midnight daily. *Shows* 8.30pm Mon-Sat; 1-3.30pm, 8.30-11pm Sun. **Admission** £5-£15. **Credit** MC, V.

This venerable, ancient Thames-side pub won a reputation for hosting modern jazz in the 1960s but today specialises in mainstream British jazz and swing. Regular guests include ace veteran pianist Stan Tracey and sax maestro Peter King.

★ Café Oto
18-22 Ashwin Street, Dalston, E8 3DL (7923 1231, www.cafeoto.co.uk). Dalston Junction or Dalston Kingsland rail. **Open** 9.30am-1am Mon-Fri; 10.30am-midnight Sat, Sun. *Shows* from 8pm; days vary. **Admission** £3-£10. **No credit cards.**

Opened in 2008, this 150-capacity café and music venue can't easily be categorised, though its website offers the tidy definition that it specialises in 'creative new music that exists outside of the mainstream'. That means Japanese noise rockers ('Oto' is Japanese for 'sound'), electronica pioneers, improvising noiseniks and artists from the stranger ends of the rock, folk and classical spectrums. *Photo p325.*

★ Charlie Wright's International Bar
45 Pitfield Street, Hoxton, N1 6DA (7490 8345, www.myspace.com/charliewrights). Old Street tube/rail. **Open** noon-1am Mon-Wed; noon-4am Thur, Fri; 5pm-4am Sat; 5pm-2am Sun. *Shows* 8-10pm daily. **Admission** £4 after 10pm Fri, Sat; £3 Sun. **Credit** MC, V. **Map** p401 Q3.

When Zhenya Strigalev and Patsy Craig began programming the line-up here in 2006, London's jazz fans were given a reason to visit what had previously been merely a rather good after-hours boozer.

Now this agreeably scruffy venue stages a fine jazz programme on every night of the week except Saturday. Gigs don't usually start until 10pm, and run late on Thursdays and Fridays.

Pizza Express Jazz Club
10 Dean Street, Soho, W1D 3RW (0845 602 7017, www.pizzaexpresslive.com). Tottenham Court Road tube. **Shows** 9-11pm daily. **Admission** £15-£25. **Credit** AmEx, DC, MC, V. **Map** p416 W2.

The upstairs restaurant (7437 9595) is jazz-free, but the 120-capacity basement is one of the best mainstream jazz venues in town. Singers such as Kurt Elling and Lea DeLaria join instrumentalists from home and abroad on the nightly bills.

★ Ronnie Scott's
47 Frith Street, Soho, W1D 4HT (7439 0747, www.ronniescotts.co.uk). Leicester Square or Tottenham Court Road tube. **Shows** 7.30pm daily. **Admission** (non-members) £15-£46. **Credit** AmEx, MC, V. **Map** p416 W2.

Opened (on a different site) by the British saxophonist Ronnie Scott in 1959, this jazz institution was completely refurbished in 2006. The capacity was expanded to 250, the food got better and the bookings became drearier. Happily, though, Ronnie's has got back on track, with jazz heavyweights dominating in place of the mainstream pop acts who held sway for a while. Perch by the rear bar or get table service at the crammed side-seating or more spacious (but noisier) central tables in front of the stage.

606 Club
90 Lots Road, Chelsea, SW10 0QD (7352 5953, www.606club.co.uk). Imperial Wharf rail or bus 11, 211. **Shows** 9pm Mon; 7.30pm Tue, Wed; 8pm Thur; 9.30pm Fri, Sat; 8.30pm Sun. **Admission** £8-£12. **Credit** AmEx, MC, V.

Since 1976, Steve Rubie has run this spot, which relocated to this 150-capacity club in 1987. Alongside its Brit-dominated bills, expect informal jams featuring musos who've come from gigs elsewhere. There's no entrance fee as such; bands are funded from a music charge added to bills at the end of the night. Alcohol can only be served to non-members with food.

★ Vortex Jazz Club
Dalston Culture House, 11 Gillet Street, Dalston, N16 8JN (7254 4097, www.vortexjazz.co.uk). Dalston Kingsland rail. **Shows** 8.30pm daily. **Admission** free-£12. **Credit** MC, V.

Before Café Oto (*see left*) joined the musical fray, the Vortex was the capital's centre for leftfield jazz, avant-garde and other marginalised talent, and it retains a fearsome reputation. Since relocating to Dalston in 2005, the venue has gone from strength to strength, hosting its own strand of the London Jazz Festival (*see p324* **Festivals**) and various other forward-thinking events. The bar stays open late.

Nightlife

Hard times for the superclubs, good times for the small clubs.

Years ago, many of London's most popular venues were large and centrally located. You could rely on them for a memorable, cutting-edge clubbing experience. But recent times have seen the closure of many of the capital's historic nightlife venues. The loss of Turnmills, the Cross and the End is already ancient history when measured in clubbing years, but the loss in spring 2010 of both Matter, which had been the newest beacon for the superclub-sized party crowd, and Shoreditch favourite T Bar began to feel a little apocalyptic.

Today, although London is still at the forefront of the world's forward-thinking nightlife and dance music, finding the best clubs requires a little effort. Not least because the merry-go-round of parties sees no need to stick to just one club. This lack of consistently excellent venues means that you can often stumble across the greatest nights bubbling out of pub-clubs like the **Old Queen's Head** (*see p330*), warehouse spaces and car parks, polysexual bars such as the notorious **Dalston Superstore** (*see p313*) or makeshift clubs in the restaurant basements and former shops along Stoke Newington High Street.

SOUNDS OF THE CITY

What's hot? Big, beefy, speakerstack-destroying bass. Always. Dubstep is huge – and heavy – its reverberating beats sending dancefloors wild across the capital as it continues to morph through urban genres like funky, future house, bassline, dancehall and 2step. The popularity of disco is tailing off, but you can still find its progeny at the resurgent Chicago house- and acid-influenced parties like **Disco Bloodbath** (www.myspace.com/discobloodbathdisco) and plenty of nights at the **Horse & Groom** (*see p332*). Meanwhile, Berlin-influenced deep and glitchy sounds still work a treat at either seminal one-off nights such as **Secretsundaze** (www.secretsundaze.net) and bank holiday mini-festivals such as **Eastern Electrics** (www.easternelectrics.com).

VENUES

Fabric (*see p329*) remains the capital's best-loved superclub, despite going through administration and being sold this year – luckily, it's progressive programming remains in place – but Shoreditch is the hub of the capital's nightlife scene, especially around Brick Lane (which offers plenty of late-night bars at the northern end of the strip) and

across towards Hoxton Square. It is, however, becoming more and more commercialised (witness the trails of hen and office parties between Old Street and Spitalfields). Brand-new club **XOYO** (*see p332*) is especially welcome.

The city's cool kids now take the bus north up the Kingsland Road from Shoreditch into Dalston and further on into Stoke Newington. The former has much-improved transport connections to the rest of the city since the London Overground arrived at Dalston Junction station, but it can be difficult to find the clubs – even more so what's happening in them. Spend a few moments browsing the Clubs section of *Time Out* magazine or www.timeout.com or hunting on Facebook and you'll unearth fabulous happenings at the likes of **Dalston**

INSIDE TRACK
GETTING HOME FROM BRIXTON

Getting back to your hotel in central London from Brixton isn't easy. 'It can be tough to get a cab here, so pick a night when there's a big gig on at the Brixton Academy (*see p320*),' says one driver.

Superstore (*see p313*) and latest hipster-magnet **Alibi** (91 Kingsland High Street, E8 2PB, 7249 2733, www.thealibilondon.co.uk).

With the demise of the End and the nearby Astoria, the appeal of clubbing in the West End has steeply declined; with the exception of **Madame JoJo's** (*see p329*), there's little here besides bars, pubs and a still bustling gay scene. To the north, up in King's Cross, only **Egg** (200 York Way, N7 9AP, 7609 8364, www.egglondon.net), not much more than an

option for a late-night drink, and the **Big Chill House** (*see p330*) remain of a former clubbing nexus lost to redevelopment. Further north, Camden is still very popular – especially with tourists. Indie student hangout **Proud** (*see p330*), teeny pub-rave spot the **Lock Tavern** (*see p330*) and new bourbon-soaked gig haunt the **Blues Kitchen** (*see p323*) offer credible nights for London party people too.

There's more of interest to the south. The gay village in **Vauxhall** is just as welcoming to

ARTS & ENTERTAINMENT

The Club that Saved Shoreditch?

When all hope was lost, up popped XOYO.

The Hoxton nightlife triangle has experienced a shift in recent years: traces of its bohemian, scene-defining cool are still evident, but much of the area now more resembles the West End. Over the summer of 2010 especially, several large warehouse spaces closed abruptly and many of the better, smaller clubs found themselves threatened by licensing issues. So it's easy to see why serious clubbers are looking to **XOYO** (for listings, *see p332*), which opened in September 2010, to reinvigorate their night out.

Located behind offices at Old Street station, far from Shoreditch High Street, it stands out from its competitors because of its size (it has a 900 capacity) and because it functions as a club, a gig hub and an exhibition space, with a stark white gallery-like room upstairs and a dance basement below offset by an unusually high ceiling. 'I think wherever you go partying around the world, whether it's New York or Berlin, the best [venues] seem to be in loft spaces,' says Cymon Eckel, one of XOYO's founders. 'This is an old Victorian warehouse and, essentially, we're converting it into a disco loft-club. It suits the gigs and the parties perfectly because of its architecture. It has character: it's not just a big open room. It has the ambience of being an illegal warehouse, but actually, it's legitimate.'

It's also run by people whose jobs you wish you had. The primary XOYO collective comprises John 'Johnno' Burgess, who, among other things, runs Bugged Out! and set up music magazines *Jockey Slut* and *Dummy*. Then there's acid-house scene innovator Eckel, who helped set up its mouthpiece, the *Boys Own* fanzine, club and label, and his club partner Marcus Weedon, who founded east London festival Field Day. Finally, on the live music side is

Tom Baker, who heads up Eat Your Own Ears. They're the kinds of people whose address books you'd really like to steal.

You may not find hen parties queuing up outside in neon tutus and metallic wigs, but XOYO was built with a pleasingly open attitude to all tribes of clubber. Says Burgess: 'I always quite like the mix of young people coming down from Dalston and older clubbers who want somewhere nicer to go; that's the kind of crowd we used to get down at the End. It was never just one thing. The DJs prefer that as well: that when they're looking out at a sea of people, it's not just an identikit crowd.'

So what's on the programme? 'Nights have jumped at the chance to do something legal and less stressful than a warehouse party here,' says Burgess. 'Neon Noise Project, Shake It!, Durrr, FACT, Bloggers Delight, Eat Your Own Ears… Since the End closed, there hasn't been anywhere for Bugged Out! to call home, so as soon as we saw this club, we knew this was where we wanted to be.' No doubt, you'll feel the same way too.

open-minded, straight-rolling types, with club promoters looking more and more towards south-of-the-river venues such as **Area** (67 Albert Embankment, SE1 7TP, www.area clublondon.com) and the **New Fire Complex** (South Lambeth Road, SW8 1RT) as occasional homes for their (largely drum 'n' bass and fetish) parties. The calendar is usually even fuller at **Cable** (*see below*).

Across town, the cabaret juggernaut rolls on, smashing through into mainstream clubland. To see the best, head to **Volupté** (*see p330*), which hosts opulent burlesque nights; the always interesting **Bethnal Green Working Men's Club** (*see p331*); and the even more alternative **RVT** (*see p310*). Again, many of the best cabaret nights are one-off parties in a range of formal and informal venues – wherever you party, bring an open mind.

London rewards those who are willing to chance something new, but not all risks are worth taking. Before you head out, find which night bus gets you home and where you need to catch it (the tube doesn't start until around 7am on Sundays). If the bus network proves too mind-boggling at stupid o'clock, then check out our guide to catching a cab (*see p331 and p314* **Inside Track**). Always make sure that your cab is licensed; to find out how to tell, and for more on public transport, *see pp362-366*.

CENTRAL

Bathhouse

7-8 Bishopsgate Churchyard, the City, EC2M 3TJ (7920 9207, www.thebathhousevenue.com). Liverpool Street tube/rail. **Open** noon-midnight Mon-Wed; noon-1am Thur; noon-5am Fri; 8pm-4am Sat. **Admission** free-£7. **Credit** MC, V.
This Victorian Turkish bathhouse is now a fresh London party space. All marble and gilt mirrors, it seems almost too appropriate for decadent Thursday happening the Boom Boom Club and its showgirl burlesque and young neo-cabaret stars. Dress to the nines in vintage, then drink wildly to fit in. Friday or Saturday is usually '50s-vintage rock 'n' roll, but quality spinners of all types are drawn to the opulent DJ booth, set in a gilded birdcage.

★ Cable

33A Bermondsey Street, Borough, SE1 2EG (7403 7730, www.cable-london.com). London Bridge tube/rail. **Open** 10pm-6am Fri, Sat; 10pm-5am Sun. **Admission** £5-£15. **Credit** MC, V.
All old-style brickwork and industrial air-con ducts, this new spot has a similar feel to Fabric (*see right*). The venue has two dance arenas, a bar with a spot-and-be-spotted mezzanine, plenty of seating and a great covered smoking area out the back. The best nights are usually on Saturday, when We Fear Silence curate nights from the likes of Minus,

Cable.

Metalheadz and Chew The Fat. Don't hesitate when staff ask to take your thumbprint when you check your coat: if you lose your ticket, you won't need to wait for the club to clear before you can claim it back.

Fabric

77A Charterhouse Street, Clerkenwell, EC1M 3HN (7336 8898, www.fabriclondon.com). Farringdon tube/rail. **Open** 10pm-6am Fri; 11pm-8am Sat; 11pm-6am Sun. **Admission** £8-£18. **Credit** AmEx, MC, V. **Map** p400 O5.
Fabric is the club that most party people come to see in London, with good reason. Located in a former meatpacking warehouse, it has a well-deserved reputation as the capital's biggest and best club. The line-ups are legendary. Fridays belong to the bass: guaranteed highlights include DJ Hype, who takes over all three rooms once a month for his drum 'n' bass and dubstep night Playaz, and Switch & Sinden's Get Familiar party is a sell-out every other month. Saturdays descend into techy, minimal, deep house territory, with the world's most-famous DJs regularly making appearances. Be warned: the queues are also legendary. Blag on to the guestlist or buy tickets in advance to avoid a three-hour wait.
▶ *Matter, Fabric's 2,600-capacity dream-venue at the O2 Arena (see p320), suddenly closed in 2010. Temporarily, the organisers say.*

Madame JoJo's

8-10 Brewer Street, Soho, W1F 0SD (7734 3040, www.madamejojos.com). Leicester Square or Piccadilly Circus tube. **Open** 7.30pm-3am daily. **Admission** £4-£10. **Credit** AmEx, MC, V. **Map** p416 W3.
The red and slightly shabby basement space at JoJo's is a beacon for those seeking to escape the West End's post-work chain pubs. The most trea-

sured nights tend towards variety: the London Burlesque Social Club, Kitsch Cabaret or Finger in the Pie Cabaret's talent-spotting showcases.

Social
5 Little Portland Street, Marylebone, W1W 7JD (7636 4992, www.thesocial.com). Oxford Circus tube. **Open** noon-midnight Mon-Wed; noon-1am Thur-Sat. **Admission** free-£5. **Credit** AmEx, MC, V. **Map** p416 U1.
A discreet, opaque front hides this daytime diner and DJ bar of supreme quality, set up by Heavenly Records nearly a decade back. After drinks upstairs, its clientele of music industry workers, alt-rock nonebrities and other scenesters shamble down to an intimate basement space rocked by DJs six nights a week. The weekly Hip Hop Karaoke is a giggle.

★ Volupté
7-9 Norwich Street, Holborn, EC4A 1EJ (7831 1622, www.volupte-lounge.com). Chancery Lane tube. **Open** noon-4pm, 5pm-1am Tue-Fri; noon-3am Sat. **Admission** free-£30. **Credit** MC, V. **Map** p416 N5.
Expect to suffer wallpaper envy as you enter the ground-floor bar and then descend to the club. Punters enjoy some of the best cabaret talent and retro nights in town, from tables set beneath absinthe-inspired vines. Try nights such as the Harlem Swing Club, which turns the clock all the way back to the 1920s.

NORTH LONDON

Better known as gig venues, **Koko** (*see p313*) and **Barfly** (*see p315*) have good reputations for feisty club nights, and the live music at the **Blues Kitchen** (*see p323*) can really rock.

Paradise.

★ Big Chill House
257-259 Pentonville Road, King's Cross, N1 9NL (7427 2540, www.bigchill.net). King's Cross tube/rail. **Open** noon-midnight Mon-Wed, Sun; noon-1am Thur; noon-3am Fri, Sat. **Admission** free-£5. **Credit** MC, V. **Map** p397 M3.
A festival, a record label, a bar and now also a club venue, the Big Chill empire rolls on. A good thing too, if it keeps offering such interesting things as this three-floor space. The programme was refreshed in 2010, introducing nights such as Reggae Roast, Slipped Disco's UFO and the Playground. There's a wonderful terrace too.

Lock Tavern
35 Chalk Farm Road, Chalk Farm, NW1 8AJ (7482 7163, www.lock-tavern.co.uk). Chalk Farm tube. **Open** noon-midnight Mon-Thur; noon-1am Fri, Sat; noon-11pm Sun. **Admission** free. **Credit** AmEx, MC, V. **Map** p404 X1.
A tough place to get into at weekends, what with queues of artfully distressed rock urchins and one of the most arbitrary entry policies in Camden. It teems with aesthetic niceties inside (cosy black couches and warm wood panels downstairs; open-air terrace on the first floor), but it's the unpredictable after-party vibe that packs in the punters, with big name DJs regularly providing the tunes.

Old Queen's Head
44 Essex Road, Islington, N1 8LN (7354 9993, www.www.theoldqueenshead.com). Angel tube. **Open** noon-midnight Mon-Wed, Sun; noon-2am Fri, Sat. **Admission** £4 after 8pm Fri, Sat. **Credit** AmEx, MC, V. **Map** p400 O1.
Pulling in fun-seekers since its relaunch way back in 2006, the Old Queen's Head is another place with long queues at the weekends. No wonder, when DJs such as Freestylers, Eno and Mr Thing are on the roster. There are two floors and outside seating front and back, and during the week you can lounge on the battered sofas. Weekends are for dancing, minor league celeb-spotting and chatting up the bar staff.

★ Paradise
19 Kilburn Lane, Kensal Green, W10 4AE (8969 0098, www.theparadise.co.uk). Kensal Green tube or Kensal Rise rail. **Open** noon-midnight Mon-Wed; noon-1am Thur; noon-2am Fri, Sat; noon-11.30pm Sun. **Admission** £3 after 10pm Fri; £4 after 9pm Sat. **Credit** MC, V.
This is a star among the legion of pub-clubs, thanks to canny promotion by DJ Tayo. Themed supper clubs, vintage burlesque shows and kicking rave-ups from the likes of the Count & Sinden and Tayo himself make it more than just a good local spot – it's become a destination in its own right.

Proud
Horse Hospital, Stables Market, Camden, NW1 8AH (7482 3867, www.proudcamden.com). Chalk

ARTS & ENTERTAINMENT

Dex. *See p332.*

Farm tube. **Open** 11am-1.30am Mon-Wed; 11am-2.30am Thur-Sat; 11am-12.30pm Sun. **Admission** free-£10. **Credit** AmEx, MC, V. **Map** p404 W2.

The North London guitar-slingers have given way to dubstep, rock 'n' rave and drum-and-bass, but the debauchery at this former equine hospital is still proper rock 'n' roll. Draping yourself – cocktail in hand – over the luxurious textiles in the individual stable-style booths, sink into deckchairs on the outdoor terrace, or spin around in the main band room to Club Remix with Eddy Temple-Morris.

EAST LONDON

East London is now the heart of London's clubland, with most venues of note based in Hoxton, Shoreditch and, increasingly, Dalston. In addition to the venues below, check out gay hangout the **Dalston Superstore** (*see p313*).

Bethnal Green Working Men's Club
42-44 Pollard Row, Bethnal Green, E2 6NB (7739 7170, www.workersplaytime.net). Bethnal Green tube. **Open** hrs vary; check website for details. **Admission** free-£8. **Credit** AmEx, MC, V.

Sticky red carpet and broken lampshades perfectly suit the programme of quirky lounge, retro rock 'n' roll and fancy-dress burlesque parties here. You might get to watch a spandex-lovin' dance duo or get hip with burlesque starlets on a 1960s dancefloor. The mood is friendly, the playlist upbeat and the air full of artful, playful mischief.

Book Club
100-106 Leonard Street, Shoreditch, EC2A 4RH (7684 8618, www.wearetbc.com). Old Street tube/rail. **Open** 8am-midnight Mon-Thur; 10am-2am Fri, Sat; 10am-midnight Sun. **Admission** free-£5. **Credit** MC, V. **Map** p401 Q4.

The Book Club aims to fuse lively creative events, table tennis (there's a ping pong table upstairs) and late-night drinking seven nights a week. Events range from Big Ten Inch ('Hoxton's Premier Rock 'n' Roll Revue!') to arty think-and-drink workshops that give the nerds a good night out.

Catch
22 Kingsland Road, Hoxton, E2 8DA (7729 6097, www.thecatchbar.com). Old Street tube/rail. **Open** 6pm-midnight Mon-Wed; 6pm-2am Thur-Sat; 7pm-1am Sun. **Admission** free-£5. **Credit** AmEx, MC, V. **Map** p401 R3.

Located at the southern end of the Kingsland Road, Catch doesn't look like much and its staff can be somewhat surly, but the small upstairs room attracts adventurous young promoters. The A Rebours night is always up to scratch.

East Village
89 Great Eastern Street, Shoreditch, EC2A 3HX (7739 5173, www.eastvillageclub.com). Old Street tube/rail. **Open** *Bar* 5pm-1am Thur; 5pm-3.30am Fri; 9pm-3.30am Sat; 2pm-1am Sun. *Club* 9pm-3am Thur; 9pm-3.30am Fri, Sat; 2pm-1am Sun. **Admission** free-£10. **Credit** AmEx, MC, V. **Map** p401 Q4.

Stuart Patterson, one of the Faith crew who've been behind all-day house-music parties across London for more than a decade (they started in 1999), has transformed what was once the Medicine Bar into this two-floor, 'real house' bar-club that punches above its weight. The top-notch DJs should suit any sophisticated clubber and the programme includes our own bimonthly Nite Sessions, as well as House Not House and, on Sundays, Rootikal.

INSIDE TRACK
GETTING HOME FROM
SHOREDITCH

According to Dimi, a local cab driver, 'You'll always catch a cab where Bethnal Green Road meets Shoreditch High Street, by the members' club Shoreditch House. Many cabbies will have stopped at the Brick Lane Beigel Bake (*see p229*), so there are a lot around there. You can also find cabs at the junction of Hackney Road and Kingsland Road, by Browns bar and the church.

ARTS & ENTERTAINMENT

Horse & Groom

28 Curtain Road, Shoreditch, EC2A 3NZ (7503 9421, www.thehorseandgroom.net). Old Street tube/rail. **Open** 6pm-1am Tue-Thur, Sun; 6pm-2am Fri, Sat. **Admission** free-£7. **Credit** AmEx, MC, V. **Map** p401 R4.

This self-proclaimed 'disco pub' is home to an eclectic range of nights, ranging from house, electro and techno to contemporary classical and pub quizzes.

Old Blue Last

38 Great Eastern Street, Shoreditch, EC2A 3ES (7739 7033, www.theoldbluelast.com). Liverpool Street or Old Street tube/rail, or Shoreditch High Street rail. **Open** noon-midnight Mon-Wed; noon-12.30am Thur, Sun; noon-1.30am Fri, Sat. **Admission** free-£5. **Credit** AmEx, MC, V. **Map** p401 R4.

Klaxons, Arctic Monkeys and Lily Allen have all played secret shows to the high-fashion rock 'n' rollers in the sauna-like upper room at this shabby two-floor Victorian boozer. The programme was recently revamped, with regular club nights including pop-punk favourite What's My Age Again, Skill Wizard, Bounty and electro night Dollop.

Plastic People

147-149 Curtain Road, Shoreditch, EC2A 3QE (7739 6471, www.plasticpeople.co.uk). Old Street tube/rail. **Open** 10pm-2am Thur; 10pm-4am Fri, Sat; 7-11pm Sun. **Admission** £5-£12. **Credit** MC, V. **Map** p403 R4.

The long-established and ever-popular Plastic People subscribed to the old-school line that all you need for a kicking party is a dark basement and a sound system – then surprised everyone last year by closing for a refurb. The programming remains true to form: deep techno to house, all-girl DJ line-ups and many a star DJ squeezing through the doors for a secret gig.

XOYO

32-37 Cowper Street, Shoreditch, EC2A 4AP (7729 5959, www.xoyo.co.uk). Old Street tube/rail. **Open/admission** varies; check website for details. **Credit** AmEx, MC, V. **Map** p401 Q4. *See p328* **The Club that Saved Shoreditch?**

SOUTH LONDON

Dex

467-469 Brixton Road, Brixton, SW9 8HH (3301 4588, www.dex-london.com). Brixton tube/rail. **Open** 10pm-6am Fri, Sat. **Admission** £10. **Credit** AmEx, MC, V.

This plush members' club is a beacon for a new young professional media crowd looking for somewhere sexy for post-work and late-night drinks. Its USP is a two-tiered rooftop bar with a hot tub and panoramic views over Brixton; good nights here include Get Diverted and Disco Motel. *Photo p331.*

Dogstar

389 Coldharbour Lane, Brixton, SW9 8LQ (7733 7515, www.antic-ltd.com/dogstar). Brixton tube/rail. **Open** 4pm-2am Mon-Thur; 4pm-4am Fri; noon-4am Sat; noon-2am Sun. **Admission** £5 after 10pm Fri, Sat. **Credit** MC, V.

A Brixton institution from back when Coldharbour Lane was an uncrossed frontier, the Dogstar is a big street-corner pub that exudes the kind of urban authenticity beloved by clubbers. The atmosphere can be intense, but it's never less than vibrant and is usually pretty friendly. The music policy varies, but quality generally stays high.

Ministry of Sound

103 Gaunt Street, off Newington Causeway, Elephant & Castle, SE1 6DP (7740 8600, www.ministryofsound.com). Elephant & Castle tube/rail. **Open** 10.30pm-6am Fri; 11pm-7am Sat. **Admission** £12-£20. **Credit** AmEx, MC, V. **Map** p402 O10.

Cool it ain't (there's little naffer in London clubland than the VIP rooms here), but home to a killer sound system the Ministry most certainly is. Long-running trance and epic house night the Gallery has made its home here on Fridays, with large sets from Paul Oakenfold and Sander van Doorn; the Saturday Sessions chop and change between deep techno, fidget house, electro and more. Check out Erick Morillo's Subliminal Sessions or retire to the aptly named Baby Box, where lesser known DJs sharpen their skills.

★ Plan B

418 Brixton Road, Brixton, SW9 7AY (7733 0926, www.plan-brixton.co.uk). Brixton tube/rail. **Open** times vary Fri-Sun; check website for details. **Admission** £5-£12.50. **Credit** AmEx, MC, V.

It may be small, but Plan B is very cool. Having been refurbished after a fire, it reopened in late 2009 and the flow of hip hop and funk stars resumed with a kicking relaunch weekend that featured DJ sets from the likes of Hot Chip and Goldie. It hasn't looked back: Community, the Saturday shindig, is a beauty.

WEST LONDON

Notting Hill Arts Club

21 Notting Hill Gate, Notting Hill, W11 3JQ (7460 4459, www.nottinghillartsclub.com). Notting Hill Gate tube. **Open** hours vary, but aournd 7pm-2am Wed-Fri; 4pm-2am Sat; 6pm-1am Sun. **Admission** free-£8. **Credit** MC, V. **Map** p404 Y4.

Hip west London folk are grateful for this small, basement club. A cross between a basement arts centre and a cocktail haunt, Notting Hill Arts Club is a destination venue that pulls in a cross-London crowd of arty types and cool kids. It almost single-handedly keeps this side of town on the radar thanks to nights such as Secousse and Death2Disco.

Sport & Fitness

In the approach to London 2012, the city is starting to go sport crazy.

Right now, you can't discuss London sport without discussing the 2012 Games (*see pp41-67* **London 2012**). The venues are all begun – some are even complete – and even the Games Maker training programme has begun. Even if you can't get a place on one of the occasional and always hugely popular tours of the **Olympic Park**, there are plenty of opportunities to get a feel for the Games: key venues outside the Olympic Park, including **Wimbledon** (*see p334*), **Lord's** (*see p336*), the **O2 Arena** (*see p320*) and **Wembley Stadium** (*see p335*), will be hosting regular sporting events in the run-up to London 2012.

Alongside a multitude of week-in week-out matches featuring professional teams and a calendar dotted with major one-off events, more active types will also find plenty of easily accessible facilities to get personally involved in all manner of sporting activity.

Spectator Sports

THE SPORTING YEAR

Below is a list of major sporting events from spring 2011. For all events held in stadiums or otherwise-enclosed spaces (basically, everything except the Boat Race, the London Marathon and the cycling events), you'll have to book tickets in advance.

Spring

Rugby Union: Six Nations
Twickenham (see p337). **Date** 12 Feb, 26 Feb, 13 Mar.
England take on Italy (12 Feb), France (26 Feb) and Scotland (13 Mar) at Twickenham in this tournament, which also features Ireland and Wales.

Football: Carling Cup Final
Wembley Stadium (see p335). **Date** 27 Feb.
The League Cup is seen as the lesser of the country's domestic tournaments, though victory ensures a place in the UEFA Europa League.

★ Rowing: The Boat Race
River Thames. **Date** 26 Mar.
Blue-clad Oxbridge students race each other in a pair of rowing eights, watched by tens of millions

worldwide and 250,000 on the riverbank. This is the 157th instalment of the historic race, that was first held in 1829. *See also p280.*

Rugby Union: LV Cup Final
Twickenham (see p337). **Date** mid Mar.
The showpiece domestic knockout competition reaches its climax.

★ Athletics: Virgin London Marathon
Around London. **Date** 17 Apr.
One of the world's elite long-distance races – and a huge participation event, with 35,000 starters. If you haven't applied to run, you're too late, but it costs nothing to watch the spectacle.

INSIDE TRACK PREVIEW 2012

The first completed London 2012 venue has already hosted international competitions and events. Back in 2009, the RS:X Class Windsurfing World Championship was held at Weymouth Bay and Portland Harbour (*see p64*). If you fancy taking a trip out of London in 2011, you can come here from 1-8 July to check out the IFDS (Paralympic Sailing) World Championship.

Football: UEFA Champions League Final

Wembley Stadium (see p335). **Date** 28 May.
Wembley hosts Europe's premier club competition for the sixth time. Inter Milan are the defending champions, but fans of three London clubs – Chelsea (*see p336*), Arsenal (*see p336*) and Tottenham (*see p336*) – will both be praying (in order of increasing doubt) to see their team contest a 'home' final.

Summer

★ Cricket: Internationals

Brit Oval (see p335). **Dates** *Tests* 18 Aug: Eng v India. 9 Sept: Eng v India. *One-day international* 28 June: Eng v Sri Lanka.
Lord's (see p336). **Date** *Tests* 3-7 June: Eng v Sri Lanka. 21-25 July: Eng v India. *One-day international* 11 Sept: Eng v India.
England play a series of Test matches (the classic five-day format – most spectators only attend one day's play during the course of the match) and one-day internationals (50 overs per side).

Football: 130th FA Cup Final

Wembley Stadium (see p335). **Date** 14 May.
The climax of the world's oldest domestic knockout tournament. In 2010, Chelsea (*see p336*) retained the cup, beating 2008 winners Portsmouth and securing a rare league and cup double in the process.

★ Horse Racing: Epsom Derby

Epsom Racecourse (see p337). **Date** 4 June.
One of Britain's best-known flat races.

Tennis: Aegon Championships

Palliser Road, West Kensington, W14 9EQ (7386 3400, www.queensclub.co.uk). Barons Court tube.
Date 6-12 June.

The pros tend to treat this grass-court tournament as a summer warm-up to Wimbledon (*see below*).

Horse Racing: Royal Ascot

Ascot Racecourse (see p337). **Date** 14-18 June.
Major races include the Ascot Gold Cup on the Thursday, which is Ladies' Day. Expect sartorial extravagance and fancy hats.

★ Tennis: Wimbledon Championships

All England Lawn Tennis Club, Church Road, Wimbledon, SW19 5AE (8971 2700, www.wimbledon.org). Southfields tube.
Date 20 June-3 July.
Getting into Wimbledon requires forethought. Seats on the show courts are distributed by a ballot, which closes the previous year; enthusiasts who queue on the day may gain entry to the outer courts. You can also turn up later in the day and pay reduced rates for seats vacated by spectators who've left early.
▶ *Wimbledon (see p63) will be hosting the tennis competition during the 2012 Games.*

Rowing: Henley Royal Regatta

Henley Reach, Henley-on-Thames, Oxon RG9 2LY (01491 572153, www.hrr.co.uk). Henley-on-Thames rail. **Date** 29 June-3 July.
First held in 1839, and under royal patronage since 1851, Henley is a posh, five-day affair.

Athletics: Aviva London Grand Prix

Crystal Palace National Sports Centre (see right).
Date 12 & 13 Aug.
Big names in this annual track and field event.

Rugby Union: Middlesex Sevens

Twickenham (see p337). **Date** mid Aug.
A curtain-raiser to the rugby union season, featuring short, fast seven-a-side matches.

Brit Oval.

Rugby League:
Carnegie Challenge Cup Final
Wembley Stadium (see right). **Date** 27 Aug.
The north's big day out, drawing boisterous, convivial crowds. Warrington broke St Helens' run of
three consecutive victories by winning the title in
2009 and again in 2010.

Autumn

Cycling: Tour of Britain
Around London. **Date** mid Sept.
Join thousands on the streets for a stage of British
cycling's biggest outdoor event – in 2010, for the
first time, the race finished in Docklands.

American Football: NFL
Wembley Stadium (see right). **Date** Oct.
The NFL took a regular-season fixture out of North
America for the first time in 2007, and plans to do
so every year until 2012.

Winter

★ Darts: PDC World Championship
Alexandra Palace (www.pdcworldchampionship.
co.uk). **Date** Dec-Jan.
The raucous, good-humoured PDC Championships
are widely regarded as being of greater stature than
the rival BDO tournament in January at Frimley
Green (www.bdodarts.com).

Horse Racing:
William Hill Winter Festival
Kempton Park (see p337). **Date** 26-27 Dec.
The King George VI three-mile chase on Boxing Day
is the highlight of this festival, a Christmas staple
for racing fans.

MAJOR STADIUMS

The most important new stadiums in London
are all rapidly nearing completion in the
Olympic Park (*see p53*) near Stratford,
in the east of the city. The 2012 Games will,
however, also be making use of several pre-
built venues across London (*see pp52-65*
Explore). These include the **O2 Arena** (*see
p320*), which hosts sporadic sporting events
such as ice hockey and basketball each year;
Wembley Arena (*see p321*), used for boxing,
snooker, basketball and show jumping; and
Wembley Stadium (*see right*).

Crystal Palace National Sports Centre
Ledrington Road, Crystal Palace, SE19 2BB
(8778 0131, www.gll.org). Crystal Palace rail.
Until the Olympic Stadium (*see p53*) is completed,
this Grade II-listed building and leisure centre
remains the major athletics venue in the country,
and hosts popular summer Grand Prix events.

Wimbledon Championships.

★ Wembley Stadium
Stadium Way, Wembley, Middx HA9 0WS (0844
980 8001, www.wembleystadium.com). Wembley
Park tube or Wembley Stadium rail.
Britain's most famous sports venue reopened in early
2007 after an expensive redevelopment. Designed by
Lord Foster, the 90,000-capacity stadium is some
sight, its futuristic steel arch now an imposing feature of the skyline. England football internationals
and cup finals are played here (as well as the 2011
Champions League final; *see p334*), as are a number
of one-off sporting events. Guided tours offer alternative access (*see p336* **Inside Track**).
► *Wembley Stadium will host the finals of the*
Football for London 2012; see p63. The original
stadium also hosted the Opening Ceremony and
many of the events in the 1948 Games.

INDIVIDUAL SPORTS
Cricket

Typically, the English national team hosts Test
and one-day series against two international
sides each summer. (Test matches are the classic
five-day format; one-day internationals last 50
overs a side.) For this summer's international
fixtures, *see left*. Seats are easier to come by
for county games, both four-day and one-day
matches. The season runs from April through
to September. Surrey play at the Brit Oval
and Middlesex at Lord's, which is hosting
the Archery for London 2012; *see p59*.

Brit Oval *Kennington Oval, Kennington, SE11*
5SS (0871 246 1100, www.surreycricket.com).
Oval tube. **Tickets** *International* £53-£92.
County £10-£20.

★ **Lord's** *St John's Wood Road, St John's Wood, NW8 8QN (7432 1000, www.lords.org). St John's Wood tube.* **Tickets** *International call for details. County £5-£15.*

Football

Playing in the lucrative Barclays Premier League, **Arsenal** and **Chelsea** are the city's major players. Arsenal, who play a slick-moving, quick-passing style that gets many neutrals purring but has won few trophies of late, are based in the 60,000-capacity Emirates Stadium. The team is under considerable pressure to deliver a trophy this year. Chelsea, slowly weaning themselves off dependency on the transfer-market largesse of Russian oil tycoon Roman Abramovich, are showing real goal-scoring flair under Carlo Ancelotti – who secured the FA Cup and Premiership Double in his first season with the club. Other London-based Premier League clubs include popular **Fulham**, inconsistently brilliant **Tottenham** and troubled **West Ham**. For football stadium tours, *see right* **Inside Track**.

Tickets for Premier League games can be hard to obtain, but a visit to Fulham is a treat: a superb setting by the river, a historic ground and seats in the 'neutral' section often available on the day. For clubs in the lower leagues (the Championship, Football Leagues 1 and 2), tickets are cheaper and easier to obtain. Prices given are for adult non-members.

The English national team plays its home fixtures at **Wembley Stadium** (*see p335*). Tickets can be hard to come by.

Arsenal *Emirates Stadium, Ashburton Grove, Highbury, N7 7AF (0844 277 3625, www.arsenal.com). Arsenal tube.* **Tickets** *£35-£94. Premier League.*

Brentford *Griffin Park, Braemar Road, Brentford, Middx TW8 0NT (0845 345 6442, www.brentfrodfc.co.uk). Brentford rail.* **Tickets** *£20-£22. League 1.*

Charlton Athletic *The Valley, Floyd Road, Charlton, SE7 8BL (8333 4000, www.cafc.co.uk). Charlton rail.* **Tickets** *£17-£22. League 1.*

Chelsea *Stamford Bridge, Fulham Road, Chelsea, SW6 1HS (0871 984 1905, www.chelseafc.com). Fulham Broadway tube.* **Tickets** *£40-£73. Premier League.*

Crystal Palace *Selhurst Park, Whitehorse Lane, South Norwood, SE25 6PU (0871 200 0071, www.cpfc.co.uk). Selhurst rail or 468 bus.* **Tickets** *£23-£27. Championship.*

Dagenham & Redbridge *Victoria Road, Dagenham, Essex RM10 7XL (8592 1549, www.daggers.co.uk). Dagenham East tube.* **Tickets** *£20-£22. League 1.*

INSIDE TRACK FOOTBALL FUN

If you fail to get tickets to a Premiership game, you can still see the inside of a football stadium by going on a tour. However, you'll need to decide who to support: **Chelsea** (0871 984 1955, www.chelseafctours.com), **West Ham** (0871 222 2700, www.whufc.com), **Tottenham Hotspur** (0844 844 0102, www.tottenhamhotspur.com) and **Arsenal** (7619 5000, www.arsenal.com) all offer tours. But perhaps you'd do best instead to tour **Wembley Stadium** (0844 800 2755, www.wembleystadium.com/wembleystadiumtour; *see also p335*) – it's not only the home of English football, but the site for numerous games during the Football competition in the London 2012 Games (*see p63*).

Fulham *Craven Cottage, Stevenage Road, Fulham, SW6 6HH (0870 442 1234, www.fulhamfc.com). Putney Bridge tube.* **Tickets** *£20-£60. Premier League.*

Leyton Orient *Matchroom Stadium, Brisbane Road, Leyton, E10 5NF (8926 1111, www.leytonorient.com). Leyton tube.* **Tickets** *£20-£22. League 1.*

Millwall *The Den, Zampa Road, Bermondsey, SE16 3LN (7232 1222, www.millwallfc.co.uk). South Bermondsey rail.* **Tickets** *£22-£27. Championship.*

Queens Park Rangers *Loftus Road Stadium, South Africa Road, Shepherd's Bush, W12 7PA (0870 112 1967, www.qpr.co.uk). White City tube.* **Tickets** *£20-£35. Championship.*

Tottenham Hotspur *White Hart Lane Stadium, 748 High Road, Tottenham, N17 0AP (0844 844 0102, www.tottenhamhotspur.com). White Hart Lane rail.* **Tickets** *£29-£78. Premier League.*

West Ham United *Upton Park, Green Street, West Ham, E13 9AZ (0871 222 2700, www.whufc.com). Upton Park tube.* **Tickets** *£36-£69. Premier League.*

Greyhound racing

In the absence of Walthamstow Stadium, sold for development in 2008 (although campaigners still hope to save it for racing), **Wimbledon** (Plough Lane, 0870 840 8905, www.lovethedogs.co.uk) is the most central dog track. Further afield, head to chirpy **Romford** (London Road, 01708 762345, www.romfordgreyhoundstadium.co.uk) or relaxed **Crayford** (Stadium Way, 01322 557836, www.crayford.com). For more, visit www.thedogs.co.uk.

Horse racing

The racing year is divided into the flat-racing season, from April to September, and the National Hunt season over jumps, from October to April. For more information about the 'sport of kings', visit www.discover-racing.com.

The Home Counties around London are liberally sprinkled with a fine variety of courses, each of which offers an enjoyable day out from the city. Impressive **Epsom** hosts the Derby in June, while cultured **Royal Ascot** offers the famous Royal Meeting in June and the King George Day in July; book ahead for them all. **Sandown Park** hosts the Whitbread Gold Cup in April and the Coral Eclipse Stakes in July. There's also racing at popular **Kempton Park** and delightful **Windsor**.

Epsom *Epsom Downs, Epsom, Surrey, KT18 5LQ (01372 726311 information, 01372 460460 tickets, www.epsomdowns.co.uk). Epsom Downs or Tattenham Corner rail.* **Admission** £15-£50.
Kempton Park *Staines Road East, Sunbury-on-Thames, Middx TW16 5AQ (01932 782292, www.kempton.co.uk). Kempton Park rail.* **Admission** from £12.
★ **Royal Ascot** *Ascot Racecourse, Ascot, Berks SL5 7JX (0870 727 1234, www.ascot.co.uk). Ascot rail.* **Admission** phone for details.
Sandown Park *Portsmouth Road, Esher, Surrey KT10 9AJ (01372 464348, www.sandown.co.uk). Esher rail.* **Admission** £18-£30.
Windsor *Maidenhead Road, Windsor, Berks SL4 5JJ (01753 498400, www.windsor-race course.co.uk). Windsor & Eton Riverside rail.* **Admission** £13-£23.

Motorsport

Every other Sunday, bangers, hot rods and stock cars come together at **Wimbledon Stadium** (01252 322920, www.spedeworth. co.uk) for pedal-to-the-metal, family-oriented mayhem. **Rye House Stadium** (01992 440400) in Hoddesdon, on the northern edge of London, also hosts speedway, providing a home for the **Rye House Rockets** (www.ryehouse.com). Matches usually take place on Saturday nights.

Rugby

For more than a century, there have been two rival rugby 'codes', each with their own rules and traditions: rugby union and rugby league.

Rugby union dominates in the south of England. The Guinness Premiership runs from early September to May; most games are played on Saturday and Sunday afternoons. Look out, too, for matches in the Heineken Cup, a pan-European competition. The four local Premiership teams – including Harlequins, infamous for 2009's 'Bloodgate' scandal – are listed below; for a full list of clubs, contact the Rugby Football Union (0871 222 2120, www.rfu.com).

The English national team's home games in the Six Nations Championship (Jan-Mar; *see p333*) are held at **Twickenham** (Rugby Road, Twickenham, Middx, 8892 2000, www.rfu.com), the home of English rugby union. Tickets are almost impossible to get hold of, but other matches are more accessible. There are also internationals in October and November.

Rugby league's heartland is in the north of England: London's sole Super League club is **Harlequins RL**. However, in late summer, the sport moves south as Wembley hosts the Challenge Cup final; *see p335*.

Harlequins *Stoop Memorial Ground, Langhorn Drive, Twickenham, Middx TW2 7SX (8410 6000 information, 0871 527 1315 tickets, www.quins.co.uk). Twickenham rail.* **Tickets** £20-£40.
Harlequins Rugby League *Stoop Memorial Ground, Langhorn Drive, Twickenham, Middx TW2 7SX (8410 6000 information, 0871 527 1315 tickets, www.league.quins.co.uk). Twickenham rail.* **Tickets** £15-£35.
London Irish *Madejski Stadium, Shooters Way, Reading, Berks RG2 0FL (0844 249 1871, www.london-irish.com). Reading rail then £2 shuttle bus.* **Tickets** £20-£40.
London Wasps *Adams Park, Hillbottom Road, High Wycombe, Bucks HP12 4HJ (0844 225 2990, www.wasps.co.uk). High Wycombe rail.* **Tickets** £15-£45.
Saracens *Vicarage Road Stadium, Watford, Herts WD18 0EP (0844 847 2482, www. saracens.com). Watford High Street rail.* **Tickets** £15-£60.

Tennis

For **Wimbledon**, *see p334*; for the **Aegon Championships**, *see p334*.

Participation & Fitness

CYCLING

Cycling in London is more popular than ever and is set to grow further with the introduction of a City Hall-sponsored bike rental scheme (*see p339* **Cycle City**). This new scheme is good for short journeys, but those in need of a longer rental should try **Velorution**, who rents folding bikes, with local delivery; and the South Bank-located **London Bicycle Tour Company** (for both, *see p338*).

Sidebar: **ARTS & ENTERTAINMENT**

Serious riders have two options. They can try out the **Herne Hill Velodrome** (Burbage Rd, Herne Hill, SE24 9HE, www.hernehillvelodrome. com), the world's oldest cycling circuit and the only single-sport venue to have survived from the 1948 Games. There's also the newly opened **Redbridge Cycle Centre** (Forest Rd, Hainault, Essex IG6 3HP, 8500 9359, www.vision-rcl.org. uk), which has a road circuit, a mountain bike track and seven different circuit combinations.

London Bicycle Tour Company *1A Gabriel's Wharf, 56 Upper Ground, South Bank, SE1 9PP (7928 6838, www.londonbicycle.com). Southwark tube.* **Open** 10am-6pm daily. **Hire** £3.50/hr; £20/1st day, then £10/day. *Deposit* with credit card, or £180 cash. **Credit** AmEx, MC, V. **Map** p402 N7.
Velorution *18 Great Titchfield Street, Fitzrovia, W1W 8BD (7637 4004, www.velorution.biz). Oxford Circus tube.* **Open** 8.30am-7pm Mon-Fri; 10.30am-6.30pm Sat. **Hire** £20/day. **Credit** MC, V. **Map** p396 J5.

GOLF

You don't have to be a member to tee off at the many public courses in the London area, but you will need to book in advance. There's a list of clubs at www.englishgolfunion.org; two accessible beauties are the lovely **Dulwich & Sydenham Hill Golf Club** in Dulwich (8693 8491, www.dulwichgolf.co.uk, £40, members only Sat & Sun) and the testing **North Middlesex Golf Club** near Arnos Grove (8445 1604, www.northmiddlesexgc.co.uk, £15-£30, members only before 1pm Sat & Sun).

HEALTH CLUBS & SPORTS CENTRES

A lot of London hotels have gym facilities, some of very high quality. But if you're looking for something more serious than your hotel can offer, many health clubs and sports centres admit non-members and allow them to join classes. Some of the best are listed below; for a list of all venues in Westminster, call 7641 1846, or for Camden, call 7974 1542. Note that last entry is normally 45-60 minutes before the listed closing times. For more independent spirits, **Hyde Park/Kensington Gardens** (*see p145*) and **Battersea Park** (*see p170*) have good jogging trails.

★ Central YMCA
112 Great Russell Street, Bloomsbury, WC1B 3NQ (7343 1844, www.centralymca.org.uk). Tottenham Court Road tube. **Open** 6.30am-10pm Mon-Fri; 10am-8pm Sat; 10am-7pm Sun. **Credit** MC, V. **Map** p416 X1.

Conveniently located and user-friendly, the Y has a good range of cardiovascular and weight-training equipment, a pool and a sports hall, as well as a full timetable of excellently taught classes.

Jubilee Hall Leisure Centre
30 The Piazza, Covent Garden, WC2E 8BE (7836 4835, www.jubileehallclubs.co.uk). Covent Garden tube. **Open** 6.45am-10pm Mon-Fri; 9am-9pm Sat; 10am-5pm Sun. **Map** p416 Z3.
A reliable and very central venue that provides calm surroundings for workouts, Jubilee Hall also offers a selection of therapies and treatments. There are other centres in Southwark, Westminster and Hampstead.

Westway Sports Centre
1 Crowthorne Road, Ladbroke Grove, W10 6RP (8969 0992, www.westwaysportscentre.org). Ladbroke Grove or Latimer Road tube. **Open** 7.45am-10pm Mon-Fri; 8am-8pm Sat; 9.45am-10pm Sun.
A smart sports centre: all-weather pitches, tennis courts, a swim centre and gym, plus the largest indoor climbing facility in the country are on offer.

ICE-SKATING

There's a permanent indoor rink in Bayswater: **Queens Ice & Bowl** (17 Bayswater, W2 4QP, 7229 0172, www.queensiceandbowl.co.uk). But at Christmas, a variety of temporary rinks spring up all over town. **Somerset House** (*see p111*) set the trend; it's since been followed by **Hampton Court Palace** (*see p173*), the **Tower of London** (*see p97*) and **Kew Gardens** (*see p172*), among others. Check the weekly *Time Out* magazine for a full list.

RIDING

There are various stables in and around the city; for a list, see www.bhs.org.uk. Those below run classes for all ages and abilities.

Hyde Park & Kensington Stables *63 Bathurst Mews, Paddington, W2 2SB (7723 2813, www.hydeparkstables.com). Lancaster Gate tube.* **Open** 7.15am-5pm Mon-Wed; 9am-5pm Thur-Sun. **Lessons** *Group* £55-£59/hr. *Individual* £79-£99/hr. **Map** p393 D6.
Wimbledon Village Stables *24 High Street, Wimbledon, SW19 5DX (8946 8579, www.wv stables.com). Wimbledon tube/rail.* **Open** 9am-12.15pm Tue; 9am-5pm Wed-Sun. **Lessons** *Group* £55-£60/hr. *Individual* £75-£80/hr.

STREET SPORTS

Under the Westway in Acklam Road, W10, **Baysixty6 Skate Park** (www.baysixty6.com) has a large street course and four halfpipes, all

Cycle City

Are two-wheelers taking over London?

Since public transport at rush hour tends to resemble a sweaty mosh pit of depression, it's perhaps no surprise that cycling is undergoing a boom. In summer 2010, Mayor Boris Johnson opened a scheme first mooted by his predecessor: the **Barclays Cycle Hire Scheme** (www.tfl. gov.uk/roadusers/cycling/14808.aspx). The Boris Bike was born.

The idea, modelled on similar schemes in Paris and Montreal, is to provide bikes for people to use as an alternative to public transport for short trips in and around town. Operating in an area equivalent to Zone 1 of the tube map, there are 6,000 bikes available from 400 docking stations – that's one station roughly every 300m.

The self-service scheme operates 24 hours a day and is open to anyone over 14, but – contrary to the original plan, by which you needed only to offer credit card details at a docking station – you have to pre-register, paying £3 and allowing a few days for Transport for London (TfL) to send you a 'key' (used to unlock the bikes from the rack). You then pay an access fee (£1 a day or £5 a week), after which trips under half an hour are free, those up to an hour cost £1 and any up to two hours are £6. TfL initially hope the scheme will generate 40,000 extra bike trips a day.

There have been teething problems. As in Paris, some docking stations are more popular for taking a bike and thus often empty (near stations, say), while others are more popular for leaving a bike (at the bottom of a hill rather than the top, for example) and so are full when you try to park your bike. The redistribution vans set up to deal with this problem were initially a specially green, specially quiet all-electric fleet, but the number of vans required was heavily underestimated – operators Serco almost immediately had to hire ordinary, non-eco-friendly white vans to supplement them. There have been isolated incidents of overcharging or key malfunctions, and the first Boris Bike accident was already being reported by September 2010 – no helmets are supplied with the bikes.

Most importantly, that credit card system – essential for tourists and other casual users who don't have three days to wait for a key – wasn't working for the launch. Initially delayed until the end of September, full roll-out was quickly (and rather quietly) postponed until the beginning of 2011. We await developments.

It's all part of TfL's rather impressive £111 million investment in cycling across the capital. Barclays is sponsoring the rental scheme for its first five years, having coughed up £25 million for the privilege, part of which will go towards sponsoring a network of a dozen 'Cycle Superhighways' (*see p31*). TfL is already planning to extend the bike hire scheme, sensibly focusing the extra bikes on Stratford and the vicinity of the Olympic Park (*see p53*).

ARTS & ENTERTAINMENT

wooden and covered. **Stockwell Skate Park** (Stockwell Park Road, SW9, www. stockwellskatepark.com) is one of the city's most popular outdoor parks; it's rivalled by **Cantelowes Skatepark** (Cantelowes Gardens, Camden Road, Camden, NW1, www. cantelowesskatepark.co.uk) and **Mile End Skatepark** (corner of Burdett Road and St Pauls Way, E3), which opened in May 2009. Many skateboarders and BMXers prefer unofficial street spots such as the **South Bank** under the Royal Festival Hall. Inliners should keep an eye on www.londonskaters.com.

SWIMMING

There are indoor pools scattered all over London. The **Central YMCA** (*see p338*) and the **Oasis Sports Centre** (*see right*) are both worth a visit, but the historic **Marshall Street** baths (*see below*), reopened in 2010, are certainly the best located – the impressively restored building dates back to 1931. To find your nearest pool, see www.activeplaces.co.uk. For pools suited to children, check www.british swimming.co.uk.

If alfresco swimming is more your thing, there are open-air lidos at **Parliament Hill Fields**, the **Serpentine**, **Tooting Bec**, **Brockwell Park** and **London Fields**.

Marshall Street Leisure Centre *15 Marshall Street, Soho, W1F 7EL (7871 7222, www. nuffieldhealth.com). Oxford Circus or Piccadilly*

Marshall Street Leisure Centre.

Circus tube. **Open** 6.30am-10pm Mon-Fri; 8am-8pm Sat, Sun. **Admission** £5.25; £1.85-£2.15 reductions. **Map** p416 V2.
Oasis Sports Centre *32 Endell Street, Covent Garden, WC2H 9AG (7831 1804, www.gll.org). Holborn tube.* **Open** *Indoor* 6.30am-9.30pm Mon-Fri; 9.30am-5pm Sat, Sun. *Outdoor* 7.30am-9pm Mon-Fri; 9.30am-5pm Sat, Sun. **Admission** £4.05; £1.10-£1.50 reductions. **Map** p416 Y2.

TENNIS

Many parks around the city have council-run courts that cost little or nothing to use; keener players should try the indoor and outdoor courts at the **Islington Tennis Centre**, though non-members may only book up to five days ahead. For grass courts, phone the Lawn Tennis Association's Information Department (8487 7000, www.lta.org.uk).

Islington Tennis Centre *Market Road, Islington, N7 9PL (7700 1370, www. aquaterra.org). Caledonian Road tube or Caledonian Road & Barnsbury rail.* **Open** 7am-11pm Mon-Thur; 7am-10pm Fri; 8am-10pm Sat, Sun. **Court rental** £9-£20/hr.

TEN-PIN BOWLING

For a classier take on bowling, dine and drink cocktails while you strike at the branches of **All Star Lanes** (*see p237*).

Queens Ice & Bowl *17 Queensway, Bayswater, W2 4QP (7229 0172, www.queensiceandbowl. co.uk). Bayswater tube.* **Open** 10am-11pm daily. Bowling £6.50/game. **Lanes** 12. **Map** p392 C7.
Rowans Bowl *10 Stroud Green Road, Finsbury Park, N4 2DF (8800 1950, www.rowans.co.uk). Finsbury Park tube/rail.* **Open** 10.30am-12.30am Mon-Thur, Sun; 10.30am-2.30am Fri, Sat. Bowling £3-£4.20. **Lanes** 24.

YOGA & PILATES

For something more than just a quick stretch in your hotel room or the nearest park, check out the yoga activities and classes (and fully equipped Pilates studio) at Triyoga. You may also want to consult the **British Wheel of Yoga** (www.bwy.org.uk).

Triyoga *6 Erskine Road, Primrose Hill, NW3 3AJ (7483 3344, www.triyoga.co.uk). Chalk Farm tube.* **Open** 6am-10pm Mon-Fri; 7.30am-8.30pm Sat; 8am-9.30pm Sun. **Admission** £12-£15/session.
Other locations Wallacespace, 2 Dryden Street, Covent Garden, WC2E 9NA (7483 3344); Kingly Court, Soho, W1B 5PW (use main number).

Theatre

Even in the West End, variety is the spice of London theatrical life.

With the highest concentration of playhouses in the world, London's West End is a beacon for lovers of stage performance, drawing more theatregoers in an average year than Broadway. The biggest attractions remain the indomitable Shaftesbury Avenue musicals, some of which have been running for two decades. However, straight plays have been making something of a comeback; productions tend towards the conservative but frequently attract the biggest names in showbiz from both sides of the Atlantic. And away from the commercial sector, political debate and formal innovation are mainstays at a handful of subsidised venues and a broad variety of fringe theatres, fed by the capital's multicultural influences and cross-pollination of its various arts scenes.

THEATRE IN LONDON

Escapist entertainment thrives when times are tough, so it's no surprise that the West End has retained its rosy glow into and through the recession. Broadway import *Wicked* announced its highest-grossing year in 2009, then scooped the 2010 Olivier for most popular musical. Yet the downturn also encouraged musical producers to stick safely to the Yellow Brick Road, with a legion of new shows based on hit movies – *Flashdance, Love Story* – joining the already-established likes of **Dirty Dancing** (*see p344*) and **Billy Elliot** (*see p344*). With *Ghost* due to open at the Piccadilly in summer 2011, it would seem that the trend isn't yet running out of steam.

Drama producers continue to rely on star casting as they fight to hold the line against the overwhelming tide of big-budget musicals. The **Donmar Warehouse** (*see p347*) continues to lure extraordinarily high-profile film stars to perform at its tiny Earlham Street home, while appearances by Kevin Spacey and his stellar chums at the **Old Vic** (*see p343*) have put bums on seats there.

Shows that start life at the **National Theatre** (*see p342*) regularly transfer to the West End; the most notable production of late has been Michael Morpurgo's *War Horse* (*see p345*). On a much smaller scale, the tiny **Menier Chocolate Factory** (*see p348* **Inside Track**) achieved major success with

a sparkling revival of *La Cage aux Folles* – a trick it may well manage to repeat with its transfer in 2010 of *Sweet Charity* to Haymarket Theatre Royal. The Haymarket continues its unique practice of operating as a producing house overseen by annually changing artistic directors, while the National's only major competitor when it comes to subsidised theatre, the **Barbican Centre** (*see p342*), continues to programme visually exciting and physically expressive work from around the world, as well as from its Artistic Associates, such as Cheek by Jowl. On a smaller scale, the **Lyric Hammersmith** (*see p348*) and the **BAC** (*see p346*) are breeding grounds for young, experimental companies.

For details of what's on when you're in town, see the Theatre section of the weekly *Time Out* magazine, which offers reviews and full listings information for all notable shows.

Theatre districts

In strictly geographical terms, the **West End** refers to London's traditional theatre district, a busy area bounded by Shaftesbury Avenue, Drury Lane, the Strand and the Haymarket. Most major musicals and big-money dramas run here, alongside transfers of successful smaller-scale shows. However, the 'West End' appellation is now also applied to other major theatres elsewhere in town, including subsidised venues such as the Barbican Centre (in the City), the National Theatre (on the South Bank) and the Old Vic (near Waterloo).

Off-West End denotes theatres with smaller budgets and smaller capacities. These venues, many of them sponsored or subsidised, push the creative envelope with new writing, often brought to life by the best young acting and directing talent. The Soho Theatre and the Bush are good for up-and-coming young playwrights, while the Almeida and Donmar Warehouse offer elegantly produced shows with the occasional big star.

One rung below these venues is the **Fringe** (*see p348* **Inside Track**), a disparate collection of small theatres within which quality and style vary wildly, but enthusiasm is a given.

The Cheap Seats

Getting the most out of the box office.

At the two **Tkts** booths (Clocktower Building, Leicester Square, Soho, WC2H 7NA, www.officiallondontheatre.co.uk/ tkts; or Brent Cross Shopping Centre in north-west London), anybody can buy tickets for big shows at much-reduced rates, either on the day or up to a week in advance. You can find the best seats for blockbusters sold at half price. The Leicester Square branch opens at 10am (noon on Sundays); you can check which shows are available on any given day by checking the website. Before buying, be sure you're at the correct booth, in a stand-alone building on the south side of Leicester Square – the square is ringed with other ticket brokers, where the seats are worse and the prices are higher.

Many West End theatres also offer their own reduced-price tickets for shows that haven't sold on the night; these are known as **'standby' seats**. Some standby deals are limited to those with student ID. The time these tickets goes on sale varies from theatre to theatre: check before setting out.

If you'd rather book ahead, subsidised theatres offer better value than purely commercial playhouses. For the Travelex-sponsored season at the **National Theatre** (*see right*), two-thirds of the seats go for £10, but you can stand in the slips at the **Royal Court Theatre** (*see p343*) for as little as 10p. The Royal Court also presents 'Cheap Mondays', with all tickets at £10, while Tuesday evenings and Saturday afternoons at the **Tricycle** (*see p348*) are 'Pay What You Can'.

Buying tickets

If there's a specific show you want to see, aim to book ahead. And, if possible, always try to do so at the theatre's box office, at which booking fees are generally smaller than they are with agents such as Ticketmaster (*see p276*).

If you're more flexible about your choice of show, consider buying from one of the **Tkts** booths or taking your chances with standby seats (for both, *see left* **The Cheap Seats**).

THE WEST END
Major theatres

Barbican Centre

Silk Street, the City, EC2Y 8DS (7638 8891, www.barbican.org.uk). Barbican tube or Moorgate tube/rail. **Box office** *In person* 9am-9pm Mon-Sat; 11am-8pm Sun. **Tickets** £7-£32. **Credit** AmEx, MC, V. **Map** p400 P5.

The annual BITE (Barbican International Theatre Events) season continues to cherry-pick exciting and eclectic theatre companies from around the globe. Recent highlights have included a rare visit from the revered (and now Paris-based) director Peter Brook, an appearance from the American Merce Cunningham Dance Company and the National Theatre of Scotland's Olivier prize-winning play *Black Watch*. Watch out too for anything by Cheek By Jowl, a Barbican Artistic Associate: there's usually a queue for returns for its shows, which have included *Andromaque* and *Macbeth* in the last couple of years.

▶ *The Barbican is an all-round arts complex. For music there, see p315.*

★ National Theatre

South Bank, SE1 9PX (7452 3400 information, 7452 3000 tickets, www.nationaltheatre.org.uk). Embankment or Southwark tube, or Waterloo tube/rail. **Box office** 9.30am-8pm Mon-Sat. **Tickets** *Olivier & Lyttelton* £10-£44. *Cottesloe* £10-£32. **Credit** AmEx, MC, V. **Map** p399 M8.

This concrete monster is the flagship venue of British theatre, and no theatrical tour of London is complete without a visit. Three auditoriums allow for different kinds of performance: in-the-round, promenade, even classic proscenium arch. Nicholas Hytner's artistic directorship, with landmark successes such as Alan Bennett's *The History Boys*, has shown that the state-subsidised home of British theatre can turn out quality drama at a profit. The Travelex season ensures a widening audience by offering two-thirds of the seats for £10, as does the free outdoor performing arts stage, Watch This Space, every summer. In 2011, watch out for Zoë Wanamaker in *The Cherry Orchard*, a version of *Frankenstein* by film director Danny Boyle and the great Peter Hall's take on *Twelfth Night*.

National Theatre.

Old Vic

The Cut, Waterloo, SE1 8NB (0844 871 7628,
www.oldvictheatre.com). Southwark tube or
Waterloo tube/rail. **Box office** *In person* 10am-
7.30pm Mon-Sat. *By phone* 9am-10pm Mon-Sat;
10am-8pm Sun. **Tickets** £10-£48.50. **Credit**
AmEx, MC, V. **Map** p402 N9.

The combination of Oscar-winner Kevin Spacey,
who's been the artistic director here since 2003, and
producer David Liddiment continues to be a commercial success; it's sometimes a critical hit as well,
especially when Spacey himself or one of his stellar
Hollywood chums takes to the stage. Programming
runs from grown-up Christmas pantomimes to the
Bridge Project, a series of transatlantic collaborations on serious plays (the likes of Chekhov and, of
course, Shakespeare) directed by Sam Mendes.

▶ *From early 2010, the theatre has been operating*
an informal space in the railway arches beneath
Waterloo station. The Old Vic Tunnels has hosted
everything from immersive theatre to an 'audio
project' by genius graphic novelist Alan Moore.

Open Air Theatre

Regent's Park, Inner Circle, Marylebone, NW1
4NR (0844 826 4242, www.openairtheatre.org).
Baker Street tube. **Tickets** £10-£35. **Credit**
AmEx, MC, V. **Map** p396 G3.

The verdant setting of this alfresco theatre lends
itself perfectly to summery Shakespeare romps in a
season that runs from June to September. The standard is a world above village-green dramatics, with
the family-friendly Shakespeares joined over the last
few years by very popular musicals.

▶ *If you don't want to bring a picnic, good-value,*
tasty food can be bought at the Garden Café; or
plump for traditional tea or Pimm's on the lawn.

★ Royal Court Theatre

Sloane Square, Chelsea, SW1W 8AS (7565
5000, www.royalcourttheatre.com). Sloane
Square tube. **Box office** 10am-6pm Mon-Sat.
Tickets 10p-£25; all tickets £10 Mon. **Credit**
AmEx, MC, V. **Map** p398 G11.

From John Osborne's *Look Back in Anger*, staged in
the theatre's opening year of 1956, to the numerous
discoveries of the past decade, among them Sarah
Kane, Joe Penhall and Conor McPherson, the emphasis at the Royal Court has always been on new voices
in British theatre. Artistic director Dominic Cooke
has injected plenty of politics into the programme,
and successfully lowered the age of his audiences in
the process. Expect to find rude, lyrical new work by
first-time playwrights, as well as better established
American and European writers with a message.
Look out for quality shorts programmed at 6pm and
9pm, and more of the usual vividly produced British
and international work by young writers.

Royal Shakespeare Company

01789 403444 information, 0844 800 1110
tickets, www.rsc.org.uk. **Box office** *By phone*
9am-8pm Mon-Sat. **Tickets** £10-£48. **Credit**
AmEx, MC, V.

Britain's flagship company hasn't had a London
base since it quit the Barbican (*see p342*) in 2002,
although it may be turning its mind towards finding one now the £100m redevelopment of its home
theatres in Stratford-upon-Avon has reached completion. In the meantime, it continues its itinerant
existence, now usually appearing for three months
from December in the Roundhouse (*see p321*), as
well as popping up in smaller venues (among them
Wilton's; *see p346* **Profile**) to stage the new plays
that artistic director Michael Boyd has championed.

★ Shakespeare's Globe
21 New Globe Walk, Bankside, SE1 9DT (7401 9919, www.shakespeares-globe.org). Southwark tube or London Bridge tube/rail. **Box office** *In person* 10am-8pm Mon-Sat; 10am-7pm Sun. *By phone* 10am-6pm Mon-Sat; 10am-5pm Sun. **Tickets** £5-£35. **Credit** AmEx, MC, V. **Map** p402 O7.

Sam Wanamaker's dream to recreate the theatre where Shakespeare first staged many of his plays has become a successful reality, underpinned by outreach work (you can drop in for regular free Q&As with cast and director). The open-air, standing-room Pit tickets are excellent value, if a little marred by low-flying aircraft. Expect a range of Shakespeare classics alongside new plays on parallel themes.

Long-runners & musicals

★ Billy Elliot the Musical
Victoria Palace Theatre, Victoria Street, Victoria, SW1E 5EA (0844 248 5000, www.victoriapalace theatre.co.uk). Victoria tube/rail. **Box office** 10am-8.30pm Mon-Sat. **Tickets** £19.50-£95. **Credit** AmEx, MC, V. **Map** p398 H10.

The combination of Elton John's music and a heart-melting yarn about a northern working-class lad with an unlikely talent for ballet has scooped more awards internationally than any other British musical.

Dirty Dancing
Aldwych Theatre, Aldwych, Covent Garden, WC2B 4DF (0844 847 2330, www.dirty dancinglondon.com). Covent Garden tube or Charing Cross tube/rail. **Box office** *In person* 10am-8pm daily. *By phone* 24hrs daily. **Tickets** £15-£65. **Credit** AmEx, MC, V. **Map** p397 M6.

With its raunchy choreography, archetypal ugly duckling story and powerful hit of nostalgia, it's no wonder *Dirty Dancing* took record advance bookings. Repeated flashes of visual wit in James Powell's production and the infectious music should have you whooping and cheering by the end.

★ Ghost Stories
Duke of York's Theatre, St Martin's Lane, Covent Garden, WC2N 4BG (0871 297 5454, www.dukeofyorkstheatre.co.uk). Leicester Square tube. **Box office** *By phone* 9am-10pm Mon-Sat; 10am-8pm Sun. *In person* 10am-6pm Mon-Sat. **Tickets** £15-£42.50. **Credit** AmEx, DC, MC, V. **Map** p416 X4.

Transferred from the Lyric (*see p348*), everything about *Ghost Stories* sets out deliberately to spook you, from a warning 'to those of a nervous disposition' on the programme to the eeriness of the auditorium – all flickering lights, police tape and apparently random numbers chalked on the walls. You're in a lecture theatre, with the jovially obnoxious Professor of the Paranormal setting out to debunk ghost stories. You just know you're being lulled into a false sense of security: the subsequent jump-out-of-your-seat shocks are effective, but the real darkness isn't apparent until right at the end.

Jersey Boys
Prince Edward Theatre, 28 Old Compton Street, Soho, W1D 4HS (0844 482 5151, www.delfontmackintosh.co.uk). Leicester Square tube. **Box office** *In person* 10am-7.45pm Tue-Sat; 10am-5.45pm Sun. *By phone* 24hrs daily. **Tickets** £20-£65. **Credit** AmEx, MC, V. **Map** p416 W2.

This Broadway import had the critics singing the praises of Ryan Molloy, who hits the high notes in

Legally Blonde.

ARTS & ENTERTAINMENT

Frankie Valli & the Four Seasons' doo-wop standards. The well-trodden storyline of early struggle, success and break-up is elevated by pacy direction.

★ Legally Blonde
Savoy Theatre, the Strand, WC2R 0ET (0844 847 2345,www.legallyblondethemusical.co.uk). Covent Garden tube or Charing Cross tube/rail. **Box office** *In person* 10am-7.30pm Mon-Sat; 11am-5pm Sun. *By phone* 24hrs daily. **Tickets** £25-£85. **Credit** AmEx, MC, V. **Map** p416 Z4.
A pepped-up, candy-coloured hymn to sisterhood, in which Malibu Barbie Elle Woods takes on the overprivileged preppies at Harvard and wins. Laurence O'Keefe and Nell Benjamin's music and lyrics give the movie an irresistible makeover: highlights are super-smart rhyming dialogues that actually propel the plot, rhythmic, catchy tunelets, and a flawless British cast.

Les Misérables
Queen's Theatre, Shaftesbury Avenue, Soho, W1D 6BA (0844 482 5160, www.lesmis.com). Leicester Square or Piccadilly Circus tube. **Box office** *In person* 10am-7.30pm Mon-Sat. *By phone* 24hrs daily. **Tickets** £15-£59. **Credit** AmEx, MC, V. **Map** p416 W3.
The RSC's version of Boublil and Schönberg's musical came to the London stage in 1985 – and no fewer than three celebratory versions ran simultaneously on one October night in 2010. The version at the Queen's should manage a few more anniversaries, which has good and bad consequences. When actors have been singing these songs since their first audition, it's easy to take it that half-inch too far. Still, the voices remain lush, the revolutionary sets are film-fabulous, and the lyrics and score (based on Victor Hugo's novel) will be considerably less chirpy than whatever's on next door.

Mousetrap
St Martin's Theatre, West Street, Cambridge Circus, Covent Garden, WC2H 9NZ (0844 499 1515, www.the-mousetrap.co.uk). Leicester Square tube. **Box office** 10am-8pm Mon-Sat. **Tickets** £15-£60. **Credit** AmEx, MC, V. **Map** p416 X3.
Running in the West End since 1952, Agatha Christie's drawing-room whodunnit is a murder mystery Methuselah, and will probably still be booking when the last trump sounds.

War Horse
New London Theatre, Drury Lane, Covent Garden, WC2B 5PW (0844 412 4654, www.nationaltheatre.org.uk/warhorse). Covent Garden tube. **Box office** *In person* 11am-8pm Mon-Sat. *By phone* 24hrs daily. **Tickets** £15-£55. **Credit** AmEx, MC, V. **Map** p416 Z2.
Transferred from the National Theatre (*see p342*), *War Horse* isn't perfect, but it is a lovely piece of

War Horse.

Festivals Theatre
What not to miss this year.

The **Greenwich+Docklands International Festival** (www.festival.org) combines acrobatics, dance and theatre, with aerial performances and fireworks over the Queen's House (*see p167*) and in Woolwich among the highlights in 2010, when more than 60,000 people attended. Expect equally eye-catching stunts at this year's free street art and outdoor theatre spectacular, held over ten days from late June. At around the same time of year, **LIFT** (the **London International Festival of Theatre**; www.liftfest.org.uk) gathers an extraordinary number of performances (last year, nearly 90 in under a month) under the directorship of Mark Ball.

In July and August, the National Theatre (*see p342*) rolls out a large square of astroturf by the river for **Watch This Space** (www.nationaltheatre.org.uk), a programme of alfresco theatre, dance and circus. Also in August, an eclectic bunch of new, experimental and short shows sprint through the **Camden Fringe** (www.camdenfringe.org). Finally, more outré work can be seen at January's **London International Mime Festival** (www.mimefest.co.uk), from haunting visual theatre to puppetry for adults.

family theatre (and a massive critical and popular hit). The play is based on Michael Morpurgo's novel about a horse separated from his young master and spirited off to World War I. Bereft Albert duly signs up, to seek Joey in the mud and carnage of Flanders. The attention is, of course, hogged by the puppet horses. Each visibly manipulated by three actors, these plywood and leather frames become astonishingly expressive beasts.

OFF-WEST END THEATRES

Almeida

Almeida Street, Islington, N1 1TA (7359 4404, www.almeida.co.uk). Angel tube. **Box office** *In person* 10am-6pm Mon-Sat. *By phone* 24hrs daily. **Tickets** £8-£32. **Credit** AmEx, MC, V. **Map** p400 O1.

Well groomed and with a rather funky bar, the Almeida turns out thoughtfully crafted theatre for grown-ups. Under artistic director Michael Attenborough it has drawn top directors like Thea Sharrock and Rupert Goold, and premières from the likes of Neil LaBute.

★ Battersea Arts Centre (BAC)

Lavender Hill, Battersea, SW11 5TN (7223 2223, www.bac.org.uk). Clapham Common tube, Clapham Junction rail or bus 77, 77A, 345. **Box office** 10am-6pm Mon-Fri; 3-6pm Sat. **Tickets** £3-£10; pay what you can Tue (phone ahead). **Credit** MC, V.

Housed in the old Battersea Town Hall, the forward-thinking BAC hosts young theatre troupes; expect quirky, fun and physical theatre from the likes of cult companies Kneehigh and 1927. May's Burst Festival is a launchpad for new contemporary theatre and performance art; you can see stand-up comedians hone their Edinburgh Festival routines during the N20 season in July.

Profile Wilton's Music Hall

A delightfully decrepit old East End theatre finding fresh life.

ARTS & ENTERTAINMENT

In the last decade, a couple of London's grandest old music halls have been refurbished to something close to their former glory. Built in 1901, the Hackney Empire received a £15m restoration in 2004, the same year that the Coliseum – first a variety hall, now an opera house – benefited from a plush renovation to celebrate its centenary. However, one music hall dates back even further than this esteemed pair – and does it ever look the part.

London's last surviving example of the giant pub halls of the mid 19th century, **Wilton's Music Hall** (for listings, *see p348*) once entertained the masses with acts ranging from Chinese performing monkeys to acrobats, contortionists to opera singers. It was here that Victorian music hall star George Leybourne made his name in character as Champagne Charlie, and that the can-can first scandalised London. Roughly 150 years after opening, Wilton's still serves as a theatre – but only just.

Wilton's Music Hall started life in the 19th century as a pub

called the Prince of Denmark, nicknamed the 'Mahogany Bar' on account of its handsome wood fittings. (The theatre's current bar, which takes on its predecessor's nickname, is on the site of the old pub.) In 1853, John Wilton, the tavern's owner, turned a purpose-built concert room behind the pub into the site's first music hall, before acquiring adjoining properties to build a larger, grander theatre to the rear in 1858. The space boasts a high proscenium arch stage, a balcony supported by unusual, twisting columns, and a decorative vaulted ceiling.

★ Bush

Shepherd's Bush Green, Shepherd's Bush,
W12 8QD (8743 5050, www.bushtheatre.co.uk).
Goldhawk Road tube or Shepherd's Bush tube/rail.
Box office noon-8pm Mon-Sat (performance
days); 10am-6pm Mon-Sat (non-performance days).
Tickets £7-£20. **Credit** AmEx, MC, V.
This diminutive venue punches above its weight,
with well-designed productions and an impressive
record of West End transfers. It's famous for its
championing of new writers; alumni include Stephen
Poliakoff and David Edgar.

★ Donmar Warehouse

41 Earlham Street, Covent Garden, WC2H 9LX
(0844 871 7624, www.donmarwarehouse.com).
Covent Garden or Leicester Square tube. **Box**
office *In person* 10am-6pm Mon-Sat. *By phone*
9am-10pm Mon-Sat; 10am-8pm Sun. **Tickets**
£12-£30. **Credit** AmEx, MC, V. **Map** p416 Y2.

The Donmar is less a warehouse than a boutique
chamber. Artistic director Michael Grandage (who
is due to leave the Donmar in late 2011 after nearly
a decade in charge) has kept the venue on a fresh,
intelligent path. Its combination of artistic integrity
and intimate size, with audience right alongside the
stage, has proved hard to resist, with many high-
profile film actors appearing: among them Nicole
Kidman, Gwyneth Paltrow and Ewan McGregor.
► *2010 saw Grandage launch Donmar Trafalgar*
– an annual 12-week residency, until 2012, that
showcases work by the stars of the Donmar's
Resident Assistant Director programme.

Gate Theatre

Prince Albert, 11 Pembridge Road, Notting Hill,
W11 3HQ (7229 0706, www.gatetheatre.co.uk).
Notting Hill Gate tube. **Box office** *By phone*
10am-6pm Mon-Fri. **Tickets** £16; £11
reductions. **Credit** MC, V. **Map** p404 Z6.

Charred roof timbers bear
witness to the huge 'sun-burner'
chandelier, complete with 300
gas jets, that once lit the room.

In 1888, the hall was acquired
by the Methodist Church and
became a mission, serving the
local community for the next
seven decades. Thousands of
striking dockers were fed here
during their landmark fight
against dock owners in
1889; in the 1930s,
the hall sheltered
locals fighting
Oswald Mosley's
blackshirts. Most
notably (indeed,
almost
miraculously), it
was one of the few
buildings in the area
to survive the Blitz.

In the years after Sir
John Betjeman launched a
successful campaign for Wilton's
to be granted listed-building
status in the 1960s, saving it
from the threat of demolition,
the property fell into disrepair.
But after Fiona Shaw and
Deborah Warner brought their
interpretation of TS Eliot's *The*
Waste Land here in 1997, it was

rediscovered, and has since
hosted opera, theatre (anything
from an all-male *Pirates of*
Penzance to a biopic of Doris
Day), music (from the Kreutzer
Quartet to Marc Almond) and
even occasional film screenings.
Private-hire events such as
weddings and film shoots
help keep it afloat.

Much of the theatre's
charm is down to
its unvarnished
condition. However,
this same state
of repair is also
causing serious
problems, to the
point where the
World Monuments
Fund Britain, a
non-profit group
that is dedicated to
architectural preservation,
placed the building on its most-
endangered list in 2008. Repairs
totalling an estimated £4m
are needed to stop the hall
collapsing in the next few years,
and funding has so far proved
difficult to secure. Unless the
money is found, the long history
of this wonderful old room could
enter its final chapter.

THREE
TO SEE
More classic
auditoriums.

Coliseum
From music
hall to opera.
See p317.

Masonic
Temple
Under the
Andaz hotel.
See p185.

Wigmore Hall
Classical in
Marylebone.
See p317.

A doll's house of a theatre, with rickety wooden chairs as seats, the Gate is the only producing theatre in London dedicated to international work, often in specially commissioned new translations.

King's Head Theatre
115 Upper Street, Islington, N1 1QN (7226 8561 information, 0844 477 1000 tickets, www.kingsheadtheatre.org). Angel tube. **Box office** *In person* 10am-7.30pm daily. *By phone* 24hrs daily. **Tickets** £10-£20. **Credit** AmEx, MC, V. **Map** p400 N2.
Started in the 1970s on a shoestring budget, this theatre is a tiny space tucked away at the back of a charming if somewhat ramshackle Victorian boozer. In the past, it's launched a raft of stars, among them Hugh Grant. It's also a favourite crossover spot for television actors to exercise their comedy muscles.

★ Lyric Hammersmith
Lyric Square, King Street, Hammersmith, W6 0QL (0871 221 1722, www.lyric.co.uk). Hammersmith tube. **Box office** *By phone* 10am-5.30pm Mon-Sat. *In person* 9.30am-7.30pm on performance days. **Tickets** £10-£25. **Credit** MC, V.
Artistic director Sean Holmes launched his tenure in 2009 with a pledge to bring writers back into the building, making space for neglected modern classics and new plays alongside the cutting-edge physical and devised work for which the Lyric is known.

Soho Theatre
21 Dean Street, Soho, W1D 3NE (7478 0100, www.sohotheatre.com). Tottenham Court Road tube. **Box office** *In person* 10am-6pm Mon-Sat; 10am-7.30pm performance nights. *By phone* 10am-7pm Mon-Sat. **Tickets** £5-£20. **Credit** MC, V. **Map** p395 K6.
Its cool blue neon lights and front-of-house café help it blend it into the Soho landscape, but this theatre has made a name for itself since opening in 2000. It attracts a young, hip crowd and brings on writers with a free script-reading service and workshops.
▶ *For comedy at the Soho, see p293.*

Theatre Royal Stratford East
Gerry Raffles Square, Stratford, E15 1BN (8534 0310, www.stratfordeast.com). Stratford tube/rail/DLR. **Box office** 10am-6pm Mon-Sat. **Tickets** £6-£27. **Credit** MC, V.
The Theatre Royal is a community theatre, with many shows written, directed and performed by black or Asian artists. Musicals are big here – *The Harder They Come* went on to West End success, and *Five Guys Named Moe* played in 2010 – but there is also a Christmas pantomime and harder-hitting fare.
▶ *There's a great comedy night too; see p294.*

★ Tricycle
269 Kilburn High Road, Kilburn, NW6 7JR (7372 6611 information, 7328 1000 tickets, www.tricycle.co.uk). Kilburn tube. **Box office** 10am-9pm Mon-Sat; 2-8pm Sun. **Tickets** £8.50-£25. **Credit** MC, V.
Passionate and political, the Tricycle consistently finds original ways into difficult subjects. It has pioneered its own genre of 'tribunal' docu-dramas.

Wilton's Music Hall
Graces Alley, off Ensign Street, E1 8JB (7702 2789, www.wiltons.org.uk). Aldgate East or Tower Hill tube. **Box office** 10am-6pm Mon-Fri. **Tickets** £10-£15. **Credit** MC, V. **Map** p403 S7. *See pp346-347* **Profile.**

★ Young Vic
66 The Cut, Waterloo, SE1 8LZ (7922 2922, www.youngvic.org). Waterloo tube/rail. **Box office** 10am-6pm Mon-Sat. **Tickets** £10-£27.50. **Credit** MC, V. **Map** p402 N8.
As the name suggests, this Vic (actually now into middle-age – it opened in September 1970) has more youthful bravura than its older sister up the road, and draws a younger crowd, who pack out the open-air balcony at its popular restaurant and bar on the weekends. They come to see European classics with a modern edge, new writing with an international flavour and collaborations with leading companies.

INSIDE TRACK FRINGE VENUES

The best places to catch next-generation talent include Battersea's **Theatre 503**, above the Latchmere pub (503 Battersea Park Road, SW11 3BW, 7978 7040, www.theatre503.com), which recently won a Peter Brook Empty Space award for its work with new writers. The theatre above the **Finborough** (118 Finborough Road, SW10 9ED, 7244 7439, www.finborough theatre.co.uk), a pub in Earl's Court, attracts national critics, and last year transferred a show to the West End. Other venues worth investigating include the excellent **Arcola Theatre** (27 Arcola Street, Dalston, E8 2DJ, 7503 1646, www.arcolatheatre.com), a former textiles factory with a laudably inclusive new and local writing policy; the **Southwark Playhouse** (Shipwright Yard, corner of Tooley Street & Bermondsey Street, SE1 2TF, 7407 0234, www.southwark playhouse.co.uk), housed in refurbished railway arches at London Bridge; and the nearby **Menier Chocolate Factory** (51-53 Southwark Street, SE1 1RU, 7907 7060, www.menierchocolatefactory.com), which currently seems to have a golden touch for West End transfers – its *Sweet Charity* opened at the Haymarket in late 2010.

Escapes & Excursions

Dungeness Point. *See p357*.

Escapes & Excursions

The south of England isn't all about the Big Smoke.

There's so much in London that you could easily spend a lifetime exploring the city, which isn't at all the same as wanting to spend a lifetime exploring the city. Everyone who lives here sometimes feels an irresistible urge to leave, so why would visitors be any different? In this chapter, there are four suggested excursions that should refresh and reinvigorate you. Two are by the sea, but could otherwise hardly be more different: **Brighton** offers traditional seaside kitsch and a full-on nightlife scene, while  **Dungeness**, **Rye** and **Romney** come with cranky charm and an other-worldly atmosphere. Inland and nestling happily in the lee of the North Downs, **Canterbury** is a lively medieval city, its cathedral and ruined abbey of such historical significance that they're listed as a UNESCO World Heritage Site. And **Cambridge**, as flat as the fenlands it sits upon, is perfect for those who like to peek into cloistered courts and college chapels.

GETTING AROUND

All of the destinations included in this chapter are within easy reach of London, perfect either for a day trip or an overnight stay. **Brighton** and **Cambridge** are the easiest of the four to reach by train; they're both within an hour of London, with rail services running from early in the morning until relatively late at night; **Canterbury** is also a direct rail journey from London, taking half an hour longer. It's more of an effort to reach **Dungeness**, **Romney** and **Rye**, but worth the work. If you don't fancy negotiating the train network, and are happy to hire a car, it's a relatively easy journey by road.

For the main attractions, we've included details of opening times, admission prices and transport details, but be aware that these can change without notice: always phone to check. Major sights are open all through the year, but many of the minor ones close out of season, often from November to March.

Before setting out, drop in on the **Britain & London Visitor Centre** (*see p374*) for additional information.

By train

Notwithstanding the occasional strike or weather-related line closure, Britain's rail network is generally reliable. However, ticket prices on some services are insultingly high, and the splintering of the network caused by privatisation has made it harder to source reliable information on train times and prices.

For information on train times and ticket prices, call **National Rail Enquiries** on 0845 748 4950. Ask about the cheapest ticket for the journey you're planning; be aware that for long journeys, the price you pay for tickets may be considerably lower if you book earlier. Timetables can be found at **www.national rail.co.uk**; you can buy tickets online at **www.thetrainline.com**.

If you need extra help, there are rail travel centres in London's mainline stations, as well as at Heathrow and Gatwick airports. Staff can give you guidance on timetables and booking. We specify departure stations in the 'Getting there' section for each destination; the journey times cited are the fastest available.

Escapes & Excursions

Brighton Pier.

By coach

Coaches operated by **National Express** (0871 781 8181, www.nationalexpress.com) are scheduled to run throughout the country. Services depart from Victoria Coach Station (*see p362*), ten minutes' walk from Victoria rail and tube stations. **Green Line Travel** (0844 801 7261, www.greenline.co.uk) also operates coaches.

Victoria Coach Station
164 Buckingham Palace Road, Victoria, SW1W 9TP (7222 1234, www.tfl.gov.uk). Victoria tube/rail. **Map** p400 H11.
Britain's most wide-ranging coach services are run by National Express (*see p362*) from Victoria Coach Station, as are services run by many other companies to and from Europe; some depart from Marble Arch.

INSIDE TRACK PARK LIFE

In 1947, a government-commissioned report by Arthur Hobhouse suggested that the South Downs should be one of a dozen UK regions to be specially protected by being given National Park status. A mere six decades later, in 2009, the government announced that a 625-square-mile area stretching roughly from Winchester to Eastbourne would become the **South Downs National Park** (www.visitsouthdowns.com), with the last administrative details due to be completed in 2011.

By car

If you're in a group of three or four, it may be cheaper to hire a car (*see p365*), especially if you plan to take in several sights within an area. The road directions in the listings below should be used in conjunction with a proper map.

By bicycle

Capital Sport (01296 631671, www.capitalsport.co.uk) offers gentle cycling tours along the Thames from London. Leisurely itineraries include plenty of time to explore royal palaces, parks and historic attractions; the website contains full details. Alternatively, try **Country Lanes** (01590 622627, www.countrylanes.co.uk), which leads cycling tours all over the beautiful New Forest in Hampshire.

London-on-Sea
BRIGHTON

Britain's youngest city, England's most popular tourist destination after London and host to the nation's biggest annual arts festival outside Edinburgh, Brighton is thriving. It's also a bracingly liberal kind of place: the constituency of Brighton Pavilion elected Britain's first Green Party MP, Caroline Lucas, in the 2010 General Election. However, novelty is nothing new to Brighton, which has been evolving throughout its existence.

Brighton began life as Brighthelmstone, a small fishing village; it remained so until 1783, when the future George IV transformed it into a fashionable retreat. George kept the architect John Nash busy converting a modest abode into a bizarre piece of orientalist kitsch; it's now the **Royal Pavilion** (*see p353*), and remains an ostentatious sight. Next door, the **Brighton Museum & Art Gallery** (Royal Pavilion Gardens, 01273 292882) has entertaining displays and a good permanent art collection.

Only two of Brighton waterfront's three Victorian piers are still standing. Lacy, delicate **Brighton Pier** is a clutter of hot-dog stands, karaoke and fairground rides, filled with customers in the summertime. Still, with seven miles of coastline, Brighton retains all the traditional seaside resort trappings. Look out for the free **Brighton Fishing Museum** (201 King's Road Arches, on the lower prom between the piers, 01273 723064, www.brightonfishingmusuem.org.uk) and the **Sea-Life Centre** (*see p353*), the world's oldest functioning aquarium.

A gay hub, a major student town and a child-friendly spot, Brighton still welcomes weekend gaggles of hen parties, ravers, nudists, discerning vegetarians, surfers, sunseekers and all-around wastrels. Many are satisfied to tumble from station to seafront, calling in at a couple of bars down the hill – and, perhaps, visiting the huge number of independent shops in and around **North Laine**, and in the charming network of narrow cobbled streets known as the **Lanes** – before plunging on to the pier or the pebbles.

But to get the best out of Brighton, seek out its unusual little pockets: the busy gay quarter of **Kemp Town**, the savage drinking culture of **Hanover**, the airy terraces of **Montpelier**. Although hilly, the city has an award-winning bus network, with an all-night service on main lines, making all parts easily accessible.

★ Royal Pavilion

Brighton, BN1 1EE (01273 292820, www.royal pavilion.org.uk). Open Apr-Sept 9.30am-5.45pm daily. Oct-Mar 10am-5.15pm daily. Tours by appointment. Last entry 45mins before closing. **Admission** £9.50; £7.50 reductions; £5.40 under-15s; free under-5s. **Credit** MC, V.

Sea-Life Centre

Marine Parade, BN2 1TB (01273 604234, www.sealifeeurope.com). Open 10am-4pm Mon-Fri; 10am-5pm Sat, Sun. Admission £15.50; £10.50-£13 reductions; free under-3s; £45 family. **Credit** MC, V.

Where to eat & drink

Brighton offers a ridiculous amount of dining possibilities for a town of its size, a handful of which would hold their head up in any city in the UK. **Gingerman** (21A Norfolk Square, 01273 326688, www.gingermanrestaurants.com)

offers top-quality continental (mainly French) cuisine at accessible prices. Located in a former bank, **Seven Dials** (1 Buckingham Place, 01273 885555, www.sevendialsrestaurant.co.uk) does two-course meal deals. **Terre à Terre** (71 East Street, 01273 729051, www.terreaterre.co.uk) is an inventive vegetarian restaurant. **La Capannina** (15 Madeira Place, 01273 680839) is the best Italian in town. And **Riddle & Finns** (12B Meeting House Lane, 01273 323008, www.riddleandfinns.co.uk) is an accomplished champagne and oyster bar.

Of the city's drinking holes, **Brighton Rocks** (6 Rock Place, 01273 601139) is Kemp Town's most talked-up small bar, with a heated terrace, sparkling cocktails and superb organic cuisine. The **Hand in Hand** (33 Upper St James Street, 01273 699595) is a small, traditional boozer that attracts an older, discerning clientele thanks to its fine range of ales. The **Lion & Lobster** (24 Sillwood Street, 01273 327299) is a wonderful little pub with a nice vibe, cool and communal. The **Sidewinder** (65 Upper St James Street, 01273 679927) is a pre-club bar with DJs. Of the gay bars, the most fun is to be had at the **Amsterdam Hotel** (11-12 Marine Parade, 01273 688825, www.amsterdam.uk.com). **Doctor Brighton's** (16-17 King's Road, 01273 208113, www.doctorbrightons.co.uk), on the seafront, is also worth a punt, with regular DJs playing house and techno.

Where to stay

Given Brighton's popularity with tourists, it's unsurprising that hotel prices can be on the high side. **Drakes** (43-44 Marine Parade, 01273 696934, www.drakesofbrighton.com, doubles £105-£325) is one of Brighton's high-end

Amherst. *See p354.*

designer hotels. The in-house restaurant is run by the best chef in town: Ben McKellar, who trained at Gingerman (*see p353*). Another worthwhile option is the typically chic **myhotel Brighton** (17 Jubilee Street, 01273 900300, www.myhotels.com, doubles £94-£600), which has a penthouse suite containing a 400-year-old carousel horse.

Blanch House (17 Atlingworth Street, 01273 603504, www.blanchhouse.co.uk, doubles £130-£230) is an unassuming Georgian terrace house with a dozen rooms themed after snow-storms, plus roses, rococo decor and a 1970s disco. The pampering **Nineteen** (19 Broad Street, 01273 675529, www.hotelnineteen.co.uk, doubles £80-£250) has just eight rooms in a stylish townhouse.

Good-quality stops on Ship Street are the classy **Hotel du Vin** (nos.2-6, 01273 718588, www.hotelduvin.com, doubles £170-£480) and, next door, its slightly cheaper sister the **Pub du Vin** (no.7, 01273 718588, www.hotelduvin. com/pub-du-vin, doubles £170-£240). The **Amherst** (2 Lower Rock Gardens, 01273 670131, www.amhersthotel.co.uk, doubles £100-£130; *photo p353*) is one of the best bargains among Brighton's contemporary hotels, while the **George IV** (34 Regency Square, 01273 321196, www.georgeivbrighton.co.uk, doubles £70-£150) is surely the best bargain, offering sea views from the city.

Getting there

By train Trains for Brighton leave from Victoria (50mins; map p400 H10) or King's Cross/St Pancras and London Bridge (1hr 10mins; map p397 L3 & p403 Q8).
By coach National Express coaches for Brighton leave from Victoria Coach Station (1hr 50mins).
By car Take the A23, the M23, then the A23 again to Brighton (approx 1hr 20mins).

Tourist information

Tourist Information Centre *Royal Pavilion, Brighton, BN1 1JS (0300 300 0088, www.visit brighton.com).* **Open** *Summer* 10am-5pm Mon-Sat; 10am-4pm Sun. *Winter* 10am-5pm Mon-Sat.

Ancient History

CANTERBURY

The home of the Church of England since St Augustine was based here in 597, the ancient city of Canterbury is rich in atmosphere. Gaze up at its soaring spires, or around you at the enchanting medieval streets, and you'll soon feel blessed, even if you're not an Anglican.

The town's busy tourist trade and large university provide a colourful counterweight to the brooding mass of history present in its old buildings. And, of course, to the glorious **Canterbury Cathedral** (*see p355*); it's at its most inspirational just before dusk, especially if there's music going on within and the coach parties are long gone. Inside, you'll find superb stained glass, stone vaulting and a vast Norman crypt. A plaque near the altar marks what is believed to be the exact spot where Archbishop Thomas Becket was murdered; the Trinity Chapel contains the site of the original shrine, plus the tombs of Henry IV and the Black Prince. Be prepared to shell out for entry, but it's well worth it.

A pilgrimage to Becket's tomb was the focus of one of the earliest and finest long poems in all English literature: Geoffrey Chaucer's *Canterbury Tales*, written in the 14th century. At the exhibition named after the poem (*see p355*), visitors are given a device that they point at tableaux inspired by Chaucer's tales of a knight, a miller, a wife of Bath, and others, enabling them to hear the rollicking stories that Chaucer brought to astonishingly vivid life.

Just down the road from Christ Church Gate lies the **Royal Museum & Art Gallery** (High Street, 01227 452747), a monument to high Victorian values. It's currently closed for refurbishment, expected to reopen in early 2012, when its permanent collections of art by cattle painter Thomas Sidney Cooper, as well as work by Van Dyck and Sickert, will be on display once again.

Founded to provide shelter for pilgrims, **Eastbridge Hospital** (25 High Street, 01227 471688) retains the smell and feel of ages past. Visitors can tour the hospital and admire the undercroft with its Gothic arches, the Chantry Chapel, the Pilgrims' Chapel and the refectory with an enchanting early 13th-century mural showing Christ in Majesty (there's only one other like this, and it's in France).

The **Roman Museum** (*see p355*) has the remains of a townhouse and mosaic floor among its treasures, augmented with computer reconstructions and time tunnels. From here, you get a super view of the cathedral tower. After the Romans comes **St Augustine**, or at least the ruins of the abbey he built (Longport, 01227 767345, www.english-heritage.org.uk). It's now in the capable hands of English Heritage, which has attached a small museum and shop to the site.

Everything you want to see, do or buy in Canterbury is within walking distance. And that includes the seaside – at least, it does if you fancy a long (seven-mile) walk or cycle along the Crab & Winkle Way, a disused railway line to pretty Whitstable.

Canterbury Cathedral.

★ Canterbury Cathedral

The Precincts, CT1 2EH (01227 762862, www.canterbury-cathedral.org). **Open** *Summer* 9am-5pm Mon-Sat; 12.30-2pm Sun. *Winter* 9am-4.30pm Mon-Sat; 12.30-2pm Sun. Admission is restricted during services and special events. **Admission** £8; £7 reductions; free under-5s. **Credit** MC, V.

Canterbury Tales

St Margaret's Street, CT1 2TG (01227 479227, www.canterburytales.org.uk). **Open** 10am-5pm daily. **Admission** £7.75; £5.75-£6.75 reductions; free under-4s. **Credit** MC, V.

Roman Museum

Butchery Lane, CT1 2JR (01227 785575, www.canterbury-museums.co.uk). **Open** *Nov-May* 10am-5pm Mon-Sat. *June-Oct* 10am-5pm Mon-Sat; 1.30-5pm Sun. Last entry 1hr before closing. **Admission** £3.10; £2.10 reductions; free under-5s. **Credit** MC, V.

Where to eat & drink

Michael Caines has brought a touch of Michelin glamour to the Canterbury eating scene. A fine dining restaurant and champagne bar is at his hotel ABode (*see right*): **Michael Caines Fine Dining Restaurant** (01227 826684, www. michaelcaines.com, main courses £19.50-£23.50) has a young, two Michelin-starred chef at the helm. The most satisfying part of a meal here may be the selection of British cheeses. There's also his **Old Brewery Tavern** (Stour Street, 01227 826682, www.michaelcaines.com, mains £9-£19), where prints of grizzled coopers rolling barrels hang on the walls. Another notable restaurant is **Deeson's** (25-26 Sun Street, 01227 767854, www.deesonsrestaurant.co.uk, mains £10-£18), serving modern British seasonal dishes made with locally sourced produce (Romney Marsh lamb, Kentish wines and beers).

Elsewhere, the **Goods Shed** (Station Road West, 01227 459153, mains £10-£18) occupies a lofty Victorian building, which was formerly a railway freight store. On a raised wooden platform, diners sit at scrubbed tables and choose from the specials chalked on the board. Only ingredients on sale in the farmers' market below them are used in the restaurant. For people who care about their food and its provenance, this is heaven.

Pub-wise, Canterbury is in thrall to its students, who take over the West Gate Inn Wetherspoons when they're tired of drinking on campus. Most of the better pubs are owned by Shepherd Neame, the local brewery based up the road in the town of Faversham, and the best both happen to be in St Dunstan's Street: the **Unicorn** (no.61, 01227 463187) has a kitsch garden and real ales, while the **Bishop's Finger** (no.13, 01227 768915) attracts both students and more mature clientele. Built in 1370, the **Parrot** (1-9 Church Lane, St Radigands, 01227 762355) is the oldest pub in Canterbury and also one of the oldest buildings. A good choice of ales and cider is served in a charming setting.

Where to stay

The third in a small chain of smart hotels created by Andrew Brownsword, **ABode** (30-33 High Street, 01227 766266, www.abodehotels.co.uk, doubles £150-£425) has brought a welcome breath of chic into Canterbury's chintzy accommodation options. The 72 rooms are ordered by price and size ranging from 'comfortable', through 'desirable' and 'enviable' to 'fabulous' (a penthouse with superior views and a tennis court-sized bed). The restaurant (*see left*) is superb.

Canterbury Cathedral Lodge (the Precincts, 01227 865350, www.canterbury cathedrallodge.org, doubles £89-£119) is right inside the cathedral precincts. There is bright and comfortable accommodation in a private courtyard and, while the hotel is hardly historic (it's only a decade old), the views certainly are. Nearby, the **Cathedral Gate Hotel** (36 Burgate, 01227 464381, www.cathgate.co.uk, doubles £62-£105) is a splendid old hotel built in 1438. It pre-dates the Christ Church Gate it sits alongside. The 25 rooms, with atmospheric sloping floors and ceilings, are reached via dark narrow corridors and low doorways.

Greyfriars (6 Stour Street, 01227 456255, www.greyfriars-house.co.uk, doubles £75) is an ancient but comfortable city-centre hotel; like all the others it's booked up at graduation time and in high season. **Magnolia House** (36 St Dunstan's Terrace, 01227 765121, www. magnoliahousecanterbury.co.uk, doubles £95-£125) is compact but recommended; the breakfast is delicious and well worth lingering over. The walk to and from town takes you through peaceful Westgate Gardens. Further out, the **Ebury Hotel** (65-67 New Dover Road, 01227 768433, www.ebury-hotel.co.uk, doubles £110-£145) is really quite grand-looking, with a sweeping drive and a Gothic exterior. The best bedrooms have views of the garden, but most of them are large, light and comfortable.

Getting there

By train From Victoria to Canterbury East (1hr 20mins; map p398 H10), or from Charing Cross (map p416 Y5) to Canterbury West (1hr 30mins). A new high-speed train service from St Pancras International brings the journey time down to about an hour.
By coach National Express from Victoria Coach Station (1hr 50mins).
By car Take the A2, the M2, then the A2 again (approx 2hrs).

Tourist information

Tourist Information Centre *12-13 Sun Street, Buttermarket, Canterbury, CT1 2HX (01227 378100, www.canterbury.co.uk).* **Open** 9.30am-5pm Mon-Sat; 9.30am-4.30pm Sun.

Wild Horizons
DUNGENESS, ROMNEY & RYE

Perhaps because it's difficult to reach from London (though there are rail links to Rye and Hastings), **Romney Marsh** is other-worldly in a way that conjures up science-fiction scenarios in Tarkovsky movies; you half expect to see Steed and Mrs Peel from *The Avengers* supping ale in the eerily unchanged villages. It's a strange, appealing mix of olde-worlde cobbled streets and ancient inns, sandy beaches, the world's largest expanse of shingle and event-horizoned marshland, criss-crossed by canals and studded with tiny medieval churches and strange concrete defence constructions dating to the period after World War I. So long as the transport links remain as poor as they are, there probably – hopefully – won't be any real changes here for decades to come. **Hastings** is the ideal starting point for a circular tour (by car) that takes in the towns of Winchelsea and Rye, Romney Marsh and Dungeness.

Winchelsea was built on a never-completed medieval grid pattern, first laid out by King Edward I, when the 'old' settlement was swept into the sea in the storms of 1287. The place is proud of its status as England's smallest town, but really it's a sleepy village of 400 residents. It's almost too quaint to be true – like **Rye**, which is a photogenic jumble of Norman, Tudor and Georgian architecture perched on one of the

Dungeness Point.

area's few hills. It's worth taking a look at the medieval Landgate gateway and the **Castle Museum** and 13th-century **Ypres Tower** (*see below*). The **Rye Art Gallery** (107 High Street, 01797 222433, www.ryeartgallery.co.uk) offers a changing series of excellent exhibitions, mostly by local artists.

East from Rye lies **Romney Marsh**, flat as a pancake and laced with cycle paths. Bikes can be hired from **Rye Hire** (1 Cyprus Place, Rye, 01797 223033); it's an ideal way to explore the lonely medieval churches that dot the level marsh. Heading out of Rye along the coast road takes you to **Camber Sands**, a vast sandy beach that's a great spot for kite-flying, riding, sand-yachting and invigorating walking.

Beyond is **Dungeness Point**, a huge beach of flint shingle stretching miles out into the sea. Clustered on this strange promontory are a lighthouse that offers wonderful views and a good café. The light on this remote, gloriously bleak patch of land is odd, reflected from the sea on both sides. The oddness of the landscape is enhanced by the presence of the massive Dungeness nuclear power station that dominates the horizon; such man-made wonders are set against a magnificent natural backdrop.

When the miniature **Romney, Hythe & Dymchurch Railway** train (01797 362353, www.rhdr.org.uk) barrels by, you know you're in an episode of *The Prisoner*. Proudly proclaiming to be the 'world's smallest public railway', it's fully functioning but one-third of the standard size. The diminutive train, built by millionaire racing driver Captain Howey in 1927, even includes a buffet car. Sitting in one of the tiny carriages is a surreal experience, as you meander from the wide-open shingle of the Point behind back gardens and caravan parks, through woodland and fields to arrive at **Hythe** (roughly 13 miles away).

Rye Castle Museum & Ypres Tower

3 East Street, TN31 7JY (01797 226728, www.ryemuseum.co.uk). **Open** *Museum* Easter-Oct 10.30am-5pm Sat, Sun. *Tower* Easter-Oct 10.30am-5pm daily. **Admission** *Museum* £2.50; £2 reductions. *Tower* £3; £2.50 reductions. *Both* £5; £4 reductions. **No credit cards**.

Where to eat & drink

You'll find some of the finest food on the south-east coast here. In Rye, the **Landgate Bistro** (5-6 Landgate, Rye, 01797 222829, www.landgatebistro.co.uk, mains £12.80-£18) once ruled the roost with its attractive, inventive and pleasingly unfussy dishes, but now faces real competition from the **George in Rye** (98 High Street, 01797 222114, www.thegeorgeinrye.com, mains £14.50-£18), where the chef is the

Australian, Paul Gordon. It's also a hotel – luxurious, stylish, welcoming and altogether very likeable. The light and informal **Fish Café** (17 Tower Street, 01797 222226, www.thefishcafe.com, mains £10-£19) serves some of the best seafood in town. If you're looking for lovingly prepared food with an emphasis on locally sourced ingredients, there are few better places to eat on the peninsula than the **Romney Bay House Hotel** (*see p358*).

If fancy isn't your thing, Rye has plenty of simpler eateries: pasta at **Simply Italian** (the Strand, 01797 226024, www.simplyitalian.co.uk, mains £5-£13) or sound pub food at any number of lovely boozers in town.

The finest option on the seaside is the **Place** (New Lydd Road, 01797 225057, www.theplacecambersands.co.uk, mains £10.50-£17.50) at Camber Sands, which prides itself on its use of locally sourced and eco-friendly produce. Further east, Lydd's **Pilot** (Battery Road, 01797 320314, www.thepilot.uk.com, mains £7-£13) serves some of the best fish and chips in Kent. For dinner with a difference, try the Sunday Fly 'n' Dine at **Lydd Airport** (Lydd, Romney Marsh, 01797 322207, www.lyddair.com), a low-level 15-minute flight over the Kent coast and a three-course carvery meal – £49.95, all in.

Of the many pubs, the **Woolpack Inn** near Brookland (Beacon Lane, 01797 344321, mains £5-£24) is one of the best, with low ceilings and original 15th-century beams sourced, enterprisingly, from local shipwrecks. The tiny, multi-award-winning **Red Lion** (Snargate, 01797 344648) is something of a Romney Marsh institution, famed for the fact that its interior hasn't been touched since World War II. It doesn't offer food, but you're welcome to bring your own.

Where to stay

Even in the winter months, accommodation in Rye needs to be booked as far in advance as possible. If the tweeness of many of the B&Bs isn't to your taste, but you want somewhere with character and some individuality, the **Hope Anchor Hotel** (Watchbell Street, 01797 222216, www.thehopeanchor.co.uk, doubles

£95-£170) is set in a lovely location at the end of a pretty, cobbled street. The **White Vine House** (24 High Street, 01797 224748, www.whitevinehouse.co.uk, doubles £140-£190) has seven tastefully decorated rooms.

Wonderfully located on Rye's quaintest cobbled street, the atmospheric 17th-century **Jeake's House** (Mermaid Street, 01797 222828, www.jeakeshouse.com, doubles £90-£125) has nearly a dozen individually decorated rooms; the 'gold room' features an impressive inglenook fireplace in which nestles a splendid wood stove. The 16th-century **Mermaid Inn** (Mermaid Street, 01797 223065, www.mermaid inn.com, doubles £160-£200) offers olde-worlde tradition at its finest. Think stone fireplaces, four-poster beds, wonky floors and secret passages. The Mermaid also has an accomplished restaurant.

In Winchelsea, **Strand House** (Tanyard's Lane, 01797 226276, www.thestrandhouse. co.uk, doubles £70-£140) dates to the 15th century, and there's a delightful garden. The **Romney Bay House Hotel** (Coast Road, Littlestone-on-Sea, New Romney, 01797 364747, doubles £84-£164) is a ten-bedroom mansion designed for Hollywood gossip columnist Hedda Hopper by Sir Clough Williams-Ellis of Portmeirion fame. In Hastings, the **Zanzibar International Hotel** (9 Eversfield Place, 01424 460109, www.zanzibarhotel.co.uk, doubles £99-£215) is a tall, thin seafront house that feels like a private house rather than a boutique hotel.

Getting there

By train From London Bridge or Cannon Street to Rye via Ashford International (approx 1hr 45mins; map p403 Q8 & p402 P7). From Charing Cross, Waterloo East or London Bridge to Hastings (approx 1hr 30mins; map p416 Y5, p399 M8 & p403 Q8).
By car Take the A20, the M20, then the A259 (approx 2hrs 30mins).

Tourist information

Folkestone Tourist Office *20 Bouverie Place Shopping Centre, Folkestone, CT20 1AU (01303 258 594, www.discoverfolkestone.co.uk).* **Open** (email and phone enquiries only) 9am-5pm Mon-Fri.
Hastings Tourist Information *Queen Square, Hastings, TN34 1TL (01424 451111, www. visit1066country.com).* **Open** 8.30am-6.15pm Mon-Fri; 9am-5pm Sat; 10.30am-4pm Sun.
Rye Tourist Information *4 Lion Street, Rye, TN31 7LB (01797 229049, www.visitrye.co.uk).* **Open** *Apr-Sept* 10am-5pm daily. *Oct-Mar* 10am-4pm daily.

Colleges & Culture

CAMBRIDGE

Gorgeous, intimidating Cambridge has the feel of an enclosed city. With the narrow streets and tall old buildings of the town centre, it has a way of conveying disapproval to visitors architecturally – and that's before you even reach the 'Keep off the Grass' signs. But pluck up the courage to pass through those imposing gates with their stern porters: within and behind the colleges are pretty green meadows and the idle River Cam, a place where time seems to have stopped back in the 18th century.

Cambridge first became an academic centre when a fracas at Oxford – involving a dead woman, an arrow and a scholar holding a bow – led to some of the learned monks bidding a hasty farewell to Oxford and a hearty hello to Cambridge. Once the dust settled, the monks needed somewhere to peddle their knowledge: the first college, **Peterhouse** (01223 338200, www.pet.cam.ac.uk), was established in 1284. The original hall survives, though most of the present buildings are from the 19th century. Up the road is **Corpus Christi** (01223 338000, www.corpus.cam.ac.uk), founded in 1352. Its Old Court dates from that time and is linked by a gallery to the 11th-century **St Bene't's Church** (Bene't Street, www.stbenetschurch. org), the oldest surviving building in town.

Past Corpus Christi, grand **King's College** (01223 331100, www.kings.cam.ac.uk) was founded by Henry VI in 1441. Its chapel (01223 331155), built between 1446 and 1515 on a scale that would humble many cathedrals, has breathtaking interior fan vaulting and the original stained glass. Attend a service in term-time to hear its wonderful choirboys.

Continue north to find pretty **Trinity** (01223 338400, www.trin.cam.ac.uk), a college founded in 1336 by Edward III and then refounded by Henry VIII in 1546. A fine crowd of Tudor buildings surrounds the Great Court where, legend has it, Lord Byron would bathe naked in the fountain with his pet bear. Wittgenstein studied and taught here, and the library (a cool and airy design by Wren) is open to visitors at certain times (01223 331232). Within, covered cases contain such treasures as a lock of Newton's hair, a Shakespeare first folio and Otto Robert Frisch's crisp and moving account of the first atomic bomb test. From behind the library, you can see the neo-Gothic Bridge of Sighs that connects the major courts of **St John's** (01223 338600, www.joh.cam.ac.uk) across the Cam.

Each of the 31 Cambridge colleges is an independent entity, so entry times (and, for the

Cambridge.

more famous ones, prices) vary considerably: www.cam.ac.uk/colleges has the details. But Cambridge isn't only about the colleges. Behind its impressive neoclassical façade, the **Fitzwilliam Museum** (*see p360*) has a superb collection of paintings and sculpture (masterpieces by Titian, Modigliani and Picasso), as well as ancient artefacts from Egypt, Greece and Rome. A short walk south, the 40 relaxing acres of the **Botanic Gardens** (*see below*) have 8,000 plants, among them delightfully modest alpine plants in a glasshouse and, at the entrance, a descendant of Sir Isaac Newton's apple tree.

Fans of eccentric and ghoulish museums should head to Downing Street. On the south side are both the towering totem poles and toucan-shaped 'lime scoop' of the **Museum of Archaeology & Anthropology** (01223 333516, www.maa-cambridge.org) and the fossils and scintillating gemstones of the **Sedgwick Museum of Earth Sciences** (01223 333456, www.sedgwickmuseum.org). On the north side, you'll find the strange scientific devices and grand orreries of the **Whipple Museum of the History of Science** (01223 330906, www.hps.cam.ac. uk/whipple) and, beneath a suspended whale skeleton, the animal skeletons and stuffed birds of the **Museum of Zoology** (01223 336650, www.zoo.cam.ac.uk/museum).

One of the real treats during a visit to Cambridge is **Kettle's Yard** (*see p360*), once Tate curator Jim Ede's home and now a magnificently atmospheric collection of early 20th-century artists – Miró, Brancusi, Hepworth – arranged just as he left it. Ring the doorbell and you can settle in one of Ede's chairs and read a book from his shelves.

Behind the main colleges, the beautiful meadows bordering the willow-shaded Cam are known as the **Backs**. Carpeted with crocuses in spring, the Backs are idyllic for summer strolling and 'punting' (pushing flat boats with long poles). Punts can be hired; **Scudamore's Boatyard** (01223 359750, www.scudamores.com) is the largest operator. If you get handy at the surprisingly difficult skill of punting, you can boat down to the **Orchard Tea Rooms** (45-47 Mill Way, CB3 9ND, 01223 551 125, www.orchard-grantchester.com), where Ted Hughes and Sylvia Plath courted and Rupert Brooke lodged as a student.

Cambridge University Botanic Gardens

1 Brookside, CB2 1JE (01223 336265, www.botanic.cam.ac.uk). **Open** *Apr-Sept* 10am-6pm daily. *Oct, Feb, Mar* 10am-5pm daily. *Nov-Jan* 10am-4pm daily. **Admission** £4; £3.50 reductions.

ESCAPES & EXCURSIONS

FREE Fitzwilliam Museum
Trumpington Street, CB2 1RB (01223 332900, www.fitzmuseum.cam.ac.uk). **Open** 10am-5pm Tue-Sat; noon-5pm Sun. **Admission** free.

★ **FREE Kettle's Yard**
Castle Street, CB3 0AQ (01223 748100, www.kettlesyard.co.uk). **Open** *House* 1.30-4.30pm Tue-Sun & bank hol Mon in summer; 2-4pm Tue-Sun & bank hol Mon in winter. *Gallery & bookshop* 11.30am-5pm Tue-Sun & bank hol Mon. **Admission** free.

Where to eat & drink

Occupying an enviable riverside spot, **Midsummer House** (Midsummer Common, 01223 369299, www.midsummerhouse.co.uk, £55 2 courses, £72.50 3 courses) produces Michelin-starred French food that rises to the occasion. Service is as fussy as you'd expect, but the food is perfectly presented and meticulously prepared in flavour combinations that are never less than intriguing.

The **Cambridge Chop House** (1 King's Parade, 01223 359506, www.chophouses.co.uk, mains £9-£17) is a great come-one-come-all bistro opposite King's College, where you can tuck into British comfort food and draught ales. Nearby, the busy subterranean **Rainbow Café** (9A King's Parade, 01223 321551, www.rainbowcafe.co.uk, mains £8-£10) serves cheap, hearty vegetarian food. A branch of **Jamie's Italian** (Old Library, Wheeler Street, 01223 654094, www.jamieoliver.com/italian) opened in 2010 in the historic Guildhall, which is just off the central market square. For a teatime treat, follow the example of generations of students and tuck into a Chelsea bun from **Fitzbillies** (52 Trumpington Street, 01223 352500, www.fitzbillies.co.uk).

Cambridge has many creaky old inns in which to settle down and enjoy one of the city's decent local ales. The **Eagle** on Bene't Street (01223 505020) is the most famous – Crick and Watson drank here after fathoming the mysteries of DNA – but there are many others,

including the **Pickerel Inn** (30 Magdalene Street, 01223 355068) and, down a back alley a little off the beaten track, the sweet little **Free Press** (Prospect Row, 01223 368337, www.freepresspub.com).

Where to stay

Because of the university's prominence in the city, there are plenty of guesthouses, with a cluster of B&Bs nicely located just across the Cam from the centre of town to the north of Midsummer Common. **Harry's** (39 Milton Road, 01223 503866, www.welcometoharrys. co.uk, doubles £75), **Worth House** (152 Chesterton Road, 01223 316074, www.worth-house.co.uk, doubles £60) and **Victoria Guest House** (57 Arbury Road, 01223 350086, www.victoria-guesthouse.co.uk, doubles £65-£75) are all good value.

The pick of the luxury hotels is the **Hotel du Vin** (15-19 Trumpington Street, 01223 227330, www.hotelduvin.com, doubles £180-£200), a cheerfully but carefully run operation, painstakingly converted from listed terraced houses. A basement bar (with wine cellar) extends the whole length of the hotel, the busy all-day restaurant occupies one end of the ground floor and there's a heated and covered cigar 'room' outside.

DoubleTree by Hilton (Granta Place, Mill Lane, 01223 259988, www.doubletreeby hilton.co.uk, doubles £159-£180) is located right on the Cam behind Peterhouse, and has an indoor swimming pool. Finally, the **Hotel Felix** (Whitehouse Lane, Huntingdon Road, 01223 277977, www.hotelfelix.co.uk, doubles £180-£230), a modern hotel centred on a characterful 1852 Victorian mansion, is a little remote for walkers, but it has loads of parking space and a good decked area outside its twinkly bar-restaurant.

Getting there

By train Trains to Cambridge leave from King's Cross (50mins; map p397 L3) or Liverpool Street (map p401 R5; 1hr 15mins).
By coach National Express coaches to Cambridge leave from Victoria Coach Station (1hr 50mins).
By car Take Junction 11 or Junction 12 off the M11.

Tourist information

Cambridge Tourist Information Centre
Peas Hill, CB2 3AD (0871 226 8006, www. visitcambridge.org). **Open** *May-Sept* 10am-5.30pm Mon-Fri; 10am-5pm Sat; 11am-3pm Sun. *Oct-Apr* 10am-5pm Mon-Sat.

INSIDE TRACK DING! DING!

Apart from punts, the classic Cambridge mode of transport is the bicycle: staff at **Cambridge Station Cycles** (01223 307125, www.stationcycles.co.uk) in the car park to the right out of the train station are very helpful (and will store luggage at a reasonable rate). Wind on a long scarf and toss some books in your basket, and you'll feel like a proper student.

Directory

Getting Around

ARRIVING & LEAVING

For information on short breaks outside London, *see pp350-360*.

By air

Gatwick Airport *0844 335 1802, www.gatwickairport.com. About 30 miles south of central London, off the M23.*
Of the three rail services that link Gatwick to London, the quickest is the **Gatwick Express** (0845 850 1530, www.gatwickexpress.com) to Victoria; it takes 30mins and runs 3.30am-12.30am daily. Tickets cost £16.90 single or £28.70 for an open return (valid for 30 days). Under-15s pay £8.45 for a single and £11.50 for returns; under-5s go free.

Southern (0845 748 4950, www.southernrailway.com) also runs a rail service between Gatwick and Victoria, with trains every 5-10mins (every 30mins between 1am and 4am). It takes about 35mins, and costs £11.30 for a single, £11.40 for a day return (after 9.30am) and £23.60 for an open period return (valid for one month). Under-16s get half-price tickets; under-5s go free.

If you're staying in King's Cross or Bloomsbury, consider trains run by **Thameslink** (0845 748 4950, www.firstcapitalconnect.co.uk) to St Pancras. Tickets are £9.50 day return (after 9.32am); £17 for a 30-day open return.

A **taxi** to the centre costs about £100 and takes a bit over an hour.

Heathrow Airport *0844 335 1801, www.heathrowairport.com. About 15 miles west of central London, off the M4.*
The **Heathrow Express** train (0845 600 1515, www.heathrow express.co.uk) runs to Heathrow every 15mins (5.10am-11.25pm daily), and takes 15-20mins. The train can be boarded at the tube station that serves Terminals 1, 2 and 3 (aka Heathrow Central; Terminal 2 is currently closed for rebuilding), or the separate station serving the new Terminal 5; for passengers travelling to or from Terminal 4, a shuttle train connects with Heathrow Central. Tickets cost £16.50 single or £32 return (£1 less online, £2 more if you buy on

board); under-16s go half-price. Many airlines have check-in desks at Paddington.

The journey by tube into central London is longer but cheaper. The 50-60min **Piccadilly line** ride into central London costs £4.50 one way (£2.50 under-16s). Trains run every few minutes from about 5am to 11.57pm daily (6am-11pm Sun).

The **Heathrow Connect** (0845 678 6975, www.heathrowconnect. com) rail service offers direct access to Hayes, Southall, Hanwell, West Ealing, Ealing Broadway and Paddington stations in west and north-west London. The trains run every half-hour, terminating at Heathrow Central (Terminals 1 and 3). From there to Terminal 4 get the free shuttle; between Central and Terminal 5, there's free use of the Heathrow Express. A single from Paddington is £7.90; an open return is £15.80.

National Express (0871 781 8181, www.nationalexpress.com) runs daily coach services to London Victoria (90mins, 5am-9.35pm daily), leaving Heathrow Central bus terminal every 20-30mins. It's £5 for a single (£2.50 under-16s) or £9 (£4.50 under-16s) for a return.

A **taxi** into town will cost £45-£65 and take 30-60mins.

London City Airport *7646 0000, www.londoncityairport.com. About 9 miles east of central London.*
The **Docklands Light Railway (DLR)** now includes a stop for London City Airport. The journey to Bank station in the City takes around 20mins, and trains run 5.30am-12.30am Mon-Sat or 7.30am-11.30pm Sun. By road, a taxi costs around £30 to central London; less to the City or to Canary Wharf.

Luton Airport *01582 405100, www.london-luton.com. About 30 miles north of central London, J10 off the M1.*
It's a short bus ride from the airport to Luton Airport Parkway station. From here, the **Thameslink** rail service (*see left*) calls at many stations (St Pancras International and City among them); journey time is 35-45mins. Trains leave every 15mins or so and cost £13.50 single one-way and £23 return, or £14.50 for a cheap day return (after 9.30am

Mon-Fri, all day weekends). Trains between Luton and St Pancras run at least hourly all night.

By coach, the Luton to Victoria journey takes 60-90mins. **Green Line** (0870 608 7261, www.green line.co.uk) runs a 24hr service. A single is £14 and returns cost £19; under-16s £11 single, £15 return.

A **taxi** to London costs £70-£80.

Stansted Airport *0844 335 1803, www.stanstedairport.com. About 35 miles north-east of central London, J8 off the M11.*
The **Stansted Express** train (0845 748 4950, www.stansted express.com) runs to and from Liverpool Street station; the journey time is 40-45mins. Trains leave every 15mins, and tickets cost £19.80 single, £28.70 return; under-16s travel half-price, under-5s free.

Several companies run coaches to central London. The **Airbus** (0871 781 8181, www.nationalexpress. com) coach service from Stansted to Victoria takes at least 80mins. Coaches run roughly every 30mins (24hrs daily), more at peak times. A single is £10 (£5 for under-16s), return is £17 (£8.50 for under-16s).

A **taxi** into the centre of London costs around £100.

By coach

Coaches run by **National Express** (0871 781 8181, www. nationalexpress.com), the biggest coach company in the UK, arrive at **Victoria Coach Station** (164 Buckingham Palace Road, SW1W 9TP, 0843 222 1234, www.tfl.gov. uk), a good 10min walk from Victoria tube station. This is where companies such as Eurolines (01582 404511, www.eurolines.com) dock their European services.

By rail

Trains from mainland Europe run by Eurostar (0843 218 6186, www.eurostar.com) arrive at **St Pancras International** (Pancras Road, King's Cross, NW1 2QP, 7843 7688, www.stpancras.com).

PUBLIC TRANSPORT

Getting around London on public transport is easy – but not cheap.

Information

Details on timetables and other travel information are provided by **Transport for London** (0843 222 1234, www.tfl.gov.uk/journey planner). Complaints or comments on most forms of public transport can also be taken up with **London TravelWatch** (7505 9000, www.londontravelwatch.org.uk).

Travel Information Centres

TfL's Travel Information Centres provide help with the tube, buses and Docklands Light Railway (DLR; see p364). You can find them in Camden Town Hall, opposite St Pancras (9am-5pm Mon-Fri), and in the stations below. Call 0843 222 1234 for more information.

Euston station 7.15am-9.15pm Mon-Fri; 7.15am-6.15pm Sat; 8.15am-6.15pm Sun.
Heathrow Terminals 1, 2 & 3 tube station 6.30am-9pm daily.
Liverpool Street tube station 7.15am-9.15pm Mon-Sat; 8.15am-8pm Sun.
Piccadilly Circus tube station 9.15am-7pm daily.
Victoria station 7.15am-9.15pm Mon-Sat; 8.15am-8.15pm Sun.

Fares & tickets

Tube and DLR fares are based on a system of six zones, stretching 12 miles out from the centre of London. A flat cash fare of £4 per journey applies across zones 1-4 on the tube, and £4.50 for zones 1-6; customers save up to £2.50 per journey with a pre-pay Oyster card (see below). Anyone caught without a ticket or Oyster card is subject to a £50 on-the-spot fine (reduced to £25 if you pay within three weeks).

Oyster cards A pre-paid smart-card, Oyster is the cheapest way of getting around on public transport. You can charge up standard Oyster cards at tube stations, Travel Information Centres (see above), some rail stations and newsagents. There is a £3 refundable deposit payable on each card; to collect your deposit, call 0845 330 9876.
　Visitor Oyster cards are available from Gatwick Express outlets, National Express coaches, Superbreak, visitlondon.com, visit britaindirect.com, Oxford Tube coach service and on Eurostar services. The only difference between Visitor Oysters and 'normal' Oysters is that they come pre-loaded with money.

A tube journey in zone 1 using Oyster pay-as-you-go costs £1.80 (65p for under-16s), compared to the cash fare of £4. A single tube ride within zones 2, 3, 4, 5 or 6 costs £1.30 (65p for under-16s); single journeys from zones 1 through to 6 using Oyster are £4.20 (7am-7pm Mon-Fri) or £2.40 (all other times), or £1.10 for children. Up to four children pay just £1 each for their fares when accompanied by an adult with a Travelcard.
　If you make a number of journeys using Oyster pay-as-you-go on a given day, the total fare deducted will always be capped at the price of an equivalent Day Travelcard. However, if you only make one journey using Oyster pay-as-you-go, you will only be charged a single Oyster fare.

Day Travelcards If you're only using the tube, DLR, buses and trams, using Oyster to pay as you go will always be capped at the same price as an equivalent Day Travelcard. However, if you're also using National Rail services, Oyster may not be accepted: opt, instead, for a Day Travelcard, a standard ticket with a coded stripe that allows travel across all networks.
　Anytime Day Travelcards can be used all day. They cost from £7.20 for zones 1-2 (£3.60 child), up to £14.80 for zones 1-6 (£7.40 child). Tickets are valid for journeys begun by 4.30am the next day. The cheaper **Off-Peak Day Travelcard** allows travel after 9.30am Mon-Fri and all day at weekends and public holidays. It costs from £5.60 for zones 1-2 up to £7.50 for zones 1-6.

Children Under-5s travel free on buses and trams without the need to provide any proof of identity. Five- and 10-year-olds can also travel free, but need to obtain a 5-10 Oyster photocard. For details, visit www.tfl.gov.uk/fares or call 0845 330 9876.
　An 11-15 Oyster photocard is needed by 11- to 15-year-olds to pay as they go on the tube/DLR and to buy 7-Day, monthly or longer period Travelcards, and by 11- to 15-year-olds if using the tram to/from Wimbledon.

Photocards Photocards are not required for 7-Day Travelcards or Bus Passes, adult-rate Travelcards or Bus Passes charged on an Oyster card. For details of how to obtain 5-10, 11-15 or 16+ Oyster photocards, see www.tfl.gov.uk/fares or call 0845 330 9876.

London Underground

Delays are fairly common, with lines closing at weekends for engineering works. Trains are hot and crowded in rush hour (8-9.30am and 4.30-7pm Mon-Fri). Even so, the 12 colour-coded lines that together comprise the underground rail system – also known as 'the tube' – remain the quickest way to get around London (for a map of the Underground, see pp414-415), carrying some 3.5 million passengers every weekday. Comments or complaints are dealt with by **LU Customer Services** on 0845 330 9880 (8am-8pm daily); for lost property, see p370.

Using the system You can get Oyster cards from www.tfl.gov.uk/oyster, by calling 0845 330 9876, at tube stations, Travel Information Centres, some rail stations and newsagents. Single or day tickets can be bought from ticket offices or machines. You can buy most tickets and top up Oyster cards at self-service machines. Some ticket offices close early (around 7.30pm); carry a charged-up Oyster card to avoid being stranded.
　To enter and exit the tube using an Oyster card, simply touch it to the yellow reader, which will open the gates. Make sure you also touch the card to the reader when you exit the tube, or you'll be charged a higher fare when you next use your card to enter a station. On certain lines, you'll see a pink 'validator' – touch this reader in addition to the yellow entry/exit readers and on some routes it will reduce your fare.
　To enter using a paper ticket, place it in the slot with the black magnetic strip facing down, then pull it out of the top to open the gates. Exiting is done in much the same way; however, if you have a single journey ticket, it will be retained by the gate as you leave.

Timetables Tube trains run daily from around 5am (except Sunday, when they start an hour or so later, and Christmas Day, when there's no service). You shouldn't have to wait more than 10mins for a train; during peak times, services should run every 2-3mins. Times of last trains vary; they're usually around 12.30am daily (11.30pm on Sun). The tubes run all night only on New Year's Eve; otherwise, you're limited to night buses (see p364).

Fares The single fare for adults across the network is £4. Using Oyster pay-as-you-go, the fare

DIRECTORY

varies by zone: zone 1 costs £1.80; zones 1-2 costs £1.80 or £2.30, depending on the time of day; zones 1-6 is £2.40 or £4.20. The single fare for children aged 5-15 is 65p for any journey. Under-5s travel free (*see also p363*).

National Rail & London Overground services

Independently run commuter services co-ordinated by **National Rail** (0845 748 4950, www.national rail.co.uk) leave from the city's main rail stations. Visitors heading to south London, or to more remote destinations such as Hampton Court Palace, will need to use these overground services. Travelcards are valid on these services within the right zones, but not all routes accept Oyster pay-as-you-go; check before you travel.

Operated by Transport for London, meaning it does accept Oyster, the **London Overground** is a fabulously useful new service. Originally the rail line ran through north London from Stratford in the east to Richmond in the south-west, with spurs connecting Willesden Junction in the north-west to Clapham Junction in the south-west, and Gospel Oak in the north to Barking in the east, as well as heading north-west from Euston. Then, in 2010, the reopened East London line was incorporated into the Overground network, connecting trains south of the river to trains to the north: effectively, Crystal Palace, West Croydon and New Cross are now connected (via useful, brand-new intermediate stations such as Shoreditch High Street) to Dalston Junction and the northerly extent of the Overground. Trains run about every 20mins (every 30mins on Sun).

For lost property, *see p370*.

Docklands Light Railway (DLR)

DLR trains (7363 9700, www.tfl. gov.uk/dlr) run from Bank station (where they connect with the tube system's Central and Waterloo & City lines) or Tower Gateway, close to Tower Hill tube (Circle and District lines). At Westferry station, the line splits east and south via Island Gardens to Greenwich and Lewisham; a change at Poplar can take you north to Stratford. The easterly branch forks after Canning Town to either Beckton or London City Airport; the latter is due to extend across the river to Woolwich

Arsenal this year. Trains run 5.30am-12.30am daily. For lost property, *see p370*.

Fares Adult single fares on the DLR are the same as for the tube (*see p363*) except for DLR-only journeys in zones 2-3, which cost £3.50 (£1.30 with Oyster pay-as-you-go) or £1.40 for 11-15s (65p with Oyster pay-as-you-go).

The DLR also offers one-day Rail & River Rover tickets, which add one day's DLR travel to hop-on, hop-off travel on **City Cruises** riverboats (10am-6pm; *see p366*) between Westminster, Waterloo, Tower and Greenwich Piers. Starting at Tower Gateway, trains leave hourly from 10am for a special tour, with a guide adding commentary. It costs £14.50 for adults or £7.25 for kids; a family pass (two adults and up to three under-16s), which must be bought in person from the piers, costs £37. Under-5s go free.

Buses

You must have a ticket or valid pass before boarding any bus in zone 1, and before boarding any articulated, single-decker bus ('bendy buses', which are in the process of being phased out) anywhere in the city. You can buy a ticket (or a 1-Day Bus Pass) from machines at bus stops, although they're often not working; better to travel with an Oyster card or some other pass (*see p363*). Inspectors patrol buses at random; if you don't have a ticket or pass, you may be fined £50.

All buses are now low-floor vehicles that are accessible to wheelchair-users and passengers with buggies. The only exceptions are Heritage routes 9 and 15, which are served by the world-famous open-platform Routemaster buses.

For lost property, *see p370*.

Fares Using Oyster pay-as-you-go costs £1.20 a trip; your total daily payment, regardless of how many journeys you take, will be capped at £3.90. Paying with cash at the time of travel costs £2 for a single trip. Under-16s travel for free (using an Under-11 or 11-15 Oyster photocard as appropriate; *see p363*). A 1-Day Bus Pass gives unlimited bus and tram travel for £3.90.

Night buses Many bus routes operate 24hrs a day, seven days a week. There are also some special night buses with an 'N' prefix, which run from about 11pm to 6am.

Most night services run every 15-30mins, but busier routes run a service around every 10mins. Fares are the same as for daytime buses; Bus Passes and Travelcards can be used at no extra fare until 4.30am of the morning after they expire.

Green Line buses Green Line buses (0844 801 7261, www.green line.co.uk) serve the suburbs within 40 miles of London. Its office is opposite **Victoria Coach Station** (*see p362*); services run 24hrs.

Tramlink

In south London, trams run between Beckenham, Croydon, Addington and Wimbledon. Travelcards that cover zones 3, 4, 5 or 6 are valid, as are Bus Passes. Cash fares are £2 (£1.20 with Oyster pay-as-you-go).

For lost property, *see p370*.

Water transport

Most river services operate every 20-60mins between 10.30am and 5pm, and may run more often and later in summer. For commuters, **Thames Clippers** (0870 781 5049, www.thamesclippers.com) runs a service between Embankment Pier and Royal Arsenal Woolwich Pier; stops include Blackfriars, Bankside, London Bridge, Canary Wharf and Greenwich. A standard day roamer ticket (valid 10am-5pm) costs £12, while a single from Embankment to Greenwich is £5.30, or £4.80 for Oyster cardholders. **Thames Executive Charters** (www. thamesexecutivecharters.com) also offers Travelcard discounts on its River Taxi between Putney and Blackfriars, calling at Wandsworth, Chelsea Harbour, Cadogan Pier and Embankment, meaning a £4.50 standard single becomes £3.

Westminster Passenger Service Assocation (7930 2062, www.wpsa.co.uk) runs a daily service from Westminster Pier to Kew, Richmond and Hampton Court from April to October. At around £12 for a single, it's not cheap, but it is a lovely way to see the city, and there are discounts of 30%-50%for Travelcard holders.

Thames River Services (www.westminsterpier.co.uk) operates from the same pier, offering trips to Greenwich, Tower Pier and the Thames Barrier. A trip to Greenwich costs £9.50, though £13 buys you a Rivercard, which allows you to hop on and off at will. Travelcard holders get a third off.

For commuter service timetables, plus a full list of leisure operators and services, see www.tfl.gov.uk.

For lost property, *see p370*.

TAXIS

Black cabs

The licensed London taxi, aka 'black cab' (although, since on-car advertising, they've come in many colours), is a much-loved feature of London life. Drivers must pass a test called 'the Knowledge' to prove they know every street in central London, and the shortest route to it.

If a taxi's orange 'For Hire' sign is lit, it can be hailed. If a taxi stops, the cabbie must take you to your destination if it's within seven miles. It can be hard to find an empty cab, especially just after the pubs close. Fares rise after 8pm on weekdays and at weekends.

You can book black cabs from the 24hr **Taxi One-Number** (0871 871 8710, a £2 booking fee applies, plus 12.5% if you pay by credit card), **Radio Taxis** (7272 0272) and **Dial-a-Cab** (7253 5000; credit cards only, with a booking fee of £2). Comments or complaints about black cabs should be made to the **Public Carriage Office** (0845 602 7000, www.tfl.gov.uk/pco). Note the cab's badge number, which should be displayed in the rear of the cab and on its back bumper.

For lost property, *see p370*.

Minicabs

Minicabs (saloon cars) are generally cheaper than black cabs, but can be less reliable. Only use licensed firms (look for a disc in the front and rear windows), and avoid those that illegally tout for business in the street: drivers may be unlicensed, uninsured and dangerous.

Trustworthy and fully licensed firms include **Addison Lee** (7387 8888), which will text you when the car arrives, and **Lady Cabs** (7272 3300), **Ladybirds** (8295 0101) and **Ladycars** (8558 9511), which employ only women drivers. Otherwise, text HOME to 60835 ('60tfl'). Transport for London will then text you the numbers of the two nearest licensed minicab operators and the number for Taxi One-Number, which provides licensed black taxis in London. The service costs 35p plus standard call rate. No matter who you choose, always ask the price when you book and confirm it with the driver.

Motorbike taxis

Passenger Bikes (0844 561 6147, www.passengerbikes.com) and **Taxybikes** (7255 4269, www.addisonlee.com/services/taxybikes) have a minimum £25 charge, and offer fixed airport rates; the bikes are equipped with panniers, and can carry a small to medium suitcase. You pay a premium for the thrill: central London to Gatwick currently costs £110-£120.

DRIVING

London's roads are often clogged with traffic and roadworks, and parking (*see right*) is a nightmare. Walking or using public transport are better options. If you hire a car, you can use any valid licence from outside the EU for up to a year after arrival. Speed limits in the city are generally 20 or 30mph on most roads. Don't use a mobile phone (unless it's hands-free) while driving or you risk a £1,000 fine.

Car hire

All firms below have branches at the airport; several also have offices in the city centre. Shop around for the best rate; always check the level of insurance included in the price.

Alamo *UK: 0870 400 4562, www.alamo.co.uk. US: 1-877 222 9075, www.alamo.com.*

Avis *UK: 0844 581 0147, www.avis.co.uk. US: 1-800 331 1212, www.avis.com.*

Budget *UK: 0844 544 3439, www.budget.co.uk. US: 1-800 472 3325, www.budget.com.*

Enterprise *UK: 0870 350 3000, www.enterprise.co.uk. US: 1-800 261 7331, www.enterprise.com.*

Europcar *UK: 0871 384 1087, www.europcar.co.uk. US: 1-877 940 6900, www.europcar.com.*

Hertz *UK: 0870 844 8844, www.hertz.co.uk. US: 1-800 654 3001, www.hertz.com.*

National *UK: 0870 400 4552, www.nationalcar.co.uk. US: 1-800 222 9058, www.nationalcar.com.*

Thrifty *UK: 01494 751500, www.thrifty.co.uk. US: 1-800 847 4389, www.thrifty.com.*

Congestion charge

Drivers coming into central London between 7am and 6pm Monday to Friday have to pay £8 (perhaps rising to £10 from early 2010), a fee known as the congestion charge. The congestion charge zone is bordered by Marylebone, Euston and King's Cross (N), the Old Street roundabout (NE), Tower Bridge (E), Elephant & Castle (S), Vauxhall, Chelsea, Kensington (SW), and Holland Park, Bayswater, Paddington (W); see the map on p390. You'll know when you're about to drive into the charging zone from the red 'C' signs on the road. You can also enter the postcode of your destination at http://cclondon.tfl.gov.uk/cclondon/zone/default.aspx to discover if it's within the charging zone.

The thoroughfare formed by Vauxhall Bridge Road, Grosvenor Place and Park Lane is the sole toll-free route through the zone. If you stick to this road while crossing central London, you won't have to pay. After a consultation period, Mayor Boris Johnson announced in late 2008 that he would be removing the Western Extension Zone (essentially, the area west of Park Lane), although the change wouldn't take place until 2010. The decision wasn't confirmed until autumn 2010 – for the very end of 2010; see www.tfl.gov.uk for all the latest details.

There are no tollbooths – the scheme is enforced by numberplate recognition from CCTV cameras. Passes can be bought from some newsagents, garages and NCP car parks; you can also pay online at www.cclondon.com, by phone on 0845 900 1234 or by SMS (you'll need to pre-register at the website for the latter option). You can pay any time during the day; payments are also accepted until midnight on the next charging day, although the fee is £10 if you pay then. Expect a fine of £50 if you fail to pay, rising to £100 if you delay payment.

Breakdown services

AA (Automobile Association) *0870 550 0600 information, 08457 887766 breakdown, www.theaa.com.*

ETA (Environmental Transport Association) *0845 389 1010, www.eta.co.uk.*

RAC (Royal Automobile Club) *0870 572 2722 information, 0800 828282 breakdown, www.rac.co.uk.*

Parking

Central London is scattered with parking meters, but free spots are rare. Meters cost £1.10 for 15mins, and are limited to 2hrs. Parking on a single or double yellow line, a red line or in residents' parking areas

DIRECTORY

during the day is illegal, and you may be fined, clamped or towed.

However, in the evening (from 6pm or 7pm in much of central London) and at various times at weekends, parking on single yellow lines is legal and free. If you find a clear spot on a single yellow line during the evening, look for a sign giving the local regulations. Meters also become free at certain times during evenings and weekends. Parking on double yellow lines and red routes is illegal at all times.

NCP 24hr car parks (0845 050 7080, www.ncp.co.uk) are numerous but pricey (£2-£7.20 for 2hrs). Central ones include Arlington House, Arlington Street, St James's, W1; Snowsfields, Southwark, SE1; and 4-5 Denman Street, Soho, W1.

Clamping & vehicle removal

The immobilising of illegally parked vehicles with a clamp is common in London. There will be a label on the car telling you which payment centre to phone or visit. You'll have to stump up an £80 release fee and show a valid licence. The payment centre will de-clamp your car within four hours. If you don't remove your car at once, it may get clamped again, so wait by your vehicle.

If your car has disappeared, it's either been stolen or, if it was parked illegally, towed to a car pound by the local authorities. A release fee of £200 is levied for removal, plus £40 per day from the first midnight after removal. To add insult to injury, you'll also probably get a parking ticket of £60-£100 when you collect the car (reduced by a 50% discount if paid within 14 days). To find out how to retrieve your car, call the **Trace Service** hotline (7747 4747).

CYCLING

London isn't the friendliest of towns for cyclists, but the **London Cycle Network** (www.londoncycle network.org.uk) and **London Cycling Campaign** (7234 9310, www.lcc.org.uk) help make it better. **Transport for London** (0843 222 1234) offers a printable route-finder for cyclists, and Mayor Boris Johnson has put a lot of weight behind developing cycling. His 'Cycle Superhighways' have had a mixed reception and, designed for residents to use for getting into central London, are of limited use for tourists looking to get between the major sights. The Barclays Cycle Hire ('Boris's Bikes') scheme has been hugely popular, however,

notwithstanding a few teething problems (see p339 **Cycle City**). For details of other London **cycle hire** companies, see pp337-338.

WALKING

The best way to see London is on foot, but the city's street layout is very complicated – even locals often carry maps. We've included street maps of central London in the back of this book (starting on p392), with essential locations clearly marked; the standard Geographers' *London A-Z* and Collins' *London Street Atlas* are useful supplements. There's also route advice at www.tfl.gov.uk/gettingaround.

GUIDED TOURS

By bicycle

The **London Bicycle Tour Company** (see p338) runs a range of tours in central London.

By boat

City Cruises: Rail River Rover *7740 0400, www.citycruises.com.* **Rates** £14.50; £7.25 reductions. Combines hop-on, hop-off travel on any regular City Cruise route (pick-ups at Westminster, Waterloo, Tower and Greenwich Piers) with free travel on the DLR.
Jason's Trip Canal Boats *www.jasons.co.uk.* **Rates** £8.50 return; £7.50 reductions. These 90min narrowboat tours between Little Venice and Camden are unremittingly popular.
Thames RIB Experience *7930 5746, www.thamesribexperience. com.* **Rates** £29-£45; £16-£27 reductions.
Our favourite of the growing number of Thames RIB tours (a RIB is a powerful speedboat) zooms you from the Embankment, either to Canary Wharf (50mins) or the Thames Barrier (80mins), and back. You'll need to book in advance.
Thames River Adventures *07931 845345, http://thamesriver adventures.co.uk.* **Tours** from £59. Want to investigate Tower Bridge, Hampton Court Palace or Regent's Canal under your own steam? Guided kayak tours are offered between March and October.

By bus

Big Bus Company *7233 9533, www.bigbustours.com.* **Rates** £26; £10 reductions; free under-5s. These open-top buses (8.30am-6pm,

or until 4.30pm in winter) cover more than 70 stops in town, among them Haymarket, Green Park (near the Ritz) and Marble Arch. There's live commentary in English, and recorded commentary in eight other languages. Passengers can hop on and off as many stops as they like. Tickets include a river cruise.
Original London Sightseeing Tour *8877 1722, www.theoriginal tour.com.* **Rates** £25; £12 reductions; £86 family; free under-5s. OLS's hop-on, hop-off bus tours cover 90 stops in central London, including Marble Arch and Trafalgar Square. Commentary comes in seven languages. Tickets include a free river cruise.
London Duck *7928 3132, www. londonducktours.co.uk.* **Rates** £20; £14-£16 reductions; £58 family. Tours of Westminster in an amphibious vehicle. The 75min road/river trip starts on Chicheley Street (behind the London Eye) and enters the Thames at Vauxhall.

By helicopter

Cabair *8953 4411, www.cabair helicopters.com.* **Rates** £150/person. Cabair runs half-hour tours (Sun, some Sat) that depart from Elstree Aerodrome in north London and follow the Thames.

By car

Black Taxi Tours of London *7935 9363, www.blacktaxitours.co.uk.* **Rates** £100-£115. Tailored 2hr tours for up to five people.
Small Car Big City *7585 0399, www.smallcarbigcity.com.* **Rates** £99-£179. Feeling a little retro? Tour town in a classic Mini Cooper.

On foot

Head to **www.walklondon.org. uk** for free walks and events. Good choices for paid group tours include **And Did Those Feet** (8806 3742, www.chr.org.uk), **Performing London** (01234 404774, www. performinglondon.co.uk), **Silver Cane Tours** (07720 715295, www. silvercanetours.com) and **Urban Gentry** (8149 6253, www.urban gentry.com). **Original London Walks** (7624 3978, www.walks. com) provides an astonishing 140 different walks on a variety of themes. More idiosyncratic walks can be downloaded from **www. citiesinsound.com**. And if walking is too slow for you, go for a guided run with **www.london sightseeingruns.com**.

Resources A-Z

ADDRESSES

London postcodes are less helpful than they could be for locating addresses. The first element starts with a compass point – N, E, SE, SW, W and NW, plus the smaller EC (East Central) and WC (West Central). However, the number that follows relates not to geography (unless it's a 1, which indicates central) but to alphabetical order. So N2 is way out in the boondocks (East Finchley), while W2 covers the very central Bayswater.

AGE RESTRICTIONS

Buying/drinking alcohol 18.
Driving 17.
Sex 16.
Smoking 18.

ATTITUDE & ETIQUETTE

Don't mistake reserve for rudeness or indifference: strangers striking up a conversation are likely to be foreign, drunk or mad. The weather is a safe subject on which to broach a conversation. Avoid personal questions or excessive personal contact beyond a handshake.

If you want to really rile a Londoner in the Underground, stand blocking the escalator during rush hour (stand on the right, walk on the left).

BUSINESS

As the financial centre of Europe, London is well equipped to meet the needs of business travellers. The financial action is increasingly centred on Canary Wharf.

Marketing, advertising and entertainment companies have a strong presence in the West End.

Conventions & conferences

Visit London *7234 5800, www.visitlondon.com.* Enquiries.
Queen Elizabeth II Conference Centre *Broad Sanctuary, Westminster, SW1P 3EE (7222 5000, www.qeiicc.co.uk). Westminster tube.* **Open** 8am-6pm Mon-Fri. *Conference facilities* 24hrs daily. **Map** p399 K9.
Excellent conference facilities.

Couriers & shippers

DHL *0844 248 0999, www.dhl.co.uk.*
FedEx *0845 607 0809, www.fedex.com.*

Office services

British Monomarks *27 Old Gloucester Street, Holborn, WC1N 3XX (7419 5000, www.britishmono marks.co.uk). Holborn tube.* **Open** 9am-5.30pm Mon-Fri. **Credit** AmEx, MC, V. **Map** p397 L5.

CONSUMER

Consumer Direct *0845 4040 506, www.consumerdirect.gov.uk.* Funded by the government's Office of Fair Trading, this is a good place to start for consumer advice on all goods and services.

CUSTOMS

Citizens entering the UK from outside the EU must adhere to duty-free import limits:

● 200 cigarettes or 100 cigarillos or 50 cigars or 250g of tobacco
● 2 litres still table wine plus either 1 litre spirits or strong liqueurs (above 22% abv) or 2 litres fortified wine (under 22% abv), sparkling wine or other liqueurs
● 60cc/ml perfume
● 250cc/ml toilet water
● other goods to the value of no more than £300

The import of meat, poultry, fruit, plants, flowers and protected animals is restricted or forbidden; there are no restrictions on the import or export of currency.

People over the age of 17 arriving from an EU country are able to import unlimited goods for their own personal use, if bought tax-paid (so not duty-free). For more details, see www.hmrc.gov.uk.

DISABLED

As a city that evolved long before the needs of disabled people were considered, London is difficult for wheelchair users, though access and facilities are slowly improving. The capital's bus fleet is now low-floor for easier wheelchair access; there are no steps for any of the city's trams; and all DLR stations have either lifts or ramp access. However, steps and escalators to the tube and overland trains mean they are often of only limited use to wheelchair users. A blue symbol on the tube map (*see pp414-415*) indicates stations with step-free access. The *Tube Access Guide* booklet is free; call 0843 222 1234 for more details. For London Overground, call 0845 601 4867.

DIRECTORY

Most major attractions and hotels offer good accessibility, though provisions for the hearing- and sight-disabled are patchier. Enquire about facilities in advance. *Access in London* is an invaluable reference book for disabled travellers, with a new edition due in 2011. It's available for a £10 donation (sterling cheque, cash US dollars or via PayPal to gordon.couch@virgin.net) from **Access Project** (39 Bradley Gardens, W13 8HE, www. accessproject-phsp.org).

Artsline *www.artsline.org.uk.* Information on disabled access to arts and culture.
Can Be Done *11 Woodcock Hill, Harrow, Middx HA3 0XP (8907 2400, www.canbedone.co.uk). Kenton tube/rail.* **Open** 9.30am-5pm Mon-Fri. Disabled-adapted holidays and tours in London, around the UK and worldwide.
Royal Association for Disability & Rehabilitation *12 City Forum, 250 City Road, Islington, EC1V 8AF (7250 3222, 7250 4119 textphone, www.radar.org.uk). Old Street tube/rail.* **Open** 9am-5pm Mon-Fri. **Map** p400 P3.
A national organisation for disabled voluntary groups that also publishes books and the bimonthly magazine *New Bulletin* (£35/yr).
Tourism for All *0845 124 9971, www.tourismforall.org.uk.* **Open** *Helpline* 9am-5pm Mon-Fri. Information for older people and people with disabilities in relation to accessible accommodation and other tourism services.
Wheelchair Travel & Access Mini Buses *1 Johnston Green, Guildford, Surrey GU2 9XS (01483 233640, www.wheelchair-travel.co.uk).* **Open** 9am-5pm Mon-Fri; 9am-noon Sat. Hires out converted vehicles (driver optional), plus cars with hand controls and wheelchair-adapted vehicles.

DRUGS

Illegal drug use remains higher in London than the UK as a whole, though it's becoming less visible on the streets and in clubs. Despite fierce debate, cannabis has been reclassified from Class C to Class B (where it rejoins amphetamine), but possession of a small amount might attract no more than a warning for a first offence. More serious Class B and A drugs (ecstasy, LSD, heroin, cocaine and the like) carry stiffer penalties, with a maximum of seven years in prison for possession.

ELECTRICITY

The UK uses the European 220-240V, 50-cycle AC voltage. British plugs use three pins, so travellers with two-pin European appliances should bring an adaptor, as should anyone using US appliances, which run off 110-120V, 60-cycle.

EMBASSIES & CONSULATES

American Embassy *24 Grosvenor Square, Mayfair, W1A 2LQ (7499 9000, http://london.usembassy.gov). Bond Street or Marble Arch tube.* **Open** 8.30am-5.30pm Mon-Fri. **Map** p398 G7.
Australian High Commission *Australia House, Strand, Holborn, WC2B 4LA (7379 4334, www. uk.embassy.gov.au). Holborn or Temple tube.* **Open** 9am-5pm Mon-Fri. **Map** p399 M6.
Canadian High Commission *38 Grosvenor Street, Mayfair, W1K 4AA (7258 6600, www.canada. org.uk). Bond Street or Oxford Circus tube.* **Open** 8am-4pm Mon-Fri. **Map** p398 H7.
Embassy of Ireland *17 Grosvenor Place, Belgravia, SW1X 7HR (7235 2171, 7225 7700 passports & visas, www.embassyofireland.co.uk). Hyde Park Corner tube.* **Open** 9.30am-5pm Mon-Fri. **Map** p398 G9.
New Zealand High Commission *New Zealand House, 80 Haymarket, St James's, SW1Y 4TQ (7930 8422, www.nzembassy.com). Piccadilly Circus tube.* **Open** 9am-5pm Mon-Fri. **Map** p416 W4.

EMERGENCIES

In the event of a serious accident, fire or other incident, call 999 – free from any phone, including payphones – and ask for an ambulance, the fire service or police. For hospital Accident & Emergency departments, *see right*; for helplines, *see p369*; for police stations, *see p372*.

GAY & LESBIAN

Time Out Gay & Lesbian London (£12.99) is the ultimate handbook to the capital. The phonelines below offer help and information; for HIV and AIDS, *see p369.*

London Friend *7837 3337, www.londonfriend.org.uk.* **Open** 7.30-9.30pm Tue, Wed, Fri.
London Lesbian & Gay Switchboard *7837 7324, www. llgs.org.uk.* **Open** 10am-11pm daily.

HEALTH

British citizens or those working in the UK can go to any general practitioner (GP). People ordinarily resident in the UK, including overseas students, are also permitted to register with a National Health Service (NHS) doctor. If you fall outside these categories, you will have to pay to see a GP. Your hotel concierge should be able to recommend one.

A pharmacist may dispense medicines on receipt of a prescription from a GP. NHS prescriptions cost £7.20; under-16s and over-60s are exempt from charges. Contraception is free for all. If you're not eligible to see an NHS doctor, you'll be charged cost price for any medicines prescribed.

Free emergency medical treatment under the NHS is available to:
● EU nationals and those of Iceland, Norway and Liechtenstein; all may also be entitled to state-provided treatment for non-emergency conditions with an EHIC (European Health Insurance Card)
● nationals of New Zealand, Russia, most former USSR states and the former Yugoslavia
● residents (irrespective of nationality) of Anguilla, Australia, Barbados, the British Virgin Islands, the Falkland Islands, Iceland, the Isle of Man, Montserrat, Poland, Romania, St Helena and the Turks & Caicos Islands
● anyone who has been in the UK for the previous 12 months, or who has come to the UK to take up permanent residence
● students and trainees whose courses require more than 12 weeks in employment in the first year
● refugees and others who have sought refuge in the UK
● people with HIV/AIDS at a special STD treatment clinic

There are no NHS charges for services including:
● treatment in A&E wards
● emergency ambulance transport to a hospital
● diagnosis and treatment of certain communicable diseases
● family planning services
● compulsory psychiatric treatment

Accident & emergency

Listed below are most of the central London hospitals that have 24-hour Accident & Emergency (A&E) departments.

Charing Cross Hospital *Fulham Palace Road, Hammersmith, W6 8RF (8846 1234, www.imperial. nhs.uk). Barons Court or Hammersmith tube.*

Chelsea & Westminster Hospital *369 Fulham Road, Chelsea, SW10 9NH (8746 8000, www.chelwest.nhs.uk). South Kensington tube.* **Map** p394 C12.

Royal Free Hospital *Pond Street, Hampstead, NW3 2QG (7794 0500, www.royalfree.nhs.uk). Belsize Park tube or Hampstead Heath rail.*

Royal London Hospital *Whitechapel Road, Whitechapel, E1 1BB (7377 7000, www.bartsandthe london.nhs.uk). Whitechapel tube.*

St Mary's Hospital *Praed Street, Paddington, W2 1NY (7886 6666). Paddington tube/rail.* **Map** p393 D5.

St Thomas' Hospital *Lambeth Palace Road, Lambeth, SE1 7EH (7188 7188, www.guysandstthomas. nhs.uk). Westminster tube or Waterloo tube/rail.* **Map** p399 L9.

University College Hospital *235 Euston Road, NW1 2BU (0845 155 5000, www.uclh.nhs.uk). Euston Square or Warren Street tube.* **Map** p396 J4.

Complementary medicine

British Homeopathic Association *0870 444 3950, www.trust homeopathy.org.* **Open** *Enquiries* 9am-5pm Mon-Fri. Referrals.

Contraception & abortion

Family planning advice, contraceptive supplies and abortions are free to British citizens on the NHS, and to EU residents and foreign nationals living in Britain. Phone 0845 310 1334 or visit www.fpa.org.uk for your local Family Planning Association. The 'morning after' pill (around £25), effective up to 72 hours after intercourse, is available over the counter at pharmacies.

British Pregnancy Advisory Service *0845 730 4030, www. bpas.org.* **Open** *Helpline* 8am-9pm Mon-Fri; 8.30am-6pm Sat; 9.30am-2.30pm Sun. Callers are referred to their nearest clinic for treatment.

Brook Advisory Centre *7284 6040, 0808 802 1234 helpline, www.brook.org.uk.* **Open** *Helpline* 9am-7pm Mon-Fri. Information on sexual health, contraception and abortion, plus free pregnancy tests for under-25s.

Marie Stopes House *Family Planning Clinic/Well Woman Centre, 108 Whitfield Street,*

Fitzrovia, W1T 5BE (0845 300 8090, www.mariestopes.org.uk). Warren Street tube. **Open** *Clinic* 8.30am-5pm Mon, Wed, Fri; 9.30am-6pm Tue, Thur; 9am-4pm Sat. *Helpline* 24hrs daily. **Map** p396 J4.
Contraceptive advice, emergency contraception, pregnancy testing, an abortion service, cervical and health screening or gynaecological services. Fees may apply.

Dentists

Dental care is free for resident students, under-18s and people on benefits. All others must pay. To find an NHS dentist, contact the local Health Authority or a Citizens' Advice Bureau (*see right*).

Dental Emergency Care Service *Guy's Hospital, St Thomas Street, Borough, SE1 9RT (7188 0511). London Bridge tube/rail.* **Open** 9am-5pm Mon-Fri. **Map** p402 Q8.
Queues start forming at 8am; arrive by 10am if you're to be seen at all.

Hospitals

For a list of hospitals with Accident & Emergency departments, *see left*; for other hospitals, consult the *Yellow Pages* directory.

Opticians

See p272.

Pharmacies

Also called 'chemists' in the UK. Branches of Boots and larger supermarkets have a pharmacy, and there are independents on the high street (*see p272*). Staff can advise on over-the-counter medicines. Most pharmacies keep shop hours (9am-6pm Mon-Sat).

STDs, HIV & AIDS

NHS Genito-Urinary Clinics (such as the Centre for Sexual Health) are affiliated to major hospitals. They provide free, confidential treatment of STDs and other problems, such as thrush and cystitis, offer counselling about HIV and other STDs, and can conduct blood tests.

The 24-hour **Sexual Healthline** (0800 567 123, www.playing safely.co.uk) is free and confidential. See online for your nearest clinic. For other helplines, *see right*; for abortion and contraception, *see left*.

Mortimer Market Centre for Sexual Health *Mortimer Market, off Capper Street, Bloomsbury, WC1E 6JB (3317 5100). Goodge Street or Warren Street tube.* **Open** 9am-6pm Mon, Thur; 9am-7pm Tue; 1-6pm Wed; 8.30am-3pm Fri. **Map** p396 J4.

Terrence Higgins Trust Lighthouse *314-320 Gray's Inn Road, King Cross, WC1X 8DP (0845 122 1200, www.tht.org.uk). King's Cross tube/rail.* **Open** *Helpline* 10am-10pm Mon-Fri; noon-6pm Sat, Sun. **Map** p397 M5.
Advice for those with HIV/AIDS, their relatives, lovers and friends. It also offers free leaflets about AIDS and safer sex.

HELPLINES

Helplines dealing with sexual health issues are listed under STDs, HIV & AIDS (*see above*).

Alcoholics Anonymous *0845 769 7555, www.alcoholics-anonymous.org.uk.* **Open** 10am-10pm daily.

Citizens' Advice Bureaux *www.citizensadvice.org.uk.* The council-run CABs offer free legal, financial and personal advice. Check the phone book or see the website for your nearest office.

Missing People *0500 700 700, www.missingpeople.org.uk.* **Open** 24hrs daily. Information on anyone reported missing.

NHS Direct *0845 4647, www.nhsdirect.nhs.uk.* **Open** 24hrs daily.
A free, first-stop service for medical advice on all subjects.

Rape & Sexual Abuse Support Centre *0808 802 9999, www.rapecrisis.org.uk.* **Open** noon-2.30pm, 7-9.30pm daily. Information and support.

Samaritans *0845 790 9090, www.samaritans.org.uk.* **Open** 24hrs daily. General helpline.

Victim Support *0845 303 0900, www.victimsupport.org.uk).* **Open** 9am-9pm Mon-Fri; 9am-7pm Sat, Sun. **Map** p396 H5.
Emotional and practical support to victims of crime.

ID

You're unlikely to be asked for ID in London when buying alcohol or tobacco, although many shops and some bars check anyone who looks 21 or under. Passports and photographic driver's licences are acceptable forms of ID.

DIRECTORY

DIRECTORY

INSURANCE

Insuring personal belongings can be difficult to arrange once you have arrived, so do so before you leave home. Medical insurance is usually included in travel insurance packages. Unless your country has an arrangement with the UK (*see p368*), it's important to ensure you have adequate health cover.

INTERNET

Many hotels now have high-speed internet access, whether via a cable or as wireless. Many cafés have wireless access; see below for four central establishments. You'll also find internet terminals in public libraries (*see right*).

Benugo Bar & Kitchen *BFI Southbank, Belvedere Road, South Bank, SE1 8XT (7401 9000, www.benugo.com). Waterloo tube/rail.* **Open** 11am-11pm Mon-Sat; 11am-10.30pm Sun.
5th View *Waterstone's, 203-206 Piccadilly, W1J 9HA (7851 2433, www.5thview.co.uk). Piccadilly Circus tube.* **Open** 9am-9pm Mon-Sat; noon-5pm Sun.
Hummus Brothers *88 Wardour Street, Soho, W1F 0TH (7734 1311, www.hbros.co.uk). Oxford Circus tube.* **Open** noon-10pm Mon-Wed, Sun; noon-11pm Thur-Sat.
Peyton & Byrne *Wellcome Collection, 183 Euston Road, Bloomsbury, NW1 2BE (7611 2138, www.peytonandbyrne.com). Euston tube/rail.* **Open** 10am-6pm Mon-Wed, Fri, Sat; 10am-10pm Thur; 11am-6pm Sun.

LEFT LUGGAGE

Airports

Gatwick Airport *01293 502014 South Terminal, 01293 569900 North Terminal.*
Heathrow Airport *8745 5301 T1, 8759 3344 T3, 8897 6874, T4, 8759 3344 T5.*
London City Airport *7646 0162.*
Stansted Airport *01279 663213.*

Rail & bus stations

Security precautions mean that London stations tend to have left-luggage desks rather than lockers. Call 0845 748 4950 for details.

Charing Cross *7930 5444.*
Open 7am-11pm daily.
Euston *7387 8699.*
Open 7am-11pm daily.

King's Cross *7837 4334.*
Open 7am-11pm daily.
Paddington *7313 1514.*
Open 9am-5.30pm Mon-Fri.
Victoria *7963 0957.*
Open 9am-5.30pm Mon-Fri.

LEGAL HELP

Those in difficulties can visit a Citizens' Advice Bureau (*see p369*) or contact the groups below. Try the **Legal Services Commission** (0845 345 4345, www.legalservices. gov.uk) for information. If you're arrested, your first call should be to your embassy (*see p368*).

Law Centres Federation *7839 2998, www.lawcentres.org.uk.*
Open 10am-5.30pm Mon-Fri. Free legal help for people who can't afford a lawyer and live or work in the immediate area; this office connects you with the nearest centre.

LIBRARIES

Unless you're a resident, you won't be able to join a lending library. At the British Library (*see p105*), only exhibition areas are open to non-members, but the libraries below can be used for reference by all.

Barbican Library *Barbican Centre, Silk Street, the City, EC2Y 8DS (7638 0569, www.cityof london.gov.uk/barbicanlibrary). Barbican tube.* **Open** 9.30am-5.30pm Mon, Wed; 9.30am-7.30pm Tue, Thur; 9.30am-2pm Fri; 9.30am-4pm Sat. **Map** p400 P5.
Holborn Library *32-38 Theobald's Road, Bloomsbury, WC1X 8PA (7974 6345). Chancery Lane tube.* **Open** 10am-7pm Mon-Fri; 10am-5pm Sat. **Map** p397 M5.
Kensington Central Library *12 Philimore Walk, Kensington, W8 7RX (7361 3010, www.rbkc.gov.uk/libraries). High Street Kensington tube.* **Open** 9.30am-8pm Mon, Tue, Thur; 9.30am-5pm Wed, Fri, Sat.
Marylebone Library *109-117 Marylebone Road, Marylebone, NW1 5PS (7641 1300, www.westminster.gov.uk/libraries). Baker Street tube or Marylebone tube/rail.* **Open** 9.30am-8pm Mon, Tue, Thur, Fri; 10am-8pm Wed; 9.30am-5pm Sat; 1.30-5pm Sun. **Map** p393 F4.
Victoria Library *160 Buckingham Palace Road, Belgravia, SW1W 9UD (7641 1300, www. westminster.gov.uk/libraries). Victoria tube/rail.* **Open** 9.30am-8pm Mon; 9.30am-7pm Tue, Thur,

Fri; 10am-7pm Wed; 9.30am-5pm Sat. **Map** p398 H10.
Westminster Reference Library *35 St Martin's Street, Westminster, WC2H 7HP (7641 1300, www. westminster.gov.uk/libraries). Leicester Square tube.* **Open** 10am-8pm Mon-Fri; 10am-5pm Sat. **Map** p416 X4.
Women's Library *25 Old Castle Street, Whitechapel, E1 7NT (7320 2222, www.thewomens library.ac.uk). Aldgate tube or Aldgate East tube.* **Open** *Reading room* 9.30am-5pm Tue, Wed, Fri; 9.30am-8pm Thur. **Map** p403 S6.

LOST PROPERTY

Always inform the police if you lose anything, if only to validate insurance claims; *see left* or the *Yellow Pages* for police station locations. Only dial 999 if violence has occurred; use 0300 123 1212 for non-emergencies. Report lost passports both to the police and to your embassy (*see p368*).

Airports

For items left on the plane, contact the relevant airline. Otherwise, phone the following:

Gatwick Airport *0844 335 1802.*
Heathrow Airport *8745 7727.*
London City Airport *7646 0000.*
Luton Airport *01582 395219.*
Stansted Airport *01279 663293.*

Public transport

If you've lost property in an overground station or on a train, call 0870 000 5151, and give the operator the details.

Transport for London *Lost Property Office, 200 Baker Street, Marylebone, NW1 5RZ (7918 2000, www.tfl.gov.uk). Baker Street tube.* **Open** 8.30am-4pm Mon-Fri. **Map** p396 G4. Allow three working days from the time of loss. If you lose something on a bus, call 0843 222 1234 and ask for the numbers of the depots at either end of the route. For tube losses, pick up a lost property form from any station.

Taxis

The Transport for London office (*see above*) deals with property found in registered black cabs. Allow seven days from the time of loss. For items lost in a minicab, contact the relevant company.

MEDIA
Magazines

Time Out remains London's only quality listings magazine. Widely available in central London every Tuesday, it gives listings for the week from Thursday. If you want to know what's going on and whether it's any good, look here.

Nationally, *Loaded*, *FHM* and *Maxim* are big men's titles, while women often buy *Glamour* and *Grazia* alongside *Vogue*, *Marie Claire* and *Elle*. The appetite for gossip rags such as *Heat*, *Closer* and *OK* has abated only slightly.

The *Spectator*, *Prospect*, the *Economist* and the *New Statesman* are at the serious, political end of the market, with the satirical *Private Eye* bringing some levity to the subject. The *London Review of Books* ponders life and letters in considerable depth. The laudable *Big Issue* is sold across the capital by registered homeless vendors.

For webzines, *see p377*.

Newspapers

London's main daily paper is the sensationalist *Evening Standard*, published Monday to Friday. It became a freesheet in 2009, after a major revamp under a new owner failed to bring in enough sales. In the mornings, in tube station dispensers and discarded in the carriages, you'll still find *Metro*, a free *Standard* spin-off that led a deluge of low-quality free dailies.

Quality national dailies include, from right to left of the political spectrum, the *Daily Telegraph* (best for sport), *The Times*, the *Independent* (which launched a cheap daily digest, *i*, in 2010) and the *Guardian* (best for the arts). All go into overdrive on Saturdays and all have bulging Sunday equivalents bar the *Guardian*, which instead has a sister Sunday paper, the *Observer*. The pink *Financial Times* (daily except Sunday) is the best for business.

In the middle market, the leader is the right-wing *Daily Mail* (and *Mail on Sunday*); the *Daily Express* (and *Sunday Express*) competes.

The tabloid leader is the *Sun* (and Sunday's *News of the World*), with the *Daily Star* and the *Mirror* its main lowbrow contenders.

Radio

The stations below are broadcast on standard wavebands as well as digital, where they are joined by some interesting new channels (mostly from the BBC). The format is not yet widespread, but you may be lucky enough to have digital in your hotel room or hire car.

Absolute *105.8 FM*. Laddish rock.
BBC Radio 1 *98.8 FM*. Youth-oriented pop, indie and dance.
BBC Radio 2 *89.1 FM*. Bland during the day; better after dark.
BBC Radio 3 *91.3 FM*. Classical music dominates, but there's also discussion, world music and arts.
BBC Radio 4 *93.5 FM, 198 LW*. The BBC's main speech station is led by news agenda-setter *Today* (6-9am Mon-Fri, 7-9am Sat).
BBC Radio 5 Live *693, 909 AM*. Rolling news and sport. Avoid the morning phone-ins.
BBC London *94.9 FM*. Danny Baker (3-5pm Mon-Fri) is brilliant.
BBC World Service *648 AM*. Some repeats, some new shows, transmitted globally.
Capital FM *95.8 FM*. Pop and chat.
Classic FM *100.9 FM*. Easy-listening classical.
Heart FM *106.2 FM*. Capital for grown-ups.
Kiss *100 FM*. Dance music.
LBC *97.3 FM*. Phone-ins and talk.
Magic *105.4 FM*. Familiar pop.
Smooth *102.2 FM*. Aural wallpaper.
Resonance *104.4 FM*. Arts radio – an inventively oddball mix.
Xfm *104.9 FM*. Alternativish rock.

Television

With a multiplicity of formats, there are plenty of pay-TV options. However, the relative quality of free TV keeps subscriptions from attaining US levels.

The five main free-to-air networks are as follows:

BBC1 The Corporation's mass-market station. Relies too much on soaps, game shows and lifestyle TV, but does have quality offerings. As with all BBC stations, there are no commercials.
BBC2 A reasonably intelligent cultural cross-section, but now upstaged by BBC4 (*see below*).
ITV1 Monotonous weekday mass-appeal shows. ITV2 does much the same on digital.
Channel 4 Extremely successful US imports (the likes of *Ugly Betty* and *ER*), more or less unwatchable home-grown entertainments and the occasional great documentary.
Five From high culture to lowbrow filth. A strange, unholy mix.

Satellite, digital and cable channels include the following:

BBC3 Often appalling home-grown comedy and dismal documentary.
BBC4 Highbrow stuff, including fine documentaries and dramas.
BBC News Rolling news.
BBC Parliament Live debates.
CBBC, CBeebies Children's programmes, the latter is younger.
Discovery Channel Science and nature documentaries.
E4, More4, Film4 Channel 4's entertainment and movie channels.
Fiver US comedy and drama, plus Australian soaps.
ITV2, ITV3, ITV4 US shows on 2, British reruns on 3 and 4.
Sky News Rolling news.
Sky One Sky's version of ITV.
Sky Sports Three channels.

MONEY

Britain's currency is the pound sterling (£). One pound equals 100 pence (p). Coins are copper (1p, 2p), silver (round: 5p, 10p; seven-sided: 20p, 50p), yellowy-gold (£1) or silver in the centre with a yellowy-gold edge (£2). Paper notes are blue (£5), orange (£10), purple (£20) or red (£50). You can exchange foreign currency at banks, bureaux de change and post offices; there's no commission charge at the last of these (for addresses of the most central, *see p372*). Many large stores also accept euros (€).

Western Union *0800 833833, www.westernunion.co.uk.* The old standby. Chequepoint (*see right*) also offers this service.

Banks & ATMs

ATMs can be found inside and outside banks, in some shops and in larger stations. Machines in many commercial premises levy a charge for each withdrawal, usually £1.50. If you're visiting from outside the UK, your card should work via one of the debit networks, but check charges in advance. ATMs also allow you to make withdrawals on your credit card if you know your PIN; you'll be charged interest plus, usually, a currency exchange fee. Generally, getting cash with a card is the cheapest form of currency exchange but there are hidden charges, so do your research.

Credit cards, especially Visa and MasterCard, are accepted in most shops (except small corner shops) and restaurants (except caffs). However, American Express and

DIRECTORY

DIRECTORY

Diners Club tend to be accepted only at more expensive outlets. You will usually have to have PIN number to make a purchase. For more, see www.chipandpin.co.uk.

No commission is charged for cashing sterling travellers' cheques if you go to one of the banks affiliated with the issuing company. You do have to pay to cash travellers' cheques in foreign currencies, and to change cash. You will always need to produce ID to cash travellers' cheques.

Bureaux de change

You'll be charged for cashing travellers' cheques or buying and selling foreign currency at bureaux de change. The commission varies. Major stations have bureaux, and there are many in tourist areas and on major shopping streets. Most open 8am-10pm.

Chequepoint *550 Oxford Street, Marylebone, W1C 1LY (7724 6127, www.chequepoint.com). Marble Arch tube.* **Open** 24hrs daily. **Map** p396 G6. **Other locations** throughout the city.
Garden Bureau *30A Jubilee Market Hall, Covent Garden, WC2E 8BE (7240 9921). Covent Garden tube.* **Open** 9.30am-6pm daily. **Map** p416 Z3.
Thomas Exchange *13 Maddox Street, Mayfair, W1S 2QG (7493 1300, www.thomasexchange.co.uk). Oxford Circus tube.* **Open** 9am-5.30pm Mon-Fri. **Map** p416 U3.

Lost/stolen credit cards

Report lost or stolen credit cards both to the police and the 24-hour phone lines listed below. Inform your bank by phone and in writing.

American Express *01273 696933, www.americanexpress.com.*
Diners Club *0870 190 0011, www.dinersclub.co.uk.*
MasterCard *0800 964767, www.mastercard.com.*
Visa *7795 5777, www.visa.com.*

Tax

With the exception of food, books, newspapers and a few other items, purchases in the UK are subject to Value Added Tax (VAT), aka sales tax. The rate of 17.5% was set to rise to 20% at the beginning of 2011. VAT is included in all prices quoted by mainstream shops, although it may not be included in hotel rates.

Foreign visitors may be able to claim back the VAT paid on most goods that are taken out of the EC (European Community) as part of a scheme generally called 'Tax Free Shopping'. To be able to claim a refund, you must be a non-EC visitor to the UK, or a UK resident emigrating from the EC. When you buy the goods, the retailer will ask to see your passport, and will then ask you to fill in a simple refund form. You need to have one of these forms to make your claim; till receipts alone will not do. If you're leaving the UK direct for outside the EC, you must show your goods and refund form to UK customs at the airport/port from which you're leaving. If you're leaving the EC via another EC country, you must show your goods and refund form to customs staff of that country.

After customs have certified your form, get your refund by posting the form to the retailer from which you bought the goods, posting the form to a commercial refund company or handing your form at a refund booth to get immediate payment. Customs are not responsible for making the refund: when you buy the goods, ask the retailer how the refund is paid.

OPENING HOURS

Government offices close on bank (public) holidays (*see p375*), but big shops often remain open, with only Christmas Day sacrosanct. Most attractions remain open on the other public holidays.

Banks 9am-4.30pm (some close at 3.30pm, some 5.30pm) Mon-Fri; some also Sat mornings.
Businesses 9am-5pm Mon-Fri.
Post offices 9am-5.30pm Mon-Fri; 9am-noon Sat.
Pubs & bars 11am-11pm Mon-Sat; noon-10.30pm Sun.
Shops 10am-6pm Mon-Sat, some to 8pm. Many also open on Sun, usually 11am-5pm or noon-6pm.

POLICE

London's police are used to helping visitors. If you've been robbed, assaulted or involved in a crime, go to your nearest police station. (We've listed a handful in central London; look under 'Police' in Directory Enquiries or call 118 118, 118 500 or 118 888 for more.)

If you have a complaint, ensure that you take the offending officer's identifying number (it should be displayed on his or her epaulette). You can then register a complaint

with the **Independent Police Complaints Commission** (90 High Holborn, WC1V 6BH, 0845 300 2002, www.ipcc.gov.uk). In non-emergencies, call 0300 123 1212; for emergencies, *see p368.*

Belgravia Police Station *202-206 Buckingham Palace Road, Pimlico, SW1W 9SX (0300 123 1212). Victoria tube/rail.* **Map** p398 H10.
Camden Police Station *60 Albany Street, Fitzrovia, NW1 4EE (0300 123 1212). Great Portland Street tube.* **Map** p396 H4.
Charing Cross Police Station *Agar Street, Covent Garden, WC2N 4JP (0300 123 1212). Charing Cross tube/rail.* **Map** p416 Y4.
Chelsea Police Station *2 Lucan Place, Chelsea, SW3 3PB (0300 123 1212). South Kensington tube.* **Map** p395 E10.
Islington Police Station *2 Tolpuddle Street, Islington, N1 0YY (0300 123 1212). Angel tube.* **Map** p400 N2.
Kensington Police Station *72 Earl's Court Road, Kensington, W8 6EQ (0300 123 1212). Earl's Court tube.* **Map** p394 B11.
Marylebone Police Station *1-9 Seymour Street, Marylebone, W1H 7BA (0300 123 1212). Marble Arch tube.* **Map** p393 F6.
West End Central Police Station *27 Savile Row, Mayfair, W1S 2EX (0300 123 1212). Piccadilly Circus tube.* **Map** p416 U3.

POSTAL SERVICES

The UK has a fairly reliable postal service. If you have a query, contact Customer Services on 08457 740740. For business enquiries, call 08457 950950.

Post offices are usually open 9am-5.30pm during the week and 9am-noon on Saturdays, although some post offices shut for lunch and smaller offices may close for one or more afternoons each week. Some central post offices are listed below; for others, call the **Royal Mail** on 0845 722 3344 or check online at www.royalmail.com.

You can buy individual stamps at post offices, and books of four or 12 first- or second-class stamps at newsagents and supermarkets that display the appropriate red sign. A first-class stamp for a regular letter costs 41p; second-class stamps are 32p. It costs 67p to send a postcard abroad. For details of other rates, see www.royalmail.com.

See also p367 **Business: Couriers & shippers**.

Post offices

Post offices are usually open 9am-6pm Mon-Fri and 9am-noon Sat, with the exception of Trafalgar Square Post Office (24-28 William IV Street, WC2N 4DL, 0845 722 3344), which opens 8.30am-6.30pm Mon-Fri and 9am-5.30pm Sat. Listed below are the other main central London offices. For general enquiries, call 0845 722 3344 or consult www.postoffice.co.uk.

Albemarle Street *nos.43-44, Mayfair, W1S 4DS. Green Park tube.* **Map** p416 U5.
Baker Street *no.111, Marylebone, W1U 6SG. Baker Street tube.* **Map** p396 G5.
Great Portland Street *nos.54-56, Fitzrovia, W1W 7NE. Oxford Circus tube.* **Map** p396 H4.
High Holborn *no.181, Holborn, WC1V 7RL. Holborn tube.* **Map** p416 Y1.

Poste restante

If you want to receive mail while you're away, you can have it sent to Trafalgar Square Post Office (*see above*), where it will be kept for a month. Your name and 'Poste Restante' must be clearly marked on the letter. You'll need ID to collect it.

RELIGION

Times may vary; phone to check.

Anglican & Baptist

Bloomsbury Central Baptist Church *235 Shaftesbury Avenue, Covent Garden, WC2H 8EP (7240 0544, www.bloomsbury.org.uk). Tottenham Court Road tube.* **Services & meetings** 11am, 5.30pm Sun. **Map** p397 Y1.
St Paul's Cathedral *For listings, see p87.* **Services** 7.30am, 8am, 12.30pm, 5pm Mon-Sat; 8am, 10.15am, 11.30am, 3.15pm, 6pm Sun. **Map** p402 O6.
Westminster Abbey *For listings, see p133.* **Services** 7.30am, 8am, 12.30pm, 5pm Mon-Fri; 8am, 9am, 12.30pm, 3pm Sat; 8am, 10am, 11.15am, 3pm, 5.45pm, 6.30pm Sun. **Map** p399 K9.

Buddhist

Buddhapadipa Thai Temple *14 Calonne Road, Wimbledon, SW19 5HJ (8946 1357, www.buddhapadipa.org). Wimbledon tube/rail then 93 bus.* **Open** *Temple* 9-6pm

Sat, Sun. *Meditation retreat* 7-9pm Tue, Thur; 4-6pm Sat, Sun.
London Buddhist Centre *51 Roman Road, Bethnal Green, E2 0HU (0845 458 4716, www.lbc.org.uk). Bethnal Green tube.* **Open** 10am-5pm Mon-Fri.

Catholic

Brompton Oratory *For listings, see p142.* **Services** 7am, 8am (Latin mass), 10am, 12.30am, 6pm Mon-Fri; 7am, 8am, 10am, 6pm Sat; 7am, 8am, 9am (tridentine), 10am, 11am (sung Latin), 12.30pm, 4.30pm, 7pm Sun. **Map** p395 E10.
Westminster Cathedral *For listings, see p135.* **Services** 7am, 8am, 10.30am, 12.30pm, 1.05pm, 5.30pm Mon-Fri; 8am, 9am, 10.30am, 12.30pm, 6pm Sat; 8am, 9am, 10.30am, noon, 5.30pm, 7pm Sun. **Map** p398 J10.

Islamic

East London Mosque *82-92 Whitechapel Road, Whitechapel, E1 1JQ (7650 3000, www.eastlondonmosque.org.uk). Aldgate East tube.* **Services** *Friday prayer* 1.30pm (1.15pm in winter). **Map** p403 S6.
Islamic Cultural Centre & London Central Mosque *146 Park Road, Marylebone, NW8 7RG (7725 2213, www.iccuk.org). Baker Street tube or bus 13, 113, 274.* **Services** times vary; check website for details.

Jewish

Liberal Jewish Synagogue *28 St John's Wood Road, St John's Wood, NW8 7HA (7286 5181, www.ljs.org). St John's Wood tube.* **Services** 6.45pm Fri; 11am Sat.
West Central Liberal Synagogue *21 Maple Street, Fitzrovia, W1T 4BE (7636 7627, www.wcls.org.uk). Warren Street tube.* **Services** 3pm Sat. **Map** p396 J4.

Methodist & Quaker

Methodist Central Hall *Central Hall, Storey's Gate, Westminster, SW1H 9NH (7222 8010, www.c-h-w.co.uk). St James's Park tube.* **Services** 12.45pm Wed; 11am, 6.30pm Sun. **Map** p399 K9.
Religious Society of Friends (Quakers) *173-177 Euston Road, Bloomsbury, NW1 2BJ (7663 1000, www.quaker.org.uk). Euston tube/rail.* **Meetings** 7pm Mon; 6.30pm Thur; 11am Sun. **Map** p397 K3.

SAFETY & SECURITY

There are no real 'no-go' areas in London, and despite endless media coverage of teenage stabbings, you're much more likely to get hurt in a car accident than as a result of criminal activity, but thieves haunt busy shopping areas and transport nodes as they do in all cities.

Use common sense and follow some basic rules. Keep wallets and purses out of sight, and handbags securely closed. Never leave bags or coats unattended, beside, under or on the back of a chair – even if they aren't stolen, they're likely to trigger a bomb alert. Don't put bags on the floor near the door of a public toilet. Don't take short cuts through dark alleys and car parks. Keep your passport, cash and credit cards in separate places. Don't carry a wallet in your back pocket. And always be aware of your surroundings.

SMOKING

July 2007 saw the introduction of a ban on smoking in all enclosed public spaces, including pubs, bars, clubs, restaurants, hotel foyers and shops, as well as on public transport. Smokers now face a penalty fee of £50 or a maximum fee of £200 if they are prosecuted for smoking in a smoke-free area. Many bars and clubs offer smoking gardens or terraces.

TELEPHONES

Dialling & codes

London's dialling code is 020; standard landlines have eight digits after that. You don't need to dial the 020 from within the area, so we have not given it in this book.

If you're calling from outside the UK, dial your international access code, then the UK code, 44, then the full London number, omitting the first 0 from the code. For example, to make a call to 020 7813 3000 from the US, dial 011 44 20 7813 3000. To dial abroad from the UK, first dial 00, then the relevant country code from the list below. For more international dialling codes, check the phone book or see www.kropla.com/dialcode.htm.

Australia 61
Canada 1
New Zealand 64
Republic of Ireland 353
South Africa 27
USA 1

DIRECTORY

Mobile phones

Mobile phones in the UK operate on the 900 MHz and 1800 MHz GSM frequencies common throughout most of Europe. If you're travelling to the UK from Europe, your phone should be compatible; if you're travelling from the US, you'll need a tri-band handset. Either way, check your phone is set for international roaming, and that your service provider at home has a reciprocal arrangement with a UK provider.

The simplest option may be to buy a 'pay-as-you-go' phone (about £50-£200); there's no monthly fee, you top up talk time using a card. Check before buying whether it can make and receive international calls. **Phones4u** (www.phones4u. co.uk) and **Carphone Warehouse** (www.carphonewarehouse.com), which both have stores throughout the city, offer options. For phone rental, *see also p260*.

Operator services

Call 100 for the operator if you have difficulty in dialling; for an alarm call; to make a credit card call; for information about the cost of a call; and for help with international person-to-person calls. Dial 155 for the international operator if you need to reverse the charges (call collect) or if you can't dial direct; this service is very expensive.

Directory enquiries

This service is now provided by various six-digit 118 numbers. They're pretty pricey to call: dial (free) 0800 953 0720 for a rundown of options and prices. The best known is 118 118, which charges 49p per call, then 14p per minute thereafter; 118 888 charges 49p per call, then 9p per minute; 118 180 charges 25p per call, then 30p per minute. Online, the www.ukphone book.com offers five free credits a day to UK residents; overseas users get the same credits if they keep a positive balance in their account.

Yellow Pages This 24-hour service lists the phone numbers of thousands of businesses in the UK. Dial 118 247 (81p connection charge plus 30p/min) and identify the type of business you require, and in which area of London.

Public phones

Public payphones take coins or credit cards (sometimes both). The minimum cost is 60p (including a 40p connection charge), which buys a 110-second local call. Some payphones, such as the counter-top ones found in pubs, require more. International calling cards, offering bargain minutes via a freephone number, are widely available.

Telephone directories

There are several telephone directories for London, divided by area, which contain private and commercial numbers. Available at post offices and libraries, these hefty tomes are also issued free to all residents, as is the invaluable *Yellow Pages* directory (also online at www.yell.com), which lists businesses and services.

TIME

London operates on Greenwich Mean Time (GMT), five hours ahead of the US's Eastern Standard time. In spring (27 March 2011) the UK puts its clocks forward by one hour to British Summer Time. In autumn (30 October 2011), the clocks go back to GMT.

TIPPING

In Britain it's accepted that you tip in taxis, minicabs, restaurants (some waiting staff rely heavily on tips), hotels, hairdressers and some bars (not pubs). Around 10% is normal, but some restaurants add as much as 15%. Always check whether service has been included in your bill: some restaurants include an automatic service charge, but also leave space for a gratuity on your credit card slip.

TOILETS

Pubs and restaurants generally reserve the use of their toilets for customers. However, all mainline rail stations and a few tube stations – Piccadilly Circus, for one – have public toilets (you may be charged a small fee). Department stores usually have loos that you can use free of charge, and museums (most of which no longer charge an entry fee) generally have good facilities. At night, options are worse. The coin-operated toilet booths around the city may be your only option.

TOURIST INFORMATION

In addition to the tourist offices below, there is a brand-new centre by **St Paul's** (*see p81*).

Britain & London Visitor Centre
1 Regent Street, Piccadilly Circus, SW1Y 4XT (7808 3800, www.visitbritain.com). Piccadilly Circus tube. **Open** 9.30am-6.30pm Mon; 9am-6.30pm Tue-Fri; 9am-5pm Sat; 10am-4pm Sun. **Map** p416 W4.
Greenwich Tourist Information Centre *Discover Greenwich, Pepys House, 2 Cutty Sark Gardens, SE10 9LW (0870 608 2000, www.greenwichwhs.org.uk). Cutty Sark DLR.* **Open** 10am-5pm daily. **Map** p405 X1.
London Information Centre *Leicester Square, Soho, WC2H 7BP (7292 2333, www.london town.com). Leicester Square tube.* **Open** 10am-6pm daily. *Helpline* 8am-10pm Mon-Fri; 9am-8pm Sat, Sun.
Richmond Tourist Information Centre *Old Town Hall, Whittaker Avenue, Richmond, Surrey TW9 1TP (8734 3363, www.visit richmond.co.uk). Richmond tube/ rail.* **Open** 10am-5pm Mon-Sat.

VISAS & IMMIGRATION

EU citizens do not require a visa to visit the United Kingdom; citizens of the USA, Canada, Australia, South Africa and New Zealand can also enter with only a passport for tourist visits of up to six months as long as they can show they can support themselves during their visit and plan to return. Go online to www.ukvisas.gov.uk to check your visa status well before you travel, or contact the British embassy, consulate or high commission in your own country. You can arrange visas online at www.fco.gov.uk. For work permits, *see below.*

Home Office Immigration & Nationality Bureau *Lunar House, 40 Wellesley Road, Croydon, CR9 1AT (0870 606 7766 enquiries, 0870 241 0645 applications, www.homeoffice.gov.uk).*

WEIGHTS & MEASURES

It has taken a considerable amount of time, and some heavy-handed intervention from the European authorities, but the UK is moving towards full metrication. Distances are still measured in miles but all goods are officially sold in metric quantities, with no legal requirement for the imperial equivalent to be given. We've used the still more common imperial measurements in this guide.

THE LOCAL CLIMATE

Average temperatures and monthly rainfall in London.

	High (°C/°F)	Low (°C/°F)	Rainfall (mm/in)
Jan	6 / 43	2 / 36	54 / 2.1
Feb	7 / 44	2 / 36	40 / 1.6
Mar	10 / 50	3 / 37	37 / 1.5
Apr	13 / 55	6 / 43	37 / 1.5
May	17 / 63	8 / 46	46 / 1.8
June	20 / 68	12 / 54	45 / 1.8
July	22 / 72	14 / 57	57 / 2.2
Aug	21 / 70	13 / 55	59 / 2.3
Sept	19 / 66	11 / 52	49 / 1.9
Oct	14 / 57	8 / 46	57 / 2.2
Nov	10 / 50	5 / 41	64 / 2.5
Dec	7 / 44	4 / 39	48 / 1.9

Below are listed some useful conversions, first into the metric equivalents from the imperial measurements, then from the metric units back to imperial:

1 inch (in) = 2.54 centimetres (cm)
1 yard (yd) = 0.91 metres (m)
1 mile = 1.6 kilometres (km)
1 ounce (oz) = 28.35 grams (g)
1 pound (lb) = 0.45 kilograms (kg)
1 UK pint = 0.57 litres (l)
1 US pint = 0.8 UK pints
or 0.46 litres

1 centimetre (cm) = 0.39 inches (in)
1 metre (m) = 1.094 yards (yd)
1 kilometre (km) = 0.62 miles
1 gram (g) = 0.035 ounces (oz)
1 kilogram (kg) = 2.2 pounds (lb)
1 litre (l) = 1.76 UK pints or 2.2 US pints

WHEN TO GO

Climate

The British climate is famously unpredictable, but Weathercall on 0906 857 5751 (60p/min) can offer some guidance. *See also below* **The Local Climate**. The best websites for weather news and features include www.metoffice.gov.uk, www.weather.com and www.bbc.co.uk/london/weather, which all offer good detailed long-term forecasts and are easily searchable.

Spring extends from March to May, though frosts can last into April. March winds and April showers may be a month early or a month late, but May is often very pleasant.

Summer (June, July and August) can be very unpredictable, with searing heat one day followed by sultry greyness and violent thunderstorms the next. There

are usually pleasant sunny days, though they vary greatly in number from year to year. High temperatures, humidity and pollution can create problems for those with hay fever or breathing difficulties, and temperatures down in the tube can be uncomfortably hot in rush hour. Do as the locals do and carry a bottle of water.

Autumn starts in September, although the weather can still have a mild, summery feel. Real autumn comes with October, when the leaves start to fall; on sunny days, the red and gold leaves can be breathtaking. When the November cold, grey and wet set in, though, you'll be reminded that London is situated on a northerly latitude.

Winter can have some delightful crisp, cold days, but don't bank on them. The usual scenario is for a disappointingly grey, wet Christmas, followed by a cold snap in January and February, when London may even see a sprinkling of snow, and immediate public transport chaos.

Public holidays

On public holidays (bank holidays), many shops remain open, but public transport services generally run to a Sunday timetable. On Christmas Day, almost everything, including public transport, closes down. All dates below are for 2011.

Good Friday Fri 22 Apr
Easter Monday Mon 25 Apr
May Day Holiday Mon 2 May
Spring Bank Holiday Mon 30 May
Summer Bank Holiday
  Mon 29 Aug
Christmas Day Mon 26 Dec
(holiday in lieu of Sun 25 Dec)
Boxing Day Tue 27 Dec (holiday in lieu of Mon 26 Dec)

New Year's Day Mon 2 Jan 2012 (holiday in lieu of Sun 1 Jan 2012)

WOMEN

London is home to dozens of women's groups and networks; www.gn.apc.org and www.wrc.org.uk provide information and many links. It also has Europe's largest women's studies archive, the Women's Library (*see p370*).

For helplines, *see p369*; for health issues, *see pp368-369*.

WORK

Finding short-term work in London can be a full-time job. Temporary jobs are posted on the Jobs section of Gumtree (www.gumtree.com). It's also worth trying recruitment agencies such as Reed (www.reed.co.uk) or Tate (www.tate.co.uk), or the various London markets for work manning the stalls.

Work permits

With few exceptions, citizens of non-European Economic Area (EEA) countries have to have a work permit before they can legally work in the United Kingdom. Permits are issued only for high-level jobs. A youth mobility scheme is open to young residents of Australia, Canada, Japan and New Zealand, however. The **UK Border Agency** website (www.ukba.home office.gov.uk) has details.

Useful addresses

BUNAC *16 Bowling Green Lane, Clerkenwell, EC1R 0QH (7251 3472, www.bunac.org.uk). Farringdon tube/rail.* **Open** 9.30am-5.30pm Mon-Thur; 9.30am-5pm Fri. **Map** p400 N4.
Council on International Educational Exchange *300 Fore Street, Portland, ME 04101, USA (+1-207 553 4000, www.ciee.org).* **Open** 9am-5pm Mon-Fri. BUNAC and the CIEE help young people to study, work and travel abroad.
Home Office *Border & Immigration Agency, Lunar House, 40 Wellesley Road, Croydon, Surrey CR9 2BY (0870 606 7766, www.ind.home office.gov.uk).* **Open** *Enquiries by phone* 9am-4.45pm Mon-Thur; 9am-4.30pm Fri.
Advice on whether or not a work permit is required. If it is, application forms can be downloaded from the website.

DIRECTORY

Further Reference

BOOKS

Fiction & poetry

Peter Ackroyd *Hawksmoor*;
The House of Doctor Dee;
The Great Fire of London
Intricate studies of the arcane city.
Monica Ali *Brick Lane*
Arranged marriage in east London.
Martin Amis *London Fields*
Darts and drinking way out east.
Anthony Burgess
Dead Man in Deptford
A fictionalised life of Marlowe.
Norman Collins
London Belongs to Me
A witty saga of 1930s Kennington.
Sir Arthur Conan Doyle
The Complete Sherlock Holmes
Reassuring sleuthing shenanigans.
Joseph Conrad *The Secret Agent*
Anarchism in seedy Soho.
Charles Dickens *Oliver Twist*;
David Copperfield; *Bleak House*
Three of the Victorian master's
most London-centric novels.
Jane Draycott *The Night Tree*
Poems inspired by conversations
with Thames watermen.
Anthony Frewin *London Blues*
Kubrick assistant explores the
1960s Soho porn movie industry.
Graham Greene
The End of the Affair
Adultery, Catholicism and the Blitz.
Patrick Hamilton *Twenty
Thousand Streets Under the Sky*
Dashed dreams at the bar of the
Midnight Bell in Fitzrovia.
Neil Hanson
The Dreadful Judgement
The embers of the Great Fire.
Alan Hollinghurst *The Swimming
Pool Library; The Line of Beauty*
Gay life around Russell Square;
metropolitan debauchery.
BS Johnson *Christie Malry's
Own Double Entry*
A London clerk plots revenge on…
everybody.
Doris Lessing *The Golden
Notebook; The Good Terrorist*
Nobel winner's best London books.
Colin MacInnes *City of Spades*;
Absolute Beginners
Coffee 'n' jazz, Soho 'n' Notting Hill.
Michael Moorcock
Mother London
A roomful of psychiatric patients
live a love letter to London.
Alan Moore *From Hell*
Dark graphic novel on the Ripper.

Derek Raymond
I Was Dora Suarez
The blackest London noir.
Nicholas Royle *The Matter of
the Heart; The Director's Cut*
Abandoned buildings and secrets.
Iain Sinclair *Downriver; White
Chappell/Scarlet Tracings*
Heart of Darkness on the Thames;
the Ripper and book dealers.
Sarah Waters *The Night Watch*
World War II Home Front.
HG Wells *War of the Worlds*
SF classic with Primrose Hill finale.
Robert Westerby
Wide Boys Never Work
Reissued 1930s noir.
Virginia Woolf *Mrs Dalloway*
A kind of London *Ulysses*.

Non-fiction

Peter Ackroyd *London: The
Biography*; *Thames: Sacred River*
Loving and obscurantist histories
of the city and its river.
Richard Anderson *Bespoke:
Savile Row Ripped and Smoothed*
Inside story of a Savile Row tailor.
Nicholas Barton
The Lost Rivers of London
Classic studies of old watercourses.
James Boswell *Boswell's
London Journal 1762-1763*
Rich account of a ribald literary life.
Paul Du Noyer *In the City*
London in song.
Ed Glinert *A Literary Guide to
London; The London Compendium*
Essential London minutiae.
Janie Hampton *The Austerity
Olympics: When the Games Came
to London in 1948*
The characters and craziness of the
'make do and mend' Games.
Sarah Hartley *Mrs P's Journey*
Biography of Phyllis Pearsall, the
woman who created the *A–Z*.
Rebecca Jenkins *The First
London Olympics: 1908*
How William Grenfell, Lord
Desborough, saved the Games.
**Edward Jones & Christopher
Woodward** *A Guide to the
Architecture of London*
A brilliant exploration.
Jenny Landreth *The Great Trees
of London* Ancient trees in famous
and unlikely city locations.
Jenny Linford
The London Cookbook
Unsung producers and chefs share
their food secrets.

Jack London
The People of the Abyss
Poverty in the East End.
HV Morton *In Search of London*
A tour of London from 1951.
George Orwell *Down and Out
in Paris and London*
Waitering, begging and starving.
Samuel Pepys *Diaries*
Plagues, fires and bordellos.
Cathy Phillips (ed) *London
through a Lens; Londoners through
a Lens* Captivating photographs of
the city from the Getty archive.
Roy Porter
London: A Social History
An all-encompassing work.
Steen Eller Rasmussen
London: The Unique City
London buildings through a
visitor's eyes.
Sukhdev Sandhu *Night Haunts*
London at night.
Iain Sinclair *Lights Out for
the Territory; London Orbital*
Time-warp visionary crosses and
then circles London.
Adrian Tinniswood
His Invention So Fertile
Biography of Sir Christopher Wren.
**Richard Trench & Ellis
Hillman** *London under London:
A Subterranean Guide*
Tunnels, lost rivers, disused tube
stations, military bunkers.
**Ben Weinreb &
Christopher Hibbert (eds)**
The London Encyclopaedia
Indispensable reference guide.
Jerry White *London in the 19th
Century; London in the 20th Century*
How London became a global city.
Patrick Wright *Journey through
Ruins: The Last Days of London*
Thatcherite urban blight and
redevelopment in east London.

FILMS

Alfie *dir Lewis Gilbert, 1966*
What's it all about, Michael?
Bigga than Ben
dir Suzie Halewood, 2008
Draft-dodging Muscovites in rude
immigrants-in-London comedy.
Blow-Up *dir Michelangelo
Antonioni, 1966*
Swinging London caught in
unintentionally hysterical fashion.
Bourne Ultimatum
dir Paul Greengrass, 2007
Pacy thriller with brilliantly staged
CCTV scene in Waterloo Station.

Death Line
dir Gary Sherman, 1972
The last of a Victorian cannibal
race is found in a lost tube station.
Derek *dir Isaac Julien, 2008*
Shorts by and memories of director
Derek Jarman.
Dirty Pretty Things
dir Stephen Frears, 2002
Body organ smuggling.
Fires Were Started
dir Humphrey Jennings, 1943
Drama-doc war propaganda about
the London Fire Brigade.
Fish Tank *dir Andrea Arnold,
2009* Violent yet cheerful film
about a rough Essex council estate.
**Harry Potter & the Order of the
Phoenix** *dir David Yates, 2007*
Overlong, but with stunning aerial
shots of London.
Jump London
dir Mike Christie, 2003
Insane free-runners hop all over the
city's landmarks.
The Krays *dir Peter Medak, 1990*
The life and times of the most
notorious of East End gangsters.
The Ladykillers *dir Alexander
Mackendrick, 1951*
Classic Ealing comedy.
**Life is Sweet; Naked; Secrets
& Lies; Vera Drake; Happy-Go-
Lucky** *dir Mike Leigh, 1990-2008*
Metroland; urban misanthropy;
familial tensions; sympathy for
post-war abortionist; day and night
with a north London optimist.
**Lock, Stock & Two Smoking
Barrels; Snatch; RocknRolla**
dir Guy Ritchie, 1998-2008
Former Mr Madonna's cheeky
London faux-gangster flicks.
**London; Robinson in Space;
Robinson in Ruins** *dir Patrick
Keiller, 1994, 1997, 2010*
Arthouse trilogy of documentary
fiction tracing London's byways.
London River *dir Rachid
Bouchareb, 2010* French African
man and Guernsey widow brought
together by 7 July 2005 bombings.
The Long Good Friday
dir John MacKenzie, 1989
Bob Hoskins in the classic London
gangster flick.
Oliver! *dir Carol Reed, 1968*
Fun musical Dickens adaptation.
Peeping Tom
dir Michael Powell, 1960
Powell's creepy murder flick.
Performance *dir Nicolas Roeg
& Donald Cammell, 1970*
Cult movie to end all cult movies.
Sex & Drugs & Rock & Roll
dir Mat Whitecross, 2009 No-holds-
barred, dark and delirious biopic of
splenetic musical genius Ian Drury.
28 Days Later
dir Danny Boyle, 2002

Post-apocalyptic London, with
bravura opening sequence.
We Are the Lambeth Boys
dir Karel Reisz, 1959
'Free cinema' classic doc on
Teddy Boy culture.
Withnail & I
dir Bruce Robinson, 1987
Classic Camden lowlife comedy.
Wonderland *dir Michael
Winterbottom, 1999*
Love, loss and deprivation in Soho.

MUSIC

Lily Allen *Alright, Still*
Feisty, urban reggae-pop.
Blur *Modern Life is Rubbish*;
Parklife
Modern classics by Essex exiles.
Billy Bragg *Must I Paint You a
Picture? The Essential Billy Bragg*
The bard of Barking's greatest hits.
Burial *Untrue*
Beautiful, menacing dubstep ode to
the brooding city.
Chas & Dave
Don't Give a Monkey's
Cockney singalong revivalists.
The Clash *London Calling*
Era-defining punk classic.
Dizzee Rascal *Boy in Da Corner*
Rough-cut sounds and inventive
lyrics from a Bow council estate.
Ian Dury *New Boots & Panties!!*
Cheekily essential listening from
the Essex pub maestro.
Hot Chip *The Warning*
Wonky electro-pop.
The Jam *This is the Modern World*
Weller at his fiercest and finest.
Jamie T *Kings & Queens*
Wimbledon's Mockney beats
troubadour comes good.
The Kinks *Something Else*
'Waterloo Sunset' and all.
Linton Kwesi Johnson
*Dread, Beat an' Blood; Forces of
Victory; Bass Culture*
Angry reggae from the man Brixton
calls 'the Poet'.
Madness *The Liberty of
Nolton Folgate*
Nutty Boys' psychogeographical
concept album.
Micachu *Jewellery*
Weird sounds make songs on a
precocious debut.
Saint Etienne *Tales from
Turnpike House*
Kitchen-sink opera by London-
loving indie dance band.
Squeeze *Greatest Hits*
Lovable south London geezer pop.
The Streets *Original
Pirate Material*
Pirate radio urban meets Madness
on Mike Skinner's first and best.
The xx *xx* Slinky alternative indie
from 2010 Mercury Prize winners.

WEBSITES

www.bbc.co.uk/london
News, travel, weather, sport.
www.britishpathe.com
Newsreels, from spaghetti-eating
contests to pre-war Soho scenes.
http://thecabbiescapital.co.uk
London's best blogging cabbie.
www.classiccafes.co.uk
The city's best 1950s and '60s caffs.
**http://diamondgeezer.
blogspot.com**
Fascinating London blogger.
www.filmlondon.org.uk
London cinema.
**http://foodsnobblog.
wordpress.com**
Funny tales of fine dining.
**www.getlondonreading.co.uk/
books-in-london**
Map of London books by district.
**http://greatwenlondon.word
press.com** Fun, engaged and often
thought-provoking blog.
www.hidden-london.com
Undiscovered gems.
www.londoneater.com
Passionate food reviews.
www.london-footprints.co.uk
Free walks.
www.london.gov.uk
The Greater London Assembly.
http://londonist.com
News, culture and things to do.
**http://london.randomness.
org.uk**
Want to find Finnish food near a
music shop? Brilliant review site-
cum-wiki for interesting places.
**http://londonreconnections.
blogspot.com**
Transport projects.
www.londonremembers.com
Plaques and statues.
**http://londonreviewof
breakfasts.blogspot.com**
Start the day in style.
www.london2012.com The
official website – all you need to
know about tickets and events.
**http://london-underground.
blogspot.com**
Daily tube blog.
www.nickelinthemachine.com
Terrific blog on history, culture and
music of 20th-century London.
http://onabus.com
Enter a bus number to map its route.
www.theworldin202meals.com
Discovering if it's possible to eat
around the world without leaving.
www.timeout.com
A vital source: eating and drinking
reviews, features and events listings.
www.tfl.gov.uk/tfl
Transport for London information,
journey planners and maps.
http://wildweb.london.gov.uk
Wildlife in the city.

DIRECTORY

Content Index

INDEX

INDEX

Venue Index

★ **indicates a**
critic's choice.

A

Abeno Too 214
Academy Hotel 187
Accommodation Outlet
208
Adam Phones 260
Aesop 270
Agent Provocateur 265
Albam 261
Albannach 241
Albemarle 219
Albert Memorial 37, **143**
★ Albion 228
Alexander Fleming
Laboratory Museum
122
Alexander McQueen 263
Alfie's Antique Market
274
★ Algerian Coffee Stores
267
Alibi 328
Alice & Astrid 265
Alison Jacques Gallery
302
All Hallows by the Tower
96
All Saints 106
★ All Star Lanes 237
★ Ally Capellino 266
Almeida 346
Amaya 223
Amused Moose Soho
292
Anchor & Hope 209
Anchor Bankside 76
Andaz Liverpool Street
185
Anglesea Arms 244
Anthropologie 262
★ Apartment C 265
Aperture Photographic
260
Apex London Wall 185
Apple Store 108, 260
Approach 305
Apsley House 128
★ Arbutus 216
Arch 468 165
Architectural Association
307
Arcola Theatre 348
Area 329
Artesian 240
Artillery Arms 236
Artwords 257
Ask 260
Assaggi 224
Aster House 202

At Home in London 208
Aubin & Wills 270
★ Autre Pied, L' 218

B

★ b store 260
B+B Belgravia 199
Balans 309
Baltic 210
Banana Cabaret 294
Bank of England Museum
92
Banqueting House 36
★ Bar Boulud 223
Bar Italia 113
Barbican Centre 39, 299,
315 ★, 342
Barbican Art Gallery 89
Barcode Vauxhall 312
Barfly 323
Barshu 217
Base2Stay 206
Bastard Batty Bass 309
Bathhouse 329
★ Battersea Arts Centre
(BAC) 346
Battersea Park Children's
Zoo 289
Baysixty6 Skate Park 338
BBC Television Centre
177
Bear, the 165
Ben Southgate 274
★ Benjamin Pollock's
Toyshop 259
Benito's Hat 213
Benjamin Franklin House
110
★ Bentley's Oyster Bar
& Grill 219
Bermondsey Square Hotel
183
Bernstock Speirs 264
Berry Bros & Rudd 267
Bethnal Green Working
Men's Club 331
★ Beyond Retro 264
Bevis Marks Restaurant
95
Bevis Marks Synagogue
95
BFI IMAX 301
★ BFI Southbank 300
★ Big Chill House 330
★ Billy Elliot the Musical
344
★ Bingham 206
★ Bistrot Bruno Loubet
212
Black Truffle 266
Blackwell 256
Blakes 201

Bloomberg Space 302
Bloomsbury Bowling
Lanes 323
Blue Anchor 178
Blue Bar 244
Blue Elephant 296
Blue Posts 115
Blues Kitchen 323
Bocca di Lupo 217
Bodean's 211
Boisdale of Belgravia 242
Book Club 331
Books for Cooks 257
★ Borderline 323
★ Borough Market 268
Botanist on the Green 249
Boundary 204
Box 312
Bradley's Spanish Bar 237
★ Brick Lane Beigel Bake
229
Brilliant 231
Brit Oval 335
British Invisible Mending
Service 264
★ British Museum 39, 102
British Music Experience
165
Broadcasting House 38
Brompton Oratory 142
Brown's 196
Browns 260
Brunel Museum 164
Buckingham Palace 37
Buddhapadipa Temple
173
Bull's Head 326
Burberry Factory Shop
263
★ Burlington Arcade 253
★ Busaba Eathai 218
★ Bush 347
★ Bush Hall 323

C

★ Cable 329
Cadenhead's Whisky
Shop & Tasting Room
267
★ Cadogan Arms 242
Cadogan Hall 315
★ Café Anglais, Le 224
Café Kick 236
★ Café Oto 326
★ Callooh Callay 246
Calvert 22 305
Camberwell College
of Arts 165
★ Camden Arts Centre
304
Camden Market 148
Camden Passage 274

Camino 213
Camley Street Natural
Park 290
★ Candy Bar 310
Canteen 210
Cantelowes Skatepark 340
Caramel Baby & Child
259
Caravan 212
Caravan 270
Carlyle's House 141
Carpenter's Arms 246
Cartoon Museum 102
Catch 331
Celebrity Cleaners 264
★ Central YMCA 337
Centre of the Cell 155
Cha Cha Moon 217
Chappell of Bond Street
275
Chariots 314
Charles Dickens Museum
104
★ Charlie Wright's
International Bar 326
★ Charlotte Street Hotel
186
Chelsea Brasserie 222
Chelsea Old Church 141
★ Chelsea Physic Garden
141
Chessington World of
Adventures 291
Chez Bruce 232
Chin Chin Laboratorists
226
Chisenhale Gallery 305
Chisou 219
Chiswick House 178
Chris Kerr 263
Christ Church Spitalfields
153
Church Street Hotel 205
Ciné Lumière 300
Cinnamon Club 220
City Hall 39
City Inn Westminster 198
City of London
Information Centre 81
★ Claridge's 196
★ Clarke's 233
Clarks 266
Clink78 188
Clockmakers' Museum
& Guildhall Library 92
Club Kali 310
Coach & Horses 114
★ Coco de Mer 271
College of Arms 87
Colonnade 202
Columbia Road Market
255
Comedy Café 294

INDEX

INDEX

Maps

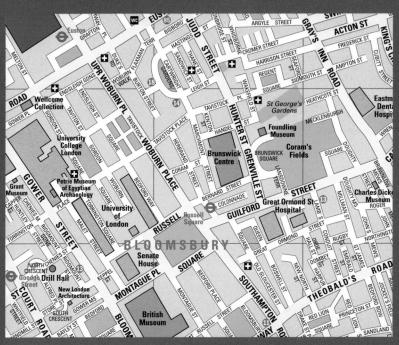

Major sight or landmark	▭
Railway or coach station	▭
Underground station	⊖
Park	▭
Hospital or place of learning	▭
Casualty unit	⊞
Church	✚
Synagogue	✡
Congestion-charge zone	Ⓒ
District	MAYFAIR
Theatre	●

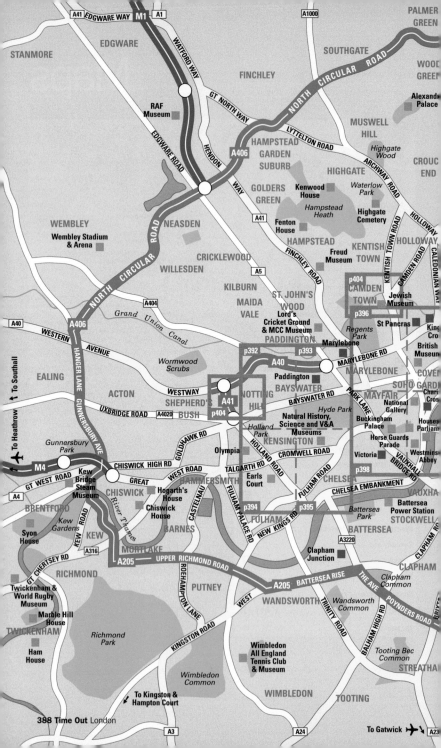

London Overview

Central London
by Area

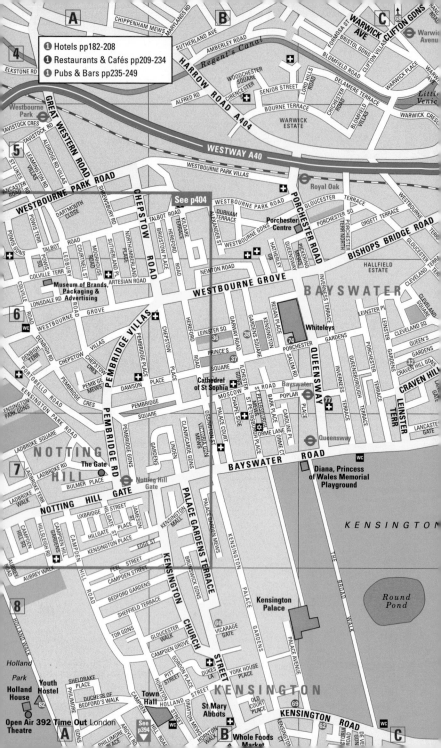

1 Hotels pp182-208
1 Restaurants & Cafés pp209-234
1 Pubs & Bars pp235-249

CHIPPENHAM MEWS

MARYLANDS RD

SUTHERLAND AVE

AMBERLEY ROAD

Regent's Canal

WARWICK AVE

CLIFTON GDNS

Warwic
Avenu

WARWICK AVE

FORMOSA ST

BRISTOL GDNS

RANL

CLIFTON VILLAS

WOODCHESTER
SQUARE

CIRENCESTER ST

SENIOR STREET

LORD HILLS ROAD

BLOMFIELD ROAD

DELAMERE TERRACE

WARWICK PLACE

WARWICK
AVE

HARROW ROAD A404

ALFRED RD

BOURNE TERRACE

WARWICK
ESTATE

CHICHESTER
ROAD

BLOMFIELD
VILLAS

Little
Venic

WARWICK CRESC

Westbourne
Park

GREAT WESTERN ROAD

WESTWAY A40

WESTBOURNE PARK VILLAS

Royal Oak

PORCHESTER ROAD

GLOUCESTER
TERRACE

WESTBOURNE
TERRACE

TAVISTOCK CRES

TAVISTOCK RD

ALDRIDGE RD VILLAS

ST LUKES RD

LEAMINGTON VILLAS

LANCASTER
ROAD

WESTBOURNE PARK ROAD

See p404

WESTBOURNE PARK ROAD

PORCHESTER SQ

PORCHESTER
TERR NORTH

ORSETT TERRACE

BISHOPS BRIDGE ROAD

POWIS GDNS

DARTMOUTH
CLOSE

SHREWSBURY RD

TALBOT ROAD

KILDARE
TERRACE

DURHAM
TERRACE

ALEXANDER ST

WESTBOURNE GDNS

Porchester
Centre

HATHERLEY
GR

QUEENSWAY

PICKERING
MEWS

HALLFIELD
ESTATE

GLOUCESTER TERR

WESTBOURNE TERR

WESTBOURNE PARK ROAD

WESTBOURNE
CHEPSTOW ROAD

TALBOT ROAD

POWIS
SQ
POWIS TERR

COLVILLE TERR

NORTHUMBERLAND
PLACE

MOORHOUSE
ROAD

ARTESIAN ROAD

SUTHERLAND
PL

HEREFORD
ROAD

BRIDSTOW
PLACE

NEWTON ROAD

WESTBOURNE GROVE

BAYSWATER

COLVILLE
ROAD

LONSDALE ROAD

COURTNELL ST

Museum of Brands,
Packaging &
Advertising

WESTBOURNE

GROVE

PEMBRIDGE VILLAS

CHEPSTOW
PLACE

LEINSTER SQ

GARWAY ROAD

KENSINGTON GDNS SQUARE

REDAN PLACE

Whiteleys

LEINSTER TERRACE

INVERNESS TERRACE

LEINSTER PL

PORCHESTER GARDENS

QUEEN'S

CLEVELAND SQ

CLEVELAND SQUARE

DENBIGH
TERR

DENBIGH RD

WESTBOURNE

36

PRINCE'S
SQUARE

38

74

GARDENS

QUEENSWAY

CRAVEN HILL

CRAVEN HILL GDNS

32

LEINSTER
TERR

PORTOBELLO ROAD

PEMBRIDGE
MEWS

CHEPSTOW
CRES

PEMB'GE
MEWS

DAWSON
PLACE

CHEPSTOW
PLACE

Cathedral
of St Sophia

37

ILCHESTER GDNS

MOSCOW RD

CHAPEL SIDE

ST PETERSBURGH PL

Bayswater

POPLAR
PLACE

77

INVERNESS TERRACE

QUEENSBOROUGH TERRACE

LANCASTER
GATE

KENSINGTON
PARK GDNS

PEMBRIDGE CRES

PEMBRIDGE
SQUARE

PEMBRIDGE PLACE

BARK PLACE

ST PETERSBURGH PL

PALACE COURT

CARS PL

CAROLINE PL

ORME LANE

NOTTING

HILL

LADBROKE SQUARE

LADBROKE RD

The Gate

BULMER PLACE

PEMBRIDGE RD

PEMBRIDGE GDNS

LINDEN
GARDENS

CLANRICARDE GDNS

VICTORIA
GDNS

OSSINGTON ST

THORNE LANE CT

BAYSWATER ROAD

WC

Queensway

Diana, Princess
of Wales Memorial
Playground

LADBROKE
WALK

LADBROKE
ROAD

CAMPDEN
HILL SQ

NOTTING HILL GATE

Notting Hill
Gate

GATE

PALACE GARDENS TERRACE

PALACE GARDEN MEWS

KENSINGTO

UXBRIDGE STREET

HILLGATE PLACE

JAMESON PLACE

KENSINGTON MALL

KENSINGTON

CAMPDEN HILL GARDENS

HILLGATE ST

KENSINGTON PLACE

EDGE ST

CAMPDEN
HILL ROAD

AUBREY WALK

PEEL STREET

CAMPDEN STREET

BRUNSWICK GDNS

KENSINGTON

KENSINGTON CHURCH STREET

PALACE
GARDENS

PALACE AVENUE

THE BROAD WALK

KENSINGTO

Round
Pond

CAMPDEN GARDENS

BEDFORD GARDENS

Kensington
Palace

SHEFFIELD TERRACE

HILLSLIDE RD

Holland
Park

DUCHESS OF
BEDFORD'S WALK

Holland
House

Youth
Hostel

82

GLOUCESTER
WALK

CAMPDEN GROVE

C6

VICARAGE
GATE

YORK HOUSE
LA

CAMPDEN HILL ROAD

SHELDRAKE
PLACE

PHILIMORE

PITT
STREET

GORDON PLACE

HOLLAND ST

DUKES LA

KENSINGTON

Open Air
Theatre

392 Time Out London

See
p394

WC

Town
Hall

St Mary
Abbots

DRAYTON MEWS

OLD
COURT
PLACE

KENSINGTON ROAD

69

62

WC

DE VE

GUN

HOLLAND WALK

HORNTON STREET

HORNTON ST

PHILLIMORE
ST PLACE

Whole Foods
Market

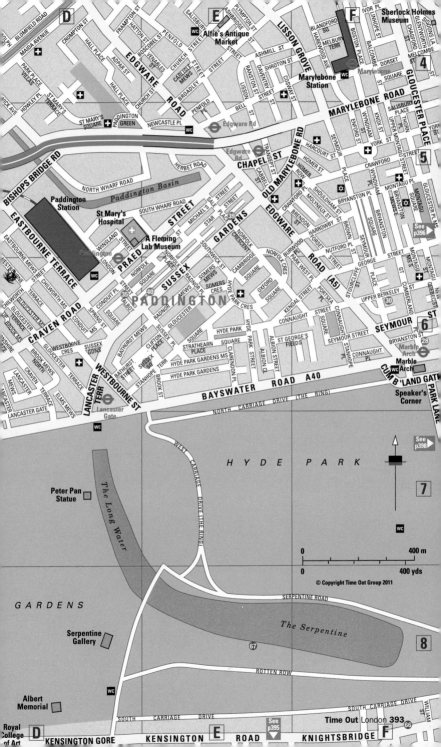

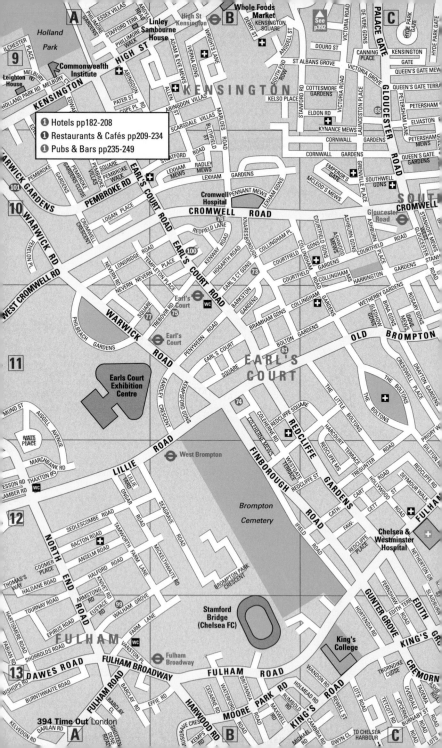

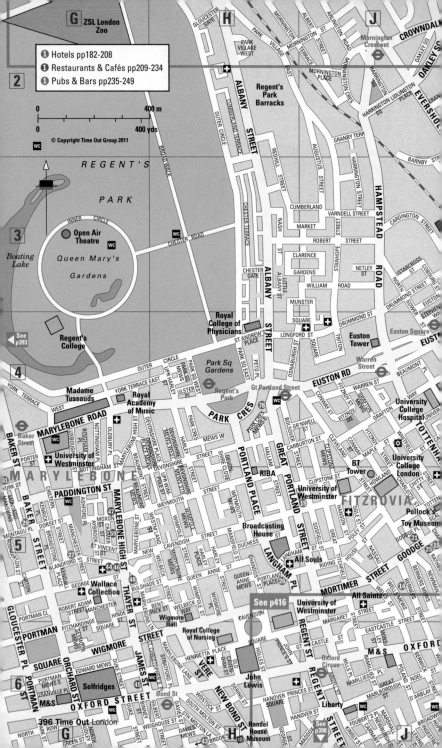

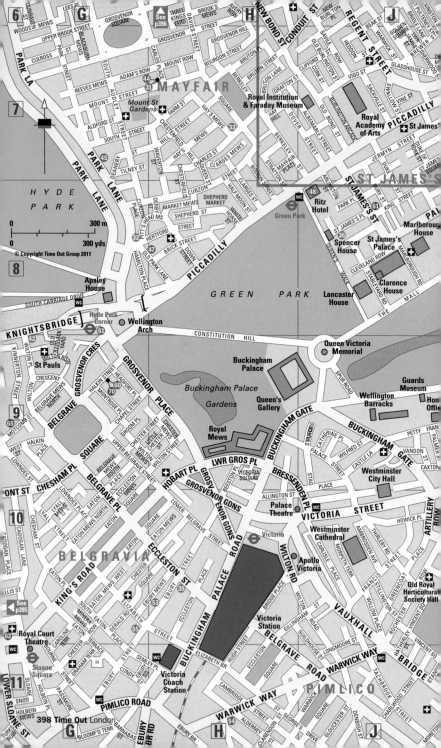

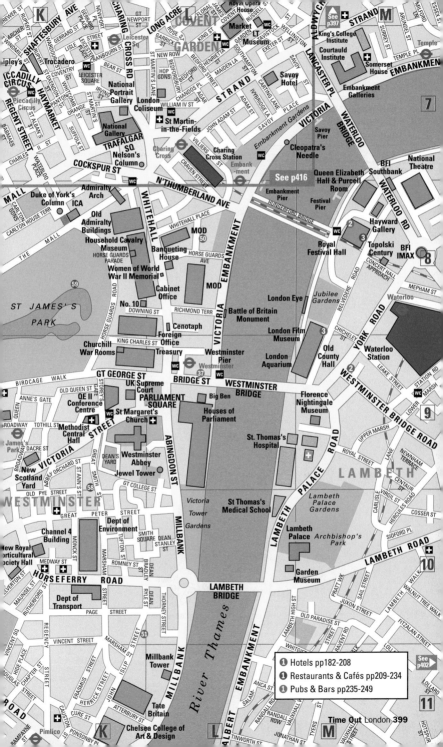

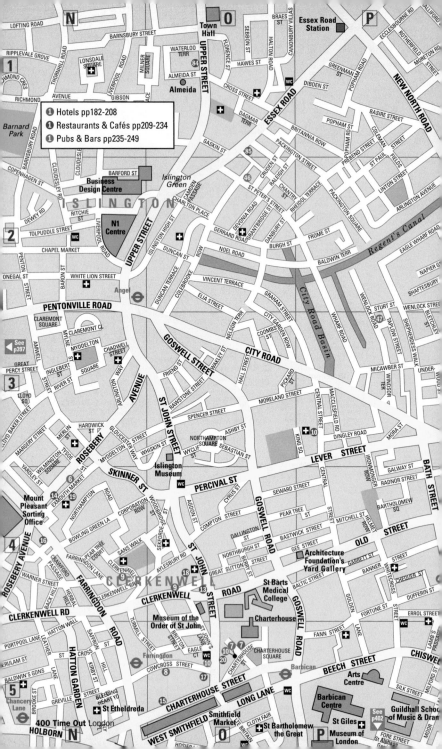

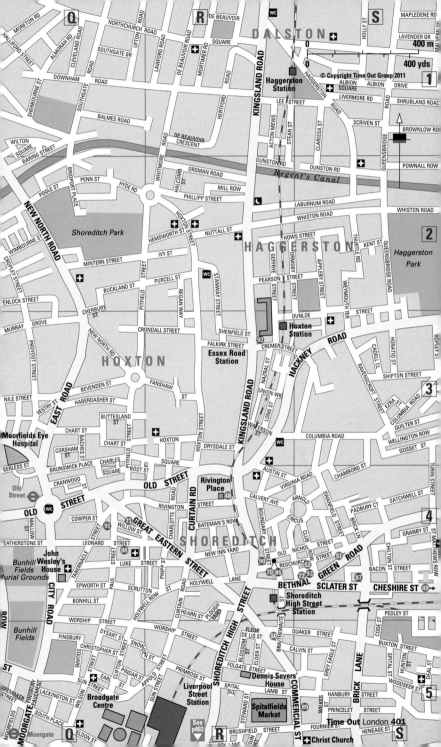

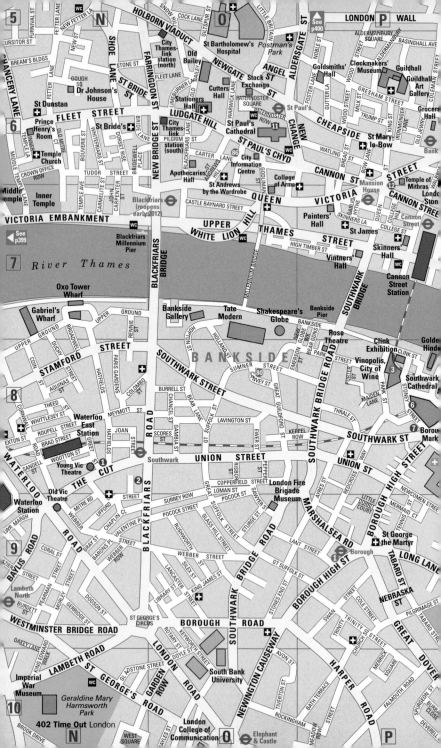

Moorgate

See
p401

Q

LIVERPOOL ST

Liverpool St

R

WHITE'S ROW

FASHION ST

CHICKSAND STREET

BRICK LANE

5

BLOMFIELD ST

LONDON WALL

BISHOPSGATE

NEW ST

TOYNBEE ST

COMMERCIAL ST

OSBORN ST

S

Carpenters' Hall

GT SWAN ALLEY

COPTHALL AV

Drapers' Hall

AUSTIN FRIARS

Bank of England

Museum

Royal Exchange

THREADNEEDLE ST

Mansion House

CORNHILL

KING WILLIAM ST

LOMBARD ST

CITY

BROAD STREET

OLD BROAD STREET

GT WINCHESTER STREET

THROGMORTON ST

THROGMORTON AV

Tower 42

BISHOPSGATE

St Helen

UNDERSHAFT

St Andrew Undershaft

Lloyd's Building

LEADENHALL ST

St Katharine Cree

Leadenhall Market

GRACECHURCH ST

FENCHURCH STREET

CAMOMILE ST

HOUNDSDITCH

BEVIS MARKS

DEVONSHIRE SQUARE

DEVONSHIRE ROW

St Helen's PLACE

ST MARY AXE

30 St Mary Axe

CREECHURCH LA

MITRE ST

DUKE'S PL

ST BOTOLPH STREET

ALDGATE

Aldgate

Aldgate East

Whitechapel Gallery

WHITECHAPEL RD

WHITE CHURCH LANE

OLD MONTAGU STREET

WHITECHAPEL HIGH ST

BRAHAM ST

COMMERCIAL ROAD

WHITECHAPEL

LEMAN STREET

GOWER'S WALK

6

7

8

9

10

© Copyright Time Out Group 2011

River Thames

London Bridge Experience

London Bridge Hospital

DUKE'S HILL

Hay's Galleria

London Dungeon

Old Operating Theatre

Guy's Hospital

BOROUGH

LONG LANE

ST THOMAS STREET

Winston Churchill's Britain at War Experience

London Bridge Station

TOOLEY STREET

City Hall

HMS Belfast

Tower Bridge Experience

St Katharine's Pier

TOWER BRIDGE

Design Museum

St Saviour's Dock

JAMAICA RD

BERMONDSEY

CRUCIFIX LA

Fashion & Textile Museum

TOWER BRIDGE RD

GRANGE ROAD

Tower Pier

Tower of London

White Tower

St Katharine Docks

TOWER BRG APPROACH

EAST SMITHFIELD

ROYAL MINT STREET

Tower Hill

TOWER HILL

All Hallows by the Tower

Custom House

Old Billingsgate Market (site of)

LOWER THAMES ST

St Magnus the Martyr

The Monument

EASTCHEAP

0   400 m
0   400 yds

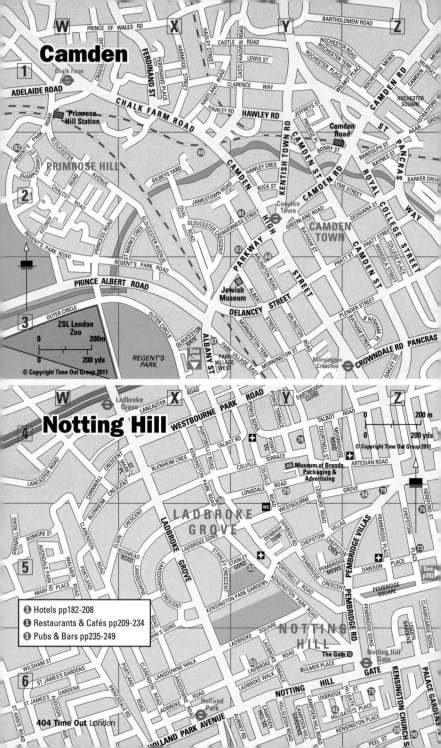

Camden

Chalk Farm

PRINCE OF WALES RD

BARTHOLOMEW ROAD

ADELAIDE ROAD

CHALK FARM ROAD

HAWLEY RD

Primrose Hill Station

PRIMROSE HILL

REGENT'S PARK

GLOUCESTER AVENUE

CHALCOT ROAD

PRINCESS ROAD

FITZROY ROAD

GLOUCESTER AVENUE

REGENT'S PARK ROAD

PRINCE ALBERT ROAD

Outer Circle

ZSL London Zoo

0   200m
0   200 yds

© Copyright Time Out Group 2011

OUTER CIRCLE

GLOUCESTER GATE

REGENT'S PARK

GILBEYS YARD

JAMESTOWN ROAD

GLOUCESTER CRESCENT

OVAL ROAD

INVERNESS STREET

PARKWAY

ALBANY ST

See p356

ALBERT STREET

DELANCEY STREET

Jewish Museum

MORNINGTON TERR

MORNINGTON STREET

PARK VILLAGE EAST

PARK VILLAGE WEST

Mornington Crescent

CAMDEN HIGH STREET

HAWLEY CRES

BUCK ST

Camden Town

ARLINGTON ROAD

ARLINGTON ROAD

KENTISH TOWN RD

GREENLAND ROAD

BAYHAM STREET

CAMDEN ST

CAMDEN RD

Camden Road

BONNY ST

RANDOLPH ST

BAYNES ST

LYME STREET

GEORGIANA ST

PRATT STREET

PRATT STREET

PLENDER STREET

BAYHAM STREET

CAMDEN ST

CAMDEN TOWN

COLLEGE PLACE

MANDELA STREET

BAYNHAM ST

CROWNDALE ROAD

OAKLEY SQ

CASTLE ROAD

CASTLEHAVEN ROAD

LEWIS ST

CLARENCE WAY

HARTLAND ROAD

HAWLEY RD

JEFFREYS ST

PROWSE PL

ROCHESTER ROAD

ROCHESTER TERR

ROCHESTER PLACE

WILMOT PLACE

ROCHESTER MEWS

CAMDEN RD

ROYAL COLLEGE STREET

AGAR GROVE

ROCHESTER SQUARE

BARKER DRIVE

PANCRAS WAY

PANCRAS

STRATFORD VILLAS

CAMDEN SQUARE

MURRAY ST

Notting Hill

Ladbroke Grove

LANCASTER ROAD

WESTBOURNE PARK ROAD

POWIS TERRACE

DARTMOUTH CLOSE

TALBOT ROAD

0   200 m
0   200 yds

© Copyright Time Out Group 2011

LANCASTER ROAD

PORTOBELLO ROAD

BLENHEIM CRES

KENSINGTON PARK ROAD

CORNWALL CRESCENT

BLENHEIM CRESCENT

ST MARK'S ROAD

CLARENDON ROAD

ELGIN CRESCENT

ROSMEAD ROAD

LANSDOWNE ROAD

LADBROKE GROVE

LADBROKE GROVE

LADBROKE GDNS

LANSDOWNE CRESCENT

LANSDOWNE WALK

STANLEY CRESCENT

STANLEY GDNS

KENSINGTON PARK GARDENS

KENSINGTON PARK ROAD

LADBROKE GARDENS

LADBROKE GROVE

COLVILLE TERRACE

COLVILLE ROAD

LONSDALE ROAD

WESTBOURNE GROVE

DENBIGH TERR

DENBIGH ROAD

PORTOBELLO ROAD

PEMBRIDGE MEWS

PEMBRIDGE CRESCENT

PEMBRIDGE VILLAS

CHEPSTOW CRES

CHEPSTOW VILLAS

LEDBURY ROAD

POWIS SQ

POWIS GDNS

COLVILLE ROAD

Museum of Brands Packaging & Advertising

ARTESIAN ROAD

MOORHOUSE ROAD

COURTNELL ROAD

HEREFORD ROAD

CHEPSTOW PLACE

PEMBRIDGE PLACE

PEMBRIDGE SQUARE

DAWSON PLACE

See p392

LADBROKE GROVE

GRENFELL ROAD

BOMORE ST

AVONDALE PARK ROAD

WALMER ROAD

PORTLAND ROAD

MARY PLACE

WILSHAM ST

ST JAMES'S GARDENS

ST JAMES'S GARDENS

ST ANN'S ROAD

ADDISON AVENUE

PRINCEDALE ROAD

PORTLAND ROAD

CLARENDON CROSS

LANSDOWNE WALK

LADBROKE ROAD

LADBROKE WALK

LADBROKE TERRACE

BULMER PLACE

HOLLAND PARK AVENUE

Holland Park

NOTTING HILL

NOTTING HILL GATE

The Gate

Notting Hill Gate

LINDEN GARDENS

CLANRICARDE GDNS

KENSINGTON CHURCH ST

PALACE GARDENS

UXBRIDGE ST

CAMPDEN ST

HILLGATE PLACE

HILLGATE ST

CAMPDEN HILL ROAD

HILLSLEIGH ROAD

KENSINGTON PLACE

PEEL ST

KENSINGTON GARDENS

❶ Hotels pp182-208
❶ Restaurants & Cafés pp209-234
❶ Pubs & Bars pp235-249

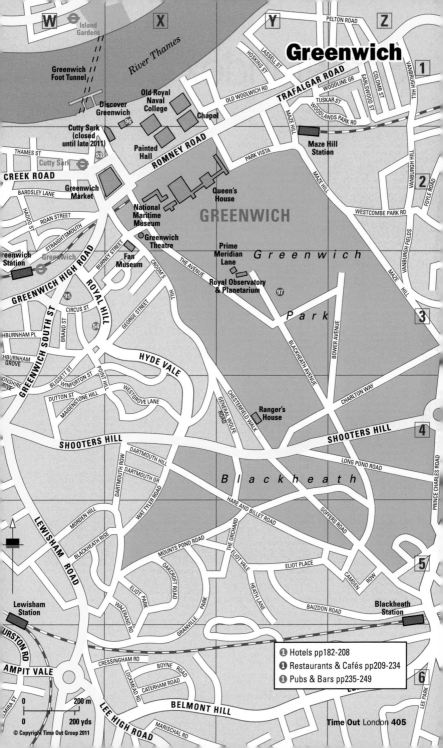

Greenwich

W X Y Z

PELTON ROAD

River Thames

Island Gardens

Greenwich Foot Tunnel

Discover Greenwich

96

Old Royal Naval College

Chapel

Cutty Sark (closed until late 2011)

Painted Hall

53

Cutty Sark

THAMES ST

CREEK ROAD

BARDSLEY LANE

Greenwich Market

ROAN STREET

HADDO ST

STRAIGHTSMOUTH

Greenwich Station

Greenwich

GREENWICH HIGH ROAD

95

CIRCUS ST

BRAND ST

54

Greenwich South St

HBURNHAM PL

HBURNHAM GROVE

ONSHIRE DRIVE

BLISSETT ST

DUTTON ST

WINFORTON ST

POINT HILL

MAIDENSTONE HILL

MORDEN HILL

BLACKHEATH RISE

LEWISHAM ROAD

Lewisham Station

THURSTON RD

AMPIT VALE

LAMIRA ST

LASSELL ST

HOSKINS ST

OLD WOOLWICH RD

TRAFALGAR ROAD

WOODLINE GR

TUSKAR ST

WOODLANDS PARK RD

MAZE HILL

Maze Hill Station

EARLSWOOD ST

COLOMBE ST

VANBRUGH HILL

WESTCOMBE PARK RD

FOYLE RD

VANBURGH FIELDS

MAZE HILL

ROMNEY ROAD

PARK VISTA

Queen's House

National Maritime Museum

GREENWICH

BURNEY STREET

Greenwich Theatre

Fan Museum

CROOM'S HILL

THE AVENUE

Prime Meridian Lane

Royal Observatory & Planetarium

97

G r e e n w i c h

P a r k

BLACKHEATH AVENUE

BOWER AVENUE

CHARLTON WAY

GEORGE STREET

HYDE VALE

SHOOTERS HILL

WESTGROVE LANE

DARTMOUTH HILL

DARTMOUTH ROW

DARTMOUTH GR

WAT TYLER ROAD

GENERAL WOLFE ROAD

CHESTERFIELD WALK

Ranger's House

SHOOTERS HILL

LONG POND ROAD

PRINCE CHARLES ROAD

B l a c k h e a t h

HARE AND BILLET ROAD

THE ORCHARD

MOUNTS POND ROAD

OAKCROFT ROAD

ELIOT PARK

ELIOT VALE

ELIOT PLACE

GOFFERS ROAD

CAMDEN ROW

ELIOT PARK

WALERAND RD

GRANVILLE PARK

HEATH LANE

BAIZDON ROAD

Blackheath Station

LEE PARK

CRESSINGHAM RD

BOYNE ROAD

LOCKMEAD RD

CATERHAM ROAD

BELMONT HILL

LEE HIGH ROAD

MARISCHAL RD

0 200 m
0 200 yds

❶ Hotels pp182-208
❶ Restaurants & Cafés pp209-234
❶ Pubs & Bars pp235-249

© Copyright Time Out Group 2011

1

2

3

4

5

6

Street Index

STREET INDEX

STREET INDEX

London Underground

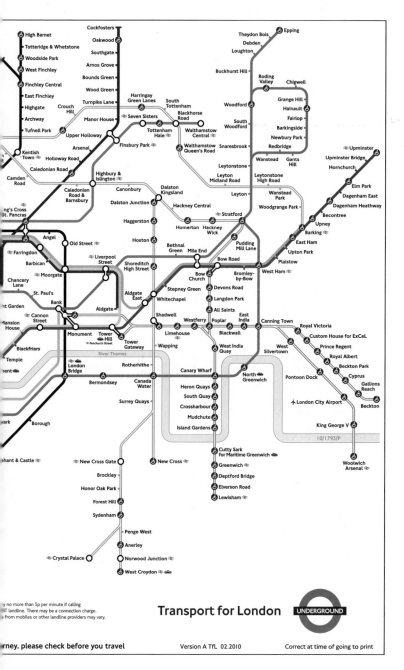

Transport for London

UNDERGROUND

Version A TfL 02.2010

Correct at time of going to print

West End

① Hotels pp182-208
① Restaurants & Cafés pp209-234
① Pubs & Bars pp235-249